**THE
COLONIAL HISTORY
SERIES**

General Editor
D. H. Simpson
Librarian of the Royal Commonwealth Society

VOYAGES AND ADVENTURES
of
FERNAND MENDEZ PINTO

THE

VOYAGES

and

ADVENTURES

of

FERNAND MENDEZ PINTO

Translated into

English

by

H. Cogan

1653

1969

DAWSONS OF PALL MALL

LONDON

First published in London 1653
Reprinted 1969
Dawsons of Pall Mall
16 Pall Mall, London, S.W.1
SBN: 7129 0377 1

Reprinted by Photo-Lithography by Warren and Son Ltd., Winchester.

THE
VOYAGES
AND
ADVENTURES,
OF
Fernand Mendez Pinto,

A *Portugal*: During his

TRAVELS

for the space of one and twenty years in
The Kingdoms of Ethiopia, China, Tartaria, Cauchinchina, Calaminham, Siam, Pegu, Japan, and a
great part of the East-Indiaes.

With a *Relation* and *Description* of most of the Places
thereof; their Religion, Laws, Riches, Customs, and
Government in time of Peace and War.

Where he five times suffered Shipwrack, was sixteen times sold,
and thirteen times made a Slave.

Written Originally by himself in the Portugal Tongue,
and Dedicated to the
Majesty of Philip King of Spain.

Done into English by *H. C.* Gent.

LONDON,
Printed by *J. Macock,* for *Henry Cripps,* and *Lodowick Lloyd,* and are to
be sold at their shop in *Popes head Alley* neer *Lumbar-street.* 1653.

TO THE

Right Noble Lord, and worthy of all Honor,

William, Earl of Strafford,

Vicount *Wentworth*, Baron *Wentworth* of
*Wentworth, Woodhouſe, Newmarſh,
Overſley*, and *Raby*.

My Lord,

Urchas, a Writer of good credit here in *England*, gives this teſtimony of my Author, that no man before him, to his knowledg, hath ſpoken ſo much, and ſo truly, of thoſe Oriental parts of the World, which are ſo little known to us, as he hath done : And that too, not upon hearſay, and report, but for the moſt part as an ocular Witneſs, and perſonal Actor, of, and in, all that he hath related, which is ſo full of Variety, and ſtrange Occurrences, that, as another Writer affirms, the like will hardly be met withall elſewhere : So that the moſt curious Wits, which delight in reading of rare Books, will, I beleeve, find all the ſatisfaction they can deſire in this ſame of his ; where, without ſo much as ſtirring out of their Studies, or running the danger of Shipwrack, they may traverſe the Seas, view the good-

lieſt

lieſt Provinces of the World, entertain themſelves with ſtupendious and unheard-of things, conſider in the manner of thoſe peoples living, whom we term *Barbarians*, their Laws, their Riches, their Government in time of Peace and War ; and, in a word, repreſent unto themſelves, as in a picture, all that is moſt exquiſite, and of greateſt marvel, in the extent of *Europe, Affrica,* and *Aſia.* Theſe, together with many other remarkable matters, are contained in this Work, which I have taken the preſumption to preſent unto your Honor, being invited thereunto by the example of two Tranſlators of it into the *Spaniſh* and *French* Tongues, whereof the one dedicated it to the Archbiſhop of *Toledo* in *Spain*, and the other to the Cardinal *Richelieu* of *France*, both of them, the moſt eminent perſons, of their time, in thoſe Kingdoms : And with whom your Honor may juſtly be ranked, eſpecially in reſpect of the Nobility of your Birth, as well as for the great Hope, which your many preſent Vertues, and Abilities, do give unto the World, of your future Worth, and Eſtimation. Be pleaſed then, my Lord, to receive it favorably, as a tender of the great deſire I have to appear in all occaſions,

Your Honors moſt humble,

and devoted Servant,

HENRY COGAN.

AN

AN
Apologetical Defence
OF
FERNAND MENDEZ PINTO
HIS
HISTORY.

F it be true that *Authors do render themselvs commendable by their Works, there is no doubt*, but that Fernand Mendez Pinto *hath by this same of his justly acquired such reputation, as will make him be esteemed for ever.* He was *a man of a strong wit, and sound judgment, and indued with a most rare, and extraordinory memory, as appears in the Relation of his Voyages and Adventures, which sufficiently testifie how far he excelled therein, retaining in his remembrance an infinitie of such strange and wonderful things*, (whereof to his cost he was for the most part an eye witnes) *as many great Personages of* Asia *and* Europe *took no little delight in hearing him recount them; especially* Philip the second King of Spain, *who at several times spent many houres in discoursing with him there about, which questionles he would never have done, being a Prince, in the opinion of all the world, of a most exact and profound judgment, had he not been verily perswaded that what he delivered was true. Neverthelesse since there may be some who in regard of the stupendious things which he delivers, wil seem to give no credit thereunto; I have held it very necessary to cite here many several authentick Authors, that in their writings have confirmed the verity of his Narrations, as followeth.*

Of the Riches and Grandeurs of these Orientall Countries, and perticularly of the Kingdome of China, Nicholas Trigault, *the Jesuite treates diffusedly in his book intituled*, De Christiana expeditione apud Sinas, *in the first part thereof, principally in the* 6th *Chapter.* Gasper de la Cruz, *in his book of* China, *the third, fourth, fifth, and nineteen Chapters.* John de Lucena, *in the life of* Francis Xavier *the Jesuite, in the tenth Book, from the seventeenth to the twenty fourth Chapter.* Anthony Galuan *in his Treatise of the Discovery of those Parts, fol.* 39. *and in his History of* Florida. Mendoza, *in his History of* China, *the second Chapter of the third Book.* Trigault, *in his first Book, the seventh Chapter, Palatii Regis.* Doctor Babia, *in the third part of his Pontifical History, the* 18 *Chapter, in the life of* Sixtus Quintus. Boterus, *in his Relations.* John de Sanctis, *in his Orientall Æthiopian History, Chap.* 8. *and in the Ecclesiastical History of* Rebullosa. Ribadeneyra, Mathew, *and* Lewes Gusman, *in divers Chapters of the Orientall Histories.* Josephus de Acosta, Peter *of* Leon, Zarate, Michael Vazquez de Padilla, Peter Martyr, Cefas *Bishop of* Chiapa, Francesco Lopez de Gomorra, Hierosme du Pré, Ferdinand de Cordoua, Hierosme Romain, Illescas,
Antonio

An Apologetical Defence.

Antonio de Herrera, Pineda, Prudentius de Sandobal, *and* Garcilaſſo *in divers places of his Royal Commentaries, and in the* 20th *Chapter of his third Book.*

Touching that which Fernand Mendez *writes of the Governors of thoſe King-domes, of the ſtrict obſervation of Juſtice, of the Names of the Judges, Vice-Royes, Magiſtrates, Captains, Governours, and Miniſters of the State,* Boterus, *in his univerſal Relations, ſayes the ſame.* Trigault, *in divers places, particularly in the ſixth Chapter of the firſt book,* de Senenſis Reipublicæ adminiſtratione. Gaſpar de la Cruz, *in the* 16. 17. 18. *and* 19. *Chapters.* Babia, *in the third page of his Ponticall book, in the life of* Sixtus Quintus. Lucena, *in the life of* Francis Xavier, *the tenth book.* Mendoza, *in the ninth and tenth chapters of his third Book, and in many other Chapters of his new world.* Mafeus, *in his Oriental Hiſto-ry ; and in the Letters of* China, *written by* Guerrier *the Jeſuit. Concerning the great number of priſons, and other particularities, the ſame may be ſeen at large in the Hiſtory of* China. Mendoza, *in the twelfth Chapter of his firſt book.* Gaſ-par de la Cruz, *Chapter ninth and twenty ſecond.* Trigault, *in divers places of his Hiſtory.* Lucena, *in the twenty firſt Chapter of his tenth book. and* Alexan-der Valignario, *in his Letters miſſive.*

That which he ſpeaks *of the great multitudes of people that are in thoſe Countries, read in* Lucena, *the nineteenth Chapter of his tenth Book.* Trigault, *in ſundry places, chiefly in the ſecond Chapter,* de nomine, ſitu, et magnitudine Regni Sinarum.

Fernand Mendez *in the eighty ninth Chapter writes of a Temple built upon a great company of pillars ; Read* de la Cruz, *the ſeventh Chapter.* Mendoza, *the third Chapter of his firſt Book.* Mafeus ; Anthony de St Romain ; *and* George Bruno, *in his book of the City of the World.*

In this Hiſtory are ſet forth huge Statues of Braſs and Iron. *See the firſt, third, fourth, fifth, Chapters of the firſt book of* Gaſper de la Cruz. Mendoza, *the ninth and tenth Chapters of his firſt Book. The ſecond Book of* Boterus, *in his relation of* Siam. Rebulloſa, *in his Eccleſiaſtical Hiſtory,* fol. 117. *and* 118. John de San-ctis, *in his Æthiopian Hiſtory, the ſeventh, and twelfth Chapters.* Lucena, *in the* 1. 6. 8. *and* 9. *Chapters of his ſeventh book.* Trigault, *in the ninth and eighteenth Chapters of his firſt Book.* Mafeus, *and* S. Romain, *in the* 90th *Chapter.* Men-doza, *in the ſeventh Chapter of his firſt Book, and in the fourteenth Chapter of his ſecond Part, as alſo in divers places of his Itinerary.* Lucena, *in the nineteenth Chapter of his nineteenth Book ; and many other Authors.*

Touching *the manner of breeding and keeping of wilde Ducks in Rivers, men-tioned in the* 97. *Chapter. See* De la Cruz, *the* 7. *and* 8. *Chapters.* Mendo-za, *the* 21. *Chapter.* Trigault, *the ſecond chapter of his firſt Book ; and divers others.*

As for that which he writes *of the Towns that are made on Rivers and the Sea, with an infinite company of ſhips in the* 98. *Chap. read* Lucena, *in the* 19. *chapter of his* 10. *Book.* Mendoza, *in his Itineraries the* 17. *chap.* De la Cruz, *in the* 8. *and* 12. *Chapters.* Trigault, *in the third Chapter of his firſt Book,* Navium Capia. Lucena, *in his firſt Book the* 19. *Chapter.*

For ſo much as is ſpoken *of the Wall which ſeparates* Tartaria *from* China : *See* Lucena, *in the* 21. *Chapter of his tenth Book.* Gaſper de la Cruz, *the ſecond and fourth Chapters.* Trigault, *in the ſecond Chapter of his firſt Book, and in the* 12. *Chapter of his fifth Book.* Galvan, *in his Commentaries* fol. 70. Mendoza, *the firſt part, in the fifth chapter of his firſt book, and in the ſeventeenth chapter of the*

ſecond

second part. Babia, *in the second part of his Pontifical History, chap.* 18. *and generally all that write of those parts of* China.

Concerning that which Fernand *sayes of the Treasure of the Dead,* read Lucean, *in the eighth chapter of the seventh Book.* De la Cruz, *and* Mendoza. Paulus Jovius, *in his History of the Turks. But that which* Passavinus *delivers in the Description of the* Persians, *and* Belorus, *in his Chronologie of the Kings of* Persia, *is yet a greater mervel. The like do* Celius *and* Augustinus Corion *write of the War of the* Cimbrians, *wherein such an infinite number of* Saracens *were slain, neer to* Marseilles, *as they made up the fences of their fields with the bones of them.* Anthony Boussin *in his Decades of* Hungary.

Our Author imploys many Chapters in the description of the stately edifices of those Eastern Countries ; The same may be seen in all the other Writers, that intreat of those parts of Asia, *who set them forth strangely rich and great.* Lucena, *in the fifth Book of the life of* Frances Xavier. *Father* Lewis *in his Letters. The same* Lucena, *in the eighth Chapter.*

For the innumerable company of Religious men and women (as they term them) which serve for the worship of their false Gods, it shall suffice to read De la Cruz, *in his first Chapter.*

And for a full clearing thereof read Damien De Gois, *in the History of King* Don Emanuel. Mafeus, *in his eleventh and fourteenth Books.* St Romain, *and* Trigault. *As also for the removing of all doubt in the reading of those things, as incridible, look on the sixteenth Chapter of the Book of Prester John, written by* Francesco Alvarez. John de Sanctis, *in his Ethiopian History, the* 17th *Chapter.* Levis de Parama, de Origine Inquisitionis, *the nineteenth Chapter of his second Book, entituled* In sexta ætate Mundi Razis, *in his Chronicle* Sancti Dominice, *folio* 299. Galvan, *in his Discoveries, folio* 70. Lucena, *in divers places of his Book.* Mendoza, *in the eighteenth, nineteenth, twentieth, and twenty third Chapters, and throughout his first and second Books.* Gaspar de la Cruz, *the fifth, seventh, and nineth Chapters.* Boterus, *in his Relations of* China, Narsingua, Japon, *and* Siam. Rebullosa, *fol* 141. Leonard Abel *in his Relations.* Paul Maria, *in his Journey into* Egypt ; *and many others.*

Concerning the setting forth, sumptuousness, and magnificence of those peoples Banquets ; their Comedies, Feasts, Dances, Musick, and diversity of Instruments ; see Lucena, *in the thirteenth Chapter of his tenth Book.* Mendoza, *in the twenty fourth and twenty eighth Chapters of his first Book ; as also in the fourteenth and eighteenth Chapters of his third Book.* Trigault, *in the seventh Chapter of his first Book,* Conrinia. *Touching their Feasts read* Mafeus, *in the sixth Book of his History,* St Romain *in his, and generally* Trigault, de expeditione apud Chinas.

For the manner of their sacrificing, see de Sanctis, *in the eighth Chapter of his* Ethiophia. Damen de Gois, *in the History of King* Emanuel. Mendoza, *in the twenty sixt Chapter of his* Itenerairy. Trigault, *throughout the whole tenth Chapter of his first Book.* Lucena, *in several places of his seventh Book.* De la Cruz, *the thirteenth Chapter.* Boterus, *in his Relations. The Maps of* Japon, *and* China. Mathew Ricio, St Romain, *and* Mafeus.

In the 116. *and* 117. *Chapters of the present Book, the Author treats of the Castle of* Nixiancoo, *for which peruse* Trigault, de Christiana expeditione, *the eleventh Chapter of his fourth Book.* Polenus, *in his Book of* Stratagems. Vegetius, de re militari ; Vanitius, *and* Vasionzelos.

A

Touching

An Apologetical Defence.

Touching that which Fernand *speaks of the* Chineses, *their penances and mortifications in the Temple of* Tinagoogoo; *as also of their processions, and the sacrificing of themselves there,* reade John de Sanctis, *in the eighth Chapter of his* Ethiopian *History.* Mendoza, *in the twenty eighth Chapter of his Itinerary.* Trigault, *in the tenth Chapter of his.first Book; and in the second part of the History of* China. Galvan, *in his discoveries, fol.* 56. Mafeus, S.t Romain, Boterus, *and* Anthony de Govea, *in the Archbishop of Goa his Voyage.*

Of that which is said concerning the great number of Idols and Statues; Mendoza *speaks amply, in the ninth Chapter of his first Book, in the seventh Chapter of his second Book, and in many other places;* de sanctis, *in the second part of his* Æthiopian History, *the seventh Chapter.* Lucena, *throughout his whole seventh Book.* Trigault, *in the tenth Chapter of his first Book,* §. Idolorum multitudo. Rebullosa; *from folio* 116. *to folio* 120. De la Cruz, *in many places of his Book.* Damien de Gois; Boterus, *in his relations of* Pegu : Babia, *in the third part of his Pontifall History, the eighteenth Chapter,* In vita Sexti Quinti.

Fernand *makes a narration of certain men, whom he calls* Caloges, *and* Fingaos, *which have their feet round, like unto those of* Cows, *and hands all over hairy; for the clearing of the truth whereof* read Galvan, *in his discoveries, folio* 32. *and* 72. Gaspar de la Cruz, *the seventh Chapter.*

Touching the tryumphant Arches, *which they have in their streets, together with their manner of accommodating, and inriching them, when as they solemnised certain Feasts,* read de la Cruz, *the seventh chapter.*

Of the Universities, *which they have in* China, *see* Trigault, *in the third and fifth Chapters of his first Book,* De Artibus apud Sinas liberalibus, ac Scientiis, &c. *And in another, entituled,* De Artibus apud Sinas mechanicis.

For a Confirmation of that which our Author says of the strange Ceremonies and Complements, used by them at their saluting one another, when they meet together by chance in the streets, and in their visits, read Mafeus, *in the sixth Book of his* Indian History, *folio* 134. *beginning with these words,* Salutandi ritus miter plebeios, &c. *Ana* Mendoza, *in divers places of his Book declares the same.* Trigault, *in the seventh Chapter of his first Book, at the title,* De Sinarum ritibus non nullis, *describes their manner of Salutations.* Babia, *in the third Part of his Pontifical History, in the life of* Gregory the thirteenth.

The History of the King of Bramaa, *together with his Victories and Conquests, may be found in the Relations of* Boterus. De la Cruz, *in the second and fourth Chapters.* Mafeus, *and* S.t Romain.

Of the entrance of the Tartars into China, *and their besieging of* Pequin : Boterus *in his Relations;* De la Cruz, *the fourth Chapter;* Paulus Jovius, Antonius Armenius, *and* Mathias de Micuy, *discourse at large.*

That which is written of the subversion of the Provinces of Cuy, and Sansii, *and of the doleful and dreadful events ensuing thereupon,* Gaspar de la Cruz *hath spoken of sufficiently in the* 29.th *Chapter of his Book.*

As for that which Fernand *says of their Gods,* Fatoquis, Amida, Xaca, Gizon, *and* Canom ; *as also of the fooleries, dreams, and leasings, which they recount of them ; and of their original, and the respects and reverences they bear unto them ; it may be all seen in the twelfth Book of* Mafeus *his Indian History ; and in the first and fourth Chapters of his Epistles.* Trigault, *in his first and second Book.* Boterus, *in his Relations.* S.t Romain, *and many others.*

By

An Apologetical Defence.

By all this now is my *Author* throughly vindicated from all *aspersions* of *falshood*, that may be cast upon this his *Work*, which, were it otherwise, and meerly devised, yet is it so full of variety, and of such strange, both *Comick* and *Tragick Events*, as cannot chuse but delight far more then any *Romance*, or other of that kind. But being accompanyed with the truth, as I have sufficiently proved, it will no doubt give all the satisfaction and content, that can be desired of the Reader.

A 2   The

The Contents.

CHAP.

The Contents.

CHAP.

The Contents.

CHAP.

The Contents.

CHAP.

2

The Contents.

THE
Travels, Voyages & Adventures
OF
Ferdinand Mendez Pinto.

CHAP. I.

After what manner I past my Youth in the Kingdom of Portugal, *until my going to the Indiaes.*

SO often as I represent unto my self the great and continual Travels that §. 1. have accompanied me from my birth, and amidst the which I have spent my first years, I find that I have a great deal of reason to complain of Fortune, for that she seemeth to have taken a particular care to persecute me, and to make me feel that which is most insupportable in her, as if her glory had no other foundation then her cruelty. For not content to have made me be born, and to live miserably in my Country during my youth, she conducted me, notwithstanding the fear I had of the dangers that menaced me, to the *East Indiaes*, where in stead of the relief which I went thither to seek, she made me find an increase of my pains, according to the increase of my age. Since then it hath pleased God to deliver me from so many dangers, and to protect me from the fury of that adverse Fortune, for to bring me into a Port of safety and assurance, I see that I have not so much cause to complain of my Travels past, as I have to render him thanks for the benefits which until now I have received of him, seeing that by his divine bounty he hath preserved my life, to the end I might have means to leave this rude and unpolished Discourse unto my children for a memorial and an inheritance. For my intention is no other but to write it for them, that they may behold what strange fortunes I have run for the space of one and twenty years, during the which I was thirteen times a captive, and seventeen times sold in the *Indiaes*, in *Æthiopia*, in *Arabia*, in *China*, in *Tartaria*, in *Madagascar*, in *Sumatra*, and in divers other Kingdoms and Provinces of that Oriental Archipalage upon the Confines of *Asia*, which the *Chineses, Siames, Gueos,* and *Lecquios* name, and that with reason in their Geography, the eye-lids of the World, whereof I hope to entreat more particularly and largely hereafter. Whereby men, for the time to come, may take example, and a resolution not to be discouraged for any crosses that may arrive unto them in the course of their lives. For no disgrace of Fortune ought to esloign us never so little from the duty which we are bound to render unto God, because there is no adversity, how great soever, but the nature of man may well undergo it, being favored with

B

the

the afliftance of Heaven. Now that others may help me to praife the Lord Almighty for the infinite mercy he hath fhewed me, without any regard to my fins, which I confefs were the caufe and original of all my mif-fortunes, and that from the fame divine Power I received ftrength and courage to refift them, efcaping out of fo many dangers with my life faved, I take for the beginning of my Voyage the time which I fpent in this Kingdom of *Portugal*, and fay, That after I had lived there till I was about eleven or twelve years old in the mifery and poverty of my fathers houfe within the Town of *Monte-mor Ovelho*, an Uncle of mine, defirous to advance me to a better fortune then that whereunto I was reduced at that time, and to take me from the careffes and cockering of my Mother, brought me to this City of *Lifbon*, where he put me into the fervice of a very honorable Lady : To the which he was carried out of the hope he had, that by the favor of her felf and her friends he might attain to his defire for my advancement, and this was in the fame year, that the funeral pomp of the deceafed King *Emanuel* of happy memory was celebrated at *Lifbon*, namely Saint *Luces* day, the thirteenth of *December*, 1521. which is the furtheft thing I can remember. In the mean time my Uncles defign had a fuccefs clean contrary to that which he had promifed to himfelf in favor of me ; For having been in the fervice of this Lady about a year and an half, an accident befell me, that caft me into manifeft peril of my life, fo that to fave my felf I was conftrained to abandon her houfe with all the fpeed that poffibly I could. Flying away then in very great fear, I arrived before I was aware at the Ford of *Pedra*, which is a fmall Port fo called ; There I found a Carvel of *Alfama*, that was laden with the horfes and ftuff of a Lord, who was going to *Setuval*, where at that inftant King *Joana* the Third kept his Court by reafon of a great plague that raigned in divers parts of the Kingdom.

Perceiving then that this Carvel was ready to put to Sea, I imbarqued my felf in her, and departed the next day. But alas ! a little after we had fet fail, having gotten to a place named *Cezmibra*, we were fet upon by a *French* Pirate, who having boarded us, caufed fifteen or fixteen of his men to leap into our Veffel, who finding no refiftance made themfelves Mafters of her : Now after they had pillaged every one of us, they emptied all the Merchandife wherewithall ours was laden, which amounted to above fix thoufand duckets, into their fhip, and then funk her ; fo that of feventeen of us that remained alive, not fo much as one could efcape flavery, for they clapped us up all bound hand and foot under hatches, with an intent to go and fell us at *La Rache* in *Barbary*, whither alfo, as we found by being amongft them, they carried Arms to the *Mahometans* in way of Trade ; for this purpofe they kept us thirteen days together, continually whipping us ; but at the end thereof it fortuned that about Sun fet they difcovered a fhip, unto which they gave chafe all the night, following her clofe, like old Pirates long ufed to fuch Theeveries ; Having fetcht her up by break of day, they gave her a volley of three pieces of Ordnance, and prefently invefted her with a great deal of courage ; Now though at firft they found fome refiftance, yet they quickly rendred themfelves Mafters of her, killing fix *Portugals*, and ten or eleven flaves. This was a goodly Veffel, and belonged to a *Portugal* Merchant of the Town of *Condé*, named *Silveftre Godinho*, which divers other Merchants of *Lifbon* had laden at Saint *Tome* with great ftore of Sugar and Slaves ; In fuch fort that thofe poor people feeing themfelves thus taken and robbed fell to lament their lofs, which they eftimated to be forty thoufand Duckets. Whereupon thefe Pirates, having gotten fo rich a booty, changed their defign for going to *la Rache*, and bent their courfe for the Coaft of *France*, carrying with them fuch of ours for flaves, as they judged fit for the fervice of their Navigation. The remainder of us they left at night in the Road, at a place called *Melides*, where we were landed miferably naked, our bodies covered with nothing but with the ftripes of the lafhes which fo cruelly we had received the days before. In this pitiful cafe we arrived the next morning at Saint *Jago de Cacen*, where we were relieved by the inhabitants of the place, efpecially by a Lady, that was there at that time, named *Donna Beatrix*, daughter to the Earl of *Villanova*, and wife to *Alonfo Perez Pantoia*, Commander and grand Provoft of the Town. Now after the fick and wounded were recovered, each of us departed, and got him where he hoped to find beft affiftance ; for my felf, poor wretch, I went with fix or feven that accompanied me in my mifery to *Setuval* : Thither I was no fooner come, but my good fortune placed me in the fervice of *Francifco de Faria*, a Gentleman belonging to the great Commander of Saint *Jago*, who in recompence of four years fervice, that I did him, put me to the faid Commander to wait on him in his chamber, which I performed for an year and an half after. But in regard the entertainment, which was given at that time in Noble-mens houfes, was fo fmall as I was not

able

able to live on it, neceffity conftrained me to quit my Mafter, with a defign to imbarque my felf by his favor to go to the *Indiaes* ; for that I thought was the beft way I could take to free me of my poverty. So albeit I were but meanly accommodated I imbarqued my felf notwith-ftanding, fubmitting my felf to whatfoever fortune fhould arrive unto me in thofe far Countries, either good or bad.

Chap. II.

My departure from Portugal for the Indiaes, and my imbarquing there for the Straight of Mecqua.

IT was in the year 1537. and the eleventh of *March*, that I parted from this Kingdom in a Fleet of five Ships, whereof there was no General ; for each of thofe Veffels was com-manded by a particular Captain : For example, in the fhip named the Queen, commanded *Don Pedro de Silva*, furnamed the Cock, fon to the Admiral *Don Vafco de Gama* ; In the fhip, called St Rock, commanded *Don Fernando de Lima*, fon to *Diego Lopez de Lima*, grand Pro-voft of the Town of *Guimaranes*, who dyed valiantly in defence of the Fortrefs of *Ormuz*, whereof he was Captain the year following, 1538. In the S. *Barba*, commanded *Don Fernando de Lima*, who was to be Governor of the Town of *Chaul* ; Of that, which was called the *Flower of the Sea*, *Lope Vaz Vagado* was Captain ; And in the fifth and laft fhip, named *Ga-lega*, commanded *Martim de Freitas*, born in the Ifle of *Madera*, who the fame year was flain at *Damao*, together with five and thirty men that followed him. Thefe Veffels, failing different ways, arrived at length at a good Port called *Mozambique* ; There we met with the S. *Michel*, that wintered there, and was commanded by *Duart Triftao*, who parted thence richly laden for to return into *Portugal* ; Howbeit I beleeve fhe was taken, or fuffered fhip-wrack, as it happens but too often in this Voyage to the *Indiaes*, for he was never heard of fince. After our five Veffels were equipped with all that was neceffary for them, and ready to fet fail from *Mozambique*, the Lievtenant of the Fortrefs, called *Vincent Pegado*, fhew-ed the Captains of the faid five fhips a Mandate from the Governor, named *Nunho de Cunha*, whereby he exprefly commanded that all *Portugal* fhips, which did arrive in that Port this year, fhould go to *Diu*, and leave their men there for the guard of the Fortrefs, becaufe of the fear they were in of the *Turkifh* Army, which was every hour expected in the *Indiaes*, by reafon of the death of *Sultan Bandur* King of *Cambaya*, whom the faid Governor had put to death the Summer before. In regard this affair was of great importance, it was the caufe that all the Captains affembled together to deliberate thereupon ; At length to meet with the prefent ne-ceffity they concluded, that three of thofe five fhips, appertaining to the King, fhould go to *Diu*, conformable to the contents of the faid Mandate, and that the other two, which belonged to particular Merchants, fhould purfue their courfe to *Goa* : The Kings three fhips failing to *Diu*, and the other two Merchants towards *Goa*, it pleafed God to conduct them fafe thither. Now as foon as the Kings three fhips came to the mouth of the River of the Port of *Diu*, which fell on the fifth of *September* the fame year, 1538. *Antonio de Silvera*, the Brother of *Lovys Silvera*, Earl of *Sortelha*, who was Captain there at that time, gave them all the teftimony that poffibly he could of the joy he took at this their arrival ; For proof whereof he beftowed liberally on every one, keeping a fet table for above feven hundred perfons which they brought along with them, befides his fecret rewards, and extraordinary gifts, whereby he fupplyed the neceffities they had fuffered during their Voyage. Whereupon the Soldiers confidering how this Captain entreated them very royally, that he payed them before-hand, diftributed their pay and munition unto them with his own hands, caufed the fick to be carefully tended, and fhew-ed himfelf moft ready to affift every one, it fo wrought upon them, that of their own accord they offered to ftay there for to ferve him, being no way conftrained thereunto, as they ufe to be in thofe Countries in all the Fortreffes which expect a fiege. This done, as foon as the three fhips had fold the Merchandife they had brought, they fet fail for *Goa*, carrying none with them but the Officers of the Veffels, and fome Sea-men to conduct them ; where they abode till fuch time as the Governor had given them difpatches for to go to *Cochin*, where being arrived they took in their lading, and returned all five fafe into *Portugal*.

Seventeen days after we were arrived at the Fortrefs of *Diu*, where at that time two Foifts were ready prepared to go to the Streight of *Mecqua*, for to difcover, and find out the defign of the *Turkifh* Army, whofe coming was greatly feared in the *Indiaes*, becaufe one of thofe

§.1.

§.2.

Foifts was commanded by a Captain that was a great friend of mine, who gave me good hope of the Voyage he was bound for, I imbarqued my self with him ; Relying then on the promifes which the Captain made me, that by his favor and means I fhould quickly be rich, the only thing in the world that I moft defired, and fuffering my felf to be deceived by my hopes, I imagined that I was already Mafter of great wealth, never confidering how vain and uncertain the promifes of men are, and that I could not reap much benefit by the Voyage I was going to undertake, by reafon it was dangerous, and unfeafonable for Navigation in that Country. Now being departed from *Diu*, we failed in a time full of ftorms, becaufe it was about the end of Winter, which feemed to begin anew, fo impetuous were the winds, and fo great was the rain : Neverthelefs, how violent foever the Tempeft was, and dark the weather, we letted not to difcover the Ifles of *Curia*, *Muria*, and *Avedalcuria*, at the fight whereof we thought our felves quite loft, and without hope of life. Whereupon to decline the danger we turned the prow of our Veffel to the South-eaft, knowing no other mean then that to avoyd fhipwrack ; But by good fortune for us, it pleafed God, that we let fall an anchor at the point of the Ifland of *Socotora* ; there we prefently anchored, a league below the place, where *Don Francifco d'Almeyda* caufed a Fortrefs to be built in the year 1507. when he came from *Portugal*, as the firft Victory that ever was in the *Indiaes*. In the faid place we took in frefh water, and fome provifion of Victuals, that we bought of the Chriftians of the Country, which are the defcendants of thofe, whom the Apoftle S. *Thomas* converted in thofe parts. Being refrefhed thus, we parted from thence with a purpofe to enter the *Straight*, fo that after we had failed nine days with a favorable wind we found our felves right againft *Mazua* ; There about Sun fet we defcryed a fail at Sea, whereunto we gave fo hard chace, that before the firft watch of the night we came up clofe to her, and then to fatisfie the defire we had for to learn fomething of the Captain by gentlenefs touching the *Turkifh* Army, we demanded of him whether it was parted from *Sues*, or whether he had not met with it in any place ; and that we might be the better informed we fpake aloud to all thofe that were in the fhip. But in ftead of anfwer, without fpeaking a word, and in contempt of us, they gave us a dozen pieces of Ordnance, whereof, five were fmall, and the other feven, field Pieces, together with good ftore of Mufquet fhot ; And withall, in a kind of jollity, and as it were beleeving that we were already theirs, they made all the ayr about refound again with their confufed cries ; After this, to brave and terrifie us the more, they flourifhed a many flags and ftreamers up and down, and from the top of their poop they brandifhed a number of naked Scymitars, commanding us with great threatening to come aboard and yield our felves unto them. At the firft view of fo many Rhodomontades and bravings we were in fome doubt and amaze, which caufed the Captains of our Foifts to call the Soldiers to Councel for to know what they fhould do, and the conclufion was to continue fhooting at them till the next morning, that fo by day-light they might be the better fought withall and invefted, it being agreed upon of all fides that they were not to be let go unpunifhed for their prefumption : Which accordingly was performed, and all the reft of the night we gave them chace, plying them with our Ordnance. So morning come, their fhip being fhot through and through in many places, and cruelly battered all over, they rendred themfelves into our hands. In the incounter there were threefcore and four of their men killed, and of fourfcore that remained, the moft part, feeing themfelves reduced to extremity, caft themfelves into the Sea, choofing rather there to be drowned, then to be burnt in their fhip with the artificial fires that we had hurled into her, fo that of all the fourfcore there efcaped but five very fore hurt, whereof one was the Captain. This fame, by force of torture, whereunto he was expofed by the Command of our two Captains, confeffed that he came from *Judaa*, and that the *Turkifh* Army was already departed from *Sues*, with a defign to take in *Adem*, and then to build a Fortrefs there before they attempted any thing in the *Indiaes*, according to an exprefs charge fent by the great *Turk* from *Conftantinople* to the *Baffa* of grand *Cairo*, who was going to be General of the Army : Befides this, he confeffed many other things conformable to our defire, amongft the which he faid, that he was a renegado Chriftian, a *Maliorquin* by Nation, born at *Cerdenha*, and fon to one named *Paul Andrez*, a Merchant of that Ifland, and that about four years before growing enamored of a very fair *Greekifh Mahumetan*, that was then his wife, for the love of her he had abjured Chriftianity, and embraced the Law of *Mahomet*. Our Captains much amazed hereat, gently perfwaded him to acquit this abominable belief, and become a Chriftian again, whereunto the wicked Caytiff made anfwer with a brutifh obftinacy, that at no hand he would yield to forfake his Law, fhewing himfelf fo hardened in the refolution to continue therein, as if he had been born in it, and never had profest any other. By these speeches of his, the Captains, perceiving there was no hope of recalling him from his damnable error, caused him to be bound hand and foot, and so with a great stone tyed about his neck to be cast alive into the Sea, sending him to participate with the torments of his *Mahomet,* and to be his companion in the other world, as he had been his confident in this. This Infidel being executed in this sort, we put the other prisoners into one of our Foists, and then sunk their Vessel with all the goods that were in her, which consisted most in packs of stained Cloths, whereof we had no use, and a few pieces of Chamlet that the Soldiers got to make them apparel.

CHAP. III.

Our travelling from Mazua by land to the Mother of Prester John; as also our re-imbarquing at the Port of Arquico, and that which befell us by the incounter of three Turkish Vessels.

WE departed from this place with an intent to go to *Arquico,* the Territory of *Prester* §.1. *John,* Emperor of *Æthiopia,* for we had a Letter to deliver, which *Antonio de Sylvera* sent to a Factor of his, named *Anrique Barbosa,* who had been three years resident in that Country by the Commandment of the Governor *Nuno de Cunha.* When we were arrived at *Gottor,* a league lower then the Port of *Mazua,* we were all received there very courteously, as well by the Inhabitants, as by a *Portugal,* called *Vasco Martins de Seixas,* born in the Town of *Obidos,* who was come thither by *Henrico Barbosa's* order, and had been there a month attending the arrival of some *Portugal* ship. The cause of that his abode was to deliver a Letter from the said *Henrico,* as accordingly he did to the Captains of our Foists; By this Letter he certified the estate of the *Turkish* Army, and besought them at any hand to send him some *Portugals,* to induce them whereunto, he remonstrated unto them how it much imported the service both of God and the King, and that for his own part he could not come unto them, because he was employed with forty other *Portugals* in the Fort of *Gileytor* for the guard of the person of the Princess of *Tigremahon,* Mother to *Prester John.* The two Captains, having perused this Letter, communicated it to the chiefest of the Soldiers, and sat in Council upon it, where it was determined that four of them should go along with *Vasco Martins* to *Barbosa,* and that they should carry the Letter which *Antonio de Sylvera* had sent him: This was no sooner resolved then executed, for the next day three other *Portugals,* and my self, departed accordingly, and we went by Land mounted upon good Mules, which the *Ciquaxy,* Captain of the Town, sent us by the Command of the Princess, the Emperors Mother, together with six *Abissins* to accompany us. The first night we lay at a very fair Monastery, called *Satilgaon;* The next day before the Sun rose we travelled along by a River, and by that time we had rode five leagues we arrived at a place, named *Bitonte,* where we spent that night in a Convent of religious persons, dedicated to S. *Michael;* there we were very well entertained both by the Prior, and the Fryers: A little after our arrival, the son of *Bernagais,* Governor of that Empire of *Æthiopia,* a very proper and courteous Gentleman, about seventeen years old, came to see us, accompanied with thirty men, all mounted upon Mules, and himself on a horse furnished after the *Portugal* manner; the furniture was of Purple Velvet trimmed with Gold fringe, which two years before the Governor *Nuno de Cunha* sent him from the *Indies,* by one *Lopez Chanoca,* who was afterwards made a slave at *Gran Cario,* whereof this young Prince being advertised, he presently dispatched away a *Jewish* Merchant of *Azabiba* to redeem him, but as ill fortune would he dyed before the Jew could get thither, which so grieved this Prince when he understood of it, as the said *Vasco Martins* assured us that in the said Monastery of S. *Michael* he caused the most honorable funerals to be celebrated for him that ever he saw, wherein assisted above four thousand Priests, besides a greater number of Novices, which in their language are called *Santilcos :* Nor was this all, for this Prince hearing that the deceased had been married at *Goa,* and likewise that he had left three daughters there behind him, which were very young and poor, he bestowed on them three hundred *Oqueas* of Gold, that are worth twelve *Crusadoes* of our mony a piece, a liberality truly royal, and which I relate here, as well to amplifie the noblenes of this Prince, as that it may serve for an example to others, and render them more charitable upon like occasions.

The next morning we continued our journey, making all the haste that possibly we could, to which end we got upon good Horses, that were given us by this Prince, and withall he appointed

pointed four of his servants to accompany us, who during our Voyage entertained us every where very sumptuously. That day our lodging was at a goodly place, called *Betenigus*, which signifies a royal house, and in-truth it was not without reason so named, for on whatsoever part one cast an eye it was invironed with gallant high Trees for three leagues about, nor is it to be credited how pleasing this Wood was, for that it was composed all of Cedars, Cypres, Palm, Date Trees, and Cocos, like to those in the *Indiaes*; Here we past the night with all kind of contentment; In the morning we proceeded on our journey, and travelling after five leagues a day we past over a great Plain, all full of goodly Corn; Then we arrived at a Mountain, named *Vangaleu*, inhabited by Jews, which were very white and handsom; Two days and an half after we came to a good Town, called *Fumbau*, not above two leagues distant from the Fort of *Gileytor*, there we found *Barbosa*, and the forty *Portugals* aforesaid, who received us with great demonstrations of joy, but not without shedding of some tears, for though they lived there at their ease, and were absolute Masters of all the Country, as they said, yet the consideration how they were as men banished from their Country into this place, did very much trouble them.

Now because it was night when we arrived, and that we had all need of rest, *Barbosa* was of the opinion that we should not see the Emperors Mother till the next morning, which was a Sunday, the fourth of *October*; that come, and we well refreshed, we went, accompanied with *Barbosa* and his forty *Portugals*, to the Princesses Palace, where we found her at Mass in her Chappel : A while after being advertised of our arrival, she caused us to be admitted into her presence ; Whereupon we fell on our knees before her, and with all kind of humility kissed the Ventilow that she held in her hand ; To these submissions we adjoyned many other Ceremonies according to their fashion, conformable to the instructions we had taken from the *Portugals* that conducted us thither. She received us with a smiling countenance, and to testifie how much she was pleased with our coming; *Verily*, said she, *you cannot imagine how glad I am to see you, that are right Christians, for it hath been a thing which I have always as much desired, as a fair garden enameled with flowers doth the mornings dew, wherefore you are most welcome come, and may your entrance into my house be as propitious, as that of the vertuous Queen* Helena's *was into blessed Jerusalem.* Herewith she made us to sit down upon mats, not above five or six paces distant from her ; Then shewing her self exceedingly contented, she questioned us about certain matters, of which, she assured us, that she very much longed to be satisfied : First she asked us the name of our holy Father the Pope, also how many Kings there were in Christendom, and whether any of us had ever been in the holy Land ; whereupon she much condemned the Christian Princes, for their neglect and want of care in seeking to ruine the power of the *Turk*, who, she said, was the common Enemy of them all. Likewise she would know of us whether the King of *Portugal* was great in the *Indiaes*, what Forts he had there, in what places they were seated, and how defended. She made us many other like demands, to the which we answered the best we could for to content her ; whereupon she dismissed us, and we returning to our lodging, continued there nine days, which we spent in waiting on this Princess, with whom we had much discourse on several subjects : That Term expired, we went to take our leaves of her, and in kissing of her hands she seemed to be somewhat troubled at our departure. *Truly*, said she, *it grieves me that you will be gone so soon, but since there is no remedy, I wish your Voyage may be so prosperous, that at your arrival in the Indiaes you may be as well received by yours, as the* Queen *of* Sheba *was heretofore by King* Solomon *in the admirable Palace of his greatness.* Now before we departed she bestowed on us twenty four *Oqueas* of Gold, which make two hundred forty Duckets of our mony ; She caused us also to be conducted by a *Naique*, and twenty *Abissins*, as well to serve us for Guides, and guard us from Robbers, whereof that Country was full, as to furnish us with Victuals and Horses until such time as we got to *Arquico*, where our Foists attended for us. This Princess also sent a rich present of divers Jewels of Gold and Stones by *Vasco Martins de Seixas* unto the Governor of the *Indiaes*, which by ill fortune was lost in this Voyage, as shall be declared hereafter.

§.2.   After we were returned to the Port of *Arquico*, where we found our companions caulking of our Foists, and furnishing them with all that was necessary for our Voyage, we fell to work with them for the space of nine days. At length all things being ready, we set sail, and parted from thence on Tuesday, the sixth of *November*, 1538. We carried with us both *Vasco Martins de Seixas*, that had the Present and a Letter from the Princess to the Governor of the

Indiaes,

Indiaes, as also an *Abiffin* Bishop, who was bound for *Portugal*, with an intent to go from thence to *Galicia*, *Rome*, and *Venice*, and afterwards to travel to *Jerufalem*, which especially he desired to see in regard of the holiness of the place. An hour before day we left the Port, and sailed along the Coast afore the wind, until such time as about noon we reached the point of the Cape of *Coçam*, and before we arrived at the Island of Rocks, we discerned three Vessels on the other side, that seemed to us to be *Gelvas* or *Terrades*, which are the names of the Vessels of that Country; Whereupon we gave them chace, and with the strength of our oars, because the wind was then somewhat down, we pursued them in such sort, that in less then two hours, having gotten up to them, we might easily perceive them to be *Turkish* Gallies, whereof we were no sooner assured, but that we presently betook our selves to flight, and made towards the Land with all the haste that might be, so if it were possible to escape the danger that inevitably threatned us: But whether the *Turks* suspected our design, or knew it, in less then a quarter of an hour they hoisted up all their sails, and having the wind favorable they followed us very hard, so as in a little while getting within a small faulcon shot of us, they discharged all their Ordnance upon us, wherewith they not only killed nine of our men, and hurt six and twenty, but so battered our Foists, that we were fain to cast a great part of our goods into the Sea; Mean while the *Turks* lost no time, but joyned us so close, that from their poop they hurt us easily with their pikes: Now there were four and forty good Soldiers remaining yet unhurt in our Foists, who knowing that upon their valor, and the force of their arms, depended the lives both of themselves, and all the rest, they determined to fight it out; With this resolution they set couragiously upon the Admiral of the three Gallies, wherein was *Solyman Dragut*, General of the Fleet; Their onset was so furious, as they invested her from poop to prow, and killed seven and twenty *Janizaries*, nevertheless she being instantly succored with fresh men by the other two Gallies, which had stayed a little behind, we were so wearied and oppressed with numbers, that we were not able to make any further resistance, for of four and fifty that we were at first, there was but eleven left alive, whereof two also dyed the next day, whom the *Turks* caused to be cut in quarters, which they hung at the end of their main yards for a sign of their Victory, and in that manner carried them to the Town of *Mocaa*, whereof the Father-in-law of the said *Solyman Dragut*, that had taken us, was Governor; who with all the Inhabitants waited the coming of his Son-in-law at the entry into the Port, to receive and welcome him for his Victory. In his Company he had a certain *Cacis*, who was *Moulana*, the chiefest Sacerdotal dignity, and because he had been a little before in pilgrimage at the Temple of their Prophet *Mahomet* in *Mecca*, he was held by all the people for a very holy man: This Imposter rode up and down the Town in a triumphant Charret, covered all over with Silk Tapestry, and with a deal of Ceremony blessed the people as he went along, exhorting them to render all possible thanks unto their Prophet for the Victory, which *Solyman Dragut* had obtained over us. As soon as they arrived at this place, we nine that remained alive were set on shore, tyed altogether with a great chain, and amongst us was the *Abiffin* Bishop, so pitifully wounded that he dyed the next day, and in his end shewed the repentance of a true Christian, which very much encouraged and comforted us. In the mean time all the Inhabitants, that were assembled about us, hearing that we were the Christians which were taken Captives, being exceedingly transported with choller, fell to beating of us in that cruel manner, as for my own part I never thought to have escaped alive out of their hands, whereunto they were especially incited by the wicked *Cacis*, who made them believe that they should obtain the more favor and mercy from their *Mahomet*, the worse they intreated us. Thus chained all together, and persecuted by every one, we were led in triumph over all the Town, where nothing was heard but acclamations and shouts, intermingled with a world of musick, as well of instruments, as voyces. Moreover, there was not a woman, were she never so retired, that came not forth then to see us, and to do us some outrage; for from the very least children to the oldest men, all that beheld us pass by cast out of the windows and balcons upon us pots of piss, and other filth, in contempt and derision of a name of a Christian, wherein every one strived to be most forward, in regard their cursed Priest continued still preaching unto them, that they should gain remission of their sins by abusing us. Having been tormented in this sort until the evening, they went and layd us bound as we were in a dark Dungeon, where we remained seventeen days, exposed to all kind of misery, having no other victual all that time, but a little oatmeal, which was distributed to us every morning to serve us all the day: Sometimes they gave us the same measure in dry Peason a little soaked in water, and this was all the meat we had.

CHAP.

CHAP. IV.

A Mutiny happening in the Town of Mocaa, *the occasion thereof, that which befell thereupon, and by what means I was carried to* Ormuz ; *as also my sailing from thence to* Goa, *and what success I had in that Voyage.*

§.1. THe next day, in regard that we had been so miserably moiled, and our hurts, that were great, but ill looked unto, of us nine there dyed two, whereof one was named *Nuno Delgado*, and the other *Andre Borges*, both of them men of courage, and of good families. The Jaylor, which in their language is called *Mocadan*, repairing in the morning to us, and finding our two companions dead, goes away in all haste therewith to acquaint the *Gauzil*, which is as the Judg with us, who came in person to the prison, attended by a great many of Officers, and other people ; Where having caused their irons to be striken off, and their feet to be tyed together with a rope, he commanded them so to be dragged from thence clean through the Town, where the whole multitude, to the very children, pursued and palted them with staves and stones, until such time as being wearied with harrying those poor bodies in such fashion, they cast them all battered to pieces into the Sea. At last we seven, that were left alive, were chained all together, and brought forth into the publique place of the Town, to be sold to them that would give most : There all the people being met together, I was the first that was put to sale ; whereupon, just as the Cryer was offering to deliver me unto whomsoever would buy me, in comes that very *Cacis Moulana*, whom they held for a Saint, with ten or eleven other *Cacis* his Inferiors, all Priests like himself of their wicked Sect, and addressing his speech to *Heredrin Sofo*, the Governor of the Town, who sate as President of the Portsale, he required him to send us, as an alms, unto the Temple of *Mecqua*, saying, that he was upon returning thither, and having resolved to make that pilgrimage in the name of all the people, it were not fit to go thither without carrying some offering to the Prophet *Noby*, (so they termed their *Mahomet*,) a thing, said he, that would utterly displease *Razaadat Moulana*, the Chief Priest of *Medina Talnab*, who without that would grant no kind of grace or pardon to the Inhabitants of this Town, which by reason of their great offences stood in extream need of the favor of God, and of his Prophet.

The Governor having heard the *Cacis* speak thus, declared unto him that for his particular he had no power to dispose with any part of the booty, and that therefore he should apply himself to *Solyman Dragut* his Son-in-law, who had made us slaves, so that in right it appertained only unto him to do with us as he pleased ; and I do not think, added he, that he will contradict so holy an intention as this is. Thou hast reason for it, answered the *Cacis*, but withall thou must know, that the things of God, and the alms that are done in his name, lose their value and force, when they are sifted through so many hands, and turmoiled with such humane opinions, for which very cause seldom doth any divine resolution follow thereupon, especially in a subject such as this is, which thou mayst absolutely dispose of, as thou art soveraign Commander of this people : Moreover, as there is no body can be displeased therewith, so I do not see how it can bring thee any discontent. For besides that, this demand is very just, it is also most agreeable to our Prophet *Noby*, who is the absolute Lord of this prize, in regard the Victory came solely from his holy hand, though with as much falshood as malice thou goest about to attribute the glory of it to the valor of thy Son-in-law, and the courage of his Soldiers. At this instant a *Janizary* was present, Captain of one of the three Gallies that took us, a man that for his exceeding valor was in great esteem amongst them, called *Copa Geynal*, who netled with that which he heard the *Cacis* speak, so much in contempt both of himself, and the rest of the Soldiers, that had carried themselves very valiantly in the fight with us, returned him this answer. Certainly you might do better for the Salvation of your Soul, to distribute some part of the excessive riches you possess amongst these poor Soldiers, then seek with feigned speeches, full of hypocrisie and deceit, to rob them of these slaves, which have cost the lives of so many brave men, their fellows in arms, and have been dearly bought by us that survive, even with our dearest blood, as the wounds we have upon us can but too well witness ; so can it not be said of your Cabayage (a Sacerdotal Robe after their fashion,) which for all it sits so trim and neat upon you, covers a pernicious habit you have of purloyning other mens estates from them : Wherefore I would wish you to desist from the damnable plot you have layd against the absolute Masters of this Prize, whereof you shall not have so much as a token, and

seek

seek out some other Present for the *Cacis* of *Mecqua*, to the end he may conceal your theeveries, and impiety, provided it be not done with the expence of our lives and blood, but rather with the goods you have so lewdly gotten by your wicked and cunning devices.

This *Cacis Moulana* having received so bold an answer from this Captain, found it very rude, and hard of digestion, which made him in bitter terms, and voyd of all respects, exceedingly to blame the Captain, and the Soldiers that were there present, who, as well *Turks* as *Saracens*, being much offended with his ill language, combined together and mutined against him, and the rest of the people, in whose favor he had spoken so insolently; nor could this mutiny be appeased by any kind of means, though the Governor of the Town, Father-in-law to the said *Solyman Dragut*, together with the Officers of Justice, did all that possibly they could. In a word, that I may not stand longer upon the particulars of this affair, I say, that from this small mutiny did arise so cruel and enraged a contention, as it ended not but with the death of six hundred persons, of the one and the other side: But at length the Soldiers party prevailing, they pillaged the most part of the Town, especially the said *Cacis Moulana*'s house, killing seven wives and nine children that he had, whose bodies together with his own were dismembered, and cast into the Sea with a great deal of cruelty. In the same manner they intreated all that belonged unto him, not so much as giving life to one that was known to be his. As for us seven *Portugals*, which were exposed to sale in the publique place, we could find out no better expedient to save our lives, then to return into the same hole, from whence we came, and that too without any Officer of Justice to carry us thither; neither did we take it for a small favor that the Jaylor would receive us into the prison. Now this Mutiny had not ceased but by the authority of *Solyman Dragut*, General of the Gallies aforesaid; For this man with very gentle words gave an end to the sedition of the people, and pacified the Mutiners, which shews of what power courtesie is, even with such as are altogether ignorant of it. In the mean time *Heredrin Sopho*, Governor of the Town, came off but ill from this hurly burly, by reason that in the very first incounter he had one of his arms almost cut off. Three days after this disorder was quieted we were led all seven again to the Market place, there to be sold with the rest of the booty, which consisted of our Stuff, and Ordnance, that they had taken in our Foists, and were sold at a very easie rate: For my self, miserable that I was, and the most wretched of them all, Fortune, my sworn enemy, made me fall into the hands of a *Greek* renegado, whom I shall detest as long as I have a day to live, because that in the space of three Months I was with him, he used me so cruelly, that becoming even desparate, for that I was not able to endure the evil he did me, I was seven or eight times upon the point to have poysoned my self, which questionless I had done, if God of his infinite mercy and goodness had not diverted me from it, whereunto I was the rather induced to make him lose the mony he payd for me, because he was the most covetous man in the world, and the most inhumane, and cruellest enemy to the name of a *Christian*. But at the end of three Months it pleased the Almighty to deliver me out of the hands of this Tyrant, who for fear of losing the mony I cost him, if I should chance to make my self away, as one of his neighbors perswaded him I would, telling him that he had discovered so much by my countenance, and manner of behavior, wherefore in pity of me he counselled him to sell me away, as he did not long after unto a *Jew*, named *Abraham Muça*, Native of a Town, called in those quarters *Toro*, not above a league and an half distant from Mount *Sinay*: This man gave for me the value of three hundred Reals in Dates, which was the Merchandise that this *Jew* did ordinarily trade in with my late Master, and so I parted with him in the company of divers Merchants for to go from *Babylon* to *Cayxem*, whence he carried me to *Ormuz*, and there presented me to *Don Fernand de Lima*, who was at that time Captain of the Fort, and to Doctor *Pedro Fernandez*, Commissary General of the *Indiaes*, that was then residing at *Ormuz* for the service of the King by order from the Governor *Nunho de Cunha*. These two, namely *Fernandez* and *de Lima* gave the Jew in recompence for me two hundred *Pardaos*, which are worth three shillings and nine pence a piece of our coyn, whereof part was their own mony, and the rest was raised of the alms which they caused to be gathered for me in the Town, so we both remained contented, the Jew for the satisfaction he had received from them, and I to find my self at full liberty as before.

Seeing my self by Gods mercy delivered from the miseries I had endured; after I had been seventeen days at *Ormuz*, I imbarqued my self for the *Indiaes* in a ship that belonged to one *Jorge Fernandez Taborda*, who was to carry Horses to *Goa*. In the course that we held we sailed with so prosperous a gale, that in seventeen days we arrived in view of the Fort of *Diu*; §.2.

There

There, by the advice of the Captains, coasting along by the Land for to learn some news, we descryed a great number of fires all that night, also at times we heard divers Pieces of Ordnance discharged, which very much troubled us, by reason we could not imagine what those fires, or that shooting in the night should mean, in so much that we were divided into several opinions. During this incertainty our best advice was, to sail the rest of the night with as little cloth as might be, until that on the next morning by the favor of day light we perceived a great many sails, which invironed the Fort on all sides. Some affirmed that it was the Governor newly come from *Goa* to make peace for the death of *Sultan Bandur*, King of *Cambaya*, that was slain a little before. Others said that it was the Infant, Brother to the King *Dom Jovan*, lately arrived there from *Portugal*, because he was every day expected in the *Indiaes*. Some thought that it was the *Patemarcaa*, with the King of *Cabicuts* hundred Foists of *Camorin*. And the last assured us, how they could justifie with good and sufficient reasons that they were the *Turks*. As we were in this diversity of minds, and terrified with that which we discerned before our eyes, five very great Gallies came forth of the midst of this Fleet, with a many of banners, flags, and streamers, which we saw on the tops of their Masts, and the ends of their sailyards, whereof some were so long that they touched even the very water. These Gallies, being come forth in this sort, turned their prows towards us in such a couragious and confident manner, that by their sailing we presently judged them to be *Turks*; Which we no sooner knew to be so indeed, but we clapt on all our cloth, for to avoyd them, and to get into the main Sea, not without exceeding fear, lest for our sins we should fall into the like estate, from whence I was so lately escaped. These five Gallies having observed our flight, took a resolution to pursue us, and chased us till night, at which time it pleased God that they tacked about, and returned to the Army from whence they came. Seeing our selves freed from so great a danger we went joyfully on, and two days after arrived at the Town of *Chaul*, where our Captain and the Merchants only landed for to visit the Captain of the Fort, named *Simon Guedez*, unto whom they reported that which had befallen them. Assuredly, said he, you are very much bound to give God thanks for delivering you from one of the greatest perils that ever you were in, for without his assistance it had been impossible for you ever to have declined it, or to tell me of it with such joy as now you do: Thereupon he declared unto them, that the Army they had incountred was the very same, which had held *Antonio de Silveyra* twenty days together besieged, being composed of a great number of *Turks*, whereof *Solyman* the *Bassa*, Vice-roy of *Caire*, was General, and that those Sails they had seen, were eight and fifty Gallies great and small, each of which carried five Pieces of Ordnance in her prow, and some of them were Pieces of Battery, besides eight other great Vessels, full of *Turks*, that were kept in reserve to succor the Army, and supply the places of such as should be killed; Moreover he added, that they had great abundance of victuals, amongst the which there was twelve Basilisks. This news having much amazed us, we rendered infinite praise to the Lord for shewing us such grace, as to deliver us from so imminent a danger.

§.3. We stayed at *Chaul* but one day, and then we set sail for *Goa*; Being advanced as far as to the River of *Carapatan*, we met with *Fernand de Morais*, Captain of three Foists, who by the command of the Vice-roy, *Dom Garcia de Noronha*, was going to *Dabul*, to the end he might see whether he could take or burn a *Turkish* Vessel, which was in the Port, laden with Victuals by order from the *Bassa*. This *Fernand de Morais* had no sooner gotten acquaintance of our ship, but he desired our Captain to lend him fifteen men, of twenty that he had, for to supply the great necessity he was in that way, by reason of the Vice-roys hastening him away upon the sudden, which, said he, would much advance the service both of God, and his Highness. After many contestations of either part upon this occasion, and which, to make short, I will pass under silence, at length they were agreed, that our Captain should let *Fernand de Morais* have twelve, of fifteen men, that he requested, wherewithall he was very well satisfied: Of this number I was one, as being always of the least respected. The ship departing for *Goa*, *Fernand de Morais* with his three Foists continued his Voyage towards the Port of *Dabul*, where we arrived the next day about nine of the clock in the morning, and presently took a Patach of *Malabar*, which laden with Cotton Wool and Pepper, rode at anchor in the midst of the Port. Having taken it we put the Captain and Pilot to torture, who instantly confessed that a few days before a ship came into that Port expresly from the *Bassa* to lade Victuals, and that there was in her an Embassador, who had brought *Hidalcan* a very rich *Cabaya*, that is a garment worn by the Gentlemen of that Country, which he would not accept of, for that

thereby

thereby he would not acknowledg himself subject to the *Turk*, it being a custom among the *Mahumetans*, for the Lord to do that honor to his Vassal; and further, that this refusal had so much vexed the Embassador, as he returned without taking any kind of provision of Victuals, and that *Hidalcan* had answered, he made much more esteem of the King of *Portugals* amity, then of his, which was nothing but deceit, as having usurped the Town of *Goa* upon him, after he had offered to ayd him with his favor and forces to regain it. Moreover they said, that it was not above two days since the ship, they spake of, parted from the Port, and that the Captain of her, named *Cide Ale*, had denounced War against *Hidalcan*, vowing that as soon as the Fort of *Diu* was taken, which could not hold out above eight days, according to the estate wherein he had left it, *Hidalcan* should lose his Kingdom, or life, and that then he should to his cost know how little the *Portugals*, in whom he put his confidence, could avail him. With these news Captain *Morais* returned towards *Goa*, where he arrived two days after, and gave accompt to the Vice-roy of that which had past. There we found *Gonçallo vaz Coutinho*, who was going with five Foifts to *Onor*, to demand of the Queen thereof one of the Gallies of *Solymans* Army, which by a contrary wind had been driven into her Ports: Now one of the Captains of those Foifts my special friend, seeing me poor and necessitous, perswaded me to accompany him in this Voyage, and to that end got me five duckets pay, which I very gladly accepted of, out of the hope I had that God would thereby open me a way to a better fortune. Being imbarqued then, the Captain and Soldiers pitying the case I was in, bestowed such spare clothes as they had upon me, by which means being reasonably well pieced up again, we parted the next morning from the Road of *Bardees*, and the Monday following we cast anchor in the Port of *Onor*; where, that the inhabitants of the place might know how little account we made of that mighty Army, we gave them a great peal of Ordnance, putting forth all our fights, beating our Drums, and sounding our Trumpets, to the end that by these exterior demonstrations they might conclude we regarded not the *Turks* awhit.

CHAP. V.

Gonçallo vaz Coutinho's Treaty with the Queen of Onor; *his assaulting of a Turkish Galley, and that which hapned unto us as we were upon our return to* Goa.

OUr Fleet making a stand upon the discharging of our peal of Ordnance, the General *Gonçallo vaz Coutinho* sent *Bento Cassanho*, a very discreet and eloquent man, to the Queen of *Onor*, to present her with a Letter from the Vice-roy, and to tell her that he was come to complain of her, for that she had sworn a peace and amity with the King of *Portugal*, and yet suffered the *Turks*, mortal enemies to the *Portugals*, to abide in her Ports. Hereunto she returned this answer; *That both himself and his company were very welcome, that she greatly esteemed of them, because they were Vassals to the King of* Portugal, *and as touching that he said of the peace which she had with the King, and his Governors, it was most true, and that she desired to maintain it as long as she lived: For that which he said of the Turks, she took her God to witness how much against her will she had received and suffered them in her Ports, but that finding her self too weak for to resist such powerful enemies, she was constrained to dissemble, which she would never have done had she been furnished with sufficient forces; furthermore, to clear her self the better unto them, she offered both her power and people for to repel them out of her Ports, and whereas he had brought men enough to chace them thence, she requested him to do it, wherein she would assist him all that possibly she could, which she confirmed with oaths, swearing by the golden Sandals of the Soveraign God whom she adored:* To this speech she added, *that she should be as well pleased if God would give him the victory over them, as if the King of* Narsingua, *whose slave she was, should set her at the table with his wife.* *Gonçallo vaz Coutinho* having received this Embassage, and other complements from the Queen, though he had little hope of any performance on her part, yet did he wisely dissemble it. Afterwards being fully informed by the people of the Country of the *Turks* intention, of the place where they were, and what they did at that instant, he called a Councel thereupon, and having throughly debated and considered all things, it was unanimously concluded, that both for the King of *Portugal* their Masters honor, and his own, it was expedient to set upon this Galley, either for to take, or fire it, wherein it was hoped that God, for whose glory we fought, would be assisting to us against those enemies of his holy Faith. This resolution being made, and signed by us all, he entered some two faulcons shot within the River, where he had

C 2 scarce

scarce anchored, when as a little Boat, which they call an *Almadia,* came aboard us, with a *Brachman* that spake very good *Portugueze :* This man delivered a message from the Queen unto our Captain, whereby she earnestly desired him, that for the Vice-roys sake he would desist from the enterprize he had undertaken, and not to assault the *Turks* any manner of way, which, said she, could not be done without great disadvantage, for that she had been advertised by her Spies, that they had fortified themselves with a good Trench, which they had cast up near the place where they had moored their Galley, in regard whereof it seemed to her almost impossible for him with no more Forces then he had to be able to prevail in so great an attempt : wherefore she took her God to witness how much she was troubled with the fear she was in lest some misfortune should betide him. Hereunto our Captain returned an answer full of wisdom and courtesie, saying, that he kissed her Highness hands for the extraordinary favor she did him in giving him so good advice : but as for his Combat with the *Turks* he could not follow her counsel, and therefore would proceed in his determination, it being always the custom of the *Portugals* not to enquire whether their Enemies were few, or many, since the more they were, the more should be their loss, and the greater his profit and honor. Thus was the *Brachman* dismissed, our Captain bestowing on him a piece of green Chamlet, and an Hat lined with red Sattin, wherewith he returned very well contented.

§.2.   The *Brachman* dismist, *Gonçallo vaz Coutinho* resolved to fight with the *Turks* but before he proceeded any further he was advertised by Spies what stratagems the Enemy would use against us, and that the precedent night by the favor of the Queen they had moored up the Galley, and by it raised up a platform, whereupon they had flanked five and twenty Pieces of Ordnance, but all that stayed him not from advancing towards the Enemy ; Seeing himself then within a Cannon shot of them, he went out of his Foist, and with fourscore men only landed, the rest which he had brought with him from *Goa* for this enterprize, being but an hundred more, he left for the guard of the Foists. So after he had set his men in Battel array, he marched couragiously against his adversaries, who perceiving us making towards them valiantly resolved to defend themselves, to which end they sallied some five and twenty or thirty paces out of their Trenches, where the fight began on either side with such fury, that in less then a quarter of an hour five and forty lay dead in the place, amongst the which there was not above eight of ours ; Hereupon our General, not contented with this first charge, gave them a second, by means whereof it pleased God to make them turn their backs, in such sort that they retired pell-mell, as men routed and in fear of death : Mean while we pursued them to their very Trenches, where they turned upon us, and made head anew, in the heat hereof we were so far engaged and intangled together, that we knocked one another with the pummels of our swords; Mean while our Foists arrived, which were come along by the shore to succor us, and accordingly they discharged all their Ordnance upon our Enemies, to such good purpose, as they killed eleven or twelve of the valiantest *Janizaries,* which wore green Turbants, as a mark of their Nobility. The death of these so terrified the rest, that they presently forsook the field, by means whereof we had leasure to set the Galley on fire upon the express command of our General *Gonçallo,* so that having cast into her five pots of powder, the fire took hold on her with such violence, as it was apparant it could not be long before she were utterly consumed, for the mast and sail yards were all of a flame, had not the *Turks,* knowing the danger she was in, most couragiously quenched the fire ; but we labored all that possibly we could to hinder them from it, and to make good that we had so bravely begun, which the enemies perceiving, as their last refuge they gave fire to a great Piece of Ordnance, which charged with stones, and other shot, killed six of ours, whereof the principal was *Diego vas Coutinho,* the Generals son, besides a dozen others were hurt, that put us quite in disorder; Whereupon the Enemies finding how they had spoiled us, fell to shouting in sign of Victory, and to rendring of thanks to their *Mahomet ;* at the naming of this their false Prophet, whom they invoked, our General the better to encourage his Soldiers, *Fellows in arms,* said he, *seeing these Dogs call upon the Devil to ayd them, let us pray unto our Saviour Jesus Christ to assist us.* This said, we once more assaulted the Trench, which the Enemies no sooner perceived, but they craftily turned their backs, and took their flight towards the Galley, but they were instantly followed by some of ours, who within a while made themselves Masters of all their Trenches, in the mean time the Infidels gave fire to a secret myne, which they had made a little within their Trenches, and blew up six of our *Portugals,* and eight Slaves, maiming many others besides ; Now the smoak was such and so thick, as we could hardly discern one another, in regard

whereof

whereof our General, fearing leaſt ſome greater loſs then the former ſhould befall him, re-treated to the water ſide, carrying along with him both the dead bodies, and all the hurt men, and ſo went where his Foiſts lay, into the which every one being imbarqued, we returned with ſtrength of rowing to the place from whence we came, where with extream ſorrow he cauſed the ſlain to be interred, and all that were hurt to be dreſt, which were a very great number.

The ſame day that was ſo fatal to us, a liſt being taken of all the ſurviving Soldiers, that ſo it might be known how many had been loſt in the laſt fight upon aſſaulting of the Trench, we found that of fourſcore which we were, there was fifteen ſlain, fifty four hurt, and nine quite maimed for ever : The reſt of the day, and the night following, we kept very good watch to avoyd all ſurprizes of the Enemy. As ſoon as the next morning appeared, there came an Embaſſador from the Queen of *Onor* to the General *Gonçallo*, with a Preſent of Hens, Chickens, and new layd Eggs for the relief of our ſick men ; Now though we had great need of thoſe things, yet in ſtead of receiving our General utterly refuſed them, and ſhewing himſelf very much dis-pleaſed with the Queen he could not forbear laſhing out ſome words, that were a little more harſher then was requiſite ; ſaying, that the Vice-roy ſhould ere long be advertiſed of the bad Offices ſhe had rendred the King of *Portugal*, and how much he was obliged to pay her that debt, when occaſion ſhould ſerve : Further he bid him tell her, that for an aſſurance of that which he ſaid, he had left his ſon dead and buried in her Land, together with the other *Portu-gals*, who had been miſerably ſlaughtered through her practiſes, by aſſiſting the *Turks* againſt them : and in a word, that he would thank her more fully another time for the Preſent ſhe had ſent, the better to diſſemble what ſhe had executed againſt him, for which he would one day return her a recompence according to her merit.

The Embaſſador, very much terrified with this ſpeech, departed ; and being come to the Queen his Miſtreſs, he ſo throughly repreſented *Gonçallo's* anſwer unto her, as ſhe greatly doubted that this Galley would be an occaſion of the loſs of her Kingdom ; wherefore to decline ſo great a miſchief ſhe thought it neceſſary to ſeek by all means poſſible to maintain the League with our General, to which end ſhe aſſembled her Councel, by whoſe advice ſhe diſpatched another Embaſſador unto him, who was a *Brachman*, a grave and reverent perſonage, and her neareſt kinſman. At his arrival where our Foiſts lay, our General gave him very good enter-tainment, and after the ordinary ceremonies and complements the *Brachman* having demand-ed permiſſion to deliver his Embaſſage ; *Signior*, ſaid he to out Governor, *if you will give me audience, I will declare the cauſe of my coming hither from the Queen of* Onor *my Mi-ſtreſs.* Hereunto *Gonçallo* replyed, *That Embaſſadors had always aſſurance for their per-ſons, and permiſſion freely to deliver the particulars of their Embaſſy, ſo that he might boldly ſay what he would.* The *Brachman* having thanked him, *Verily,* continued he, *I am not able to expreſs unto you, how ſenſible the Queen my Miſtreſs is of the death of your ſon, and of thoſe other* Portugals, *that were yeſterday ſlain in the fight ; And without lying I ſwear un-to you by her life, and by this ſtring of a Brachman that I wear, the mark of my Prieſtly dig-nity, and only proper to thoſe which are of that profeſſion, wherein I have been exerciſed from my youth, that ſhe was ſo exceedingly afflicted at the notice of your diſaſter, and the un-luckie ſucceſs of your conflict, as ſhe could not have been more vexed if ſhe had been made to eat Cows fleſh (which is the greateſt ſin committed amongſt us) at the principal gate of the Temple, where her father is interred : Whereby you may judg, Signior, what a ſhare ſhe bears of your ſorrow. But ſince there is no remedy for things done, ſhe deſireth, and very inſtantly beſeecheth you to confirm the Peace unto her anew which other Governers have al-ways granted her heretofore ; Whereunto ſhe the rather intreats you, becauſe ſhe knows of what power you are with the Vice-roy : Now that confirmed unto her, ſhe aſſures you, and faithfully promiſeth, within four days to burn the Galley, that hath put you to ſo much pain, and turn the Turks out of the limits of her Kingdom, which is all that ſhe can do, and which you may be moſt confident ſhe will not fail to execute accordingly.*

Our General knowing of what importance this affair was, preſently accepted of the *Brach-mans* offer, and told him that he was contented that the League ſhould be renewed betwixt them, according whereunto it was inſtantly publiſhed on either part with all the ceremonies accuſtomed in ſuch caſes ; Thereupon the *Brachman* returned to the Queen, who afterwards labored all ſhe could to make good her word ; But becauſe *Gonçallo* could not ſtay the four days, which ſhe had demanded, in regard of the extream danger he ſhould thereby have expoſed

our

our hurt men unto, he refolved to be gone, and fo the fame day after dinner we departed; Howbeit he firft left one, named *Georgio Neogueyra*, there, with exprefs order exactly to obferve all that was done concerning that affair, and thereof to give certain intelligence to the Vice-roy, as the Queen her felf had requefted.

CHAP. VI.

What paffed till fuch time as Pedro de Faria *arrived at* Malaca; *his receiving an Embaffador from the King of* Batas; *with his fending me to that King, and that which arrived to me in that Voyage.*

§.1. THe next day our General *Gonçallo vaz Coutinho* arrived at *Goa*, with fo many of us as remained alive; There he was exceedingly welcomed by the Vice-roy, unto whom he rendred an accompt of his Voyage, as alfo of that which he had concluded with the Queen of *Onor*, who had promifed to burn the Galley within four days, and to chace the *Turks* out of all the Confines of her Kingdom, wherewith the Vice-roy was very well fatisfied. In the mean time after I had remained three and twenty days in the faid Town of *Goa*, where I was cured of two hurts which I had received in fight at the *Turks* Trenches, the neceffity whereunto I faw my felf reduced, and the counfel of a Fryer, my Friend, perfwaded me to offer my fervice unto a Gentleman, named *Pedro de Faria*, that was then newly preferred to the Charge of Captain of *Malaca*, who upon the firft motion was very willing to entertain me for a Soldier, and promifed me withall to give me fomething over and above the reft of his Company during the Voyage which he was going to make with the Vice-roy. For it was at that very time when as the Vice-roy *Dom Garcia de Noronha* was preparing to go to the fuccor of the Fortrefs of *Diu*, which he certainly knew was befieged, and in great danger to be taken, by reafon of the great Forces wherewithall it was invefted by the *Turk*, and to relieve it the Vice-roy had affembled a mighty Fleet at *Goa*, confifting of about two hundred and twenty five Veffels, whereof fourfcore and three were great ones, namely Ships, Gallions, Carvels, and the reft Brigantins, Foifts, and Galleys, wherein it was faid there were ten thoufand Land-men, and thirty thoufand Mariners, befides a great number of Slaves. The time of fetting fail being come, and the Foifts provided of all things neceffary, the Vice-roy imbarqued himfelf on *Saturday* the fourteenth of *November*, 1538. Howbeit five days paft away before he put out of the Haven, in regard he ftayed for his men that were not all ready to imbarque, the mean while a Catur arrived from the Town of *Diu* with a Letter from *Antonio de Silveyra*, Captain of the Fortrefs, whereby he advertifed the Vice-roy, that the *Turks* had raifed the fiege, and were retired. Now though thefe were good news, yet was the whole Fleet grieved thereat for the great defire every one had to fight with the Enemies of our Faith. Hereupon the Vice-roy abode there five days longer, during the which he took order for all things neceffary to the confervation of his Government of the *Indiaes*, and then commanding to hoift fail he departed from *Goa* on a Thurfday morning the fixteenth of *December*: The fourteenth of his Navigation he went and caft anchor at *Chaul*, where he remained three days, during the which he entred into conference with *Inezamuluco*, a *Mahometan* Prince, and took order for certain affairs very much importing the furety of the Fortrefs: After that he canfed fome of the Veffels of the Fleet to be rigged, which he furnifhed with Soldiers and Victuals, and then departed for to go to *Diu*; But it was his ill fortune, as he was crofing the Gulph, to be fuddenly overtaken by fuch a furious Tempeft, that it not only feparated his Fleet, but was the lofs of many Veffels, chiefly of the Baftard Galley, which was caft away at the mouth of the River *Dabul*, whereof *Dom Alvaro de Noronha*, the Vice-roys fon, and General of the Sea-forces, was Captain; In the fame Gulph alfo perifhed the Galley named *Efpinheyro*, commanded by *Jovan de Sonfa*, howbeit the moft part of their men were faved by *Chriftophilo de Gama*, who came moft opportunely to their fuccor. During this Tempeft there were feven other fhips likewife caft away, the names of which I have forgotten, in fo much that it was a month before the Vice-roy could recover himfelf of the lofs he had fuftained, and re-affemble his Fleet again which this ftorm had fcattered in divers places: At length the fixteenth of *January*, 1539. he arrived at the Town of *Diu*, where he caufed the Fortrefs to be re-built, the greater part whereof had been demolifhed by the *Turks*, fo as it feemed that it had been defended by the befieged, rather by miracle, then force: Now to effect it the better he made proclamation, that all the Captains with their Soldiers fhould each of them take in charge to re-build that quarter, which fhould be allotted

lotted them; and because never a Commander there had more then *Pedro de Faria*, he thought fit to appoint him the Bulwark, which looked to the Sea, for his quarter, together with the out-wall that was on the Lands side; wherein he bestowed such care and diligence, that in six and twenty days space, both the one and the other were restored to a better state then before, by the means of three hundred Soldiers that were employed about it. This done, for that it was the fourteenth of *March*, and a fit time for Navigation to *Malaca*, *Pedro de Faria* set sail for *Goa*, where by vertue of a Pattent granted him by the Vice-roy he furnished himself with all things necessary for his Voyage; Departing then from *Goa* on the thirteenth of *April* with a Fleet of eight Ships, four Foists, and one Galley, wherein there were five hundred men, he had so favorable a wind, that he arrived at *Malaca* the fifth day of *June* in the same year, 1539.

Pedro de Faria succeeding *Dom Estevano de Gama* in the Charge of Captain of *Malaca*, §.2. arrived there safely with his Fleet, nothing hapning in his Voyage worthy of writing. Now because at his arrival, *Estevan de Gama* had not yet ended the time of his Commission, he was not put into the possession of that Government until the day that he was to enter upon his Charge. Howbeit, in regard *Pedro de Faria* was ere long to be Governor of the Fortress, the neighboring Kings sent their Embassadors to congratulate with him, and to make a tender of their amity, and of a mutual conservation of Peace with the King of *Portugal*. Amongst these Embassadors there was one from the King of *Batas*, who raigned in the Isle of *Samatra*, where it is held for a surety that the Island of Gold is, which the King of *Portugal*, *Dom Joana* the Third, had resolved should have been discovered by the advice of certain Captains of the Country. This Embassador, that was Brother-in-law to the King of *Batas*, named *Aquarem Dabolay*, brought him a rich Present of Wood of *Aloes*, *Calambaa*, and five quintals of *Benjamon* in flowers, with a Letter written on the bark of a Palm tree, where these words were inserted.

More ambitious then all men of the service of the crowned Lyon, seated in the dreadful Throne of the Sea, the rich and mighty Prince of Portugal, thy Master and mine, to whom, in thee Pedro de Faria, I do now render obedience with a sincere and true amity, to the end I may become his Subject with all the purity and affection which a Vassal is obliged to carry unto his Master; I Angeessiry Timorraia, King of Batas, desiring to insinuate my self into thy friendship, that thy Subjects may be inriched with the fruits of this my Country, I do offer by a new Treaty to replenish the Magazins of thy King, who is also mine, with Gold, Pepper, Camfire, Benjamon, and Aloes, upon condition that with an entire confidence thou shalt send me a safe conduct, written and assigned with thine own hand, by means whereof all my Lanchares and Jurupanges may navigate in safety. Furthermore, in favor of this new amity, I do again beseech thee to succor me with some Powder and great Shot, whereof thou hast but too much in thy Store-houses, and therefore mayst well spare them; for I had never so great need of all kind of warlike munitions as at this present. This granted, I shall be much indebted to thee if by thy means I may once chastise those perjured Achems, the mortal and eminent Enemies of thy Malaca, with whom, I swear to thee, I will never have peace as long as I live, until such time as I have had satisfaction for the blood of my three children, which call upon me for vengeance, and that therewith I may asswage the sorrow of their noble Mother, who having given them suck, and brought them up, hath seen them since miserably butchered by that cruel Tyrant of Achem in the Towns of Jacur and Lingua, as thou shalt be more particularly informed by Aquarem Dabolay, the Brother of those childrens desolate Mother, whom I have sent unto thee for a confirmation of our new amity, to the end, Signior, that he may treat with thee about such things as shall seem good unto thee, as well for the service of God, as for the good of thy people. From Paniau the fifth day of the eighth Moon.

This Embassador received from *Pedro de Faria* all the honor that he could do him after their manner, and as soon as he had delivered him the Letter it was translated into the *Portugal* out of the *Malayan* Tongue wherein it was written. Whereupon the Embassador by his Interpreter declared the occasion of the discord, which was between the Tyrant of *Achem*, and the King of *Batas*, proceeding from this, that the Tyrant had not long before propounded unto this King of *Batas*, who was a Gentile, the imbracing of *Mahomets* Law, conditionally that he would wed him to a Sister of his, for which purpose he should quit his wife, that was also a Gentile, and married to him six and twenty years; Now because the King of *Batas* would by no means condescend thereunto, the Tyrant, incited by a *Cacis* of his, immediately denounced

3

denounced War against him : So each of them having raised a mighty Army, they fought a most bloody Battel, that continued three hours, and better, during the which the Tyrant perceiving the advantage the *Bataes* had of him, after he had lost a great number of his people, he made his retreat into a Mountain, called *Cagerrendan*, where the *Bataes* held him besieged by the space of three and twenty days, but because in that time many of the Kings men fell sick, and that also the Tyrants Camp began to want Victuals, they concluded a Peace, upon condition that the Tyrant should give the King five bars of Gold (which are in value two hundred thousand crowns of our mony) for to pay his Soldiers, and that the King should marry his eldest son to that sister of the Tyrant, who had been the cause of making that War. This accord being signed by either part, the King returned into his Country, where he was no sooner arrived, but relying on this Treaty of Peace he dismist his Army, and discharged all his Forces. The tranquillity of this Peace lasted not above two months and an half, in which time there came to the Tyrant three hundred *Turks*, whom he had long expected from the Straight of *Mecqua*, and for them had sent four Vessels laden with Pepper, wherein also were brought a great many Cases full of Muskets and Hargebusezes, together with divers Pieces both of Brass and Iron Ordnance. Whereupon the first thing the Tyrant did was to joyn those three hundred *Turks* to some Forces he had still afoot, then making as though he would go to *Pacem* for to take in a Captain that was revolted against him, he cunningly fell upon two places, named *Jacur* and *Lingua*, that appertained to the King of *Batas*, which he suddenly surprized when they within them least thought of it, for the Peace newly made between them took away all the mistrust of such an attempt, so as by that means it was easie for the Tyrant to render himself Master of those Fortresses. Having taken them he put three of the Kings sons to death, and seven hundred *Ouroballones*, so are the noblest and the valiantest of the Kingdom called. This while the King of *Batas*, much resenting, and that with good cause, so great a Treachery, sware by the head of his god *Quiay Hocombinor*, the principal Idol of the Gentiles sect, who hold him for their god of Justice, never to eat either fruit, salt, or any other thing, that might bring the least gust to his palate, before he had revenged the death of his children, and drawn reason from the Tyrant for this loss; protesting further, that he was resolved to dye in the maintenance of so just a War. To which end, and the better to bring it to pass, the King of *Batas* straightway assembled an Army of fifteen thousand men, as well natives, as strangers, wherewithall he was assisted by some Princes his friends : and to the same effect he emplored the Forces of us Christians, which was the reason why he sought to contract that new amity, we have spoken of before, with *Pedro de Faria*, who was very well contented with it, in regard he knew that it greatly imported, both the service of the King of *Portugal*, and the conservation of the Fortress, besides that by this means he hoped very much to augment the Revenue of the Customs, together with his own particular, and all the rest of the *Portugals* profit, in regard of the great Trade they had in those Countries of the *South*.

§.3.   After that the King of *Batas* Embassador had been seventeen days with us, *Pedro de Faria* dismissed him, having first granted whatsoever the King his Master had demanded, and something over and above, as fire-pots, darts, and murdering Pieces, wherewith the Embassador departed from the Fortress so contented, that he shed tears for joy, nay, it was observed, that passing by the great door of the Church, he turned himself towards it, with his hands and eyes lift up to Heaven, and then as it were praying to God ; *Almighty Lord,* said he openly, *that in rest and great joy livest there above seated on the Treasure of thy Riches, which are the spirits formed by thy Will, here I promise thee, if it may be thy good pleasure to give us the victory against this Tyrant of Achem, and to permit us to regain that from him, which with such notable treachery he hath taken from us in those places of* Jacur *and* Lingua, *We will always most faithfully and sincerely acknowledg thee according to the Law of the* Portugals, *and according to that holy Verity, Wherein consists the Salvation of all that are born in the World : Furthermore, in our Country we will build fair Temples unto thee, perfumed with sweet odours, Where all living Souls shall on their bended knees adore thee, as it hath been always used to be done unto this present in the Land of* Portugal. *And hear what besides I promise, and swear unto thee with all the assuredness of a good and faithful servant, that the King my Master shall never acknowledg any other King then the great* Portugal, *Who is now Lord of* Malaca.

Having made this protestation, he presently imbarqued himself in the same *Lanchara*, wherein he came thither, being accompanied with eleven or twelve *Balons*, which are small

Barques, and so went to the Isle of *Upa*, distant not above half a league from the Port. There the *Bandara* of *Malaca* (who is as it were chief Justicer amongst the *Mahometans*) was present in person by the express commandment of *Pedro de Faria* for to entertain him; And accordingly he made him a great Feast, which was celebrated with Hoboys, Drums, Trumpets, and Cymbals, together with an excellent consort of voyces framed to the tune of Harps, Lutes, and Viols after the *Portugal* manner. Whereat this Embassador did so wonder, that he would often put his finger on his mouth, an usual action with those of that Country when they marvel at any thing. About twenty days after the departure of this Embassador, *Pedro de Faria* being informed, that if he would send some Commodities from the *Indiaes* to the Kingdom of *Batas*, he might make great profit thereof, and much more of those which should be returned from thence, he to that effect set forth a *Jurupango*, of the bigness of a small Carvel, wherein he ventured a matter of some ten thousand duckets; In this Vessel he sent, as his Factor, a certain *Mahometan*, born at *Malaca*, and was desirous to have me to accompany him, telling me that thereby I should not only much oblige him, but that also under pretext of being sent as Embassador thither, I might both see the King of *Batas*, and going along with him in his journey against the Tyrant of *Achem*, which some way or other would questionless redound to my benefit. Now to the end that upon my return out of those Countries I might make him a true relation of all that I had seen, he prayed me carefully to observe whatsoever should pass there, and especially to learn whether the Isle of Gold, so much talked of, was in those parts, for that he was minded, if any discovery of it should be made, to write unto the King of *Portugal* about it. To speak the truth, I would fain have excused my self from this Voyage, by reason those Countries were unknown to me, and for that the inhabitants were by every one accounted faithless and treacherous, having small hope besides to make any gain by it, in regard that all my stock amounted not to above an hundred duckets; But because I durst not oppose the Captains desire I imbarqued my self, though very unwillingly, with that Infidel who had the charge of the Merchandise. Our Pilot steered his course from *Malaca* to the Port of *Sorotilau*, which is in the Kingdom of *Aaru*, always coasting the Isle of *Samatra* towards the *Mediterranean* Sea, till at length we arrived at a certain River, called *Hicandure*; After we had continued five days sailing in this manner we came to an Harbor, named *Minhatojey*, distant some ten leagues from the Kingdom of *Peedir*. In the end finding our selves on the other side of the Ocean we sailed on four days together, and then cast anchor in a little river, called *Gaateamgim*, that was not above seven fathom deep, up the which we past some seven or eight leagues. Now all the while we sailed in this River with a fair wind, we saw athwart a Wood, which grew on the bank of it, such a many Adders, and other crawling creatures, no less prodigious for their length, then for the strangeness of their forms, that I shall not marvel if they that read this History will not beleeve my report of them; especially such as have not travelled, for they that have seen little beleeve not much, whereas they that have seen much beleeve the more. All along this River, that was not very broad, there were a number of Lizards, which might more properly be called Serpents, because some of them were as big as an *Almadia*, with scales upon their backs, and mouths two foot wide. Those of the Country assured us, that these creatures are so hardy, as there be of them that sometimes will set upon an *Almadia*, chiefly when they perceive there is not above four or five persons in her, and overturn it with their tails, swallowing up the men whole, without dismembering of them. In this place also we saw strange kind of creatures, which they call *Caquesseitan*; They are of the bigness of a great Goose, very black, and scaly on their backs, with a row of sharp pricks on their chins, as long as a writing pen: Moreover, they have wings like unto those of Bats, long necks, and a little bone growing on their heads resembling a Cocks spur, with a very long tail spotted black and green, like unto the Lizards of that Country; These creatures hop and fly together, like Grashoppers, and in that manner they hunt Apes, and such other beasts, whom they pursue even to the tops of the highest Trees. Also we saw Adders, that were copped on the crowns of their heads, as big as a mans thigh, and so venomous, as the *Negroes* of the Country informed us, that if any living thing came within the reach of their breath, it dyed presently, there being no remedy nor antidote against it. We likewise saw others, that were not copped on the crowns, nor so venomous as the former, but far greater and longer, with an head as big as a Calves. We were told that they hunt their prey in this manner: They get up into a tree, and winding their tails about some branch of it, let their bodies hang down to the foot of the tree, and then laying one of their ears close to the ground, they harken whether they can hear any thing stir during the still-

ness

neſs of the night, ſo that if an Ox, a Boar, or any other beaſt doth chance to paſs by, they pre-ſently ſeize on it, and ſo carries it up into the tree where he devours it. In like ſort we de-ſcryed a number of Baboons, both grey and black, as big as a great Maſtiff, of whom the *Ne-groes* of the Country are more afraid, then of all the other beaſts, becauſe they will ſet upon them with that hardineſs, as they have much ado to reſiſt them.

CHAP. VII.

What happened to me at Penaiu *with the King of* Batas *expedition againſt the Tyrant of* Achem; *and what he did after his Victory over him.*

§.1. BY that time we had ſailed ſeven or eight leagues up the River, at the end we arrived at a little Town, named *Botterrendan*, not above a quarter of a mile diſtant from *Panaiu*, where the King of *Batas* was at that time making preparation for the War he had undertaken againſt the Tyrant of *Achem*. This King underſtanding that I had brought him a Letter and a Preſent from the Captain of *Malaca*, cauſed me to be entertained by the *Xabandar*, who is he that with abſolute power governs all the affairs of the Army: This General, accompanied with five *Lanchares*, and twelve *Ballons*, came to me to the Port where I rode at anchor; Then with a great noiſe of Drums, Bells, and popular acclamations, he brought me to a certain Key of the Town, called *Campalator*; There the *Bendara*, Governor of the Kingdom, ſtayed for me in great ſolemnity, attended by many *Ourobalons* and *Amborraias*, which are the nobleſt perſons of his Court, the moſt part of whom, for all that, were but poor and baſe, both in their habit, and manner of living, whereby I knew that the Country was not ſo rich as it was thought to be in *Malaca*. When I was come to the Kings Palace, and had paſt through the firſt Court, at the entrance of the ſecond I found an old woman, accompanied with other per-ſons far nobler, and better apparelled then thoſe that marched before me, who beckoning me with her hand, as if ſhe had commanded me to enter:

Man of Malaca, ſaid ſhe unto me, Thy arrival in the King my Maſters Land, is as agreeable unto him, as a ſhowre of rain is to a crop of Rice in dry and hot weather; Wherefore enter boldly, and be afraid of nothing, for the people, which by the goodneſs of God thou ſeeſt here, are no other then thoſe of thine own Country, ſince the hope which we have in the ſame God makes us believe that he will maintain us all together unto the end of the world. Having ſaid ſo, ſhe carried me where the King was, unto whom I did obeyſance according to the man-of the Country, then I delivered him the Letter and the Preſent I had brought him, which he graciouſly accepted of, and asked me what occaſion drew me thither. Whereunto I anſwered, as I had in commiſſion, that I was come to ſerve his Highneſs in the Wars, where I hoped to have the honor to attend on him, and not to leave him till ſuch time as he returned Conqueror of his Enemies: Hereunto I likewiſe added, that I deſired to ſee the City of *Achem*, as alſo the ſcituation and fortifications of it, and what depth the River was of, whereby I might know whether it would bear great Veſſels and Gallions, becauſe the Captain of *Malaca* had a deſign to come and ſuccor his Highneſs, as ſoon as his men were returned from the *Indiaes*, and to deliver his mortal Enemy, the Tyrant of *Achem*, into his hands. This poor King preſently believed all that I ſaid to be true, and ſo much the rather, for that it was conformable to his deſire, in ſuch ſort, that riſing out of his Throne where he was ſet, I ſaw him go and fall on his knees before the carcaſs of a Cows head, ſet up againſt the wall, whoſe horns were guilt, and crowned with flowers; Then lifting up his hands and eyes, *O thou, ſaid he, that not con-ſtrained by any material love, whereunto Nature hath obliged thee, doſt continually make glad all thoſe that deſire thy milk, as the own mother doth him whom ſhe hath brought into the world, without participating either of the miſeries, or pains, which ordinarily ſhe ſuffers from whom we take our Being, be favorable unto the prayer which now with all my heart I offer up unto thee: and it is no other but this, that in the meadows of the Sun, where with the payment and recompence which thou receiveſt, thou art contented with the good that thou doſt here below, thou wilt be pleaſed to conſerve me in the new amity of this good Captain, to the end he may put in execution all that this man here hath told me.* At theſe words all the Courtiers, which were likewiſe on their knees, ſaid three times as it were in anſwer, *How happy were he that could ſee that, and then dye incontinently?* Whereupon the King aroſe, and wiping his eyes, which were all beblubbered with the tears that proceeded from the zeal of the prayer he had made, he queſtioned me about many particular things of the *Indiaes*, and

Malaca.

Malaca. Having spent some time therein, he very courteously dismissed me, with a promise to cause the Merchandise, which the *Mahometan* had brought in the Captain of *Malaca's* name, to be well and profitably put off, which indeed was the thing I most desired. Now for as much as the King at my arrival was making his preparations for to march against the Tyrant of *Achem,* and had taken order for all things necessary for that his Voyage, after I had remained nine days in *Panaiu,* the Capital City of the Kingdom of *Batas,* he departed with some Troops towards a place, named *Turban,* some five leagues of, where he arrived an hour before Sun-set, without any manner of reception, or shew of joy, in regard of the grief he was in for the death of his children, which was such as he never appeared in publique, but with great demonstrations of sorrow.

The next morning the King of *Batas* marched from *Turban* towards the Kingdom of *A-* §.2. *chem,* being eighteen leagues thither : He carried with him fifteen thousand men of War, whereof eight thousand were *Bataes,* and the rest *Menancabes, Lusons, Andraguires, Jambes,* and *Bournees,* whom the Princes his neighbors had assisted him with, as also forty Elephants, and twelve Carts with small Ordnance, namely, Faulcons, Bases, and other field Pieces, amongst the which there were three that had the Arms of *France,* and were taken in the year 1526. at such time as *Lopo Vaz de Sampayo* governed the State of the *Indies.* Now the King of *Batas* marching five leagues a day came to a River, called *Quilem* ; There by some of the Tyrants Spies, which he had taken, he learnt that his Enemy waited for him at *Tonda-cur,* two leagues from *Achem,* with a purpose to fight with him, and that he had great store of strangers in his Army, namely *Turks, Cambayans,* and *Malabars* : Whereupon the King of *Batas* assembling his Councel of War, and falling into consultation of this affair, it was concluded as most expedient to set upon the Enemy before he grew more strong. With this resolution having quit the River he marched somewhat faster then ordinary, and arrived about ten of the clock in the night at the foot of a Mountain, half a league from the Enemies Camp, where, after he had reposed himself a matter of three hours, he marched on in very good order, for which effect having divided his Army into four Squadrons, and passing along by a little hill, when he came to the end thereof he discovered a great Plain sowed with Rice, where the Enemy stood ranged in two Battalions. As soon as the two Armies descryed one another, and that at the sound of their Trumpets, Drums, and Bells the Soldiers had set up a terrible cry, they encountred very valiantly together, and after the discharge of their shot on both sides, they came to fight hand to hand with such courage, that I trembled with fear to behold their fury. The Battel continued in this manner above an hour, and yet could it not possibly be discerned which party had the better. At last the Tyrant foreseeing, that if he persisted in the fight, he should lose the day, because he perceived his men to grow faint and weary, he retreated to a rising ground, that lay South of the *Bataes,* and about a Faulcons shot distant from them. There his intention was to fortifie himself in certain Trenches which before he had caused to be cast up against a Rock in form of a garden, or tilth of Rice ; But a brother to the King of *An-draguire* interrupted his design, for stepping before him with two thousand men, he cut off his way, and stopt him from passing further, in so much that the medly grew to be the same it was before, and the fight was renewed between them with such fury, as cruelly wounding one another, they testified sufficiently how they came but little short of other Nations in courage. By this means the Tyrant, before he could recover his Trenches, lost fifteen hundred of his men, of which number were the hundred and threescore *Turks,* that a little before were come to him from the Straight of *Mecqua,* with two hundred *Sarrazins, Malabars,* and some *Abissins,* which were the best men he had ; Now because it was about mid-day, and therefore very hot, the King of *Batas* retired towards the Mountain, where he spent the rest of the day in causing those that were wounded to be looked unto, and the dead to be buried. Hereupon, not being well resolved what to do, in regard he was altogether ignorant of the Enemies design, he took care to have good watch kept all that night in every part. The next morning no sooner began the Sun to appear but he perceived the Valley, wherein the *Achems* had been the day before, to be quite abandoned, and not one of them to be seen there, which made him think the Enemy was defeated : In this opinion, the better to pursue the first point of his Victory, he dismissed all the hurt men, as being unfit for service, and followed the Tyrant to the City, where arriving two hours before Sun-set, to shew that he had strength and courage enough to combat his Enemies, he resolved to give them proof of it by some remarkable action before he would encamp himself ; To which effect he fired two of the Suburbs of the Town, as also four Ships, and

two

two Gallions, which were drawn on Land, and were those that had brought the *Turks* from the Straight of *Mecqua*: And indeed the fire took with such violence on those six Vessels, as they were quite consumed in a very little time, the Enemy not daring to issue forth for to quench it. After this, the King of *Batas* seeing himself favored by Fortune, to lose no opportunity began to assault a Fort, called *Penacao*, which with twelve Pieces of Ordnance defended the entry of the River, to the Scalado of this he went in person, his whole Army looking on, and having caused some seventy or eighty ladders to be planted, he behaved himself so well, that with the loss only of seven and thirty men he entred the place, and put all to the sword that he found in it, to the number of seven hundred persons, without sparing so much as one of them. Thus did he on the day of his arrival perform three memorable things, whereby his Soldiers were so heartned, as they would fain have assaulted the City the very same night if he would have permitted them, but in regard it was very dark, and his men weary, he gave thanks to God, and contented himself with that which he had done.

§.3.   The King of *Batas* held the City besieged by the space of three and twenty days, during the which two sallies were made, wherein nothing past of any reckoning, for there were but ten men slain on either part; Now as victories and good success in War do ordinarily encourage the victorious, so oftentimes it happens that the weak become strong, and cowards so hardy, as laying aside all fear they dare undertake most difficile and dangerous things, whence also it as often falls out, that the one prospers, and the other is ruined, which appeared but too evidently in that which I observed of these two Princes; For the King of *Batas*, seeing that the Tyrant had shut himself up in his City, thereby as it were confessing that he was vanquished, grew to such an height of confidence, that both he and his people beleeving it was impossible for them to be resisted, and trusting in this vain opinion, that blinded them, were twice in hazard to be lost by the rash and inconsiderate actions which they entred into. In the third sally, made by the inhabitants, the King of *Batas* people encountred them very lustily in two places, which those of *Achem* perceiving, they made as though they were the weaker, and so retreated to the same Fort, that was taken from them by the *Bataes* the first day of their arrival, being closely followed by one of the Kings Captains, who taking hold of the opportunity, entred pell-mell with the *Achems*, being perswaded that the Victory was sure his own; But when they were all together in the Trenches the *Achems* turned about, and making head afresh defended themselves very couragiously: At length in the heat of their medley, the one side endeavoring to go on, and the other to withstand them, those of *Achem* gave fire to a Myne they had made, which wrought so effectually, as it blew up the Captain of the *Bataes*, and above three hundred of his Soldiers, with so great a noise, and so thick a smoak, as the place seemed to be the very portraiture of Hell: In the mean time the Enemies giving a great shout, the Tyrant sallied forth in person, accompanied with five thousand resolute men, and charged the *Bataes* very furiously; Now for that neither of them could see one another by reason of the smoak proceeding from the Myne, there was a most confused and cruel conflict between them, but to speak the truth I am not able to deliver the manner of it, sufficeth it that in a quarter of an hours space, the time this fight endured, four thousand were slain in the place on both sides, whereof the King of *Batas* lost the better part, which made him retire with the remainder of his Army to a Rock, called *Minaçaleu*, where causing his hurt men to be drest, he found them to be two thousand in number, besides those that were killed, which because they could not be so suddenly buried were thrown into the current of the River. Hereupon the two Kings continued quiet for four days after, at the end whereof one morning, when nothing was less thought of, there appeared in the midst of the River on *Penaticans* side a Fleet of fourscore and six Sails, with a great noise of musick, and acclamations of joy: At first this object much amazed the *Bataes*, because they knew not what it was, howbeit the night before their scouts had taken five fishermen, who put to torture confessed, that this was the Army which the Tyrant had sent some two months before to *Tevassery*, in regard he had War with the *Sornau*, King of *Siam*, and it was said that this Army was composed of five thousand *Lussons* and *Sornes*, all choyce men, having to their General a *Turk*, named *Hametecam*, Nephew to the *Bassa* of *Cairo*: Whereupon the King of *Batas* making use of these fishermens confession, resolved to retire himself in any sort whatsoever, well considering that the time would not permit him to make an hours stay, as well because his Enemies Forces were far greater then his, as for that every minute they expected succors from *Pedir* and *Pazen*, whence, as it was reported for certain, there were twelve ships full of strangers coming. No sooner was the King fortified

in

in this refolution, but the night enfuing he departed very fad, and ill contented for the bad fuccefs of his enterprize, wherein he had loft above three thoufand and five hundred men, not comprifing the wounded, which were more in number, nor thofe that were burnt with the fire of the Myne. Five days after his departure he arrived at *Panaiu*, where he difmiffed all his Forces, both his own fubjects and ftrangers; That done, he imbarqued himfelf in a fmall *Lanchara*, and went up the River without any other company then two or three of his Favorites: With this fmall retinue he betook himfelf to a place, called *Pachiffaru*, where he fhut himfelf up for fourteen days, by way of pennance, in a Pagod of an Idol, named *Ginnaffereo*, which fignifies *the God of Sadnefs*. At his return to *Panaiu* he fent for me, and the *Mahometan* that brought *Pedro de Faria's* Merchandife; The firft thing that he did was to enquire particularly of him whether he made a good fale of it, adding withall, that if any thing were ftill owing to him he would command it to be prefently fatisfied; Hereunto the *Mahometan* and I anfwered, that through his Highnefs favor all our bufinefs had received a very good difpatch, and that we were well payd for that we had fold, in regard whereof the Captain of *Malaca* would not fail to acknowledg that courtefie, by fending him fuccor for to be revenged on his Enemy the Tyrant of *Achem*, whom he would inforce to reftore all the places, which he had unjuftly ufurped upon him. The King hearing me fpeak in this manner ftood a while mufing with himfelf, and then in anfwer to my fpeech, *Ah Portugal*, faid he, *fince thou conftraineft me to tell thee freely what I think, beleeve me not hereafter to be fo ignorant, as that thou mayft be able to perfwade me, or that I can be capable to imagine, that he, which in thirty years fpace could not revenge himfelf, is of power to fuccor me at this prefent in fo fhort a time; or if yet thou thinkeft I deceive my felf, tell me I pre-thee now whence comes it that thy King and his Governors could not hinder this cruel King of Achem from gaining from you the Fort of Pazem, and the Galley which went to the Molucquaes, as alfo three Ships in Queda, and the Gallion of Malaca, at fuch time as Garcia was Captain there, befides the four Foifts that were taken fince at Salengor, with the two Ships that came from Bengala, or Lopo Chanoca's Jounk and Ship, as likewife many other Veffels, which I cannot now remember, in the which, as I have been affured, this Inhumane hath put to death above a thoufand Portugals, and gotten an extream rich booty. Wherefore if this Tyrant fhould happen to come once more againft me, how canft thou have me rely upon their word which have been fo often overcome? I muft of neceffity then continue as I am with three of my children murdered, and the greateft part of my Kingdom deftroyed, feeing you your felves are not much more affured in your Fortrefs of Malaca.* I muft needs confefs that this anfwer, made with fo much refentment, rendred me fo afhamed, knowing he fpake nothing but truth, that I durft not talk to him afterwards of any fuccor, nor for our honor reiterate the promifes which I had formerly made him.

CHAP. VIII.

What paff between the King of Batas and me, until fuch time as I imbarqued for Malaca; *my Arrival in the Kingdom of* Queda, *and my return from thence to* Malaca.

THe *Mahometan* and I returning to our lodging, departed not in four days after, employing that time in fhipping an hundred Bars of Tin, and thirty of Benjamin, which were ftill on Land. Then being fully fatisfied by our Merchants, and ready to go, I went to wait upon the King at his *Paffeiran*, which was a great place before the Palace, where thofe of the Country kept their moft folemn Fairs; There I gave him to underftand, that now we had nothing more to do but to depart if it would pleafe his Majefty to permit us: The entertainment that he gave me then was very gracious, and for anfwer he faid to me, I am very glad for that *Hermon Xabandar* (who was chief General of the Wars) affured me yefterday that your Captains commodities were well fold, but it may be that that which he told me was not fo, and that he delivered not the truth for to pleafe me, and to accommodate himfelf to the defire he knew I had to have it fo, wherefore, continued he, I pre-thee declare unto me freely whether he dealt truly with me, and whether the *Mahometan* that brought them be fully fatisfied, for I would not that to my difhonor thofe of *Malaca* fhould have caufe to complain of the Merchants of *Panaiu*, faying, that they are not men of their word, and that there is not a King there who can conftrain them to pay their debts; and I fwear to thee by the faith of Pagan,

§.1.

that

that this affront would be no lefs infupportable to my condition, then if I fhould chance to make peace with that Tyrant, and perjured Enemy of mine, the King of *Achem*. Whereunto having replyed, that we had difpatched all our affairs, and that there was nothing due to us in his Country; Verily, faid he, I am very well pleafed to hear that it is fo, wherefore fince thou haft nothing elfe to do here, I hold it requifite, that without any further delay thou fhouldft go, for the time is now fit to fet fail, and to avoyd the great heats that ordinarily are endured in paffing the Gulph, which is the caufe that fhips are many times caft upon *Pazem* by foul weather at Sea, from which I pray God deliver thee, for I affure thee that if thy ill fortune fhould carry thee thither, the men of *Achem* would eat thee alive, and the Tyrant himfelf would have the firft bite at thee, there being nothing in the world thefe Inhumanes fo much vaunt of, as to carry on the creft of their Arms the device of *Drinkers of the troubled blood of miferable Caffers*, who they fay are come from the end of the world, calling them *Tyrannical men, and Ufurpers in a foveraign degree of other mens Kingdoms in the Indiaes, and Ifles of the Sea*. This is the title wherein they glory moft, and which they attribute particularly to themfelves, as being fent them from *Mecqua* in recompence of the golden Lamps, which they offered to the Alcoran of their *Mahomet*, as they ufe to do every year. Furthermore, although heretofore I have often advifed thy Captain of *Malaca* to take careful heed of this Tyrant of *Achem*, yet do not thou omit to advertife him of it once more from me; for know that he never had, nor fhall have other thoughts then to labor by all means to expel him out of the *Indiaes*, and make the *Turk* Mafter of them, who to that end promifeth to fend him great fuccors; but I hope that God will fo order it, as all the malice and cunning of this difloyal wretch fhall have a contrary fuccefs to his intentions. After he had ufed this language to me, he gave me a Letter in anfwer to my Embaffage, together with a prefent, which he defired me to deliver from him to Captain *de Faria*; this was fix fmall Javelins headed with Gold, twelve *Cates* of *Calambuca* Wood, every one of them weighing twenty ounces, and a box of exceeding value, made of a Tortoife fhell, beautified with Gold, and full of great feed pearl, amongft the which there were fixteen fair pearls of rich account: For my felf, he gave me two *Cates* of Gold, and a little Courtelace garnifhed with the fame. Then he difmiffed me with as much demonftration of honor as he had always ufed to me before, protefting to me in particular, that the amity which he had contracted with our Nation fhould ever continue inviolable on his part. Thus I imbarqued my felf with *Aquarem Dabolay*, his Brother-in-law, who was the fame he had fent Embaffador to *Malaca*, as I have related before. Being departed from the Port of *Panaiu*, we arrived about two hours in the night at a little Ifland, called *Apofingua*, diftant fome league and an half from the mouth of the River, and inhabited by poor people, who lived by the fifhing of Shads.

§.2.   The next morning, leaving that Ifland of *Apofingua*, we ran along by the coaft of the Ocean Sea for the fpace of five and twenty leagues, until fuch time as at length we entered into the Straight of *Minhagaruu*, by which we came; then paffing by the contrary coaft of this other *Mediterranean* Sea, we continued our courfe along by it, and at laft arrived near to *Pullo Bugay*: There we croft over to the firm Land, and paffing by the Port of *Junçalan*, we failed two days and an half with a favorable wind, by means whereof we got to the River of *Parles* in the Kingdom of *Queda*, there we rode five days at anchor in expectation of a fit wind to carry us on. During that time, the *Mahometan* and my felf, by the counfel of certain Merchants of the Country, went to vifit the King with an *Odiaa*, or Prefent of divers things, that we thought were convenient for our defign, which was received with much demonftration of being very well pleafed therewith. When we came to his Court we found, that with a great deal of pomp, excellent mufick, dancing, and largefs to the poor, he was folemnizing the funerals of his Father, whom he himfelf had poynarded, of purpofe for to marry his own mother, after he had gotten her with child: Wherewithall not being contented, to decline the murmur, which fo wicked and horrible an act might provoke unto, he had made proclamation, that on pain of a moft rigorous death no perfon whatfoever fhould be fo daring, as to fpeak a word of that which had paft, and it was told us there, how for that caufe he had moft tyrannically put the principal Perfonages of his Kingdom, and a number of Merchants already to death, whofe goods he had confifcated to his own ufe, and thereby enriched his Coffers with two millions of Gold; So that upon our arrival we perceived fuch a general fear to be amongft the people, as not the moft hardy of them all durft fo much as make the leaft mention in the world of it. Now in regard the *Mahometan*, my companion, named *Coia Ale*, was a man liberal of his tongue,

and

and that would say any thing which came into his head, he perswaded himself, in regard he was a stranger, and the Captain of *Malaca's* Factor, that he might with more liberty then those of the Country talk what he listed, and the King not punish him for it, as he did his Subjects; But he found himself far short of his account, and this presumption cost him his life: For being invited to a feast by another *Mahometan* like himself, a Merchant stranger, born at *Patana*, when as they were both of them high with wine and meat, as I learned since, they began to talk boldly, and without any respect of the Kings Brutality and Parracide, whereof the King, being incontinently advertised by Spies, which he had in every corner for that purpose, he caused the house to be presently invested, and all the guests to be apprehended, to the number of seventeen persons; These poor wretches were no sooner brought bound before him, but immediately, without observing any form of Justice, or hearing what they could say for themselves either good or bad, he commanded them to be put to a most cruel kind of death, called by them *Gregoge*, which is, to saw off the feet, hands, and heads of them that are condemned to it, as I beheld afterwards my self. This execution done, the King, fearing lest the Captain of *Malaca* should be offended for that he had executed his Factor thus with the rest, and therefore might arrest some goods that he had at *Malaca*, sent the night following for me to the *Jurupango*, where I was sleeping, and altogether ignorant of that which had past: understanding the Kings pleasure away I went, and coming about midnight to the Palace I perceived in the outward Court a great many men in arms; the sight whereof I must confess put me into a mighty amazement and mistrust, because I could not imagine what should be the cause of it, and doubting lest it might be some such Treason as at other times they had practised against us, I would fain have returned, but they that accompanied me, judging that my fear proceeded from the Soldiers which I beheld there, bid me be afraid of nothing, for these men were only going forth to apprehend an offendor by the Kings commandment; Having said thus with an intent to confirm me, I could not for all that be satisfied, but was seized with so terrible a fear, as I was not able to utter a word, howbeit at length recollecting my self a little, I signified to them the best I could, how if they would permit me to return to my Skiff for to fetch a thing which I had forgotten, I would give them forty Crowns in Gold; whereunto they answered, that if I would give them all the Silver in *Malaca* they would not let me go, for if they should, they were sure to lose their heads: This speech of theirs redoubled my fear, which yet increased when I saw my self invironned with twenty more of those armed men, who guarded me all that night. The next morning the King being advertised that I was there, commanded me to be brought unto him, into the next Court, where I found him mounted on an Elephant, and accompanied with an hundred persons besides those of his guard, which were far more in number; When he saw me coming towards him, much troubled, and indeed more dead then alive, he said twice to me, *Be not afraid, but come nearer to me, and thou shalt know the cause why I sent for thee.* Thereupon having made a sign to me with his hand that I should look that way he pointed me to, I turned me about and beheld a great many bodies extended on the place, and weltring in their own blood, amongst the which I presently knew the *Mahometan, Coia Ale,* with whom I came, which I no sooner perceived, but like a man distraught of his wits I cast my self at the feet of the Elephant whereupon the King rode, and with tears in my eyes cryed out, O Sir, have pity on me, and take me for thy slave, rather then cause me to end my days with the torments which have taken those out of the world whom I see here; I swear unto thee by the faith of a Christian, that I have not deserved death, as having no way offended thee; Consider likewise, I beseech thee, that I am Nephew to the Captain of *Malaca*, who will give thee any ransom for me thou wilt desire, as also that thou hast the *Jurupango*, wherein I came, in thy Port, full of goods, all which thou mayst take it if thou pleasest. Hearing me speak in this sort, *God forbid,* said he, *that ever I should do any such thing, no, no, be not afraid, but stand up, and recollect thy self, for I see well thou art much troubled, and when thou art in better case to hear me I will tell thee wherefore I caused the Moor, that came with thee, to be executed; and in good faith if he had been either a Portugal, or a Christian, I would not have put him to death, no, though he had killed mine own son.* Howbeit perceiving, that all which he could say would not rid me of my fear, he commanded a pot of fresh water to be brought me, whereof I drunk a pretty quantity, and withall made one of his followers to fan me with a ventilow for to refresh me: A quarter of an hour, or thereabouts, was spent in this action, at the end thereof finding that I was so well recovered, as I was able with good sence to answer unto the questions he should ask me; *Portugal*, said he unto me, I know that

thou

thou haft bern told, since thy coming hither, how I killed my Father, as indeed I did, becauſe I was ſure he would have killed me, incited thereunto by the falſe reports of ſome of his ſlaves, would have made him believe that I had gotten my mother with child, whereof I had never ſo much as the leaſt thought, whereby thou mayſt ſee what ill tongues can do. Indeed it is true, that being moſt aſſured he had without all reaſon given ſuch credit to thoſe ſlanderous reports, as he was fully reſolved to have taken away my life, to decline that imminent peril I prevented him, and caught him in the ſame ſnare he had layd for me ; But God knows how much againſt my mind this fell out, and how I always made it my chiefeſt glory to render him the dutiful offices of a moſt obedient ſon, as it may well appear now at this preſent : for to keep my mother from being a ſad and deſolate widow, as many others are, ſeeing my ſelf to be the cauſe of her miſery, and obliged to comfort her, I have taken her to wife ; judg then whether I have been wrongfully blamed, or no, ſince that for her I have refuſed many great parties, that have been propounded unto me from *Patacia, Berdio, Tanauçarin, Siaca, Jamba,* and *Andragia,* who were no leſs then Siſters and Daughters of Kings, and offered unto me with very rich dowries. Now being informed that ſuch falſe reports had been diſperſed abroad of me, for to arreſt the tongues of Detractors, which are ſo audacious as to talk of any thing comes in their heads, I cauſed it to be proclaimed, that none ſhould dare to ſpeak of that affair ; But for as much as without any regard at all of this my Injunction, this fellow of thine, which lies there in the company of thoſe other Dogs, like unto himſelf, ſpoke yeſterday of me moſt reproachfully in publique, ſaying, I was an Hog, or worſe then a very Hog, and my mother a ſalt Bitch ; as well to puniſh his ſlanders, as to preſerve my honor, I was conſtrained to put him to death, together with theſe other Dogs, who were no leſs ſlanderous then he : Wherefore I am to deſire thee, that as my friend thou wilt not think this procedure of mine any way ſtrange. Now if thou ſhouldſt happen to think, that I have done it on purpoſe to ſeize upon the Captain of *Malaca*'s goods, be confident that I never meant it, & thou mayſt truly certifie him ſo much; For I ſwear unto thee by my Law, that I have ever been a great friend to the *Portugals,* and ſo will continue all my life. Hereupon being ſomewhat recovered from the fear I was in a little before, I anſwered him, How his Highneſs had much obliged his very good friend, and brother, the Captain of *Malaca,* by the execution of that *Mahometan,* who had imbezelled away a great part of the goods committed to his charge, and underſtanding that I had diſcovered his knavery he had twice gone about to poyſon me ; whereunto alſo I added, how this Dog when he was drunk would bark at every one, and ſpeak his pleaſure at large. This anſwer made upon the ſudden, and not knowing well what I ſaid, very much pleaſed the King, who commanding me to come nearer to him, Verily, continued he, by this ſpeech of thine I perceive thou art an honeſt man, and my friend, and being ſo I doubt not but thou wilt give a good interpretation to my actions, contrary to thoſe maſtiff Dogs that lie there weltring in their own blood. Having ſaid ſo, he took a purſe from his girdle trimmed with gold, and gave it me, as alſo a Letter directed to *Pedro de Faria,* whereupon I took my leave of him, with a promiſe that I would ſtay there a week longer ; howbeit getting ſpeedily aboard my *Jurupango,* I made not a minutes ſtay, but inſtantly cauſed the Mariners to hoiſt ſail, and away, ſtill imagining that ſome were following to apprehend me, by reaſon of the extream fear I was in, having ſo lately eſcaped, as I thought, the danger of a moſt cruel death.

§. 3.   Being departed from the River of *Parles* on a Saturday about Sun-ſet, I made all the ſpeed that poſſibly I could, and continued my courſe until the Tueſday following, when it pleaſed God that I reached to the Iſles of *Pullo Sambalin,* the firſt Land on the Coaſt of *Mallayo.* There by good fortune I met with three *Portugal* ſhips (whereof two came from *Bengala,* and the other from *Pegu*) commanded by *Triſtan de Gaa,* who had ſometimes been Governor of the perſon of *Don Lorenzo,* ſon to the Vice-roy *Don Franceſco d'Almeda,* that was afterward put to death by *Miroocem* in *Chaul* Roade, as is at large delivered in the Hiſtory of the Diſcovery of the *Indiaes.* This ſame *Triſtan* furniſhed me with many things that I had great need of, as tackle, and Mariners, together with two Soldiers, and a Pilot ; moreover, both himſelf and the other to ſhips had always a care of me until our arrival at *Malaca* where diſ-imbarquing my ſelf, the firſt thing I did was to go to the Fortreſs for to ſalute the Captain, and to render him an account of the whole ſucceſs of my Voyage, where I diſcourſed unto him at large what Rivers, Ports, and Havens I had newly diſcovered in the Iſle of *Samatra,* as well on the *Mediterranean,* as on the Ocean Seas ſide, as alſo what commerce the inhabitants of the Country uſed ; Then I declared unto him the manner of all that Coaſt, of all thoſe Ports,

and

and of all those Rivers; whereunto I added the scituations, the heights, the degrees, the names, and the depths of the Ports, according to the direction he had given me at my departure. Therewithall I made him a description of the Rode wherein *Rosado*, the Captain of a *French* ship, was lost, and another, named *Matelote de Brigas*, as also the Commander of another ship, who by a storm at Sea was cast into the Port of *Diu* in the year 1529. during the raign of *Sultan Bandur*, King of *Cambaya*. This Prince having taken them all, made fourscore and two of them abjure their faith, who served him in his Wars against the great *Mogor*, and were every one of them miserably slain in that expedition. Moreover I brought him the description of a place fit for anchorage in *Pullo Botum* Roade, where the *Bisquayn* Ship suffered shipwrack, which was said to be the very same, wherein *Magellan* compassed the World, and was called the *Vittoria*, which traversing the Isle of *Jooa* was cast away at the mouth of the River of *Sonda*. I made him a recital likewise of many different Nations, which inhabit all along this Ocean, and the River of *Lampon*, from whence the Gold of *Menancabo* is transported to the Kingdom of *Campar*, upon the waters of *Jambes* and *Broteo*. For the inhabitants affirm out of their Chronicles, how in this very Town of *Lampon* there was anciently a Factory of Merchants, established by the Queen of *Sheba*, whereof one, named *Nausem*, sent her a great quantity of Gold, which she carried to the Temple of *Jerusalem*, at such time as she went to visit the wise King *Solomon*; From whence, some say, she returned with child of a son, that afterwards succeeded to the Empire of *Æthiopia*, whom now we call *Prester-John*, of whose race the *Abissins* vaunt they are descended. Further, I told him what course was usually held for the fishing of seed pearl betwixt *Pullo Tiquos* and *Pullo Quenim*, which in times past were carried by the *Bataes* to *Pazem* and *Pedir*, and exchanged with the *Turks* of the Straight of *Mecqua*, and the Ships of *Judaa*, for such Merchandise as they brought from *Grand Cairo*, and the Ports of *Arabia Fælix*. Divers other things I recounted unto him, having learnt them of the King of *Batas*, and of the Merchants of *Panaiu*: And for conclusion, I gave him an information in writing, as he had formerly desired me, concerning the Island of Gold: I told him, how this Island is beyond the River of *Calandor* five degrees to the Southward, invironed with many shelfs of sand, and currents of water, as also that it was distant some hundred and threescore leagues from the point of the Isle of *Samatra*. With all which reports *Pedro de Faria* remained so well satisfied, that he made present relation thereof to the King *Dom Jovan* the Third of happy memory, who the year after ordained *Francesco d' Almeida* for Captain to discover the Isle of Gold, a Gentleman of merit, and very capable of that charge, who indeed had long before petitioned the King for it in recompence of the services by him performed in the Islands of *Banda*, of the *Molucques*, of *Ternate*, and *Geilolo*: But by ill fortune this *Francesco d' Almeida*, being gone from the *Indiaes* to discover that place, dyed of a feaver in the Isles of *Nicubar*; Whereof the King of *Portugal* being advertised, he honored one *Diego Cabral*, born at the *Maderaes*, with that Command, but the Court of Justice deprived him of it by express order from *Martinez Alphonso de Sousa*, who was at that time Governor, which partly proceeded, according to report, for that he had murmured against him; Whereupon he gave it to *Jeronimo Figuereydo*, a Gentleman belonging to the Duke of *Braganca*, who in the year 1542. departed from *Goa* with two Foists, and one Carvel, wherein there were fourscore men, as well Soldiers, as Mariners; But it is said, that his Voyage was without effect, for that, according to the apparances that he gave of it afterward, it seemed that he desired to enrich himself too suddenly: To which end he passed to the Coast of *Tanassery*, where he took certain Ships, that came from *Mecqua*, *Adem*, *Alcosser*, *Judaa*, and other places upon the Coast of *Persia*. And verily this booty was the occasion of his undoing, for upon an unequal partition thereof falling at difference with his Soldiers, they mutined in such sort against him, as after many affronts done him they bound him hand and foot, and so carried him to the Isle of *Ceilan*, where they set him on Land; and the Carvel, with the two Foists, they returned to the Governor *Don Joano de Castra*, who in regard of the necessity of the time pardoned them the fault, and took them along with him in the Army, which he led to *Diu* for the succor of *Don Joana Mascarenhas*, that was then straitly besieged by the King of *Cambaya's* Forces. Since that time there hath been no talk of the discovery of this Island of Gold, although it seems very much to import the common good of our Kingdom of *Portugal*, if it would please God it might be brought to pass.

E

The Arrival of an Embassador at Malaca *from the King of* Aaru *to the Captain thereof; his sending me to the said King, my coming to* Aaru, *and that which happend to me after my departing from thence.*

§.1. FIve and twenty days after my coming to *Malaca, Dom Stephano de Gama* being still Captain of the Fortress, an Embassador arrived there from the King of *Aaru,* for to demand succor of men from him, and some munitions of War, as Powder, and Bullets, for to defend himself from a great Fleet that the King of *Achem* was setting forth against him, with an intention to deprive him of his Kingdom, and so be a nearer neighbor unto us, to the end that having gained that passage, he might afterwards send his forces the more easily against our Fortress of *Malaca :* whereof *Pedro de Faria* was no sooner advertised, but representing unto himself how important this affair was for the service of the King, and preservation of the Fortress, he acquainted *Dom Stephano de Gama* with it, in regard his Command of the place was to continue yet six weeks longer ; howbeit he excused himself from giving the succor, which was required, saying, that the time of his Government was now expiring, and that his being shortly to come in the duty of his charge did oblige him to take care of this business, and to think of the danger that menaced him. Hereunto *Pedro de Faria* made answer,that if he would relinquish his Government for the time he had yet to come in it, or give him full power to dispose of the publique Magazins, he would provide for the succor that he thought was necessary. In a word, and not to stand long on that which past betwixt them, it shall suffice to say, that this Embassador was utterly denyed his demand by these two Captains, whereof the one alledged for excuse, that he was not yet entered upon his Charge, and the other that he was upon the finishing of his : whereupon he returned very ill satisfied with this refusal, and so far resented injustice,which he thought was done unto his King,as the very morning wherein he imbarqued himself, having met by chance with the two Captains at the gate of the Fortress, he said aloud before them publiquely with the tears in his eyes ; *O God ! that with a soveraign Power and Majesty raignest in the highest of the Heavens, even with deep sighs fetch'd from the bottom of my heart, I take thee for Judg of my cause, and for Witness of the just occasion I have to make this request to these Captains here, and that in the name of my King, the faithful Vassal of the great King of* Portugal, *upon homage sworn by his Ancestors to the famous* Albuque.que, *who promised us, that if the Kings of our Kingdom did always continue true and loyal Subjects to his Master, that then both he and his successors would oblige themselves to defend them against all their enemies, as belonged to their soveraign Lord to do ; wherefore since we have continued still loyal to this day, what reason have you, my Masters, not to accomplish this obligation, wherein your King and you are so deeply engaged, especially seeing you know that only in respect of you this perfidious Tyrant of* Achem *takes our Country from us ; For there is nothing he so much reproacheth us withall, as that my King is as good a Portugal,and Christian, as if he had been born in* Portugal ; *and yet now that he desires you to succor him in his need, as allyes and true friends ought to do, you excuse your selves with reasons that are of no validity. The succor we require of you for to secure us, and to keep this faithless wretch from seizing on our Kingdom, is a very small matter, namely, forty or fifty* Portugals, *that may instruct us in the military art, together with four barrels of Powder, and two hundred Bullets for field Pieces ; a poor thing in comparison of that you have. Now if you can yet be perswaded to grant us this little ayd, you shall thereby so much oblige our King, as he will ever remain a faithful slave to the mighty Prince of* Portugal, *your Master and ours, in whose name I beseech you, once, twice, nay an hundred times, that you will perform that appertains unto your duty to do, for this which I thus publiquely demand of you is of so great importance, that therein consists, not so much the preservation of the Kingdom of* Aaru, *as the safety of this your Fortress of* Malaca, *which that Tyrant of* Achem *our enemy so extreamly desires to possess,and to that purpose he hath gotten the assistance of divers strange Nations ; but because he finds that our Kingdom is a let to the execution of his design, he endeavors to usurp it upon us, and then he intends to guard this Straight in such sort, as he will quite exclude you from all Commerce with the Spices of* Banda *and the* Molucques, *and from all the Trade and Navigation of the Seas of* China, Sunda, Borneo, Timor, *and* Jappon, *and this his own people stick not to boast of even already,being also further manifested by the accord,*
which

which he hath lately made with the *Turk*, through the interposure of the *Bassa* of grand Cairo, who in consideration thereof hath promised to ayd him with great Forces : Wherefore at length give ear unto the request which I have made unto you in the name of my King, and that so much concerns the service of yours, for since you may yet give a remedy to the mischief, which you see is ready to fall, I desire you to do it speedily ; And let not one of you excuse himself by alledging that the time of his Government is almost at an end, nor the other, that he is not as yet entered upon his Charge, for it is sufficient that you know you are both of you equally obliged thereunto.

Having finished this speech in form of a request, which availed him nothing, he stooped down to the ground, from whence taking up two stones, he knocked with them upon a Piece of Ordnance, and then the tears standing in his eyes he said, *The Lord, who hath created us, will defend us if he please*, and so imbarquing himself he departed greatly discontented for the bad answer he carried back. Five days after his departure *Pedro de Faria* was told how all the Town murmured at the small respect, that both he and *Dom Stephano* had carried to that poor King, who had ever been a friend both to them, and the whole *Portugal* Nation, and continually done very good offices to the Fort, for which cause his Kingdom was now like to be taken from him : This advice causing him to see his fault, and to be ashamed of his proceeding, he labored to have palliated it with certain excuses, but at last he sent this King by way of succor fifteen quintals of fine Powder, an hundred pots of Wild-fire, an hundred and fifty Bullets for great Ordnance, twelve Harquebuzes, forty sacks of stones, threescore Headpieces, and a Coat of guilt Mail, lined with Crimson Sattin for his own person, together with many other garments of divers sorts, as also twenty pieces of *Caracas*, which are stained linnen, or Cotten Tapestry, that come from the *Indiaes*, and cloth of *Malaya*, wherewith they usually apparel themselves in that Country, as well for his wife, as his daughters. All these things being laden aboard a *Lanchara* with oars, he desired me to conduct and present them from him to the King of *Aaru*, adding withall, that this business greatly concerned the King of *Portugals* service, and that at my return, besides the recompence I should receive from him, he would give me an extraordinary pay, and upon all occasions employ me in such Voyages, as might redound to my profit ; whereupon I undertook it, in an ill hour as I may say, and for a punishment of my sins, in regard of what arrived unto me thereupon, as shall be seen hereafter. So then I imbarqued my self on Tuesday morning, the fifth of *October*, 1539. and used such speed, that on Sunday following I arrived at the River of *Panetican*, upon which the City of *Aaru* is scituated.

I no sooner got to the River of *Panetican*, but presently landing I went directly to a Trench, §.2. which the King in person was causing to be made at the mouth of the River for to impeach the Enemies dis-imbarquing ; Presenting my self unto him, he received me with great demonstration of joy, whereupon I delivered him *Pedro de Faria's* Letter, which gave him some hope of his coming in person to succor him, if need required, with many other complements, that cost little the saying, wherewith the King was wonderfully contented, because he already imagined that the effect thereof would infallibly ensue ; But after he saw the Present I brought him, consisting of Powder, and Ammunitions, he was so glad, that taking me in his arms, My good friend, said he unto me, I assure thee that the last night I dreamt how all these things, which I behold here before me, came unto me from the King of *Portugal*, my Masters Fortress, by means whereof, with Gods assistance, I hope to defend my Kingdom, and to serve him, in the manner I have always hitherto done, that is, most faithfully, as all the Captains can very well testifie, which have heretofore commanded in *Malaca*. Hereupon questioning me about certain matters, that he desired to know, as well concerning the *Indiaes*, as the Kingdom of *Portugal*, he recommended the finishing of the Trench to his people, who wrought very earnestly and chearfully in it, and taking me by the hand, on foot as he was, attended only by five or six Gentlemen, he led me directly to the City, that was about some quarter of a league from the Trench, where in his Palace he entertained me most magnificently, yea and made me to salute his wife, a matter very rarely practised in that Country, and held for a special honor, which when I had done with abundance of tears he said unto me, *Portugal*, here is the cause that makes me so much to redoubt the coming of mine Enemies, for were I not withheld by my wife I swear unto thee by the Law of a good and true Moor, that I would prevent them in their designs without any other ayd then of my own Subjects ; for it is not now that I begin to know what manner of man the perfidious *Achem* is, or how far his power extends ; Alas ! it is the

great

great store of Gold, which he possesseth, that covers his weaknes, and by means whereof he wageth such forces of strangers, wherewith he is continually served : But now that thou mayst on the other side understand how vile and odious poverty is, and how hurtful to a poor King, such as I may be, come thee along with me, and by that little which I will presently let thee see thou shalt perceive, whether it be not too true, that Fortune hath been exceeding niggardly to me of her goods ; Saying so, he carried me to his Orsenal, which was covered with thatch, and shewed me all that he had within it, whereof he might say with reason, that it was nothing in comparison of what he needed for to withstand the attempts of two hundred and thirty Vessels, replenished with such warlike people, as the *Achems* and *Mulabar Turks* were ; Moreover, with a sad countenance, and as one that desired to discharge his mind of the grief he was in for the danger was threatned him, he recounted unto me, that he had in all but six thousand men *Aaruns*, without any other forraign succor, forty Pieces of small Ordnance, as Falconets, and Bases, and one cast Piece, which he had formerly bought of a *Portugal*, named *Antonio de Garcia*, sometimes Receiver of the Toll and Customs of the Ports of the Fortress of *Pacem*, whom *Georgio d' Albuqurque* caused since to be hanged and quartered at *Malaca*, for that he treated by Letters with the King of *Bintham* about a plot of Treason, which they had contrived together ; He told me besides, that he had also forty Muskets, six and twenty Elephants, fifty Horsemen for the guard of the place, eleven or twelve thousand staves hardened in the fire, called *Salignes*, whose points were poysoned, and for the defence of the Trench fifty Lances, good store of Targets, a thousand pots of unslack'd Lime made into Powder, and to be used in stead of pots of Wild-fire, and three or four Barques full laden with great flints; In a word, by the view of these, and such other of his miseries, I easily perceived he was so unprovided of things necessary for his defence, that I presently concluded the Enemy would have no great ado to seize on this Kingdom : Nevertheless he having demanded of me what I thought of all this Ammunition in his Magazin, and whether there were not enough to receive the guests he expected, I answered him, that it would serve to entertain them ; but he understanding my meaning stood musing a pretty while, and then shaking his head, Verily, said he unto me, if your King of *Portugal* did but know what a loss it would be to him, that the Tyrant of *Achem* should take my Kingdom from me, doubtless he would chastise the little care of his Captains, who, blinded as they are, and wallowing in their avarice, have suffered my Enemy to grow so strong, that I am much afraid they shall not be able to restrain him when they would, or if they could, that then it must be with an infinite expence. I labored to answer this which he had said unto me with such resentment, but he confuted all my reasons with so much truth, as I had not the heart to make any farther reply; withall he represented divers foul and enormous actions unto me, wherewithall he charged some particulars amongst us, which I am contented to pass by in silence, both in regard they are nothing pertinent to my discourse, and that I desire not to discover other mens faults ; For a conclusion of his speech, he related unto me the little punishment which was ordained for such as were culpable of these matters, and the great rewards that he had seen conferred on those which had not deserved them ; whereunto he added, that if the King desired throughly to perform the duty of his Charge, and by Arms to conquer people so far distant from his Kingdom, and to preserve them, it was as necessary for him to punish the wicked, as to recompence the good. This said, he sent me to lodg in a Merchants house, who for five days together, that I remained there, entertained me bravely, though to speak truth I had rather have been at that time in some other place with any poor victuals, for here I was always in fear, by reason of the Enemies continual alarms, and the certain news that came to the King the next day after my arrival, how the *Achems* were already marching towards *Aaru*, and would be there within eight days at the farthest, which made him in all haste to give directions for such things as he had not taken order for before, and to send the women, and all that were unfit for War, out of the City five or six leagues into the Wood, amongst the which the Queen her self made one, mounted on an Elephant. Five days after my arrival, the King sent for me, and asked me when I would be gone, whereunto I replyed, at such time as it would please his Greatness to command me, though I should be glad it might be with the soonest, for that I was to be employed by my Captain with his Merchandise to *China:* Thou hast reason, answered he ; then taking two Bracelets of massy Gold off from his wrists, worth some thirty Crowns, I pre-thee now, said he, giving them to me, do not impute it to miserableness that I bestow so little on thee, for thou mayst be assured, that it hath been always my desire for to have much for to give much ; withall I must desire thee to present this Letter, and

this

this Diamond from me to thy Captain, to whom thou ſhalt ſay, that whatſoever I am further engaged to him in for the pleaſure he hath done me by ſuccoring me with thoſe Ammunitions he hath ſent me by thee, I will bring it to him my ſelf hereafter, when I ſhall be at more liberty then now I am.

Having taken leave of the King of *Aaru*, I preſently imbarqued my ſelf, and departed about §.3. Sun-ſet, rowing down the River to an Hamlet, that is at the entrance thereof, compoſed of ten or eleven houſes covered with ſtraw : This place is inhabited with very poor people, that get their living by killing of *Lezards*, of whoſe livers they make a poyſon, wherewith they anoint the heads of their arrows ; For the poyſon of this place, chiefly that, which is called *Pocauſilim*, is held by them the beſt of thoſe Countries, becauſe there is no remedy for him that is hurt with it. The next day, having left this ſmall Village, we ſailed along the coaſt with a land wind until evening, that we doubled the Iſlands of *Anchepiſan*, then the day and part of the night following we put forth ſomewhat farther to Sea : But about the firſt watch the wind changed to the North-eaſt, for ſuch winds are ordinary about the Iſle of *Samatra*, and grew to be ſo tempeſtuous, that it blew our maſt over board, tore our ſails in pieces, and ſo ſhattered our Veſſel, that the water came in that abundance into her at two ſeveral places, as ſhe ſunk in-continently to the bottom, ſo that of eight & twenty perſons, which were in her, three and twen-ty were drowned in leſs then a quarter of an hour. For as five that eſcaped by the mercy of God, we paſſed the reſt of the night upon a Rock, where the waves of the Sea had caſt us. There all that we could do was with tears to lament our ſad fortune, not knowing what counſel or courſe to take, by reaſon the Country was ſo moorish, and invironned with ſo thick a Wood, that a bird, were ſhe never ſo little, could hardly make way through the branches of it, for that the trees grew ſo cloſe together ; We ſat crouching for the ſpace of three whole days upon this Rock, where for all our ſuſtenance we had nothing but Snails, and ſuch filth, as the foam of the Sea produced there. After this time, which we ſpent in great miſery and pain, we walked a whole day along by the Iſle of *Samatra*, in the owze up to the girdle-ſtead, and about Sun-ſet we came to the mouth of a little River, ſome Croſsbow-ſhot broad, which we durſt not un-dertake to ſwim over, for that it was deep, and we very weak and weary ; ſo that we were forced to paſs all that night, ſtanding up to the chin in the water. To this miſery was there adjoyned the great affliction which the Flies and Gnats brought us, that coming out of the neighboring Woods, bit and ſtung us in ſuch ſort, as not one of us but was gore blood. The next morning as ſoon as we perceived day, which we much deſired to ſee, though we had lit-tle hope of life, I demanded of my four companions, all Mariners, whether they knew the Country, or whether there was any habitation thereabout ; Whereupon the eldeſt of them, who had a wife at *Malaca*, not able to contain his tears, Alas ! anſwered he, the place that now is moſt proper for you, and me, is the houſe of death, where ere it be long we muſt give an account of our ſins, it therefore behoves us to prepare our ſelves for it without any further delay, and patiently to attend that which is ſent us from the hand of God : For my part, let me intreat thee to be of a good courage whatſoever thou ſeeſt, and not be terrified with the fear of dying, ſince, every thing well conſidered, it matters not whether it be to day, or to morrow. This ſpoken, he embraced me, and with tears in his eyes deſired me to make him a Chriſtian, becauſe he beleeved, as he ſaid, that to be ſo was ſufficient to ſave his Soul, which could not otherwiſe be done in the curſed ſect of *Mahomet*, wherein he had lived till then, and for which he craved pardon of God. Having finiſhed theſe laſt words, he remained dead in mine arms, for he was ſo weak, as he was not able to ſubſiſt any longer, as well for that he had not eaten ought in three or four days before, as in regard of a great wound the wrack of the *Lanchara* had given him in his head, through which one might ſee his brains all putrefied and corrupted, occaſion'd both for want of looking unto, as by ſalt water and flies that were gotten into it. Verily this accident grieved me very much, but for my ſelf I was in little better caſe, for I was likewiſe ſo weak, that every ſtep I made in the water I was ready to ſwoon, by reaſon of cer-tain hurts on my head and body, out of which I had loſt a great deal of blood. Having buried him in the owze the beſt we could, the other three Mariners and my ſelf reſolved to croſs the River, for to go and ſleep on certain great Trees, that we ſaw on the other ſide, for fear of the Tygers and Crocodiles, whereof that Country is full, beſides many other venomous creatures, as an infinite of thoſe copped Adders I have ſpoken of before in the ſixth Chapter, and divers ſorts of Serpents with black and green ſcales, whoſe venom is ſo contagious, as they kill men with their very breath. This reſolution being thus taken by us, I deſired two of them to ſwim

over

over firſt, and the other to ſtay with me for to hold me up in the water, for that in regard of my great weakneſs I could hardly ſtand upon my legs: whereupon they two caſt themſelves preſently into the water, exhorting us to follow them, and not be afraid; But alas! they were ſcarce in the midſt of this River, when as we ſaw them caught by two great Lezards, that before our faces, and in an inſtant tearing them in pieces, dragged them to the bottom, leaving the water all bloody, which was ſo dreadful a ſpectacle to us, as we had not the power to cry out; and for my ſelf, I knew not who drew me out of the water, nor how I eſcaped thence, for I was gone before into the River as deep as my waſte, with that other Mariner which held me by the hand.

CHAP. X.

By what means I was carried to the Town of Ciaca, *and that which befell me there; my going to* Malaca *with a Mahometan Merchant; and the Tyrant of* Achems *Army marching againſt the King of* Aaru.

§.1. FInding my ſelf reduced to that extremity I have ſpoken of, I was above three hours ſo beſides my ſelf, as I could neither ſpeak, nor weep; At length the other Mariner and I went into the Sea again, where we continued the reſt of that day. The next morning having diſcovered a Barque, that was ſeeking the mouth of the River, as ſoon as it was near we got out of the water, and falling on our knees with our hands lift up we deſired them to come and take us up; whereupon they gave over rowing, and conſidering the miſerable ſtate we were in they judged immediately that we had ſuffered ſhipwrack, ſo that coming ſomewhat nearer they asked us what we deſired of them; we anſwered, that we were Chriſtians, dwelling at *Malaca,* and that in our return from *Aaru* we were caſt away by a ſtorm about nine days before, and therefore prayed them for Gods ſake to take us away with them whitherſoever they pleaſed. Thereupon one amongſt them, whom we gueſſed to be the chiefeſt of them, ſpake to us thus, By that which I ſee, you are not in caſe to do us any ſervice, and gain your meat, if we ſhould receive you into our Barque, wherefore if you have any mony hidden, you ſhall do well to give it us aforehand, and then we will uſe towards you that charity you require of us, for otherwiſe it is in vain for you to hope for any help from us: Saying ſo, they made ſhew as though they would be gone; whereupon we beſought them again weeping, that they would take us for ſlaves, and go ſell us where they pleaſed; hereunto I added, how they might have any ranſom for me they would require, as having the honor to appertain very nearly unto the Captain of *Malaca.* Well, anſwered he then, we are contented to accept of thy offer, upon condition, that if that which thou ſayſt be not true, we will caſt thee, bound hand and foot, alive into the Sea. Having replyed, that they might do ſo if they found it otherwiſe, four of them got preſently to us, and carried us into their Barque, for we were ſo weak at that time, as we were not able to ſtir of our ſelves. When they had us aboard, imagining that by whipping they might make us confeſs where we had hid our mony, for ſtill they were perſwaded that we had ſome, they tyed us both to the foot of the Maſt, and then with two double coards they whipped us till we were nothing but blood all over. Now becauſe that with this beating I was almoſt dead, they gave not to me, as they did to my companion, a certain drink, made of a kind of Lime, ſteeped in Urine, which he having taken it, made him fall into ſuch a furious vomiting, as he caſt up both his lungs and his liver, ſo as he dyed within an hour after. And for that they found no gold come up in his vomit, as they hoped, it pleaſed God that that was the cauſe why they dealt not ſo with me, but only they waſhed the ſtripes they had given me with the ſaid liquor, to keep them from feſtering, which notwithſtanding put me to ſuch pain, as I was even at the point of death. Being departed from this River, which was called *Ariſſumbea,* we went the next day after dinner aſhore at a place, where the houſes were covered with ſtraw, named *Ciaca,* in the Kingdom of *Jambes,* there they kept me ſeven and twenty days, in which time by the aſſiſtance of Heaven I got my ſelf throughly cured of all my hurts. Then they that had a ſhare in my perſon, who were ſeven in number, ſeeing me unfit for their Trade, which was fiſhing, expoſed me to ſale three ſeveral times, and yet could meet with no body that would buy me; whereupon being out of hope of ſelling me, they turned me out of doors, becauſe they would not be at the charge of feeding me. I had been ſix and thirty days thus abandoned by theſe Inhumanes, and put a graſing like a caſt Horſe, having no other means to live but what I got by begging from door to door, which God knows was very little, in regard

thoſe

those of the Country were extream poor, when as one day, as I was lying in the Sun upon the sand by the Sea side, and lamenting my ill fortune with my self, it pleased God that a *Mahometan*, born in the Isle of *Palimban*, came accidentally by : This man, having been sometimes at *Malaca* in the company of *Portugals*, beholding me lie naked on the ground, asked me if I were not a *Portugal*, and willed me to tell him the truth ; whereunto I answered, that indeed I was one, and descended of very rich parents, who would give him for my ransom whatsoever he would demand, if he would carry me to *Malaca*, where I was Nephew to the Captain of the Fortress, as being the son of his sister. The *Mahometan* hearing me say thus, If it be true, replyed he, that thou art such as thou deliverest thy self to be, what so great sin hast thou committed that could reduce thee to this miserable estate wherein I now see thee ? Then I recounted to him from point to point how I was cast away, and in what sort the fishermen had first brought me thither in their Barque, and afterwards had turned me out to the wide world, because they could not find any body that would buy me. Hereat he seemed to be much astonished, so that musing a pretty while by himself, Know stranger, said he unto me, that I am but a poor Merchant, all whose wealth amounts not to above an hundred *Pardains* (which are worth two shillings a piece of our mony) with which I trade for the rows of Shads, thereby hoping to get my living ; Now I am assured that I might gain something at *Malaca*, if so be the Captain, and the Officers of the Custom-house there, would not do me the wrong, which I have heard say they do to many Merchants that come thither to traffique ; wherefore if thou thinkst that for thy sake I should be well used there, I could be contented to redeem thee from the fishermen, and go thither with thee. Thereunto I answered him, with tears in mine eyes, that considering the state I was in at the present, it was not likely he could give credit to any thing I said, because it was probable that to free my self out of my miserable captivity I would prize my person at a far higher value then it would be esteemed for at *Malaca* ; howbeit if he would lend any belief to my oaths, since I had no other assurance to give him, I would swear to him, and also set it under my hand, that if he would carry me to *Malaca*, the Captain should do him a great deal of honor for my sake, and besides the exempting of his Merchandise from paying of custom, he should receive ten times as much as he should disburse for me. Well, replyed the *Mahometan*, I am contented to redeem, and reconduct thee to *Malaca*, but thou must take heed that thou speakest not a word of that we have concluded on, for fear thy Masters hold thee at so dear a rate, as I shall not be able to draw thee out of their hands though I would never so fain ; whereupon I gave him my faith to do nothing but what he would have me do, especially in that particular, which I held to be most necessary for the better effecting of our desire.

Four days after this agreement, the *Mahometan* Merchant, that he might the more easily §.2. redeem me, used the interposure of a man born in the Country, who under hand went to the fishermen, and carried the business so cunningly with them, as they quickly consented to my redemption, for they were already very weary of me, as well in regard that I was sickly, as for that I could no way stand them in any stead, and therefore, as I delivered before, they had turned me out of doors, where I had continued a month and better ; so by the means of this third person, whom the *Mahometan* had employed, the fishermen sold me to the Merchant for the sum of seven *mazes* of gold, which amounts in our mony to seventeen shillings and six pence. The *Mahometan* as soon as he had redeemed me, brought me to his house, where I was five days out of the tyranny of these fishermen, and in a far better captivity then the former ; At the end whereof my new Master went five leagues off to a place, named *Sorobaya*, where he got his Merchandise aboard, which, as I said before, was nothing but the rows of Shads ; For there is such great abundance of them in that River, as the Inhabitants do therewith every year lade above two thousand Vessels, which carry at least an hundred and fifty, or two hundred Barrels, whereof each one contains a thousand rows, the rest of the fish not yielding them a peny. After that the *Mahometan* had laden a *Lanchara* with this commodity, he presently set sail for *Malaca*, where within a while he safely arrived, and carrying me to the Fortress presented me to the Captain, relating unto him what agreement we had made together. *Pedro de Faria* was so amazed to see me in such a lamentable plight, as the tears stood in his eyes, whereupon he bade me speak out aloud, that he might know whether it was I that he beheld, for that I did not seem to be my self, in regard of the strange deformity of my face. Now because that in three months space there had been no news of me, and that every one thought me to be dead, there came so many folks to see me, as the Fortress could scarce hold them :

4

Here

Here being demanded the occasion of my misfortune, and who had brought me into that miserable case, I recounted the adventures of my Voyage, just in the same manner as I have already delivered them, whereat the whole company were so astonished, that I saw some go away without speaking a word, and others shrink up their shoulders, and bless themselves in admiration of that which they had heard from me; but in conclusion their compassion towards me was such, that with the very alms they bestowed on me I became far richer then I was before I undertook that unlucky Voyage. As for *Pedro de Faria*, he caused threescore duckets to be given to the *Mahometan* Merchant that brought me, besides two pieces of good *China* Damask; moreover he freed him of all the duties he was to pay for the custom of his Merchandise, which amounted to very near a like sum, so as he remained exceeding well satisfied of the bargain he had made with me. After this, to the end I might be the better used and looked unto, the Captain commanded me to be lodged in the Registers house of the Kings Customs, where for that he was married there he thought I might be better accommodated then in any other place, as indeed I was very well entreated by him and his wife, so that having kept my bed about the space of a month, it pleased God to restore me unto my perfect health.

§.3.   When I had recovered my health, *Pedro de Faria* sent for me to the Fortress, where he questioned me about that which had past betwixt me and the King of *Aaru*, as also how and in what place I was cast away, whereupon I made him an ample relation thereof. But before I proceed any further, it is requisite I should here report what was the success of the War between the Kings of *Aaru* and *Achem*, to the end, that the desolation, which I have so often foretold, of our Fortress of *Malaca*, may the more evidently appear, it being a matter of too much importance for to be so neglected as it is by those, who ought to have more care of it. For this is certain, that either the power of the King of *Achem* is utterly to be ruined, or by it we shall be miserably expelled out of all the Countries we have conquered all along the Southern Coast, as *Malaca*, *Banda*, *Maluco*, *Sunda*, *Borneo*, and *Timor*, and Northwards, *China*, *Japan*, and the *Lequios*, as also many other parts and Ports, where the *Portugals* are very much interessed by reason of the Traffique which they dayly use there, and where they reap more profit then in any other place, that is yet discovered, beyond the Cape of good hope, the extent thereof being so great, that it contains along the Coast above three thousand leagues, as may easily be seen by the cards and globes of the world, if so be their graduation be true. Besides, if this loss should happen, which God of his infinite mercy forbid, though we have but too much deserved it for our carelessness and sins, we are in danger in like manner to lose the Customs of *Mandorim* of the City of *Goa*, which is the best thing the King of *Portugal* hath in the *Indiaes*, for they are Ports and Islands, mentioned heretofore, whereon depends the greatest part of his Revenue, not comprehending the Spices, namely, the Nutmegs, Cloves, and Maces, which are brought into this Kingdom from those Countries. Now to return to my discourse, I say, that the Tyrant of *Achem* was advised by his Councel how there was no way in the world to take *Malaca*, if he would assail it by Sea, as he had done divers times before, when as *Dom Stephano de Gama* and his Predecessors were Captains of the Fortress, but first to make himself Master of the Kingdom of *Aaru*, to the end he might afterwards fortifie himself on the River of *Panetican*, where his Forces might more commodiously and nearly maintain the War he intended to make: For then he might have means with less charge to shut up the Straights of *Cincapura*, and *Sabaon*, and so stop our Ships from passing to the Seas of *China*, *Sunda*, *Banda*, and the *Molucques*, whereby he might have the profit of all the Drugs which came from that great Archipelague; And verily this counsel was so approved by the Tyrant, that he prepared a Navy of an hundred and threescore Sails, whereof the most part were *Lanchares* with oars, Galiots, *Calabuzes* of *Jaoa*, and fifteen Ships high built, furnished with Munition and Victual. In these Vessels he imbarqued seventeen thousand men, namely twelve thousand Soldiers, the rest Sailers and Pioners. Amongst these were four thousand Strangers, *Turks*, *Abissins*, *Malabares*, *Gusurates*, and *Lusons* of the Isle of *Borneo*. Their General was one, named *Heredin Mahomet*, Brother-in-law to the Tyrant, by marriage with a Sister of his, and Governor of the Kingdom of *Baarros*. This Fleet arrived safely at the River of *Panetican*, where the King of *Aaru* attended them with six thousand of his own natural Subjects, and not a forraigner amongst them, both in regard he wanted mony for to entertain Soldiers, and that also he had a Country unprovided of victual to feed them. At their arrival the Enemies found them fortifying of the Trench, whereof I spake heretofore; Whereupon

without

without any further delay they began to play with their Ordnance, and to batter the Town on the Sea side with great fury, which lasted six whole days together. In the mean time the besieged defended themselves very valiantly, so as there was much blood spilt on either side: The General of the *Achems*, perceiving he advanced but little, caused his Forces to Land, and mounting twelve great Pieces he renewed the battery three several times with such impetuosity, that it demolished one of the two Forts that commanded the River, by means whereof, and under the shelter of certain packs of Cotton which the *Achems* carried before them, they one morning assaulted the principal Fortress: In this assault an *Abissin* commanded, called *Mamedecan*, who a month, or thereabout, before was come from *Juda*, to confirm the new League made by the Bassa of *Caire* on the behalf of the grand *Signior* with the Tyrant of *Achem*, whereby he granted him a Custom-house in the Port of *Pazem*. This *Abissin* rendered himself Master of the Bulwark, with threescore *Turks*, forty *Janizaries*, and some *Malabar* Moors, who instantly planted five Ensigns on the walls; In the mean time the King of *Aaru*, encouraging his people with promises, and such words as the time required, wrought so effectually, that with a valorous resolution they set upon the Enemy, and recovered the Bulwark which they had so lately lost, so as the *Abissin* Captain was slain on the place, and all those that were there with him. The King following his good fortune, at the same instant caused the gates of the Trench to be opened, and sallying out with a good part of his Forces, he combated his Enemies so valiantly, as he quite routed them; In like manner he took eight of their twelve Pieces of Ordnance, and so retreating in safety he fortified himself the best he could for to sustain his Enemies future assaults.

CHAP. XI.

The Death of the King of Aaru, *and the cruel Justice that was executed on him by his Enemies; the going of his Queen to* Malaca, *and her reception there.*

THe General of *Achem*, seeing the bad success which he received in this incounter, was §.т. more grieved for the death of the *Abissin* Captain, and the loss of those eight Pieces of Ordnance, then for all them that were slain besides; whereupon he assembled his Councel of War, who were all of opinion that the commenced siege was to be continued, and the Trench assailed on every side, which was so speedily put in execution, that in seventeen days it was assaulted nine several times, in so much as by divers sorts of fire-works, continually invented by a *Turkish* Engineer, that was in their Camp, they demolished the greater part of the Trench; Moreover they overthrew two of the principal Forts on the South side, together with a great Platform, which in the manner of a false-bray defended the entry of the River, notwithstanding all the resistance the King of *Aaru* could make with his people, though they behaved themselves so valiantly, as the *Achems* lost above two thousand and five hundred men, besides those that were hurt, which were far more then the slain, whereof the most part dyed shortly after for want of looking to. As for the King of *Aaru*, he lost not above four hundred men, howbeit for that his people were but few, and his Enemies many, as also better ordered, and better armed, in the last assault, that was given on the thirteenth day of the Moon, the business ended unfortunately by the utter defeat of the King of *Aaru*'s Forces; For it was his ill hap, that having made a salley forth by the advice of a *Cacis* of his, whom he greatly trusted, it fell out that this Traytor suffering himself to be corrupted with a bar of gold, weighing about forty thousand duckets, which the *Achem* gave him, whereof the King of *Aaru* being ignorant, set couragiously on his Enemies, and fought a bloody battel with them, wherein the advantage remained on his side in all mens judgment, but that Dog, the perfidious *Cacis*, whom he had left Commander of the Trench, sallied forth with five hundred men, under colour of seconding the King in his pursuit of so prosperous a beginning, and left the Trench without any manner of defence, which perceived by one of the Enemies Captains, a *Mahometan Malabar*, named *Cutiale Marcaa*, he presently with six hundred *Gusarates* and *Malabars*, whom he had led thither for that purpose, made himself Master of the Trench, which the traytrous *Cacis* for the bar of gold he had received had left unguarded, and forthwith put all the sick and hurt men that he found there to the sword, amounting to the number of about fifteen hundred, whereof he would not spare so much as one. In the mean time the unhappy King of *Aaru*, who thought of nothing less then the treachery of his *Cacis*, seeing his Trench taken, ran to the succoring of it, being a matter that most imported him: But finding himself the weaker, he was constrained to quit the place, so that as he was making his retreat to the Town ditch, it was his ill fortune to be killed by a shot of an Harquebuse from a *Turk* his enemy. Upon this death of his ensued the loss of all the rest, by reason of the great disorder it brought amongst them. Whereat the Enemies exceedingly rejoycing, took up the Corps of that wretched King, which they found amongst the other dead bodies, and having imbowelled and salted him they put him up in a Case, and so sent him as a Present to the Tyrant, who, after many ceremonies of Justice, caused him to be publiquely sawed into sundry pieces, and then boiled in a great Cauldron full of Oyl and Pitch, with a dreadful Publication, the tenor whereof was this:

See here the Justice, which Sultan Laradin, *King of the Land of the two Seas, hath caused to be executed, whose will and pleasure it is, that as the body of this miserable Mahometan hath been sawed in sunder, and boiled here on Earth, so his Soul shall suffer worse torments in Hell, and that most worthily, for his transgressing of the Law of Mahomet, and of the perfect belief of the* Musselmans *of the House of* Mecqua: *For this execution is very just, and conformable to the holy Doctrine of the Book of Flowers, in regard this Miscreant hath shewed himself in all his works to be so far without the fear of God, as he hath incessantly from time to time betrayed the most secret and important affairs of this Kingdom to those accursed Dogs of the other end of the world, who for our sins, and through our negligence, have with notorious Tyranny made themselves Lords of* Malaca. This Publication ended, a fearful noise arose amongst the people, who cryed out, *This punishment is but too little for so execrable a crime.* Behold truly the manner of this passage, and how the loss of the Kingdom of *Aaru* was joyned with the death of that poor King, who lived in such good correspondence with us, and that in my opinion might have been succored by us with very small charge and pains, if at the beginning of the War he had been assisted with that little he demanded by his Embassador; Now who was in the fault hereof, I will leave to the judgment of them which most it concerns to know it.

§.2.   After that this infortunate King of *Aaru* had miserably ended his days, as I have before related, and that his whole Army was utterly defeated, both the Town and the rest of the Kingdom were easily and quickly taken in. Thereupon the General of the *Achems* repaired the Trenches, and fortified them in such manner as he thought requisite for the conservation and security of all that he had gained: which done, he left there a Garison of eight hundred of the most couragious men of his Army, who were commanded by a certain *Lusan Mahometan,* named *Sapetù de Raia,* and incontinently after departed with the rest of his Forces. The common report was that he went to the Tyrant of *Achem,* who received him with very much honor for the good success of this enterprize; For, as I have already delivered, being before but Governor and *Mandara* of the Kingdom of *Baarros,* he gave him the title of King, so that ever after he was called *Sultan* of *Baarros,* which is the proper denomination of such as are Kings amongst the *Mahometans.* Now whilest things passed in this sort, the desolate Queen remained some seven leagues from *Aaru,* where being advertised and assured of the death of the King her husband, and of the lamentable issue of the War, she presently resolved to cast her self into the fire, for so she had promised her husband in his life time, confirming it with many and great oaths; But her friends and servants, to divert her from putting so desperate a design in execution, used many reasons unto her, so that at length, overcome by their perswasions, *Verily,* said she unto them, *although I yield to your request, yet I would have you know, that neither the considerations you have propounded, nor the zeal you seem to shew of good and faithful Subjects, were of power to turn me from so generous a determination, as that is which I promised to my King, my Husband, and my Master, if God had not inspired me with this thought, that living I may better revenge his death, as by his dear blood I vow unto you to labor as long as I live to do, and to that end I will undergo any extremity whatsoever, nay if need be turn Christian a thousand times over, if by that means I may be able to compass this my desire.* Saying so, she immediately got up on an Elephant, and accompanied with a matter of seven hundred men, she marched towards the Town with a purpose to set it on fire, where incountring some four hundred *Achems,* that were busie about pillaging of such goods as were yet remaining, she so encouraged her people with her words and tears, that they cut them all presently in pieces; This execution done, knowing her self too weak for to hold the Town, she returned into the Wood, where she sojourned twenty days, during which time she made War upon the Townsmen, surprising and pillaging them as often as they issued forth to get water, wood, or other necessaries, so as they durst not stir out of the Town to provide them-

themselves such things as they needed, in which regard if she could possibly have continued this War other twenty days longer, she had so famished them, as they would have been constrained to render the Town: But because at that time it rained continually by reason of the Climate, and that the place was boggy and full of bushes, as also the fruits, wherewithall they nourished themselves in the Wood, were all rotten, so that the most part of her people fell sick, and no means there to relieve them, the Queen was constrained to depart to a River, named *Minha-çumbaa,* some five leagues from thence, where she imbarqued her self in sixteen Vessels, such as she could get, which were fishermens *Paroos,* and in them she went to *Malaca,* with a belief that at her Arrival there she should not be denyed any thing she would ask.

Pedro de Faria, being advertised of the Queens coming, sent *Alvaro de Faria,* his son, §.3. and General of the Sea-forces, to receive her with a Galley, five Foists, two Catures, twenty Balons, and three hundred men, besides divers persons of the Country. So she was brought to the Fortress, where she was saluted with an honorable peal of Ordnance, which lasted the space of a good hour. Being landed, and having seen certain things, which *Pedro de Faria* desired to shew her, as the Custom-house, the River, the Army, the Manufactures, stores of Powder, and other particulars, prepared before for that purpose, she was lodged in a fair house, and her people, to the number of six hundred, in a field, called *Ilber,* in Tents and Cabbins, where they were accommodated the best that might be. During all the time of her abode, which was about a matter of five months, she continued soliciting for succor, and means to revenge the death of her husband. But at length perceiving the small assistance she was likely to have from us, and that all we did was but a meer entertainment of good words, she determined to speak freely unto *Pedro de Faria,* that so she might know how far she might trust to his promises; To which end, attending him one Sunday at the gate of the Fortress, at such time as the place was full of people, and that he was going forth to hear Mass, she went to him, and after some complements between them, she said unto him; *Noble and valiant Captain, I beseech you by the generosity of your race, to give me the hearing in a few things I have to represent unto you. Consider, I pray you, that albeit I am a Mahometan, and that for the greatness of my sins I am altogether ignorant in the knowledg of your holy Law, yet in regard I am a woman, and have been a Queen, you ought to carry some respect to me, and to behold my misery with the eyes of a Christian.* Hereunto at first *Pedro de Faria* knew not what to answer, in the end putting off his cap, he made her a low reverence, and after they had both continued a good while without speaking, the Queen bowed to the Church gate, that was just before them, and then spake again to *Pedro de Faria. Truly,* said she, *the desire I have always had to revenge the death of my husband, hath been, and still is, so great, that I have resolved to seek out all the means that possibly I may to effect it, since by reason of the weakness of my sex Fortune will not permit me to bear arms; Being perswaded then that this here, which is the first I have tryed, was the most assured, and that I more relyed upon then any other, as trusting in the ancient amity which hath always been betwixt us and you Portugals, and the obligation wherein this Fortress is engaged to us, passing by many other considerations well known to you, I am now to desire you with tears in mine eyes, that for the honor of the high and mighty King of Portugal, my soveraign Lord, and unto whom my husband was ever a loyal Subject and Vassal, you will ayd and succor me in this my great adversity, which in the presence of many noble Personages you have promised me to do; howbeit now I see that in stead of performing the promises which you have so often made me, you alledg for an excuse that you have written unto the Vice-roy about it, whereas I have no need of such great Forces as you speak of, for that with an hundred men only, and such of my own people as are flying up and down in hope and expectation of my return, I should be able enough, though I be but a Woman, in a short space to recover my Country, and revenge the death of my husband, through the help of Almighty God, in whose Name I beseech and require you, that for the service of the King of Portugal, my Master, and the only refuge of my widowhood, you will, since you can, assist me speedily, because expedition is that which in this affair imports the most, and so doing you shall prevent the plot which the wicked enemy hath upon this Fortress, as too well you may perceive by the means he hath used to effect it. If you will be pleased to give me the succor I demand of you, say so; if not, deal clearly with me, for that you will prejudice me as much in making me lose time, as if you refused me that which so earnestly I desire, and which as a Christian you are obliged to grant me, as the Almighty Lord of Heaven and Earth doth well know, whom I take to witness of this my request.*

*The Queen of Aaru's departure from Malaca; her going to the King of Jantana;
his summoning the Tyrant of Achem to restore the Kingdom of Aaru,
and that which past between them thereupon.*

§.1. PEdro de Faria, having heard what this desolate Queen said openly unto him, convinced by
his own conscience, and even ashamed of having delayed her in that fashion, answered her,
that in truth, and by the faith of a Christian, he had recommended this affair unto the Vice-
roy, and that doubtless there would some succor come for her ere it were long, if so be there
were no trouble in the *Indiaes* that might hinder it, wherefore he advised and prayed her to
stay still in *Malaca*, and that shortly she should see the verity of his speeches. Thereunto this
Princess having replyed upon the uncertainty of such succor, *Pedro de Faria* grew into choller,
because he thought she did not believe him, so that in the heat of his passion he lashed out some
words that were more rude then was fit. Whereupon the desolate Queen, with tears in her
eyes, and beholding the Church gate, which was just against her, and sobbing in such manner
as she could scarcely speak; *The clear Fountain, said she, is the God which is adored in that
house, out of whose mouth proceeds all truth, but the men of the Earth are sinks of troubled
water, wherein change and faults are by nature continually remaining, wherefore accursed
is he that trusts to the opening of their lips; For I assure you, Captain, that ever since I knew
my self to this present I have neither heard, nor seen ought, but that the more such unhappy
wretches, as my late husband was, and my self now am, do for you Portugals, the less you regard them, and the more you are obliged, the less you acknowledg, whence I may well conclude
that the recompence of the* Portugal *Nation consists more in favor, then in the merits of persons; And would to God, my deceased husband had nine and twenty years ago but known what
now for my sins I perceive too well, for then he had not been so deceived by you as he was:
But since it is so, I have this only left to comfort me in my misery, that I see many others
scandalized with your amity as well as my self; For if you had neither the power nor the will
to succor me, why would you so far engage your self to me, a poor desolate widow, concerning
that which I hoped to obtain from you, and so beguile me with your large promises?* Having
spoken thus, she turned her back to the Captain, and without harkening to what he might say
she instantly returned to her lodging, then caused her Vessels, wherein she came thither, to be
made ready, and the next day set sail for *Bintan*, where the King of *Jantana* was at that time,
who, according to the report was made of it to us afterward, received her with great honor
at her arrival. To him she recounted all that had past betwixt her and *Pedro de Faria*, and
how she had lost all hope of our friendship; Unto whom, it is said, the King made this answer,
*That he did not marvel at the little faith she had found in us, for that we had shewed it but too
much upon sundry occasions unto all the world.* Now the better to confirm his saying, he recited some particular examples of matters, which he said had befallen us, conformable to his
purpose; and like a *Mahometan*, and our Enemy, he made them appear more enormous then
they were: So after he had recounted many things of us very ill done, amongst the which he
interlaced divers Treacheries, Robberies, and Tyrannies, at length he told her, that as a good
King, and a good *Mahometan*, he would promise her, that ere it were long she should see her
self by his means restored again to every foot of her Kingdom; and to the end she might
be the more assured of his promise, he told her that he was content to take her for his wife, if
so she pleased, for that thereby he should have the greater cause to become the King of *Achems*
Enemy, upon whom for her sake he should be constrained to make War, if he would not by
fair means be perswaded to abandon that which he had unjustly taken from her. Whereunto
she made answer, that albeit the honor he did her was very great, yet she would never accept
of it, unless he would first promise, as in way of a dowry, to revenge the death of her former
husband, saying, it was a thing she so much desired, as without it she would not accept of the
Soveraignty of the whole world. The King condescended to her request, and by a solemn Oath taken on a Book of their Sect confirmed the promise which to that effect he made
her.

§.2. After that the King of *Jantana* had taken that Oath before a great *Cacis* of his, called *Raia
Moulana*, upon a festival day when as they solemnized their *Ramadan*, he went to the Isle of
Compar, where immediately upon the celebration of their Nuptials he called a Councel for to
                                                                                         advise

advise of the course he was to hold for the performance of that whereunto he had engaged himself, for he knew it was a matter of great difficulty, and wherein he should be forced to hazard much of his Estate. The resolution that he took hereupon was before he enterprized any thing to send to summon the Tyrant of *Achem* to surrender the Kingdom of *Aaru*, which in the right of his new wife belonged now unto him, and then according to the answer he should receive to govern himself. This Council seemed so good to the King, that he presently dispatched an Embassador to the Tyrant, with a rich Present of Jewels, and Silks, together with a Letter containing these words. *Sibri Laya quendou, pracama de Raia, lawful King by a long succession of* Malaca, *which by strong hand, and the injustice of the faithless Kings of* Jantana *and* Bintan *hath been usurped from me, To thee* Sity Sultan Aaradin, *King of Achem, and of all the Land of the two Seas, my true Brother by the ancient Amity of our forefathers. I, thine Ally in flesh and in blood, do give thee to understand by my Embassador, that about the seventh Moon of this present year the noble Widow* Anchesiny, *Queen of Aaru, came to me full of grief and tears, and prostrating her self on the ground before me, she told me that thy Captains had taken her Kingdom from her, as also the two Rivers of* Lava *and* Panetican, *and slain* Alibonic *car her husband, together with five thousand* Amborraias *and* Ouroballons, *all men of mark, that were with him, and made three thousand children slaves, which had never offended, tying their hands behind them, and scourging them continually without pity, as if they had been the sons of unbelieving mothers. Wherefore being moved with compassion I have received her under the protection of my faith, to the end that I might with more certainty inform my self of the reason and right thou hadst so to do, and perceiving by her oaths that thou hadst none, I have taken her to my Wife, that I might the more freely before God demand that which is hers. I desire thee then, as being thy true Brother, that thou wilt render that thou hast taken from her, and thereof make her a good and full restitution; And touching the proceeding that is to be held in this restitution which I demand of thee, it is to be done according to the manner that* Syribican *my Embassador will shew thee. And not doing thus conformable to what in justice I require of thee, I declare my self thine Enemy in the behalf of this Lady, unto whom I am obliged by a solemn Oath to defend her in her affliction.* This Embassador being come to *Achem*, the Tyrant received him very honorably, and took his Letter; But after he had opened it, and read the contents, he would presently have put him to death, had he not been diverted by his Council, who told him, that in so doing he would incur great infamy: Whereupon he instantly dismissed the Embassador with his Present, which in contempt of him he would not accept of, and in answer of that he brought him he returned him a Letter, wherein it was thus written. *I* Sultan Aaradin, *King of Achem,* Baarros, Pedir, Paacem, *and of the Signories of* Dayaa, *and* Batas, *Prince of all the Land of the two Seas, both Mediterranean and Ocean, and of the Mynes of* Menencabo, *and of the Kingdom of Aaru newly conquered upon just cause, To thee-King, replenished with joy, and desirous of a doubtful heritage: I have seen thy Letter, written at the table of thy Nuptials, and by the inconsiderate words thereof have discerned the drunkenness of thy Councellors and Secretaries, whereunto I would not have vouchsafed an answer, had it not been for the humble prayers of my servants. As touching the Kingdom of Aaru, do not thou dare to speak of it if thou desirest to live, sufficeth it that I have caused it to be taken in, and that it is mine, as thine also shall be ere long, if thou hast married* Anchesiny *with a purpose upon that occasion to make claim to a Kingdom, that now is none of hers; Wherefore live with her as other husbands do with their wives, that tilling the ground are contented with the labor of their hands. Recover first thy* Malaca, *since it was once thine, and then thou mayst think of that which never belonged to thee. I will favor thee as a Vassal, and not as a Brother, as thou qualifiest thy self. From my great and Royal House of rich* Achem, *the very day of this thy Embassaders arrival, whom I have presently sent away without further seeing or hearing of him, as he may tell thee upon his return to thy presence.*

The King of *Jantana's* Embassador, being dismissed with this Answer the very same day §.3. that he arrived, which amongst them they hold for a mighty affront, carried back the Present, which the Tyrant would not accept of in the greater contempt both of him that sent, and he that brought it, and arrived at *Compar*, where the King of *Jantana* was at that instant, who upon the understanding of all that had past grew by report so sad and vext, that his servants have vowed they have divers times seen him weep for very grief that the Tyrant should make so little reckoning of him; Howbeit he held a Council there upon the second time, where it was concluded,

cluded, that at any hand he should make War upon him, as on his mortal Enemy, and that the first thing he should undertake, should be the recovery of the Kingdom of *Aaru*, and the Fort of *Panetican*, before it was further fortified. The King accordingly set forth a Fleet of two hundred Sails, whereof the most part were *Lanchares*, *Calaluses*, and fifteen tall Juncks, furnished with Munition necessary for the enterprize; And of this Navy he made General the great *Laque Xemena*, his Admiral, of whose valor the History of the *Indiaes* hath spoken in divers places. To him he gave two thousand Soldiers, as also four thousand Mariners and gally slaves, all choyce and trained men. This General departed immediately with his Fleet, and arrived at the River of *Panetican* close by the Enemies Fort, which he assaulted five several times, both with scaling ladders, and divers artificial fires, but perceiving he could not prevail that way, he began to batter it with four hundred great Pieces of Ordnance, which shot continually for the space of seven whole days together, at the end whereof the most part of the Fort was ruined, and overthrown to the ground, whereupon he presently caused his men to give an assault to it, who performed it so valiantly, that they entered it, and slew fourteen hundred *Achems*, the most of which came thither but the day before the Fleet arrived under the conduct of a *Turkish* Captain, Nephew to the *Bassa* of *Caire*, named *Mora do Arraiz*, who was also slain there with four hundred *Turks* he had brought along with him, whereof *Laque Xemena* would not spare so much as one. After this he used such diligence in repairing that which was fallen, wherein most of the Soldiers labored, that in twelve days the Fort was rebuilt, and made as strong as before, with the augmentation of two Bulwarks. The news of this Fleet, which the King of *Jantana* prepared in the Ports of *Bintan* and *Compar*, came to the Tyrants ears, who fearing to lose that which he had gotten, put instantly to Sea another Fleet of fourteen hundred and twenty Sails, Foists, Lanchares, Galiots, and fifteen Galleys of five and twenty banks of oars a piece, wherein he caused fifteen thousand men to be imbarqued, namely, twelve thousand Soldiers, and the rest Mariners, and such as were for the service of the Sea; Of this Army he made the same *Heredin Mahomet* General, who had before (as I have already declared) conquered the Kingdom of *Aaru*, in regard he knew him to be a man of a great spirit, and fortunate in War, who departing with this Army arrived at a place, called *Aapessumhee*, within four leagues of the River of *Panetican*, where he learnt of certain fishermen, whom he took and put to torture, all that had past concerning the Fort and the Kingdom, and how *Laque Xemena* had made himself Master both of the Land and Sea in expectation of him. At this news, it is said, that *Heredin Mahomet* was much perplexed, because intruth he did not believe the Enemy could do so much in so little time; By reason whereof he assembled his Councel, where it was concluded, that since both the Fort and Kingdom were regained, and all the men he had left there cut in pieces, as likewise for that the Enemy was very strong, both at Sea and Land, and the season very unfit for their design, therefore they were to return back: Nevertheless *Heredin Mahomet* was of a contrary opinion, saying, that he would rather dye like a man of courage, then live in dishonor, and that seeing the King had made choyce of him for that purpose, by the help of God he would not lose one jot of the reputation he had gotten; wherefore he vowed and swore by the bones of *Mahomet*, and all the Lamps that perpetually burn in his Chappel, to put all those to death as Traytors that should go about to oppose this intent of his, and that they should be boiled alive in a Cauldron of Pitch, in such manner as he meant to deal with *Laque Xemena* himself; and with this boiling resolution he parted from the place where he rode at anchor, with great cries, and noise of Drums, and Bells, as they are accustomed to do upon like occasions. In this sort by force of oars and sails they got into the entry of the River, and coming in sight of *Laque Xemena*'s Navy, who was ready waiting for him, and well reinforced with a great number of Soldiers, that were newly come to him from *Pera*, *Bintan*, *Siaca*, and many other places thereabout, he made towards him, and after the discharging of their Ordnance afar off, they joyned together with as much violence as might be. The fight was such, that during the space of an hour and an half there could no advantage be discerned on either part, until such time as *Heredin Mahomet*, General of the *Achems*, was slain with a great shot, that hit him just in the brest, and battered him to pieces. The death of this Chieftain discouraged his people in such manner, as laboring to return unto a Point, named *Baroquirin*, with a purpose there to unite and fortifie themselves until night, and then by the favor thereof to fly away, they could not execute their design, in regard of the great currant of the water, which separated and dispersed them sundry ways, by which means the Tyrants Army fell into the power of *Laque Xemena*, who defeated it, so that but fourteen Sails of them escaped,

escaped, and the other hundred threescore and six were taken, and in them were thirteen thousand and five hundred men killed, besides the fourteen hundred that were slain in the Trench. These fourteen Sails that so escaped returned to *Achem*, where they gave the Tyrant to understand how all had past, at which, it is reported, he took such grief, as he shut up himself for twenty days without seeing any body, at the end whereof he struck off the heads of all the Captains of the fourteen Sails, and commanded all the Soldiers beards that were in them to be shaved off, enjoyning them expresly upon pain of being sawed asunder alive, to go ever after attired in womens apparel, playing upon Timbrels in all places where they went, and that whensoever they made any protestation, it should be in saying, *So may God bring me back my husband again, as this is true,* or, *So may I have joy of the children I have brought into the World.* Most of these men seeing themselves inforced to undergo a chastisement so scandalous to them, fled their Country, and many made themselves away, some with poyson, some with halters, and some with the sword. A relation altogether true, without any addition of mine. Thus was the Kingdom of *Aaru* recovered from the Tyrant of *Achem*, and remained in the hands of the King of *Jantana* until the year 1574. At which time the said Tyrant with a Fleet of two hundred Sails, feigning as though he would go to take in *Patava*, fell cunningly one night on *Jantana*, where the King was at that time, whom, together with his wife, children, and many others, he took prisoners, and carried into his Country, where he put them all to most cruel deaths, and for the King himself he caused his brains to be beaten out of his head with a great club. After these bloody executions he possest the Kingdom of *Aaru*, whereof he presently made his eldest son King, the same that was afterward slain at *Malaca*, coming to besiege it in the time of *Don Lionis Pereyra*, son to the Earl of *Feyra*, Captain of the Fortress, who defended it so valiantly, that it seemed to be rather a miracle then any natural work, by reason the power of that Enemy was so great, and ours so little in comparison of theirs, as it may be truly spoken how they were two hundred *Mahometans* against one *Christian*.

CHAP. XIII.

My departure from Malaca *to go to* Pan; *that which fortuned after my arrival there; with the murther of the King of* Pan, *and the cause thereof.*

TO return unto the Discourse where I left, I say, that when I was recovered of the sickness §.1. which I got in my Captivity at *Siaca*, *Pedro de Faria*, desiring to find out some occasion to advance and benefit me, sent me in a *Lanchara* to the Kingdom of *Pan* with goods of his, to the value of ten thousand duckets, for to consign them into the hands of a Factor of his, that recided there, named *Tome Lobo*, and from thence to go to *Patava*, which is an hundred leagues beyond that. To that purpose he gave me a Letter and a Present for the King, and an ample Commission to treat with him about the redemption of five *Portugals*, who in the Kingdom of *Siam* were Slaves to *Monteo de Bancha* his Brother-in-law. I parted then from *Malaca* upon this employment, and the seventh day of our Voyage, just as we were opposite to the Island of *Pullo Timano*, which may be distant from *Malaca* some ninety leagues, and ten or twelve from the mouth of the River of *Pan*, a little before day we heard at two several times great lamentations at Sea, and being not able in regard of the darkness of the night to know what it was, we were all suspended into divers opinions, for that we could not imagine what it should be, in so much that to learn the certainty thereof I caused them to hoist up sail, and row towards that part where we heard the lamentation, every one looking down round about close to the water, the better to discern and hear that of which we were in such doubt. After we had continued a pretty while in this manner, we perceived far from us a black thing that floated on the Sea, and unable at first to discover what it was, we advised together about it. Now there being but four *Portugals* of us in the *Lanchara*, we were all of different minds, so that I was told how I was to go directly to the place whither *Pedro de Faria* had sent me, that losing but an hours time I might endanger the Voyage, and hazard the goods, and so for want of performing the duty of my charge I might very much wrong him. Whereunto I answered, that happen what might, I would not leave off laboring to know what it was, and that if in so doing I committed any fault, the *Lanchara* appertained to none but *Pedro de Faria*, unto whom my self was to render an account of the goods in it, and not they, that had nothing else in the Vessel but their persons, which were in no more danger then mine: During this debate it pleased God that the day appeared, by the light whereof we perceived people that
were

were caft away, who floated pell-mell together upon planks, and other pieces of wood: Whereupon without further fear we turned our prow towards them, and with force of fails and oars we made to them, hearing them cry fix or feven times, without ufing any other fpeech, *Lord have mercy upon us.* At the fight of this ftrange and pitiful fpectacle we remained fo a-mazed, that we were almoft befides our felves, and caufing fome of the Mariners to get with all fpeed into the Cock-boat, they fetcht three and twenty perfons of them into the Lanchara, namely fourteen *Portugals,* and nine Slaves, which were all fo dif-figured in the face, as they made us afraid to look on them, and fo weak as they could neither fpeak nor ftand. After they had been thus taken up by us, and entreated in the beft manner we could, we demanded of them the caufe of their mif-fortune, whereunto one of the company weeping anfwered, My Mafters, I am named *Fernand Gil Porcalho,* and the eye, which you behold I want, was ftrucken out by the *Achems* at the fiege of *Malaca,* when as the fecond time they came to fur-prize *Dom Eftevano de Gama,* who defiring to do fomething for me, becaufe he faw me poor, as I was at that time, gave me leave to go to the *Molucques,* where would to God I had ne-ver been, fince my Voyage was to have fo bad a fuccefs: for after I departed from the Port of *Talagame,* which is the Roade of our Fort at *Ternate,* having failed three and twenty days with a favorable gale in a Junck that carried a thoufand bars of Cloves, worth above an hundred thoufand duckets, my ill fortune would, that at the point of *Surabaya* in the Ifle of *Java,* there arofe fo impetuous a North-wind, that our Junck brake in the prow, which conftrained us to lighten the hatches; So we paffed that night by the fhoar, without bearing fo much as a rag of fail, by reafon the Sea was exceedingly moved, and the waves moft infupportable. The next day we perceived that our Junk fank, fo that of an hundred forty and feven perfons that were in her there were faved but fix and twenty, and now it is fourtain days that we have been upon thefe planks, having during all that time eaten nothing but a flave of mine that dyed, with whom we have fuftained our felves eight days, and the very laft night two *Portugals* more dyed, on whom we would not feed, although we were very much preft to it by our hunger, becaufe we hoped that this or the next day would give an end both to our lives and mifery.

§.2. The relation, which this man made us, having rendred us all very penfive, and full of amaze-ment to fee him and his companions reduced to fo deplorable an eftate, we greatly wondered at the means, whereby God had fo miraculoufly delivered them, wherefore we gave him moft humble thanks for it, and comforted our new guefts, in reprefenting unto them all thofe things which the duty of true Chriftians and our poor captivity obliged us to tell them. After that we beftowed part of our clothes on them, and layd them in our ordinary beds, then we apply-ed thofe remedies to them, which we thought neceffary for their recovery; for not having flept of a long time, they were fo exceeding dizzy in the head, that they would fall down ftunned in fuch fort, as they continued without any knowledg for an hour together. This done, we went to feek out the Port of *Pan,* where we arrived near about midnight, cafting anchor in the Roade, juft againft a little inhabited place, called *Campalaru.* The next morning by break of day we rowed up the River about fome league to the Town, where we found *Tome Lobo,* who, as I have already declared, refided there, as Factor for the Captain of *Malaca,* into whofe hands I configned all the Merchandife that I brought along with me. The fame day three of the fourteen *Portugals,* which we took up at Sea, dyed, whereof the afore-named *Fernando Gil Porcalho* was one, as alfo five young men that were Chriftians, whom we caft all into the Sea, with great ftones tyed to their feet and about their necks for to make them fink to the bottom, in regard we could not be permitted to bury them in the Town, although *Tome Lobo* offered them forty duckets for that purpofe, the reafon they alledged was, that if they fhould fuffer it, their Country would remain accurfed, and incapable of nourifhing any thing, becaufe the deceafed were not purged from the Hogs flefh they had eaten, it being the moft de-teftable and enormous fin of all others; As for thofe which refted alive, *Tome Lobo* gave them very good entertainment, and furnifhed them with all things that they wanted, until fuch time as they recovered and returned to *Malaca.* Not long after, preparing my felf for my Voyage to *Patana, Tome Lobo* very earneftly defired me not to go thither, and told me that he held not himfelf fafe in that Town, by reafon he was advertifed that one *Taan Nerrafa,* a man of reputation, and of the chiefeft of the Town, had fworn to burn him in his houfe, with all the goods that were in it, faying, that at *Malaca* the Captains Factor had taken from him the va-lue of five thoufand duckets in Benjamin, Silk, and wood of Aloes, at a far lower rate then it was worth, and that he had payd him at his own pleafure, and therewith not contented had

in

in part of payment given him rotten stuffs, which he could make nothing of; moreover, that for all his five thousand duckets worth of Commodities, that in *Malaca* would have yielded him ten thousand, and by exchange of vendible wares, he might easily have returned, would have made him ten thousand more, he never could get above seven hundred duckets; and therefore to be revenged of this wrong, he had picked quarrels of purpose to tole him forth to kill him, in regard whereof he instantly desired me to stay, and not abandon him and the Captains stock to such apparant danger: Whereupon having used all the reasons I could to facilitate my voyage, he would by no means approve of them, but contradicted me in all my propositions. For conclusion, I remonstrated unto him, that if it were his ill fortune, as he said he feared, to be killed for that which he had, I should be in no better case, and therefore I marvelled why he would let those eleven *Portugals* go, with whom rather he should have imbarqued himself for *Malaca*. Hereunto after a little pause he made answer, that he was very sorry he had not done so, but since it was now too late, he intreated me not to forsake him in this extremity, and that for the Captains sake, who he knew would not take it well I should leave him so alone with his goods, which were no less worth then thirty thousand duckets, besides those belonging to himself, that amounted to almost as much more. This request of his made to me with such instance on the one side, somewhat perplexed me, and on the other considering the extream hazard I ran if I stay'd, I knew not what to resolve; At length after I had well thought of the matter, I was constrained to come to this accord with him, that in case he did not within fifteen days imbarque himself with me in my *Lanchara* for *Patana*, with all his Commodities reduced into gold, or stones, whereof there was great plenty in the Town, that then I might go where I pleased without him; an offer that he was forced to accept of, and so we remained agreed.

The fear *Tome Lobo* was in, lest that wherewithall he was threatened should befall him, made §.3. him use such diligence in selling away of his commodities, that by means of the good peny-worths he afforded them at, in less then eight days he cleared his Warehouse, and the other places wherein they lay; so that utterly refusing Pepper, Cloves, and such other Drugs, which took up too much room, he trucked all away for gold of *Menencabo*, for Diamonds of *Lavo* and *Taucampura*, and Pearls of *Borneo*. Now having made a full dispatch of all, and that we were resolved to imbarque the next day, by ill fortune a most terrible accident happened the night ensuing, which was, that one, named *Coia Geinal*, the King of *Borneo's* Embassador, who had been three or four years resident in the King of *Pan's* Court, and a marvelous rich man, killed the King upon finding him in bed with his wife, which caused such a commotion in the Town, that it seemed to be a Tumult of Hell rather then any humane business; Whereupon certain rogues and vagabonds, that wished for nothing more then such like occasions, to the end they might do what before for fear of the King they durst not enterprize, made a Troop of five or six hundred, which separated into three bands, went directly to the house, where *Tome Lobo* dwelt. Having assaulted it in six or seven places, they entred by force, notwithstanding all the resistance we could make, and that in defending it we lost eleven men, whereof the *Portugals*, which came with me from *Malaca*, were three. During this violence, all that *Tome Lobo* could do was to escape away with six great blows of a sword, one of the which had cut his right cheek almost away, so as he was like to dye of that hurt. We were both of us then constrained to abandon the house to them, together with all the goods that were in it, and retire to the *Lanchara*, where we remained with five Boys and eight Mariners, not having so much as the worth of a peny left of all our merchandize, which amounted to fifty thousand crowns in gold and stone only. In this *Lanchara* we past away all the night very much afflicted, and still harkening what might be the end of this mutiny, which was risen among the people, as I have before related. At length perceiving the matters grew worse and worse, and that there was no hope for us to recover any part of our goods, we thought it a far safer course to go away to *Patana*, then by staying to run a hazard of being killed, as above four thousand persons were. With this resolution we parted from this place, and in six days arrived at *Patana*, where we were very well received by the *Portugals* which were in that Country, unto whom we recounted all that had past at *Pan*, and the pitious estate wherein we had left that miserable Town. This accident very much afflicted them, so that desiring to give some remedy thereunto, with a true affection of charitable Christians they went all to the Palace of the King, and complained to him of the wrong that had been done to the Captain of *Malaca*, beseeching him thereupon they might be permitted to recover, if it were possible, the loss they had sustained, and have leave granted to right themselves upon any merchants goods belonging to the

Kingdom

Kingdom of *Pan*, to the value of the sum they had been despoyled of. The King having heard their complaint, and presently granting what they demanded; It is reasonable, said he, that you should do as you have been done unto, and that you should spoyl them that first have spoyled you, especially in a matter that concerns the Captain of *Malaca*, unto whom all of you are so much obliged. The *Portugals*, having rendred him very humble thanks for this grace, returned to their houses, where they concluded to seize upon all the goods they could meet with belonging to the Kingdom of *Pan*, until such time as they had fully recovered their loss. It hapned then about nine days after they being advertised, that some ten leagues off, in the river of *Calantan*, were three Junks of *China*, very rich, and appertaining to *Mahometan* Merchants, Natives of the Kingdom of *Pan*, that by foul weather at Sea were constrained to put in there, our people resolved to fall upon them: To which effect, out of three hundred *Portugals*, that were then in the Country, we chose out fourscore, with whom we imbarqued our selves in two Foysts, and one round ship, well provided of all things we thought to be necessary for this enterprize. So we departed three days after with all speed, for fear lest the *Mahometans* of the Country, having discovered our design, should advertise them of it whom we went to seek; Of these three vessels one *Joano Fernandez Dabrea*, born in the Isle of *Madera*, was General, who with forty Soldiers went in the round ship, and the other two Foysts were commanded by *Laurenco de Goes*, and *Vasco Sermento*, both of them of the City of *Braganca* in *Portugal*, and very well experienced in Sea-service. The next day we arrived at the river of *Calentan*, where as soon as we decryed the three Junks riding at anchor, which we had been told of, we set very valiantly upon them, and albeit those that were in them did at first do their best endevor to defend themselves, yet at length all their resistance was in vain, for in less then an hour we reduced them all under our power, so as seventy and four of theirs were slain, and but three of ours, though we had many men hurt. I will not hold you here with any particular discourse of what was done on either side, let it suffice, that after the three Junks had rendred themselves, we presently set sail, and carryed them away with us in all haste, because the whole Country thereabout was in an uproar, directing our course towards *Patana*, where by the favor of a fair wind we arrived the next day in the afternoon: Having then cast anchor, we saluted the Town with a peal of Ordnance in sign of joy, which put the *Mahometans* of the Country out of all patience; for though we stood in the terms of good friends with them, yet they left not to use all possible means, both of Presents which they gave to the Governors and the Kings Favorites, and otherwise, for to make our prizes voyd, and that the King would expel us out of his dominions, whereunto he would at no hand consent, saying, that he would not for any thing in the world break the peace, which his Ancestors had made with the Christians of *Malaca*, and that all that he could do therein was to become a third betwixt them: Whereupon he desired us, that the three *Necodas* of the Junks, so are the Commanders of them called in that Country, restoring unto us what had been taken from the Captain of *Malaca*, we would likewise render unto them as well their vessels free, as the overplus, a matter which *Joano Fernandez Dabrea*, and the rest of the *Portugals* very willingly agreed unto, to testifie the desire they had to content him; As indeed he was exceedingly well pleased with them for it, which he expressed both in courteous language, and many promises of his future favor. Thus were the fifty thousand duckets recovered, that *Pedro de Faria* and *Tome Lobo* had lost, and the *Portugals* were in great esteem over all that Country, so that their valor rendred them very formidable to the *Mahometans*. A little after the Soldiers assured us, that in the three Junks we had taken, there was only in lingots of silver, besides the other merchandize wherewithall they were laden, to the value of two hundred *Taieis*, which in our mony amounts to an hundred thousand duckets.

CHAP. XIV.

The Misfortune that befell us at the entry into the River of Lugor; *our hiding our selves in a Wood, with that which happened unto us afterwards; and our return unto* Malaca.

§.I. HAving sojourned six and twenty days at *Patana* for to sell away some few commodities of *China* that I had, there arrived a Foyst from *Malaca*, commanded by one *Antonio de Faria*, who came thither by the express commandment of *Pedro de Faria* to treat with the King about some accord, as also to confirm the ancient league anew which he had with *Malaca*,

laca, and withall to give him thanks for the good entertainment he gave in his Kingdom to those of the *Portugal* Nation. This businefs was carryed with a fair fhew of an Embaffie, accompanyed with a Letter and a Prefent of Jewels, fent in the name of the King of *Portugal* our Mafter, and taken out of his Coffers, as all the Captains of that place ufed to do. Now for as much as the faid *Antonio de Faria* had brought along with him fome ten or twelve thoufand crowns worth of *Indian* woolen and linnen cloth, which he had taken up on his credit at *Malaca,* and that he faw there was fo little utterance of that commodity, as he could not meet with any Merchant that would deal for it, he was fain to refolve for to fpend the winter there until fuch time as he might meet with fome opportunity to put it off; Howbeit he was advifed by fome of the beft experienced of the Country to fend it unto *Lugor,* which is a great Town in the Kingdom of *Siam,* an hundred leagues lower towards the North, for they alledged that this Port was very rich, and of great vent, by reafon of a world of Junks that arrived there dayly from the Ifle of *Jaoa,* from *Lava, Taniampura, Japara, Demaa, Panaruca Sydayo, Paffarvan, Solor,* and *Borneo,* whofe Merchants were ufed to give a good rate for fuch like commodities, in exchange of gold, or ftone. This advice was well approved of by *Antonio de Faria,* who inftantly went about to put it in execution; To which end he took order for the providing of a veffel, by reafon the Foyft wherein he came was altogether unfit for a further voyage: Matters thus difpofed of, he deputed one, named *Chriftovano Borhalho,* for his Factor, a man exceeding well vers'd in bufinefs of Traffique, with whom there imbarqued fome fixteen men, as well Soldiers as Merchants, with a hope that one crown would yield them fix or feven, what in the commodities they fhould carry, as in thofe they fhould return. Hereupon, wretched I being one of the fixteen, we parted from the Port on a Saturday, and failed with a favorable wind along the coaft till Thurfday next in the morning, that we arrived at *Lugor* Road, and anchored at the mouth of the River; There it was thought fit to pafs the reft of the day, to the end we might inform our felves of what was behoveful for us to do, as well for the fale of our commodities, as for the fafety of our perfons: And to fay truth, we learnt fuch good news, that we were confident of gaining above fix times double, and to be fure of freedom and liberty during all the month of *September,* according to the Ordinance of the King of *Siam,* becaufe it was the month of the Kings *Sumbayas.* Now the better to clear this, you muft know, that all along this coaft of *Malaya,* and within the Land, a great King commands, who for a more famous and recommendable Title above all other Kings, caufeth himfelf to be called *Prechau Saleu,* Emperor of all *Sornau,* which is a Country wherein there are thirteen Kingdoms, by us commonly called *Siam,* to the which fourteen petty Kings are fubject, and yield homage, that were anciently obliged to make their perfonal repair unto *Odiaa,* the Capital City of this Empire, as well to bring their Tribute thither, as to do the *Sumbaya* to their Emperor, which was indeed to kifs the Courtelas that he ware by his fide; Now becaufe this City was feated fifty leagues within the Land, and the Currents of the Rivers fo ftrong, as thefe Kings were oftentimes forced to abide the whole winter there to their great charge, they petitioned the *Prechau,* King of *Siam,* that the place of doing this their homage might be altered, whereupon he was pleafed to ordain, that for the future there fhould be a Viceroy refident in the Town of *Lugor,* which in their language is called *Poyho,* unto whom every three years thofe fourteen Kings fhould render that duty and obedience they were accuftomed to do unto himfelf, and that during that time they fpent there in performing the fame, being the whole month of *September,* both their own merchandize, and that of all others, as well natives as ftrangers, that either came in, or went out of the Country, fhould be free from all manner of impofts whatfoever: So that we arriving in the time of this freedom, there was fuch a multitude of Merchants that flocked thither from all parts, as we were affured there was no lefs then fifteen hundred Veffels in the Port, all laden with an infinity of Commodities of very great value: And this was the good news we learnt at fuch time as we arrived at the mouth of the River; wherewith we were fo well pleafed, that we prefently refolved to put in as foon as the wind would permit us. But alafs! we were fo unfortunate, that we could never come to fee what we fo much defired; for about ten of the clock, juft as we had dined, and were preparing to fet fail, we faw a great Junk coming upon us, which perceiving us to be *Portugals,* few in number, and our Veffel fmall fell clofe with our prow on the larboard fide, and then thofe that were in her threw into us great Cramp-irons, faftened unto two long chains, wherewithall they grappled us faft unto them, which they had no fooner done, but ftraightway fome feventy or eighty *Mahometans* came flying out from under their hatches, that till then had lien lurking

                                                                                   there,

there, who with a mighty cry cast so many stones, darts, and lances, which fell as thick as hail
upon us, that of us sixteen *Portugals* twelve rested dead in the place, together with six and
thirty others, as well Boys as Mariners. Now for us four remaining *Portugals*, after we had
escaped so dreadful an incounter, we leapt all of us into the Sea, where one was drowned, and
we three that were left getting to land as well as we could, being dangerously hurt, and wading
up to the wast in mud, went and hid our selves in the next adjoyning wood. In the mean time
the *Mahometans* of the Junk, entring into our Frigot, not contented with the slaughter they
had made of our men, like mad dogs they killed six or seven Boys out-right, whom they found
wounded on the Deck, not sparing so much as one of them : That done, they imbarqued all
the goods of our Vessel into their Junk, then made a great hole in her, and so sunk her : Immediately whereupon, leaving their anchor in the Sea, and the Cramp-irons wherewithall they
had grappled us unto them, they set sail, and made away as fast as ever they could for fear of being discovered.

§. 2.   After this our escape, seeing our selves all sore hurt, and without any hope of help, we did
nothing but weep and complain, for in this disaster we knew not what to resolve on, so much
were we amazed with that which had befaln us within the space of half an hour. In this desolation we spent the rest of that sad day, but considering with our selves, that the place was
moorish, and full of Adders and Lizards, we thought it our safest course to continue there all
the night too, as accordingly we did, standing up to the middle in the Owze : The next morning as soon as it was day we went along by the Rivers side, until we came unto a little channel,
which we durst not pass, as well for that it was very deep, as for fear of a great number of
Lizards that we saw in it, so that in great pain we stayd not only that night there, but five days
after, being not able either to go forward, or turn aside, by reason of the bogs round about us,
all covered over with rushes : In the mean time one of our companions dyed, whose name was
Bastian Anriques, a rich man, and that had lost eight thousand crowns in the *Lauchara*, in
so much that of all the company we were before there remained none but *Christovano Borralho* and my self, that with tears sat lamenting over the poor dead mans body, which we had
covered with a little earth as well as we could, for we were then so weak, that we could hardly stir, or almost speak, so as we had set up our rest to make an end of those few hours we
hoped to live in that place. The next day, being the seventh of our disaster, about Sun-set we
espyed a great Barque coming rowing up the River, whereupon as soon as it was near us, we
prostrated our selves on the ground, beseeching those that were aboard her to take us in ; They
wondering at us, presently made a stand, seeming much amazed to see us so on our knees, and
our hands lift up to Heaven, as though we were at our prayers ; neverthelefs without speaking
at all to us, they made as if they would go on, which constrained us afresh to cry aloud to them
with tears that they would not suffer us for want of succor to dye miserably there. Upon those
our cries and lamentations an ancient woman came forth from under the hatches, whose grave
countenance represented her to be such as afterwards we found her to be ; she seeing us in so
pitiful a plight, moved with our misfortune, and our wounds that we shewed her, she took up
a stick, and therewith struck three or four of the Mariners because they would not take us in,
whereupon approaching to the bank, five or six of them leapt on shore, and by her commandment took us upon their shoulders, and carryed us into the Barque. This honorable woman,
much grieved to behold us so hurt, and our shirts and linnen drawers all bloody and mired,
caused them straightway to be washed, and having given each of us, a linnen cloth to cover us
withall, she would needs have us to sit down by her, where commanding meat to be brought
us, she her self presenting it to us with her own hand, *Eat, eat,* said she, *poor strangers, and
be not afflicted to see your selves reduced unto the estate you are in ; for I, whom now you look
upon, and that am but a woman, not having as yet attained to the age of fifty years, have seen
my self a slave, and despoyled of above an hundred thousand duckets worth of goods : Nor is
that all, for to this misfortune was the death of three of my sons adjoyned, and that of my
husband, whom I held far more dearer then these eyes of mine, these eyes, alass ! wherewith
I beheld both the father and the sons torn in pieces by the King of* Siams *Elephants, together
with two brothers, and a son-in-law I had ; Ever since I have had a languishing life, and to
all these miseries have many others far greater succeeded, for so implacable hath fortune been
unto me, that I have seen three daughters of mine ready to be marryed, as also my father,
mother, and two and thirty of my kinsmen, nephews, and cousins, thrown into burning furnaces, where their cries and lamentations could not chuse but reach unto Heaven, for God to*
                                                                                    succor

fuccor them in the violence of that infupportable torment; but alafs! the enormity of my fins no doubt fo ftopped the ears of the clemency of the Lord of Lords, that he would not hear our requeft, which feemed very juft to me; neverthelefs I deceived my felf, fince nothing is juft but what it pleafeth his divine Majefty to ordain. Hereunto we anfwered, that the fins which we alfo had committed againft him were the caufe of our calamities. Seeing it is fo, replyed fhe, mingling her tears with ours, it is always good in your adverfities to acknowledg, that the touches of the hand of God are evermore righteous, for both in that, as alfo in a confeffion of the mouth, in a forrow for having offended, and in a firm refolution to do fo no more, confifteth all the remedy of your fufferings and mine. Having entertained us thus with the difcourfe of her misfortune, fhe enquired of us the occafion of ours, and by what means we came to be in that miferable eftate, whereupon we recounted unto her all that had paft, and that we neither knew who it was that had fo ill intreated us, nor wherefore he did it; Her people, hearing us, faid, that the great Junk, whereof we fpake, belonged to a *Mahometan*, a *Guzarat* by Nation, named *Coia Acem*, who the fame morning went out of the River laden with Brazil, and was bound for the Ifle of *Ainan* : Hereat the good woman fmote her breft, and feeming to be much moved, *Let me not live*, faid fhe, *if it be not fo, for I have heard that* Mahometan, *of whom you fpeak, vaunt publiquely before all that would give ear unto him, that he had flain a great number of the race of thofe of* Malaca, *and that he hated them in fuch fort, as he had promifed to his* Mahomet *to kill more of them in time.* Being amazed hereat, we defired her to declare unto us who that man was, and why he was fo much our enemy, whereunto fhe anfwered, that fhe knew no other reafon, but for that a great Captain of our Nation, named *Hector de Sylveira*, had killed his father and two of his brothers in a fhip, which he took from them in the ftraight of *Mecqua*, that was going from *Judas* to *Dabul*. Thus much did this good Matron tell us, and many other things afterwards concerning the great hatred this *Mahometan* bore us, as alfo what lyes he devifed to render us infamous.

This honorable woman, departing from the place where fhe found us, went fome two §.3. leagues up the River, till fhe came to a little Village, where fhe lay that night; The next morning parting from thence, fhe made directly to the Town of *Lugor*, which was above five leagues further. Arriving there about noon, fhe landed, and went to her houfe, whither fhe carryed us with her, and kept us there three and twenty days, during which time we were very well looked unto, and plentifully accommodated with all that was neceffary for us. This woman was a widow, and of an honorable family, as afterwards we learnt, and that had been marryed to the Captain General, which they call *Xabandar* of *Prevedim*, whom the *Pata* of *Lafapara* King of *Quaijuan* had put to death in the Ifle of *Jaoa* the year 1538. At the time fhe met with us, as I have related, fhe came from a Junk of hers, that lay at the Road laden with Salt; and becaufe it was great, and could not pafs up by reafon of the fhelves, fhe caufed it to be unladen by little and little with that Barque. By that time the three and twenty days, I fpake of, were expired, it pleafed God to reftore us to our perfect health, fo that this virtuous Dame feeing us able to travel, recommended us to a Merchant, her kinfman, that was bound for *Patana*, with whom, after we had taken our leave of that noble Matron, unto whom we were fo much obliged, we imbarqued our felves in a *Cataluz* with Oars, and failing on a River, called *Sumhechitano*, we arrived feven days after at *Patana*. Now for as much as *Antonio de Faria* looked every day for our return, with a hope of good fuccefs in his bufinefs, as foon as he faw us, and underftood what had paft, he remained fo fad and difcontented, that he continued above an hour without fpeaking a word; in the mean time fuch a number of *Portugals* came in, as the houfe was fcarce able to contain them, by reafon the greateft part of them had ventured goods in the *Lanchara*, whofe lading in that regard amounted to feventy thoufand duckets and better, the moft of it being in filver coyn, of purpofe with it to return gold. *Antonio de Faria* feeing himfelf ftripped of the twelve thoufand duckets he had borrowed at *Malaca*, refolved not to return thither, becaufe he had no means to pay his Creditors, but rather thought it fitter to purfue thofe that had robbed him of his goods; fo that he took a folemn Oath upon the holy Evangelifts to part incontinently from that place for to go in queft of thofe Pyrats, for to revenge upon them the death of thofe fourteen *Portugals*, and thirty fix *Chriftians*, Boys and Mariners, killed by them as aforefaid; Adding withall, that if fuch a courfe were not taken, they fhould every day be ufed fo, nay far worfe. All the Affiftants very much commended his valorous refolution, and for the execution thereof there were many young Soldiers amongft them that offered to accompany him in that voyage; fome

likewife

likewife prefented him with mony, and others furnifhed him with divers neceffaries : Having accepted thefe offers and prefents of his friends, he uf ed fuch diligence, that within eighteen days he made all his preparations, and got together five and fifty Soldiers, amongft whom poor unfortunate I was fain to be one ; for I faw my felf in that cafe, as I had not fo much as a fingle token, nor knew any one that would either give or lend me one, being indebted befides at *Malaca* above five hundred duckets, that I had borrowed there of fome of my friends, which, with as much more, that dog had robbed me of amongft others, as I have related before, having been able to fave nothing but my miferable carcafs, wounded in three places with a Javelin, and my skull crackt with a ftone, whereby I was three or four times at the point of death ; But my companion *Chriftovan Borralho* was yet far worfe entreated then my felf, and that with more hurts, which he received in fatisfaction of five and twenty hundred duckets that he was robbed of as the reft.

CHAP. XV.

Antonio de Faria's fetting forth for the Ifle of Ainan, *his arrival at the River of* Tinacoren ; *and that which befell us in this Voyage.*

§.1. AS foon as *Antonio de Faria* was ready, he departed from *Patana* on a Saturday the ninth of *May,* 1540. and fteered North North-weft, towards the Kingdom of *Champaa,* with an intent to difcover the Ports and Havens thereof, as alfo by the means of fome good booty to furnifh himfelf with fuch things as he wanted ; for his hafte to part from *Patana* was fuch, as he had not time to furnifh himfelf with that which was neceffary for him, no not with victual and warlike ammunition enough. After we had failed three days we had fight of an Ifland, called *Pullo Condor,* at the height of eight degrees and three quarters, on the North Coaft, and almoft North-weft towards the mouth of the River of *Camboia,* fo that having rounded all the Coaft, we difcovered a good Haven Eaftward, where in the Ifland of *Camboia,* diftant fome fix leagues from the firm Land, we met with a Junk of *Lequios,* that was going to the Kingdom of *Siam* with an Embaffador from the *Nautauquim* of *Lindau,* who was Prince of the Ifland of *Tofa,* and that had no fooner difcovered us but he fent a meffage by a *Chinefe* Pilot to *Antonio de Faria,* full of complements, whereunto was added thefe words from them all: *That the time would come when as they fhould communicate with us in the true love of the Law of God, and of his infinite clemency, who by his death had given life to all men, and a perpetual inheritance in the houfe of the good, and that they beleeved this fhould be fo, after the half of the half time was paft.* With this complement they fent him a Courtelas of great value, whofe handle and fcabbard was of gold, as alfo fix and twenty Pearls in a little Box likewife of gold, made after the fafhion of a Salt-feller, whereat *Antonio de Faria* was very much grieved, by reafon he was not able to render the like unto this Prince, as he was obliged to do, for when the *Chinefe* arrived with this meffage they were diftant above a league at Sea from us. Hereupon we went afhore, where we fpent three days in taking in frefh water, and fifhing. Then we put to Sea again, laboring to get to the firm Land, there to feek out a River, named *Pullo Cambim,* which divides the State of *Camboia* from the Kingdom of *Champaa,* in the height of nine degrees, where arriving on a Sunday the laft of *May,* we went up three leagues in this River, and anchored juft againft a great Town, called *Catimparu,* there we remained twelve days in peace, during the which we made our provifion of all things neceffary. Now becaufe *Antonio de Faria* was naturally curious, he endevored to underftand from the people of the Country what Nation inhabited beyond them, and whence that mighty River took its fource ; whereunto he was anfwered, that it was derived from a lake, named *Pinator,* diftant from them Eaftward two hundred and fixty leagues in the Kingdom of *Quitirvan,* and that it was invironed with high mountains, at the foot whereof, upon the brink of the water, were eight and thirty villages, of which thirteen were very great, and the reft fmall, and that only in one of the great ones, called *Xincaleu,* there was fuch a huge myne of gold, as by the report of thofe that lived thereabout, there was every day a bar and a half drawn out of it, which, according to the value of our mony, makes two and twenty millions in a year, and that four Lords had fhare in it, who continually were in war together, each one ftriving to make himfelf mafter of it ; I, and that one of them, named *Raiahitau,* had in an inner yard of his houfe, in pots under ground, that were full to the very brims, above fix hundred bars of gold in powder, like to that of *Menancabo* of the Ifland of *Samatra* ; And that if three hundred

Harquebufiers

Harquebufiers of our Nation fhould go and affault it, without doubt they would carry it : Moreover that in another of thofe Villages, called *Buaquirim*, there was a quarry, where out of an old Rock they digged a great quantity of Diamonds, that were very fine, and of greater value then thofe of *Lava* and *Taniampura* in the Ifle of *Jaoa*. Whereupon *Antonio de Faria* having queftioned them about many other particularities, they made him a relation of the fertility of the Country, which was further up this River, no lefs fit to be defired, then eafie to be conquered, and that with little charge.

Being departed from this River of *Pullo Cambim*, we failed along the Coaft of the Kingdom §.2. of *Champaa*, till we came to an Haven, called *Saleyzacau*, feventeen leagues farther on towards the North, whereinto we entred. Now becaufe there was nothing to be gotten there, we went out of this place about fun-fetting, and the next morning we came to a River, named *Toobafoy*, without the which *Antonio de Faria* caft anchor, becaufe the Pilot would not venture to enter into it, for that he had never been there before, and therefore knew not the depth of it. As we were contefting hereabout, fome for to enter, and others gainfaying it, we difcerned a great fail making towards this Port from the main Sea. Hereupon, without ftirring from the place where we were, we prepared to receive them in a peaceable manner, fo that as foon as they came neer us, we faluted them, and hung up the flag of the Country, called *Charachina*, which is a fign of friendfhip, ufed among them in fuch like occafions. They of the fhip, in ftead of anfwering us in the fame manner, as in reafon it feemed they fhould have done, and knowing that we were *Portugals*, to whom they wifhed not well, gave us very vile and bafe words, and from the top of their poup made a capher flave hold up his arfe bare to us with a mighty noife and din of Trumpets, Drums, and Bells, by way of fcorn and derifion of us. Whereat *Antonio de Faria* was fo offended, that he gave them a whole broad fide, to fee if that would make them more courteous; To this fhot of ours they returned us an anfwer of five pieces of Ordnance, namely three Faulcons, and two little field-pieces; whereupon confulting together what we fhould do, we refolved to abide where we were, for we held it not fit to undertake fo doubtful an enterprize, until fuch time as the next days light might difcover the forces of this Veffel unto us, that fo we might afterwards either fet upon her with the more fecurity, or let her pafs by : This counfel was approved both by *Antonio de Faria*, and us all, fo that keeping good watch, and giving order for all that was neceffary, we continued in that place expecting day; now about two of the clock in the morning we perceived three black things clofe to the water coming towards us, which we could not well difcern, whereupon we wakened *Antonio de Faria*, who was then afleep on the hatches, and fhewed him what we had difcovered, being by that time not far from us; He fearing, as we did, left they were Enemies, cryed out prefently, *Arm, Arm, Arm*, wherein he was ftraightway obeyed; for now plainly perceiving that they were Veffels rowing towards us, we betook us to our Arms, and were beftowed by our Captain in places moft neceffary to defend our felves. We conceived by their filent approaching to us, that they were the Enemies we had feen over night, fo that *Antonio de Faria* faid unto us, *My mafters, this is fome Pyrat coming to fet upon us, who thinks we are not above fix or feven at the moft, as the manner is in fuch kinde of Veffels; wherefore let every man ftoop down, fo as they may not fee any of us, and then we fhall foon know their defign; in the mean time let the pots of powder be made ready, with which, and our fwords, I hope we fhall give a good end to this adventure : Let every one alfo hide his match in fuch fort, as they may not be difcovered, whereby they may be perfwaded that we are afleep :* all which, as he had prudently ordained, was incontinently executed. Thefe three Veffels, being come within a flight fhoot of ours, went round about her, and after they had viewed her well, they joyned all clofe together, as if they had entred into fome new confultation, continuing fo about a quarter of an hour; that done, they feparated themfelves into two parts, namely the two leffer went together to our poup, and the third, that was greater, and better armed, made to the ftarboard of us; Hereupon they entred our Lorch where moft conveniently they could, fo that in lefs then half a quarter of an hour above forty men were gotten in, which feen by *Antonio de Faria*, he iffued out from under the hatches with fome forty Soldiers, and invoking Saint *James* our Patron, he fell fo couragioufly upon them, that in a fhort time he killed them almoft all; Then with ayd of the pots of powder, that he caufed to be caft in amongft thofe that were remaining in the three Veffels which he prefently took, he made an end of defeating them, the moft of them being conftrained to leap into the Sea, where they were all drowned but five, whom we took up alive, whereof one was the capher flave that

fhewed

shewed us his tail, and the other four were one *Turk*, two *Achems*, and the Captain of the Junk, named *Similau*, a notorious Pyrat, and our mortal Enemy. *Antonio de Faria* commanded them instantly to be put to torture, for to draw out of them who they were, from whence they came, and what they would have had of us, whereunto the two *Achems* answered most brutishly; and when as we were going about to torment the slave in like maner, he began with tears to beseech us to spare him, for that he was a Christian as we were, and that without torture he would answer truly to all our demands; whereupon *Antonio de Faria* caused him to be unbound, and setting him by him, gave him a piece of Bisket, and a glass of wine, then with fair words he perswaded him to declare the truth of every thing to him, since he was a Christian, as he affirmed; To which he replyed in this sort, *If I do not speak the truth unto you, then take me not for such as I am; my name is* Sebaſtian, *and I was ſlave to* Gaſpar de Mello, *whom this dog* Similau, *here preſent, ſlew about two years ago in* Liampao, *with five and twenty other* Portugals *that were in his ſhip.* *Antonio de Faria* hearing this, cryed out, like a man amazed, and said, Nay now I care not for knowing any more; is this then that dog *Similau*, that slew thy master? Yes, answered he, *it is he, and that meant likewiſe to have done as much to you, thinking that ye were not above ſix or ſeven, for which effect he came away in haſte with a purpoſe, as he ſaid, to take you alive, for to make your brains fly out of your heads with a frontal of cord, as he did to my Maſter, but God I hope will pay him for all the miſchief he hath committed.* *Antonio de Faria* being also advertised by this slave, that this dog *Similau* had brought all his men of war along with him, and left none in his Junk but some *Chineſe* Mariners, he resolved to make use of this good fortune, after he had put *Similau* and his companions to death, by making their brains fly out of their heads with a cord, as *Similau* had done to *Gaſpar de Mello*, and the other *Portugals* in *Liampao*: Wherefore he presently imbarqued himself with thirty Soldiers in his Boat, and the three *Machnas*, wherein the Enemies came, and by means of the flood and a favorable wind, he arrived withless then an hour, where the Junk rode at anchor within the River about a league from us, whereupon he presently boarded her, and made himself master of the poup, from whence, with only four pots of powder, which he cast in among the Rascals that were asleep upon the hatches, he made them all leap into the Sea, where nine or ten of them were drowned, the rest crying out for help were taken up and saved, because we stood in need of them for the navigation of the Junk, that was a great tall Vessel. Thus you see how it pleased God out of his divine justice to make the arrogant confidence of this cursed dog a means to chastise him for his cruelties, and to give him by the hands of *Portugals* a just punishment for that which he had done unto them. The next morning, taking an inventory of this prize, we found six and thirty thousand *Taeis* in silver of *Japan*, which amounts in our mony to fifty four thousand duckets, besides divers other good commodities, that were not then praised for want of time, because the Country was all in an uproar, and fires every where kindled, whereby they use to give warning one to another upon any alarm or doubt of Enemies, which constrained us to make away with all speed.

§.3.   *Antonio de Faria* parted from this River of *Toobaſoy* on a Wednesday morning, being *Corpus Chriſti* Eve, in the year 1540. and sailed along by the Coast of the Kingdom of *Champaa*, fearing to abandon it, the wind being Easterly, which in that place is oftentimes very impetuous, especially in the conjunction of the new and full Moons. The Friday following we found our selves just against a River, called by the inhabitants of the Country *Tinacoreu*, and by us *Varella*, whereinto we thought fit to enter, as well to be informed of certain things *Antonio de Faria* desired to know, as also to see whether he could learn any news of *Coia Acem* whom he sought for, in regard that all the Junks of *Siam*, and of all the Coast of *Malaya*, that sail to *China*, use to trade in this River, where many times they sell their commodities well in exchange of gold, *Calembouc* wood, and Ivory, whereof there is abundance in that Kingdom; and having cast anchor a little within the mouth of the River, over against a Village, named *Taquileu*, there came a number of *Paroos*, and many other small Boats with fishermen, full of refreshments, who having never seen men made like unto us, said one to another; *Lo, this is a ſtrange novelty wherewithall God doth viſit us, let us beſeech him he will be pleaſed, that theſe bearded men may not be ſuch as for their particular profit do ſpy Countries like Merchants, and afterwards rob them like Theeves. Let us get to the woods for fear leſt the ſparks of theſe firebrands do not burn up our houſes, and reduce the fields of our labors into aſhes, as they uſe to do unto the Lands of other men.* Whereunto some of them

made

made anſwer, God forbid it ſhould be ſo ; but if by misfortune they ſhould come amongſt us, let us carry our ſelves in ſuch ſort, as they may not perceive we fear them as Enemies, for ſo they would ſet upon us with the more confidence ; wherefore the beſt courſe for us will be, in a fair way, and with gentle words, to endevor to learn of them what they would have of us, that upon knowledg thereof we may certifie it unto *Hoyaa Paquir,* who is now at *Congrau.* *Antonio de Faria,* making as though he did not underſtand them, although all that they ſaid was delivered to him by an Interpreter, received them very courteouſly, and bought the refreſhments, which they brought, of them at their own price, wherewithall they were very well ſatisfied ; And they demanding of him from whence he came, and what he would have, he anſwered them, that he was of the Kingdom of *Siam,* and as a Merchant was going to traffique in the Iſle of *Lequios,* being come into that place only to learn ſome news of a friend of his named *Coia Acem,* that was alſo bound thither : whereupon he enquired of them whether he were paſt by, or no ; howſoever he intended to depart thence ſuddenly, both for to loſe no time, as for that he knew he could not ſell his commodities there. To which they replyed, You ſay true, for in this village of ours there is nothing but nets and fiſher Boats, wherewith we get our living, and that poorly enough God knows. Howbeit, added they, if thou wilt go up the River to the Town of *Pilaucacem,* where the King is, thou wilt ſell not only the commodities which are in thy ſhips, be they never ſo rich, but likewiſe more then ten ſuch ſhips as thine could carry, by reaſon that there are Merchants in that place ſo wealthy, and that drive ſo great a trade, as they go with whole Troops of Elephants, Oxen, and Camels, whom they ſend laden with goods to the Lands of the *Lauhos, Paſuaas,* and *Gueos,* which are inhabited by very rich people. *Antonio de Faria* ſeeing a good occaſion offered to inform himſelf of that he deſired to know, queſtioned them at large concerning many things, whereunto ſome of them, that ſeemed to be of more authority then the reſt, anſwered very aptly, how the River, where we rode at anchor, was called *Tinacoreu,* and that it extended to *Moncalor,* a mountain diſtant from thence ſome fourſcore leagues, and that further upwards it was far broader, but not ſo deep, where in many places there was great ſhelves of ſand, and a world of land overflown with water, in the which were ſuch a multitude of fowls, as they covered all the Country thereabout ; And how beyond that it was all mountainous and rocky, and ſo full of Elephants, Rhinoceroſes, Lions, wilde Boars, Buffles, and ſuch other wilde beaſts, as men could not poſſibly live there for them ; And moreover, how in the midſt of that continent there was a great Lake, which the inhabitants thereof called *Cunebetea,* and others *Chiammay,* from whence this River took its beginning, as alſo three others, that watered a good part of this Country ; And that the ſaid Lake, according to the report of thoſe who have written of it, was threeſcore Jaos about, each Jao containing three Leagues, all along the which there were many Mynes of Silver, Copper, Tin, and Lead, from whence great quantities thereof were continually drawn, which the Merchants carryed away with Troops of Elephants and Rhinoceroſes, for to tranſport it into the Kingdoms of *Sornau,* by us called *Siam, Paſſiloco, Sarady, Tangu, Prom, Calaminham,* and other Provinces, that are very far within land, and diſtant from theſe Coaſts two or three months journey. Further, they told us, that theſe Countries were divided into Kingdoms, and Regions inhabited with people, that were white, tawny, and others ſomewhat blacker ; and that in exchange of thoſe commodities they returned Gold, Diamonds, and Rubies. Having thereupon demanded of them whether thoſe people had Arms, they anſwered none, but ſtaves hardened in the fire, and daggers with blades two ſpans long ; They alſo aſſured us that from hence one could not go thither by the River in leſs then half two months, or two months and an half, by reaſon of the impetuoſity of the waters deſcending with a great and ſtrong current the moſt part of the year, and that one might return in eight or ten days at the moſt. After theſe demands *Antonio de Faria* made them divers others, wherein they alſo gave him good ſatisfaction, and reported many other particulars unto him, whereby it may be gathered, that if the Country could be taken, it would, without ſo much labor and loſs of blood, be of greater profit, and leſs charge, then the *Indiaes.*

The Friday following we left this River of *Tinacoreu,* and by our Pilots advice we went §.4. to find out *Pullo Champeiloo,* which is an inhabited Iſland, ſcituate in the entrance to the Bay of *Cauchenchina* in forty degrees and a third to the Northward ; Being come to it, we caſt anchor in an Haven, where there was good and ſafe riding, and there we remained three days, accommodating our artillery in the beſt manner we could ; That done, we ſet ſail towards the Iſle of *Ainan,* hoping to meet with the Pyrat *Coia Acem* there whom we ſought for, and arriving

H riving

riving at *Pullo Capas*, which was the first land that we saw of it, we sailed close to the shoar, the better to discover the Ports and Rivers on that side, and the entries into them. Now because the Lorch, wherein *Antonio de Faria* came from *Patana*, leaked very much, he commanded all his Soldiers to pass into another better Vessel, which was immediately performed, and arriving at a River, that about evening we found towards the East, he cast anchor a league out at Sea, by reason his Junk was great, and drew much water, so that fearing the sands, which he had often met withall in this Voyage, he sent *Christovano Borralho* with fourteen Soldiers in the Lorch up the River to discover what fires those might be that he saw. Being gone then about a league in the River, he incountred a Fleet of forty very great Junks, whereupon fearing lest it was the *Mandarims* Army, whereof we had heard much talk, he kept aloof off from them, and anchored close by the shoar; now about midnight the tyde began to come in, which *Borralho* no sooner perceived, but he presently without noise weighed anchor, and declining the Junks he went on to that part where he had seen the fires, that by this time were almost all out, there being not above two or three that gave any light, and which served to guide him. So continuing his course very discreetly, he came to a place where he beheld a mighty company of great and small Ships, to the number as he guessed of thousand Sails, passing through the which very stilly he arrived at a Town of above ten thousand housholds, enclosed with a strong wall of Brick, with Towers and Bulwarks after our manner, and with Curtains full of water. Here five of the fourteen Soldiers, that were in the Lorch, went on shoar with two of those *Chineseses*, that were saved out of *Similaus* Junk, who had left their wives as hostages with us for their return; These having spent three hours in viewing and surveying the Town on the outside, reimbarqued themselves without any notice taken of them at all, and so went back very quietly as they came to the mouth of the River, where they found a Junk riding at anchor, that was come thither since their departure in the evening. Being returned to *Antonio de Faria*, they related unto him what they had seen, particularly the great Army that lay up in the River, as also the Junk, which they had left riding at anchor at the entrance into it, telling him that it might well be the Dog *Coia Acem* whom he sought for. These news so rejoyced him, that instantly he weighed anchor, and set sail, saying, his mind gave him that it was undoubtedly he; and if it proved so, he assured us all that he was contented to lose his life in fighting with him, for to be revenged of such a Rogue as had done him so much wrong. Approaching within sight of the Junk, he commanded the Lorch to pass unto the other side of her, to the end they might board her both together at once, and charged that not a Piece should be shot off, for fear they should be heard of the Army that lay up in the River, who might thereupon come to discover them. As soon as we were come to the Junk, she was presently invested by us, and twenty of our Soldiers leaping in made themselves Masters of her without any resistance, for the most of her men threw themselves into the Sea, the rest that were more couragious valiantly made head against our people; but *Antonio de Faria* presently getting in with twenty Soldiers more made an end of defeating them, killing above thirty of theirs, so as there remained none alive but those which voluntarily cast themselves into the Sea, whom he caused to be drawn up to serve for the Navigation of his Vessels, and for to learn who they were, and from whence they came, to which purpose he commanded four of them to be put to torture, whereof two chose rather to dye so then to confess any thing; and as they were about to do the like to a little boy, an old man, his father, that was layd on the deck, cryed out with tears in his eyes for to give him the hearing before they did any hurt to the child; *Antonio de Faria* made the Executioner stay, and bade the old man say what he would, provided he spake truth, for otherwise he vowed, that both he and the boy should be thrown alive into the Sea, whereas on the contrary, if he dealt truly, he promised to set them both at liberty on shoar, and restore unto him whatsoever he would take his oath did appertain unto him: Whereunto the old *Mahometan* answered, *I accept of the promise which thou makest me, and I very much thank thee for sparing the life of this child, for as for mine, as a thing unprofitable, I make no reckoning of it, and I will rely on thy word, although the course thou holdest may well divert me from it, in regard it is no way conformable to the Christian Law, which thou hast profest in thy Baptism:* An answer, that rendred *Antonio de Faria* so confounded and amazed, as he knew not what to reply; Howbeit he caused him to come nearer to him, and questioned him gently without any further threatening.

§.5.　This old man then sat him down by *Antonio de Faria*, who seeing him white like unto us, asked him whether he were a *Turk*, or a *Persian*? whereunto he answered, that he was neither,

ther, but that he was a Chriſtian, born at Mount *Sinai. Antonio de Faria* thereupon replyed, how he wondred much, being a Chriſtian, as he ſaid, that he lived not amongſt Chriſtians. To which the old man anſwered, that he was a Merchant of a good family, named *Tome Moſtanguo*, and that riding one day at anchor in a Ship of his in the Port of *Judaa*, in the year one thouſand five hundred thirty and eight, *Soliman* the Baſſa, Vice-roy of *Cairo*, took his, and ſeven others Ships, to carry Victual and Munition for his Army of threeſcore Galleys, wherewith he went by the Command of the grand *Signior* to reſtore *Sultan Bandur* to his Kingdom of *Cambaya*, which the great *Mogul* had deprived him of ; And that at the end of the Voyage going to demand the freight which they had promiſed him, the *Turks*, that were ever cruel and faithleſs, took his wife, and a young daughter he had, and forced them before his face, and becauſe his ſon wept at the ſight of this injury they threw him bound hand and foot into the Sea ; as for himſelf, they layd him in Irons, and continually ſcourging him they ſtript him of all his goods, to the value of ſix thouſand duckets and better, ſaying, that it was not lawful for any to enjoy the bleſſings of God, but the holy and juſt *Mouſſilimans*, ſuch as they were : And that his wife and daughter dying not long after, he found means one night to caſt himſelf into the Sea with that little boy, which was his ſon, at the mouth of the River of *Diu*, from whence he went by Land to *Surrat*, and ſo to *Malaca* in a ſhip of *Garcia de Saas*, Captain of *Bacaim* ; then how by the commandment of *Eſtevano de Gama*, going to *China* with *Chriſtovano Sardinha*, which had been Factor at the *Molucques*, one night as they rode at anchor in *Cincaapura*, *Quiay Taijano*, Maſter of the Junk, ſurprized them, and killed the ſaid *Sardinha*, together with ſix and twenty *Portugals* more ; as for him, becauſe he was a Gunner they ſaved his life. At this report *Antonio de Faria* ſtriking himſelf on the breſt, as a man amazed at this diſcourſe, *Lord, Lord*, ſaid he, *this ſeems to be a dream that I hear* ; then turning himſelf to his Soldiers that ſtood about him, he related the life of this *Quiay* unto them, and further affirmed, that he had ſlain at times in ſtrayed Veſſels above an hundred *Portugals*, and deſpoyled them of an hundred thouſand duckets at leaſt ; And though his name was ſuch, as this *Armenian* delivered, to wit, *Quiay Taijano*, yet after he had killed *Chriſtovano Sardinha* in *Cincaapura*, in a vain-glory of that which he had done he cauſed himſelf to be called Captain *Sardinha*. Whereupon having demanded of the *Armenian* where he was, he told us, that he was very ſore hurt, and hidden in the hold of the Junk amongſt the Cables with five or ſix others. Hereat *Antonio de Faria* aroſe, and went directly to the place where this Dog was hidden, followed by the greateſt part of his Soldiers, which opened the ſcuttle where the Cables lay to ſee whether the *Armenian* ſpake true or no ; in the mean time the Dog, and the ſix others that were with him, got out at another ſcuttle, and moſt deſperately fell upon our men, who were above thirty in number, beſides fourteen boys. Then began there ſo furious and bloody a fight, that in leſs then a quarter of an hour we made a clean diſpatch of them all, but in the mean while two *Portugals*, and ſeven boys were ſlain, beſides I know not how many hurt, whereof *Antonio de Faria* received two downright blows on his head, and one on his arm, which put him to very much pain. After this defeat, and that the wounded men were dreſt, he ſet ſail, for fear of the forty Junks that were in the River : So getting far from Land, about evening we went and anchored on the other ſide of *Cauchenchina*, where *Antonio de Faria* cauſing an Inventory to be taken of all that was in this Pyrats Junk, there was found in her five hundred Bars of Pepper, after fifty quintals to the Bar, forty of Nutmegs and Mace, fourſcore of Tin, thirty of Ivory, twelve of Wax, and five of Wood of fine Aloes, which might be worth according to the rate of the Country ſeventy thouſand duckets ; beſides a little field Piece, four Faulcons, and thirty Baſes of Braſs, the greateſt part of which Artillery had been ours, for this *Mahometan* had taken them in the ſhips of *Sardinha, Oliveyra*, and *Bartolemeu de Matos* : There were alſo found three Coffers covered with Leather, full of Silk quilts, and the apparel of *Portugals*, with a great Baſon and Ewer ſilver and guilt, and a Salt-ſeller of the ſame, two and twenty Spoons, three Candleſticks, five guilt Cups, eight and fifty Harquebuzes, twelve hundred twenty and two pieces of *Bengala* Cloth, all which were *Portugals* goods, eighteen quintals of Powder, and nine Children about ſeven or eight years of age, chained together by the hands and the feet, moſt lamentable to behold, for that they were ſo weak and lean, that one might eaſily through their skins have counted all the bones in their bodies.

CHAP. XVI.

Antonio de Faria's Arrival at the Bay of Camoy, *where was the fishing of Pearls for the King of* China; *the Relation made to him of the Isle of* Ainan; *with that which happened to him by the means of a renegado Pyrat, and otherwise.*

§.1. THe next day after noon, *Antonio de Faria* parted from the place where he rode at anchor, and returned towards the Coast of *Ainan*, by the which he kept all the rest of that day, and the next night with five and twenty or thirty fathom water. In the morning he came to a Bay, where there were many great Boats fishing for Pearls, and being unresolved what course to take, he bestowed all the forenoon in counsel with his company thereabout, whereof some were of the opinion that he should seize upon the Boats that were fishing for Pearls, and others opposed it, saying, it was a safer way to treat with them as Merchants, for that in exchange of the great store of Pearls, which were in that place, they might easily put off the most part of their Commodities. This appearing to be the best and safest advice, *Antonio de Faria* caused the Flag of Trade to be hung out, according to the Custom of *China*, so that instantly there came two Lanteaas from Land to us, which are Vessels like to Foists, with great abundance of refreshments, and those that were in them, having saluted us after their manner, went aboard the great Junk wherein *Antonio de Faria* was; but when they beheld men, such as we were, having never seen the like before, they were much amazed, and demanded what people we were, and wherefore we came into their Country. Whereunto we answered by an Interpreter, that we were Merchants born in the Kingdom of *Siam*, and were come thither to sell or barter our Commodities with them, if so be they would permit us. To this, an old man, much respected of all the rest, replyed, that here was no Traffique used, but in another place further forward, called *Guamboy*, where all strangers that came from *Cantan*, *Chincheo*, *Lamau*, *Comhay*, *Sumbor*, *Liampau*, and other Sea-coast Towns, did ordinarily trade: Wherefore he counselled him to get him suddenly from thence, in regard this was a place destined only to the fishing of Pearls for the Treasure of the house of the son of the Sun, to the which, by the Ordinance of the *Tutan* of *Comhay*, who was the soveraign Governor of all the Country of *Cauchenchina*, no Vessel was permitted to come, but only such as were appointed for that service, and that all other ships, which were found there, were by the Law to be burnt, and all that were in them; but since he, as a stranger, and ignorant of the Laws of the Country, had transgressed the same, not out of contempt, but want of knowledg, he thought fit to advertise him of it, to the end he might be gone from thence before the arrival of the *Mandarim* of the Army, which we call General, to whom the Government of that fishing appertained, and that would be within three or four days at the most, being gone not above six or seven leagues from thence to a Village, named *Buhaquirim*, for to take in Victual. *Antonio de Faria* thanking him for his good advice, asked him how many Sails, and what Forces the *Mandarim* had with him: Whereunto the old man answered, that he was accompanied with forty great Junks, and twenty five *Vancans* with oars, wherein there were seven thousand men, namely, five thousand Soldiers, and the rest Slaves and Mariners; and that he was there every year six Months, during the which time was the fishing for Pearls, that is to say, from the first of *March* to the last of *August*. Our Captain desiring to know what duties were payd out of this fishing, and what revenue it yielded in those six Months, the old man told him, that of Pearls which weighed above five Carats they gave two thirds, of the worser sort half less, and of seed Pearl the third part; and that this Revenue was not always alike, because the fishing was sometimes better in one year, then in another, but that one with another he thought it might yield annually four hundred thousand *Taeis*. *Antonio de Faria* made very much of the old man, and gave him two cakes of Wax, a bag of Pepper, and a tooth of Ivory, wherewith both he and the rest were exceedingly well pleased. He also demanded of them, of what bigness this Isle of *Ainan* might be, whereof so many wonders were spoken. Tell us first, replyed they, who you are, and wherefore you are come hither, then will we satisfie you in that you desire of us; for we vow unto you, that in all our lives we never saw so many young fellows together in any Merchants ships, as we now see in this of yours, nor so spruce and neat; and it seems that in their Country *China* Silks are so cheap as they are of no esteem, or else that they have had them at so easie a rate, as they have given nothing near the worth for them, for we see them play away a piece of Damask at one cast at Dice, as those that come

lightly

lightly by them : A speech that made *Antonio de Faria* secretly to smile, for that thereby he well perceived how these fishermen had a shrewd guess that the same were stollen, which made him tell them, that they did this like young men, who were the sons of very rich Merchants, and in that regard valued things far under that they were worth, and had cost their fathers ; dissembling then what they thought, they answered in this manner, It may very well be as you say. Whereupon *Antonio de Faria* gave a sign to the Soldiers to leave off their play, and to hide the pieces of Silk that they were playing for, to the end they might not be suspected for Robbers by these folks, which immediately they did, and the better to assure these *Chineses* that we were honest men, and Merchants, our Captain commanded the scuttles of the Junk to be opened, that we had taken the night before from Captain *Sardinha*, which was laden with Pepper, whereby they were somewhat restored to a better opinion then they had of us before, saying one to another, Since now we find that they are Merchants indeed, let us freely answer to their demand, so as they may not think, though we be rude, that we know nothing but how to catch fish and Oysters.

The old man desiring to satisfie *Antonio de Faria's* demand, *Sir,* said he, *since now I know* §.2. *what you are, and that only out of curiosity you fairly require to learn this particular of me, I will clearly tell you all that I know thereof, and what I have heard others deliver concerning it, that have been elder then my self, and which have a long time governed this Archipelague ; They said then, that this Island was an absolute State under a very rich and mighty King, who, for an higher and more transcendent title then other Monarchs his Contemporaries carried, caused himself to be stiled* Prechau Gamuu ; *He dying without heirs, so great a discord arose amongst the people about the succession to the Crown, as encreasing by little and little it caused such effusion of blood, that the Chronicles of those times affirm, how only in four years and an half sixteen* Lacazaas *of men were slain, every* Lacazaa *containing an hundred thousand, by means whereof the Country remained so deserted of people, that unable to defend it self the King of* Cauchin *conquered it, only with seven thousand* Mogores, *which the King of* Tartarie *sent him from the City of* Tuymican, *that then was Metrapolitan of all his Empires. This Island of* Ainan *being conquered, the King of* Cauchin *returned into his Country, and for Governor thereof left behind him a Commander of his, named* Hoyha Paguarol, *who revolted from him for certain just causes, as he pretended, that invited him thereunto. Now to have the assistance and support of the King of* China, *he became his Tributary for four hundred thousand* Taeis *by the year, which amount to six hundred thousand duckets, in consideration whereof the King of* China *obliged himself to defend him against all his enemies, whensoever he should have need : This accord continued between them the space of thirteen years, during the which the King of* Cauchin *was five several times defeated in open Battel ; At length this* Hoyha Paguarol *coming to dye without issue, in regard of the good offices that in his life time he had received from the King of* China, *he by his testament declared him for his Successor and lawful Heir, so that ever since, being now two hundred thirty and five years ago, to this present, this Isle of* Ainan *hath remained annexed to the Scepter of the great* Chinese. *And touching that you have further demanded of me concerning the Treasures, and Revenue of this Island, I am able to say no more then what I have learnt of some ancient Personages, who, as I have related before, have governed it in quality of* Teutons, *and* Chaems, *and I remember they said, that all the Revenues thereof, as well in* Mynes *of Silver,* Customs, *and otherways, amounted unto two Millions and an half* Taeis *yearly ;* And perceiving that our Captain was amazed to hear him speak of so mighty a riches, continuing his discourse, *Truly, my Masters,* said he laughing, *if you make such a matter of that little I have spoken of, what would you do if you saw the great City of* Pequin, *where the son of the Sun* (the name they give to their King) *with his Court is always resident, and where the Revenues of two and thirty Kingdoms, that depend on this Monarchy, are received, of which out of fourscore and six* Mynes *of Gold and Silver only is annually drawn above fifteen thousand* Picos, *which according to our weight comes to twenty thousand quintals ?* After *Antonio de Faria* had given him many thanks for satisfying him so fully in his demands, he desired him to tell him in what Port he would advise him to go and sell his Commodities, seeing the season was not proper to set sail for *Liampoo.* Whereunto he answered, that we were not to go into any Port of that Country, nor to put trust in any *Chinese* whatsoever ; for I assure you, said he, there is not one of them will speak truth in any thing he says to you, and believe me, for I am rich, and will not lye to you like a poor man ; besides, I would wish you to go in this Straight always with the plummet in your

hand

hand for to found your way, becaufe there are very many dangerous fhelvs all along till you come to a River called *Tanauquir*, and there is a Port where is very good anchoring, and where you may be as fafe as you can defire, as alfo you may there, in lefs then two days, put off all your commodities, and much more if you had them. Neverthelefs I will not counfel you to dif-imbarque your goods on land, but to fell them in your Veffels, in regard that many times the fight caufeth defire, and defire diforder amongft peaceable perfons, much more with them that are mutinous and of an evil confcience, whofe wicked inclination carries them rather to take away another mans goods from him, then give of their own to the needy for Gods fake. This faid, both he that fpake, and thofe that accompanyed him, took leave of our Captain, and us, with many complements and promifes, whereof they are not ordinarily very fparing in thofe parts, beftowing on *Antonio de Faria*, in return of that he had given them, a little Box made of a Tortoife fhell, full of feed-pearl, and twelve pearls of a pretty bignefs, craving his par-don for that they durft not traffique with him in this place, for fear left if they fhould do fo, to be all put to death, conformably to the Law of the rigorous juftice of the Country; and they again intreated him to make hafte away before the *Mandarims* arrival with his Army, for if he found him there, he would burn both his Veffel, and him and all his company. *Antonio de Faria* unwilling to neglect the counfel of this man, left that which he told him fhould prove true, he fet fail immediately, and paffed to the other fide towards the South, and in two days with a Wefterly wind he arrived at the River of *Tanauquir*, where juft over againft a little village, called *Neytor*, he caft anchor.

§.3.   We remained all that day, and the next night, at the mouth of the River of *Tanauquir*, in-tending the next morning to fail up to the Town, which was fome five leagues from thence in the River, to fee if by any means we might put off our commodities there, for our Veffels were fo heavy laden with them, as there was fcarce a day wherein we ran not twice or thrice on fome fhelve or other, which in divers places were four or five leagues long, wherefore it was con-cluded that before we did any thing elfe we were to fell away our commodities, fo that we la-bored with all our might to get into the River, whofe current was fo ftrong, that though we had all our fails up, yet could we prevail but very little againft it; As we were in this pain we perceived two great Junks in warlike manner come out of the River upon us, which chaining themfelves together for the more ftrength, attaqued us fo lively, as we had fcarce the leafure to defend our felves, fo that we were conftrained to throw into the Sea all that ftood in our way to make room for our artillery, being that we had then moft need of: The firft falutation we had from them was a peal of fix and twenty pieces of Ordnance, whereof nine were Falconets, and field-pieces: *Antonio de Faria*, as a man verft in fuch affairs, feeing them chained one to another, perceived their drift, and therefore made as though he fled, as well to win time to prepare himfelf, as to make them beleeve that they were no Chriftians; whereupon they, like cunning thieves, defiring that the prey, which they held to be furely their own, fhould not efcape out of their hands, loofed themfelves the one from the other the better to fet upon us, and approaching very near to us, they fhot fo many arrows and darts into our Junk, as no man was able to appear upon the deck: *Antonio de Faria*, to avoyd this ftorm, retired under the half deck, with five and twenty Soldiers, and fome ten or twelve others, Slaves and Mariners; there he entertained the Enemy with Harquebufe fhot the fpace of half an hour, in which time, having ufed all their munitions of war, fome forty of them, that feemed to be more va-liant then the reft, longing to finifh their enterprize, leaped into our Junk, with a purpofe to make themfelves mafter of the prow; but to hinder them from it, our Captain was conftrained to go and receive them, fo that there began a moft bloody fight, wherein it pleafed God with-in an hour to give us the upper hand by the flaughter of four and twenty of their forty in the place: Thereupon twenty of ours, purfuing this good fuccefs, boarded the Enemies Junk, where finding but fmall refiftance, by reafon the principals were already flain, all that were in her quickly rendred themfelves unto us. That done, *Antonio de Faria* went with all fpeed to fuccor *Chriftovano Borralbo*, who was boarded by the other Junk, and very doubtful of the victory, in regard the greateft part of his men were hurt, but at our approach the Enemies threw themfelves all into the Sea, where moft of them were drowned, and fo both the Junks remained in our power. After this we took a furvey of our company, the better to underftand what this victory had coft us, and we found there was one *Portugal*, five Boys, and nine Mariners killed, befides thofe that were hurt: and on the Enemies part fourfcore were flain, and almoft as many taken. Having given order then for the dreffing and accommodating of our

wounded

wounded men in the best manner that could be, *Antonio de Faria* caused as many Mariners to be taken up as could be saved, and commanding them to be brought into the great Junk where he was, he demanded of them what those Junks were, how the Captain of them was named, and whether he were alive or dead, whereunto not one of them would make any answer, but chose rather to dye in torments like mad dogs, when as *Christovano Borralho* cryed out from the Junk where he was, *Signior, Signior, come hither quickly, for we have more to do then we think of*; whereat *Antonio de Faria*, accompanyed with fifteen or sixteen of his men, leapt into his Junk, asking what the matter was? *I hear a many talking together*, said he, *towards the prow, which I doubt are hidden there*; hereupon opening the scuttle, they heard divers cry out, *Lord Jesu have mercy upon us*; and that in such a woful manner, as struck us all with pity: *Antonio de Faria* approaching to the scuttle, and looking down, could perceive some persons there shut up, but not able to discern what they might be, he made two of his boys to go down, who a little after brought up seventeen Christians, namely two *Portugals*, five small children, two girls, and eight boys, which were in such a lamentable case, as would have grieved any heart to have beheld them; The first thing he did was to cause their Irons to be strucken off, and then he enquired of one of the *Portugals* (for the other was like a man dead) unto whom those children appertained, and how they fell into the hands of this Pyrat, as also what his name was. Whereunto he answered, that the Pyrat had two names, the one Christian, the other Pagan, and that his Pagan name, wherewith he used to be called of late, was *Necoda Nicaulem*, and his Christian name *Francisco de Sàa*, being Christned at *Malaca*, at such time as *Garcia de Saa* was Captain of the Fortress, and for that he was his godfather, and had caused him to be baptized, he gave him that name, and marryed him to an orphan maid, a very handsom wench, the daughter of an honorable *Portugal*, to oblige him the more to our Religion and Country; but in the year 1534. setting sail for *China* in a great Junk of his, wherein there accompanyed him twenty of the wealthiest *Portugals* of *Malaca*, as also his wife, and arriving at the Island of *Pullo Catan*, they stayd two days to take in fresh water, during which time he and his Company, who were all *Chineses* like himself, and no better Christians, conspired the death of the poor *Portugals* for to despoyl them of their goods, so that one night whil'st the *Portugals* were asleep, and little dream'd of such Treason, they killed them all with their little hatchets, and their servants likewise, not sparing the life of any one that bore the name of a Christian; after which, he perswaded, with his wife, to turn Pagan, and adore an Idol, that *Tucan*, Captain of the Junk, had concealed in his chest, and that then being free from the Christian Religion he would marry her to *Tucan*, who in exchange would give him a sister of his to wife, that was a *Chinese*, and there with him. But in regard she would neither adore the Idol, nor consent to the rest, the dog struck her over the head with his hatchet till her brains flew out, and then departing from thence went to the Port of *Liampoo*, where the same year before he had traded; and not daring to go to *Patana*, for fear of the *Portugals* that resided there, he wintered at *Siam*, and the year following he returned to the Port of *Chincheo*, where he took a little Junk that came from *Sunda*, with ten *Portugals* in her, all which he slew; And because the wickedness that he had done us was known over all the Country, doubting to encounter some *Portugal* forces, he had retired himself into this straight of *Cauchenchina*, where as a Merchant he traded, and as a Pyrat robbed those he met withall that were weaker then himself. It being now three years since he had taken this River for a refuge of his Robberies, thinking himself secure here from us *Portugals*, by reason we have not used to traffique in the Ports of this straight, and Island of *Ainan*. *Antonio de Faria* asked of him whether those children belonged to the *Portugals* he had mentioned before; whereunto he answered, that they did not, but that both they, and the boys and girls, were the children of *Nuno Preto*, *Gian de Diaz*, and of *Pero Borges*, whom he had killed at *Mompollacota*, near the mouth of the River of *Siam* in *Joano Oliveyra's* Junk, where he also put sixteen *Portugals* more to death, only he saved their two lives, because one was a shipwright, and the other a Caulker, and had carryed them along with him in this manner, continually whipping, and almost famishing of them; further he said, that when he set upon us, he did not think we had been *Portugals*, but some *Chinese* Merchant, like such as he had accustomed to rob when he found them at advantage, as he thought to have found us. *Antonio de Faria* demanded of him, whether he could know the Pyrat amongst those other dead bodies? Having replyed that he could, the Captain presently arose, and taking him by the hand, went with him into the other Junk, that was fastned to his, and having made him view all that lay dead upon the hatches, he

said

said that it was none of them. Whereupon he commanded a Manchuas, which is a little boat, to be made ready, wherein he and this man went and fought for him amongst the other dead bodies that floated on the water, where they found him with a great cut over his head, and a thrust quite through the body; so causing him to be taken up, and layd upon the hatches, he demanded of that man again, if he were sure that this was he, who answered, how without doubt it was he. Whereunto *Antonio de Faria* gave the more credit, by reason of a great chain of gold he had about his neck, to which was fastned an Idol of gold with two heads, made in the form of a Lizard, having the tail and paws enammelled with green and black, and commanding him to be drawn towards the prow, he caused his head to be chopt off, and the rest of the body to be cut in pieces, which were cast into the Sea.

§.4. Having obtained this victory in the manner I have before declared, caused our hurt men to be drest, and provided for the guard of our Captains, we took an Inventory of the goods that were in these two Junks, and found that our prize was worth forty thousand *Taeis*, which was immediately committed to the charge of *Antonio Borges*, who was Factor for the Prizes. Both the Junks were great and good, yet were we constrained to burn one of them for want of Mariners to man it: There was in them besides seventeen pieces of brass Ordnance, namely four Faulconets, and thirteen small pieces, the most part whereof had the Royal Arms of *Portugal* upon them, for the Pyrat had taken them in the three ships where he killed the forty *Portugals*. The next day *Antonio de Faria* went about once more to get into the River, but he was advised by fishermen, which he took a little before, that he should beware of going to the Town, because they were advised there of all that had passed betwixt him and the renegado Pyrat, for whose death the people were in an uproar, in so much that if he would let them have his commodities for nothing, yet would they not take them, in regard that *Chileu*, the Governor of that Province, had contracted with him, to give him the third part of all the prizes he took, in lieu whereof he would render him a safe retreat in his Country; so that his loss now being great by the death of the Pyrat, he should be but badly welcomed by him, and to that purpose had already commanded two great Rafts, covered with dry wood, barrels of pitch, and other combustible stuff, to be placed at the entering into the Port, that were to be kindled and sent down upon us, as soon as we had cast anchor, for to fire us, besides two hundred *Paraos*, full of shot, and men of war were also in readiness to assault us. These news made *Antonio de Faria* conclude to make away unto another Port, named *Mutipinan*, distant from thence above forty leagues towards the East, for that there were many rich Merchants, as well Natives as Strangers, which came in great Troops from the Countries of *Lanhos, Pafuaas*, and *Gueos*, with great sums of mony. So we set sail with the three Junks, and the Lorch, wherein we came from *Patana*, coasting the Land from one side to the other, by reason of a contrary wind, until we arrived at a place called *Tilaumera*, where we anchored, for that the current of the water ran very strong against us. After we had continued so three days together, with a contrary wind, and in great want of victual, our good fortune about Evening brought four *Lanteaas* unto us, that are like unto Foysts, in one of the which was a Bride, that was going to a Village, named *Pandurea*: Now because they were all in jollity, they had so many Drums beating aboard them, as it was almost impossible to hear one another for the noise they made. Whereupon we were in great doubt what this might be, and wherefore there was such triumphing; some thought that they were spies sent from the Captain of *Tanauquir's* Army, who insulting, for that we were already in their power, gave this testimony thereof. *Antonio de Faria* left his anchors in the Sea, and preparing himself to sustain all that might happen unto him, he displayed all his Banners and Flags, and with demonstration of joy attended the arrival of these *Lanteaas*, who when they perceived us to be all together, imagining it was the Bridegroom that stay'd to receive them, they came joyfully towards us. So after we had saluted one another after the manner of the Country, they went and anchored by the shore. And because we could not comprehend the mystery of this affair, all our Captains concluded that they were spies from the Enemies Army, which forbore assaulting us in expectation of some other Vessels that were also to come; In this suspicion we spent the little remainder of that Evening, and almost two hours of the night: But then the Bride, seeing that her Spouse sent not to visit her, as was his part to do, to shew the love she bore him she sent her Uncle in one of the *Lanteaas* with a Letter to him, containing these words. *If the feeble sex of a woman would permit me to go from the place where I am for to see thy face, without reproach to mine honor, assure thy self that to kiss thy tardy feet my body would fly as doth the hungry Faulcon*

after

after the fearful Heron; But since I am parted from my fathers house, for to seek thee out here, come thy self hither to me, where indeed I am not, for I cannot see my self, but in seeing thee; Now if thou dost not come to see me in the obscurity of this night, making it bright for me, I fear that to morrow morning when thou arrivest here, thou shalt not find me living. My Uncle Licorpinau *will more particularly acquaint thee with what I keep concealed in my heart, for I am not able to say any more, such is my grief to be so long deprived of thy so much desired sight; Wherefore I pray thee come unto me, or permit me to come unto thee, as the greatness of my love to thee doth deserve, and as thou art obliged to do unto her, whom now thou art to possess in marriage until death, from which Almighty God of his infinite goodness keep thee as many years, as the Sun and Moon have made turns about the World since the beginning of their birth.* This *Lanteaa* being arrived with the Brides Uncle and Letter, *Antonio de Faria* caused all the *Portugals* to hide themselves, suffering none to appear but our *Chinese* Mariners, to the end they might not be afraid of us; To our Junk then they approached with confidence, and three of them coming aboard us, asked where the Bridegroom was? All the answer we made them was to lay hold of them, and clap them presently under hatches; now because the most part of them were drunk, those that were in the *Lanteaa* never heard our bustling with them, nor if they had, could they have had time to escape, for suddenly from the top of our poup we fastned a cable to their mast, whereby they were so arrested, as it was impossible for them to get loose of us; whereupon casting in some pots of powder amongst them, the most of them leapt into the Sea, by which time six or seven of our Soldiers, and as many Mariners, got into the *Lanteaa*, and straight rendred themselves masters of her, where the next thing they did was to take up the poor wretches, who cryed out that they drowned: Having made them sure, *Antonio de Faria* went towards the other three *Lanteaas*, that anchored some quarter of a league from thence, and coming to the first, wherein was the Bride, he entred her without any resistance, in regard there were none other in her but a few Mariners, and six or seven men, that seemed to be of good reckoning, all of kin to the Bride, being there only to accompany her, together with two little boys her brothers, that were very white, and certain ancient women, of such as in *China* are hired for mony to dance, sing, and play of instruments upon like festival occasions. The other two *Lanteaas* beholding this sad success, left their anchors in the Sea, and fled in such haste, as if the Devil had been in them, but for all that we took one of them, so that we had three of the four: This done, we returned aboard our Junk, and by reason it was now midnight, we did nothing for the present but take our prisoners, and shut them up under the hatches, where they remained until day, that *Antonio de Faria* came to view them, and seeing they were most of them aged, full of sorrow, and fit for nothing, he caused them to be set a shore, retaining only the Bride, and her two brothers, because they were young, white, and well-favored, and some twenty Mariners, which afterwards were of great use to us for the navigation of our Junks. This Bride, as since we learned, was daughter to the *Anchary* of *Colem* (which signifies Governor) and betrothed to a youth, the son of the *Chifuu*, Captain of *Pandurea*, who had written unto her that he would attend her in this place with three or four Junks of his fathers, who was very rich, but alass! we shamefully cozened him. After dinner, being departed from thence, the Bridegroom arrived, seeking for his Bride with five sail full of Flags, Streamers, and Banners; Passing by us, he saluted us with great store of musick, and shews of gladness, ignorant of his misfortune, and that we carryed away his wife. In this jollity he doubled the Cape of *Tilanmera*, where the day before we took this prize, and there anchored attending his Bride, according as he had written to her, whil'st we sailing on arrived three days after at the Port of *Mutipiman*, which was the place we aymed at, in regard of the advice that *Antonio de Faria* had, that there he might sell off his commodities.

I

CHAP. XVII.

Antonio de Faria's Arrival at the Port: The Information that Antonio de Faria *had of the Country; some passages between him and the* Nautarel *of the Town; his going to the River of* Madel; *with his incountring a Pyrat there, and that which passed betwixt them.*

§. I. BEing arrived at this Port we anchored in a Rode, which the Land makes near to a little Island on the South side of the mouth of the River, at the entry whereinto we remained without saluting the Port, or making any noise, intending as soon as it was night to send for to sound the River, and to be informed of that we desired to know. Upon the appearing of the Moon, which was about eleven of the clock, *Antonio de Faria* sent away one of his *Lanteaas*, well furnished, and twelve Soldiers in her, besides the Captain, named *Valentino Martins Dalpoem*, a discreet man, and of great courage, that at other times had given good proof of himself in like occasions, who departing went always sounding the depth of the River, until he arrived where divers Vessels rode at anchor; There he took two men that were sleeping in a Barque laden with earthen ware, and returning aboard undiscovered he rendred *Antonio de Faria* an accompt of what he had found touching the greatness of the place, and the fewness of the Ships that were in the Port, wherefore his opinion was, that he might boldly enter into it, and if it happened he could not trade there as he desired, no body could hinder him from issuing forth whensoever he pleased, by reason the River was very large, clean, and without any shelves, sands, or other things that might endanger him. Having consulted then with his company, he concluded by their advice, not to put the two *Mahometans*, that were taken, to torture, as was before ordained, because there was no need of it; Day being come, *Antonio de Faria* desiring, before he stirred, to be informed from those two *Mahometans* of some particulars he would fain know, and thinking he might sooner prevail with them by fair means, then by menaces and torment, he made very much of them, and then declared his mind: Whereupon both of them with one accord said, that touching the entrance of the River there was nothing to be feared, in regard it was one of the best in all that Bay, and that ordinarily far greater Vessels then his went in and out there, for that the shallowest place was fifteen fathom at the least, and as for the people of the Country he was not to stand in any doubt of them, by reason they were naturally weak, and without arms; And that the strangers, which were at that instant there, arrived some nine days before from the Kingdom of *Benan* in two Companies of fifty Oxen a piece, laden with store of Silver, Wood of Aloes, Cloth, Silk, Linnen, Ivory, Wax, Lacre, Benjamin, Camphire, and Gold in Powder, like to that of the Island of *Samatra*, who were come with this Merchandise to buy Pepper, Drugs, and Pearls of the Isle of *Ainan*. Being demanded whether there was any Army in those parts, they answered No, because most of the Wars, which the *Prechau*, that is, the Emperor of the *Cauchins*, made, or were made against him, were by Land; and that when any was made upon the Rivers it was always with little Vessels, and not with such great Ships as his, for that they were not deep enough for them: Further being asked, whether the *Prechau* was near to that place, they replyed, that he was twelve days journey from thence, at the City of *Quangepaaru*, where most commonly he with his Court resided, governing his Kingdom in Peace and Justice, and that the Mynes, reserved for his Crown, rendred him in yearly rent fifteen thousand *Picos* of Silver, every *Pico* weighing five quintals, the moyety whereof by the divine Law, inviolably observed in his Countries, was for the poor Laborers, that tilled the ground, to sustain their families withall, but that all his people by a general consent had freely relinquished that right unto him, upon condition, that from thence-forward he should not constrain them to pay tribute, or any other thing that might concern them, and that the ancient *Prechaus* had protested to accomplish it as long as the Sun should give light to the Earth. *Antonio de Faria* further demanded of them, what belief they were of, whereunto they answered, that they hold the very verity of all verities, and that they believed there was but one God Almighty, who as he had created all, so he preserved all; howbeit if at any time our understandings were intangled with the disorder and discord of our desires, that no way proceeded from the soveraign Creator, in whom was no imperfection, but only from the sinner himself, that out of his impatience judged according to the wicked inclination of his heart. Moreover asking of them, whether in their Law they believed, that the great God, which governeth this All, came at any time

into

into the world, clothed with a humane form, they said No, because there could be nothing that might oblige him to so great an extremity, in regard he was through the excellency of the divine Nature delivered from our miseries, and far esloigned from the Treasures of the Earth, all things being more then base in the presence of his splendor. By these answers of theirs, we perceived that these people had never attained to any knowledg of our truth, more then their eyes made them to see in the picture of Heaven, and in the beauty of the day, for continually in their *Combayes*, which are their prayers, lifting up their hands they say, *By thy works, Lord, we confess thy greatness.* After this *Antonio de Faria* set them at liberty, and having given them certain presents, wherewith they were very well pleased, he caused them to be conveyed to Land; that done, the wind beginning a little to rise he set sail, having all his Vessels adorned with divers coloured Silks, their Banners, Flags and Streamers displayed, and a Standart of Trade hung out after the manner of the Country, to the end they might be taken for Merchants, and not for Pyrats, and so an hour after he anchored just against the Key of the Town, which he saluted with a little peal of Ordnance, whereupon ten or eleven *Almadiaes* came presently to us with good store of refreshments; Howbeit finding us to be strangers, and discerning by our habits that we were neither *Siams*, *Jaos*, nor *Malayos*, nor yet of any other Nation that ever they had seen, they said one to another, *Please Heaven, that the dew of the fresh morning may be as profitable to us all, as this evening seems fair with the presence of these whom our eyes behold.* Having said thus, one of the *Almadiaes* asked leave to come aboard us, which they were told they might do, because we were all their brothers, so that three of nine, which were in that *Almadia*, entred into our Junk, whom *Antonio de Faria* received very kindly, and causing them to sit down upon a Turky Carpet by him, he told them, that he was a Merchant of the Kingdom of *Siam*, and going with his goods towards the Isle of *Ainan* he had been advertised, that he might better and more securely sell off his Commodities in this Town, then in any other place, because the Merchants thereof were juster and truer of their word, then the *Chineses* of the Coast of *Ainan*; Whereunto they thus answered, *Thou art not deceived in that which thou sayst, for if thou be a Merchant, as thou affirmest, beleeve it, that in every thing and every where thou shalt be honored in this place, wherefore thou mayst sleep without fear.*

§.2.

Antonio de Faria mistrusting some intelligence might come over Land concerning that which he had done to the Pyrat upon the River of *Tanauquir*, and so might work him some prejudice, would not dis-imbarque his goods, as the Officers of the Custom-house would have had him, which was the cause of much displeasure and vexation to him afterward, so that his business was twice interrupted by that means, wherefore perceiving that good words would not serve to make them consent to his Propositions, he sent them word by a Merchant, who dealt between them, that he knew well enough they had a great deal of reason to require the landing of his goods, because it was the usual course for every one so to do; But he assured them, that he could not possibly do it, in regard the season was almost past, and therefore he was of necessity to hasten his departure as soon as might be, the rather too for the accommodating of the Junk wherein he came, for as much as she took in so much water, that threescore Mariners were always laboring at three pumps to clear her, whereby he ran a great hazard of losing all his goods; And that touching the Kings Customs he was contented to pay them, not after thirty in the hundred, as they demanded, but after ten, as they did in other Kingdoms, and so much he would pay presently and willingly. To this offer they rendred no answer, but detained him that carried the message prisoner; *Antonio de Faria*, seeing that his messenger returned not, set sail immediately, hanging forth a number of flags, as one that cared not whether he sold or no; Whereupon the Merchants strangers, that were come thither to trade, perceiving the Commodities, of which they hoped to make some profit, to be going out of the Port, through the perversness and obstinacy of the *Nautarel* of the Town, they went all to him, and desired him to recall *Antonio de Faria*, otherwise they protested to complain to the King of the injustice he did them, in being the cause of hindring their Traffique. The *Nautarel*, that is the Governor, with all the Officers of the Custom-house, fearing lest they might upon this occasion be turned out of their places, condescended to their request, upon condition, since we would pay but ten in the hundred, that they should pay five more, whereunto they agreed, and instantly sent away the Merchant, whom they had detained prisoner, with a Letter full of complements, wherein they declared the agreement they had made. *Antonio de Faria* answered them, that since he was out of the Port, he would not re-enter it upon any terms,

by

by reason he had not leasure to make any stay, howbeit if they would buy his Commodities in grofs, bringing lingots of filver with them for that purpose, he would fell them to them, and in no other manner would deal, for he was much diftasted with the little respect the *Nautarel* of the Town had carried towards him, by despising his messages; and if they were contented to accept thereof, that then they should let him know so much within an hour at the farthest, otherwise he would fail away to *Ainan*, where he might put off his Commodities far better then there. They finding him so resolved, and doubting to lose so fair an occasion, as this was, for them to return into their Country, embarqued themselves in five great Lighters with forty chests full of lingots of filver, and a many facks to bring away the Pepper, and arriving at *Antonio de Faria*'s Junk, they were very well received by him, unto whom they represented anew the agreement they had made with the *Nautarel* of the Town, greatly complaining of his ill Government, and of some wrongs, which without all reason he had done them; but since they had pacified him by consenting to give him fifteen in the hundred, whereof they would pay five, they defired him to pay the ten, as he had promised, for otherways they could not buy his Commodities. Whereunto *Antonio de Faria* answered, that he was contented so to do, more for the love of them, then for any profit he hoped to reap thereby, for which they gave him many thanks, and so being on all fides agreed they used such diligence in discharging the goods, as in three days the most of it was weighed and consigned into the hands of the owners thereof; whereupon the accompts were made up, and the lingots of filver received, amounting in all to an hundred and thirty thousand *Taeis*, after the rate of seven shillings and six pence the *Taei*, as I have said elsewhere. And though all possible speed was used herein, yet before all was finished, news came of that which we had done to the Pyrat in the River of *Tananquir*, in so much that not one of the inhabitants would come near us afterward, by reason whereof *Antonio de Faria* was conftrained to set fail in all hafte.

§.3.   After we had quit the River of *Mutepinan*, directing our course Northward, *Antonio de Faria* thought good to make to the Coaft of the Ifland of *Ainan*, for to feek out a River, named *Madel*, with a purpofe there to accommodate the great Junk, wherein he was, becaufe it took in much water, or provide himfelf of a better in exchange upon any terms whatfoever; So having failed for the fpace of twelve days with a contrary wind, at length he arrived at the Cape of *Pullo Hinhor*, which is the Ifland of Cocos; There hearing no news of the Pyrat he fought for, he returned towards the South Coaft, where he took certain Prizes, which were of good value, and well gotten as we thought. For it was the main intention of this Captain to deal with the Pyrat, which frequented this Coaft of *Ainan*, as they before had done with divers Chriftians in depriving them of their lives and goods; For as God doth ordinarily draw good out of evil, so it pleafed him out of his divine Juftice to permit, that *Antonio de Faria* in revenge of the Robbery, committed by *Coia Acem* upon us in the Port of *Lugor*, fhould in the purfuit of him chaftife other Theeves, that deferved to be punifhed by the hands of the *Portugals*. Now having for certain days together with much labor continued our Navigation within this Bay of *Cauchenchina*, as we were newly entred into a Port, called *Madel*, upon the day of the nativity of our Lady, being the eight of *September*, for the fear that we were in of the new Moon, during the which there oftentimes happens in this Climate fuch a terrible ftorm of wind and rain, as it is not poffible for fhips to withftand it, which by the *Chinefes* is named *Tufan*, and that the Sky charged full with Clouds had four days together threatened that which we feared, it pleafed God amongft many other Junks that fled into this Port for fhelter, there came in one belonging to a notorious *Chinefe* Pyrat, named *Hinimilau*, who of a Gentile, that he had been, was not long before become a *Mahometan*, induced thereunto (as it was faid) by a *Cacis* of that accurfed Sect, who had made him fuch an Enemy to the Chriftian name, as he vaunted publiquely, that God did owe Heaven unto him for the great fervice he had done him upon Earth, in depopulating it by little and little of the *Portugal* Nation, who from their mothers wombs delighted in their offences, as the very Inhabitants of the fmoaky Houfe, a name which they give to Hell; And thus did he with fuch fayings, and other like blafphemies, fpeak as villanoufly and abominably of us as could be imagined. This Pyrat, entring into the River in a very great and tall Junk, came up to us where we rode at anchor, and faluted us after the cuftom of the Country, whereunto we returned the like, as it is the manner there to do at the entry into any of the Ports, they neither knowing us to be *Portugals*, nor we what they were; for we thought they had been *Chinefes*, and that they came into the Port to fhrewd themfelves from the ftorm as others did, whereupon, behold,

five

five young men, that were Chriſtians, whom this Robber held as Slaves in his Junk, gueſſing us to be *Portugals*, fell a crying out three or four times together, *Lord, have mercy upon us.* At theſe words we all ſtood up to ſee who they were, and perceiving them to be Chriſtians, we called aloud to the Mariners for to ſtay their courſe, which they would not do, but contrarily beating up a Drum, as it were in contempt of us, they gave three great ſhouts, and withall brandiſhed their naked Scymitars in the ayr in a way of threatening us, and then caſt anchor ſome quarter of a league beyond us. *Antonio de Faria* deſiring to learn the reaſon hereof, ſent a *Baion* to them, which no ſooner arrived near them, but the barbarous Rogues pelted them with ſo many ſtones, that the Veſſel was almoſt overwhelmed, ſo that they were glad to return, both Mariners and Soldiers being very ſore hurt ; *Antonio de Faria* ſeeing them come back all bloody, demanded the cauſe of it : *Sir,* anſwered they, *we are not able to tell you, only you behold in what plight we are* ; ſaying ſo, and ſhewing him the hurts on their heads, they declared unto him in what manner they had been entertained. At firſt this accident much troubled *Antonio de Faria,* ſo that he ſtood muſing a good while upon it, but at length turning himſelf to them that were preſent, *Let every one here,* ſaid he, *prepare himſelf, for I cannot be perſwaded but this is that Dog Coia Acem, who I hope this day ſhall pay for all the wrong he hath done us.* Whereupon he commanded preſently to weigh anchor, and with all the ſpeed that might be he ſet ſail with the three Junks and Lanteas. Being come within a Muſket ſhot of them, he ſaluted them with ſix and thirty Pieces of Ordnance, whereof twelve were Faulconets, and other Field-pieces, amongſt the which was one of Battery, that carried caſt Bullets, wherewith the Enemies were ſo amated, as all the reſolution they could take for the inſtant was to leave their anchors in the Sea, not having leaſure to weigh them, and to make to the ſhoar, wherein alſo they failed of their deſire ; for *Antonio de Faria* perceiving their deſign got before them, and boarded their Junk with all the Forces of his Veſſels ; hereupon began a moſt furious Combat both with Pikes, Darts, and pots full of Powder thrown from either ſide, ſo that for half an hour it could not be diſcerned who had the better: But at length it pleaſed God to favor us ſo much, that the Enemies, finding themſelves weary, wounded, and hurt, threw themſelves into the Sea. *Antonio de Faria,* ſeeing theſe wretches ready to ſink by reaſon of the impetuouſneſs and ſtrength of the current, he imbarqued himſelf with ſome Soldiers in two Balons, and with much ado ſaved ſixteen men, whereunto he was induced by the great need he ſtood in of them for the maning of his *Lanteas,* becauſe he had loſt a great many of his people in the former fights.

Chap. XVIII.

What Antonio de Faria *did with the Captain of the Pyrats Junk ; that which paſt between him and the people of the Country ; with our caſting away upon the Iſland of Theeves.*

ANtonio de Faria having obtained this Victory in the manner I have related, the firſt thing §.1. he did was to ſee his hurt men dreſt, as that which chiefly imported him ; then being given to underſtand that the Pyrat *Hinimilau,* the Captain of the Junk he had taken, was one of the ſixteen he had ſaved, he commanded him to be brought before him, and after he had cauſed him to be dreſt of two wounds that he had received, he demanded of him what was become of the young *Portugals* which he held as Slaves? Whereunto the Pyrat, being mad with rage, having anſwered that he could not tell, upon the ſecond demand that was made him with menaces, he ſaid, that if firſt they would give him a little water, in regard he was ſo dry as he was not able to ſpeak, that then he would conſider what anſwer to make. Thereupon having water brought him, which he drunk ſo greedily as he ſpilt the moſt part of it without quenching his thirſt, he deſired to have ſome more given him, proteſting, that if they would let him drink his fill, he would oblige himſelf by the Law of *Mahomets Alçoran* voluntarily to confeſs all that they deſired to know of him. *Antonio de Faria,* having given him as much as he would drink, queſtioned him again about the young Chriſtians, whereto he replyed, that he ſhould find them in the chamber of the prow ; thereupon he commanded three Soldiers to go thither and fetch them, who had no ſooner opened the ſcuttle to bid them come up, but they ſaw them lie dead in the place with their throats cut, which made them cry out, *Jeſu, Jeſu, come hither we beſeech you, Sir, and behold a moſt lamentable ſpectacle* ; hereat *Antonio de Faria,* and thoſe that were with him, ran thither, and beholding thoſe youths lying ſo ore

upon

upon another, he could not forbear shedding of tears; having caused them then to be brought upon the deck, together with a woman and two pretty children, about seven or eight years old, that had their throats also cut, he demanded of the Pyrat why he had used such cruelty to those poor innocents: Whereunto he answered, that it was because they were Traytors, in discovering themselves to those, which were such great Enemies to him as the *Portugals* were, and also for that having heard them call upon their Christ for help, he desired to see whether he would deliver them; as for the two infants, there was cause enough to kill them, for that they were the children of *Portugals*, whom he ever hated: with the like extravagancy he answered to many other questions, which were propounded to him, and that with so much obstinacy as if he had been a very Devil. Afterwards being asked whether he were a Christian, he answered, no, but that he had been one at such time as *Don Paulo de Gama* was Captain of *Malaca*. Whereupon *Antonio de Faria* demanded of him, what moved him, since he had been a Christian, to forsake the Law of *Jesus Christ*, wherein he was assured of his salvation, for to embrace that of the false Prophet *Mahomet*, from whence he could hope for nothing but the loss of his Soul. Thereunto he answered, that he was induced so to do, for that so long as he was a Christian, the *Portugals* had always contemned him, whereas before when he was a *Gentile* they called him *Quiay Necoda*, that is to say, *Signior* Captain, but that respect immediately upon his Baptism forsook him, which he verily believed did arrive to him by *Mahomets* express permission, to the end it should open his eyes to turn *Mahometan*; as after he did at *Bintan*, where the King of *Jantana* was in person present at the ceremony, and that ever since he had much honored him, and that all the *Mandarins* called him brother, in regard of the vow he had made upon the holy Book of Flowers, that as long as he lived he would be a sworn Enemy to the *Portugals*, and of all others that profess the Name of Christ, for which both the King and the *Cacis Moulana* had exceedingly comended him, promising that his Soul should be most blessed if he performed that vow. Being likewise demanded how long ago it was since he revolted, what *Portugal* Vessels he had taken, how many men he had put to death, and what Merchandize he had despoyled them of? He answered, that it was seven years since he became a *Mahometan*; that the first Vessel he took was *Luiso de Pavia's* Junk, which he surprized in the River of *Liampoo* with four hundred Bars of Pepper only, and no other spice, whereof having made himself master, that he had put to death eighteen *Portugals*, besides their slaves, of whom he made no reckoning, because they were not such as could satisfie the Oath he had made; That after this prize he had taken four ships, and in them put to death above an hundred persons, amongst whom there was some threescore and ten *Portugals*, and that he thought the Merchandize in them amounted to fifteen or sixteen hundred Bars of Pepper, whereof the King of *Pan* had the better moity for to give him a safe retrait in his Ports, and to secure him from the *Portugals*, giving him to that purpose an hundred men, with commandment to obey him as their King. Being further demanded, whether he had not killed any *Portugals*, or lent an hand for the doing thereof, he said no, but that some two years before, being in the River of *Choaboquec* on the Coast of *China*, a great Junk arrived there with a great many *Portugals* in her, whereof an intimate friend of his, named *Ruy Lobo*, was Captain, whom *Don Estevan de Gama*, then Governor of the Fortress of *Malaca*, had sent thither in the way of commerce, and that upon the sale of his commodities going out of the Port, his Junk about five days after took so great a leak, as not being able to clear her, he was constrained to return towards the same Port from whence he parted, but that by ill fortune clapping on all his sails to get the sooner to Land, she was overset by the violence of the wind, so as all were cast away saving *Ruy Lobo*, seventeen *Portugals*, and some slaves, who in their skiff made for the Island of *Laman*, without sail, without water, or any manner of victual; That in this extremity *Ruy Lobo*, relying on the ancient friendship that was between them, came with tears in his eyes, and pray'd him on his knees to receive him and his into his Junk, which was then ready to set sail for *Patana*, whereunto he agreed upon condition that therefore he should give him two thousand duckets, for the performance whereof he bound himself by his Oath of a Christian. But that after he had taken them in, he was counselled by the *Mahometans* not to trust unto the friendship of Christians, lest he might endanger his own life, for when they had recovered strength, they would without doubt seize upon his Junk, and all the goods that were in her, it being their usual custom so to do in all places where they found themselves the strongest: wherefore fearing lest that which the *Mahometans* suggested should befall him, he slew them all on a night as they slept, for the which notwithwithftanding he was forry afterwards. This declaration fo much incenfed *Antonio de Faria,* and all that were about him, as indeed the enormity of fo wicked a fact did require, that prefently, without queftioning or hearing of him further, he commanded him to be put to death with four more of his company, and fo they were all thrown into the Sea.

This juftice being executed on the Pyrat and his four companions, *Antonion de Faria* caufed **§.2.** an Inventory to be taken of all that was in the Junk, which was adjudged to amount unto forty thoufand *Taeis* in raw and twifted Silk, pieces of Sattin, Damask, Musk, fine Pourcelains, and other lefs valuable commodities, which with the Junk we were conftrained to burn, becaufe we wanted Mariners for our navigation. With thefe valorous exploits the *Chinefes* were fo amazed, as they ftood in dread of the very mention of the name of the *Portugals,* in fo much that the *Necodaes,* or Mafters, of the Junks, that were in the Port, fearing the like might be done to them, affembled all together in councel; and there making Election of two of the principal amongft them, whom they held moft capable of performing their charge, they fent them as Embaffadors unto *Antonio de Faria,* defiring him, that as King of the Sea he would protect them upon the affurance of his word, fo as they might pafs fafely out of the place where they were, for to make their voyage whil'ft the feafon ferved; in confideration whereof, as his Tributaries, fubjects, and flaves, they would give him twenty thoufand *Taeis* in Ingots of Silver, wherof payment fhould be made out of hand by way of acknowledging him to be their Lord. *Antonio de Faria* received them very courteoufly, and granting their requeft, protefted and fware to perform the fame, and upon his word to protect them for the future from having any of their goods taken from them by any Pyrat. Whereupon one of the Embaffadors remained as furety for the twenty thoufand *Taeis,* and the other went to fetch the Ingots, which he brought an hour after, together with a rich prefent of many feveral things fent him over and above by the *Necodaes.* This done, *Antonio de Faria* defiring to advance a fervant of his, named *Cofta,* made him Clark of the Patents that were to be granted to the *Necodaes,* whereof he prefently fet a rate, namely five *Taeis* for a Junk, and two *Taeis* for a *Vanco, Lantea,* and fmall Barque, which proved fo beneficial to him, that in the fpace of thirteen days, wherein thefe Patents were difpatched, he got (according the report of thofe that envyed him) above four thoufand *Taeis* in filver, befides many good gratuities that were given him for expedition: The form of thefe Patents was thus. *I give affurance upon my word to* Necoda *fuch a one, that he fhall fail fafely all about the Coaft of* China *without any difturbance of any that belongs to me, upon condition that wherefoever he meets with any* Portugals *he fhall entreat them as brethren*; and underneath he figned, *Antonio de Faria*: All which Patents were moft exactly obferved, and by that means he was fo redoubted all along this Coaft, as the *Chaem* himfelf of the Ifland of *Ainan,* who is the Viceroy thereof, upon the report which he heard of him, fent to vifit him by his Embaffador, with a rich prefent of Pearls and Jewels, as alfo a Letter, whereby he defired him to take entertainment from the fon of the Sun, a name which they give to the Emperor of this Monarchy, for to ferve him as Commander General of all the Coaft from *Laman* to *Liampoo,* with ten thoufand *Taeis* Penfion yearly, and that if he carryed himfelf well, according to the renown went of him, he affured him that upon the expiration of his three years charge he fhould be advanced into the rank of the *Chaems* of the State, and that fuch men as he, if they were faithful, might attain to be one of the twelve *Tutoens* of the Empire, whom the foveraign fon of the Sun, being the Lion crowned on the Throne of the World, admitted to his bed and board, as members united to his perfon by means of the honor, power, and command that he gave them, with an annual Penfion of an hundred thoufand *Taeis.* *Antonio de Faria* gave him many thanks for this offer, and excufed himfelf with complements after their manner; faying, that he was not capable of fo great favor as he would honor him withall, but that without any regard at all of mony he would be ready to ferve him as often as the *Tutoens* of *Pequin* would be pleafed to command him. After this going out of the Port of *Madel,* where he had been fourteen days, he ran all along the Coaft of that Country for to find out *Coia Acem,* it being the main defign of all his voyage, as I have declared before: Imagining then that he might meet with him in fome of thefe places, he ftayd there above fix months, with much pain and hazard of his perfon; At length he arrived at a very fair Town, named *Quangiparu,* wherein were goodly buildings and Temples: In this Port he abode all that day and the night following, under colour of being a Merchant, peaceably buying that which was brought him aboard; And becaufe it was a Town of fifteen hundred fires, as we gueffed, the next morning by break

of

of day we set sail without any great notice taken of us. So returning to Sea, although it were with a contrary wind, in twelve days with a troublesom navigation he visited the shores both of the South and North Coasts, without incountring any thing worthy the observation, although they were replenished with a many of little Villages, whereof divers were inclosed with walls of brick, but not strong enough to withstand the force of thirty good Soldiers, the people of themselves being very weak, and having no other Arms but staves hardned in the fire; howsoever the scituation of this Country was under one of the best and fertilest Climates on the Earth, abounding with great store of cattel, and many goodly large fields, sowed with Wheat, Rice, Barly, Millet, and sundry other kinds of grain; as also replenished with many great groves of Pine, and *Angeline* trees, as in the *Indiaes*, able to furnish a world of shiping: Moreover, by the relation of certain Merchants, *Antonio de Faria* was informed, that in this Land there were many Mynes of Copper, Silver, Tin, Saltpeter, Sulphur, and an infinite deal of untilled, but excellently good ground, altogether neglected by this weak Nation, which were it in our power, we might in all probability be more advanced in the *Indiaes*, then now we are through the unhappiness of our sins.

§.3.   After we had been seven months and an half in this Country, sometimes on the one side, sometimes on the other, from River to River, and on both Coasts, North and South, as also in the Isle of *Ainan*, without hearing any news of *Coia Acem*, the Soldiers, weary of so long and tedious travel, assembled all together, and desired *Antonio de Faria* to make a partition of that which had been gotten, according to a promise before made to them by a note under his hand, saying that thereupon they would return unto the *Indiaes*, or where else they thought good, whereby a great deal of stir arose amongst us; At length it was agreed, that we should go and winter in *Siam*, where all the goods which were in the Junk should be sold, and being reduced into gold, division should be made of it, as was desired. With this accord, sworn and signed by all, we went and anchored in an Island, called the Island of Thieves, in regard it was the outermost Island of all that Bay, to the end that from thence we might make our voyage with the first fair wind that should blow. So having continued there twelve days with an earnest desire to effect the agreement we had made together, it fortuned, that by the conjunction of the new Moon in *October*, which we had always feared, there arose such a tempest of rain and wind, as seemed to be no natural thing, in so much that lying open to the South wind, as we traverst the Coast, the waves went so high, that though we used all means possible to save our selves, cutting down our Masts, and all the dead works from poop to prow, as also casting into the Sea even the most part of our merchandize, reducing our great Ordnance into their places again, out of which they had been toss'd, and strengthening our Cables, that were half rotten, with ropes; But all this was not able to preserve us, for the night was so dark, the weather so cold, the sea so rough, the wind so high, and the storm so horrible, that in these extremities nothing could deliver us but the meer mercy of God, whom with continual cries and tears we called upon for help: But for as much as in regard of our sins we did not deserve to receive this grace at his hands, his divine justice ordained, that about two hours after midnight there came such a fearful gust of wind, as drove our four vessels foul one of another upon the shore, where they were all broken to pieces, so that four hundred and fourscore men were drowned, amongst which were eight *Portugals*, and it pleased God that the remainder, being fifty three persons, were saved, whereof three and twenty were *Portugals*, the rest slaves and Mariners. After this lamentable shipwrack we got half naked, and most of us hurt, into a Marish hard by, where we stay'd till the next morning, and as soon as it was day we returned to the Sea side, which we found all strewed with dead bodies, a spectacle of that dread and horror as scarce any one of us could forbear swooning to behold it; over them we stood lamenting a great while, till such time an *Antonio de Faria*, who by the mercy of God was one of those that remained alive, whereof we were all very glad, concealing the grief which we could not dissemble, came where we were, having on a scarlet coat, that he had taken from one of the dead, and with a joyful countenance, his eyes dry and voyd of tears, he made a short speech unto us, wherein he remonstrated how variable and uncertain the things of this world were, and therefore he desired us as Brethren, that we would endevor to forget them, seeing the remembrance of them was but a means to grieve us; for considering the time and miserable estate whereunto we were reduced, we saw how necessary his counsel was: And how he hoped that God would in this desolate place present us with some good opportunity to same our selves, and how we might be assured that he never permitted any evil but for a greater

good;

good ; moreover how he firmly believed, that though we had now loft five hundred thoufand crowns, we fhould ere it were long get above fix hundred thoufand for them. This brief exhortation was heard by us all with tears and difcomfort enough, fo we fpent two days and an half there in burying the dead, during which time we recovered fome wet victuals and provifions to fuftain us withall, but they lafted not above five days of fifteen that we ftayed there, for by reafon of their wetnefs they corrupted prefently, and did us little good. After thefe fifteen days it pleafed God, who never forfakes them that truly put their truft in him, miraculoufly to fend us a remedy, whereby we efcaped out of that mifery we were in, as I will declare hereafter.

CHAP. XIX.

In what fort we efcaped miraculoufly out of this Ifland; our paffage from thence to the River of Xingrau; our incountring with a Chinefe Pyrat, and the agreement we made with him.

BEing efcaped from this miferable fhipwrack, it was a lamentable thing to fee how we §.1. walked up and down almoft naked, enduring fuch cruel cold and hunger, that many of us talking one to another fell down fuddenly dead with very weaknefs, which proceeded not fo much from want of victuals, as from the eating of fuch things as were hurtful to us, by reafon they were all rotten, and ftunk fo vilely, that no man could endure the tafte of them in his mouth ; But as our God is an infinite good, there is no place fo remote, or defert, where the mifery of finners can be hid from the affiftance of his infinite mercy, which I fpeak, in regard that on the day when as the feaft of S. *Michael* is celebrated, as we were drowned in tears, and without hope of any humane help, according as it feemed to the weaknefs of our little faith, a Kite came unexpectedly flying over our heads from behind a point, which the Ifland made towards the South, and by chance let fall a fifh, called a Mullet, about a foot long. This fifh falling clofe by *Antonio de Faria*, it fomewhat amazed him till he perceived what it was, fo that having confidered a little he fell on his knees, and with tears pronounced thefe words from the bottom of his heart. *O Lord Jefus Chrift, the eternal Son of God, I humbly befeech thee by the forrows of thy facred Paffion, that thou wilt not fuffer us to be overwhelmed with the unbelief, whereinto the mifery of our weaknefs hath caft us ; for I hope, and am almoft affured, that the fame fuccor which thou didft fend unto* Daniel *in the Lions den by the hand of thy Prophet* Abacuc, *thou wilt grant us at this prefent out of thy infinite goodnefs, and not only here, but in every other place, where a finner fhall invoke thy ayd with a firm and true faith ; Wherefore, my Lord, and my God, I pray thee, not for mine, but thine own fake, that thou wilt not caft thine eyes on that we have merited from thee, but on that thou haft merited for us, to the end it may pleafe thee to accord us the fuccor which we hope to receive from thee, and out of thy bleffed mercy to fend us the means whereby we may get from hence into fome Chriftian Country, where ftill perfevering in the holy Worfhip of thee, we may for ever continue thy faithful fervants.* This faid, he took the Mullet and caufed it to be broiled upon coals, and given to fuch of the fick as had moft need of it ; Then looking towards the point of the Ifland from whence the Kite came, we perceived divers others, that in their flying made many ftoopings, whence we concluded that there was fome kind of prey there whereon thefe fowls fed ; now all of us being moft defirous of relief, we went thither in all hafte, and coming to the top of the higher ground we difcovered a low valley full of divers fruit trees, and in the middle a river of frefh water, whereupon by good fortune before we went down we faw a Stag newly killed, and a Tyger beginning to eat him, therewith we made a great cry, which frighted him away into the Wood, leaving us the Stag as he was ; Then defcended we to the River, and by the bank of it ftayd all that night, making a feaft, as well with the Stag, as with divers Mullers that we took there, for there were a great number of Kites, that from the water catched a many of thofe fifhes, and oftentimes let them fall being fcared with our cries : Thus continued we by this River till Saturday following, when about the break of day we difcerned a Sail making as we thought towards the Ifland where we were, the better to be affured whereof we returned to the fhoar where we were wracked, and there ftaying about half an hour, we found it to be fo indeed, in which regard we got us prefently into the Wood to decline difcovery from thofe in the Veffel, which arriving in the Port we perceived it to be a *Lantea*, and that thofe that were in her faftened her to the fhoar with two cables, at the beak and the ftern,

K

the

the better to accommodate a plank for to pass in and out of her. Being all dif-imbarqued out of her to about the number of thirty persons, more or less, they went presently some to making provision of water and wood, some to washing of their linnen, and dressing of meat, and others to wraftling, and such like paftimes, little thinking to find any body in that place which could any way annoy them. *Antonio de Faria* seeing them altogether without fear and order, and that there was none remaining in the Veffel able to refift us ; *My Mafters, said he unto us, you behold the wretched eftate whereinto our mif-fortune hath reduced us, whereof I confefs my fins are the caufe, but the mercy of God is fo infinite, as I am verily perfwaded he will not fuffer us to perifh thus miferably here, and therefore hath as it were miraculoufly fent this Veffel hither, by feizing whereupon we may efcape from hence, which before to humane reafon feemed almoft impoffible ; wherefore I exhort you all to joyn with me in making our felves Mafters fuddenly of her ere ever we be heard or feen, and having fo done, let our only care be to poffefs our felves of the Arms we fhall find in her, that therewith we may defend our felves, and make good our poffeffion, upon which, next under God, our fafety depends ; and as foon as you fhall hear me fay three times,* Jefus, *do as you fhall fee me do :* Whereunto we anfwered, that we would diligently perform what he had enjoyned us ; fo that we ftanding all prepared to execute his defign, *Antonio de Faria* gave the fignal which he had fpoken of, and withall ran as faft as ever he could, and we along with him, till he arrived at the *Lantea*, whereinto we fuddenly entred without any contradiction ; then unloofing the two cables with which fhe was faftened, we put out to Sea about a Crofsbow fhot from Land. The *Chinefes* furprized in this manner, ran all to the Sea fide upon the noife that they heard, and feeing their Veffel taken, were much amazed, but knew not how to help it, for we fhot at them with an Iron Bafe that was in the *Lantea*, which made them fly into the Wood, where no doubt they paffed the reft of that day in lamenting the fad fuccefs of their ill fortune, as we had done ours before.

§.2.   After we were gotten into the *Lantea*, and that we were fure the deceived *Chinefes* could no way hurt us, we fat us down to eat that at leafure which they had caufed to be made ready for their dinner by an old man, that we found there, and it was a great Skillet full of Rice with hached Lard, whereunto we fell with good ftomacks, as being not a little hungry : Dinner done, and thanks rendred to God for his gracious mercy to us, an Inventory was taken of the goods that were in the *Lantea*, which was raw Silks, Damasks, Sattins, together with three great pots of Musk, amounting in all to the value of four thoufand Crowns, befides good ftore of Rice, Sugar, Gammons of Bacon, and two Coups full of Poultry, whereof we had more need then of all the reft for the recovery of our fick men, which were not a few amongft us. Hereupon we all began without fear to cut out pieces of Silk, therewith to accommodate every one with clothes. *Antonio de Faria*, having found a pretty boy in the *Lantea*, about fome twelve or thirteen years old, demanded of him from whence fhe came, and what fhe did in this place, as alfo to whom fhe belonged, and whither fhe was bound. *Alas !* anfwered the boy, *fhe not long fince belonged to my unfortunate Father, whofe ill hap it is to have that taken from him by you in lefs then an hour, which he hath been above thirty years in getting : He came from a place, called* Quoaman, *where in exchange of lingots of Silver he bought all thofe Commodities, that you have, with a purpofe to have gone and fold them to the Junks of* Siam, *which are in the Port of* Comhay ; *And wanting frefh water, it was his ill hap to come hither for to take in fome, where you have robbed him of all that he hath without any fear at all of the divine Juftice.* Whereupon *Antonio de Faria* bade him leave weeping, and making much of him promifed to ufe him as his own fon, and that he would always account him fo ; Hereat fmiling as it were in difdain, he anfwered, *Think not though I am but a child, that I am fo foolifh to beleeve, that having robbed my Father, thou canft ever ufe me like thy fon : But if thou wilt do as thou fayft, I befeech thee for the love of thy God fuffer me to fwim unto that fad Land where he remains that begot me, who indeed is my true father, with whom I had rather dye where I fee him lamenting, then live with fuch wicked people as you are.* Then fome of them that were prefent reprehending and telling him that it was not well fpoken ; *Would you know,* replyed he, *why I faid fo ? it was becaufe I faw you after you had filled your bellies praife God with lifted up hands, and yet for all that like hypocrites never care for making reftitution of that you have ftollen ; but be affured, that after death you fhall feel the rigorous chaftifement of the Lord Almighty for fo unjuftly taking mens goods from them.* *Antonio de Faria* admiring the childs fpeech, asked him whether he would become a Chriftian?
Where-

Whereunto, earnestly beholding him, he answered, *I understand not what you say, nor that you propound ; declare it first unto me, and then you shall know my mind further.* Then *Antonio de Faria* began to instruct him therein after the best manner he could, but the boy would not answer him a word, only lifting up his hands and eyes to Heaven he said weeping, *Blessed be thy Power, O Lord, that permits such people to live on the Earth, that speak so well of thee, and yet so ill observe thy Law, as these blinded Miscreants do, who think that robbing and preaching are things that can be acceptable to thee.* Having said so, he got him into a corner, and there remained weeping for three days together without eating any thing that was presented unto him. Hereupon falling to consult whether were the best course for us to hold from this place, either Northward, or Southward, much dispute arose thereabout, at length it was concluded that we should go to *Liampoo,* a Port distant from thence Northwards two hundred and threescore leagues, for we hoped that along this Coast we might happen to incounter and seize on some other greater and more commodious Vessel then that we had, which was too little for so long a Voyage, in regard of the dangerous storms that are ordinarily caused by the new Moons on the Coast of *China,* where dayly many Ships are cast away. With this design we put to Sea about Sun-set, and so went on this night with a South-west wind, and before day we discovered a little Island, named *Quintoo,* where we surprized a fisher-boat full of fresh fish, of which we took as much as we had need of, as also eight of twelve men that were in her for the service of our *Lantea,* by reason our own were so feeble as they were not able to hold out any longer. These eight fishermen, being demanded what Ports there were on this Coast to *Chincheo,* where we thought we might meet with some Ship of *Malaca,* answered, that about eighteen leagues from thence there was a good River and a good Rode, called *Xingrau,* much frequented with Junks, where we might be easily and throughly accommodated with all that we stood in need of ; that at the entring into it, there was a little Village, named *Xamoy,* inhabited with poor fishermen, and three leagues beyond that the Town, where there was great store of Silks, Musk, Pourcelains, and many other sorts of Commodities, which were transported into divers parts. Upon this advice we steered our course towards that River, where we arrived the next day immediately after dinner, and cast anchor just against it about a league in the Sea, for fear lest our ill fortune should run us into the same mischief we were in before. The night following we took a *Paroo* of fishermen, of whom we demanded what Junks there were in this River, and how they were man'd, with divers other questions proper for our design. Whereunto they answered, that at the Town up the River there was not above two hundred Junks, by reason the greatest part were already gone to *Ainan, Sumbor, Lailoo,* and other Ports of *Cauchenchina* ; moreover, that we might ride in safety at *Xamoy,* and that there we might buy any thing we wanted ; Whereupon we entred into the River, and anchored close to the Village, where we continued the space of half an hour, being much about midnight. But *Antonio de Faria* seeing that the *Lantea* wherein we sailed could not carry us to *Liampoo,* where we purposed to lie all the Winter, he concluded by the advice of his company to furnish himself with a better Vessel, and although we were not then in case to enterprise any thing, yet necessity constrained us to undertake more then our Forces would permit ; Now there being at that instant a little Junk riding at anchor fast by us alone, and no other near her, having but few men in her, and those asleep, *Antonio de Faria* thought he had a good opportunity to effect his purpose, wherefore leaving his anchor in the Sea, he got up close to this Junk, and with seven and twenty Soldiers and eight Boys boarded her on a sudden unespyed, where finding seven or eight *Chinese* Mariners fast asleep, he caused them to be taken, and bound hand and foot, threatening if they cryed out never so little to kill them all, which put them in such a fear as they durst not so much as quetch. Then cutting her cables, he got him straight out of the River, and sailing away with all the speed he could ; The next day we arrived at an Island, named *Pullo Quirim,* distant from *Xamoy* not above nine leagues, there meeting with a little favorable gale within three days we went and anchored at another Island, called *Luxitay,* where, in regard the ayr was wholesom, and the water good, we thought fit to stay some fifteen days for the recovery of our sick men : In this place we visited the Junk, but found no other commodity in her then Rice, the greatest part whereof we cast into the Sea, to make her the lighter and securer for our Voyage ; Then we unladed all her furniture into the *Lantea,* and set her on ground for to caulk her, so that in doing thereof, and making our provision of water, we spent (as I said before) fifteen days in this Island, by which time our sick men fully recovered their health ; whereupon we departed for *Liampoo,* being

given

given to underftand, that many *Portugals* were come thither from *Malaca, Sunda, Siam,* and *Patana,* as they ufed ordinarily to do about that time for to winter there.

§.3.   We had failed two days together along the Coaft of *Laman* with a favorable wind, when it pleafed God to make us incounter with a Junk of *Patana,* that came from *Lequio,* which was commanded by a *Chinefe* Pyrat, named *Quiay Panian,* a great friend of the *Portugal* Nation, and much addicted to our fafhions and manner of life, with him there were thirty *Portugals,* choyce and proper men, whom he kept in pay, and advantaged more then the reft with gifts and prefents, fo that they were all very rich. This Pyrat had no fooner difcovered us but he refolved to attaque us, thinking nothing lefs then that we were *Portugals,* fo that endeavoring to inveft us, like an old Soldier as he was, and verft in the trade of Pyrat, he got the wind of us; that done, falling down within a Musket fhot of us, he faluted us with fifteen Pieces of Ordnance, wherewith we were much affrighted, becaufe the moft of them were Faulconets; but *Antonio de Faria* encouraging his men, like a valiant Captain, and a good Chriftian, dif-pofed them on the hatches in places moft convenient, as well in the prow as the poop, referving fome to be afterwards fitted as need fhould require. Being thus refolved to fee the end of that which Fortune fhould prefent us, it pleafed God that we defcryed a Crofs in our Enemies Flag, and on the foredeck a number of red Caps, which our men were wont to wear at Sea in thofe times, whereby we were perfwaded that they might be *Portugals,* that were going from *Liampoo* to *Malaca* ; Whereupon we made them a fign for to make our felves known to them, who no fooner perceived that we were *Portugals,* but in token of joy they gave a great fhout, and withall vailing their two top fails in fhew of obedience, they fent their long boat, called a Balon, with two *Portugals* in her, for to learn what we were, and from whence we came : At length having well obferved and confidered us, they approached with fome more confidence to our Junk, and having faluted us, and we them, they came aboard her, where *Antonio de Faria* received them very courteoufly ; And for that they were known to fome of our Soldiers, they continued there a good while, during the which they recounted divers particulars unto us neceffary for our defign. That done, *Antonio de Faria* fent *Chriftovano Borralho* to accom-pany them back, and to vifit *Quiay Panian* from him, as alfo to deliver him a Letter, full of complements, and many other offers of friendfhip, wherewith this Pyrat *Panian* was fo con-tented and proud, that he feemed not to be himfelf, fuch was his vanity, and paffing clofe by our Junk he took in all his fails ; then accompanied with twenty *Portugals,* he came and vi-fited *Antonio de Faria* with a goodly rich Prefent, worth above two thoufand duckets, as well in Ambergreece and Pearls, as Jewels of Gold and Silver. *Antonio de Faria,* and the reft of us, received him with great demonftrations of love and honor : After that he and all his company were fet, *Antonio de Faria* fell to difcourfe with them of divers things according to the time and occafion, and then recited unto them his unhappy Voyage, and the lofs he had fuftained, acquainting them with his determination to go unto *Liampoo,* for to reinforce him-felf with men, and make provifion of Veffels with oars, to the end he might return again, to pafs once more into the Streight of *Cauchenchina,* and fo get to the Mynes of *Quoaniaparu,* where he had been told there were fix large houfes full of lingots of Silver, befides a far greater quantity that was continually melted all along the River, and that without any peril one might be wonderfully enriched. Whereunto the Pyrat *Panian* made this anfwer, *For mine own part, Signior Captain, I am not fo rich as many think, though it is true I have been fo heretofore, but having been beaten with the fame misfortune, which thou fayft hath befallen thee, my riches have been taken from me ; Now to return to* Patana, *where I have a wife and children, I dare not, by reafon I am affured that the King will defpoil me of all that I fhould bring thi-ther,, becaufe I departed from thence without his permiffion, which he would make a moft haynous crime, to the end he might feize upon my eftate, as he hath done to others for far leffer occafions then that wherewith he may charge me. Wherefore if thou canft be contented that I fhall accompany thee in the Voyage thou meaneft to undertaken, with an hundred men that I have in my Junk, fifteen Pieces of Ordnance, thirty Muskets, and forty Harquebufes, which thefe Signiers, the* Portugals *that are with me, do carry, I fhall moft willingly do it, upon con-dition that thou wilt impart unto me a third part of that which fhall be gotten, and to that effect I defire thee to give me an affurance under thy hand, as alfo to fwear unto me by thy Law to perform it accordingly.* *Antonio de Faria* accepted of this offer very gladly, and after he had rendred him many thanks for it, he fwore unto him upon the holy Evangelifts fully and without all fail to accomplifh what he required, and thereof likewife made him a promife under

his

his hand, to which divers of their company subscribed their names as witnesses. This accord past between them, they went both together into a River, called *Anay*, some five leagues from thence, where they furnished themselves with all that they stood in need of, by means of a Present of an hundred duckets, which they gave to the *Mandarin*, Captain of the Town.

<h2 style="text-align:center">CHAP. XX.</h2>

Our Encounter at Sea with a little Fisher-boat, wherein were eight Portugals *very sore hurt; and* Antonio de Faria's *meeting and fighting with* Coia Acem *the Pyrat.*

BEing parted from this River of *Anay*, and well provided of all things necessary for the §.I. Voyage we had undertaken, *Antonio de Faria* resolved by the advice and counsel of *Quiay Panian*, whom he much respected, to go and anchor in the Port of *Chincheo*, there to be informed by such *Portugals* as were come from *Sunda*, *Malaca*, *Timor*, and *Patana*, of certain matters requisite for his design, and whether they had any news from *Liampoo*, in regard the report went in the Country, that the King of *China* had sent thither a Fleet of four hundred Junks, wherein there were an hundred thousand men, for to take the *Portugals* that resided there, and to burn their houses, for that he would not endure them to be any longer in his dominions, because he had been lately advertised, that they were not a people so faithful and peaceable as he had been formerly given to understand. Arriving then in the Port of *Chincheo*, we found five *Portugal* ships that were come thither about a month before from the places above mentioned. These ships received us with great joy, and after they had given us intelligence of the Country, Traffique, and Tranquillity of the Ports, they told us they had no other news from *Liampoo*, but that it was said a great number of *Portugals* were come thither from many parts to winter there; and how that great Army, which we so much feared, was not thereabout; but that it was suspected to be gone for the Islands of *Goto*, to the succor of *Sucan de Pontir*, from whom the brute went a Brother-in-law of his had taken his Kingdom, and that in regard *Sucan* had lately made himself subject to the King of *China*, and his Tributary for an hundred thousand *Taeis* by the year, he had in contemplation thereof given him this great Army of four hundred Junks, with the forces aforesaid, for to restore him to his Crown and Signiories, whereof he had been despoyled. Being very glad of this news, after we had remained in this Port of *Chincheo* the space of nine days, we departed from thence for *Liampoo*, taking along with us five and thirty Soldiers more out of the five ships we found there, to whom *Antonio de Faria* gave very good pay; and after we had sailed five days with a contrary wind, coasting from one side to another, without advancing any whit at all, it happened that one night about the first watch we met with a little Fisher-boat, or *Paroo*, wherein there were eight *Portugals*, very sore hurt, two of the which were named *Mem Taborda*, and *Antonio Anriques*, men of honor, and very much renowned in those quarters, the cause why in particular I name them; These and the other six were in such a pitiful estate, and so hideous to see to, as they moved every one to compassion. This *Paroo* coming close to *Antonio de Faria*, he caused them to be taken up into his Junk, where they presently cast themselves at his feet, from whence he raised them up, weeping for pity to behold them so naked, and all bathed in their own blood with the wounds they had received, and then demanded of them the occasion of their misfortune: Whereunto one of the two made answer, that about seventeen days before they set sail from *Liampoo* for *Malaca*, and that being advanced as far as the Isle of *Sumbor* they had been set upon by a Pyrat, a *Guzarat* by Nation, called *Coia Acem*, who had three Junks, and four *Lanteaas*, wherein were fifteen hundred men, namely an hundred and fifty *Mahometans*, the rest *Luzzons*, *Jaoas*, and *Champaas*, people of the other side of *Malaya*, and that after they had fought with them from one to four in the afternoon, they had been taken with the death of fourscore and two men, whereof eighteen were *Portugals*, and as many made slaves; And that in their Junk, what of his and of others, there was lost in merchandize above an hundred thousand *Taeis*. *Antonio de Faria* remaining a good while pensive at that which these men related unto him, at length said unto them, I pray tell me how was it possible for you to escape more then the rest, the fight passing as you deliver? *After we had been fought withall about an hour and an half, the three great Junks boarded us five times, and with the force of their shot they so tore the Prow of our Vessel, that we were ready to sink; wherefore to keep out the water, and lighten*

our

our ship, we were constrained to cast the most part of our goods into the Sea, and whil'st our men were laboring to do so, our Enemies layd so close at us, as every one was fain to leave that he was about for to defend himself on the hatches: But whil'st we were thus troubled, most of our company being hurt, and many slain, it pleased God that one of the Enemies Junks came to be so furiously fired, as it caught hold likewise of another that was fastned unto it, which made the Pyrats Soldiers leave the fight for to go and save their Vessels, yet that they could not do so speedily, but that one of them was burnt down even to the very water, so that they of the Junk were compelled to leap into the Sea to save themselves from burning, where most of them were drowned: In the mean time we made shift to get our Junk close to a stock of Piles, which Fishermen had planted there against a rock, hard by the mouth of the river, where at this present is the Temple of the Siams, but the dog Coia Acem was instantly with us, and having fast grappled us, he leapt into our Vessel, being followed by a great number of Mahometans, all armed with Coats of Mail, and Buff Jerkins, who straightway killed above an hundred and fifty of ours, whereof eighteen were Portugals; which we no sooner perceived, but all wounded as we were, and spoyled with the fire, as you see, we sought for some way to save our selves, and to that end we sped us into a Manchua, that was fastned to the stern of our Junk, wherein it pleased God that fifteen of us escaped, whereof two dyed yesterday, and of the thirteen, that remain yet miraculously alive, there are eight Portugals, and five servants. In this sort we got us with all speed between this Pallisado and the land amongst the rocks, the better to preserve us from being boarded by their Junk, but they were otherwise employed in seeking to save the men of their burnt Vessel; and afterwards they entred all into our Junk, where they were so carryed away with covetousness of the booty, as they never thought of pursuing us; so that the Sun being almost set, and they wonderful glad of their victory over us, they retired into the River with great acclamations. *Antonio de Faria*, very joyful at this news, though he was as sad again on the other side for the bad success of those that had made him this relation, rendred thanks unto God for that he had found his Enemy, it being a matter so much desired of him and his: Certainly, said he unto them then, by your report they must needs be now in great disorder, and much spoiled in the River where they are, for I am perswaded, that neither your Junk, nor that of theirs, which was fastned to the burnt one, can do them any longer service, and that in the great Junk, which assaulted you, it is not possible but that you have hurt and killed a good many. Whereunto they answered, that without doubt they had killed and hurt a great number. Then *Antonio de Faria*, putting off his cap, fell down on his knees, and with his hands and eyes lifted up to Heaven he said weeping, *O Lord Jesus Christ, my God and Saviour, even as thou art the true hope of those that put their trust in thee, I, that am the greatest sinner of all men, do most humbly beseech thee in the name of thy servants, that are here present, whose Souls thou hast bought with thy precious blood, that thou wilt give us strength and victory against this cruel Enemy, the murtherer of so many* Portugals, *whom with thy favor and ayd, and for the honor of thy holy Name I have resolved to seek out, as hitherto I have done, to the end he may pay to thy Soldiers and faithful servants what he hath so long owed them.* Whereunto all that were by answered with one cry, *To them, to them, in the Name of Jesus Christ, that this dog may now render us that, which for so long together he hath taken, as well from us, as from our poor miserable companions.* Hereupon with marvelous ardor and great acclamations we set sail for the Port of *Lailoo*, which we had left eight leagues behind us, whither by the advice of some of his company *Antonio de Faria* went to furnish himself with all that was necessary for the fight he hoped to make with the Pyrat, in the quest of whom (as I have already delivered) he had spent so much time, and yet could never till then hear any news of him in all the Ports and places where he had been.

§.2.   The next morning we arrived at the Port of *Lailoo*, where *Quiay Panian* had much kinred, and many friends, so that he wanted no credit in that place; wherefore he intreated the *Mandarin* (who is the Captain of the Town) to permit us to buy for our mony such things as we stood in need of, which he instantly granted, as well for fear lest some displeasure might be done him, as for the sum of a thousand duckets, presented unto him by *Antonio de Faria*, wherewith he rested very well satisfied. Hereupon some of our Company went ashore, who with all diligence bought whatsoever we wanted, as Saltpeter and Sulphur to make powder, Lead, Bullets, Victual, Cordage, Oyl, Pitch, Rosin, Ockam, Timber, Planks, Arms, Darts, Staves hardened in the fire, Masts, Sails, Sail-yards, Targets, Flints, Pullies, and Anchors; that done, we

took

took in fresh water, and furnished our Vessels with Mariners. Now although that this place contained not above three or four hundred houses, yet was there both there, and in the villages adjoyning, such a quantity of the aforesaid things, that in truth it were hard to express it; for *China* is excellent in this, that it may vaunt to be the Country in the world most abounding in all things that may be desired. Besides for that *Antonio de Faria* was exceeding liberal, in regard he spent out of the general booty, before the partitions were made, he payd for all that he bought at the price the sellers would set, by means whereof he had more brought him by far then he had use for, so that within thirteen days he went out of this Port wonderfully well accommodated, with two other new great Junks, which he had exchanged for two little ones that he had, and two *Lanteaas* with Oars, as also an hundred and sixty Mariners, both for towing, and for governing the sails. After all these preparations were made, and we ready to weigh anchor, a general muster was taken of all that were in our Army, which in number was found to be five hundred persons, as well for fight, as for the service and navigation of our Vessels, amongst whom were fourscore and fifteen *Portugals*, young and resolute, the rest were Boys, and Mariners, and men of the other Coast, which *Quiay Panian* kept in pay, and were well practised in Sea-fight, as they that had been five years Pyrats. Moreover we had an hundred and sixty Harquebuses, forty pieces of brass Ordnance, whereof twenty were field-pieces, that carryed stone-bullets, threescore quintals of powder, namely fifty four for the great Ordnance, and six for the Harquebuses, besides what the Harquebusiers had already delivered to them, nine hundred pots of artificial fire, whereof four hundred were of powder, and five hundred of unslaked Lime after the *Chinese* manner, a great number of stones, Arrows, Half-pikes, four thousand small Javelings, store of Hatchets to serve at boarding, six Boats full of Flints, wherewith the Sailers fought, twelve Cramp-irons with their hooks fastned to great Iron chains for to grapple Vessels together, and many sorts of fire-works, which an Engineer of the *Levant* made for us. With all this equipage we departed from this Port of *Lailoo*, and within three days after it pleased God that we arrived at the fishing place, where *Coia Acem* took the *Portugals* Junk: There as soon as it was night *Antonio de Faria* sent spies into the River, for to learn whereabout he was, who took a *Paroo*, with six Fishermen in her, that gave us to understand how this Pyrat was some two leagues from thence in a River, called *Tinlau*, and that he was accommodating the Junk he had taken from the *Portugals*, for to go in her, with two others that he had, unto *Siam*, where he was born, and that he was to depart within two days. Upon this news *Antonio de Faria* called some of his company to councel, where it was concluded, that first of all the places and forces of our Enemy was to be visited and seen, because in a matter of so much hazard, it was not safe to run as it were blindfold unto it, but to advise on it well beforehand, and that upon the certainty of that which should be known, such resolution might afterwards be taken, as should seem good to all; Then drawing the fishermen out of the *Paroo*, he put some of *Quiay Panians* Mariners into her, and sending her away only with two of those fishermen, keeping the rest as hostages, he committed the charge of her to a valiant Soldier, named *Vincentio Morosa*, attired after the *Chinese* fashion, for fear of discovery; who arriving at the place where the Enemy rode, made shew of fishing as others did, and by that means espyed all that he came for, whereupon returning, he gave an account of what he had seen, and assured us that the Enemies were so weak, as upon boarding of them they might easily be taken. *Antonio de Faria* caused the most experienced men of his company to be assembled, to advise thereon, and that in *Quiay Panians* Junk, to honor him the more, as also to maintain his friendship, which he much esteemed: At this meeting it was resolved, that as soon as it was night they should go and anchor at the mouth of the River, where the Enemy lay, for to set upon him the next morning before day. This agreed unto by all, *Antonio de Faria* set down what order and course should be held at the entring into the River, and how the Enemy should be assaulted: Then dividing his men, he placed thirty *Portugals* in *Quiay Panians* Junk, such as he pleased to choose, because he would be sure to give him no distaste; Likewise he disposed six *Portugals* into each of the *Lanteaas*, and into *Christovano Borralho's* Junk twenty; the rest of the *Portugals*, being three and thirty, he retained with himself, besides slaves and divers Christians, all valiant and trusty men. Thus accommodated and ordered for the execution of his enterprize, he set sail towards the River of *Tinlau*, where he arrived about Sun-set, and there keeping good watch he past the night till three of the clock in the morning, at which time he made to the Enemy, who rode some half a league up in the River.

It

§.3. It pleased God that the Sea was calm, and the wind so favorable, as our Fleet, sailing up the River, arrived in less then an hour close to the Enemy, unperceived of any; But because they were Thieves, and feared the people of the Country, in regard of the great mischiefs and robberies which they dayly committed, they stood so upon their guard, and kept so good watch, that as soon as they discerned us, in all haste they rung an alarum with a Bell, the sound whereof caused such a rumor and disorder, as well amongst them that were ashore, as those aboard, that one could hardly hear one another, by reason of the great noise they made. Whereupon *Antonio de Faria*, seeing we were discovered, cryed out to his company, *To them, my Masters, to them in the name of God before they be succored by their Lorches*, wherewith discharging all his Ordnance, it pleased Heaven, that the shot lighted to such purpose, as it overthrew and tore in pieces the most part of the valiantest, that then were mounted and appeared on the deck, even right as we could have wished : In the neck hereof our Harquebusiers, which might be some hundred and threescore, failed not to shoot upon the signal, that had formerly been ordained for it, so that the hatches of the Junk were cleared of all those that were upon them, and that with such a slaughter as not an Enemy durst appear there afterwards ; At which very instant our two Junks boarded their two in the case they were in, where the fight grew so hot on either side, as I confess I am not able to relate in particular what passed therein, though I was present at it, for when it began it was scarce day. Now that which rendred the conflict betwixt us and our Enemies most dreadful was the noise of Drums, Basins, and Bells, accompanyed with the report of the great Ordnance, wherewith the valleys and rocks thereabouts resounded again. This fight continuing in this manner some quarter of an hour, their *Lorches* and *Lanteaas* came from the shore to assist them with fresh men, which one, named *Diego Meyrelez*, in *Quiay Panians* Junk, perceiving, and that a Gunner employed not his shot to any purpose, in regard he was so beside himself with fear, that he knew not what he did, as he was ready to give fire to a Piece, he thrust him away so rudely, as he threw him down into the scuttle, saying to him, *Away villain, thou canst do nothing, this business belongs to men, such as I am, not to thee* : whereupon pointing the Gun with its wedges of level, as he knew very well how to do, he gave fire to the Piece, which was charged with bullets and stones, and hitting the Lorch that came foremost, carryed away all the upper part of her from Poup to Prow, so that she presently sank, and all that were in her, not a man saved : The shot then having past so through the first *Lorch*, fell on the hatches of another *Lorch*, that came a little behind, and killed the Captain of her, with six or seven more that were by him, wherewith the two other *Lorches* were so terrified, that going about to fly back to Land, they fell foul one of another, so as they could not clear themselves, but remained entangled together, and not able to go forward or backward, which perceived by the Captains of our two *Lorches*, called *Gasparo d'Oliveyra*, and *Vincentio Morosa*, they presently set upon them, casting a great many artificial pots into them, wherewith they were so fired, that they burnt down to the very water, which made the most of those that were in them to leap into the Sea, where our men killed them all with their Pikes, so that in those three *Lorches* alone there dyed above two hundred persons ; and in the other, whereof the Captain was slain, there was not one escaped, for *Quiay Panian* pursued them in a *Champana*, which was the Boat of his Junk, and dispatched most of them as they were getting to Land, the rest were all battered against the rocks that were by the shore : which the Enemies in the Junks perceiving, being some hundred and fifty *Mahometans*, *Luzzons*, *Borneos*, and *Jaos*, they began to be so discouraged, that many of them threw themselves into the Sea ; whereupon the dog *Coia Acem*, who yet was not known, ran to this disorder, for to animate his men. He had on a Coat of Mail lined with Crimson Sattin, edged with gold fringe, that had formerly belonged to some *Portugal*, and crying out with a loud voyce, that every one might hear him, he said three times, *Lah bilah, bilah la Mahumed, rocol halah, Massulmens, and true Believers in the holy Law* of Mahomet, *will you suffer your selves to be vanquished by such feeble slaves, as these Christian Dogs, who have no more heart then white Pullets, or bearded women ? To them, to them, for we are assured by the Book of Flowers, wherein the Prophet* Noby *doth promise eternal delights to the* Daroezes *of the House of* Mecqua, *that he will keep his word both with you and me, provided that we bathe our selves in the blood of these dogs without Law* : With these cursed words the Devil so encouraged them, that rallying all into one body, they re-inforced the fight, and so valiantly made head against us, as it was a dreadful thing to see how desperately they ran amongst our weapons. In the mean time *Antonio de Faria* thus

exhorted

exhorted his men: *Courage valiant Chriſtians, and whileſt theſe wicked Miſcreants fortifie themſelves in their deviliſh Sect, let us truſt in our Lord Jeſus Chriſt, nailed on the Croſs for us, who will never forſake us, how great ſinners ſoever we be, for after all we are his, which theſe Dogs here are not.* With this ferver and zeal of faith flying upon *Coia Acem,* to whom he had moſt ſpleen, he diſcharged ſo great a blow on his head with a two-handed ſword, that cutting through a Cap of Mail he wore, he layd him at his feet, then redoubling with another reverſe ſtroke he lamed him of both his legs, ſo as he could not riſe, which his followers beholding they gave a mighty cry, and aſſaulted *Antonio de Faria* with ſuch fury and hardineſs, as they made no reckoning of a many of *Portugals,* by whom they were invironned, but gave him divers blows that had almoſt overthrown him to the ground : Our men ſeeing this ran preſently to his ayd, and behaved themſelves ſo well, that in half a quarter of an hour forty eight of our enemies lay ſlaughtered on the dead body of *Coia Acem,* and but fourteen of ours, whereof there were not above five *Portugals,* the reſt were ſervants and ſlaves, good and faithful Chriſtians. The remainder of them, beginning to faint, retired in diſorder towards the foredeck, with an intent to fortifie themſelves there, for prevention whereof twenty Soldiers, of thirty that were in *Quiay Panians* Junk, ran inſtantly and got before them, ſo that ere they could render themſelves Maſters of what they pretended unto, they were inforced to leap into the Sea, where they fell one upon another, and were by our men quite made an end of, ſo that of all their number there remained but only five, whom they took alive, and caſt into the Hold bound hand and foot, to the end they might afterwards be forced by torments to confeſs certain matters that ſhould be demanded of them, but they fairly tore out one anothers throats with their teeth, for fear of the death they expected, which yet could not keep them from being diſmembered by our ſervants, and after thrown into the Sea, in the company of the Dog *Coia Acem* their Captain, great *Cacis* of the King of *Bintan,* the Shedder and Drinker of the blood of *Portugals,* Titles which he ordinarily gave himſelf in his Letters, and which he publiſhed openly to all *Mahometans,* by reaſon whereof, and for the ſuperſtition of his curſed Sect, he was greatly honored by them.

CHAP. XXI.

What Antonio de Faria *did after his Victory ; his departure from the River of* Tinlau, *with his ill ſucceſs thereupon, and the ſuccor we met withall.*

§. 1. THis bloody Battel finiſhed with the honor of the Victory, before-mentioned, in the deſcription whereof I have not uſed many words ; for if I ſhould undertake to recount the particularies of it, and ſet forth all that was performed by ours, as alſo the valor wherewith the Enemies defended themſelves, beſides that I am unable to do it, I ſhould then be forced to make a far larger diſcourſe, and more ample Hiſtory then this is : but it being my intention to declare things *en paſſant*, I have labored to ſpeak ſuccinctly in divers places, where poſſibly better wits then mine would amplifie matters in a more accompliſhed manner, and this is the reaſon that I have now delivered nothing but what was needful to be written. Returning then to my former diſcourſe, I ſay, that the firſt thing *Antonio de Faria* did after this Victory was to ſee his hurt men looked unto, whereof there were about fourſcore and twelve, the moſt part *Portugals,* our ſervants being included ; As for the number of the dead, there were on our ſide forty two, amongſt which eight were *Portugals,* the loſs of whom afflicted *Antonio de Faria* more then all the reſt, and of the Enemies three hundred and eighty, whereof an hundred and fifty fell by fire and ſword, the remainder were drowned. Now albeit this Victory brought a great deal of content to us all, yet were there many tears ſhed both in general and particular for the ſlaughter of our companions, the moſt part of whoſe heads were cleft aſunder with the Enemies hatchets. After this *Antonio de Faria,* notwithſtanding he was hurt in two or three places, went preſently aſhoar with thoſe that were in caſe to accompany him, where the firſt thing he did was to give order for the burial of the dead ; thereupon he ſurrounded the Iſland for to ſee what he could diſcover : Compaſſing of it then in this ſort he lighted upon a very pleaſant Valley, wherein were many gardens, repleniſhed with ſundry kinds of fruits ; there alſo was a Village of about forty or fifty very low houſes, which the infamous *Coia Acem* had ſacked, and in them ſlain many of the inhabitants, that had not the means to eſcape his hands. Further, in the ſaid Valley, and by a delicate River of freſh water, wherein were a number of Mullets and Trouts, he met with a very fair houſe, which ſeemed

L

to be the *Pagod* of the Village, that was full of sick and hurt persons, whom *Coia Acem* had put there to be cured; amongst these were divers *Mahometans* of his kinred, and others of his best Soldiers, to the number of ninety six, who as soon as they perceived *Antonio de Faria* afar off cryed out to him for mercy and forgiveness, but he would by no means harken unto them, alledging that he could not spare those that had killed so many Christians; Saying so, he caused the house to be fired in six or seven places, which in regard it was of wood, bepitched, and covered with dry Palm tree leaves, burned in such sort as it was dreadful to behold; In the mean time it would have moved any man to pity to hear the lamentable cries made by these wretches within, and to see them cast themselves headlong out of the windows, where our men, provoked with a desire of revenge, received them upon their Pikes and Halberds. This cruelty performed, *Antonio de Faria* returned to the Sea side, where the Junk lay, that *Coia Acem* had taken a month before from the *Portugals* of *Liampoo*, and caused it to be lanched into the Sea, having been formerly repaired and caulked, which being done, and he aboard again, he restored it to *Mem Taborda*, and *Antonio Anriques*, to whom it belonged, as I have already declared; But first, causing them to lay their hands on the Book of Prayers, *Worthy Friends*, said he unto them, *for all those my companions sakes, as well living as dead, who for your Junk here have lost so much blood, and so many lives, I present you with her, and all the goods that were in her, as a free gift, to the end that thereby our Lord may receive us into his everlasting Kingdom; and besides, be pleased to grant us an abolition of all our sins in this world, and in the other everlasting life, as I trust he hath given to our brethren, that this day dyed like good Christians for the holy Catholique Faith; Howbeit, I pray and expresly enjoyn you, nay I conjure you by the oath you are now to make, that you take no other goods but such only as appertain unto you, and that you brought from* Liampoo, *both for your selves, and those other Merchants that were Venturers with you: For more I do not give you, nor were it reasonable I should, in regard it would be much against the duty of either of our consciences, for me to give, and you to receive it.* Having spoken in this manner, *Mem Taborda* and *Antonio Anriques*, who little looked for any such favor, fell down at his feet, and with tears of joy rendred him a world of thanks, and then presently went ashoar for to seek out their goods, taking with them about fifty or threescore servants, whom their Masters had lent them for to help gather up the Silks that were wet, and hanged up by the Enemies on Trees a drying, besides two great rooms full of such as had never been wet, all which amounted, as it was said, to an hundred thousand *Taeis*, wherein above an hundred Merchants had a share, as well of them that dwelt at *Liampoo*, as at *Malaca*, to whom they were consigned; The rest of their Commodities, being a third part thereof, were lost, and could never be heard of. The next morning, as soon as it was light, he went to the great Junk that he had taken, which was full of the bodies of them that were slain in her the day before, whom without further ado he caused to be thrown into the Sea; howbeit for *Coia Acems*, in regard he was of a more eminent condition then the rest, and consequently deserving a greater honor in his funerals, he commanded him clothed and armed as he was to be cut into four quarters, and so cast also into the Sea, where for the merit of his works his body was intombed in the bellies of the hungry Lizards, whereof there was a great company all about our Junk, that shewed themselves above water, allured by the appast of those formerly thrown over-board; and in precipitating him so dismembered into the Sea, *Antonio de Faria* in stead of a prayer, *Go wicked wretch*, said he, *to the bottom of Hell, where thy damned Soul doth now enjoy the promised delights of thy Mahomet, as thou didst yesterday publish to these other Dogs such as thy self.* Thereupon he commanded all the Slaves and Captives of his company, together with their Masters, before him, unto whom he made a speech like a true Christian, as indeed he was, whereby he prayed them in the Name of God to manumit these Slaves, according to the promise he had made them before the fight, engaging himself to satisfie them for it out of his own Estate: Whereunto they answered all with one consent, that since it was his desire they were wel contented, and that they did even then set them at full liberty, whereof he caused a writing to be presently made with all their hands unto it, being as much as could be done for the instant, but afterwards each of them had in particular Letters of manumission granted unto them. This done, an Inventory was taken of such Commodities as were found to be good and merchantable, over and above those which were given to the *Portugals*, and all was praised at an hundred and thirty thousand *Taeis* in Silver Lingots of *Japan*, consisting of Sattin, Damask, raw Silk, Taffety, Musk, and very fine Porcelain, for as touching the rest they were not put in writing; And all these Robberies

the

the Pyrats had committed on the Coasts between *Sumbor* and *Fucheo*, where for above a year together they had coursed up and down.

After that *Antonio de Faria* had remained four and twenty days in this River of *Tinlau*, during which time all his hurt men were cured, he set sail directly for *Liampoo*, where he purposed to pass the Winter, to the end that with the beginning of the Spring he might set forth on his Voyage to the Mynes of *Quoaniaparu*, as he had resolved with *Quiay Panian*, the *Chinese* Pyrat that was in his company, but being advanced even to the point of *Micuy*, which is at the height of six and twenty degrees, so great a Tempest arose towards the North-west, that we were fain to strike our top-sails, for fear we should be forced back again from our course; but after dinner it increased with such a terrible storm of rain, and the Sea went so high, that the two *Lanteas* were not able to brook it, so that about evening they made to Land, with an intent to recover the River of *Xilendau*, which was about a league and an half from thence, whereupon *Antonio de Faria* doubting some misfortune, carried as little sail as possibly he could, as well for that he would not outgo the *Lanteas*, as in regard of the violence of the wind, which was such, as they durst not carry more: Now by reason the night was so dark, and the billows so great, they could not discern a shelf of sand, that lay betwixt an Island and the point of a Rock, so that passing over it our Junk struck her self so rudely on it, as her upper keel cleft in two or three places, and her under keel a little, whereupon the Gunner would have given fire to a Falconet, for to have warned the other Junks to come in to succor us in this extremity, but *Antonio de Faria* would by no means permit him, saying, that since it pleased God he should be cast away in that place, there was no reason that others should be lost there also for his cause; But he desired every one to assist him, both with manual labor, and secret prayers unto God to pardon their sins: Having said so, he caused the main Mast to be cut down, whereby the Junk came to be in somewhat a better case then she was before; but alas! the fall of it cost three Mariners and one of our servants their lives, who chancing to be under it when it fell were battered all to pieces; In like manner he made all the other Masts from poop to prow to be hewed down, together with all the dead works, as the cabins and galleries without, so that all was taken away close to the hatches. And though all this was done with incredible diligence, yet it stood us in little stead, for that the weather was so foul, the sea so swoln, the night so dark, the waves so furious, the rain so great, and the violence of the storm so intolerable, that no man was able to withstand it: In the mean time the other four Junks made a sign to us, as if they also were cast away; Whereupon *Antonio de Faria* lifting up his eyes and hands to Heaven, *Lord*, said he before them all, *as through thy infinite mercy thou wast fastened upon the Cross for the Redemption of sinners, so I beseech thee, Who art all mercy, that for the satisfaction of thy Justice I alone may suffer for the offences which these men have committed, since I am the principal cause of their trespassing against thy divine goodness; permit not then, O Lord, that in this woful night they may fall into that danger wherein I see my self at this present by reason of my sins; but with a repentant Soul I most humbly beseech thee, and that in the name of all the rest, though I am most unworthy to be heard, that instead of having regard to our sins, thou wilt behold us with the eyes of that pity and infinite clemency wherewith thou art replenished.* Upon these words we all fell a crying out so lamentably, *Lord have mercy upon us*, that it would have grieved any heart in the world to have heard us; And as all men, that find themselves in the like extremity, are naturally carried to the preservation of their lives, without any regard at all of ought else, there was not one amongst us that sought not the means to safe his, so that all of us together employed our selves in discharging our Vessel, by casting our goods into the Sea; To which effect about an hundred men of us, as well *Portugals*, as Slaves and Mariners, leapt down into the Ship, and in less then an hour heav'd all over-board, without any respect in so eminent a danger of that which we did, for amongst the rest we threw twelve great chests full of lingots of Silver into the Sea, which in the last incounter we had taken from *Coia Acem*, besides many other things of great value, whereby our Junk was somewhat lightened.

Having past the night in that miserable state we were in, at length, as the day began to break, it pleased God that the wind also began to slack, whereby our Junk remained a little more at rest, though she was still in great peril, by reason of the water she had taken in, it being almost four yards deep in her, so that to avoyd the eminent danger we were threatened with, we all of us got forth, and catching hold by the tackle we hung on the out-side of the Junk, because the waves beat with such violence against her, that we feared to be drowned,

or

or cast against the Rocks, which had already happened to eleven or twelve of our company for want of taking heed : Now when the day began perfectly to appear, it pleased God that *Mem Taborda's* and *Antonio Anriquez* Junks discovered us, and presently coming up close to us, they that were in her threw us a great many staves tyed to cords, to the end we might fasten our selves to them, as we presently did, and therein an hour was spent with much ado, by reason of the extream disorder amongst us, every man desiring and striving to be first saved, by which occasion twenty men were drowned, whereof five were *Portugals*, for whom *Antonio de Faria* was more grieved, then for the loss of the Junk, and all the goods that were in her, although the value thereof was not so small, but that it amounted to above an hundred thousand *Taeis*, and that in Silver alone ; for the greatest part of the booty, taken from *Coia Acem*, had been put into *Antonio de Faria's* Junk, as that which was held to be freer from danger then all the rest : Thus after we had with much peril and pain gotten into *Taborda's* Junk, we past all that day in continual lamentation for our ill success without hearing any news of our consorts ; Nevertheless it pleased God, that about evening we discovered two Sails, which made so many short turnings from one side to another, as one might well guess they did it of purpose to spend time, whereby we were perswaded that they were of our company. Now because it was almost night, we thought it not fit to go to them for some reasons given thereupon, but having made them a sign they answered us presently with the like according to our desire, and about the end of the last watch they approached so near unto us, that after they had sadly saluted us they demanded how the Captain General and the rest did ; whereunto we replyed, that as soon as it was day we would tell them, and that in the mean time they should retire from thence till the next morning that it was light, for that the waves then went so high, as some disaster might otherwise ensue thereupon. The next day as soon as the Sun began to appeared two *Portugals* came to us from *Quiay Panians* Junk, who seeing *Antonio de Faria* in the case he was in aboard *Mem Taborda's* Junk, and understanding the bad success of his fortune, they recounted theirs unto us, which seemed to be little better then ours ; for they declared that a gust of wind had caught up and thrown three of their men a stones cast from the Vessel into the Sea, a thing never seen nor heard of before : Withall they delivered, how the little Junk was cast away, with fifty men in her, almost all Christians, amongst the which were seven *Portugals*, and the Captain, named *Nuno Preto*, an honorable man, and of great courage and wisdom, whereof he had given good proof in the former adversities : At this relation *Antonio de Faria* was very much grieved, but much more when a little after one of the two *Lanteas*, of whom no news had been heard of till then, arriving, told us what dangers they had ran, and that the other having broken their cables, and left their anchors in the Sea, was in their sight battered all to pieces on the Sea shoar, all that were in her being drowned, saving thirteen persons, whereof there were five *Portugals*, and three servants Christians, whom those of the Country had made Slaves, and carried to a place, called *Nouday* ; so that by this unlucky Tempest two Junks, and one *Lantea*, or *Lorch*, were cast away, wherein above an hundred men were lost, besides Slaves, Apparel, Commodities, Silver, Jewels, Ordnance, Arms, Victual, and Munition, worth in all above two hundred thousand Duckets, in so much that both our General, and every one of us Soldiers, found our selves destitute of all manner of relief, having nothing left us but what was upon our backs. We learnt afterwards, that suchlike fortunes at Sea do ordinarily happen on this Coast of *China*, more then in any other part, so that it is impossible to sail there a whole year together without shipwrack, unless upon the Conjunction of the new Moons one fly into the Ports for shelter, which are there so many, and so good, that without fear of any thing one may enter them easily, because they are all very clear, except those of *Laman* and *Sumbor*, which have certain Rocks lying some half a league Southward from the mouth of the River.

Chap. XXII.

Antonio de Faria hath news of the five Portugals that were made Captives ; his Letter to the Mandarin of Nouday *about them ; and his assaulting the said Town.*

§.1. AFter this furious Tempest was wholly asswaged, *Antonio de Faria* incontinently imbarqued himself in the other great Junk, that he had taken from *Coia Acem*, whereof *Pedro de Sylva* was Captain, and setting sail he departed with the rest of his Company, which con-

consisted of three Junks, and one *Loroh*, or *Lantea*, as the *Chineses* term them. The first thing he did then was to go and anchor in the Haven of *Nouday*, to the end he might learn some news of the thirteen Captives, that were carried thither; being arrived there about night he sent two small Barques, called *Baloes*, well man'd, to spy the Port, and found the depth of the River, as also to observe the scituation of the Country, and to learn by some means what Ships were riding there, together with divers other matters answerable to his design; For which effect he commanded the Mariners to endeavor all they could for to surprize some of the Inhabitants of the Town, that by them he might be truly informed what was become of the *Portugals*, by reason he was afraid they were already carried further up into the Country. These *Baloes* went away about two hours after midnight, and arrived at a little Village seated at the mouth of the River on a little stream of water, called *Nipaphau*; There it pleased God that they behaved themselves so well, as they returned before day aboard our Junk, bringing along with them a Barque laden with earthen vessel, and Sugar canes, which they had found lying at anchor in the midst of the River: In this Barque there were eight men, and two women, together with a little child some six or seven years old, who seeing themselves thus in our power, became so transported with the fear of death, that they were in a manner besides themselves, which *Antonio de Faria* perceiving labored all he could to comfort them, and began to speak them very fair, but to all his questions, he could draw no other answer from them then these words following, *Do not kill us without cause, for God will require an account of our blood from you, because we are poor folks*; and saying thus, they wept and trembled in such sort, as they could scarce pronounce a word; Whereupon *Antonio de Faria*, pitying their misery and simplicity, would importune them no further: Howbeit, the better to compass his intent, he intreated a *Chinese* woman, that was a Christian, and came along with the Pilot, to make much of them, and to assure them they should have no hurt, to the end, that being more confirmed by this means, they might answer to that should be demanded of them; Wherein the *Chinese* so well acquitted her self, and made them so tractable, as about an hour after they told her, that if the Captain would let them freely return in their boat to the place from whence they were taken, they would willingly confess all that either they had heard or seen. *Antonio de Faria* having promised them to do so, and that with many words and protestations one amongst them, that was ancienter, and that seemed to be of more authority then the rest, addressing himself to him: *Truly*, said he, *I do not rely much on thy words, because that by amplifying of them in such manner thou makest me afeard, that the affect will not be conformable to thy speech; Wherefore I beseech thee to swear unto me by this Element that bears thee, that thou wilt not fail to perform that which thou hast promised unto me: for otherwise perjuring thy self, be assured that the Lord, whose hand is Almighty, will be incensed against thee with such indignation, as the winds from above, and the Seas from below, will never cease to oppose thy desires during thy Voyages; for I vow unto thee by the beauty of these Stars, that lying is no less odious and abominable in the sight of that Soveraign Lord, then the pride of those Judges on Earth, that with scorn and contempt do answer those which demand Justice of them.* *Antonio de Faria* obliging himself by oath, as the old man required, to perform his word, the *Chinese* said he was satisfied, and then he continued in this sort: *About two days since I saw those men, whom thou enquirest after, layd in prison at* Nouday *with great irons on their legs, because it was beleeved they were notorious Theeves, that made a trade of robbing such as they met upon the Sea.* This relation very much enraged and disquieted *Antonio de Faria*, who was perswaded that it might well be as the old man delivered, so that desiring to take some course for their deliverance as soon as might be, he sent them a Letter by one of the *Chineses*, retaining all the rest in hostage for him, who departed the next morning by break of day, and because it much imported the *Chineses* to be delivered out of captivity, he that carried the Letter, and that was husband to one of the two women, which had been taken in the boat of earthen vessel, and were now aboard in our Junk, made such speed, that he returned about noon with an answer, endorsed on the Letter we sent, and signed by all the five *Portugals*; Thereby they gave *Antonio de Faria* to understand, that they were cruelly detained in prison, out of which they did not think they should ever get, unless it were to go to execution, and therefore they besought him for the passion of our Lord Jesus Christ, that he would not suffer them to perish there for want of succor, according as he had promised them at their setting forth in that Voyage, and the rather in regard it was only for his sake that they were reduced to that miserable estate; Hereunto they added many other very

pitiful

pitiful entreaties, as might well come from such poor wretches, that were Captives under the Tyranny of such fell and cruel people, as the *Chinefes* were. *Antonio de Faria*, having received this Letter, read it in the prefence of all his Company, of whom he asked counfel thereupon; but as they were many, fo were their opinions many and different, which was the occafion of much contention amongft them; whereby perceiving that nothing would be concluded concerning this affair, he said to them as it were in choller; *My Mafters and Friends, I promifed to God by a folemn oath that I have taken, never to part from hence, till by fome means or other I have recovered thefe poor Soldiers, my companions, though I fhould therefore venture my life a thoufand times, yea and all my eftate, which I make little reckoning of in regard of them; wherefore, my Mafters, I earneftly defire you, that no man go about to oppofe this refolution of mine, upon the execution whereof mine honor wholly depends, for whofoever fhall contrary me therein I muft take him for mine enemy, as one that would feek the prejudice of my Soul.* To this fpeech all made anfwer, that he was in the right, and that for the difcharge of his confcience nothing fhould ftay him from performing the fame; adding moreover, that all of them would ftand to him in that behalf to the death. The Captain hereupon giving them many thanks, and with tears in his eyes and his hat in his hand embracing them, protefted that he would when time fhould ferve acknowledg this good-will of theirs in fuch real manner as it deferved, wherewith they all remained very well fatisfied.

§.2.   This refolution being taken, they fell to councel concerning the carriage of this affair, whereupon they concluded to treat with the *Mandarin* in a gentle manner, and for that end to fend unto him to demand thefe Prifoners, with promife to give him for their ranfom whatfoever fhould be thought reafonable, and that according to his anfwer fuch further courfe fhould be taken therein as fhould feem requifite: A Petition then was prefently drawn anfwerable to the form, that was ufually prefented to the Judges, which *Antonio de Faria* fent to the *Mandarin* by two of the chiefeft of the *Chinefes* he had taken, who alfo carried him a prefent worth two hundred duckets, whereby he hoped to induce him to reftore the poor prifoners; but it fell out far otherwife then he expected: For as foon as the *Chinefes* had delivered the Petition and the Prefent, they returned the next day with an anfwer written on the back of the Petition, the tenor whereof was this: *Let thy mouth come and prefent it felf at my feet, and after I have heard thee I will do thee juftice.* *Antonio de Faria* feeing what high words the *Mandarin* gave was exceedingly troubled, becaufe he well perceived by this beginning, that he fhould have much ado to deliver his companions, wherefore having communicated this affair in particular to fome few, whom for that end he had called unto him, they were of feveral opinions; neverthelefs after good deliberation it was at length concluded to fend another Meffenger, that fhould more effectually demand the Prifoners of him, and for their ranfom offer the fum of two thoufand *Taeis* in lingots of Silver and Commodities, declaring unto him, that he would not part from that place till he had returned them; for he made account that it might be this refolution would oblige him to do that which he had refufed him another way, or that he would be carried to it by the confideration of his own gain and intereft. So the two *Chinefes* went again the fecond time with a Letter fealed up, as from one perfon to another, without any kind of ceremony or complement, which thefe Gentiles fo much ufe amongft themfelves; And this *Antonio de Faria* did of purpofe, to the end that by the fharpnefs of this Letter the *Mandarin* might know he was difpleafed, and refolved to execute what he had written. But before I proceed any further I will only relate the two main points of the contents of the Letter, which were the caufe of the utter ruine of this bufinefs. The firft was, where *Antonio de Faria* faid, that he was a Merchant ftranger, a *Portugal* by Nation, that was going by way of Traffique towards the Port of *Liampoo*, where there were alfo many other Merchants ftrangers like himfelf, who duly payd the ufual Cuftoms, without committing any manner of ill or injuftice. The fecond point was, where he faid, that the King of *Portugal* his Mafter was allyed in a brotherly amity with the King of *China*, by reafon whereof they traded in his Country, as the *Chinefes* ufed to do at *Malaca*, where they were entertained with all favor and juftice duly miniftred unto them. Now though both thefe points were diftaftful to the *Mandarin*, yet the laft, wherein he mentioned the King of *Portugal* to be brother to the King of *China*, was that which put him fo out of patience, that without any regard at all he commanded them that brought the Letter, not only to be cruelly fcourged, but to have their nofes cut off, and in that pickle he fent them back to *Antonio de Faria* with an anfwer written on a fcurvy piece of torn paper, where thefe words were written: *Stinking carrion, begotten of vile flies in the filthieft*

fink

Ank that ever was in any dungeon of a lothsom prison, what hath made thy baseness so bold, as that thou darest undertake to meddle with heavenly things? Having caused thy Petition to be read, whereby like a Lord, as I am, thou prayest me to have pity on thee, which art but a poor wretch, my greatness, out of its generosity, was even deigning to accept of that little thou presentedst me withall, and was also inclining to grant thy request, when as my ears were touched with the horrible blasphemy of thy arrogance, which made thee term thy King Brother to the son of the Sun, the Lion crowned by an incredible Power in the Throne of the World, under whose feet all the Diadems of those that govern the Universe are subjected, nay all Scepters do serve but as latches to his most rich sandals, as the Writers of the golden Temple do certifie under the Law of their Verities, and that through the whole habitable Earth: Know then, that for the great Heresie thou hast uttered, I have caused thy Paper to be burnt, thereby representing the vile effigies of thy person, which I desire to use in like manner for the enormous crime thou hast committed; wherefore I command thee to be speedily packing, that the River which bears thee may not be accursed. So soon as the Interpreter had read the Letter, and expounded the contents thereof, all that heard it were much vexed therewith, but no man was so sensible of it as *Antonio de Faria,* who was exceedingly grieved to see himself thus wholly deprived of all hope of recovering his Prisoners, wherefore after they had well considered the insolent words of the *Mandarins* Letter, and his great discourtesie, they in the end concluded to go ashoar, and attaque the Town, in hope that God would assist them, seeing their intentions were good; For this effect they instantly prepared Vessels to land with, which were the four fishermens great Barques they had taken the night before: Whereupon taking a muster of the Forces he could make for this enterprize, he found the number to be three hundred, whereof forty were *Portugals,* the rest were Slaves and Mariners, besides *Quiay Panians* men, amongst whom were an hundred and threescore Harquebusiers, the others were armed with Pikes and Lances; he had also some Pieces of Ordnance, and other things necessary for his design.

The next morning a little before day *Antonio de Faria* sailed up the River with three Junks, §.3. the *Lorches,* and the four Barques he had taken, and so went and anchored at six fathom and an half of water close by the walls of the Town; Then causing the sails to be taken down without any noise, or discharge of Ordnance, he displayed the Banner of Trade according to the fashion of *China,* to the end that by this demonstration of peace no complement should rest unperformed, although he was perswaded that nothing would prevail with the *Mandarin:* Hereupon he sent another Messenger unto him, never making shew that he had received any ill usage from him, by whom with a great deal of complement he demanded the Prisoners, and offered him a round sum of mony for their ransom, with a promise of perpetual correspondence and amity; But so far was this Dog the *Mandarin* from harkening thereunto, that contrariwise he made the poor *Chinese,* that carried the Letter, to be hewed in pieces, and so shewed him from the top of the wall to the whole Fleet, the more to despight us. This tragical act wholly deprived *Antonio de Faria* of that little hope, which some had given him for the deliverance of the Prisoners; hereupon the Soldiers, being more incensed then before, said unto him, that since he had resolved to land, he should no longer defer it, because further delay would but give his Enemies leasure to gather more strength: This counsel seeming good to him, he presently imbarqued with them he had chosen for the action, having first given order to his Junks to shoot continually at the Town, and the Enemy, wheresoever they perceived any store of people assembled, howbeit with this caution, to forbear till they saw them together by the ears with them. Having landed then about a Faulcon shot below the Rode, he marched without any let along the shoars side directly to the Town: In the mean time a number of people appeared upon the walls, with divers ensigns of different colours, where these Barbarous, made a mighty noise Fifes, Drums, and Bells, and withall hooting at us, made us signs with their caps to approach, thereby intimating the little reckoning they made of us: Now by that time we were come within a Musket shot of the walls, we discerned some thousand, or twelve hundred men, as we guessed, sally out at two several gates, of which some sixscore were mounted on horses, or to say better, on lean carrion Tits that were nothing but skin and bone, wherewith they began to course up and down the field in a skirmishing manner, wherein they shewed themselves so untoward, as they often ran one upon another, and tumbled down together; which when *Antonio de Faria* saw he was exceeding glad, and encouraging his men to the fight he stood firm attending the Enemy, who continued still wheeling about us, being perswaded, it seems,

that

that that would fuffice to skare us, and make us retire to our veffels ; But when they perceived us remain unmoved, without turning our backs as they beleeved, and as it may be, they defired we would doe, they clofed themfelves into one body, and fo in very ill order they made a ftand without advancing on.   But then our Captain, feeing them in this pofture, caufed all his Muskettiers to difcharge at one inftant, who till that time had not ftirred, which fucceeded with fuch effect, as it pleafed God that he moft part of this goodly Cavalry fell to the ground with feare ; we taking this for a good prefage ran and luftily purfued them, invoking to our aid the name of Jefus, whofe good pleafure it was though his divine mercy, to make our enemies flye before us fo amazed, and in fuch diforder, as they tumbled pell mell one upon another, in which manner arriving at a bridge that croft the town ditch, they were fo peftered together, as they could neither go forward nor backward ; in the mean time our forces coming up to them difcharged their fhot to fuch purpofe amongft them, that we laid three hundred of them on the earth, which in truth was a pittifull fight to behold, becaufe there was not one of them that had the heart fo much as to draw a fword : whereupon hotly purfuing the firft point of this victory, we ran to the gate, where we found the *Mandarin* in the front of fix hundred men, mounted upon a good Horfe, having on a cuiraffe lined with purple Velvet, which had belonged, as we knew afterwards, to a Portugal, named *Tome Perez*, whom King *Don Emanoel* of glorious memory had fent as Ambaffador to *China*, in *Fernando Perez* his fhip, at fuch time as *Lopo Suarez d' Albergaria* governed the *Indies*.   At the entrance into the gate the *Mandarin* and his people made head againft us, fo that there was a fhrewd bickering between us, this enemy fhewing another manner of courage then we had met with on the bridge ; but by good hap it fortuned that one of our fervant hit the *Mandarin* juft in the breaft with an Harquebuffe fhot, and overthrew him dead from his Horfe, wherewith all the *Chineffes* were fo terrified, as they prefently turned their backs, and in great diforder retired within the gate, not one of them having the wit to fhut it after them, fo that we chafed them before us with our Lances, as if they had been a drove of cattell : In this fort they fled pell mell together quite through a great ftreet, and iffued out at another gate, which was on the lands from whence they got all away, not fo much as one remaining behind.   Thereupon *Antonio de Faria*, affembling his men into one body, for fear of fome diforder, marched with them directly to the prifon, where our companions lay, who feeing us coming, gave a great cry, faying, *Lord have mercy upon us*, ftraightway the doors and iron grates were broken up, and our poor fellows irons knocked off their legs, which being done, and they fet at liberty, all our company had leave to make what purchafe they could, to the end that without fpeaking afterwards of partition, every one might be Mafter of what he had gotten.   Howbeit *Antonio de Faria* defired them to perform it fuddenly, and therefore he gave them but half an houres time for it, whereunto they all condefcended very willingly, and fo fell to ranfacking the houfes.   In the mean fpace *Antonio de Faria* went to that of the *Mandarin*, which he took for his part, where he met with eight thoufand *Taeis* in filver, together with eight great veffels full of Muske, and that he caufed to be referved for himfelf ; the reft he left to the fervants that were with him, who moreover found there a great deal of raw Silke, Sattin, Damask, and fine Pourcellain, whereof every one took as much as he could carry, fo as the four Barques, and the three Champanaes, that brought our men on fhore, were four feveral times laden and unladen aboard the Juncks, infomuch that the meaneft Marriner amongft us fpake not of this booty but by whole cafes, befides what each one concealed in his particular.

But when *Antonio de Faria* perceived that an hour and half had been fpent in pillaging, he commanded a furceafe thereof, but his company were fo hot upon the fpoil, that by no means they would be drawn from it, wherein the perfons of qualitie were moft faulty, in which regard our Captain fearing leaft fome difafter might happen by reafon the night approached, he caufed the Town to be fet on fire in eleven or twelve places ; Now for that moft of it was built of Firr, and other wood, it was in fuch a flame within a quarter of an hour, as to fee it burn fo, one would have taken it for a pourtraiture of Hell. This done, and all our company retired, *Antonio de Faria* embarqued without any impediment, every man being well fatisfied and contented, onely it was great pittie to behold a number of handfome maids lead away, tied four and four and five and five together with the matches of their Muskets, weeping and lamenting, whilst our people did nothing but laugh and sing.

CHAP. XXIII.

Antonio de Faria's *Navigation till he came to the Port of* Liampoo; *his arrival and gallant reception there by the Portugals.*

AFter that *Antonio de Faria* had embarqued his men, the first thing he did was to give order for the dressing of those that were hurt, which were in number fiftie, whereof eight of them were *Portugals,* and the rest slaves and Mariners : He also took care for the burial of the dead, that were not above nine, of which onely one was a *Portugal.* All that night we kept good watch, and placed Sentinels in sundry parts, for fear of the Junks that were upon the River ; The next morning as soon as it was day, our Captain went to a little Town that was on the other side of the water, where he met not with any Inhabitant, they being all fled, howbeit he found a great deal of Merchandise in their houses, together with good store of Victuals, wherewith he had laded the Junks, fearing least that which he had done in this place, should be the occasion of barring him from being furnished with any in the Ports where he should happen to arrive. Furthermore, by the advice of his company, he resolved to go and winter, during the three moneths he had yet to make his voyage in, at a certain desart Island, distant some fifteen leagues from the Sea of *Liampoo,* called *Pullo Hinhor,* where there was a good road, and good water; whereunto he was chiefly induced, because he thought that going directly to *Liampoo,* his voyage thither might bring some prejudice to the traffique of the *Portugals,* who wintered there peaceably with their goods : And indeed this advice was so approved of every one, as it was generally applauded. Being departed then from *Nouday,* after we had sailed five dayes between the Isles of *Comolem,* and the continent, we were set upon on *Saturday* about noon by a Pirate, named *Premata Gundel,* a sworn enemy to the *Portugals,* unto whom he had oftentimes done much damage, as well at *Patana,* as at *Sunda, Siam,* and many other places, when he found himself the stronger. This Rover beleeving that we were *Chineses* came and assailed us with two great Juncks, wherein there were two hundred fighting men, besides Mariners ; One of them being grappled to *Mem Taborda's* Junk had almost made her self Master of it, which *Quiay Panian* perceiving, who was a little before, he turned upon her, and with full sails running her on the Starboard side gave her so terrible a shock, that they sank both together, whereby *Mem Taborda* was delivered from the danger he was in, howbeit *Quia Panian* was instantly, and so opportunely succoured by three Lorches, which *Antonio de Faria* had taken a little before at *Nouday,* that all his men in a manner were saved, but every one of the enemies were drowned : In the mean time the Pyrate *Premata Gundel,* setting upon the great Junk, wherein *Antonio de Faria* was, the first thing he did was to grapple her poop to prow with two great cramp-irons, fastened to long chains, whereupon began such a fight betwixt them, as deserved to be seen, which for half an hour was so couragiously maintained by the Enemie, that *Antonio de Faria* and most of his men were hurt, and himself besides in danger twice to have been taken ; neverthelesse it was his good hap to be relieved in time by three Lorches, and a small Junck, commanded by *Pedro de Sylva,* by which means it pleased God that ours not onely recovered what they had lost, but pressed the Enemie in such sort, as the fight ended with the death of fourscore and six *Mahometans,* which were in *Antonio de Faria's* Junk, and had held him up so strait, that our men had nothing left them but the fore-deck in her : After this we entred into the Pirates Junck, and put all those to the edge of the Sword that we found there, not sparing so much as one, all the Mariners having cast themselves before into the Sea. Howbeit we got not this victorie so cheap, but that it cost seventeen mens lives, whereof five were *Portugals,* and of the best Souldiers we had, besides three and fourty were hurt, *Antonio de Faria* being one of them, who had one wound with a dart, and two with a sword. The fight being ended in this sort, an Inventorie was taken of all that was in the enemies Junck, and this prize was estimated at fourscore thousand *Taeis,* the better part whereof consisted in *Lingots* of silver of *Japan,* which the Pirate had taken in three Merchants Ships, that from *Firando* were bound for *Chincheo,* so that the Pirate had in this onely veffel to the value of fixfcore thoufand crowns, and it was thought that the other Junck which was funk was worth as much, to the extream grief of all our company. With this prize *Antonio de Faria* retired to a little Ifland, called *Buncalou*, which was three or four Leagues Weftward from thence, and much commended for good water, and fafe riding : Having landed in this place, we fpent eighteen dayes there, lodging in Cabbins, that were made for the accommodation of our hurt men. From this Ifland we failed towards that part, whither we had refolved before to go, namely, *Antonio de Faria* in the great Junk, *Mem Taborda*, and *Antonio Anriquez* in theirs, *Pedro de Sylva* in the little Junk, that was taken at *Nouday*, and *Quiay Panian* with all his followers in the Pyrats, laft taken, which was given him in recompence of his that he had loft, together with twenty thoufand *Taeis* out of the general booty, wherewith he refted very well contented, being done with the confent of the whole company at the requeft of *Antonio de Faria*. Sailing in this manner we arrived fix dayes after at the Ports of *Liampoo*, which are two Iflands, one juft againft another, diftant three Leagues from the place, where at that time the *Portugals* ufed their commerce; There they had built above a thoufand houfes, that were governed by Sheriffs, Auditors, Confuls, Judges, and fix or feven other kinde of Officers, where the Notaries underneath the publique Acts, which they made, wrote thus, *I, fuch a one, publique Notarie of this Town of Liampoo for the King our Soveraign Lord.* And this they did with as much confidence and affurance, as if this place had been fcituated between *Santarem* and *Lisbon*; fo that there were houfes there which coft three or four thoufand Duckats the building, but both they and all the reft were afterwards demolifhed for our fins by the *Chinefes*, as I hope to relate more amply hereafter : Whereby one may fee how uncertain our affairs are in *China*, whereof the *Portugals* difcourfe with fo much curiofity, and abufed by apparances make fuch account, never confidering what hazard they hourly run, and how they are expofed to infinite difafters.

§.2.   Between thefe two Iflands, which the Inhabitants of the Country, and they that fail in thofe Seas, call the Ports of *Liampoo*, there is a channel, fome two Harquebufe fhot over, and five and twenty fathom deep, where in certain places is very good anchoring, as alfo a pleafant River of frefh water, which takes his beginning from the top of a mountain, and paffeth by thick woods of Cedar, Oak, and Firr trees, whereof many Ships make their provifion for Sail-yards, Mafts and Planks, never cofting them a penny. At thefe Iflands *Antonio de Faria* caft anchor on Wednefday morning, and there *Mem Taborda*, and *Antonio Anriquez* defired him to give them leave to go and advertife the Town of his Arrival, as likewife to underftand the news of the Country, and whether there was any fpeech of that which he had done at *Nouday*; For in cafe his coming fhould prove never fo little prejudiciall to them, he was refolved (as I have formerly related) to winter in the Ifle of *Pullo Hinhor*, concerning the which they promifed with all diligence to advertize him fo much as they could learn : To this requeft of theirs, *Antonio de Faria* condefcended very willingly, and withall fent certain Letters by them, directed to the Principal Governours of the Town, whereby he made them a brief Recitall of the fucceffe of his Voyage, and inftantly defired them to advife him what they would have him to do, being ready to obey them accordingly, with many other complements of kindneffe, from whence oftentimes much profit arifes, without any charge at all. *Antonio Anriquez* and *Mem Taborda* departed about evening, and within two hours of night, they arrived at the Town, where as foon as the Inhabitants heard the effect of their Meffage, they prefently affembled upon the ringing of a Bell, at the Church of the conception of our Lady, being the Cathedral of fix or feven others in the Town, there they deliberated upon the Letters which *Antonio Anriquez* and *Mem Taborda* had delivered, and in the end having confidered the great liberalitie that *Antonio de Faria* had ufed, as well to them as to all the reft that had part in the Junk, they concluded to acknowledge it unto him by all demonftrations of affection; For which purpofe they returned him a Letter, figned by them all, as the Refolution of a General Affembly, and fent it him together with two *Lanteaus* full of divers refrefhments, and that by an ancient Gentleman, named *Jeronimo de Rego*, a Perfonage of great wifdome and authoritie amongft them : In this Letter they gave him thanks in very courteous termes, both for the exceeding favour he had done them by refcuing their goods out of the enemies hands, and for the noble Teftimonie he had given them of his affection by his extraordinary liberality towards them, for

which

which they hoped that God would throughly require him: As for the fear he was in touching his wintering there, by reason of what had paſt at *Nouday*, he might be confident that way, becauſe the Country was ſo full of trouble, by occaſion of a mighty uprore that was then amongſt the people thereof, as if he had razed the very Citie of *Canton* it ſelf, they would not much regard it, wherefore he might well thinke they would care much leſſe for that which he had done at *Nouday*, which in *China*, compared with many others, was no greater then *Oeyras* in *Portugal* is, being equally with *Lisbon*: And concerning the good news he had ſent them of his arrivall in their Port, they earneſtly deſired him to continue ſtill at anchor there ſix dayes longer, that they might in the mean while make ſome fit preparation for his entertaiment, ſeeing that thereby onely they ſhould be able to teſtifie their good will unto him, having not the power other wayes to acquit ſo many obligations, wherein they ſtood ingaged unto him. Theſe words of kindneſs were accompanied with many other complements, whereunto *Antonio de Faria* returned them a moſt curteous Anſwer, and condeſcending to their deſire, he ſent all his ſick men on ſhore in the two *Lanteaus*, which brought the refreſhments, whom thoſe of *Liampoo* received with great ſhew of affection and charity, for preſently they were lodged in the richeſt houſes of the Town, and plentifully accommodated with all things neceſſary for them, wanting nothing. Now during the ſix dayes *Antonio de Faria* remained in that place, there was not a man of any qualitie in all the Town, but came and viſited him with many preſents, and divers ſorts of proviſions, refreſhments, and fruits, and that in ſuch abundance, that we were amazed to behold them, the more too for the good order and magnificence wherewith every thing was accompanied.

During the ſix dayes, that *Antonio de Faria* continued in the Port according to his promiſe to them of *Liampoo*, he never budgd from his Ships, At length on Sunday morning before day, which was the time limited for our going to the Town, an excellent conſort of Muſick was heard, both of Inſtruments and Voyces, the harmony whereof was wonderfully pleaſing, and after that a Triumph of Drums and Trumpets together, according to the manner of our own country: Then ſome two houres before Sun-riſing, the night being very quiet, and the Moon exceeding bright, *Antonio de Faria* ſet ſail with his whole Fleet, having all his Ships decked with Silken Flaggs, and ſtreamers of ſundry Colours, and every *ſcuttle* both of the greater and leſſer maſts hung round about with cloth of Silver, and many brave Standards of the ſame: After theſe Veſſels followed a number of row-Barges, wherein were a great many of Trumpets, Hoboyes, Flutes, Fifes, Drums, and other ſuch Inſtruments, each one of a ſeveral Invention. §.3.

When it was broad day the winde began to calm, as we were within half a League of the Town, whereupon there came preſently to us ſome twenty *Lanteaus*, very well ſet forth, and full of Muſicians, that played on divers Inſtruments; So in leſſe then an hour we arrived at the Road, but firſt there came aboard *Antonio de Faria* about threeſcore Boats and *Manchaus*, adorned with Pavilions and Banners of Silke, as alſo with Turkie Carpets of great value; In theſe Boats were about three hundred men, all richly apparrelled, with chains of Gold, and guilt Swords, hanging in Belts after the faſhion of *Affrick*, every thing ſo well accommodated, that we which beheld this Equipage, were no leſſe contented then aſtoniſhed therewith. With this train *Antonio de Faria* came to the Town, where there ſtood ranged in excellent order twenty ſix ſhips, and fourſcore Junks, beſides a great ſort of *Vancons* and *Barcaſſes*, all in File one after another, ſo making as it were a fair long ſtreet, every where beautified with Pines, Laurels, and green Canes, with many Triumphal Arches, beſet with Cherries, Pears, Lemons, Oranges, and ſundry odoriferous green Herbs, wherewith the Maſts and Cordage were covered all over. As ſoon as *Antonio de Faria* came neer the place, which was prepared for his landing, he ſaluted the Town with a great peal of Ordnance, which was inſtantly anſwered with the like by all the Ships, Junks and Barques before mentioned, in order, a matter very pleaſing, and wherewith the *Chineſe* Merchants were ſo taken, as they demanded of us, Whether this man, unto whom we did ſo much honour, was either the brother or kinſman of our King? whereunto certain chief men of the Town anſwered, *That his Father ſtood the Horſes, whereon the King of Portugal rode, and that in that regard all this honour was done him*; adding withall, *That they thought themſelves ſcarce worthy to be his ſlaves, much leſſe his ſervants*; The *Chineſes* beleeving all this to be true, ſaid one to another, as it were in admiration; *Verily, there be great Kings in the world, whereof our ancient Historians for want of knowledge of them have made no mention in their Writings, and it seems that above them all, the King of these* Portugals *is to be most esteemed, for by that which is delivered to us of his greatnesse, he must needs be richer, more mighty, and greater then either the* Tartar, *or the* Cauchin, *as is most apparent, since he that shooes his horses, which is but an ordinary and contemptible trade in every Country, is so respected by those of his Nation*; Whereupon another that heard his Companion say thus, *Certainly,* said he, *this Prince is so great, that if it were not a blasphemy, one might almost compare him to the Son of the Sun*; The rest that were about him added, *It well appears to be so by the great riches which this bearded Nation get in every place where they come by the power of their armes, wherewith they affront all the People of the world.* This salutation being ended on either part, a *Lanteaa* came aboard *Antonio de Faria's* Junk, gallantly equipped, and covered all over with boughs of Chesnut trees, full of their bristled fruit just as they grew, and intermingled with delicate small green trees, which those of the Country call *Lechias,* stuck every where with most fragrant Roses and Violets, all plashed so close together, that we could not see the Rowers; now upon the upper end of the Deck of this Vessel, there was a kinde of State set up, made of Tynsell, under the which stood a silver chair, and about it six girles of about some ten or eleven yeares of age a piece, wonderful beautiful, and that very harmoniously accorded their voyces, to certain Instruments of Musick whereon they playd : In this *Lanteaa* then *Antonio de Faria* embarqued himselt, and so arrived at the Key with a great noyse of Hoyboys, Trumpets, Drums, Fifes, and other such like, after the manner of the *Chineses, Malayoes, Champaas, Siamites, Borneos, Lequios,* and other people, that were then in the Haven under the protection of the *Portugals,* for fear of the Pirates, which in great numbers over-ran all that Sea. Being landed he found a chair of State provided for him, like unto one of those wherein the principall *Chaems* of the Empire are usually carried ; In this, but with much refusall first on his side, was he placed, and it being supported by eight silver pillars, it was taken up by eight of the chiefest persons amongst them, apparrelled in gowns of cloth of Gold richly imbroidered, and so was he carried on their shoulders into the Town, environed with threescore Halberdeers, bravely set forth, and their Halberds Damasked with Gold and Silver ; before him also marched eight Sergeants at Armes, carrying great guilt Maces, clothed in Hongarlines of Crimson-Velvet embroidered with Gold ; In the head of them rode eight Knights mounted on gallant white Steeds, and attired in Sattin of the same colour, with white Damask Ensigns, and brave plumes of white Feathers, and foremost of all were eight other men likewise on Horseback, wearing Crimson, and green Velvet Caps, which ever and anon cryed out after the manner of *China* for people to make way. In this sort was *Antonio de Faria* carried along till alighting out of his chair he went to visit the Governours of the Town, who in way of complement prostrated themselves at his feet, wherein some small time being spent, two ancient Gentlemen, who had lived long in that place, the one named *Tristan de Gaa,* and the other *Jeronimo de Rego,* made an eloquent Oration in the commendation of him : That done, he was led from thence to the Church through a long street, adorned on both sides with Laurel and Firr Trees, below strewed with Rushes, and above hung with Sattin and Damask, amongst the which divers court-cupboards were placed, whereon stood very curious perfuming pans of Silver, from whence most pleasing and delicious odours breathed forth : Neer to the end of this street was a Tower of Deal Boards erected, painted all over, as if it had been stone, on the top whereof, under a Banner of white Damask, the Royal Arms of *Portugal* were limned in Gold ; and in a window of the same Tower, certain little Boyes were drawn, attired after the *Portugal* fashion, as also an old Woman, that seemed to weep, and hold a man lying dis-membred at her feet, whom some eleven or twelve armed *Castillians* were a killing, having their Halberds and Partizans dyed with his bloud ; All which Figures were done so to the life, that one would have thought them to have been the very persons they represented. Now this was to signifie how *Nuno Gonçalles de Faria,* chief of that Noble Family, gave for his armes his own body, at such time as he was slain in the Wars, that had been anciently between *Castile* and *Portugal.* Presently hereupon as soon as a clock, that was on the top of the said Tower, had struck thrice, and that the people upon this signal were all silent, there came a venerable old man out of the principall gate, apparrelled in a robe of Crimson Damask, accompanied with four Beadles, which

carried

carried silver Maces before him : Having made a lovv reverence to *Antonio de Faria*, he told him in termes full of respect, how much all the Inhabitants were obliged unto him, as well for the great liberality he had used towards them, as for the favour he had done them, by having been the onely cause of the recovery of their goods, in acknovvledgement whereof they all offered themselves to be his Vassals for the time to come, and to do him the Homage of Tributaries as long as he lived : And further, if he pleased to cast his eye upon that Table before him, he should behold there as in a clear Mirror, with how much fidelity his Ancestors had gained the honourable name of his Family, as it was manifest to all the people of *Spain*, whereby he might well perceive how much it was for his honour that he had performed such generous actions, in regard whereof be most earnestly besought him, and that in the Name of them all, that for a beginning of the Tribute, which they offered to give him by way of Vassallage, he would be pleased to accept of a small Present, they now had brought him, onely for to defray the charge of Match for his Souldiers, and that for the rest wherein they stood so far ingaged to him, they promised to dif-oblige themselves in time and place convenient ; whereupon they presented him with five Cases full of Lingots of Silver, to the value of ten thousand Taeis. *Antonio de Faria* having very courteously thanked the good old man for this many Honours had hitherto been done him, as also for the present they now offered unto him, excused himself from receiving of it, though he were very much importuned thereunto.

Antonio de Faria setting forward then to go to the Church, whither he was to have been conducted under a rich Canopie, which six of the chiefest and honourablest Inhabitants of *Liampoo* were there ready with for him, he would by no means accept of it, telling them that he vvas not born to have so much honour as they would do him, and so he proceeded on without other pompe then ordinary, being accompanied with a world of people, as well *Portugals* as others of divers Nations, who for commerce sake wete come to that Port, as the best and richest that was then in that Country. In the mean space wheresoever he cast his eye he saw nothing but publique rejoycings, which consisted in daunces, Masks, and Playes of several kindes, invented by those of the Country that lived amongst us ; all which became more splendidious by the Trumpets, Cornets, Hoboys, Flutes, Harps, Vials, Fifes, and Drums, that were heard in every corner, and confounded together in a Labyrinth of Voyces after the manner of *China*, which so amazed the sense, that one knew not whether it were a dream or no, so extraordinary it seemed : Being arrived at the Church door, eight Priests came forth to receive him covered vvith Copes all embroidered vvith Gold and Silver, vvho going in Procession began to sing *Te Deum*, whereunto many excellent voyces tuned to the Organs answered, which made up as harmonious Musick as could be heard in the Chappel of any great Prince : In this sort he was carried up to the High Altar, where there was a State of White Damask, and under it a Chair of Carnation Velvet, and at the foot of it a Cushion of the same ; In this Chair he sate him down and heard Masse, which was celebrated vvith a great deal of Ceremonie, and a marvellous consort both of Voyces and Instruments. Masse being ended, the Sermon followed, that was made by *Estevano Nogueyra*, an ancient man, and Curate of the place, vvho, to speak the truth through discontinuance of preaching, was but little verst in Pulpit matters, and illiterate vvithall, howbeit desiring to shew himself that day a learned man in so remarkable a solemnity, he laboured to make demonstration of his best Rhetorick ; To which effect he grounded all his Sermon on the Prayses of *Antonio de Faria*, and that in words so ill placed, and so far from his Text, as our Captain was much ashamed at it, wherefore some of his friends pluckt him three or four times by the Surplis for to make him give over, wherewith being netled, he turned him about to those that would have had him leave off, *I will not*, said he unto them, *but will rather say more, for I speake nothing but that which is as true as Gospel, in regard whereof, let me alone I pray you, for I have made a vow to God never to desist from commending this noble Captain, as he more then deserves at my hands, for saving me seven thousand Duckats venture, that* Mem Taborda *had of mine in his Junk, and was taken from him by that dog* Coia Acem, *for which let the soul of so cursed a rogue and wicked Devil be tormented in Hell for ever and ever, whereunto say all with me, Amen.* This Conclusion provoked all the Assembly so to laugh, that we could not hear one another in the Church for the noise that was made there. This tumult over, there came out of the Vestry six little Boyes, attired like Angels, with Instruments of Musick

sick in their hands guilt all over, and then the same Priest falling on his knees before the Altar of our Lady, and lifting up his hands, began to sing aloud these words, *Virgin, you are a Rose*, whereunto the little Boyes answered very melodiously with their Instruments, all being performed with such harmony and devotion, as it drew tears from most of the Assistants.

§. 5.   Masse being finished, the four principal Governours of the Town, namely, *Mateus de Brito, Lançarote Pereyra, Jeronimo de Rego*, and *Tristan de Gaa*, came unto *Antonio de Faria*, and being accompanied with all the *Portugals*, which were above a thousand in number, they conducted him into a great place before the Town Hall, that was compassed about with a small thick wood of Chesnut Trees, all full of Fruit just as they grew, adorned above with Standards and Banners of Silk, and strewed below with *Flower de luces*, and Red and White Roses, whereof there is great abundance in *China*. In this Wood were three long Tables set, under a goodly spacious Arbor, that was covered over with Myrtle, and round about were divers Conduits of Water, which ran from one to the other by certain Inventions of the *Chineses*, that were so subtile, as one could not possibly discern the secret; For by the means of a kinde of Bellows like unto that of an Organ, that was joyned to the principall Conduit, the water rebounded up so high, that when it came to descend again it fell as small as dew, so that with one onely pot full of water, they could gently moisten that great place; before these three Tables were three Court-cup boards placed, upon the which was a great deal of very fine Pourcelain, and six huge Vessels of Gold, that the *Chinese* Merchants had borrowed of the *Mandarins* of the Town of *Liampoo* ; For in that Country Persons of quality are served all in Gold, Silver being for those of meaner condition : They brought likewise divers other pieces all of Gold, as great Basons, Saltsellers and Cups. After they were dismissed which were not for the Banquet, there onely remained those that were invited, being fourscore in number, besides fiftie of *Antonio de Faria*'s Souldiers : These being set at Table were served by young Wenches, very beautiful, and finely apparrelled, according to the manner of the *Mandarins* ; At every course that was served up they sung very melodiously to the tune of certain Instruments whereon some of their companions played : As for *Antonio de Faria* he was served by eight Maidens, the Daughters of worthy Merchants, exceeding fair and comely, whom their Fathers had brought thither for that purpose at the request of *Mateus de Brito*, and *Tristan de Gaa*; They were attired like Mermaids, and carried the meat to the Table, dancing to the sound of divers Instruments, a marvellous thing to behold, and wherewithal the *Portugals* were so mightily taken, as they could not sufficiently commend the excellent Order and Gentilenesse of these Magnificencies, by which their eyes and eares were so charmed ; Remarkable it was also, that at every health, the Trumpets, Hoboys, and Drums plaid their parts. In this sort the Banquet continued two hours, during which there was alwayes one device or other after the *Portugal* or *Chinese* fashion. I will not stand here to recount the delicacy or abundance of the meats, that were served up in it, for it would be a matter not onely superfluous, but even infinite to recite every thing in particular. After they were risen from Table, they went all to another great place, that was invironed with Scaffolds, all hung with Silk, and full of People, where ten Bulls and five wild Horses were baited, being accompanied with the sound of Trumpets, Fifes, and Drums ; in sequel whereof, divers Mummeries of several Inventions were represented. Now because it was late *Antonio de Faria* would have imbarqued himself again for to have returned unto his Ships, but they of the Town would by no means suffer him, for they had prepared the Houses of *Tristan de Gaa*, and *Mateus de Brito* for his lodging, having caused a Gallerie to be built from the one to the other for that purpose ; There was he lodged very commodiously during the space of five Months that he abode in that place, alwaies entertained with new sports and delights of Fishing, Hunting, Hawking, Comedies, and Masques, as also with sumptuous Feasts, as well on Sundayes and Holydayes, as other Dayes of the Week, so that we passed these five Months in such pleasure, as at our departure we did not thinke we had been there five dayes. This term expired *Antonio de Faria* made preparation of Vessels and Men, for his Voyage to the Mines of *Quoaniaparu*, for in regard the season was then proper for it, he resolved to be gone as soon as possibly he could, but in the mean time it happened that *Quiay Panian* fell into a dangerous sicknesse, whereof not long after he died, to the extream grief of *Antonio de Faria*, who exceedingly affected him

for

for many good qualities that were in him, worthy of his friendship, and therefore he caused him to be honourably buried, as the last dutie that he could do to his Friend. After the the death of *Quiay Panian* he was counselled not to hazard himself in that Voyage, because it was reported for a certainty, how all that Country was up in arms by reason of the Wars which the *Prechau Muan* had with the Kings of *Chamay*, and *Champaa*; And withall he had Information given him of a famous Pirate, named *Similau*, whom he went presently to seek out, and having found him, the said *Similau* related strange wonders unto him of an Island, called *Calempluy*, where he assured him there were seventeen Kings of *China* interred in Tombes of Gold, as also a great number of Idols of the same Mettal, and such other immense treasures, as I dare not deliver, for fear of not being credited. Now *Antonio de Faria*, being naturally curious, and carried with that ambition, whereunto Souldiers are for the most part inclined, lent so good ear to this *Chineses* report, as looking for no other assurance of it then what he gave him, he presently resolved to undertake this Voyage, and expose himself to danger, without taking further counsel of any man, whereat many of his friends were with reason offended.

Chap. XXIV.

Antonio de Faria departs from Liampoo *for to seek out the Island of* Calempluy, *the strange things that We saw, and the hazard we ran in our voyage thither.*

THe season being now fit for Navigation, and *Antonio de Faria* furnished with all that §.1. was necessary for this new Voyage, which he had undertaken to make on *Munday* the fourteenth of *May*, in the year one thousand five hundred forty and two, he departed from this Port to go to the Island of *Calempluy*; For which purpose he imbarqued in two *Panoures*, resembling small Gallies, but that they were a little higher, by reason he was counselled not to use Junks, as well to avoid discovery, as in regard of the great currants of water that descended from the Bay of *Nanquin*, which great Vessels with all their sails were not able to stem, especially at the time wherein he set forth, for then the snows of *Tartaria* and *Nixihumflao* dissolving ran all the Months of *May*, *June*, and *July*, into these Seas with a most violent impetuosity. In these two Vessels were fiftie *Portugals*, one Priest to say Masse, and fortie eight Marriners, all Natives of *Patana*, as also two and fortie slaves, so that the whole number of our company amounted to an hundred forty and one persons, for the Pirate *Similau*, who was our Pilot, would have no more men, nor Vessels, for fear of being known, because he was to traverse the streight of *Nanquin*, and to enter into Rivers that were much frequented, whereby we might probably be subject to great hazard. That day and al the night following we imployed in getting out from amongst the Islands of *Angitur*, and pursued our course through Seas, which the *Portugals* had neither seen nor sailed on till then. The first five dayes we had the wind favourable enough, being still within sight of land till we came to the mouth of the River of the Fishings of *Nanquin*; There we crost over a Gulf of forty leagues, and discovered a very high Mountain, called *Nangafo*, towards the which bending Northerly, we sailed fiftie dayes; at length the wind abated somewhat, and because in that place the Tides were very great, *Similau* put into a little River, where was good anchoring and riding, inhabited by men that were white and handsome, having very little eyes, like to the *Chineses*, but much different from them, both in language and attire. Now during the space of three dayes, that we continued there, the Inhabitants would have no manner of communication with us, but contrariwise they came in troopes to the shore, by which we anchored, and running up and down like mad-men they howled in a most hideous fashion, and shot at us with slings and cross-bows. As soon as the weather and the sea would permit us, *Similau*, by whom all was then governed, began to set sail, directing his course East Northeast, and so proceeded seven dayes in sight of land; then traversing another Gulfe, and turning more directly to the East, he past through a straight, ten leagues over, called *Sileupaquin*; There he sailed five dayes more, still in view of many goodly Cities and Towns, this River being frequented with an infinite company of Vessels; whereupon *Antonio de Faria*, knowing that if he hapned to be discovered he should never escape with life, resolved to get from thence, and continue this course no longer, which *Similau* perceiving, and opposing the advice that every one gave him; *Signior*, said unto him, *I do not think that any of your company can accuse me for mis-performing my*

duty

duty hitherto, you know how at Liampoo I told you publiquely in the General Councel that was held in the Church before an hundred Portugals at the least, that we were to expose our selves to great dangers, and chiefly my self, because I was a Chinese and a Pilot, for all you could be made to endure but one death, whereas I should be made to endure two thousand if it were possible, whereby you may well conclude, that setting apart all treason, I must of necessity be faithful unto you, as I am, and ever will be, not only this Voyage, but in all other enterprizes, in despight of those that murmur, and make false reports unto you of me; howbeit if you fear this danger so much as you say, and are therefore pleased that we shall take some other way lesse frequented with men and vessels, and where we may sail without dread of any thing, then you must be contented to bestow a far longer time in this voyage, wherefore resolve with your company upon it without any further delay, or let us return back, for lo I am ready to do whatsoever you will. *Antonio de Faria*, embracing, and giving him many thanks, fell to discourse with him about that other safer way of which he spake : Whereupon *Similau* told him, that some hundred and forty leagues further forwards to the North, there was a River somewhat larger by half a league, called *Sumhepadano*, where he should meet with no Obstacle, for that it was not peopled like the streight of *Nanquin*, wherein they now were, but that then they should be retarded a month longer, by the exceeding much winding of this River. *Antonio de Faria* thinking it far better to expose himself to a length of time, then to hazard his life for abridgement of way, followed the counsel that *Similau* gave him ; so that going out of the streight of *Nanquin*, he coasted the land five dayes, at the end whereof we discovered a very high Mountain towards the East, which *Similau* told us was called *Fanius* ; approaching somewhat neer unto it we entred into a very fair Port, forty fathom deep, that extending it self in the form of a Crescent was sheltred from all sorts of winds, so spacious withall, as two thousand Vessels how great soever might ride there at ease. *Antonio de Faria* went ashore with some ten or eleven Souldiers, and rounded this haven, but could not meet with any one body, that could instruct him in the way he pretended to make, whereat he was very much vext, and greatly repented him for that without any kinde of consideration, or taking advice of any one, he had rashly, and out of a capacious humour, undertaken this Voyage : Howbeit he dissembled this displeasure of his the best he could for fear lest his company should tax him with want of courage. In this Haven he discoursed again with *Similau* before every one concerning this our Navigation, which he told him was made but by guesse ; whereunto the *Chinese* answered, *Signior Captain, If I had any thing I could engage to you of more value then my head, I protest unto you I would most willingly do it, for I am so sure of the course I hold, that I would not fear to give you my very children in Hostage of the promise I made you at Liampoo : Nevertheless I advertise you again, that if repenting the undertaking of this enterprise you fear to proceed any further, in regard of the tales your people are ever tatling in your ear, as I have often observed, do but command, and you shall finde how ready I am to obey your pleasure : And whereas they would make you believe that I spin out this Voyage longer then I promised you at Liampoo, the reason thereof you know well enough, which seemed not amisse when I propounded it unto you, seeing then you once allowed of it, let me intreat you to set your heart at rest, for that matter, and not to break off this design by returning back, whereby at length you shall finde how profitable this patience of yours will prove.* This speech somewhat quieted *Antonio de Faria's* minde, so that he bid him go on as he thought best, and never trouble himself with the murmuring of the Souldiers, whereof he complained, saying, that it was ever the manner of such as were idle, to finde fault with other mens actions, but if they did not mend their error the sooner, he would take a course with them to make them to do it ; wherewith *Similau* rested very well satisfied and contented.

§. 2.   After we were gone from this Haven, we sailed along the coast above thirteen dayes together, alwaies in sight of land, and at length arrived at a Port, called *Buxipalem*, in the height of fortie nine degrees. We found this Climate somewhat colder then the rest, here we saw an infinite company of Fishes and Serpents, of such strange forms, as I cannot speak of them without fear ; *Similau* told *Antonio de Faria* incredible things concerning them, as well of what he had seen himself, having been there before, as of that had been reported unto him, especially in the full Moons of the months of *November, December,* and *January*, when the storms raign there most, as indeed this *Chinese* made it appear to our own eyes, whereby he justified unto us the most of that which he had affirmed.

firmed. For in this place we saw Fishes in the shape of Thornbacks that were four fathoms about, and had a Muzzle like an Oxe ; likewise we saw others resembling great Lizards, spotted all over with green and black, having three rows of prickles on their backs, that were very sharp, and of the bignesse of an arrow ; their bodies also were full of the like, but they were neither so long, nor so great as the others : These Fishes would ever and anon bristle up themselves like Porcupines, which made them very dreadful to behold, they had Snouts that were very sharp and black, with two crooked teeth out of each jawbone, two spans long, like the tusks of a wild Boar. We also saw Fishes whose bodies were exceeding black, so prodigious and great, that their heads onely were above six spans broad. I will passe over in silence many other Fishes of sundry sorts, which we beheld in this place, because I hold it not fit to stand upon things that are out of my discourse, let it suffice me to say, that during two nights we stayed here we did not thinke our selves safe, by reason of the Lizards, Whales, Fishes and Serpents, which in great numbers shewed themselves to us. Having left this Haven of *Buxipalem,* by us called the River of Serpents, which in great numbers shewed themselves to us, *Similau* sailed fifteen leagues further to another Bay named *Calindano,* which was in form of a Crescent, six leagues in circuit, and invironed with high Mountains, and very thick woods, amidst whereof divers Brooks of fresh waters descended, which made up four great Rivers that fell all into this Bay. There *Similau* told us, that all those prodigious creatures we had both seen and heard of, as well in this Bay, as in that where we were before, came thither to feed upon such Ordure and Carrion, as the overflowing of these Rivers brought to this place. *Antonio de Faria* demanding of him thereupon, whence those Rivers should proceed, he answered that he knew not, but it was said that the Annals of *China* affirmed, how two of those Rivers took their beginnings from a great Lake, called *Moscombia,* and the other two from a Province, named *Alimania,* where there are high Mountains, that all the year long are covered with Snow, so that the Snow coming to dissolve, these Rivers swelled in that manner as we then beheld them, for now they were bigger, then at any other time of the year. Hereunto he added, that entring into the mouth of the River, before the which we rode at anchor, we should continue our course, steering Eastward, for to finde out the Port of *Nanquin* again, which we had left two hundred and threescore leagues behinde us, by reason that in all this distance we had multiplied a greater height then that of the Island was, which we were in quest of. Now although this was exceeding grievous unto us, yet *Similau* desired *Antonio de Faria* to think the time we had past well spent, because it was done for the best, and for the better securing of our lives ; being asked then by *Antonio de Faria* how long we should be in passing through this River, he answered that we should be out of it in fourteen or fifteen dayes, and that in five dayes after he would promise to land him and his Souldiers in the Island of *Calempluy,* where he hoped fully to content his desire, and to make him think his pains well bestowed, whereof he now so complained. *Antonio de Faria,* having embraced him very lovingly thereupon ; vowed to be his friend for ever, and reconciled him to his Souldiers, who were very much out with him before. Being thus reconfirmed by *Similaus* speeches, and certified of this new course we were to take, he incouraged his company, and put all things in order convenient for his design, to that end preparing his Ordnance which till then had never been charged ; he caused also his Arms to be made ready, ordained Captains, and Sentinels to keep good watch, together with all besides that he thought necessary for our defence, in case of any attempt upon us. That done, he spake unto *Diego Lobato,* who was the Priest that we carried along with us, and one that we much respected as a man of the Church, to make a Sermon unto his company for to animate them against all dangers that might happen, which he worthily performed, and by the efficacy of his words, full of sweetnesse, and excellent examples, he so revived our spirits, that before were much dejected through the apprehension of the dangers that menaced us, as there was not one amongst us, but presently took fresh heart, boldly to execute the enterprise we had undertaken : Whereupon with great devotion and zeal we sung a *Salvo,* before an Image of our Lady, every man promising without any future fear to finish the Voyage we had begun. That done, we joyfully hoysed sail, and entring into the mouth of the River, steering directly East, and with tears in our eyes invoked from the bottome of our hearts, the assistance of that Soveraign Lord which sits at the right hand of the Father everlasting, to preserve us by his Almighty power.

N

§.3.   Continuing on our course with the force of Oares and Sails, and steering divers wayes, by reason of the many turnings of the River, the next day we arrived at a very high mountain called *Botinafau*, whence sundry Rivers of fresh water ran down. In this mountain were a number Tygers, Rhinocerots, Lyons, Ounces, and such other creatures of severall kinds, which running and roaring in their wilde manner, made cruell war upon other weaker Beasts, as Stags, Boars, Apes, Monkeys, Baboons, Wolves, and Foxes, wherein we took much delight, spending a great deal of time in beholding them ; and ever and anon we cryed out from our Ships to fright them, but they were little moved with it, in regard they were not used to be hunted : We were about six dayes in passing this Mountain, it being some forty or fifty leagues long.   Within a pretty while after we had left this Mountain we came to another, named *Gangitanon*, no lesse wilde then the former, beyond the which all the Countrie was very stonie, and almost inaccessible ; moreover it was full of such thick Woods, as the Sun could not possibly pierce them with his beams : *Similau* told us, that in this mountain there were ninety leagues of desert land, altogether unfit for Tillage, and the bottome thereof onely was inhabited by certain most deformed men, called *Gigauhos*, who lived after a most brutish fashion, and fed on nothing but what they got in hunting, or some Rice, that the Merchants of *China* brought them to *Catan* in exchange of Furres ; which the said Merchants carried from thence to *Pocasser* and *Lantau*, amounting yearly as by the Books of the Customes thereof appeared, to the number of twenty thousand Cates, each Cate, or pack, containing threescore skins, wherewith the people used in winter to line their Gowns, hang their Houses, and make coverings for their Beds, to withstand the cold of the Climate, which is great there.   *Antonio de Faria* wondring at the Relation this *Chinese* made of the deformity of these *Gigauhos*, desired him if it were possible to let him see one of them, whereby he said he should more content him then if he should give him the treasures of *China* ; whereunto *Similau* made him this Answer, *Signior Captain, since it it so much imports me, as well to maintain my credit with you, as to stop their mouthes that murmur against me, and that jogging one another scoffe at me, when I recount these things unto you, which they account as so many Fables, and to the end that by the truth of the one, they may be ascertained of the other, I will promise before Sun-setting yet to shew you a couple of these people, and that you shall also speak with them, upon condition you do not go ashore, as you have still used to do hitherto, for fear some mischance should happen to you, as many times it doth to Merchants in like cases : For I assure you, that the* Gigauhos *are of so savage and brutish a nature, as they feed on nothing commonly but raw flesh and blood, like the wilde Beasts that live in this Forrest.*   So continuing our course all along the side of this Mountain, at length behinde a little point of land, we discovered a young youth, without ere an hair on his face, driving six or seven Cows before him, that pastured there by. *Similau* making a sign to him with a napkin, he presently stayed, whereupon coming a little neerer to him, *Similau* shewed him a piece of green Taffeta, which he told us was a stuffe very acceptable to these brutish men, and withall by signs demanded of him whether he would buy it ; this drew him to the banke of the River, were he answered with an hoarse voice, some words that we could not comprehend, because there was not one in all our Vessels that understood this barbarous language, so that of necessity this commerce was to be made by signs : *Antonio de Faria* commanded three or four yards of the said piece of Taffeta to be given him, as also six Pourcelains, wherewith this Salvage seemed to be very well pleased, for taking both the one and the other, transported with joy he said something to us, which we could understand no better then the former, then making a sign with his hand towards the place of his abode, he left his Cows, and ran away to the wood, clothed as he was with a Tigers skin, his arms and legs naked, bare-headed, and a staffe hardned at one end with the fire in his hand. For his person, he was well proportioned of his limbs, his hair red and curled hanging down on his shoulders; his stature by conjecture was above ten foot high, but we were amazed to see him return about a quarter of an hour to the very same place again, carrying a live Stag on his back, and having thirteen persons in his company, namely eight men and five women, leading three Cows tyed together, and dancing as they went at the sound of a kinde of Tabor, upon the which they beat five stroaks at a time, and as often clapped their hands together singing to it, with a very hoarse voice in their language. Hereupon *Antonio de Faria* caused five or six pieces of silk stuffe, and a great many of Pourcelains to be shewed them, for to make them beleeve that we were Merchants,

chants, at the fight whereof they very much rejoyced. Thefe perfons, both men and women, were apparrelled all after one and the fame fafhion, without any kinde of difference, faving that the women wore great tinnen Bracelets about the middle of their armes, and their hair a great deal longer then the mens, ftuck all about with flowers, refembling our Flower de luces; they had chains alfo of red Cockles about their necks, almoft as big as Oyfter-fhels; as for the men they carried great ftaves in their hands, covered to the middeft with the fame skins wherewith they were clothed; moreover they had all of them fierce looks, great lips, flat nofes, wide nofthrils, and were of ftature very tall, but yet not fo high as we thought they had been; for *Antonio de Faria* having caufed them to be meafured, he found that the talleft of them exceeded not ten fpans and an half, except one old man that reached to eleven. The womens ftature was not fully ten fpans: Their very countenances fhewed them to be very rude and blockifh, and leffe rational, then all the other people which we had feen in our Conquefts. Now *Antonio de Faria* being glad that we had not altogether loft our labour, beftowed on them threefcore Pourcelains, a piece of green Taffety, and a pannier full of Pepper, wherewith they feemed to be fo contented, that proftrating themfelves on the ground, and lifting up their hands to heaven, they fell to faying certain words which we took for a thanksgiving after their manner, becaufe they fell down three feveral times on the earth, and gave us the three Cows and the Stag, as alfo a great many of Herbs: Having been talking about two houres with them by figns, and no leffe wondring at us, then we at them, they returned into the wood from whence they came, and we purfued our courfe up the River by the fpace of five dayes, during the which we faw more of them along by the water fide; after we had paft all this diftance of land, which might be fome forty leagues, or thereabouts, we navigated fixteen dayes more with the force of Oars and Sails, without feeing any perfon in that defert place, onely for two nights together we difcerned certain fires a good way off at land: In the end it pleafed God that we arrived at the Gulf of *Nanquin*, as *Similau* had told us, with a hope in five or fix dayes to fee our defires accomplifhed.

Being come into the gulf of *Nanquin*, *Similau* councelled *Antonio de Faria*, that at any §. 4. hand he fhould not fuffer any *Portugal* to be feen, becaufe if fuch a thing fhould happen he feared fome uproar would follow amongft the *Chinefes*, in regard no ftrangers had ever been feen in thofe quarters; adding withall, that it would be fafer for them to keep ftill in the middle of the gulf, then by the fhore, by reafon of the great number of *Lorches* and *Lanteaas*, that inceffantly failed up and down; this advice was approved of every one, fo that having continued our courfe fome fix dayes Eaft and Eaft Northeaft, we difcovered a great Town, called *Sileupamor*, whither we directly went, and entred the Haven about two houres within night, where we found an infinite company of Veffels riding at anchor, to the number, according to our thinking, of three thoufand at the leaft, which gave us fuch an alarum, as not daring fcarce to wag we got out again with all the fecrecy that might be; croffing over the whole breadth of the River then, which was fome fix or feven leagues, we profecuted our courfe all the reft of that day, and coafted along by a great plain, with a refolution to accommodate our felves with Victuals wherefoever we could firft meet with any, for we were in fuch fcarcitie, as for thirteen dayes together, no man had more then three mouthfuls of boyled Rice allowance. Being in this extremity we arrived clofe to certain old buildings, there went afhore one morning before day, and fell upon a houfe, that ftood a little way off from the reft, where we found a great quantity of Ryce, fome Beans, divers pots ful of Honey, poudred Geefe, Onions, Garlick, and Sugar Canes, wherewith we throughly furnifhed our felves: Certain *Chinefes* told us afterwards, that this was the ftorehoufe of an Hofpital, which was fome two leagues off, where fuch were entertained, as paft that way in Pilgrimage to the Sepulchers of the Kings of *China*; Being re-imbarqued, and well provided of Victual, we continued on our voyage feven daies more, which made up two months and an half, fince we put out of *Liampoo*; Then *Antonio de Faria* began to miftruft the truth of what *Similau* had faid, fo that he repented the undertaking of this voyage, as he confeffed publiquely before us all, neverthelefle in regard there was no other remedy for it but to recommend himfelf to God, and wifely to prepare for all that might happen, he couragioufly performed it. Hereupon it fell out that *Antonio de Faria* having one morning demanded of *Similau* in what part he thought they were, he

answer-

anſwered him ſo far from the purpoſe, and like a man that had loſt his judgement, or that knew not which way he had gone, as put *Antonio de Faria* into ſuch choller, that he was going to ſtab him with a Ponyard that he wore, which without doubt he had done, had he not been diverted from it by ſome, that counſelled him to forbear, leſt it ſhould be the cauſe of his utter ruine, whereupon moderating his anger he yeelded to the advice of his friends; neverthelesse he was not for all that ſo contained, but that taking him by the Beard he ſwore, that if within three dayes at the fartheſt, he did not let him ſee, either the truth or the falſhood of what he had told him, he would Ponyard him infallibly; wherewith *Similau* was ſo exceedingly terrified , that the night following as we were abiding by the ſhore he ſlid down from the Veſſel into the River, and that ſo cloſely, as he was never diſcovered by the Sentinels or any other untill the end of the firſt Watch, when as *Antonio de Faria* was thereof advertiſed : This news put him ſo far beſides himſelf, as he loſt all patience, the rather for that he feared ſome revolt upon it from his Souldiers, who he ſaw were too much diſpoſed thereunto. But he preſently went aſhore with a great many of his company, and ſpent the moſt part of the night in ſeeking of *Similau*, without meeting him, or any other living ſoul that was able to tell any news of him, but the worſt of it yet was, that upon his return into his Junk, of forty ſix *Chineſe* Mariners, that he had aboard him, he found ſix and thirty fled away to prevent the danger they were afraid of, whereat *Antonio de Faria* and all his company were ſo amazed, that lifting up their hands and eyes to heaven, they ſtood a long time mute, their tears ſupplying the defect of their ſpeech, thereby teſtifying the ſecret ſorrow of their hearts, for conſidering well what had hapned unto them, and the great peril they were in, the leaſt that they could do in this confuſion was to loſe their courage and judgment, much more their ſpeech. Howbeit falling at length to conſult what we ſhould do for the future, after much diverſitie of opinion, it was in the end concluded, that we ſhould purſue our deſign, and labour to take ſome body that might inform us how far it was from thence to the Iſland of *Calempluy*, and this to be done as ſecretly as poſſible might be for fear the Country ſhould riſe; likewiſe that if upon the report ſhould be made us we found it would be eaſily taken, as *Similau* had aſſured us, we ſhould then proceed on, otherwiſe, that we ſhould return with the current of the water, which would bring us directly to the Sea with its ordinary courſe. This reſolution taken and approved of every one, we went on with no leſs confuſion then fear, for in ſo manifeſt a danger we could not chuſe but be very much perplexed ; the night following about break of day we diſcovered a little Barque a head of us riding at anchor in the midſt of the River ; her we boarded with as little noiſe as might be, and took five men aſleep in her, whom *Antonio de Faria* queſtioned each one apart by himſelf, to ſee how they would agree in that they ſaid : To his demands they anſwered all of them, that the Country wherein we were, was called *Temquilem*, from whence the Iſland of *Calempluy* was diſtant but ten leagues, and to many other queſtions propounded to them for our common ſecuritie, they anſwered likewiſe ſeparately one from the other to very good purpoſe, wherewith *Antonio de Faria* and his whole company, were exceedingly well ſatisfied, but yet it grieved us not a little, to think what an inconvenience the lack of *Similau* would prove to us in this attempt ; however *Antonio de Faria* cauſing the five *Chineſes* to be arreſted, and chained to oares, continued his courſe two dayes and an half more, at the end whereof it pleaſed God that doubling a cape of land, called *Guimai Tarao*, we diſcovered this Iſland of *Calempluy*, which we had been fourſcore and three dayes ſeeking for with extream confuſion of pains and labour, as I have before related.

Chap. XXV.

Our Arrival at Calempluy, *and the deſcription thereof; what hapned to* Antonio de Faria *in one of the Hermitages thereof, and how we were diſcovered.*

§.1. HAving doubled the Cape of *Guimai Tarao*, two leagues beyond it, we diſcovered a goodly levell of ground, ſcituated in the midſt of a River, which to our ſeeming was not above a league in circuit, whereunto *Antonio de Faria* approached with exceeding great joy, which yet was intermingled with much fear, becauſe he knew not to what danger he and his were expoſed ; about twelve of the clock at night he anchored within a Canon ſhot of this Iſland, and the next morning as ſoon as it was day he ſate in Councell with such of his company as he had called to it, there it was concluded that it was not possible so great and magnificent a thing should be without some kind of guard, and therefore it was resolved that with the greatest silence that might be, it should be rounded all about, for to see what advenues it had, or what Obstacles we might meet with when there was question of landing, to the end that accordingly we might deliberate more amply on that we had to do: With this Resolution, which was approved by every one, *Antonio de Faria* weighed anchor, and without any noyse got close to the Island, and compassing it about exactly observed every particular that presented it self to his sight. This Island was all inclosed with a platform of *Jasper*, six and twenty spans high, the stones whereof were so neatly wrought, and joyned together, that the wall seemed to be all of one piece, at which every one greatly marvelled, as having never seen any thing till then, either in the *Indiaes*, or elsewhere, that merited comparison with it; this Wall was six and twenty spans deep from the bottome of the River to the Superficies of the water, so that the full height of it was two and fifty spans. Furthermore the top of the Platform was bordered with the same stone, cut into great Tower-work; Upon this wall, which invironed the whole Island, was a Gallerie of Balisters of turn'd Copper, that from six to six fathom joyned to certain Pillars of the same Mettal, upon each of the which was the figure of a Woman holding a bowl in her hand; within this gallery were divers Monsters cast in mettal, standing all in a row, which holding one another by the hand in manner of a dance incompassed the whole Island, being as I have said, a league about: Amidst these monstrous Idols there was likewise another row of very rich Arches, made of sundry coloured pieces; a sumptuous work, and wherewith the eye might well be entertained and contented; Within was a little wood of Orange Trees, without any mixture of other plants, and in the midst an hundred and threescore Hermitages dedicated to the gods of the year, of whom these Gentiles recount many pleasant Fables in their Chronicles for the defence of their blindness in their false belief: A quarter of a league beyond these Hermitages, towards the East, divers goodly great Edifices were seen, separated the one from the other with seven fore-fronts of Houses, built after the manner of our Churches; from the top to the bottome as far as could be discerned, these buildings were guilt all over, and annexed to very high Towers, which in all likelihood were Steeples; their Edifices were invironed with two great streets arched all along, like unto the Frontispieces of the Houses; these Arches were supported by very huge Pillars, on the top whereof, and between every arch was a dainty Prospective; now in regard these buildings, towers, pillars and their chapters, were so exceedingly guilt all over, as one could discern nothing but Gold, it perswaded us that this Temple must needs be wonderfull sumptuous and rich, since such cost had been bestowed on the very Walls. After we had surrounded this whole Island, and observed the advenues and entries thereof, notwithstanding it was somewhat late, yet would *Antonio de Faria* needs go ashore to see if he could get any Intelligence in one of those Hermitages, to the end he might thereupon resolve, either to prosecute his design, or return back: So having left a guard sufficient for his two Vessels, and *Diego Lobato*, his Chaplain, Captain of them, he landed with fourty Souldiers, and twenty slaves, as well Pikes, as Harquebuses; He also carried with him four of the *Chineses*, which we took a while before, both for that they knew the place well, as having been there at other times, and likewise that they might serve us for truthmen and guides: Being got to the shore unespied of any one, and without noise, we entred the Island by one of the eight Advenues that it had, and marching through the middest of the little wood of Orange-trees we arrived at the gate of the first Hermitage, which might be some two Musket-shot from the place we dis-imbarqued, where that hapned unto us which I will deliver hereafter.

Antonio de Faria went directly to the next Hermitage he saw before him with the greatest silence that might be, and with no little fear, for that he knew not into what danger he was going to ingage himself; which he found shut on the inside, he commanded one of the *Chineses* to knock at it, as he did two or three times, when at last he heard one speak in this manner, *Praysed be the Creator, who hath enameled the beauty of the skies, let him that knocks at the gate go about, and he shall finde it open on the other side, where let me know what he desires.* The *Chinese* went presently about, and entring into the Hermitage by a back door, he opened the foregate to *Antonio de Faria*, and let him in with all his followvers; There

There he found an old man, that seemed to be an hundred years old; he was apparelled in a long violet coloured damask gown, and by his countenance appeared to be a man of quality, as we underſtood afterwards : Being amazed to ſee ſo many men, he fell to the ground, where he lay a good while without ſpeaking a word, howbeit at length he began to be better confirmed, and beholding us with a ſerious look, he gravely demanded of us what we were, and what we would have ; whereunto the Interpreter anſwered by the expreſs commandment of *Antonio de Faria*, that he was a Captain ſtranger, a native of the Kingdom of *Siam*, and that ſayling in a Junk of his, laden with merchandiſe, and bound for *Liampoo*, he had ſuffered ſhipwrack, whence he had miraculouſly eſcaped with all his company, and for that he had vowed to make a pilgrimage to this holy place, to praiſe God for preſerving him from ſo great a peril, he was now come to perform his vow ; alſo to crave ſomwhat of him by way of alms, whereby his poverty might be relieved, proteſting within three years to render him twice as much as he ſhould then take from him : whereupon the Hermit, named *Hiticon*, having muſed a little on the matter, and fixing his eye on *Antonio de Faria* : *Whoever thou art*, ſaid he unto him, *know that I throughly underſtand what thou ſayeſt, and that I perceive but too well thy damnable intention, wherewith out of the obſcurity of thy blindneſs, like an infernal pilot, thou carrieſt both thy ſelf, and theſe others, into the profound abiſm of the lake of night : for inſtead of rendring thanks to God for ſo great a favour, as thou confeſſeſt he hath ſhewed thee, thou comeſt hither to rob this holy houſe : But let me ask thee, if thou executeſt thy miſchievous deſigne, what will the divine Juſtice, thinkeſt thou, do with thee at the laſt gaſp of thy life ? Change then thy perverſe inclination, and never ſuffer the imagination of ſo great a ſin to enter thy thoughts ; give credit unto me that tels thee nothing but the very truth, even as I hope to thrive by it all the reſt of my life.* *Antonio de Faria* ſeeming to approve of the counſel, which the old Hermit gave him, earneſtly deſired him not to be diſpleaſed, aſſuring him that he had no other means or way left to relieve him and his, but what he could find in that place : To which the Hermit wringing his hands, and lifting up his eyes, ſaid weeping, *Praiſed be thou, O Lord, that permitteſt men to live on the earth, who offend thee under pretext of ſeeking means to live, and that vouchſafe not to ſerve thee one hour, although they know how aſſured thy glory is.* After he had uttered theſe words, he remained very penſive and much troubled to ſee the great diſorder we uſed in breaking up the coffins, and flinging them out of their places; at length looking upon *Antonio de Faria*, who ſtood leaning upon his ſword, he intreated him to ſit down by him, which he did with a great deal of compliment, not deſiſting for all that from making ſignes to his ſouldiers to perſiſt as they had begun, that was to take the ſilver which was mingled amongſt the bones of the dead in the tombs, that they brake up ; whereat the Hermit was ſo grieved as he fell down twice in a ſwoon from his ſeat, but being come to himſelf, he ſpake thus to *Antonio de Faria*, *I will declare unto thee as to a man that ſeems diſcreet, the means whereby thou mayſt obtain pardon for the ſin, which thou and thy people now commit, to the end that thy ſoul may not periſh eternally, when as the laſt breath of thy mouth ſhal go out of thy body : Seeing then, as thou ſayeſt, that it is neceſſity conſtrains thee to offend in thus grievous manner, and that thou haſt a purpoſe to make reſtitution before thou dyeſt, of that thou takeſt away from hence ; if thou haſt time and power, thou mayſt do theſe three things : Firſt, thou muſt render again what thou now carrieſt away, that the Sovereign Lord may not turn his mercy from thee : Secondly, thou muſt with tears ask him forgiveneſs for thy fault, which is ſo odious unto him, never ceaſing to chaſtiſe thy fleſh both day and night : And thirdly, thou muſt diſtribute thy goods to the poor, as liberally as to thy ſelf, giving them alms with prudence and diſcretion, to the end the ſervant of the night may have nothing to accuſe thee of at the laſt day. Now, for recompence of this counſel, I deſire thee to command thy followers to gather together the bones of the Saints, that they may not be deſpiſed on the earth.* *Antonio de Faria* promiſed him very curteouſly to perform his requeſt, wherewith the Hermit was a little better at quiet then before, but yet not fully ſatisfied, howbeit he ſpake him very fair, and aſſured him that after he had once ſeen him, he very much repented the undertaking of this enterpriſe, but his ſouldiers had threatned to kill him, if he returned without executing of it, and this he told him as a very great ſecret, *God grant it be ſo*, replyed the Hermit, *for that thou ſhalt not be ſo blame-worthy as theſe other monſters of the night, which are ſo greedy, like to famiſhed dogs, that it ſeems all the ſilver in the world is not able to ſatiate them.*

§ 3.   After we had gathered all the ſilver together, that was in the graves amongſt the dead mens

bones,

bones, and carryed it abord our ships, we were all of opinion not to go any farther to the reft of the Hermitages, as well becaufe we knew not the Countrey, as for that it was almoft night, upon hope that the next day we might continue our enterprife more at leifure. Now before he reinbarqued himfelfe, *Antonio de Faria* took leave of the Hermit, and giving him very good words, he defired him for Gods fake not to be offended with that his followers had done, being conftrained thereunto by meer neceffity : for as his for particular he exceedingly abhorred fuch like actions, adding withall, that at the firft fight of him, he would have returned back, out of the remover of confcience, and true repentance ; but that his company had hindered him, faying, that if he did fo, they would furely kill him ; fo that for to have his life he was compelled to yeild and confent thereunto, though he plainly faw that it was a very great fin, in regard whereof he was refolved, as foon as he could rid his hands of them, to go up and down the world to perform fuch penance as was requifite for the purging of him from fo enormous a crime. Hereunto the Hermit anfwered, *Pleafeth the Lord, who living, reigneth above the beauty of the Stars, that the knowledge, which by this difcourfe, thou fheweft to have, be not prejudiciall unto thee ; For I be affured, that he who knows thefe things, and doth them not, runs a far greater danger, then he that fins through ignorance.* Then one of ours, named *Nuno Coelho,* who would needs have an oar in our talk, told him, that he was not to be angry for a matter of fo fmall importance ; whereunto the Hermit beholding him with fo ftern a countenance, anfwered, *Certainly, the fear which thou haft of death is yet leffe, fince thou imployeft thy felfe in actions as infamous and black as the foul that is in thy body ; and for my part, I cannot but be perfwaded, that all thy ambition is wholly placed upon money, as but too well appears by the the thirft of thy infatiable avarice, whereby thou wilt make an end of heaping up the meafure of thine infernal appetite : Continue then thy theeveries, for feeing then thou muft go to hell far that which thou haft already taken out of this holy houfe, thou fhalt alfo go thither for thofe things which thou fhalt fteal otherwife, fo the heavier the burden fhall be that thou beareft, the fooner fhalt thou be precipitated into the bottom of hell, where already thy wicked works have prepared thee an everlafting abode.* Hereupon *Nuno de Coelho* prayed him to take all things patiently, affirming that the Law of God commanded him fo to do. Then the Hermit lift up his hand by way of admiration, and as it were fmiling at what the fouldier had faid, *Truly,* anfwered he, *I am come to fee, that I never thought to fee or hear, namely, evil actions difguifed with a fpecious pretext of vertue, which makes me believe that thy blindneffe is exceeding great, fince trufting to good words, thou fpendeft thy life fo wickedly, wherefore it is not poffible thou fhouldeft ever come to Heaven, or give any account to God at the laft day, as of neceffity they muft do.* Saying fo, he turned him to *Antonio de Faria,* without attending further anfwer from him, and earneftly defired him not to fuffer his company to fpit upon and prophane the altar, which he vowed was more grievous to him, then the induring of a thoufand deaths ; whereupon to fatisfie him, he prefently commanded the forbearance of it ; wherewith the Hermit was fomewhat comforted ; Now becaufe it grew late, *Antonio de Faria* refolved to leave the place, but before he departed he held it neceffary to inform himfelf of certain other particulars, whereof he ftood in fome doubt, fo that he deferved of the Hermit how many perfons there might be in all thofe Hermitages : whereunto *Hiticon* anfwered, that there were about three hundred and threefcore *Talagrepos,* befides forty *Menigrepos,* appointed to furnifh them with things requifite for their maintenance, and to attend them when they were fick : moreover he asked him, whether the King of *China* came not fomtimes thither ; he told him, No, for, faid he, the King cannot be condemned by any body, he is the fon of the Sun, but contrarily he had power to abfolve every one. Then he enquired of him if there were any arms in their Hermitages ? O no, anfwered the Hermit, *for all fuch as pretend to go to heaven have more need of patience to indure injuries, then of arms to revenge themfelves :* Being alfo defirous to know of him the caufe why fo much filver was mingled with the bones of the dead. *This filver,* replied the Hermit, *comes of the alms that the deceafed carry with them out of this into the other life, for to ferve them at their need in the heaven of the Moon, where they live eternally : In conclufion,* having demanded of him whither they had any women, he faid, *That they which would maintain the life of their fouls, ought not to tafte the pleafures of the flefh, feeing experience made it apparent, that the Bee which nourifheth her felf in an hony-comb, doth often fting fuch as offer to meddle with that fweetneffe.* After *Antonio de Faria* had propounded all thefe queftions, he took his leave of him, and fo went directly to his ships, with an intenti-

8

on

on to return again the next day, for to set upon the other Hermitages, where, as he had been told, was great abundance of silver, and certain Idols of gold, but our sins would not permit us to see the effect of a business, which we had been two months and an halfe a purchasing with so much labor and danger of our lives, as I will deliver hereafter.

§.4.　At the clearing up of the day, *Antonio de Faria*, and all of us, being embarqued, we went and anchored on the other side of the Island, about a faulcon shot from it, with an intent, as I have before declared, to go a shore again the next morning, and set upon the Chappels where the Kings of *China* were interred, that so we might the more commodiously lade our two vessels with such treasures, which peradventure might have succeeded according to our desires, if the business had been well carried, and that *Antonio de Faria* had followed the counsel was given him, which was, that since we had not been as yet discovered, that he should have carried the Hermit away with him, to the end he might not acquaint the House of the *Bonzos* with what we had done; howbeit he would never hearken to it, saying, that we were to fear nothing that way, by reason the Hermit was so old, and his legs so swoln with the gout, as he was not able to stand, much less to go: But it fell out clean contrary to his expectation, for the Hermit no sooner saw us imbarqued, as we understood afterwards, but he presently crawled as well as he could to the next Hermitage, which was not above a flight shoot from his, and giving intelligence of all that had past, he bad his companion, because himself was not able, to go away with all speed to the *Bonzoes* house to acquaint them with it, which the other instantly performed; so that about midnight we saw a great many of fires lighted on the top of the wall of the Temple, where the Kings were buried, being kindled to serve for a signal to the Countrey about, of some extraordinary danger towards: This made us ask of our *Chineses*, what they might mean, who answered, that assuredly, we were discovered, in regard whereof they advised us without any longer stay to set sail immediatly; Herewith they acquainted *Antonio de Faria*, who was fast asleep, but he straightway arose, and leaving his anchor in the sea, rowed directly, afraid as he was, to the Island, for to learn what was done there: Being arrived near to the Key, he heard many bels ringing in each Hermitage, together with a noise of men talking, whereupon the *Chineses* that accompanied him, said, Sir, never stand to hear or see more, but retire, we beseech you, as fast as you may, and cause us not to be all miserably slain with your further stay; Howbeit little regarding, or afraid of their words, he went ashore only with six souldiers, having no other arms but swords and targots, and going up the stairs of the Key, whither it were that he was vext for having lost so fair an occasion, or carried thereunto by his courage, he entered into the gallery, that invironed the Island, and ran up and down in it like a mad man, without meeting any body; That done, and being returned abord his vessel, much grieved and ashamed, he consulted with his company about what they should do, who were of opinion that the best course we could take, was to depart, and therefore they required him to put it accordingly in execution; Seeing them all so resolved, and fearing some tumults among the souldiers, he was fain to answer, that he was also of their mind, but first he thought it fit to know for what cause they should fly away in that manner, and therefore he desired them to stay for him a little in that place, because he would trie whether he could learn by some means or other the truth of the matter, whereof they had but a bare suspition; for which, he told them, he would ask but half an hour at the most, so that there would be time enough to take order for any thing before day; some would have alledged reasons against this, but he would not hear them, wherefore having caused them all to take their oaths, upon the holy Evangelists, that they would stay for him, he returned to land with the same souldiers, that had accompanied him before, and entering into the little wood, he heard the sound of a bell, which addressed him to another Hermitage, far richer then that wherein we were the day before: There he met with two men, apparaled like Monks, with large hoods, which made him think they were Hermits, of whom he presently laid hold, wherewith one of them was so terrified, as he was not able to speak a good while after: Hereupon four of the six souldiers past into the Hermitage, and took an Idol of silver from the altar, having a crown of gold on its head, and a wheel in its hand; they also brought away three candlesticks of silver, with long chains of the same belonging to them: This performed, *Antonio de Faria* carrying the two Hermits along with him, went abord again, and sailing away, he propounded divers questions to him, of the two, that was least affraid, threatning to use him in a strange fashion if he did not tell the truth. This Hermit seeing himself so menaced, answered, That an holy man, named *Pilau Angiroo* came about midnight to the house of the Kings Sepultures,

wher

where knocking in haste at the gate, he cryed out, saying ; *O miserable men, buried in the drunkenneſs of carnal ſleep, Who by a ſolemn vow, have profeſt your ſelves to the honour of the Goddeſs* Amida, *the rich reward of our labours , hear, hear, hear, O the moſt wretched men that ever were born ; There are ſtrangers come into our Iſland, from the further end of the World, which have long beards, and bodies of Iron, theſe wicked creatures have entred into the Holy Houſe of the ſeven and twenty Pillars, of whoſe ſacred Temple an holy man is keeper, that hath told it me, where after they had ranſacked the rich treaſures of the Saints, they contemptedly threw their bones to the ground, which they prophaned with their ſtinking and infectious ſpitting, and made a mockerie of them like Devils, obſtinate and hardned in their wretched ſins, wherefore I adviſe you to look well to your ſelves, for it is ſaid, that they have ſworn to kill us all as ſoon as it is day : Fly away then, or call ſome people to your ſuccour, ſince being Religious men you are not permitted to meddle with any thing that may ſhed the blood of man.* Herewith they preſently aroſe and ran to the gate, where they found the Hermite laid on the ground, and half dead with grief and wearineſſe through the imbecillity of his age ; whereupon the *Grepos* and *Meingrepos* made thoſe fires that you ſaw, and withall ſent in all haſte to the Towns of *Corpilem,* and *Fonbana,* for to ſuccour them ſpeedily with the Forces of the Country, ſo that you may be aſſured it will not be long before they fall upon this place with all the fury that may be. *Now this is all that I am able to ſay concerning the truth of this affair, wherefore I deſire you to return us both unto our Hermitage with our lives ſaved, for if you do not ſo you will commit a greater ſin, then you did yeſterday : Remember alſo that God, in regard of the continuall penance we perform, hath taken us ſo far into his protection, as he doth viſit us almoſt every hour of the day, wherefore labour to ſave your ſelves as much as you will, yet ſhall you hardly do it ; For be ſure, that the earth, the air, the winds, the waters, the beaſts, the fiſhes, the fowls, the trees, the plants, and all things created will purſue and torment you ſo cruelly, as none but he that lives in heaven will be able to help you.* Antonio *de* Faria being hereby certainly informed of the truth of the buſineſſe ſailed inſtantly away, tearing his hair and beard for very rage, to ſee that through his negligence and indiſcretion he had loſt the faireſt occaſion, that ever he ſhould be able to meet withall.

C H A P. XXVI.

Our caſting away in the Gulf of Nanquin, *with all that befell us after this lamentable Shipwrack.*

WE had already ſailed ſeven dayes in the Gulf of *Nanquin,* to the end that the force §.1. of the Current might carry us the more ſwiftly away, as men whoſe ſafety conſiſted wholly in flight, for we were ſo deſolate and ſad, that we ſcarce ſpake one to another ; In the mean time we arrived at a Village, called *Suſequerim,* where no news being come either of us, or what we had done, we furniſhed our ſelves with ſome Victual, and getting Information very covertly of the courſe we were to hold, we departed within two hours after, and then with the greateſt ſpeed we could make we entred into a ſtraight, named *Xalingau,* much leſſe frequented then the gulf, that we had paſt ; here we navigated nine dayes more, in which time we ran an hundred and fourty leagues, then entring again into the ſaid Gulf of *Nanquin,* which in that place was not above ten or eleven leagues broad, we ſailed for the ſpace of thirteen dayes from one ſide to another with a Weſterly winde, exceedingly afflicted, both with the great labour we were fain to indure, and the cruel fear we were in, beſides the want we began to feel of Victuals : In this caſe being come within ſight of the mountains of *Conxinacau,* which are in the height of forty and one degrees, there aroſe ſo terrible a Southwind, called by the *Chineſes Tufaon,* as it could not poſſibly be thought a natural thing, ſo that our Veſſels being low built, weak, and without Mariners, we were reduced to ſuch extremity, that out of all hope to eſcape we ſuffered our ſelves to be driven along the coaſt, as the current of the water would carry us, for we held it more ſafe to venture our ſelves amongſt the Rocks, then to let us be ſwallowed up in the midſt of the Sea, and though we had choſen this deſign, as the better and leſſe painful, yet did it not ſucceed, for after dinner the winde turned to the North-weſt, whereby the Waves became ſo high, that it was moſt dreadful to behold ; Our fear then was ſo extream, as we began to caſt all that we had into the Sea, even to the Cheſts full of

O

Silver :

Silver : That done, we cut down our two Mafts, and so without Mafts and Sails we floated along all the reft of the day ; at length about midnight we heard them in *Antonio de Faria*'s Veffel cry, *Lord have mercy upon us*, which perfwaded us that they were caft away, the apprehenfion whereof put us in fuch a fright, as for an hour together no man fpake a word. Having paft all this fad night in fo miferable a plight, about an hour before day our Veffel opened about the Keel, fo that it was inftantly full of water eight fpans high, whereupon perceiving our felves to finke, we verily beleeved, it was the good pleafure of God that in this place we fhould finifh both our lives and labours : As foon then as it was day we looked out to Sea, as far as poffibly we could difcern, but could no way difcover *Antonio de Faria*, which put us quite out of heart, and fo continuing in this great afflidion till about ten of the clock, with fo much terror and amazement, as words are not able to expreffe, at laft we ran againft the coaft, and even drowned as we were, the Waves rouled us towards a point of Rocks, that ftood out into the Sea, where we were no fooner arrived but that all went to pieces, infomuch that of five and twenty *Portugals*, which we were, there were but fourteen faved, the other eleven being drowned, together with eighteen Chriftian Servants, and feven *Chinefe* Mariners. This miferable difafter hapned on a Munday, the fifth of *Auguft*, in the year one thoufand five hundredforty and two, for which the Lord be prayfed everlaftingly.

§.2.   We fourteen *Portugals*, having efcaped out of this fhipwrack by the meer mercy of God, fpent all that day, and the night following, in bewailing our mif-fortune, and the wretched eftate whereunto we were reduced, but in the end confulting together, what courfe to take for to give fome remedy thereunto, we concluded to enter into the Country, hoping that far or neer we fhould not fail to meet with fome body, that taking us for flaves, would relieve us with meat, till fuch time as it fhould pleafe Heaven to terminate our travels with the end of our lives. With this Refolution we went fome fix or feven leagues over rocks and hills, and on the other fide difcovered a great Marfh, fo large and void, as it paft the reach of our fight, there being no appearance of any land beyond it, which made us turn back again, towards the fame place where we were caft away ; being arrived there the day after about Sun-fet, we found upon the fhore the bodies of our men, which the Sea had caft up, over whom we recomenced our forrow and lamentations, and the next day we buried them in the fand, to keep them from being devoured by the Tygers, whereof that Country is full, which we performed with much labour and pain, in regard we had no other tools for that purpofe but our hands and nails ; After thefe poor bodies were interred we got us into a Marfh, where we fpent all the night, as the fafeft place we could chufe to preferve us from the Tygers: From thence we continued our journey towards the North, and that by fuch Precipes and thick woods, as we had much adoe to pafs through them. Having travelled in this manner three dayes, at length we arrived at a little ftraight, without meeting any body, over the which refolving to fwim, by ill fortune the four firft that entred into it, being three *Portugals* and a young youth, were miferably drowned, for being very feeble, and the ftraight fomewhat broad, and the current of the water very ftrong, they were not able to hold out any longer when they came to the midft ; fo we eleven with three fervants that remained, feeing the infortunate fucceffe of our companions, could do nothing but weep and lament, as men that hourly expected fuch or a worfe end. Having fpent all that dark night, expofed to the winde, cold, and rain, it pleafed our Lord that the next morning before day we difcovered a great fire towards the Eaft, whereupon as foon as the day broke, we marched fair and foftly that way, recomending our felves to that Almighty God from whom alone we could hope for a remedy to our miferies, and fo continuing our journey all along the River, the moft part of that day, at laft we came to a little wood, where we found five men making of coals, whom on our knees we befought for Gods fake to direct us to fome place where we might get fome relief ; *I would*, faid one of them, beholding us with an eye of pitie, *it lay in our power to help you, but alas ! all the comfort we can give you is to beftow fome part of our Supper on you, which is a little rice, wherewith you may paffe this night here with us if you will, though I hold it better for you to proceed on your way, and recover the place you fee a little below, where you fhall finde an Hofpital that ferves to lodge fuch Pilgrims, as chance to come into thefe quarters.* Having thanked him for his good addreffe, we fell to the Rice they gave us, which came but to two mouthfuls a piece, and fo took our leaves of them, going directly to the place they had fhewed us, as well as our weaknefs would permit.   About

About an hour within night, we arrived at the Hospital, where we met with four men, that had the charge of it, who received us very charitably: The next morning as soon as it was day they demanded of us, what we were, and from whence we came? Thereunto we answered, that we were strangers, natives of the Kingdom of *Siam*, and that coming from the Port of *Liampoo* to go to the fishing of *Nanquin*, we were cast away at sea by the violence of a storm, having saved nothing out of this shipwrack, but those our miserable and naked bodies. Whereupon demanding of us again, what we intended to do, and whither we would go; we replyed, that we purposed to go to the City of *Nanquin*, there to imbarque our selves as rowers in the first *Lanteaa*, that should put to sea, for to pass unto *Cantan*, where our countreymen by the permission of the *Aito of Panquin*, exercised their traffique under the protection of the son of the Sun, and *Lyon* crowned in the throne of the world, wherefore we desired them for Gods cause to let us stay in that Hospital, until we had recovered our healths, and to bestow any poor clothes of us to cover our nakednedness. After they had given good ear unto us; It was reason, answered they, to grant you that which you require with so much earnestness, and tears; but in regard the House is now very poor, we cannot so easily discharge our duties unto you as we should, howbeit we will do what we may with a very good will; Then quite naked, as we were, they lead us all about the Village, containing some forty or fifty fires, more or less; the inhabitants whereof were exceeding poor, having no other living but what they got by the labour of their hands, from whom they drew by way of alms some two *Taeis* in mony, half a Sack of rice, a little meal, aricot beans, onions, and a few old rags, wherewith we made the best shift we could; over and above this they bestowed two *Taeis* more on us out of the Stock of the Hospital: But whereas we desired that we might be permitted to stay there, they excused themselves, saying, that no poor might remain there above three days, or five at the most, unless it were sick people, or women with child, of whom special care was to be had, because in their extremities they could not travel without endangering their lives, wherefore they could for no other persons whatsoever transgress that Ordinance, which had of ancient time been instituted by the advice of very learned and religious men; nevertheless, that three leagues from thence, we should in a great Town, called *Sileyiacau*, find a very rich hospital, where all sorts of poor people were entertained, and that there we should be far better looked unto then in their house, which was poor, and agreeable to the place of its scituation, to which end they would give us a letter of recommendation, by means whereof we should incontinently be received. For these good offices we rendred them infinite thanks, and told them that God would reward them for it since they did it for his sake, whereupon an old man, one of those four, taking the Speech upon him, *It is for that consideration alone we do it*, answered he, *and not in regard of the world; for God and the world are greatly different in matters of works, and of the intention which one my have in the doing of them: For the world being poor and miserable as it is, can give nothing that is good, whereas God is infinitely rich, and a friend to the poor, that in the heighth of their afflictions praise him with patience and humility; The world is revengeful, but God is suffering; the world is wicked, God is all goodness; the world is gluttonous, God is a lover of abstinence; the world is mutinous and turbulent, God is quiet and peaceable; the world is a lyar and full of dissimulation to them that belong to it, God is always true, free, and merciful to them that invoke him by prayer; the world is sensual and covetous, God is liberal, and purer then the light of the Sun, or stars, or then those other lamps which are far more excellent then they that appear to our eyes, and are always present before his most resplendent face; the world is full of irresolution and falshood, wherewith it entertains it self in the smoak of its vain glory, whereas God is constant in his truth, to the end that thereby the humble may possess glory in all sincerity of heart; In a word, the world is full of folly and ignorance, contrarily God is the fountain of wisdom; wherefore my friends, although you be reduced to so pitiful an estate, do you not for all that distrust his promises; for be assured he will not fail you, if you do not render your selves unworthy of his favours, in regard it was never found that he was at any time wanting to his; albeit they, that are blinded by the world, are of another opinion, when as they see themselves oppressed with poverty, and despised of every body.* Having used this Speech to us, he gave us a letter of recommendation to the Brotherhood of the other Hospital, whither we were to go, and so we departed about noon, and arrived at the town an hour or two before sun-set. The first thing we did, was to go to the house of the repose of the poor, for so the *Chineses* call the Hospitals; There we delivered our letters to the Masters of that Society, which they term *Tanigories*, whom we found altogether in a chamber, where they were assembled about the affairs of the poor; After they had received the letter with a kind of compliment, that seemed very strange to us, they commanded the Register to read it, whereupon he stood up and read thus to them that were sitting at the Table : *We the poorest of the poor, unworthy to serve that Sovereign Lord, whose works are so admirable, as the Sun, and the stars that twinckle in the skie, during the darkness of the night do testifie : Having been elected to the succession of this his house of Buatendoo, scituated in this Village of Catihorau, with all manner of respect and honour, do beseech your humble persons, admitted to the service of the Lord, that out of a zeal of charity, you will lodg and favour these fourteen strangers, whereof three are tawny, the other eleven somewhat whiter, whose poverty will manifestly appear to your eyes, whereby you may judg how much reason we have to present this request unto you, for that they have been cast away with all their merchandise in the impetuous waters of the sea, that with their accustomed fury have laid the execution of the Almighty hand upon them, which for a just punishment doth often permit such like things to happen ; for to shew us how dreadful his judgments are, from which may it please him to deliver us all at the day of death, to the end we may not see the indignation of his face.* This letter being read, they caused us presently to be lodged in a very neat chamber, accommodated with a Table, and divers Chairs, where after we had been served with good meat, we rested our selves that night : The next morning the Register came along with the rest of the officers, and demanded of us who we were, of what Nation, and whereabout we had suffered shipwrack, whereunto we answered as we had done before to those of the Village from whence we came, that we might not be found in two tales, and convinced of lying ; whereupon having further enquired of us what we meant to do, we told them that our intention was to get our selves cured in that house, if it pleased them to permit us, in regard we were so weak and sickly as we could scarce stand upon our legs : To which they replyed, that they would very willingly see that performed for us, as a thing that was ordinarily done there for the service of God ; for the which we thanked them weeping, with so much acknowledgment of their goodness and charity, as the tears stood in their eyes, so that presently sending for a Physician, they bid him look carefully to us, for that we were poor flocks, and had no other means but what we had from the house ; That done he took our names in writing, and set them down in a great book, whereunto we all of us set our hands, saying, it was necessary it should be so, that an accompt might be rendred of the expence was to be made for us.

§.4.   Having spent eighteen days in this Hospital, where we were sufficiently provided for with all things necessary, it pleased God that we throughly recovered our healths, so that feeling our selves strong enough to travel, we departed from thence for to go to a place, called *Zuzoangances*, some five leagues from that Hospital, where we arrived about sun-set ; Now in regard we were very weary, we sat us down upon the side of a fountain, that stood at the entrance of that Village, being much perplexed and unresolved what way to take : In the mean time, they which came to fetch water, seeing us set there in so sad an equipage, returned with their pitchers empty, and advertising the inhabitants of it, the most of them came presently forth to us ; Then wondering much, because they had never seen men like unto us, they gathered altogether, as if they would consult thereupon, and after they had a good while debated one with another, they sent an old woman to demand of us what people we were, and why we sat so about that fountain, from whence they drew all the water they used : Hereunto we answered, that we were poor strangers, natives of the Kingdom of *Siam*, who by a storm at sea were cast upon their Countrey, in that miserable plight wherein they beheld us. Tell me, replyed she, what course would you have us to take for you, and what resolve you to do, for here is no house for the repose of the poor whereinto you may be received ? To these words one of our company answered with tears in his eyes, and a gesture conformable to our designe, that God, being that which he was, would never abandon us with his Almighty hand, but would touch their hearts to take compassion of us, and our poverty ; and further, that we were resolved to travel in that miserable case we were in till we had the good fortune to arrive at the City of *Nanquin*, where we desired to put our selves into the *Lanteaas*, there to serve for rowers to the Merchants that ordinarily went from thence to *Cantano*, and so to get to *Comhay*, where great store of our Country Junks usually lay, in which we would imbarque our selves. Thereupon having somewhat a better opinion of us then before ; Seeing you are, said she, such as you deliver, have a little patience till I come again, and tell you what these folks resolve to do with you ;

you; wherewith she returned to those country people, which were about some hundred persons, with whom she entred into a great contestation, but at length she came back with one of their Priests, attired in a long gown of red damask, which is an ornament of chiefest dignity among them, in this equipage he came to us with an handful of ears of corn in his hand; Then having commanded us to approach unto him, we presently obeyed him with all kind of respect, but he little regarded it, seeing us so poor; whereupon after he had thrown the ears of corn into the fountain, he willed us to put our hands upon them, which we accordingly having done: *You are to confess*, said he unto us, *by this holy and solemn oath, that now you take in my presence upon these two substances of bread and water, which the high Creator of all things hath made by his holy will to sustain and nourish all that is born into the world, during the pilgrimage of this life, whether that which you told this woman but now be true, for upon that condition we will give you lodging in this village conformably to the charities we are bound to exercise towards Gods poor people ; whereas contrarily, if it be not so, I command you in his Name that you presently get you gone, upon pain of being bitten and destroyed by the teeth of the gluttenous Serpent, that makes his abode in the bottom of the house of smoak.* Hereunto we answered, that we had said nothing but what was most true, wherewith the Priest remaining satisfied ; since you are, said he, such as you say, come you along boldly with me, and rely on my word : Then returning with us to the inhabitants of the place, he told them that they might bestow their alms upon us without offence, and that he gave them permission so to do, whereupon we were presently conducted into the Village, and lodged in the porch of their *Pagode*, or Temple, where we were furnished with all that was needful for us, and had two mats given us to lie upon : The next morning as soon as it was day, we went up and down the street, begging from door to door, and got four *Taeis* in silver, wherewith we supplied our most pressing necessities. After this we went away to another place, called *Xiangnulea*, that was not above two leagues from that, with a resolution to travel in that sort, as it were in pilgrimage, to the City of *Nanquin*, to which it was then some hundred and forty leagues ; for we thought that from thence we might go to *Cantano*, where our ships traded at that time, and it may be our designe had succeeded, had it not been for ill fortune. About even-song we arrived at that village, where we sat us down under the shadow of a great tree that stood by it self, but it was our ill hap to meet with three boyes that kept certain cattel there, who no sooner perceived us, but betaking them to their heels, they cried out, Thieves, thieves, whereat the inhabitants came instantly running out, armed with lances and crossbowes, crying out, stop the thieves, stop the thieves ; and so perceiving us, that fled from them, they mauld us cruelly with stones and staves, in such manner as we were all of us grievously hurt, especially one of our boyes that died upon it ; Then seizing on us, they tied our arms behind us, and leading us like prisoners into the village, they so beat and buffeted us with their fists, as they had almost killed us, then they plunged us into a cistern of standing water, that reached up to our wasts, wherein were a great number of horse-leeches ; In this miserable place we remained two days, which seemed two hundred years to us, having neither rest, nor any thing to eat all that time : At last, it was our good fortune, that a man of *Zuzoangance*, from whence we came, passing by, chanced to understand how we had been used by those of the Village, and thereupon went and told them, that they did us great wrong to take us for thieves, for that we were poor strangers, which had been cast away by a storm at sea, wherefore they had committed a great sin to imprison, and handle us in that sort ; The report of this man wrought so effectually with them, that we were presently taken out of the cistern, being all gore blood with the sucking of the horse-leeches, and I verily believe that if we had stayed there but one day longer, we had all of us been dead : So we departed from this place about evening, and bewailing our bad fortune, continuing on our voyage.

After our departure from *Xiangnulea* we arrived at a Village, inhabited by very poor people, where we met with three men that were pilling Flax, who as soon as they saw us forsook their work, and fled hastily away into a wood of Firr trees, there they cryed out to those that passed by to take heed of us for that we were thieves, whereupon fearing to incur the same danger whence we so lately escaped, we got us away presently from that place, although it was almost night, and continued our journie, in the rain and the dark, without knowing whither we went, till we came to a gate where Cattel were kept, and there we lay the rest of the night upon a little heap of dung ; the next morning as soon as

S.5.

it

it was day we got again into the way which we had left, and not long after we difcover-ed from the top of a little hill a great plain full of trees, and in the midft thereof a very fair Houfe hard by a River, whither forthwith we went, and fate us down by a fountain that was before the outer gate, where we remained two or three hours without feeing any bo-dy, at length a young Gentleman about fixteen or feventeen years of age came riding up-on a very good Horfe, accompanied with four men on foot, whereof one carried two Hares, and another five *Nivatores*, which are Fowls refembling our Phefants, with a Gof-Hawk on his fift, and three or four couple of Spaniels at their heels; when this Gentleman came at us he ftaid his Horfe, to ask us who we were, and whether we would have any thing with him.   Hereunto we anfwered as well as we could, and made him an ample Relati-on of the whole event of our fhipwrack, whereat he feemed to be very forry, as we could gather by his countenance, fo that ere he went, Stay there, faid he unto us, for by and by I will fend you what you have need of, and that for his fake that with a glory of great riches lives raigning in the higheft of all the Heavens.   A little after he fent an old woman for us, which was apparelled in a long garment, with a Chaplet hanging down on her neck, the good Dame coming to us, The fon of him faid fhe, whom me hold for Mafter in this houfe, and whofe Rice we eat, hath fent for you, follow me then with all humlity, to the end you may not feem idle fellows to thofe that fhall fee you, and fuch as beg onely to be exempted from getting your living by the labour of your hands; This faid, we entred with her into an outward court, all about invironed with Galleries, as if it had been fome Cloifter of Religious perfons, on the walls whereof were painted divers women on Horfe-back going on hunting with Hawks on their fifts; over the gate of this Court was a great arch very richly engraven, in the midft whereof hung a Scutcheon of Arms, in the fafhion of a fhield, faftned to a filver chain, within it was a man painted almoft in the form of a *Tortois*, with the feet up, and the head downwards, and round about it thefe words were read for a device, *Ingualec finguau, potim aquarau*, that is to fay, *So is it with all that appertains to me*; We learnt afterwards, that by this Monfter the Figure of the world was reprefented, which the *Chinefes* depaint in this manner to demonftrate that there is nothing in it but falfhood, and fo to dif-abufe all them that make fuch account of it by making them to fee how all things in it are turned upfide down.   Out of this Court we went up a broad pair of ftairs, made of fair hewed ftone, and entred into a great Hall, where a woman of about fiftie years of age, was fet upon a Tapeftry Carpet, having two young Gentlewomen by her fide, that were exceeding fair, and richly apparelled, with chains of Pearl about their necks, and hard by them was a reverend old man laid upon a little bed, whom one of the two Gentlewomen fanned with a Vintiloe; at his Beds head ftood the young Gentleman that had fent for us, and a little further off upon another Car-pet nine young maids, clothed in Crimfon and white Damask, fate fowing; as foon as we came before the old man we fell on our knees, and asked an almes of him, beginning our fpeech with tears, and in the beft terms that the time and our neceffities could infpire us with, whereupon the old Lady beckning to us with her hand, *Come, weep no more*, faid fhe, *for it grieves me much to fee you fhed fo many tears, it is fufficient that I know you defire an almes of us*; then the old man that lay in the bed fpake unto us, and demanded whe-ther any of us knew what was good for a Fever? Whereat the young Gentlewoman that fan-ned him, not able to forbear fmiling: *Sir*, faid fhe, *they have more need that you would be pleafed to give order for the fatisfying of their hunger, then to be queftioned about a matter which it is likely they are ignorant of, wherefore me thinks it were better firft to give them what they want, and afterwards to talk with them about that which concerns them leffe*; For thefe words the Mother reprehending her, *Go to*, faid fhe, *you will ever be prating when you fhould not, but furely I fhall make you leave this cuftome*; whereunto the daughter fmiling, replied, *That you fhall when you pleafe, but in the mean time I befeech you, let thefe poor ftrangers have fomething to eat*: For all this the old man would not give over queftioning us, for he demanded of us who we were, of what country, and whither we were going, be-fides many other fuch like things? To which we anfwered as occafion required, and re-counted unto him, how, when, and in what place we had fuffered fhipwrack, as alfo how many of our company were drowned, and that thus wandring we travelled up and down not knowing whither to addreffe our felves.   This anfwer rendred the old man pen-five for a while, until at length turning him to his fon, Well now, faid he unto him, **what**
                                                                                                                    thinkeft

thin'cest thou of that which thou hast heard these strangers deliver ? It were good for thee to inprint it well in thy memory, to the end it may teach thee to know God better, and give him thanks for that he hath given thee a Father, who to exempt thee from the labours and necessities of this life hath parted with three of the goodliest things in this Country, whereof the least is worth above a hundred thousand *Taeis*, and bestowed them on thee, but thou art of a humour more inclined to hunt a Hare, then to retain this which I now tell thee ; The young Gentleman made no reply, but smiling looked upon his Sisters. Then the old man caused meat to be brought unto us before him, and commanded us to fall to it, as we most willingly did, whereat he took great pleasure, in regard his stomack was quite gone with his sickness, but his young daughters much more, who with their brother did nothing but laugh to see us feed our selves with our hands, for that is contrary to the custome which is observed throughout the whole Empire of *China*, where the Inhabitants at their meat carry it to their mouthes with two little sticks made like a pair of Cizers ; After we had given God thanks, the old man that had well observed us, lifting up his hands to heaven, with tears in his eyes, *Lord*, said he, *that livest raigning in the tranquility of thy high Wisdome, I laud thee in all humility for that thou permittest men that are strangers, come from the farthest end of the world, and without the knowledge of thy doctrine, to render thee thanks, and give thee praise according to their weak capacity, which makes me beleeve that thou wilt accept of them with as good a will, as if it were some great offering of melodious musick agreeable to thine eares.* Then he caused three pieces of linnen cloth, and four *Taeis* of Silver to be given us, willing us withall to passe that night in his house, because it was somewhat too late for us to proceed on our journey ; This offer we most gladly accepted, and with complements, after the manner of the Country we testified our thankfulness to him, wherewith himself, his wife, and his son rested very well satisfied.

CHAP. XXVII.
Our arrival at the Town of Taypor, *where we were made Prisoners, and so sent to the Citie of* Nanquin.

THe next morning by break of day parting from that place, we went to a Village called *Finginilau*, which was some four leagues from the old Gentlemans house, where we remained three dayes, and then continuing travelling from one place to another, and from Village to Village, ever declining the great Towns, for fear lest the Justice of the country should call us in question in regard we were strangers; in this manner we spent almost two months without receiving the least damage from any body. Now there is no doubt but we might easily have got to the Citie of *Nanquin* in that time if we had had a guide, but for want of knowing the way we wandred we knew not whither, suffering much, and running many hazards ; At length we arrived at a Village, named *Chancer*, at such a time as they were solemnizing a sumptuous Funeral of a very rich woman, that had disinherited her kindred, and left her estate to the Pagod of this Village, where she was buried, as we understood by the Inhabitants ; We were invited then to this Funeral, as other poor people were, and according to the custome of the Country we did eat on the grave of the deceased : At the end of three dayes that we stayed there, which was the time the funeral lasted, we had six *Taeis* given us for an Alms, conditionally that in all our Oraisons we should pray unto God for the soul of the departed. Being gone from this place we continued on our journey to another Village, called *Guinapalir*, from whence we were almost two months travelling from country to country, untill at last our ill fortune brought us to a Town, named *Taypor*, where by chance there was at that time a *Chumbrin*, that is to say, one of those Super-intendents of Justice, that every three years are sent throughout the Provinces for to make report unto the King of all that passeth there : This naughty man seeing us go begging from door to door called to us from a window where he was, and would know of us who we were, and of what Nation, as also what obliged us to run up and down the World in that manner? Having asked us these questions in the presence of three Registers, and of many other persons, that were gathered together to behold us, we answered him, that we were strangers, Natives of the Kingdom of *Siam*, who being cast away by a storm at Sea went thus travelling and begging our living, to the end we might sustain our selves with the charity of good people, untill such time as we could arrive at *Nanquin,*

S.1

quin, whither we were going with an intent to imbarque our selves there in some of the Merchants *Lanteaas* for *Canton*, where the shipping of our Nation lay. This answer we made unto the *Chumbim*, who questionless had been well enough contented with it, and would have let us go, had it been for one of his Clarks, for he told them that we were idle vagabonds, that spent our time in begging from door to door, and abusing the alms that were given us, and therefore he was at no hand to let us go free, for fear of incurring the punishment, ordained for such as offend in that sort, as is set forth in the seventh of the twelve books of the Statutes of the Realm; wherefore as his faithful servant he counselled him to lay us in good and sure hold, that we might be forth-coming to answer the Law: The *Chumbim* presently followed his Clarks advice, and carried himself toward us with as much barbarous cruelty, as could be expected from a Pagan, such as he was, that lived without God or religion; To which effect after he had heard a number of false witnesses, who charged us with many foul crimes, whereof we never so much as dreamt, he caused us to be put into a deep dungeon, with irons on our hands and feet, and great iron collars about our necks; In this miserable place we endured such hunger, and were so fearfully whipped, that we were in perpetual pain for six and twenty days together, at the end whereof we were by the sentence of the same *Chumbim* sent to the Parliament of the *Cheam* of *Nanquin*, because the Jurisdiction of this extended not to the condemnation of any prisoner to death.

§.2   We remained six and twenty days in that cruel prison, whereof I spake before, and I vow we thought we had been six and twenty thousand years there, in regard of the great misery we suffered in it, which was such, as one of our companions called *Joano Roderiguez Bravo*, died in our arms, being eaten up with lice, we being no way able to help him, and it was almost a miracle that the rest of us escaped alive from that filthy vermine; At length, one morning, when we thought of nothing less, loden with irons as we were, and so weak that we could hardly speak, we were drawn out of that prison, and then being chained one to another, we were imbarqued with many others, to the number of thirty or forty, that having been convicted for sundry hainous crimes, were also sent to the Parliament of *Nanquin*, where, as I have already declared, is always residing a *Chaem* of Justice, which is like to the Sovereign Title of the Vice-roy of *China*: There is likewise a Parliament of some five and twenty *Gerozemos* and *Ferucuas*, which are as those we call Judges with us, and that determine all causes, as well civil as criminal: So as there is no appeal from their sentence, unless it be unto another Court, which hath power even over the King himself, whereunto if one appeals, it is as if he appealed to heaven: To understand this the better, you must know that although this Parliament, and others such like, which are in the principal Cities of the Realm, have an absolute power from the King, both over all criminal & civil causes, without any opposition or appeal whatsoever, yet there is another Court of Justice, which is called the Court of the Creator of all things, whereunto it is permitted to appeal in weighty and important matters: In this Court are ordinarily assisting four & twenty *Menigrepos*, which are certain religious men, very austere in their manner of living, (such as the *Capuchins* are amongst the Papists, & verily if they were Christians, one might hope for great matters from them in regard of their marvellous abstinence, & sincerity: There are none admitted into this rank of Judges under seventy years of age, & are elected thereunto by the suffrages of their chiefest Prelates, most incorruptible men, & so just in all the causes, whereof there are appeals before them, as it is not possible to meet with more upright, for were it against the King himself, and against all the powers that may be imagined in the world, no consideration, how great soever, is able to make them swerve never so little from that they think to be justice. Having been imbarqued in the manner I spake of, the same day at night we went & lay at a great tower, called *Potinleu*, in one of the prisons whereof were mained nine days, by reason of the much rain that fell then upon the conjunction of the New-moon: There we happened to meet with a *Russian* prisoner, that received us very charitably, of whom demanding in the *Chinese* tongue, which he understood as well as we, what countrey-man he was, and what fortune had brought him thither; he told us, that he was of *Moscovy*, born in a town, named *Hiquegens*, and that some five years past, being accused for the death of a man, he had been condemned to a perpetual prison, but as a stranger he appealed from that sentence to the tribunal of the *Aytau* of *Batampina*, in the City of *Pequin*, who was the highest of the two and thirty Admirals, established in this Empire, that is, for every Kingdom one: He added further, that this Admiral by a particular Jurisdiction, had absolute power over all strangers, whereupon he hoped to find some relief from him, intending to go and die a Christian among the Christians, if he might have the

good

good hap to be set at liberty. After we had passed those nine days in this prison, being reinbarqued, we sayled up a great river seven days together, at the end whereof we arrived at *Nanquin*. As this City is the second of all the Empire, so is it also the Capital of the three Kingdoms of *Liampoo*, *Fanius*, and *Sambor*: Here we lay six weeks in prison, and suffered so much pain and misery, as reduced to the last extreamities, we died incensibly for want of succour, not able to do any thing, but look up to heaven with a pitiful eye; for it was our ill fortune to have all that we had stoln from us the first night we came thither: This prison was so great, that there were four thousand prisoners in it at that time, as we were credibly informed, so that one should hardly sit down in any place without being robbed, and filled full of lice: having layn there a month and an half, as I said, the Anchacy, who was one of the Judges before whom our cause was to be pleaded, pronounced our sentence at the Suit of the Atturny General, the tenor whereof was, That having seen and considered our process, which the *Chumbin* of *Taypor* had sent him, it appeared by the accusations laid to our charge, that we were very hainous malefactors, & though we denied many things, yet in justice no credit was to be given unto us, & therefore that we were to be publickly whipped, for to teach us to live better in time to come, and that withall our two thumbs should be cut off, wherewith it was evident by manifest suspicions, that we used to commit robberies, and other vile crimes; & furthermore, that for the remainder of the punishment we deserved, he referred us to the *Aytau* of *Bataupina*, unto whom it appertained to take cognisance of such causes, in regard of the Jurisdiction that he had of life and death. This Sentence was pronounced in the prison, where it had been better for us to have suffered death, then the stripes that we received, for all the ground round about us ran with blood upon our whiping, so that it was almost a miracle, that of the eleven which we were, nine escaped alive, for two of our company died three days after, besides one of our servants.

After we had been whipped in that manner, I have declared, we were carried into a great Chamber, that was in the prison, where were a number of sick, and diseased persons, lying upon beds, and other ways; There we had presently our stripes washed, and things applyed unto them, whereby we were somewhat eased of our pain, and that by men, much like unto the fraternity of mercy among the Papists, which only out of charity, and for the honour of God, do tend those that are sick, and liberally furnish them with all things necessary. Hereafter some eleven or twelve days, we began to be pretily recovered, and as we were lamenting our ill fortune, for being so rigorously condemned to lose our thumbs, it pleased God one morning, when as we little dreamt of it, that we espied two men come into the chamber, of a good aspect, clothed in long gowns of violet coloured satin, & carrying white rods in their hands; As soon as they arrived, all the sick persons in the Chamber cried out, *Blessed be the Ministers of the Works of God:* whereunto they answered, holding up their rods, *May it please God to give you patience in your adversity:* whereupon having distributed clothes and money to those that were next to them, they came unto us, and after they had saluted us very courteously, with demonstration of being moved at our tears, they asked us who we were, and of what countrey, as also why we were imprisoned there: whereunto we answered weeping, that we were strangers, natives of the Kingdom of *Siam*, and of a country called *Malaca*, that being Merchants and well to live, we had imbarqued our selves with our goods, and being bound for *Liampoo*, we had been cast away just against the Isles of *Lamau*, having lost all that we had, and nothing left us but our miserable bodies in the case they now saw us; moreover we added, that being thus evil intreated by fortune, arriving at the City of *Taypor*, the *Chumbin* of Justice had caused us to be apprehended without any cause, laying to our charge, that we were thieves and vagabonds, who to avoid pains-taking went begging from door to door, entertaining our idle laziness with the alms that were given us unjustly, whereof the *Chumbin* having made informations at his pleasure, as being both Judg and party, he had laid us in irons in the prison, where for two and forty days space, we had indured incredible pain and hunger, and no man would hear us in our justifications, as well because we had not wherewithall to give presents for to maintain our right, as for that we wanted the language of the Country. In conclusion, we told them, how in the mean time, without any cognisance of the cause, we had been condemned to be whipped, as also to have our thumbs cut off, like thieves, so that we had already suffered the first punishment, with so much rigour and cruelty, that the marks thereof remained but two visibly upon our wretched bodies, and therefore we conjured them by the charge they had to serve God in assisting the afflicted, that they would not abandon us in this need, the rather for that our extream poverty rendred as odious to all the world, and ex-

§. 3.

P

posed

posed us to the induring of all affronts. These two men having heard us attentively, remained very pensive and amazed at our speech; at length lifting up their eyes, all bathed with tears, to heaven, and kneeling down on the ground, *O almighty Lord,* said they, *that governest in the highest places, and whose patience is incomprehensible, be thou evermore blessed, for that thou art pleased to harken unto the complaints of necessitous and miserable men, to the end that the great offences committed against thy divine goodness by the Ministers of Justice may not rest unpunished, as we hope that by thy holy Law they will be chastised at one time or other.* Whereupon they informed themselves more amply by those who were about us, of what we had told them, and presently sending for the Register, in whose hands our sentence was, they straitly commanded him, that upon pain of grievous punishment he should forthwith bring them all the proceedings which had been used against us, as instantly he did; now the two Officers, seeing there was no remedy for the whipping that we had suffered, presented a Petition in our behalf unto the *Chaem,* whereunto this Answer was returned by the Court; *Mercy hath no place, where Justice looseth her name, in regard whereof your request cannot be granted.* This Answer was subscribed by the *Chaem,* and eight *Conchacis,* that are like criminal Judges. This hard proceeding much astonished these two Proctors for the poor, so named from their office, wherefore carried with an extream desire to draw us out of this misery, they presently preferred another Petition to the Soveraign Court of Justice, of which I spake in the precedent Chapter, where the *Menigrepos* and *Talegrepos* were Judges, an Assembly which in their language is called, *The breath of the Creator of all things.* In this Petition, as sinners, confessing all that we were accused of, we had recourse to mercy, which sorted well for us; for as soon as the Petition was presented unto them, they read the Processe quite through, and finding that our right was overborn for want of succour, they instantly dispatched away two of their Court, who with an expresse Mandate under their hands and Seals, went and prohibited the *Chaems* Court from intermedling with this cause, which they commanded away before them. In obedience to this Prohibition the *Chaems* Court made this Decree, *We, that are assembled in this Court of Justice of the Lyon crowned in the throne of the world, having perused the Petition presented to the four and twenty Judges of the austere life, do consent, that those nine strangers be sent by way of appeal to the Court of the Aytau of Aytaus in the Citie of Pequin, to the end that in mercy the sentence pronounced against them may be favourably moderated: Given the seventh day of the fourth Moon, in the three and twentieth year of the raign of the Son of the Sun.* This Decree, being signed by the *Chaem,* and the eight *Conchacis,* was presently brought us by the two Proctors for the poor, upon the Receit whereof we told them, that we could but pray unto God to reward them for the good they had done us for his sake; whereunto beholding us with an eye of pitie, they answered, *May his Celestial goodness direct you in the knowledge of his Works, that thereby you may with patience gather the fruit of your labours, as they which fear to offend his holy Name.*

S.4.　　After we had past all the adversities and miseries, whereof I have spoken before, we were imbarqued in the company of some other thirty or forty Prisoners, that were sent, as we were, from this Court of Justice to that other Soveraign one by way of appeal, there to be either acquitted or condemned, according to the crimes they had committed, and the punishment they had deserved. Now a day before our departure, being imbarqued in a *Lanteaa,* and chained three and three together, the two Proctors for the poor came to us, and first of all furnishing us with all things needful, as clothes, and Victuals, they asked us whether we wanted any thing else for our Voyage? Whereunto we answered, that all we could desire of them was, that they would be pleased to convert that further good they intended to us into a Letter of Recommendation unto the Officers of that holy Fraternity of the Citie of *Pequin,* thereby to oblige them to maintain the right of our cause, in regard (as they very well knew) they should otherwise be sure to be utterly abandoned of every one, by reason they were strangers and altogether unknown. The Proctors hearing us speak in this manner: *Say not so,* replyed they, *for though your ignorance discharges you before God, yet have you committed a great sin, because the more you are abased in the world through poverty, the more shall you be exalted before the eyes of his divine Majesty, if you patiently bear your crosses, whereunto the flesh indeed doth always oppose it self, being evermore rebellious against the Spirit, but as a Bird cannot fly without her wings, no more can the soul meditate without works: As for the Letter you require of us, we will give it you most willingly, knowing it will*

be

be very neceſſary for you, to the end that the favour of good people be not wanting to you in your need. This ſaid they gave us a ſack ful of Rice, together with four *Taeis* in ſilver, and a Coverlet to lay upon us ; Then having very much recommended us unto the *Chifuu,* who was the Officer of juſtice that conducted us, they took their leaves of us in moſt courteous manner ; The next morning as ſoon as it was day they ſent us the Letter, ſealed with three Seals in green Wax, the Contents whereof were theſe ; *Ye ſervants of that high Lord, the reſplendent mirrour of an uncreated light, before whom our merits are nothing in compariſon of his, we the leaſt ſervants of that holy houſe of Tauhinarel, that was founded in favour of the fifth priſon of Nanquin, with true words of reſpect, which we owe unto you, we give your moſt humble perſons to underſtand, that theſe nine ſtrangers, the bearers of this Letter, are men of a far country, whoſe bodies and goods have been ſo cruelly intreated by the furie of the ſea, that according to their report, of ninety and five that they were, they only have eſcaped ſhipwrack, being caſt by the tempeſt on the ſhore of the Iſles of Tautaa, upon the coaſt of the Bay of Sumbor : In which pitious and lamentable caſe, as we have ſeen them with our own eyes, begging their living from place to place of ſuch, as charitie obliged to give them ſomething after the manner of good folkes, it was their ill fortune without all reaſon or juſtice to be apprehended by the Choumbin of Taypor, and ſent to this fifth priſon of Faniau, where they were condemned to be whipped, which was immediatly executed upon them by the Miniſters of the diſpleaſed arm, as by their Proceſs better appeareth : But afterwards, when as through too much crueltie their thumbs were to be cut off, they with tears beſought us, for that Soveraign Lords ſake, in whoſe ſervice we are imployed, to be aſſiſting unto them, which preſently undertaken by us we preferred a Petition in their behalf, whereunto this Anſwer was made by the Court of the crowned Lyon, That mercy had no place where juſtice loſt her name ; whereupon provoked by a true zeal to Gods honour, we addreſſed our ſelves to the Court of thoſe four and twenty of the auſtere life, who carried by a bleſſed devotion inſtantly aſſembled in the Holy Houſe of the remedy for the poor, and of an extream deſire they had to ſuccour theſe miſerable creatures, they interdicted that great Court from proceeding any further againſt them, and accordingly the ſucceſs was agreeable to the mercy of ſo great a God, for theſe laſt Judges revoking the others firſt Sentence, ſent the cauſe by way of Appeal to your Citie of Pequin with amendment of the ſecond puniſhment, as you may ſee more at large by the proceedings ; In regard whereof, moſt reverend and humble Brethren, We beſeech you all in the Name of God to be favourable unto them, and to aſſiſt them with whatſoever you ſhall thinke neceſſary for them, that they may not be oppreſſed in thier right which is a very great ſin, and an eternal infamy to us, who again intreat you to ſupply them with your Alms, and beſtow on them means to cover their nakedneſs, to the end they may not periſh for want of help, which if you do there is no doubt but that ſo pious a work will be moſt acceptable to that Lord above, to whom the poor of the earth do continually pray, and are heard in the Higheſt of Heavens, as we hold for an Article of Faith ; On which earth may it pleaſe that divine Majeſtie, for whoſe ſake we do this, to preſerve us till death, and to render us worthy of his preſence in the houſe of the Sun, where he is ſeated with all his.* Written in the Chamber of the zeal of Gods honour, the ninth day of the ſeventh Moon, and the three and twentieth year of the Raign of the Lyon crowned in the Throne of the World.

CHAP. XXVIII.

The Marvels of the Citie of Nanquin, our departure from thence towards Pequin, and that which hapned unto us, till we arrived at the Town of Sempitay.

THis Letter being brought to us very early the next morning, we departed in the manner before declared, and continued our voyage till Sun-ſet, when as we anchored at a little Village, named *Minbacutem,* where the *Chifuu,* that conducted us, was born, and where his Wife and Children were at that time, which was the occaſion that he remained there three dayes, at the end whereof he imbarqued himſelf with his family, and ſo we paſſed on in the company of divers other Veſſels, that went upon this River unto divers parts of this Empire : Now though we were all tyed together to the bank of the *Lanteaa,* where we rowed, yet did we not for all that loſe the view of many Towns and Villages that were ſcituated along this River, whereof I hold it not amiſſe to make ſome deſcriptions ; To which effect, I will begin with the Citie of *Nanquin* from whence we laſt parted ; This

City is under the North in nine and thirty degrees, and three quarters, scituated upon the river of *Batampina*, which signifies, *The flower of fish*. This river, as we were told then, and as I have seen since, comes from *Tartaria*, out of a lake, called *Faniftor*, nine leagues from the City of *Lancama*, where *Tamberlan*, King of the *Tartarians* usually kept his Court ; Out of the same lake, which is eight and twenty leagues long, twelve broad, and of a mighty depth, the greatest rivers, that ever I saw, take their source ; The first is the same *Batampina*, that passing through the midst of this Empire of *China* three hundred and threescore leagues in length, disimboques into the sea at the bay of *Nanquin* in thirty six degrees ; The second, named *Lechuna*, runs with great swiftness all along by the mountains of *Pancruum*, which separate the Country of *Cauchim*, and the State of *Catebenan*, in the height of sixteen degrees ; The third is called *Tauquida*, signifying the *Mother of Waters*, that going North-west, traverseth the Kingdom of *Nacataas*, a Country where *China* was anciently seated, as I will declare hereafter, and enters into the sea in the Empire of *Sornau*, vulgarly stiled *Siam*, by the mouth of *Cuy*, one hundred and thirty leagues below *Patana* ; The fourth, named *Batobasoy*, descends out of the Province of *Sansim*, which is the very same that was quite overwhelmed by the sea in the year 1556. as I purpose to shew else-where, and renders it self into the sea at the mouth of *Cofmim*, in the Kingdom of *Pegu* ; The fifth and last, called *Leyfacotay*, crosseth the Country by *East* as far as to the *Archipelago* of *Xinxipou*, that borders upon *Mocovye*, and fals, as is thought, into a sea that is not navigable, by reason the clymate there is in the height of seventy degrees. Now to return to my discourse, the City of *Nanquin*, as I said before, is seated by this river of *Batampina*, upon a reasonable high hill, so as it commands all the plains about it ; The climate thereof is somewhat cold, but very healthy, and it is eight leagues about, which way soever it is considered, three leagues broad, and one long ; The houses in it are not above two stories high, and all built of wood, only those of the *Mandarins* are made of hewed stone, and also invironed with walls and ditches, over which are stone bridges, whereon they passe to the gates, that have rich and costly arches, with divers sorts of inventions upon the towers, all which put together, make a pleasing object to the eye, and represent a certain kind of I know not what Majesty. The houses of the *Chaems, Anchacys, Aytaus, Tutons,* and *Chumbims,* which are all Governours of Provinces or Kingdoms, have stately towers, six or seven stories high, and guilt all over, wherein they have their magazines for arms, their Wardrobes, their treasuries, and a world of rich houshold stuff, as also many other things of great value, together with an infinite of delicate and most fine porcelain, which amongst them is prised and esteemed as much as precious stone, for this sort of porcelain never goes out of the Kingdom, it being expresly forbidden by the laws of the Country, to be sold, upon pain of death to any stranger, unlesse to the *Xatamaas,* that is, the *Sophyes* of the *Persians,* who by a particular permission buy of it at a very dear rate. The *Chineses* assured us, that in this City there are eight hundred thousand fires, fourscore thousand *Mandarins* houses, threescore and two great market places, an hundred and thirty butchers shambles, each of them containing fourscore shops, and eight thousand streets, whereof six hundred that are fairer and larger then the rest, are compassed about with ballisters of copper ; we were further assured, that there are likewise two thousand and three hundred *Pagodes,* a thousand of which were *Monestaries* of religious persons, professed in their accursed Sect, whose buildings were exceeding rich and sumptuous, with very high steeples, wherein there were between sixty and seventy such mighty huge bels, that it was a dreadful thing to here them rung ; There are moreover in this City thirty great strong prisons, each whereof hath three or four thousand prisoners ; and a charitable Hospital, expresly established to supply the necessities of the poor, with Proctors ordained for their defence, both in civil and criminal causes, as is before related ; At the entrance into every principal street, there are arches and great gates, which for each mans security, are shut every night, and in most of the streets are goodly fountains whose water is excellent to drink ; Besides, at every full and new moon, open fayrs are kept in several places, whither Merchants resort from all parts, and where there is such abundance of all kind of victual, as cannot well be exprest, especially of flesh and fruit ; It is not possible to deliver the great store of fish that is taken in this river, chiefly Soles and Mullets, which are all sold alive, besides a world of sea-fish, both fresh, salted, and dried ; we were told by certain *Chineses,* that in this City there are ten thousand trades for the working of silks, which from thence are sent all over the Kingdom ; The City it self is invironed with a very strong wall, made of fair hewed stone ; The gates of it are an hundred and thirty, at each of which there is a Porter, and

two

two Halberdiers, who are bound to give an account every day of all that paſſes in and out; There are alſo twelve Forts or Cittadels, like unto ours, with bulwarks and very high towers, but without any ordinance at all; The ſame *Chineſes* alſo affirmed unto us, that the City yeilded the King daily two thouſand *Taeis* of ſilver, which amount to three thouſand duckats, as I have delivered heretofore; I will not ſpeak of the Pallace royal, becauſe I ſaw it but on the outſide, howbeit the *Chineſes* tell ſuch wonders of it, as would amaze a man, for it is my intent to relate nothing ſave what we beheld here with our own eyes, and that was ſo much as I am afraid to write it, not that it would ſeem ſtrange to thoſe that have ſeen and read the marvels of the Kingdom of *China*, but becauſe I doubt, that they, which would compare thoſe wondrous things that are in the countrys, they have not ſeen with that little they have ſeen in their own will make ſome queſtion of it, or it may be give no credit at all to theſe truth, becauſe they are not conſormable to their underſtanding, and ſmall experience.

Continuing our courſe up this river, the firſt two days we ſaw not any remarkable town §.2. or place, but only a great number of Villages, and little hamlets of two or three hundred fires a piece, which by their buildings ſeemed to be houſes of fiſher men, and poor people, that live by the labour of their hands; For the reſt, all that was within view in the countrey, was great woods of Firr, Groves, Forreſts, and Orange trees, as alſo plains full of wheat, rice, beans, peaſe, millet, panick, barley, rye, flax, cotton wool, with great incloſures of gardens, and goodly houſes of pleaſure, belonging to the *Mandarins*, and Lords of the Kingdom: There was likewiſe all along the river ſuch an infinite number of cattel of all ſorts, as I can aſſure you there is not more in *Æthiopia*, nor in all the dominions of *Preſter John*; upon the top of the mountains many houſes of their Sects of *Gentiles* were to be ſeen, adorned with high Steeples guilt all over, the gliſtering whereof was ſuch, and ſo great, that to behold them a far off was an admirable ſight: The fourth day of our voyage we arrived at a town, called *Pocaſſer*, twice as big as *Cantano*, compaſſed about with ſtrong wals of hewed ſtone, and towers and bulwarks almoſt like ours, together with a key on the river ſide, twice as long as the ſhot of a falconet, and incloſed with two rows of iron grates, with very ſtrong gates, where the Junks and veſſels that arrived there were unladen; This place abounds with all kinds of merchandiſe, which from thence is tranſported over all the Kingdom, eſpecially with copper, ſugar, and allum, whereof there is very great ſtore; Here alſo in the middeſt of a carrefour, that is almoſt at the end of the town, ſtands a mighty ſtrong caſtle, having three bulwarks and five towers, in the higheſt of which the preſent Kings Father, as the *Chineſes* told us, kept a King of *Tartaria* nine years priſoner, at the end whereof he killed himſelf with poyſon, that his ſubjects ſent him, becauſe they would not be conſtrained to pay that ranſome, which the King of *China* demanded for his deliverance: In this town the *Chifuu* gave three of us leave to go up and down for to crave the alms of good people, accompanied with four *Hupes*, that are as Sergeants, or Bailiffs amongſt us, who led us, chained together, as we were, through ſix or ſeven ſtreets, where we got in alms to the value of above twenty duckats, as well in clothes, as mony, beſides fleſh, rice, meal, fruit, and other victuals, which was beſtowed on us, whereof we gave the one half to the *Hupes* that conducted us, it being the cuſtom ſo to do. Afterwards we were brought to a *Pagode*, whither the people flocked from all parts that day, in regard of a very ſolemn feaſt that was then celebrated there: This Temple, or *Pagode*, as we were told, had ſomtime been a Pallace royal, where the King then reigning was born, now becauſe the Queen his Mother died there in child-birth, ſhe commanded her ſelf to be buried in the very ſame chamber where ſhe was brought to bed, wherefore to honour her death the better, this Temple was dedicated to the invocation of *Tauhinaret*, which is one of the principal Sects of the *Pagans* in the Kingdom of *China*, as I will more amply declare, when as I ſhall ſpeak of the *Labyrinth* of the two and thirty laws that are in it; All the buildings of this Temple, together with all the gardens, and walks, that belong to it, are ſuſpended in the ayr upon three hundred and threeſcore pillars, every one of the which is of one intire ſtone of a very great bigneſs; Theſe three hundred and threeſcore pillars, are called by the names of three hundred and threeſcore days of the year, and in each of them is a particular feaſt kept there with many alms, gifts, and bloody ſacrifices, accompanied with muſick, dancing, and other ſports; Under this *Pagode*, namely between thoſe pillars, are eight very fair ſtreets, incloſed on every ſide with grates of copper, and gates for the paſſage of pilgrims, and others, that run continually to this feaſt, as it were to a Jubilee; The Chamber above, where the Queen lay, was made in the form of a Chappel, but round, and from the top to the bottom all garniſhed

nished with silver, the workmanship whereof was of greater cost then the matter it self; In the midst of it stood a kind of Tribunal, framed round, like the Chamber, some fifteen steps high, compassed about with six graves of silver, on the top whereof was a great bowl, and upon that a Lion of silver, that with his head supported a shrine of gold, three hand-bredths square, wherein they said, the bones of the Queen were, which these blinded ignorants reverenced as a great relique; Below this Tribunal in equal proportion were four bars of silver, that traversed the Chamber, whereon hung three and forty lamps of the same mettal, in memory of the three and forty years that this Queen lived, and seven lamps of gold in commamoration of seven sons that she had; moreover at the entry into the Chappel, just against the door, were eight other bars of iron, whereon also hung a very great number of silver lamps, which the *Chineses* told us were offered by some of the Wives of the *Chaems, Aytaos, Tutoens,* and *Anchacys,* who were assistant at the death of the Queen, so that in aknowledgment of that honour they sent those lamps thither afterwards; without the gates of the Temple, and round about six ballisters of copper that invironed it, were a great many Statues of Giants, fifteen foot high, cast in brass, all well proportioned with halberts or clubs in their hands, and some of them with battle-axes on their shoulders, which made so brave and majestical a shew, as one could never be satisfied enough with looking on them; Amongst these Statues, which were in number twelve hundred, as the *Chineses* affirmed, there were four and twenty very great Serpents also of brass, and under every one of them a woman seated, with a sword in her hand, and a silver crown on her head; It was said, that those four and twenty women carried the Titles of Queens, because they sacrificed themselves to the death of this Queen, to the end their souls might serve hers in the other life, as in this their bodies had served her body, a matter which the *Chineses,* that draw their extraction from these women, hold for a very great honour, insomuch as they inrich the crests of their coats of arms with it; round about this row of Giants was another of triumphant arches, guilt all over, whereon a number of silver bels hung by chains of the same mettal, which moved with the air kept such a continual ringing, as one could hardly hear one another for the noise they made; Without these arches there were likewise at the same distance two rows of copper grates, that inclosed all this huge work, and among them certain pillars of the same mettal, which supported Lions rampant, mounted upon bowls, being the arms of the Kings of *China,* as I have related elsewhere. At each corner of the Carrefour was a monster of brass, of so strange and unmeasurable an heighth, and so deformed to behold, as it is not possible almost for a man to imagine, so that I think it best not to speak of them, the rather for that I confess I am not able in words to express the form wherein I saw their prodigies; Howbeit as it is reasonable to conceal these things without giving some knowledg of them, I will say, as much as my weak understanding is able to deliver. One of these Monsters which is on the right hand, as one comes into the Carrefour, whom the *Chineses* call, the Serjeant *Gluttom* of the hollow or profound house of smoak, and that by their histories is held to be *Lucifer,* is represented under the figure of a Serpent of an excessive heighth, with most hideous and deformed adders coming out of his stomack, covered all over with green and black scares, and a number of prickles on their backs above a span long, like unto Porcupins quils; each of these Adders had a woman between his jaws, with her hair all dishevelled, and standing an end, as one affrighted; The monster carried also in his mouth, which was unmeasurable great, a Vizard that was above thirty foot long, and as big as a tun, with his nostrils & chaps so full of blood, that all the rest of his body was besmeared with it; this Vizard held a great Eliphant between his paws, and seemed to gripe him so hard, as his very guts came out of his throat, and all this was done so proportionably, and to the life, that it made a man tremble to behold such a deformed figure, and which was scarce possible for one to imagine: His tail might be some twenty fathom long, was entortilled about such another Monster, that was the second of the four, whereof I spake, in the figure of a man, being an hundred foot high, and by the *Chineses* called *Turcamparoo,* who they say was the son of that Serpent; besides that he was very ugly, he stood with both his hands in his mouth, that was as big as a great gate, with a row of horrible teeth, and a foul black tongue, hanging out two fathom long, most dreadfull to behold: As for the other two Monsters, one was in the form of a woman, named by the *Chineses, Magdelgau,* seventeen fathom high, and six thick; This same about the girdlesteed before had a face made proportionable to her body, above two fathom broad, and she breathed out of her mouth and nostrils great flakes, not of artificial, but true fire, which proceeded, as they told us, from

her

her head, where fire was continually kept, that in like manner came out of the said face below. By this Figure these Idolaters would demonstrate that she was the Queen of the fiery sphear, which according to their belief is to burn the earth at the end of the World. The fourth Monster was a man, set stooping, which with great swoln cheeks, as big as the main sail of a Ship, seemed to blow extreamly; this Monster was also of an unmeasurable height, and of such an hideous and gastly aspect, that a man could hardly endure the sight of it; the *Chineses* called it *Vzinguenahon*, and said, that it was he which raised Tempests upon the Sea, and demolished Buildings, in regard whereof the people offred many things unto him, to the end he should do them no harm, and many presented him with a piece of money yearly, that he might not drown their Junks, nor do any of theirs hurt that went by Sea; I will omit many other abuses which their blindness makes them beleeve, and which they hold to be so true, as there is not one of them but would endure a thousand deaths for the maintenance thereof.

The next day being gone from the Town of *Pocasser* we arrived at another fair and great §.3. Town, called *Xinligau*; there we saw many Buildings inclosed with walls of Brick, and deep ditches about them, and at one end of the Town two Castles, very well fortified with Towers and Bulwarks after our fashion; at the gates were draw Bridges, suspended in the air with great Iron chains, and in the midst of them a Tower five Stories high, very curiously painted with several Pictures; the *Chineses* assured us, that in those two Castles there was as much Treasure, as amounted to fifteen thousand pieces of silver, which was the revenue of all this *Archipelage*, and laid up in this place by the Kings Grandfather now raigning, in Memorial of a Son of his that was born here, and named *Leuquinau*, that is to say, *The joy of all*; those of the Country repute him for a Saint, because he ended his dayes in Religion, where also he was buried in a Temple, dedicated to *Quiay Varatel*, the God of all the Fishes of the Sea, of whom these miserable Ignorants recount a world of Fooleries, as also the Laws he invented, and the precepts which he left them, being able to astonish a man, as I will more amply declare when time shall serve. In this Town and in another five leagues higher the most part of the Silks of this Kingdome are dyed, because they hold that the waters of these places make the colours far more lively then those of any other part, and these Dyers, which are said to be thirteen thousand, pay unto the King yearly three hundred thousand *Taeis*. Continuing our course up the River the day after about evening we arrived at certain great plains, where were great store of Cattle, as Horses, Mares, Colts, and Cows, guarded by men on Horsback, that make sale of them to Butchers, who afterwards retail them indifferently as any other flesh: Having past these plains containing some ten or eleven Leagues, we came to a Town called *Junquileu*, walled with Brick, but without Battlements, Bulwarks, or Towers, as others had, whereof I have spoken before; at the end of the Suburbs of this Town we saw divers houses built in the water upon great Piles, in the form of Magazines; Before the gate of a little street stood a Tombe made of stone, invironed with an Iron grate, painted red and green, and over it a steeple framed of pieces of very fine Pourcelain, sustained by four pillars of curious stone; upon the top of the Tombe were five Globes, and two others that seemed to be of cast iron, and on the one side thereof were graven in Letters of gold, and in the *Chinese* language, words of this substance. *Here lyes* Trannocem Mudeliar, *Uncle to the King of* Malaca, *whom death took out of the World before he could be revenged of Captain* Alphonso Albuquerque, *the Lyon of the robberies of the Sea.* We were much amazed to behold this Inscription there, wherefore enquiring what it might mean, a *Chinese*, that seemed more honourable then the rest, told us; that about some fortie years before, this man which lay buried there, came thither as Embassador from a Prince, that stiled himself King of *Malaca*, to demand succour from the son of the Sun against men of a Country, that hath no name, which came by Sea from the end of the World, and had taken *Malaca* from him; this man recounted many other incredible things concerning this matter, whereof mention is made in a printed Book thereof, as also that this Embassador having continued three years at the Kings Court suing for this succour, just as it was granted him, and that preparations for it were a making, it was his ill fortune to be surprised one night at Supper with an Apoplexie, whereof he dyed at the end of nine dayes, so that extreamly afflicted to see himself carried away by a suddain death before he had accomplished his business, he expressed his earnest desire of revenge by the Inscription which he caused to be graven on his

Tombe,

9

tombe, that posterity might know wherefore he was come thither. Afterwards we departed from this place, and continued our voyage up the river, which thereabouts is not so large as towards the City of *Nanquin*, but the Country is here better peopled with Villages, Boroughs, and Gardens, then any other place, for every stones cast we met still with some *Pagode*, Mansion of pleasure, or Countrey house; Passing on about some two leagues further, we arrived at a place encompassed with great iron gates, in the midst whereof stood two mighty Statues of brass upright, sustained by pillars of cast mettal of the bigness of a bushel, and seven fathom high, the one of a man, and the other of a woman, both of them seventy four spans in heighth, having their hands in their mouths, their cheeks horribly blown out, and their eyes so staring, as they affrighted all that looked on them. That which represented a man, was called *Quiay Xingatalor*, and the other in the form of a woman, was named *Apancapatur*; Having demanded of the *Chineses* the explication of these figures, they told us that the male was he, which with those mighty swoln cheeks blew the fire of hell for to torment all those miserable wretches, that would not liberally bestow alms in this life; and for the other monster, that she was Porter of hell gate, where she would take notice of those that did her good in this world, and letting them fly away into a river of very cold water, call'd *Ochilenday*, would keep them hid there from being tormented by the Divels, as other damned were: Upon this Speech one of our company could not forbear laughing at such a ridiculous and diabolical foolery, which three of their Priests, or *Banzoes*, then present observing, they were so exceedingly offended therewith, as they perswaded the *Chifuu*, which conducted us, that if he did not chastise us in such manner, as those gods might be well contented with the punishment inflicted on us for our mockery of them, both the one and the other would assuredly torment his soul, and never suffer it to go out of hell; which threatning so mightily terrified this dog, the *Chifuu*, that without further delay, or hearing us speak, he caused us all to be bound hand and foot, and commanded each of us to have an hundred lashes given him with a double cord, which was immediately executed with so much rigour, as we were all in a gore bloud, whereby we were taught not to jeer afterwards at any thing we saw, or heard. At such time as we arrived here we found twelve *Bonzoes* upon the place, who with silver censors full of perfumes of aloes and beniamin, censed those two divelish Monsters, and chanted out aloud, *Help us, even as We serve thee*; whereunto divers other Priests answered in the name of the Idol with a great noise, *So I promise to do like a good Lord*: In this sort they went as it were in procession round about the place, singing with an ill tuned voice to the sound of a great many bels, that were in Steeples thereabouts; In the mean time there were others, that with Drums and Basins made such a dinne, as I may truly say, put them all together, was most horrible to hear.

CHAP. XXIX.

Our Arrival at Sempitay, *our encounter there with a Christian woman, together with the Original and Foundation of the Empire of China; and who they were that first peopled it.*

FRom this place we continued our voyage eleven days more up the river, which in those parts is so peopled with Cities, Towns, Villages, Boroughs, Forts and Castles, that commonly they are not a flight shot distant one from another, besides a world of houses of pleasure, and temples, where Steeples were all guilt, which made such a glorious shew, as we were much amazed at it; In this manner we arrived at a Town, named *Sempitay* where we abode five days, by reason the *Chifuus* wife, that conducted us, was not well: Here by his permission we landed, and chained together, as we were, we went up and down the streets craving of alms, which was very liberally given us by the Inhabitants, who wondering to see such men as we, demanded of us what kind of people we were, of what Kingdom, and how our countrey was called? Hereunto we answered conformably to that we had often said before, namely that we were natives of the Kingdom of of *Siam*, that going from *Liampoo* to *Nanquin*, we had lost all our goods by shipwrack, and that although they beheld us then in so poor a case, yet we had been forme ly very rich; whereupon a woman who was come thither amongst the rest to see us; It is very likely, said she, speaking to them about her, that what these poor strangers have related is most true, for daily experience doth shew how those that trade by sea, do oftentimes make it their grave, wherefore it is best and surest to travel upon the earth, and

to

to esteem of it, as of that, whereof it hath pleased God to frame us; saying, so she gave us two mizes, which amounts to about sixteen pence of our mony, advising us to make no more such long voyages, since our lives were so short: Hereupon she unbottoned one of the sleeves of a red Satin Gown she had on, and baring her left arm, she shewed us a crosse imprinted on it, like to the mark of a slave, saying, Do any of you know this signe, which amongst those, that follow the way of truth, is called a crosse? or have any of you ever heard it named? To this falling down on our knees, we answered, with tears in our eyes, that we know exceeding well; Then lifting up her hands, she cried out, *Our Father, which art in heaven, hallowed be thy Name,* speaking these words in the *Portugal* tongue, and because she could speak no more of our language, she very earnestly desired us in *Chinese* to tell her whether we were Christians; we replyed that we were, and for proof thereof, after we had kissed that arm, whereon the cross was, we repeated all the rest of the Lords prayer, which she had left unsaid, wherewith being assured that we were Christians indeed, she drew aside from the rest there present, and weeping said to us; Come along Christians of the other end of the world, with her that is your true Sister in the faith of Jesus Christ, or peradventure a kinswoman to one of you, by his side that begot me in this miserable exile, and so going to carry us to her house, the *Hupes* which guarded us, would not suffer her, saying, that if we would not continue our craving of alms, as the *Chifuu* had permitted us, they would return us back to the ship; but this they spake in regard of their own interest, for that they were to have the moitie of what was given us, as I have before declared, and accordingly they made as though they would have lead us thither again, which the woman perceiving, I understand your meaning, said she, and indeed it is but reason you make the best of your places, for thereby you live, so opening her purse, she gave them two *Taeis* in silver, wherewith they were very well satisfied; whereupon with the leave of the *Chifuu,* she carried us home to her house, and there kept us all the while we remained in that place, making exceeding much of us, and using us very charitably; Here she shewed us an Oratory, wherein she had a cross of wood guilt, as also candlesticks, and a lamp of silver: Furthermore she told us, that she was named, *Inez de Leyria,* and her Father *Tome Pirez,* who had been great Ambassadour from *Portugal* to the King of *China,* and that in regard of an insurrection with a *Portugal* Captain, made at *Canton,* the *Chineses* taking him for a Spye, & not for an Ambassodor, as he termed himself, clapped him and all his followers up in prison, where by order of Justice five of them were put to torture, receiving so many, and such cruel stripes on their bodies, as they died instantly, and that the rest were all banished into several parts, together with her father into this place, where he married with her mother, that had some means, and how he made her a Christian, living so seven and twenty years together, and converting many *Gentiles* to the faith of Christ, whereof there were above three hundred then abiding in that Town; which every *Sunday* assembled in her house to say the Catechisme: whereupon demanding of her what were their accustomed prayers, she answered, that she used no other but these, which on their knees, with their eyes and hands lift up to heaven, they pronounced in this manner, *O Lord Jesus Christ, as it is most true that thou art the very Son of God, conceived by the Holy Ghost in the womb of the Virgine Mary for the salvation of sinners, so thou wilt be pleased to forgive us our offences, that thereby we may become worthy to behold thy face in the glory of thy Kingdom, where thou art sitting at the right hand of the Almighty. Our Father which art in heaven, hallowed be thy Name. In the Name of the Father, the Son, and the Holy Ghost, Amen.* And so all of them kissing the Crofs, imbraced one another, and thereupon returned every one to his own home. Moreover she told us, that her Father had left her many other prayers, which the *Chineses* had stollen from her, so that she had none left but those before recited; whereunto we replyed, that those we had heard from her were very good, but before we went away we would leave her divers other good and wholsome prayers; do so then, answered she, for the respect you owe to so good a God, as yours is, and that hath done such things for you, for me, and for all in general: Then causing the cloth to be laid, she gave us a very good and plentiful dinner, and treated us in like sort every meal, during the five days we continued in her house, which as I said before, was permitted by the *Chifuu* in regard of a present that this good woman sent his wife, whom she earnestly intreated so to deal with her husband, as we might be well intreated, for that we were men of whom God had a particular care, as the *Chifuus* wife promised her to do with many thanks to her for the present she had received; In the mean space, during the five days we remained in her Houfe, we read the Catechifm feven times to the Chriftians, wherewithall they were very much edifyed, befide, *Chriftophoro Borkalho* made them a little Book in the *Chinefe* tongue, containing the *Pater Nofter*, the Creed, the Ten Commandments, and many other good Prayers. After thefe things we took our leaves of *Inez de Leyria*, and the Chriftians who gave us fifty *Taeis* in Silver, which ftood us fince in good ftead, as I fhall declare hereafter, and withall *Inez de Leyria* gave us fecretly fifty *Taeis* more, humbly defiring us to remember her in our Prayers to God.

§.2. After our departure from the Town of *Sempitay* we continued our courfe upon the River of *Batanpina*, unto a place, named *Lequinpau*, containing about eleven or twelve thoufand fires, and very well built, at leaft we judged fo by that we could difcern, as alfo inclofed with good Walls, and Curtains round about it : Not far from it was an exceeding long Houfe ; having within it thirty Furnaces on each fide, where a great quantity of Silver was melted, which was brought in carts from a Mountain, fome five leagues off, called *Tuxenguim* : The *Chinefes* affured us, that above a thoufand men wrought continually in that Mine to draw out the Silver, and that the King of *China* had in yearly Revenue out of it about five thoufand *Picos*; This place we left about Sun-fet, and the next day in the evening we arrived juft between two little Towns, that ftood oppofite one to another, the River onely between, the one named *Pacau*, and the other *Nacau*, which although they were little, yet were they fairly built, and well walled with great hewed ftone, having a number of Temples, which they call Pagods, all guilt over, and enriched with Steeples and Fanes of great price, very pleafing and agreeable to the eye. Now in regard of that they recounted unto us here of thefe two Towns, I hold it not amiffe to difcourfe it in this place, the rather for that I have heard it confirmed fince, and that thereby one may come to know the Original and Foundation of this Empire of *China*, whereof ancient Writers have fpoken little till this prefent. It is written in the firft Chronicle, of fourfcore which have been made of the Kings of *China*, the thirteenth Chapter, as I have heard it many times delivered, That fix hundred thirty and nine years, after the Deluge there was a Country called then *Guantipocau*, which as may be judged by the height of the Climate where it is fcituated, being in fixty two degrees to the Northward, abutts on the backfide of our *Germany* ; In this Country lived at that time a Prince, named *Turbano*, whofe ftate was not very great : It is faid of him, that being a youth he had three children by a Woman, called *Nancaa* whom he extreamly affected, although the Queen his Mother then a Widow, was exceedingly difpleafed at it. This King being much importuned by the principal Perfons of his Kingdom to marry, always excufed himfelf alledging fome Reafons for it, which they did not well allow of, but incited by his Mother, they preffed him fo far, that at length they perceived he had no intent to condefcend unto them, for indeed his minde was to legitimate the eldeft Son he had by *Nancaa*, and to refign his Kingdome unto him ; to which effect he not long after put himfelf into Religion in a Temple named *Gifon*, which feems to have been the Idol of a certain Sect that the *Romans* had in their time, and that is ftill at this prefent in the Kingdomes of *China*, *Jappon*, *Cauchenchina*, *Cambaya*, and *Siam*, whereof I have feen many Pagods in thofe Countries : But firft having declared his faid fon King, the Queen his Mother would by no means approve of it, faying, *That fince the King her Son would needs profefs himfelf into that Religion, and leave the Kingdom without a lawful Heir, fhe would labour to remedy fo great a diforder*, as indeed fhe did by inftantly marrying her felf, being fifty years of age, to a Prieft of hers, called *Silau*, that was but fix and twenty, whom fhe proclaimed King, notwithftanding all oppofition made to the contrary ; whereof *Turbano* being prefently advertifed, and knowing that his Mother had done it of purpofe to defeat his Son of the Crown, he got him forthwith out of his Religion for to repoffefs himfelf of it, and to that end ufed all the means and diligence he could, whereupon the Queen Mother, and *Silau*, fearing that which might follow thereof to both their deftructions, if he were not in time, and that fpeedily prevented, they fecretly affembled fome of their partakers, to the number of thirty Horfe, and fourfcore Foot, who going one night where *Turbano* was, flew him, and all his Company ; Howbeit *Nancaa* faved her felf, with her three Sons, and accompanied with certain of her Domeftical Servants, fhe imbarqued her felf in a fmall *Lanteaa*, and fled away down the River to a place fome feventy leagues from thence, where fhe landed with thofe few followers fhe had : There affifted with fome others that reforted unto her, fhe fortified her felf in a little Ifland, that was in the middeft of the River, and

and which fhe named *Pilaunere*, that fignifies, *The retrait of the poor*, with an intent there to end the reſt of her dayes; now having lived five years in that poor and miſerable eſtate, the Tyrant *Silau* whom the people hated, doubting leaſt the three young Princes coming to age, might expell him out of what he had iniuſtly uſurped upon them, or at leaſt wiſe diſturbe him with Wars, by reaſon of the right they pretended to the Kingdom, he ſent a Fleet of thirty *Jengas*, wherein as it is ſaid, were ſixteen hundred men, for to ſeek them out, and deſtroy them, whereof *Nancaa* receiving Intelligence fell to conſult what ſhe ſhould do, and at length reſolved by no means to attend theſe Forces, in regard her ſons were but Infants, her ſelf a weak Woman, her men few in number, and unprovided of all that was neceſſary to make any defence againſt ſo great a number of enemies, and ſo well furniſhed; whereupon taking a view of her people ſhe found they were but thirteen hundred in all, and of them onely five hundred men, the reſt being women and children, for all which company there were but three little *Lanteas*, and one *Jangaa*, in the whole River, and they not able to carry an hundred perſons, ſo that *Nancaa* ſeeing no means to tranſport them away, the Hiſtory ſaith, *ſhe aſſembled all her people, and declaring the fear ſhe was in, deſired them to adviſe her what ſhe ſhould do, but excuſing themſelves they ingeniouſly confeſſed they knew not what counſel to give her in that extremity*, whereupon according to their ancient cuſtome they reſolved to caſt lots, to the end that on whom the lot did fall to ſpeak, he ſhould freely deliver what God would be pleaſed to inſpire him with: For which purpoſe they took three dayes time, wherein with faſting, cryes, and tears, they would all with one voyce crave the favour and aſſiſtance of the Lord Almighty, in whoſe hands was all the hope of their deliverance; this advice being approved of all in general *Nancaa* made it to be proclaimed, that upon pain of death no perſon whatever ſhould eat above once during thoſe three dayes, to the end that by this abſtinence of the body, the Spirit might be carried with the greater attention towards God.

The three dayes abſtinence being expired, lots were caſt five times one after another, and all thoſe five times the lot fell ſtill on a little Boy of ſeven years of age, named as the Tyrant was *Silau*, whereat they were all exceedingly amazed, in regard that in the whole Troop there was not another of this ſame name: After that they had made their Sacrifices with all the accuſtomed Geremonies of Muſick, Perfumes, and ſweet Odours, to render thanks unto God, they commanded the little Boy to lift up his hands unto Heaven, and then to ſay what he thought was neceſſary for the remedying of ſo great an affliction, as that wherein they were; whereupon the little Boy *Silau* beholding *Nancaa*, the Hiſtory affirms he ſaid theſe words: *O feeble and wretched woman, now that ſorrow and affliction makes thee more troubled and perplexed then ever thou art, in regard of the ſmall relief that humane underſtanding doth repreſent unto thee, ſubmit thy ſelf with humble ſighs to the omnipotent hand of the Lord; Eſloign then, or at leaſt wiſe labour to eſloign thy mind from the vanities of the earth, lifting up thine eyes with Faith and Hope, and thou ſhalt ſee what the prayers of an innocent, afflicted and purſued before the juſtice of him that hath created thee, can do; For as ſoon as in all humility thou haſt declared the weakneſs of thy power unto the Almighty, victory will incontinently be given thee from above over the Tyrant* Silau; *wherefore I command thee in his Name to imbarque thy ſelf, thy children, and all thy followers in thine enemies veſſels, wherein amidſt the confuſed murmur of the waters thou ſhalt wander ſo long, till thou arriveſt at a place, where thou art to lay the foundation of a Houſe of that reputation, as the mercy of the moſt High ſhall be publiſhed there from generation to generation by the voice of a ſtrange people, whoſe cryes ſhall be as pleaſing to him, as thoſe of ſucking children that lye in the cradle.* This ſaid, the little Boy, according to the Hiſtory, fell down ſtark dead to the ground, which much aſtoniſhed *Nancaa*, and all hers: The ſaid Hiſtory further delivers, and as I have often heard it read, that five dayes after this ſucceſs the thirty *Jangaas* were one morning ſeen coming down the River in very good Equipage, but not ſo much as one man in them; the reaſon hereof, by the report of the Hiſtory, which the *Chineſes* hold to be moſt true, was, that all theſe Ships of War being joyned together for to execute unmercifully upon *Nancaa* and her children, the cruel and damnable intentions of the Tyrant *Silau*, one night as this Fleet rode at anchor in a place, called *Catebaſoy*, a huge dark cloud came over them, whereout iſſued ſuch horrible thunder and lightning accompanied with mighty rain, the drops whereof were ſo hot, that falling upon them which were aſleep in the veſſels, it made them leap into the River, ſo as within leſſe then an hour they periſhed

§.3.

all; And it is said that one drop of this rain coming to fall upon a body it burnt in such sort, as it penetrated to the very marrow of the bone with most insupportable pain, no cloths, nor arms, being able to resist it. *Nancaa* receiving this favour from the hand of the Lord, with abundance of tears, and humble thanks, embarqued her self, her children, and all her company in the said thirty *Jangaas*, and sailing down the river was carried by the strength of the curant, which for her sake, the History saith, redoubled then, in seven and forty days to the very place where now the City of *Pequin* is built; There she, and all hers landed, and doubting least the Tyrant *Silau*, whose cruelty she feared, might still pursue her, she fortified her self in this place the best she could.

C H A P. XXX.

The Foundation of the four chief Cities of China; *together with which of the Kings of* China *it was that built the* Wall *between* China *and* Tartaria; *and many things that* We *saw as* We *past along.*

§. 1. THe said History delivers, that few days after the poor *Nancaa*, and her followers were setled on shore, she caused them to swear fealty unto her eldest Son, and to acknowledg him for their lawful Prince; Now the very same day that he received the Oath of Allegiance from these few Subjects of his, he made election of the place where the Fortress should be erected, together with the inclosure of the wall; Afterwards as soon as the first foundations were laid, which was speedily done, he went out of his Tent, accompanied with his Mother, who governed all, together with his brothers, and the chiefest of his company, attired in festival robes, with a great stone carried before him by the noblest Personages, which he had caused to be wrought aforehand, and arriving at the said foundations he laid his hand upon the stone, and on his knees, with his eyes lifted up to heaven, he said to all that were present, *Brethren, and worthy friends, know that I give mine own Name, that is,* Pequin, *to this Stone, upon which this new place is to be built, for I desire, that hereafter it should be so called; wherefore I pray you all, as friends, and command you as your King, not to call it otherwise, to the end the memory thereof may remain immortal to those that shall come after us to the end of the world; By which means it shall be manifested to all men, that the thirteenth day of the eighth Moon, in the year one thousand, six hundred, and thirty nine, after the Lord of all things created had made those that lived upon the earth, see how much he abhorred the sins of men, for the which he drowned the whole world with waters, that he sent down from heaven, in satisfaction of his divine justice, it shall, I say, be manifested to them, that the new Prince* Pequin *built this Fortress, whereunto he gave his Name; And so conformable to the Prophesie, which the dead child hath delivered, it shall be published over all, by the voice of strange people, in what manner the Lord is to be feared, and what sacrifices are to be made, that may be just and acceptable unto him.* Now this was that which King *Pequin* said unto his Vassals, and which is at this day to be seen engraven on a silver Scutchion, fastened to an arch of one of the principal gates of the City, called *Pommicotay*, where in memory of this Prophecy, there is ordinarily a guard of forty Halberdiers, with their Captain, whereas there are but only four in all the rest, who are bound to render an account of all that passe in and out there daily; And because the Histories relate, that this new King laid the first foundation of this City on the third of the month of *August* the Kings of *China* do on that day usually shew themselves to the people, and that with such Pomp and Majesty, that I profess I am not able to declare the least part of it, much less to describe the whole. Now in regard of this first Kings words, which the *Chineses* hold for an infallible prophecy, his descendants do so fear the accomplishment thereof, that by a Law expresly made by them, the admittance of any strangers into this Kingdom, saving Ambassadors and Slaves, is forbidden upon most grievous pains; So that when any do chance to arrive there, they banish them presently from one place to another, not permitting them to settle any where, as they practised it towards me, and my eight companions. And thus, as I have succinctly delivered, was this Empire of *China* founded, and peopled by the means of this Prince, named *Pequin*, the eldest of *Nancaas* three Sons; As for the other two, called *Pacan* and *Nacan*, they afterwards founded the other two Towns aforesaid, and withall gave them their own Names. It is also the general opinion, that their Mother *Nancaa* founded the City of *Nanquin*, which took its denomination from her, continuing it so to this day; and is the second City of this great Monarchy.

narchy. The Hiſtories further affirm, that from the time of this firſt founder, the Empire of *China* augmented always from one King to another, by a juſt ſucceſſion till a certain age, which according to our computation, was in the year of our Lord, one thouſand, one hunded, and thirty; After which a King that then reigned, named *Xixipau*, incloſed the City of *Pequin*, within the ſpace of three and twenty years, in ſuch manner as it is ſeen at this day, and and that fourſcore and two years after another King, his Grand-child, called *Jumbileytay*, made the like, ſo that both together were ſixty leagues in circuit, namely, each of them thirty; ten in length, and five in breadth : Now it is certain, and I have often times read it, that each of theſe incloſures or walls, hath a thouſand and threeſcore round bulwarks, as alſo two hundred and forty towers, very fair, ſtrong, large, and high, with guilt Lions upon globes, being the Arms of the Kings of *China*, which are very pleaſing to the eye. Without the laſt Incloſure, is an exceeding great ditch round about it, ten fathom deep, and forty broad, continually repleniſhed with many barques and boats, covered over head as if they were houſes, where both proviſions, and all ſorts of merchandiſe are ſold. This City, according to the *Chineſes* report, hath above three hundred and threeſcore gates, in each of which, as I have before recited, there are always four Halberdiers, who are obliged to render an account of all that go in and out daily. There are alſo certain chambers in it, whither it is the cuſtome to bring ſuch children as wander and go aſtray, in the Town ; to the end their Parents that loſe them may be ſure to hear of them there. I will referre my ſpeaking more largely of the magnificences of this goodly City to another place, for that which I have now delivered in haſt, and as it were *en paſſant*, was but to make a brief relation of the original of this Empire, and of the firſt founder of the City of *Pequin*, (which may be truely ſaid to be the chifeſt of all in the world for greatneſs, policy, riches, and abundance of all things that can be deſired of man) as alſo of the foundation of the ſecond City of this mighty Kingdom, that is *Nanquin*, and of the other two, *Pacan* and *Nacau*, whereof I have heretofore ſpoken, and in which the founders of them are buried in very ſtately and rich Temples, within tombs of white and green alabaſter, all garniſhed with gold, and erected upon Lions of ſilver, with a world of Lamps, and perfuming pans full of divers ſorts to ſweet odours round about them.

Now that I have ſpoken of the Original and Foundation of this Empire , together with the circuit of the great City of *Pequin*, I hold it not amiſs to entreat as ſuccinctly as I may of another particular, which is no leſs admirable then thoſe whereof I have made mention before : It is written in the fifth Book of the Scituation of all the remarkable places of this Empire, or rather Monarchy, (for to ſpeak truly, there is no appellation ſo great but may be well attributed unto it) that a King, named *Criſnagol Dicotay*, who according to the computation of that book, reigned in the year of our Lord five hundred and eighteen, happened to make war with the *Tartar*, about ſome difference between them concerning the State of *Xenxinapau*, that borders on the Kingdom of *Lauhos*, and ſo valiantly demeaned himſelf in a battail againſt him, that he defeated his Army, and remained Maſter of the field ; whereupon the *Tartar* confederating himſelf with other Kings, his friends, did by their aſſiſtance aſſemble together greater forces then the former, and therewith invaded the Kingdom of *China*, where it is ſaid, he took three and thirty very important towns, of which (the principal was *Panquilor*, inſomuch that the *Chineſe* fearing he ſhould not be well able to defend himſelf concluded a peace with him upon condition to relinquiſh his right, which he pretended to that in queſtion, betwixt them, and to pay him two thouſand *Picos* of Silver for to defray the charges of thoſe ſtrangers the *Tartar* had entertained in this War ; by this means *China* continued for a good while quiet, but the King doubting leaſt the *Tartar* might in time to come return to annoy him again, reſolved to build a wall, that might ſerve for a Bulwark to his Empire, and to that end calling all his Eſtates together he declared this his determination unto them , which was preſently not onely well approved of, but held moſt neceſſary, ſo that to enable him for the performance of a buſineſs, ſo much concerning his ſtate they gave him ten thouſand *Picos* of ſilver, which amount according to our account unto fifteen Millions of Gold, after the rate of fifteen hundred Duckets each *Pico*, and moreover they entertained him two hundred and fifty thouſand men to labour in the work, whereof thirty thouſand were appointed for Officers, and all the reſt for Manual ſervices ; Order being taken then for whatſoever was thought fit for ſo prodigious an enterpriſe they fell to it in ſuch ſort, as by the report of the Hiſtory all that huge wall was in ſeven and twenty years quite finiſhed from one end to the other , which if credit may be given to the ſame Chronicle is ſeventy *Jaos* in length, that is ſix hundred and

§.2.

fifteen

fifteen miles after nine miles every *Jao* ; wherein that which seemed most wonderful and most exceeding the belief of man , was that seven hundred and fifty thousand men laboured incessantly for so long a time in that great work, whereof the Commonalty , as I delivered before, furnished one third part; the Priests, and Isles of *Aynan*, another third ; and the King assisted by the Princes, Lords, *Chaems*, and *Anchacys* of the Kingdom, the rest of the building, which I have both seen and measured, being thirty foot in height, and ten foot in breadth, where it is thickest : It is made of lime and sand,and plaistered on the outside with a kind of Bitumen,which renders it so strong,that no Canon can demolish it : Instead of Bulwarks it hath Sentries,or Watch-Towers,two stages high,flanked with Buttresses of Carpentry made of a certain black wood,which they call *Caubesy*,that is to say, wood of iron, because it is exceeding strong and hard, every Buttress being as thick as an Hogshead, and very high, so that these Sentries are far stronger then if they were made of Lime and Stone. Now this wall, by them termed *Chaufacan*, which signifies, *strong resistance* , extends in height equall to the mountains, whereunto it is joyned, and that those Mountains also may serve for a wall they are cut down very smooth and steep, which renders them far stronger then the Wall it self, but you must know that in all this extent of land there is no Wall but in the void spaces from hill to hill, so that the hills themselves make up the rest of the wall and fence : Further it is to be noted, that in this whole length of an hundred and fifteen leagues, which this fortification contains, there are but onely five Entries wherby the Rivers of *Tartaria* do pass, which are derived from the impetuous Torrents, that descend from these mountains, and running above five hundred leagues in the Country, render themselves into the Seas of *China* and *Cauchenchina* ; howbeit one of these Rivers, being greater then the rest, disemboques by the Bar of *Cuy* in the Kindom of *Sornnau*, commonly called *Siam*. Now in all these five Passages both the King of *China*, and the King of *Tartaria* keep Garrisons; the *Chinese* in each of them entertains seven thousand men giving them great pay,whereof six thousand are Horse, the rest foot, being for the most part strangers, as *Mogores, Pancrus, Champaas, Coraçones, Gizares* of *Persia*, and other different Nations, bordering upon this Empire, and which in consideration of the extraordinary pay they receive,serve the *Chineses*; who to speak truth are nothing couragious, as being but little used to the Wars, and ill provided of Arms and Artillery. In all this length of wall there are three hundred and twenty companies, each of them containing five hundred Souldiers, so that there are in all one hundred and threescore thousand men , besides Officers of Justice, *Anchacis, Chaems*, and other such like persons necessary for the government,and entertainment of these forces; so that all joyned together make up the number of two hundred thousand, which are all maintained at the Kings onely charge,by reason the most of them are Malefactors condemned to the reparations and labour of this Wall, as I shall more amply declare when I come to speak of the prison destined to this purpose,in the Citie of *Pequin*, which is also another Edifice, very remarkable, wherein there are continually above thirty thousand Prisoners,the most of them from eighteen to forty five years of age, appointed to work in this Wall.

§.3.   Being departed from those two Towns *Pacan* and *Nacau* we continued our course up the River, and arrived at another Town, called *Mindoo*, somwhat bigger then those from whence we parted, where about half a mile of was a great lake of Salt-water, and a number of Salt-houses round about it : The *Chineses* assured us, that this Lake did ebbe and flow like the Sea, and that it extended above two hundred Leagues into the country, rendring the King of *China* in yearly revenue one hundred thousand *Taeis*, only for the third of the salt was drawn out of it ; as also that the Town yielded him one other hundred thousand *Taeis* for the silk alone that was made there, not speaking at all of the Camphire, Sugar, Pourcelain, Vermilion, and Quick-silver , whereof there was very great plenty, moreover, that some two leagues from this Town were twelve exceeding long houses, like unto Magazines, where a world of people laboured in casting and purifying of Copper, and the horrible din which the Hammers made there was such, and so strange, as if there were any thing on earth that could represent Hell this was it, wherefore being desirous to understand the cause of this extraordinary noyse, we would needs go to see from whence it proceeded, and we found that there were in each of these Houses forty Furnaces, that is twenty of either side, with forty huge Anvills, upon every of which eight men beat in order, and so swiftly, as a mans eye could hardly discern the blows, so as three hundred and

twenty

twenty men wrought in each of thefe twelve Houfes, which in all the twelve Houfes made up three thoufand eight hundred and forty workmen, befide a great number of other perfons that laboured in other particular things; whereupon we demanded how much Copper might be wrought every year in each of thefe Houfes, and they told us, one hundred and ten, or fixfcore thoufand *Picos*, whereof the King had two thirds, becaufe the Mines were his, and that the Mountain from whence it was drawn was called *Corotum baga*, which fignifies a River of Copper, for that from the time fince it was difcovered, being above two hundred years, it never failed, but rather more and more was found. Having paft about a league beyond thofe twelve Houfes up the River, we came to a place inclofed with three ranks of Iron grates, where we beheld thirty Houfes, divined into five rows, fix in each row, which were very long and compleat, with great Towers full of Bells of caft mettle, and much carved work, as alfo guilt Pillars, and the Frontifpieces of fair hewed ftone, whereupon many Inventions were engraved : At this place we went afhore by the *Chifuus* permiffion, that carried us, for that he had made a Vow to this Pagod, which was called *Bigay potim*, that is to fay, *God of an hundred and ten thoufand Gods, Corchoo fungane ginaco ginaca*, which according to their report fignifies, *ftrong and great above all others*, for one of the Errors wherewith thefe wretched people are blinded is, *that they beleeve every particular thing hath its God, who hath created it, and preferves its natural being, but that this Bigay potim brought them all forth from under his arm-pits, and that from him as a father, they derive their being, by a filial union, which they term* Bira Porentafay ; *And in the Kingdom of* Pegu, *where I have often been, I have feen one like unto this, named by thofe of the country* Ginocoginans, *the God of all greatnefs, which Temple was in times paft built by the* Chinefes, *when as they commanded in the* Indiaes, *being according to their fupputation from the year of our Lord* Jefus Chrift 1013. *to the year* 1072. *by which account it appears that the* Indiaes *were under the Empire of* China *but onely fifty and nine years, for the fucceffor of him that conquered it, called* Exiragano, *voluntarily abandoned it in regard of the great expence of mony and bloud that the unprofitable keeping of it coft him :* In thofe thirty Houfes, whereof I formerly fpake, were a great number of Idols of guilt Wood ; and a like number of Tin, Latten, and Pourcelain, being indeed fo many, as I fhould hardly be believed to declare them. Now we had not paft above five or fix leagues from this place but we came to a great Town, about a league in circuit, quite deftroyed and ruinated, fo that asking the *Chinefes* what might be the caufe thereof, they told us, that this Town was anciently called *Cohilouza*, that is, *The flower of the field*, and had in former times been in very great profperity, and that about one hundred forty and two years before, a certain ftranger, in the company of fome Merchants of the Port of *Tanacarim* in the Kingdom of *Siam*, chanced to come thither, being as it feems an holy man, although the *Bonzes* faid he was a Sorcerer, by reafon of the wonders he did, having raifed up five dead men, and wrought many other Miracles, whereat all men were exceedingly aftonifhed ; and that having divers times difputed with the Priefts he had fo fhamed and confounded them, as fearing to deal any more with him, they incenfed the Inhabitants againft him, and perfwaded them to put him to death, affirming that otherwife God would confume them with fire from Heaven, whereupon all the Townfmen went unto the Houfe of a poor Weaver, where he lodged, and killing the Weaver, with his fon and two fons in Law of his, that would have defended him, the Holy man came forth to them, and reprehending them for this uproar, he told them amongft other things, *That the God of the Law, whereby they were to be faved was called* Jefus Chrift, *who came down from heaven to the earth for to become a man, and that it was needful he fhould dye for men, and that with the price of his precious bloud, which he fhed for finners upn the Croffe, God was fatisfied in his juftice, and that giving him the charge of Heaven, and Earth, he had promifed him, that whofoever profeffed his Law with Faith and good Works fhould be faved, and have everlafting life* ; *and withall, that the gods whom the Bonzes ferved and adored with facrifices of bloud, were falfe, and Idols, wherewith the Devil deceived them* ; Here at the Churchmen entred into fo great furie, that they called unto the people faying, *Curfed be he that brings not wood and fire for to burn him*, which was prefently put in execution by them, and the fire beginning exceedingly to rage the Holy man faid certain Prayers, by vertue whereof the fire incontinently went out, wherewith the people being amazed cryed out, faying, *Doubtleffe the God of this man is moft mighty, and worthy to be adored throughout the whole World*, which one of the *Bonzes* hearing, who was

ringleader

ring-leader of this mutiny, and seeing the Town-men retire away in consideration of that they had beheld, he threw a stone at the holy man, saying, *They which do not as I do, may the Serpent of the night ingulf them into hell fire.* At these words all the other *Bonzes* did the like, so that he was presently knock'd down dead with the stones they flung at him, whereupon they cast him into the river, which most prodigiously staid its course from running down, and so continued for the space of five days together that the body lay in it ; By means of this wonder many imbraced the law of that holy man, whereof there are a great number yet remaining in that country : Whilest the *Chineses* were relating this history unto us, we arrived at a point of land, where going to double Cape, we descryed a little place environed with trees, in the midst whereof was a great cross of stone very well made, which we no sooner espied, but transported with exceeding joy, we fell on our knees before our Conductor, humbly desiring him to give us leave to go on shoar, but this Heathen dog refused us, saying, that they had a great way yet to the place where they were to lodge, whereat we were mightily grieved ; Howbeit God of his mercy, even miraculously so ordered it, that being gone about a league further, his wife fell in labour, so as he was constrained to return to that place again, it being a Village of thirty or forty houses, hard by where the Cross stood : Here we went on land, and placed his wife in an house, where some nine days after she died in Child-bed, during which time we went to the Cross, and prostrating our selves before it with tears in our eyes ; The people of the Village beholding us in this posture, came to us, and kneeling down also, with their hands lift up to heaven, they said, *Christo Jesu, Jesu Christo, Maria micauvidau late impone model,* which in our tongue signifies, *Jesus Christ, Jesus Christ, Mary always a Virgine conceived him, a Virgine brought him forth, and a Virgine still remained* ; whereunto we weeping answered, that they spake the very truth ; Then they asked us if we were Christians, we told them we were, which as soon as they understood they carried us home to their houses, where they entertained us with great affection ; Now all these were Christians, and descended of the Weaver, in whose house the holy man was lodged, of whom demanding whether that which the *Chineses* had told us was true ; they shewed us a book that contained the whole history thereof at large, with many other wonders wrought by that holy man, who they said was named *Matthew Escandel,* and that he was an Hermit of Mount *Sinai,* being an *Hungarian* by nation, and born in a place called *Buda* : The same book also related that nine days after this Saint was buried, the said Town of *Cohilouzaa,* where he was murthered, began to tremble in such sort, as all the people thereof in a mighty fright, ran out into the fields, and there continued in their tents, not daring to return unto their houses, for they cried out all with one common consent, *The blood of this stranger craves vengeance for the unjust death the Bonzes hath given him, because he preached the truth unto us* ; But the *Bonzes* rebuked and told them, that they committed a great sin in saying so, Nevertheless, they willed them to be of good cheer, for they would go all to *Quiay Tiguarem,* God of the night, and request him to command the earth to be quiet, otherwise we would offer him no more sacrifices: Immediately whereupon all the *Bonzes* went accordingly in procession to the said Idol, which was the chiefest in the Town, but none of the people durst follow them, for fear of some earthquake, which the very next night, about eleven of the clock, as those divelish monsters were making their sacrifices, with odoriferous perfumes, and other ceremonies, accustomed amongst them, increased so terribly, that by the Lords permission, and for a just punishment of their wickedness, it quite overthrew all the Temples, houses, and other edifices of the Town to the ground, wherewith all the *Bonzes* were killed, not so much as one escaped alive, being in number above four thousand, as the book delivereth, wherein it is further said, that afterwards the earth opening such abundance of water came forth, as it clean overwhelmed and drowned the whole Town, so that it became a great lake, and above an hundred fathom deep ; moreover they recounted many other very strange particulars unto us, and also however since that time the place was named *Fiunganorsee,* that is, *the chastisement of heaven,* whereas before it was called *Cohilouzaa,*
§.4. which signifies, *the flower of the field,* as I have declared heretofore.

After our Departure from the ruines of *Fiunganorsee,* we arrived at a great Town, called *Junquinilau,* which is very rich, abounding with all kind of things, fortified with a strong Garrison of Horse and Foot, and having a number of Junks and Vessels riding before it : Here we remained five days to celebrate the Funeral of our *Chifuus* wife ; for whose soul he gave us by way of alms both meat and clothes, and withall freeing us from the oar, permitted us to go ashore without irons, which was a very great ease unto us. Having left this place, we

con-

continued our courfe up the river, beholding ftill on either fide a world of goodly great Towns, inuironed with ftrong walls, as alfo many Fortreffes and Caftles all along the waters fide; we faw likewife a great number of Temples, whofe Steeples were all guilt, and in the fields fuch abundance of cattel that the ground was even covered over with them, fo far as we could well difcern : Moreover there were fo many veffels upon this river, efpecially in fome parts, where Fairs were kept, that at firft fight one would have thought them to be populous Towns, befides other leffer companies of three hundred, five hundred, fix hundred, and a thoufand boats, which continually we met withall on both fides of the river, wherein all things that one could imagine were fold ; Moreover the *Chinefes* affured us, that in this Empire of *China*, the number of thofe which levied upon the rivers, was not lefs, then thofe that dwelled in the Towns, and that without the good order which is obferved to make the common people work, and to conftrain the meaner fort to fupply themfelves unto trades, for to get their living, they would eat up one another. Now it is to be noted, that every kind of traffique and commerce is divided among them into three or four forms, as followeth : They which trade in Ducks, whereof there are great quantities in this Countrey, proceed therein diverfly ; fome caufe their egs to be hatched for to fell the Ducklings, others fat them when they are great for to fell them dead after they are falted; Thefe traffique only with the egs, others with the feathers, and fome with the heads, feet, gizards, and intrails, no man being permitted to trench upon his companions fale, under the penalty of thirty lafhes, which no priviledg can exempt them from : In the fame manner, concerning hogs, fome fell them alive, and by whole fale, others dead, and by retail, fome make bacon of them, others fell their pigs, and fome again fell nothing but the chitterlings, the fweet-breads, the blood, and the haflets ; which is alfo obferved for fifh, for fuch a one fels it frefh, that cannot fell it either falted or dried, and fo of other Provifions, as flefh, fruit, fowls, venifon, pulfe, and other things, wherein fuch rigour is ufed, as there are chambers exprefly eftablifhed, whofe officers have commiffion and power to fee, that they which trade in one particular may not do it in another, if it be not for juft and lawful coufes, and that on pain of thirty lafhes. There be others likewife that get their living by felling fifh alive, which to that purpofe they keep in great well-boats, and fo carry them into divers countrys, where they know there is no other but falt fifh. There are likewife all along this river of *Batampina*, whereon we went from *Nanquin* to *Pequin*, which is diftant one from the other one hundred and fourfcore leagues, fuch a number of engines for fugar, and preffes for wine and oyl, made of divers forts of pulfe and fruit, as one could hardly fee any other thing on either fide of the water. In many other places alfo there were an infinite company of Houfes, and Magazines full of all kinds of provifion, that one could imagine, where all forts of flefh are falted, dried, fmoaked, and piled up in great high heaps, as gammons of Bacon, Pork, Lard, Geefe, Ducks, Cranes, Buftards, Oftriches, Stags, Cows, Buffles, wild Goats, Rhinocerofes, Horfes, Tygers, Dogs, Foxes, and almoft all other creatures that one can name, fo that we faid many times amongft our felves, that it was not poffible for all the people of the world to eat up all thofe provifions. We faw likewife upon the fame river, a number of Veffels, which they call *Paneuras*, covered from the poup to the prow with nets, in manner of a cage, three inches high, full of ducks and geefe, that were carried from place to place to be fold ; when the Owners of thofe boats would have thefe fowl to feed, they approach to the Land, and where there are rich medows, or marfhes, they fet forth Planks, penning the doors of thofe cages, they beat three or four times upon a Drum, which they have exprefly for that purpofe, whereupon all thefe fowl, being fix or feven thoufand at the leaft, go out of the boat with a mighty noife, & fo fall to feeding all along the waters fide; Now when the Owner perceives, that thefe fowl have fed fufficiently, and that it is time to return them, he beats the drum the fecond time, at the found whereof they gather all together, and re-enter with the fame noife, as they went out, wherein it is ftrange to obferve, that they return all in again, not fo much as one miffing. That done, the Mafter of the boat parts from that place, and afterwards when he thinks it is time for them to lay, he repairs towards land, and where he finds the grounds dry, and good grafs, he opens the doors, and beats the drum again, at which all the fowl of the boat come forth to lay, and then at fuch time as the Mafter judges that thefe fowl have laid, he beats his drum afrefh, and fuddenly in hafte they all throng in to the boat, not fo much as one remaining behind; Thereupon two or three men get afhore, with baskets in their hands, whereinto they gather up the egs, till they have gotten eleven or twelve baskets full, and fo they proceed on their voyage to make fale of their war, which being almoft fpent, to ftore themR selves anew, they go for to buy more unto them that breed them, whose trade it is to sell them young, for they are not suffered to keep them when they are g eat, as the others do, by reason, as I have said before, no man may deal in any commodity for which he hath not permission from the Governors of the Towns. They that get their living by breeding of Ducks have neer to their Houses certain Ponds, where many times they keep ten or eleven thousand of these duckings, some bigger, some lesser. Now for to hatch the Eggs, they have in very long galleries twenty and thirty furnaces full of dung, wherein they bury two hundred, three hundred, and five hundred Eggs together, then stopping the mouth of each furnace that the dung may become the hotter, they leave the Eggs there till they think the young ones are disclosed, whereupon putting into every several furnace a Capon half pulled, and the skin stript from off his breast, they leave him shut up therein for the space of two dayes, at the end whereof being all come out of the shell, they carry them into certain places under ground made for that purpose, setting them bran soaked in liquor, and so being left there loose some ten or eleven dayes, they go afterwards of themselves into the ponds, where they feed and bring them up for to sell them unto those former Merchants, who trade with them into divers parts, it being unlawfull for one to trench upon anothers traffick, as I have before related, so that in the Markets and publique places, where provisions for the mouth are sold, if any that sell Goose Eggs do chance to be taken seazed with Hens Eggs and it is suspected that they sell of them, they are presently punished with thirty lashes on the bare Buttocks, without hearing any justification they can make for themselves, being as I have said, found seazed of them, so that if they will have Hens Eggs for their own use, to avoid incurring the penalty of the Law they must be broken at one end, whereby it may appear that they keep them not to sell, but to eat. As for them that sell Fish alive, if any of their Fish chance to die, they cut them in pieces, and salting them sell them at the price of salt-fish, which is lesse then that of fresh-fish, wherein they proceed so exactly, that no man dares passe the limits, which are prescribed and ordained by the *Conchalis* of the State, upon pain of most severe punishment, for in all this Country the King is so much respected, and Justice so feared, as no kinde of person, how great soever, dares murmur, or look awry at an Officer, no not at the very *Huppes*, which are as the Bayliffs or Beadles amongst us.

C H A P. XXXI.
The order which is observed in the moving Towns that are made upon the Rivers, and that which further befell us.

§.1. WEe saw likewise all along this great River a number of Hogs both wilde and domestick, that were kept by certain men on horseback, and many herds of tame red Deer, which were driven from place to place like Sheep, to feed, all lamed of their right legs, to hinder them from running away, and they are lamed so, when they are but Calves, to avoid the danger, that otherwise they might incur of their lives: We saw also divers Parks, wherein a world of Dogs were kept to be sold to the Butchers, for in these Countries they eat all manner of Flesh, whereof they know the price, and of what creatures they are, by the choppings they make of them; moreover we met with many small Barques, whereof some, were full of Pigs, others of Tortoises, Frogs, Otters, Adders, Eeeles, Snails, and Lizards, for as I have said, they buy there of all that is judged good to eat; now to the end that such provisions may passe at an easier rate, all that sell them are permitted to make traffick of them in several fashions; true it is, that in some things they have greater Franchises, then in others, to the end that by means thereof no Merchandise may want sale: And because the Subject I now treat of dispences me to speak of all, I will relate that which we further observed there, and whereat we were much abashed, judging thereby how far men suffer themselves to be carried by their Interests, and extream avarice; you must know then that in this Country there are a many of such as make a trade of buying and selling mens Excrements, which is not so mean a Commerce amongst them, but that there are many of them grow rich by it, and are held in good account; now these Excrements serve to manure grounds that are newly grubb'd, which is found to be far better for that purpose then the ordinary dung: They which make a trade of buying it go up and down the streets with certain Clappers, like our Spittle men, whereby they give to understand what they
desire,

defire without publifhing of it otherwife to people, in regard the thing is filthy of it felf; whereunto I will adde thus much, that this commodity is fo much efteemed amonft them, and fo great a trade driven of it, that into one fea port, fometimes there comes in one tyde two or three hundred Sayls laden with it : Oftentimes alfo there is fuch ftriving for it, as the Governours of the place are fain to enterpofe their authority for the diftribution of this goodly commodity, and all for to manure their grounds, which foyled with it, bears three crops in one year. We faw many boats likewife laden with dryed orange pills, wherewith in victualing houfes they boyl dogs flefh, for to take away the rank favour and humidity of it, as alfo to reader it more firm : In brief, we faw fo many *Vaucans, Lanteaas,* and *Barcaffes,* in this river, laden with all kinds of provifion, that either the fea or land produces, and that in fuch abundance, as I muft confefs I am not able to expreffe it in words ; for it is not poffible to imagne the infinite ftore of things that are in this Country, of each whereof you fhall fee two or three hundred Veffels together at a time, all full, efpecially at the Fairs, and Markets, that are kept upon the folemn feftival days of their *Pagodes,* for then all the fairs are free, and the *Pagodes* for the moft part are fcituated on the banks of rivers, to the end all commodities may the more commodioufly be brought thither by water. Now when all thefe veffels come to joyn together, during thefe Fairs, they take fuch order, as they make as it were a great and fair Town of them, fo that fometimes you fhall have of them a league in length, and three quarters of a league in bredth, being compofed of above twenty thoufand veffels, befides *Balons, Guedees,* and *Manchuas,* which are fmall boats, whofe number is infinite ; For the Government hereof there are threefcore Captains appointed, of which thirty are to fee good order kept, and the other thirty are for the guard of the Merchants that come thither, to the end they may fail in fafety ; Moreover there is above them a *Chaem,* who hath abfolute power both in civil, and criminal caufes, without any appeal or oppofition whatfoever, during the fifteen days, that this Fair lafts, which is from the new to the full Moon ; And indeed more come to fee the policy, order, and beauty of this kind of Town, then otherwife ; for to fpeak the truth, the framing of it in that manner with veffels, makes it more to be admired then all the Edifices that can be feen upon the land ; There are in this moving Town two thoufand ftreets, exceeding long, & very ftrait, inclofed on either fide with fhips, moft of which are covered with filks, and adorned with a world of banners, flags, and ftreamers, wherein all kind of commodities that can be defired, are to be fold ; In other ftreets are as many trades to be feen, as in any Town on the Land, amidft the which they that traffique, go up and down in little *Manchuas,* and that very quietly, and without any diforder : Now if by chance any one is taken ftealing, he is inftantly punifhed according to his offence ; As foon as it is night, all thefe ftreets are fhut up with cords athwart them, to the end none may paffe after the retreat founded ; In each of thefe ftreets there are at leaft a duzen of lanthorns, with lights burning, faftened a good heighth on the Mafts of the veffels, by means whereof all that go in and out are feen, fo that it may be known who they are, from whence they come, and what they would have, to the end the *Chaem* may the next morning receive an account thereof ; And truly to behold all thefe lights together in the night, is a fight fcarce able to be imagined, neither is there a ftreet without a Bell, and a Sentinel, fo as when that of the *Chaems* fhip is heard to ring, all the other bels anfwer it, with fo great a noife of voices adjoyned thereunto, that we were almoft befides our felves, at the hearing of a thing, which cannot be well conceived ; and that was ruled with fuch good order : In every of thefe ftreets, even in the pooreft of them, there is a Chappel to pray in, framed upon great *Barcaffes,* like to Gallies, very neat, and fo well accommodated, that for the moft part they are enriched with filks, and cloth of gold ; In thefe Chappels are their Idols, and Priefts which adminifter their facrifices, and receive the offerings that are made them, wherewith they are abundantly furnifhed for their living ; Out of each ftreet, one of the moft account, or chiefeft Merchant is chofen to watch all night in his turn with thofe of his Squadron, befides the Captains of the government, who in Ballons, walk the round without, to the end no thiefe may efcape by any avenue whatfoever, and for that purpofe thefe guards cry as loud as they can that they may be heard. Amongft the moft remarkable things, we faw one ftreet, where there were above an hundred veffels, laden with Idols of guilt wood, of divers fafhions, which were fold for to be offered to the *Pagodes,* together with a world of feet, thighs, arms, and heads, that fick folks bought to offer in devotion ; There alfo we beheld other fhips, covered with filk hangings, where Comedies, and other playes were reprefented to entertain the people withall, which in great numbers

　　flocked

flocked thither; In other places, Bils of exchange for Heaven were fold, whereby thefe Priefts of the Divel promifed them many merits, with great intereft, affirming that without thefe bils they could not poffibly be faved, for that God, fay they, is a mortal enemy to all fuch as do not fome good to the *Pagodes*, whereupon they tell them fuch fables and lies, as thefe unhappy wretches do often times take the very bread from their mouths to give it them; There were alfo other veffels all laden with dead mens skuls, which divers men bought for to prefent as an offering, at the tombs of their friends, when they fhould happen to dye; for, fay they, as the deceafed is laid in the grave in the company of thefe skuls, fo fhall his foul enter into Heaven, attended by thofe unto whom thofe skuls belonged, wherefore when the Porter of Paradife fhall fee fuch a Merchant, with many followers, he will do him honour, as to a man that in this life hath been a man of quality, for if he be poor, and without a train, the Porter will not open to him, whereas contrarily the more dead mens skuls he hath buried with him, the more happy he fhall be efteemed; There were many boats likewife, where there were men that had a great many of Cages, full of live birds, who playing on divers inftruments of mufick, exhorted the people with a loud voice, to deliver thofe poor creatures of God, that were there in captivity, whereupon many came and gave them mony for the redemption of thofe prifoners, which prefently they let out of the cages, and then as they flew away, the redeemers of them cried out to the birds, *Pichau pitavel catan vacaxi*, that is, *Go, and tell God, how we ferve him here below.* In imitation of thefe, there are others alfo, who in their fhips, kept a great many of little live fifhes in great pots of water, and like the fellers of birds invite the people, for Gods caufe to free thofe poor innocent fifhes, that had never finned, fo that divers bought many of them, and cafting them into the river, faid, *Get ye gone, and tell there below, the good I have done you for Gods fake.* To conclude all, the veffels where thefe things are expofed to fale, are feldom lefs in number then two hundred, befides thoufands of others, which fell fuch like wares in a far greater quantity.

§. 2.   We faw likewife many *Barcaffes* full of men and women; that played upon divers forts of inftruments, and for mony gave them mufick that defired it; There were other veffels laden with horns, which the Priefts fold, therewith to make feafts in Heaven, for they fay, that thofe were the horns of feveral beafts, which were offered in facrifice to the Idols out of devotion, and for the performance of vows that men had made in divers kind of misfortunes, and ficknesses, wherein they had at others times been; And that as the flefh of thofe beafts, had been given here below for the honour of God to the poor, fo the fouls of them for whom thofe horns were offered, do in the other world eat the fouls of of thofe beafts to whom thofe horns belonged, and thereunto invite the fouls of their friends, as men ufe to invite others here on earth; Other veffels we faw covered with blacks, and full of tombs, torches, and great wax lights, as alfo women in them, that for money would be hired to weep and lament for the dead; others there were, called *Pitaleus*, that in great barques kept divers kinds of wild beafts to be fhewed for mony, moft dreadful to behold as Serpents, huge Adders, monftrous Lizards, Tygers, and many others fuch like; we faw in like fort a great number of Stationers, which fold all manner of books, that could be defired, as well concerning the creation of the world; whereof they tell a thoufand lies, as touching the States, Kingdoms, Iflands, and Provinces of the world, together with the Laws and Cuftoms of Nations, but efpecially of the Kings of *China*, their number, brave acts, and of all things elfe that happened in each of their reigns, Moreover we faw a great many of the light, fwift Foyfts, wherein were men very well armed, who cried out with a loud voice, that if any one had received an affront, whereof he defired to be avenged, let him come unto them, and they would caufe fatisfaction to be made him; In other veffels there were old women, that ferved for midwives, and that would bring women fpeedily and eafily a bed, as alfo a many of Nurfes, ready to be entertained for to give children fuck; There were barques likewife very well adorned, and fet forth, that had in them divers reverend old men, and grave matrons, whofe profeffion was to make marriages, and to comfort widows, or fuch as had loft their children, or fuffered any other misfortune; In others there were a number of young men and maids, that lacked Mafters, and Miftreffes, which offered themfelves to any that would hire them; There were other veffels that had in them fuch as undertook to tell fortunes, and to help folks to things loft. In a word, not to dwell any longer upon every particular, that was to be feen in this moving Town, for then I fhould never have done, it fhall fuffice me to fay, that nothing can be defired on land, which was not to be had in their veffels, and that in greater abundance then I have delivered, wherefore I

will

will paffe from it to fhew you that one of the principal caufes why this Monarchy of *China*, that contains two and thirty Kingdoms, is fo mighty, rich, and of fo great commerce, is, becaufe it is exceedingly replenifhed with rivers, and a world of Chanals that have been anciently made by the Kings, great Lords, and people thereof, for to render all the Country navigable, and fo communicate their labours with one another: The narroweft of thefe Chanals have bridges, of hewed ftone over them, that are very high, long and broad, whereof fome are of one ftone, eighty, ninety, nay, an hundred fpans long, and fifteen, or twenty broad, which doubtleffe is very marvellous, for it is almoft impoffible to comprehend by what means fo huge a maffe of ftone could be drawn out of the Quarry without breaking, and how it fhould be tranfported to the place where it was to be fet. All the ways and paffages, from Cities, Towns, and Villages, have very large caufeys made of fair ftone, at the ends whereof are coftly pillars and arches, upon which are infcriptions with letters of gold, containing the prayfers of them that erected them; moreover there are handfome feats placed all along for poor paffengers to reft themfelves on : There are likewife innumerable Aqueducks and fountains every where, whofe water is moft wholefom and excellent to drink ; And in divers parts there are certain Wenches of love, that out of charity proftitute themfelves to travellers, which have no mony, and although amongft us this is held for a great abufe and abomination, yet with them it is accounted a work of mercy, fo that many on their death-beds do by their teftaments bequeath great revenues, for the maintenance of this wickednefs, as a thing very meritorious for the falvation of their fouls ; moreover many others have left lands for the erecting and maintaining of houfes, in deferts and unhabited places, where great fires are kept all the night to guide fuch as have ftrayed out of their way, as alfo water for men to drink, and feats to repofe them in, and that there may be no default herein, there are divers perfons entertained with very good means, to fee thefe things carefully continued, according to the inftitution of him that founded them for the health of his foul. By thefe marvels which are found in the particular Towns of this Empire, may be concluded what the greatnefs thereof might be, were they joyned all together ; but for the better fatisfaction of the Reader, I dare boldly fay, if my teftimony may be worthy of credit, that in one and twenty years fpace, during which time, with a world of misfortune, labour and pain, I traverfed the greateft part of *Afia*, as may appear by this my difcourfe, I had feen in fome countrys a wonderfull abundance of feveral forts of victuals, and provifions, which we have not in our *Europe*, yet without fpeaking what each of them might have in particular, I do not think there is in all *Europe* fo much as there is in *China* alone ; And the fame may be faid of all the reft, wherewith Heaven hath favoured this clymate, as well for the temperature of the air, as for that which concerns the policy, and riches, the magnificence and greatnefs of their eftate ; Now that which gives the greateft lufter unto it, is, their exact obfervation of juftice, for there is fo well ruled a Government in this Country, as it may juftly be envied of all others in the world ; And to fpeak the truth, fuch as want this particular, have no glofs, be they otherways never fo great & commendable. Verily, fo often as I reprefent unto my felf thofe great things which I have feen in this *China*, I am on the one fide amazed to think how liberally it hath pleafed God to heap up on this people, the goods of the earth, & on the other fide I am exceedingly grieved to confider how ungratefull they are in acknowledging fuch extraordinary favours ; for they commit amongft themfelves an infinite of moft enormous fins, wherewithal they inceffantly offend the Divine Goodnefs, as well in their bruitifh and diabolical Idolatries, as in the abominable fin of *Sodomy*, which is not only permitted amongft them in publique, but is alfo accounted for a great vertue according to the inftructions of their Priefts.

CHAP. XXXII.

Our Arrival at the City of Pequin ; *together with our imprifonment, and that which moreover happened unto us there ; as alfo the great Majefty of the Officers of their Court of Juftice.*

AFter we were departed from that rare and marvellous Town, whereof I have fpoken, §. 1. we continued our courfe up the river, until at length on *Tuefday*, the nineteenth of *October*, in the year 1541. we arrived at the great City of *Pequin*, whither, as I have faid before, we had been remitted by Appeal ; In this manner chained three and three together, we were caft into a prifon, called *Gofanianferca*, where for our welcom we had at the firft dafh thirty
lafhes

laſhes a piece given us, wherewith ſome of us became very ſick: Now as ſoon as the *Chifun* who conducted us thither, had preſented the proceſs of our ſentence, ſealed with twelve ſeals, to the Juſtice of the *Aytao*, which is their Parliament, the twelve *Chonchalis* of the criminal Chamber, unto whom the cogniſance of our cauſe appertained, commanded us preſently away to priſon, whereupon one of thoſe twelve, aſſiſted by two Regiſters, and ſix or ſeven officers, whom they term *Hupes*, and are much like our Catchpoles here, terrified us not a little, as he was leading us thither, for giving us very threatning ſpeeches, *Come*, ſaid he unto us, *By the power and authority, which I have from the Aytao of Batampina, chief Preſident of the two and thirty Judges of ſtrangers, within whoſe breſt are the ſecrets of the Lyon crowned on the throne of the world incloſed, I enjoyn and command you to tell me, what people you are, as alſo of what country, and whether you have a King, who for the ſervice of God, and for the diſcharge of his dignity, is inclined to do good to the poor, and to render them juſtice, to the end that with tears in their eyes, and hands lifted up, they may not addreſſe their complaints to that Soveraign Lord, which hath made the bright Enamel of the skies, and for whoſe holy feet all they that reign with him, ſerve but for ſandals.* To this demand we anſwered him, that we were poor ſtrangers, natives of the Kingdom of *Siam*, who being imbarqued with our Merchandiſe for *Liampoo*, were caſt away in a great ſtorm at ſea, from whence we eſcaped naked with the loſs of all that we had, and how in that deplorable eſtate we were fain to get our living by begging from door to door till ſuch time as at our arrival at the Town of *Taypor*, the *Chumbim*, then reſident there, had arreſted us for priſoners without cauſe, and ſo ſent us to the City of *Nanquin*, where by his report we had been condemned to the whip, and to have our thumbs cut off, without ſo much as once daigning to hear us in our juſtifications, by reaſon whereof lifting up our eyes to Heaven, we had been adviced to have recourſe with our tears to the four and twenty Judges of auſter life, that through their zeal to God, they might take our cauſe in hand, ſince by reaſon of our poverty we were altogether without ſupport, and abandoned of all men, which with an holy zeal they incontinently effected by revoking the cauſe, and annulling the judgment that had been given againſt us, and that theſe things conſidered we moſt inſtantly beſought him, that for the ſervice of God he would be pleaſed to have regard to our miſery, and the great injuſtice that was done us, for that we had no means in this Country, nor perſon that would ſpeak one word for us. The Judg remained ſomtimes in ſuſpence upon that we had ſaid to him, at length he anſwered, that we need ſay no more to him, for it is ſufficient that I know you are poor, to the end this affair may go another way then hitherto it hath done, neverthertheleſs to acquit me of my charge, I give you five days time, conformably to the Law of the third Book, that within the ſaid term you may retain a Proctor to undertake your cauſe, but if you will be adviſed by me, you ſhall preſent your requeſt to the *Tanigores* of the ſacred Office, to the end that they carryed by an holy zeal of the honour of God, may out of compaſſion of your miſeries, take upon them to defend your right. Having ſpoken thus, he gave us a *Taeis* in way of alms, and ſaid further to us, Beware of the priſoners that are here, for I aſſure you that they make it their trade, to ſteal all that they can from any one; whereupon entring into another chamber where there were a great number of priſoners, he continued there above three hours in giving them audience, at the end whereof he ſent ſeven and twenty men, that the day before had received their judgment to execution, which was inflicted upon them by whipping to death, a ſpectacle ſo dreadful to us, and that put us in ſuch a fright, as it almoſt ſet us beſides our ſelves: The next morning, as ſoon as it was day, the Jaylors clapt irons on our feet, and manacles on our hands, and put us to exceeding great pain, but ſeven days after we had endured ſuch miſery, being laid on the ground one by another, and bewayling our diſaſter, for the extream fear we were in, of ſuffering a moſt cruel death, if that which we had done at *Calempluy* ſhould by any means chance to be diſcovered, it pleaſed God that we were viſited by the *Tanigores* of the houſe of mercy, which is of the juriſdiction of this priſon, who are called in their language *Coſilem Gnaxy*; At their arrival all the priſoners bowing themſelves, ſaid with a lamentable tone, *Bleſſed be the day wherein God doth viſit us by the miniſtery of his ſervants*; whereunto the *Tanigories* made anſwer with a grave and modeſt countenance, *The Almighty and divine hand of him that hath formed the beauty of the ſtars keep and preſerve you*; Then approaching to us, they very courteouſly demanded of us what people we were, and whence it proceeded that our impriſonment was more ſenſible to us then to others? To this ſpeech we replied with tears in our eyes, that we were poor ſtrangers, ſo abandoned of men, as in all

that

that Country there was not one that knew our names, and that all we could in our poverty say to intreat them to think of us for Gods sake, was contained in a letter, that we had brought them from the Chamber of the Society of the house of *Quiay Hinarol*, in the City of *Nanquin*; whereupon *Christophoro Borralho*, presenting them with the letter, they received it with a new ceremony, full of all curtesie, saying, *Praysed be he who hath created all things, for that he is pleased to serve himself of sinners here below, whereby they may be recompensed at the last day of all days, by satisfying them double their labour with the riches of his holy treasures, which shall be done, as we believe in as great abundance, as the drops of rain fall from the clouds to the earth.* After this, one of the four, putting up the Letter, said unto us, that as soon as the Chamber of Justice for the poor was open, they would all of them give an answer to our busine's, and see us furnished with all that we had need of, and so they departed from us: Three days after they returned to visit us in the prison, and in the next morning coming to us again, they asked us many questions answerable to a memorial which they had thereof, whereunto we replyed in every point according as we were questioned by each of them, so as they remained very well satisfied with our answers; Then calling the Register to them, who had our papers in charge, they inquired very exactly of him, touching many things that concerned us, and withall required his advice about our affair; that done, having digested all that might make for the conversation of our right into certain heads, they took our process from him, saying, they would peruse it all of them together in their Chambers of Justice with the Proctors of the house, and the next day return it him again, that he might carry it to the *Chaem*, as he was resolved before to do.

Not to trouble my self with recounting in particular all that occurred in this affair, until such time as it was fully concluded, wherein six months and an half were imployed, during the **S. 2.** which we continued stil prisoners in such misery, I will in few words relate all that befel us unto the end; when as our business was come before the twelve *Conchalis* of the criminal Court, the two Proctors of the house of mercy most willingly took upon them to cause the unjust sentence, which had been given against us, to be revoked; Having gotten then all the proceedings to be disannulled, they by petition remonstrated unto the *Chaem*, who was the President of that Court, *How we could not for any cause whatsoever be condemned to death, seeing there were no witnesses of any credit that could testifie that we had robbed any man, or had ever seen us carry any offensive weapons contrary to the prohibition made against it by the Law of the first book, but that we were apprehended quite naked, like wretched men, wandering after a lamentable shipwrack, and that therefore our poverty and misery was worthy rather of a pitiful compassion, then of that rigour, wherewith the first Ministers of the arm of wrath had caused us to be whipt; moreover that God alone was the Judg of our innocency, in whose name they required him once, twice, nay many times, to consider that he was mortal, and could not last long, for that God had given him a perishable life, at the end whereof he was to render an account of that which had been required of him, since by a solemn oath he was obliged to do all that should be manifest to his judgment, without any consideration of men of the world, whose custom it was to make the ballance sway down, which God would have to be upright, according to the integrity of his divine Justice.* To this petition the Kings Proctor opposed himself, as he that was our adverse party, and that in certain articles, which he framed against us, set forth, how he would prove by ocular witnesses, as well of the Country, as strangers, that we were publique thieves, making a common practise of robbing, and not merchants, such as we pretended to be; whereunto he added, that if we had come to the Coast of *China* with a good designe, and with an intent to pay the King his due in his Custom-houses, we would have repaired to the ports, where they were established by the Ordinance of the *Aytan* of the Government, but for a punishment, because we went from Isle to Isle, like Pirats, Almighty God, that detests sin and robbery, had permitted us to suffer shipwrack, that so falling into the hands of the Ministers of his justice, we might receive the guerdon of our wicked works, namely, the pains of death, whereof our crimes rendred us most worthy; In regard of all which, he desired we might be condemned according to the Law of the second book, that commanded it in express terms; And that if for other considerations, no way remarkable in us, we could by any law be exempted from death, yet nevertheless for that we were strangers, and vagabonds, without either faith, or knowledg of God, that alone would suffice at leastwise to condemn us to have our hands and noses cut off, and so to be banished for ever into the Country of *Ponxileytay*, whither such peo-

pla

ple as we, were wont to be exiled, as might be verified by divers sentences given and executed in like cases, and to that effect, he desired the admittance of his articles, which he promised to prove within the time, that should be prescribed him. These articles were presently excepted against by the Proctor of the Court of Justice, established for the poor, who offered to make the contrary appear within a certain term, which to that end, and for many other reasons alleadged by him in our favour, was granted him, wherefore he required that the said articles might not be admitted, especially for that they were infamous, and directly contrary to the Ordinances of Justice. Whereupon the *Chaem* ordered, that his articles should not be admitted, unless he did prove them by evident testimonies, and such as were conformable to the Divine Law, within six days next ensuing, and that upon pain in case of contravention not to be admitted to any demand of a longer delay. The said term of six days being prescribed the Kings Proctor, he, in the mean time, producing no one proof against us, nor any person that so much as knew us, came and demanded a delay of other six days, which was flatly denied him, in regard it but too well appeared, that all he did was only to win time, and therefore he would by no means consent unto it, but contrarily he gave the Proctor for the poor five days respit to alledge all that further he could in our defence; In the mean time, the Kings Proctor declaimed against us in such foul and opprobrious terms, as the *Chaem* was much offended thereat, so that he condemned him to pay us twenty *Taeis* of silver, both for his want of charity, and for that he could not prove any one of the obligations which he had exhibited against us. Three days being spent herein, four *Tanigores* of the house of the poor, coming very early in the morning to the prison, sent for us into the *Infirmirie*, where they told us that our business went very well, and how we might hope that our sentence would have a good issue, whereupon we cast our selves at their feet, and with abundance of tears desired God to reward them for the pains they had taken in our behalf. Thereunto one of them replyed, *And we also most humbly beseech him to keep you in the knowledg of his Law, wherein all the happiness of good men consists*; and so they caused two coverlets to be given us, for to lay upon our beds in the night, because the weather was cold, and withall bid us, that we should not stick to ask any thing we wanted, for that God Almighty did not love a sparing hand in the distributing of alms for his sake. A little after their departure came the Register, and shewing us the *Chaems* order, whereby the Kings Proctor was condemned to pay us twenty *Taeis*, gave us the mony, and took an acquittance under our hands for the receipt of it; For which giving him a world of thanks, we intreated him for his pains to take as much thereof as he pleased, but he would not touch a peny, saying, I will not for so small a matter lose the recompence which I hope to gain from God, for the consideration of you.

§.3.   We past nine days in great fear, still expecting to have our sentence pronounced, when as one *Saturday* morning two *Chumbims* of Justice came to the prison for us, accompanied with twenty officers, by them called *Huppes*, carrying Halberts, Portisans, and other arms, which made them very dreadfull to the beholders; These men tying us all nine together in a long iron chain, lead us to the *Caladigan*, which was the place where audience was given, and where execution was done on delinquents; Now how we got thither, to confess the truth, I am not able to relate, for we were at that instant so far besides our selves, as we knew not what we did, or which way we went, so as in that extremity all our thought was how to conform our selves to the will of God, and beg of him with tears, that for the merit of his sacred passion, he would be pleased to receive the punishment, that should be inflicted on us for the satisfaction of our sins. At length after much pain, and many affronts, that were done us by many which followed after us, with loud cries, we arrived at the first Hall of the *Caladigan*, where were four and twenty Executioners, whom they call, *The Ministers of the arm of justice*, with a great many of other people, that were there about their affairs. Here we remained a long time, till at length upon the ringing of a bell, other doors were opened, that stood under a great Arch of Architecture, very artificially wrought, and whereon were a number of rich figures; On the top a monstrous Lion of silver was seen, with his fore and hind feet upon a mighty great bowl, made of the same mettal, whereby the arms of the King of *China* are represented, which are ordinarily placed on the Fore-front of all the Sovereign Courts, where the *Chaems* precide, who are as Vice-roys amongst us. Those doors being opened, as I said before, all that were there present entred into a very great Hall, like the Body of a Church, hung from the top to the bottom with divers pictures, wherein strange kinds of of execution done upon perfons of all conditions, after a moft dreadful manner were conftrained, and under every picture was this infcription, *Such a one was executed with this kind of death for committing fuch a crime*; fo that in beholding the diverfity of thefe fearful pourtraitures one might fee in it, as it were, a declaration of the kind of death that was ordained for each crime, as alfo the extream rigour which the Juftice there obferved in fuch executions. From this Hall we went into another room far richer, and more coftly, for it was guilt all over, fo that one could not have a more pleafing object, at leaft wife, if we could have taken pleafure in any thing, confidering the mifery we were in. In the midft of this room there was a Tribunal, whereunto one afcended by feven fteps, invironed with three rows of ballifters of iron, copper, and ebony; the tops whereof were beautified with Mother of Pearl: At the upper end of all was a cloth of State of white damask, frenged about with a deep cawl frenge of green filk and gold; Under this State fat the *Chaem* with a world of greatnefs and majefty, he was feated in a very rich Chair of filver, having before him a little table, and about him three boys on their knees, fumptuoufly apparelled, with chains of gold, one of the which (namely, he in the middle) ferved to give the *Chaem* the pen wherewithall he figned; The other two took the petitions that were preferred, and prefented them on the Table, that they might be figned; On the right hand in another place fomewhat higher, and almoft equall with the *Chaem*, ftood a boy, fome ten or eleven years old, attired in a rich robe of white Satin, imbroidered with rofes of gold, having a chain of pearl three double about his neck, and hair as long as a womans, moft neatly plaited with a fillet of gold, all enamelled with green, and powdered over with great feed pearl; In his hand he held, as a mark of that which he reprefented, a little branch of rofes, made of filk, gold thread, and rich pearls, very curioufly intermixed; And in this manner he appeared fo gentile, handfome, and beauiful, as no woman, how fair foever, could overmatch him; this boy leaned on his elbow upon the *Chaems* chair, and figured mercy. In the like manner, on the left hand was another goodly boy, richly apparelled in a Coat of carnation Satin, all fet with rofes of gold, having his right arm bared up to the elbow, and died with a vermilion as red as blood, and in that hand holding a naked fword, which feemed alfo to be bloody: moreover, on his head he wore a crown, in fafhion like to a Myter, hung all with little razors, like unto lancets, wherewith Chyrurgions let men blood, being thus gallantly fet forth, and of moft beautiful prefence, yet he ftruck all that beheld him with fear, in regard of that he reprefented, which was Juftice. For they fay, that the Judg, which holds the place of the King, who prefents God on earth, ought neceffarily to have thofe two qualities, *Juftice*, and *Mercy*; and that he which doth not ufe them is a Tyrant, acknowledging no Law, and ufurping the power that he hath. The *Chaem* was apparelled in a long Gown of violet Satin, frenged with green filk and gold, with a kind of fcapulair about his neck, in the midft of which was a great plate of gold, wherein an hand holding a very even pair of ballance was engraven, and the infcription about it; *It is the nature of the Lord Almighty, to obferve in his juftice, weight, meafure, and true account, therefore take heed to what thou doeft, for if thou comeft to fin thou fhalt fuffer for it eternally.* Upon his head he had a kind of round bonet, bordered about with fmall fprigs of gold, all enamelled violet and green, and on the top of it was a little crowned Lion of gold, upon a round bowl of the fame mettal; by which Lion crowned, as I have delivered heretofore, is the King fignified, and by the bowl, the world, as if by thefe devices, they would denote, that the King is the Lion crowned on the throne of the world; In his right hand he held a little rod of ivory, fome three fpans long, in manner of a Scepter; upon the top of the three firft fteps of this Tribunal ftood eight Ufhers with filver maces on their fhoulders, and below were threefcore *Mogors* on their knees, difpofed into three ranks, carrying halberts in their hands, that were neatly damasked with gold; In the vantgard of thefe fame ftood, like as if they had been, the Commanders or Captains of this Squadron, the Statues of two Giants, of a moft gallant afpect, and very richly attired, with their fwords hanging in fcarfs, and mighty great halberts in their hands, and thefe the *Chinefes* in their langnage call *Gigaos*; on the two fides of this Tribunal below in the room were two very long tables, at each of which fat twelve men, whereof four were Prefidents, or Judges, two, Regifters, four, Solicitors, and two, *Conchalis*, which are as it were, Affiftants to the Couw, one of thefe Tables was for criminal, and the other for civil caufes, and all the officers of both thefe Tables were apparelled in gowns of white Satin, that were very long, and had large flieves, thereby demonftrating the latitude and purity of juftice; the Tables were covered with carpets of violet damask, and richly bordered about with gold,

S

the

the *Chaems* table, becaufe it was of filver, had no carpet on it, nor any thing elfe, but a cufhion of cloth of gold, and a Standith ; Now all thefe things put together, as we faw them, carried a wonderful fhew of State and Majefty ; But to proceed, upon the fourth ringing of a bell, one of the *Conchalis* ftood up, and after a low obeyfance made to the *Chaem*, with a very loud voice, that he might be heard of every one, he faid, *Peace there, and with all fubmiffion hearken, on pain of incurring the punifhment, ordained by the* Chaems *of the Government for thofe, that interrupt the filence of facred Juftice.* Whereupon this fame fitting down again, another arofe, and with the like reverence, mounting up to the Tribunal, where the *Chaem* fat, he took the Sentences from him that held them in his hand, and publifhed them aloud one after another, with fo many ceremonies, and compliments, as he employed above an hour therein ; At length coming to pronounce our judgment, they caufed us to kneel down, with our eyes fixed on the ground, and our hands lifted up, as if we were praying unto Heaven, to the end that in all humility we might hear the publication thereof, which was thus ; *Bitau Dicabor, the new* Chaem *of this facred Court, where juftice is rendred to ftrangers, and that by the gracious pleafure of the Son of the Sun, the Lion crowned on the throne of the world, unto whom are fubjected all the Scepters and Crowns of the Kings that govern the earth ; ye are fubjected under his feet by the grace and will of the moft High in Heaven, having viewed and confidered the Appeal made to me by thefe nine ftrangers, whofe caufe was commanded hither by the City of* Nanquin, *by the four and twenty of aufteer life, I fay, by the oath I have taken upon my entry into the Charge, which I exercife for the* Aytao *of Batampina, the chief of two and thirty that govern all the people of this Empire, that the ninth day of the feventh Moon, in the fifteenth year of the reign of the Son of the Sun, I was prefented with the accufations, which the* Cumbim *of* Taypor, *fent me againft them, whereby he chargeth them to be theeves, and robbers of other mens goods, affirming that they have long practifed that trade, to the great offence of the Lord above, who hath created all things ; and withall that without any fear of God they ufed to bathe themfelves in the blood of thofe, that with reafon refifted them, for which they have already been condemned to be whipt, and have their thumbs cut off, whereof the one hath been put in execution ; but when they came to have their thumbs cut off, the Proctors for the poor, oppofing it, alledged in their behalf, that they were wrongfully condemned, becaufe there was no proof of that wherewith they were charged, in regard whereof they required for them, that in ftead of judging them upon a bare fhew of uncertain fufpitions, voluable teftimonies might be produced, and fuch as were conformable to the divine Laws, and the Juftice of Heaven ; whereunto anfwer was made by that Court, how juftice was to give place to mercy, whereupon they that undertook their caufe made their complaint to the four and twenty of aufteer life, who both out of very juft confiderations, and the regard they had to the little fupport they could have, for that they were ftrangers, and of a Nation fo far diftant from us, as we never heard of the Country where they fay they were born, mercifully inclining to their lamentable cries, fent them and their caufe to be judged by this Court, wherefore omitting the profecution thereof here by the Kings Proctor, being able to prove nothing whereof he accufed them, affirms only that they are worthy of death for the fufpicion and jealoufie they have given of themfelves, but in regard facred juftice, that ftands upon confiderations which are pure and agreeable to God, admits of no reafons from an adverfe party, if they be not made good by evident proofs, I thought it not fit to allow of the Kings Proctors accufations, fince he could not prove what he had alledged, whereupon infifting on his demand, without fhewing either any juft caufes, or fufficient proof concerning that he concluded againft thofe ftrangers, I condemned him in twenty* Taeis *of filver amends to his adverfe parties, being altogether according to equity, becaufe the reafons alledged by him were grounded upon a bad zeal, and fuch as were neither juft, nor pleafing to God, whofe mercy doth always incline to their fide that are poor and feeble on the earth, when as they invoke him with tears in their eyes, as is daily and clearly manifefted by the pitiful effects of his greatnefs ; fo that having thereupon exprefly commanded the* Tanigores *of the houfe of mercy, to alledge whatfoever they could fay on their behalf, they accordingly did fo, within the time that was prefixed them for that purpofe ; And fo all proceedings having received their due courfe, the caufe is now come to a final Judgment : Wherefore every thing duly viewed and confidered, without regard had to any humane refpect, but only to the merit and equity of their caufe, and according to the refolution of the Laws, accepted by the twelve* Chaems *of the Government in the fifth book of the will and pleafure of the Son of the Sun, who*

in

in such cases out of his greatness and goodness hath more regard to the complaints of the poor, then to the insolent clamors of the proud of the earth; I do ordain, and decree, that these nine strangers shall be clearly quit and absolved of all that, which the Kings Proctor hath laid to their charge, as also of all the punishment belonging thereunto, condemning them only to a years exile, during which time they shall work for their living in the reparations of Quansy; and when as eight months of the said year shall be accomplished, then I expresly enjoyn all the Chumbims, Conchalis, Monteos, and other Ministers of their government, that immediately upon their presenting of this my Decree unto them, they give them a passeport and safe conduct, to the end they may freely and securely return into their Country, or to any other place they shal think fit. After this sentence was thus published in our hearing, we all cried out with a loud voice, *The Sentence of thy clear judgment is confirmed in us, even as the purity of thy heart is agreeable to the son of the Sun.* This said, one of the *Conchalis*, that sate at one of the tables, stood up, and having made a very low obeisance to the *Chaem*, he said aloud five times one after another, to all that presse of people, which were there in great number; *Is there any one in this Court, in this City, or in this Kingdom, that will oppose this Decree, or the deliverance of these nine prisoners?* Whereunto no answer being made the two boyes, that represented justice and mercy, touched the ensignes which they held in their hands together, and said aloud, *Let them be freed and discharged according to the sentence very justly pronounced for it;* whereupon one of those Ministers, whom they call *Huppes*, having rung a bell thrice, the two *Chumbims* of execution, that had formerly bound us, unlosed us from our chain, and withall took off our manacles, collers, and the other irons from our legs, so that we were quite delivered, for which we gave infinite thanks to our Lord Jesus Christ, because we always thought, that for the ill conceit men had of us, we should be condemned to death. From thence so delivered as we were, they led us back to the prison, where the two *Chumbims* signed our enlargment in the Jaylors book; nevertheless that we might be altogether discharged, we were to go two months after to serve a year according to our sentence, upon pain of becoming slaves for ever to the King, conformable to his Ordinances: Now because we would presently have gone about to demand the alms of good people in the City, the *Chifun*, who was as Grand Provost of that prison, perswaded us to stay till the next day, that he might first recommend us to the *Tanigores* of mercy, that they might do something for us.

Chap. XXXIII.

What past betwixt us, and the Tanigores of mercy, with the great favors they did us; and a brief Relation of the City of Pequin, where the King of China kept his Court.

THe next morning the four *Tanigores* of mercy came to visit the Infirmity of this prison, as they used to do; where they rejoyced with us for the good success of our Sentence, giving us great testimony, how well contented they were with it, for which we returned them many thanks, not without shedding abundance of tears, whereat they seemed to be not a little pleased, and willed us not to be troubled with the term we were condemned to serve in, for they told us that in stead of a year we should continue but eight months there, and that the other four months, which made the third part of our punishment, the King remitted it by way of alms for Gods sake, in consideration that we were poor, for otherwise if we had been rich, and of ability, we should have had no favour at all, promising to cause this diminution of punishment to be endorsed on our Sentence, and besides that they would go, and speak to a very honourable man for us, that was appointed to be the chief Marshal, or Monteo, of *Quansy*, the place where we were to serve, to the end he might shew us favour, and cause us to be truly paid for the time we should remain there: Now because this man was naturally a friend to the poor, and inclined to do them good, they thought it would be fit to carry us along with them to his house, the rather for that it might be he would take us into his charge; we gave them all very humble thanks for this good offer of theirs, and told them that God would reward this charity, they shewed us for his sake; whereupon we accompanied them to the *Monteos* house, who came forth to receive us in his outward Court, leading his wife by the hand, which he did, either out of a greater form of complement, or to do the more honour to the *Tanigo-*

res, and coming neer them he proſtrated himſelf at their feet, and ſaid : *It is now, my Lord, and holy brethren, that I have cauſe to rejoyce, for that it hath pleaſed God to permit, that you his holy ſervants ſhould come unto my houſe, being that which I could not hope for, in regard I held my ſelfe unworthy of ſuch favour.* After the *Tanigores* had uſed many complements and cereremonies to him, as is uſuall in that Country, they anſwered him thus, *May God, our Soveraign Lord, the infinite ſource of mercy, recompence the good thou acſt for the poor with bleſſing in this life ; for believe it, dear brother, the ſtrongeſt ſtaff whereon the ſoul doth lean to keep her from falling ſo often as ſhe happens to ſtumble, is the charity, which we uſe towards our neighbour, when as the vain glory of this world doth not blind the good zeal whereunto his holy Law doth oblige us, and that thou mayſt merit the bleſſed felicity of beholding his face, we have brought thee here theſe nine* Portugals, *who are ſo poor, as none in this Kingdom are like to them ; wherefore we pray thee that in the place whither thou art going now, as* Monteo, *thou wilt do for them all that thou thinkeſt will be acceptable to the Lord above, in whoſe behalf we crave this of thee.* To this Speech the *Monteo*, and his wife, replyed in ſuch courteous and remarkable terms, as we were almoſt beſides our ſelves to hear in what manner they attributed the ſucceſſe of their affairs, to the principal cauſe of all goodneſs, even as though they had the light of faith, or the knowledg of the Chriſtian verity. Hereupon they withdrew into a Chamber, into which we went not, and continued there about half an hour; then as they were about to take leave of one another, they commanded us to come in to them, where the *Tanigores* ſpake to them again about us, and recommending us unto them more then before, the *Monteo* cauſed our names to be written down in a book that lay before him, and ſaid unto us, *I do this, becauſe I am not ſo good a man, as to give you ſomething of mine own, nor ſo bad as to deprive you of the ſweat of your labour, whereunto the King hath bound you, wherefore even at this inſtant you ſhall begin to get your living, although you do not ſerve as yet, for the deſire I have that this may be accounted to me for an alms, ſo that now you have nothing to do, but to be merry in my houſe, where I will give order that you ſhall be provided of all that is neceſſary for you ; Beſides this, I will not promiſe you any thing, for the fear I am in of the ſhewing ſome vanity by my promiſe, and ſo the Divel may make uſe thereof as of an advantage, to lay hold on me, a matter that often arrives through the weakneſs of our nature ; wherefore let it ſuffice you for the preſent to know, that I will be mindful of you for the love of theſe holy brethren here, who have ſpoken to me for you.* The four *Tanigores* thereupon taking their leave, gave us four *Taeis*, and ſaid unto us, *Forget not to render thanks unto God for the good ſucceſs you have had in your buſineſs, for it would be a grievous ſin in you not to acknowledge ſo great a grace.* Thus were we very well entertained in the houſe of this Captain for the ſpace of two months, that we remained there, at the end whereof we parted from thence, for to go to *Quanſy*, where we were to make up our time, under the conduct of this Captain, who ever after uſed us very kindly, and ſhewed us many favours, untill that the *Tartars* entred into the Town, who did a world of miſchief there, as I will more amply declare hereafter.

§. 2.   Before I recount that which happened unto us, after we were imbarqued with thoſe *Chineſes* that conducted us, and that gave us great hope of ſetting us at liberty, I think it not amiſs to make a brief relation here of the City of *Pequin*, which may truly be termed the capital of the Monarchy of the world, as alſo of ſome particulars I obſerved there, as well for its arches and policy, as for that which concerns its extent, its government, the laws of the Country, and the admirable manner of providing for the good of the whole State, together in what ſort they are paid, that ſerve in the time of war, according to the Ordinances of the Kingdom, and many other things like unto theſe, though I muſt needs confeſs that herein I ſhall want the beſt part, namely, wit, and capacity, to render a reaſon in what clymate it is ſcituated, and in the heigth of how many degrees, which is a matter the learned and curious moſt deſire to be ſatisfied in ; But my deſigne having never been other (as I have ſaid heretofore) then to leave this my book unto my children, that therein they may ſee the ſufferings I have undergone, it little imports me to write otherwiſe then I do, that is, in a groſs and rude manner ; for I hold it better to treat of theſe things in ſuch ſort as nature hath taught me, then to uſe Hyperboles, and ſpeeches from the purpoſe, whereby the weakneſs of my poor underſtanding may be made more evident. Howbeit ſince I am obliged to make mention of this matter, by the promiſe i have made of it heretofore, I ſay, that this City, which we call *Pequin*, and they of the Country *Pequin*, is ſcituated in the heigth of forty and one degrees of Northerly latitude ;

the

the walls of it are in circuit (by the report of the *Chineses* themselves, and as I have read in a little book, treating of the greatness thereof, and intituled *Aquisendan*, which I brought since along with me into *Portugal*) thirty large leagues, namely ten long, and five broad ; Some others hold, that it is fifty, namely seventeen in length, and eight in bredth : and forasmuch as they that intreat of it are of different opinions, in that the one make the extent of it thirty leagues, as I have said before, and others fifty, I will render a reason of this doubt, conformable to that which I have seen my self. It is true, that in the manner it is now built, it is thirty leagues in circuit, as they say, for it is invironed with two rows of strong walls, where there are a number of towers and bulwarks after our fashion ; But without this circuit, which is of the City it self, there is another far greater, both in length and bredth, that the *Chineses* affirm was anciently all inhabited, but at this present there are only some Boroughs and Villages, as also a many of fair houses, or castles about it, amongst the which there are sixteen hundred, that have great advantages over the rest, and are the houses of the Proctors of the sixteen hundred Cities, and most remarkable Towns of the two and thirty Kingdoms of this Monarchy, who repair unto this City at the general Assembly of the Estates, which is held every three years for the publique good. Without this great inclosure, which (as I have said) is not comprehended in the City, there is in a distance of three leagues broad, and seven long, fourscore thousand Tombs of the *Mandarins*, which are little Chappels all guilded within, and compassed about with Billisters of iron and latin, the entries whereinto are through very rich and sumptuous arches : near to these Chappels there are also very great houses, with gardens and tufted woods of high trees, as also many inventions of ponds, fountains, and aqueducts ; whereunto may be added, that the walls of the inclosure are on the inside covered with fine porcelain, and on the fanes above are many Lions pourtrayed in gold, as also in the squares of the steeples, which are likewise very high, and embellished with pictures. It hath also five hundred very great Palaces, which are called *the houses of the Son of the Sun*, whither all those retire, that have been hurt in the Wars for the service of the King, as also many other souldiers, who in regard of age or sickness are no longer able to bear arms, and to the end that during the rest of their days they may be exempted from incommodity, each of them receives monthly a certain pay to find himself withall, and to live upon. Now all these men of War, as we learned of the *Chineses*, are ordinarily an hundred thousand, there being in each of those houses two hundred men according to their report. We saw also another long street of low houses, where there were four and twenty thousand oar-men, belonging to the King *Panoures* ; and another of the same structure a good league in length, where fourteen thousand Taverners that followed the Court dwelt : as also a third street like unto the other two, where live a great number of light women, exempted from the tribute, which they of the City pay, for that they are Curtisans, whereof the most part had quitted their husbands for to follow the wretched trade ; and if for that cause they come to receive any hurt, their husbands are grievously punished for it, because they are there as in a place of freedom, and under the protection of the *Tutan* of the Court, Lord Steward of the Kings house. In this inclosure do likewise remain all the Landresses, by them called *Maynates*, which wash the linnen of the City, who as we were told, are above an hundred thousand, and live in this quarter, for that there are divers rivers there, together with a number of wells, and deep pools of water, compassed about with good walls. Within this same inclosure, as the said *Aquisendan* relates, there are thirteen hundred gallant and very sumptuous houses of religious men and women, who make profession of the four principal Laws of those two and thirty which are in the Empire of *China*, and it is thought that in some of these houses there are above a thousand persons, besides the servants, that from abroad do furnish them with victuals, and other necessary provisions. We saw also a great many houses, which have fair buildings of a large extent, with spacious inclosures, wherein there are gardens, and very thick woods, full of any kind of game, either for hawking, or hunting, that may be desired ; And these houses are as it were Inns, whither come continually in great number people of all ages, and sexes, as to see Comedies, Playes, Combates, Bul-baitings, Wrastlings, and magnificent Feasts, with the *Tutons, Chaems, Conchacys, Aytaos, Bracalons, Chumbims, Monteos, Lauteas, Lords, Gentlemen, Captains, Merchants*, and other rich men, do make for to give content to their kindred and friends ; These houses are bravely furnished with rich hangings, beds, chairs, and stools, as likewise with huge cupbards of plate, not only of silver, but of gold also ; and the attendants that wait at the table, are maids ready to be married, very beautiful, and gallantly attired ; howbeit all
this

this is nothing in comparifon of the fumptuoufnefs, and other Magnificences that we faw there. Now the *Chinefes* affured us, there were fome feafts that lafted ten days after the *Carachina*, or *Chinefe* manner, which in regard of the ftate, pomp, and charge thereof, as well in the attendance of fervants and wayters, as in the coftly fare of all kind of flefh, fowl, fifh, and all delicacies in mufick, in fports of hunting, and hawking, in playes, comedies, tilts, turnayes, and in fhews both of horfe and foot, fighting and skirmifhing together, do coft above twenty thoufand *Taeis*. Thefe Inns do ftand in at leaft a million of gold, and are maintained by certain Companies of very rich Merchants, who in way of commerce and traffique employ their mony therein, whereby it is thought they gain far more, then if they fhould venture it to fea. It is faid alfo, that there is fo good and exact an order obferved there, that whenfoever any one will be at a charge that way, he goes to the *Xipaton* of the houfe, who is the fuperintendant thereof, and declares unto him what his defigne is, whereupon he fhews him a book, all divided into chapters, which treats of the ordering and fumptuoufnefs of Feafts, as alfo the rates of them, and how they fhall be ferved in, to the end, that he who will be at the charge, may chufe which he pleafes; This book, called *Pinetoreu*, I have feen, and heard it read, fo that I remember how in the three firft Chapters thereof, it fpeaks of the feafts, whereunto God is to be invited, and of what price they are; and then it defcends to the King of *China*, of whom it fayes, *That by a fpeciall grace of Heaven, and right of Soveraignty, he hath the Government of the whole earth, and of all the Kings that inhabit it.* After it hath done with the King of *China*, it fpeaks of the feafts of the *Tutons*, which are the ten Soveraign dignities, that command over the forty *Chaems*, who are as the Vice-royes of the State. Thefe *Tutons* alfo are termed the beams of the Sun, for, fay they, as the King of *China* is the Son of the Sun, fo the *Tutons*, who reprefent him, may rightly be termed his beams, for that they proceed from him, even as the rayes do from the Sun; But fetting afide the bruitifhnefs of thefe *Gentiles*, I will only fpeak of the Feaft, whereunto God is to be invited, which I have feen fome to make with much devotion, though for want of faith, their works can do them little good.

CHAP. XXXIV.

The Order which is obferved in the Feafts, that are made in certain Inns; and the State, which the Chaem of the two and thirty Univerfities keeps; with certain remarkable things in the City of Pequin.

THe firft thing whereof mention is made in the Preface of that Book, which treats of Feafts, as I have faid before, is the Feaft, that is to be made unto God here upon earth, of which it is fpoken in this manner: *Every Feaft, how fumptuous foever it be, may be paid for with a price, more or lefs, conformable to the bounty of him that makes it, who for all his charge beftowed on it reaps no other recompence, then the praife of flatterers and idle perfons; wherefore, O my Brother, faith the Preface of the faid Book, I counfel thee to imploy thy goods in feafting of God in his poor, that is to fay, fecretly to fupply the neceffities of good folks, fo that they may not perifh for want of that which thou haft more then thou needeft. Call to mind alfo the vile matter wherewith thy father ingendred thee, and that too, which is far more abject, wherewith thy mother conceived thee, and fo thou wilt fee how much inferiour thou art, even to the bruit beafts, which without diftinction of reafon apply themfelves to that whereunto they are carried by the flefh; and feeing that in the quality of a man thou wilt invite thy friends, who poffibly by to morrow may not be, to fhew that thou art good and faithful, invite the poor creatures of God, of whofe groans and neceffities he like a pitiful Father taketh compaffion, and promifeth to him that doth them good infinite fatisfaction in the houfe of the Sun, where as an Article of faith we hold, that his fervants fhall abide for evermore in eternal happinefs.* After thefe words, and other fuch like, worthy to be obferved, the *Xipaton*, who, as I told you, is the chief of them that govern this great Labyrinth, fhews him all the Chapters of the Book, from one end to the other, and bids him look what manner of men, or Lords he will invite, what number of guefts, and how many days he will have the feaft to laft; for addeth he, the *Kings*, and *Tutons*, at the feafts that are made for them, have fo many Meffes of meat, fo many Attendants, fuch Furniture, fuch Chambers, fuch veffel, fuch plate, fuch fports, and fo many days of hawking, and hunting, all which amounts to fuch a fum of mony: Then if he will not beftow fo much, the *Xipaton* fhews him in another Chapter, the feafts which

are

are ordinarily made for the *Chaems, Aytaos, Ponchacis, Bracalons, Anchacis, Conchalaas, Lanteas,* or for Captains, and rich men, whereas other kind of persons of meaner condition have nothing else to do, but to sit down, and fall to on free cost, so that there are usually fifty or threescore rooms full of men and women of all sorts; There are also in other rooms most excellent and melodious consorts of musick, namely of Harps, Viols, Lutes, Bandores, Cornets, Sackbuts, and other Instruments, which are not in use amongst us. If it be a feast of women, as it often falls out to be, then are the waytcrs on the table likewise women, or young Damosels, richly attired, who for that they are maids, and endued with singular beauty, it happens many times that men of extraordinary quality fall in love with them, and do marry them. Now for a conclusion of that which I have to say of these Inns, of all the mony, which is spent upon such feasts, four in the hundred, whereof the *Xipaton* paies the one half, and they that make the feasts the other, is set apart for the entertainment of the table of the poor, whereunto for Gods sake all manner of people are admitted that will come to it; Moreover, they are allowed a Chamber, and a good bed but that only for the space of three days, unless they be women with child, or sick persons, which are not able to travel; for in that case they are entertained a longer time, because regard is had unto the people according to the need they are in. We saw also in this outward inclosure, which, as I have delivered, invirons all the other City, two and thirty great Edifices, or Colledges, distant about a flight shoot the one from the other, where such, as apply themselves to the study of the two and thirty Laws, which are professed in the two and thirty Kingdoms of this Empire, do recide. Now in each of these Colledges, according as we could guess by the great number of persons that we saw there, there should be above ten thousand Scholers; and indeed the *Aquesendoo,* which is the Book that treats of these things, makes them amount in the whole to four hundred thousand: There is likewise somewhat apart from the rest, another far greater and fairer Edifice, of almost a league in circuit, where all those that have taken degrees, as well in their Theologie, as in the Laws of the government of this Monarchy, do live. In this University there is a *Chaem,* who commands over all the Heads of the Colledges, and is called, by a title of eminent dignity, *Xileyxitapou,* that is to say, Lord of all the Nobles. This *Chaem,* for that he is more honourable, and of an higher quality then all the rest, keeps as great a Court as any *Tuton;* for he hath ordinarily a guard of three hundred *Mogores,* four and twenty *Loshers* that go with silver Maces before him, and six and thirty women, which mounted on white ambling Nags, trapped with silk and silver, ride playing on certain very harmonious instruments of musick, and singing to the tune thereof, make a pleasing Consort after their manner. There are also led before him twenty very handsome spare horses, without any other furniture then their clothes of silver tinsel, and with headstals full of little silver bells, every horse being waited on by six Halberdiers, and four footmen very well apparelled; Before all this train goes four hundred *Huppes,* with a number of great long chains, which trailing on the ground, make such a dreadful ratling and noise, as does not a litle terrifie all that are within hearing; Then next to them marches twelve men on horsback, called *Peretandas,* each of them carrying an Umbrello of carnation Sattin, and other twelve that follow them with banners of white damask, deeply indented, and edged about with golden frenge; Now after all this pomp comes the *Chaem* sitting in a triumphant Chariot, attended by threescore *Conchalas, Chumbims,* and *Monteos,* such as amongst us are the Chancellors, Judges, and Councellors of the Courts of Justice, and these go all on foot, carrying upon their shoulders Cymiters richly garnished with gold. Last of all follow lesser officers, that are like unto our Registers, Examiners, Auditors, Clarks Atturneys, and Solicitors, all likewise on foot, and crying out unto the people with a loud voice for to retire themselves into their houses, and clear the streets, so as there may be nothing to hinder or trouble the passage of this magnificence. But the most observable thing herein is, that close to the Person of the *Chaem,* march two little boyes on horsback, one on the right hand, the other on the left, richly attired, with their ensignes in their hands, signifying *Justice,* and *Mercy,* whereof I have spoken heretofore; That on the right side representing mercy, is clothed in white, and that on the left representing justice is apparelled in red; The horses whereon these little boyes are mounted, have on them foot-clothes of the same colour their garments are, and all their furniture and trappings are of gold, with a kind of net-work over them, made of silver thread; After each of these children march six young youths, about fifteen years of age, with silver Maces in their hands, so that all these things together are so remarkable, as there is no man that beholds them, but on the one side trembles for fear, and on the other side remains astonished

ſtoniſhed at the ſight of ſo much greatneſs, and majeſty. Now that I may not longer dwel on that which concerns this great incloſure, I will paſs over in ſilence many other marvels that we ſaw there, conſiſting in rich & fair buildings in magnificent *Pagodes*, in bridges placed upon great pillars of ſtone, on either ſide whereof are rayls or grates of iron finely wrought, and in high ways, that are ſtraight, broad, and all very well paved, whereof I think fit not to ſpeak, for by that which I have already ſaid, one may eaſily judg of what I have omitted, in regard of the reſemblance and conformity that is between them; wherefore I will only intreat, and that as ſuccinctly as I can, of certain buildings, which I ſaw in this City, chiefly of four, that I obſerved more curiouſly then the reſt, as alſo of ſome other particularities, that well deſerve to be inſiſted upon.

§.2.   This City of *Pequin*, whereof I have promiſed to ſpeak more amply then yet I have done, is ſo prodigious, and the things therein remarkable, as I do almoſt repent me for undertaking to diſcourſe of it, becauſe to ſpeak the truth, I know not where to begin, that I may be as good as my word; for one muſt not imagine it to be, either as the City of *Rome*, or *Conſtantinople*, or *Venice*, or *Paris*, or *London*, or *Sevill*, or *Liſbon*, or that any of the Cities of *Europe* are comparable unto it, how famous or populous ſoever they be: Nay I will ſay further, that one muſt not think it to be like to Grand *Cairo* in *Egypt*, *Tauris* in *Perſia*, *Amadaba* in *Cambaya*, *Biſnagar* in *Narſingna*, *Goura* in *Bengala*, *Ava* in *Chaleu*, *Timplan* in *Calaminhan*, *Martaban* and *Bagou* in *Pegu*, *Guimpel* and *Tinlau* in *Siammon*, *Odia* in the Kingdom of *Sornau*, *Paſſarvan* and *Dema* in the Iſland of *Jaoa*, *Tangor* in the Country of the *Lequiens*, *Uſangea* in the *Grand Cauchin*, *Lancama* in *Tartaria*, and *Meaco* in *Jappun*, all which Cities are the Capitals of many great Kingdoms; for I dare well affirm, that all thoſe ſame are not to be compared to the leaſt part of the wonderful City of *Pequin*, much leſs to the greatneſs and magnificence of that which is moſt excellent in it, whereby I underſtand her ſtately buildings, her inward riches, her exceſſive abundance of all that is neceſſary for the entertaining of life, alſo the world of people, the infinite number of Barques and Veſſels that are there, the Commerce, the Courts of Juſtice, the Government and the State of the *Tutons*, *Chaems*, *Anchacys*, *Aytaos*, *Puchancys*, and *Bracanons*, who rule whole Kingdoms, and very ſpacious Provinces, with great pentions, and are ordinarily reſident in this City, or others for them, when as by the Kings command they are ſent about affairs of conſequence. But ſetting theſe things aſide, whereof yet I intend to ſpeak more amply, when time ſhall ſerve, I ſay that this City, (according to that which is written of it, both in the *Aqueſendoo* before mentioned, and all the Chronicles of the Kingdom of *China*) is thirty leagues in circuit, not comprehending therein the buildings of the other incloſure that is without it, and is invironed with a double wall, made of good ſtrong free-ſtone, having three hundred and threeſcore gates, each of which hath a ſmall Fort, compoſed of two high towers, with its ditches, and draw-bridges; and at every gate is a Regiſter, & four Porters with halberds in their hands, who are bound to give account of all that goes in and out. Theſe gates by the Ordinance of the *Tuton*, are divided according to the three hundred and threeſcore dayes of the year, ſo that every day in his turn hath the feaſt of the invocation of the Idol, whereof each gate bears the name, celebrated with much ſolemnity. This great City hath alſo within that large incloſure of her walls, as the *Chineſes* aſſured us, three thouſand and three hundred *Pagodes* or Temples, wherein are continually ſacrificed a great number of birds and wild beaſts, which they hold to be more agreeable unto God, then ſuch as are kept tame in houſes, whereof their Prieſts render divers reaſons to the people, therewith perſwading them to believe ſo great an abuſe for an article of faith. The ſtructures of theſe *Pagodes*, whereof I ſpeak, are very ſumptuous, eſpecially thoſe of the orders of the *Menegrepos*, *Conquiays*, and *Talagrepos*, who are the Prieſts of the four Sects of *Xaca*, *Amida*, *Gizom*, and *Canom*, which ſurpaſs in antiquity the other two and thirty of that Labyrinth of the Divel, who appears to them many times in divers forms, for to make them give more credit to his impoſtures and lies. The principal ſtreets of this City are all very long and broad, with fair houſes of two or three ſtories high, and incloſed at both ends with balliſters of iron and lattin; the entrance into them is through lanes, that croſs theſe great ſtreets, at the ends whereof are great arches, with ſtrong gates, which are ſhut in the night, and on the top of the arches, there are watch-bels; Each of theſe ſtreets hath its Captain, and officers, who walk the round in their turns, and are bound every ten dayes to make report into the Town-houſe of all that paſſeth in their quarters, to the end that the *Punchacys*, or *Chaems* of the Government, may take ſuch order therein, as reaſon requires. Moreover this great City (if credit may

be

be given to that which the said book, so often before mentioned by me, records) hath an hundred and twenty Canals, made by the Kings and people in former times, which are three fathom deep, and twelve broad, crossing through the whole length and bredth of the City, by the means of a great number of bridges, built upon arches of strong free-stone, at the end whereof there are pillars, with chains, that reach from the one to the other, and resting places for passengers to repose themselves in : It is said that the bridges of these hundred & twenty Canals, or Aqueducts, are in number eighteen hundred, and that if one of them is fair and rich, the other is yet more, as well for the fashion, as for the rest of the workmanship thereof. The said Book affirms, *That in this City there are sixscore Piatzues, or publique places, in each of the which is a Fair kept every month.* Now during the two months time that we were at liberty in this City, we saw eleven or twelve of these Fairs, where were an infinite company of people, both on horse-back, and on foot, that out of boxes hanging about their necks sold all things that well neer can be named, as the Haberdashers of small wares do amongst us, besides the ordinary shops of rich Merchants, which were ranged very orderly in the particular streets, where was to be seen a world of silk stuffs, tinsels, cloth of gold, linnen, and cotton-cloth, sables, ermyns, musk, aloes, fine pourcelain, gold and silver plate, pearl, seed pearl, gold in powder, and lingots, and such other things of value, whereat we nine *Portugals* were exceedingly astonished ; But if I should speak in particular of all the other commodities, that were to be sold there, as of iron, steel, lead, copper, tin, latin, corral, cornalin, crystal, quicksilver, vermillion, ivory, cloves, nutmegs, mace, ginger, tamarinds, cinnamon, pepper, cardamone, borax, hony, wax, sanders, sugar, conserves, acates, fruit, meal, rice, flesh, venison, fish, pulse, and herbs ; there was such abundance of them, as it is scarce possible to express it in words. The *Chineses* also assured us, that this City hath an hundred and threescore Butchers shambles, and in each of them an hundred stalls, full of all kinds of flesh that the earth produceth, for that these people feed on all, as Veal, Mutton, Pork, Goat, the flesh of Horses, Buffles, Rhinocerets, Tygers, Lions, Dogs, Mules, Asses, Otters, Shamois, Bodgers, and finally of all other beasts whatsoever. Furthermore, besides the weights which are particularly in every shambles, there is not a gate in the City that hath not its scales, wherein the meat is weighed again, for to see if they have their due weight that have bought it, to the end that by this means the people may not be deceived. Besides those ordinary Shambles, there is not scarce a street but hath five or six Butchers shops in it, where the choicest meat is sold ; there are withall many Taverns, where excellent fare is alwayes to be had, and cellers full of gammons of bacon, dried tongues, poudered geese, and other savoury viands, for to relish ones drink, all in so great abundance, that it would be very superfluous to say more of it ; but what I speak is to shew how liberally God hath imparted to these miserable blinded wretches the good things which he hath created on the earth, to the end that his holy Name may therefore be blessed for evermore.

CHAP. XXXV.

The Prison of Xinanguibaleu, *wherein those are kept, which have been condemned to serve at the reparations of the Wall of* Tartaria; *and another inclosure, called the Treasure of the dead, with the revenues whereof this prison is maintained.*

DEsisting now from speaking in particular of the great number of the rich and magnificent buildings, which we saw in this City of *Pequin*, I will only insist on some of the Edifices thereof, that seemed more remarkable to me then the rest, whence it may be easie to infer, what all those might be, whereof I will not make any mention here to avoid prolixity ; And of these neither would I speak, were it not that our Lord may one day permit, that the *Portugal* Nation, full of valour, and of lofty courage, may make use of this relation for the glory of our great God, to the end that by these humane means, and the assistance of his divine favor, it may make those barbarous people understand the verity of our holy Catholique faith, from which their sins have so far esloigned them, as they mock at all that we say to them thereof : Hereunto I will adde, that they are extravagant, and senceless, as they dare boldly affirm, that only with beholding the face of the Son of the Sun, which is their King, a soul would be more happy then with all other things of the world besides, which perswades me that if God of his infinite mercy and goodness would grant, that the King of the people might become a Christian, it would be an easie matter to convert all his Subjects, whereas otherwise I hold it difficult for

so much as one to change his belief, and all by reason of the great awe they are in of the Law, which they fear and reverence a like, and whereof it is not to be believed how much they cherish the Ministers. But to return to my discourse, the first building which I saw of those that were most remarkable, was a prison, which they call *Xinanguibaleu*, that is to say, *The inclosure of the Epiles*; the circuit of this prison is two leagues square, or little less, both in length and bredth: It is inclosed with a very high wall without any battlements; the wall on the outside is invironed with a great deep ditch full of water, over the which are a many of draw-bridges, that are drawn up in the night with certain iron chains, and so hang suspended on huge cast pillars; In this prison is an arch of strong hewed stone, abutting in two towers, in the tops whereof are six great sentinel bells, which are never rung but all the rest within the said inclosure do answer them, which the *Chineses* affirm to be above an hundred, and indeed they make a most horrible din. In this place there are ordinarily three hundred thousand prisoners, between seventeen and fifty, whereat we were much amazed, and indeed we had good cause, in regard it is a thing so unusual and extraordinary. Now desiring to know of the *Chineses* the occasion of so marvellous a building, and of the great number of prisoners that were in it; they answered us, that after the King of *China*, named *Crisnago Docotay*, had finished a wall of three hundred leagues space betwixt this Kingdom of *China*, and that of *Tartaria*, as I have declared other where, he ordained by the advice of his people, (for to that effect he caused an Assembly of his Estates to be held) that all those which should be condemned to banishment, should be sent to work in the repairing of this wall, and that after they had served six years together therein, they might freely depart, though they were sentenced to serve for a longer time, because the King pardoned them the remainder of the term by way of charity and alms; but if during those years, they should happen to perform any remarkable act, or other thing, wherein it appeared they had advantage over others, or if they were three times wounded in the Sallies they should make, or if they killed some of their enemies, they were then to be dispensed with for all the rest of their time, and that the *Chaem* should grant them a certificate thereof, where it should be declared why he had delivered them, and how he had thereby satisfied the Ordinances of War. Two hundred and ten thousand men are to be continually entertained in the work of the wall, by the first institution, whereof defalcation is made of a third part, for such are dead, maimed, and delivered, either for their notable actions, or for that they had accomplished their time: And likewise when as the *Chaem*, who is as the chief of all those, sent to the *Pitaucamay*, which is the highest Court of Justice, to furnish him with that number of men, they could not assemble them together so soon as was necessary, for that they were divided in so many several places of that Empire, which is prodigiously great, as I have delivered before, and that withall a long time was required for the assembling them together, another King, named *Gopiley Aparan*, who succeeded to that *Crisnago Dacotay*, ordained that the great inclosure should be made in the City of *Pequin*, to the end that as soon as any were condemned to the work of this wall, they should be carried to *Xinanguibaleu* for to be there altogether, by which means they might be sent away without any delay, as now is done. So soon as the Court of Justice hath committed the prisoners to this prison, whereof he that brings them hath a Certificate, they are immediately left at liberty, so that they may walk at their pleasure within this great inclosure, having nothing but a little plate of a span long, and four fingers broad, wherein these words are engraven, *Such a one of such a place hath been condemned to the general exile for such a cause, he entred such a day, such a month, such a year.* Now the reason why they make every prisoner to carry this plate for a testimony of their evil actions, is, to manifest for what crime he was condemned, and at what time he entred, because every one goes forth conformably to the length of time that shall be since he entred in. These prisoners are held for duly delivered when they are drawn out of captivity for to go and work at the wall, for they cannot upon any cause whatsoever be exempted from the prison of *Xinanguibaleu*, and the time they are there is counted to them for nothing, in regard they have no hope of liberty but at that instant when their turn permits them to work in the reparations, for then they may be sure to be delivered, according to the ordinance whereof I have made mention before. Having now delivered the occasion whereof so great a prison was made, before I leave it I hold it not amiss to speak of a Fair, which we saw there, of two that are usually kept every year, which those of the Country call, *Gunxinem, Apparan, Xinanguibaleu*, that is to say, *The rich Fair of the prison of the condemned*; These Fairs are kept in the months of *July*, and *January*, with very magnificent feasts, solemnized for the invocation of
their

their Idols ; And even, there they have their plenory indulgences, by means whereof great riches of gold and silver are promised them in the other world. They are both of them frank and free, so as the Merchants pay no duties, which is the cause that they flock thither in such great number, as they assured us that there were three millions of persons there ; And forasmuch as I said before, that the three hundred thousand that are imprisoned there, are at liberty, as well as those that go in and out, you shall see what course they hold to keep the prisoners from getting forth amongst others. Every one that is free and comes in hath a mark set on the wrist of his right arm] with a certain Confection made of Oyl, Bitumen, Lacre, Rubarb, and Alum, which being once dry cannot be any wayes defaced, but by the means of vinegar and salt mingled together very hot ; And to the end that so great a number of people may be marked, on both sides of the gates stand a many of *Chainpatoens*, who with stamps of lead, dipt in this Bitumen, imprints a mark on every one that presents himself unto them, and so they let him enter ; which is only practised on men, not upon women, because none of that Sex are ever condemned to the labour of the wall. When therefore they come to go out of the gates, they must all have their arms bared where this mark is, that the said *Chaintapoens*, who are the Porters and Ministers of this affair, may know them, and let them pass ; and if by chance any one be so unhappy as to have that mark defaced by any accident, must even have patience, and remain with the other prisoners, in regard there is no way to get him out of this place if he be found without that mark. Now those *Chaintapoens* are so dextrous and well versed in it, that an hundred thousand men may in an hour go in and out without trouble, so that by this means the three hundred thousand prisoners continue in their captivity, and none of them can slip away amongst others to get out. There are in this prison three great inclosures like great towns, where there are a number of houses, and very long streets, without any lanes ; and at the entrance into each street there are good gates, with their sentinel bells aloft, together with a *Chumbim*, and twenty men for a Guard ; within a flight shoot of those inclosures are the lodgings of the *Chaem*, who commands all this prison, and those lodgings are composed of a number of fair houses, wherein are many out-Courts, Gardens, Ponds, Halls, and Chambers, inriched with excellent inventions, able to lodge a King at his ease, how great a Court soever he have. In the two principal of these Towns there are two streets, each of them about a flight shoot long, which abut upon the *Chaems* lodgings, arched all along with stone, and covered over head like the Hospital at *Lisbon*, but that they far surpass it. Here are all things to be sold that one can desire, as well for victual, and other kind of provisions, as for all sorts of Merchandise, and rich wares. In those arched streets, which are very spacious and long, are these two Fairs kept every year, whither such an infinite multitude of people resort, as I have declared before. Moreover within the inclosure of this prison are divers woods of tall and high trees, with many small streams, and ponds of clear sweet water for the use of the prisoners, and to wash their linnen, as also sundry Hermitages, and Hospitals, together with twelve very sumptuous and rich Monasteries, so that whatsoever is to be had in a great Town, may in great abundance be found within the inclosure, and with advantage in many things, because the most part of these prisoners have their wives and children there, to whom the King gives a lodging answerable to the houshold, or family, which each one hath.

The second of those things, which I have undertaken to relate, is another inclosure we saw §.2. almost as big as the former, compassed about with strong walls, and great ditches. This place is called *Muxiparan*, which signifies *The treasure of the dead*, where are many towers of hewed carved stone, and steeples diversly painted. The walls on the top are in stead of battlements invironed with iron grates, where there are a number of idols of different figures, as of Men, Serpents, Horses, Oxen, Elephants, Fishes, Adders, and many other monstrous forms of creatures, which were never seen, some of Brass, and Iron, and others of Tin, and Copper ; so that this infinite company of several figures joyned together is one of the most remarkable and pleasantest things that can be imagined. Having past over the bridge of the ditch we arrived at a great Court that was at the first entrance, inclosed round about with huge gates, and paved all over with white and black stones in checquer work, so polished and bright, as one might see himself in them as in a looking glass ; In the midst of this Court was a pillar of Jasper six and thirty spans high, and as it seemed all of one piece, on the top whereof was an idol of silver in the figure of a woman, which with her hands strangled a Serpent, that was excellently enamelled with black and green. A little further at the entrance of another gate, which stood between two very high towers, and accompanied with four and twenty pillars of huge great

stone,

stone, there were two figures of men, each of them with an iron club in his hand, as if they had served to guard that passage, being an hundred and forty spans high, with such hideous and ugly visages, as makes them even to tremble that behold them; The *Chineses* called them *Xixipatau Xalican*, that is to say, *The blowers of the house of smoak*. At the entring into this gate there were twelve men with halberds, and two Registers, set at a table, who enrolled all that entred there, unto whom every one paid a matter of a groat : when we were entred within this gate, we met with a very large street, closed on both sides with goodly arches, as well in regard of the workmanship, as the rest, round about the which hung an infinite company of little bells of lattin, by chains of the same mettal, that moved by the air, made such a noise as one could with much ado hear one another : This street might be about half a league long, and within these arches, on both sides of the way, were two rows of low houses, like unto great Churches, with steeples all guilt, and divers inventions of painting : Of these houses the *Chineses* assured us there was in that place three thousand, all which from the very top to the bottom were full of dead mens skuls, a thing so strange, that in every mans judgment a thousand great shops could hardly contain them. Behind these houses, both on the one side and the other, were two great Mounts of dead mens bones, reaching far above the ridges of the houses, full as long as the street, and of a mighty bredth. These bones were ordered and disposed one upon another so curiously and aptly, that they seemed to grow there ; Having demanded of the *Chineses* whether any register was kept of these bones, they answered, there was, for the *Talagrepos*, unto whose charge the administration of these three thousand houses was committed, enrolled them all ; and that none of these houses yielded less then two thousand *Taeis* revenue out of such lands, as the owners of these bones had bequeathed to them for their souls health ; and that the rent of all these three thousand houses together amounted unto five millions of gold yearly, whereof the King had four, and the *Talagrepos* the other for to defray the expences of this Fabrick; and that the four appertained to the King, as their Support, who dispenced them in the maintenance of the three hundred thousand prisoners of *Xinanguibaleu*. Being amazed at this marvel, we began to go along this street, in the midst whereof we found a great *Piazza*, compassed about with two huge grates of lattin, and within it was an Adder of brass infolded into I know not how many boughts, and so big that it contained thirty fathom in circuit, being withall so ugly and dreadful, as no words are able to describe it. Some of us would estimate the weight of it, and the least opinions reached to a thousand quintals, were it hollow within, as I believe it was. Now although it was of an unmeasurable greatness, yet was it in every part so well proportioned, as nothing can be amended, whereunto also the workmanship thereof is so correspondent, that all the perfection which can be desired from a good workman is observed in it. This monstrous Serpent, which the *Chineses* call, *The gluttonous Serpent of the house of smoak*, had on the top of his head a bowl of iron, two and fifty foot in circumference, as if it had been thrown at him from some other place ; Twenty paces further was the figure of a man of the same brass in the form of a Gyant, in like manner very strange and extraordinary, as well for the greatness of the body, as the hugeness of the limbs : This Monster held an iron bowl just as big as the other aloft in both his hands, and beholding the Serpent with a frowning and angry countenance, he seemed as though he would throw this bowl at him. Round about this figure was a number of little idols all guilt on their knees, with their hands lifted up to him, as if they would adore him. All this great edifice was consecrated to the honour of this Idol, called *Mucluparon*, whom the *Chineses* affirmed to be the treasurer of all the dead mens bones, and that when the gluttonous Serpent before mentioned came to steal them away, he made at him with that bowl which he held in his hands, whereupon the Serpent in great fear fled immediately away to the bottom of the profound house of smoak, whither God had precipitated him for his great wickedness ; and further that he had maintained a combate with him three thousand years already, and was to continue the same three thousand years more, so that from three thousand to three thousand years he was to imploy five bowls, wherewith he was to make an end of killing him ; Hereunto they added, that as soon as this Serpent should be dead, the bones that were there assembled, would return into the bodies, to which they appertained formerly, and so should go and remain for ever in the house of the Moon ; To these brutish opinions they joyn many others such like, unto which they give so much faith, that nothing can be able to remove them from it, for it is the doctrine that is preached unto them by their *Bonzes*, who also tell them that the true way to make a soul happy, is to gather these bones together into this place, by means whereof there

is

is not a day paffes but that a thoufand or two of thefe wretches bones are brought thither. Now if fome for their far diftance cannot bring all the bones whole thither, they will at leaft-wife bring a tooth or two, and fo they fay that by way of an alms they make as good fa-tisfaction as if they brought all the reft; which is the reafon that in all thefe chunel houfes there is fuch an infinite multitude of thefe teeth, that one might lade many fhips with them.

We faw in a great Plain without the walls of this City another building, very fumptuous and rich, which they call *Nacapirau*, that is to fay, the Queen of Heaven, for it is the opinion of thefe blinded wretches, that our Lord above is married like the Kings here below, and that the children which he hath had by the *Nacapirau*, are the Stars we fee twinkling in the Firmament by night, and that when any exhalation comes to diffolve in the air, they fay that it is one of his children that is dead, whereof his other brothers are fo grieved, that they fhed fuch abundance of tears, as the earth is watered therewith, by which means God provides us of our living, as it were in manner of alms beftowed for the fouls of the deceafed. But letting pafs thefe and other fuch like fooleries, I will only intreat of fuch particulars, as we obferved in this great Edifice, whereof the firft was one hundred and forty Convents of this accurfed Religion, both of men and women, in each of which there are four hundred perfons, amounting in all to fix and fifty thoufand, befides an infinite number of religious fervants, that are not obliged to their vow of profeffion that are within, who for a mark of their Prieftly dignity are clothed in violet, with green ftars on them, having their head, beard, and eye-brows fhaven, and wearing beads about their necks to pray with, but for all that they crave no alms, by reafon they have revenue enough to live on. The next was an inclofure within this huge building, a league in circuit, the walls whereof were built upon arches, vaults, of ftrong hewed ftone, and underneath them were Galleries, invironed all about with ballifters of lattin; within this inclofure at a gate, through which we paft, we faw under moft deformed figures the two porters of hell, at leaft they believe fo, calling the one *Bacharon*, and the other *Quagifau*, both of them with iron clubs in their hands, and fo hideous and horrible to fee to, that it is impoffible to behold them without fear. Having paft this gate under a chain, that went a crofs from the breft of one of thefe divels to the other, we entred into a very fair ftreet, both for bredth and length, inclofed at either end with many arches, diverfly painted, on the top whereof were all along two rows of idols to the number of five thoufand; Now we could not well judg of what matter thefe idols were made, howfoever they were guilt all over, and upon their heads they wore myters of fundry inventions. At the end of this ftreet was a great fquare place, paved with black and white ftone, and compaffed about with four rows of gyants in brafs, each of them fifteen foot high, with halberds in their hands, and their hair and beards all guilt, which was not only a very pleafing object to the eye, but alfo reprefented a kind of majeftical greatnefs. At the end of this place was *Quiay Huyan*, the god of rain, which idol was fo huge, that with his head he touched the battlements of the tower, being above twelve fathom high; he was likewife of brafs, and both from his mouth, head, and breft, at fix and twenty feveral places came out ftreams of water: Having paft between his legs, which ftood ftradling at a great diftance, one from another, we entred into a large room, as long as a Church, where there were three fhips fet upon very big and high pillars of Jafper; all along the walls thereof on both fides were a many of idols, great and little in divers forms all guilt, fitted and difpofed in fuch order, as they took up all the bredth and length of the walls, and feemed at firft fight to be all gold: At the end of this room or temple upon a round Tribunal, whereunto one afcended by fifteen winding ftairs, was an altar, proportionable to the fame Tribunal, whereon ftood the image of *Nacapirau*, in the likenefs of a very fair woman, with her hair hanging upon her fhoulders, and her hands lifted up to Heaven. Now for that fhe was guilt all over with fine gold, and that with a great deal of art and care, fhe gliftered in that manner as it was unpoffible to continue looking on her, fo dazled were a mans eyes with the rayes that darted from her. Round about this Tribunal on the firft four ftairs were the Statues of twelve Kings of *China* in filver, with crowns on their heads, and maces on their fhoulders; a little lower were three rows of idols guilt, kneeling on their knees, and holding up their hands, and all about hung a number of filver candlefticks with feven branches apiece. When we were out of this, we went through another ftreet all arched like that by which we entred in, and from this we paffed through two other ftreets full of very ftately buildings, and fo came to a gate, that ftood between four high towers, where there was a *Chifuu*, with thirty Halberdiers, and

two

two Regifters, which wrot down the names of all that went in and out, as they did ours, and so we gave them about a groat for our paſſage out.

CHAP. XXXVI.

Of an Edifice, ſcituated in the midſt of the river, wherein were the hundred and thirteen Chappels of the Kings of China *; with the publique Granaries eſtabliſhed for the relief of the poor.*

TO give an end to the matter, whereof I intreat, which would be infinite if I ſhould recount every thing in particular, amongſt the great number of marvellous buildings, which we ſaw, the moſt remarkable to my ſeeming was an incloſure, ſeated in the midſt of the river of *Batampina*, containing ſome league in circuit in an Iſland, and invironed with fair hewed ſtone, which on the out-ſide was about eight and thirty foot high above the water, and on the in-ſide even with the ground, being encompaſſed with two rows of balliſters of lattin, whereof the outermoſt were but ſix foot high, for the commoditie of ſuch as would reſt themſelves there, and the innermoſt were nine foot high, having ſix Lyons of ſilver ſtanding upon huge bowls, which are the arms of the King of *China*, as I have ſaid elſewhere. Within the incloſure of theſe balliſters ſtood in very goodly order an hundred and thirteen Chappels after the faſhion of Bulwarks all round, in each of which was a rich Tomb of Alabaſter, placed with much art upon the heads of two ſilver Serpents, which in regard of the many boughts wherein they were entertained ſeemed to be ſnakes, though they had the viſages of women, and three horns on their heads, the explication whereof we could not poſſibly learn. In each of theſe Chappels were thirteen branched Candleſticks with ſeven great lights a piece in them, ſo that to compute the whole, the candleſticks of theſe hundred and thirteen Chappels amount to a thouſand, four hundred, thirty and nine. In the midſt of a great place, invironed round about with three rows of winding ſtairs, and two ranks of idols, was a very high tower, with five ſteeples diverſly painted, and ſilver Lions on the top of all : Here the *Chineſes* told us were the bones of thoſe hundred and thirteen Kings, that had been tranſported thither from theſe Chappels below : And it is the opinion of theſe brutiſh people, that theſe bones, which they hold for great reliques, do feaſt one another at every new Moon ; in regard whereof theſe *Barbarians* uſe on that day to offer unto them a great Charger full of all kind of fowl, as alſo Rice, Beef, Pork, Sugar, Hony, and all other ſorts of victual that one can name ; wherein their blindneſs is ſuch, as in recompence of theſe meats, which the Prieſts take unto themſelves, they imagine that all their ſins are forgiven them, by way as it were of a plenory indulgence. In this tower likewiſe we ſaw an exceeding rich Chamber, covered on the inſide all over from the top to the bottom with plates of ſilver. In this Chamber were the Statues of thoſe hundred and thirteen Kings of *China* all of ſilver, where in each of them were the bones of each ſeveral King incloſed ; Now they hold, according as they are made to believe by their prieſts, that theſe Kings thus aſſembled together converſe every night one with another, and paſs away the time In ſundry ſports, which none is worthy to ſee, but certain *Bonzes*, whom they term *Cabizundes*, a title amongſt them of the moſt eminent dignity, ſuch it may be as the Cardinals of *Rome*. To this beaſtly ignorance the wretches adde many other blind tales, which they are aſſuredly perſwaded are very clear and manifeſt truths : Within this great incloſure we counted in ſeventeen places three hundred and forty bells of caſt mettal, namely twenty in each place, which are all rung together on thoſe days of the Moon, wherein they ſay theſe Kings do viſit and feaſt one another. Near to this tower in a very rich Chappel, built upon ſeven and thirty pillars of fair hewed ſtone, was the image of the goddeſs *Amida*, made of ſilver, having her hair of gold, and ſeated upon a Tribunal fourteen ſteps high, that was all overlaid with fine gold ; Her face was very beautiful, and her hands were heaved up towards Heaven, at her armpits hung a many of little idols not above half a finger long filed together, whereupon demanding of the *Chineſes* what thoſe meant, they anſwered us, *That after the waters of Heaven had overflowed the earth, ſo that all mankind was drowned by an univerſal Deluge, God ſeeing that the world would be deſolate, and no body to inhabit it, he ſent the goddeſs* Amida, *the chief Lady of honour to his wife* Nacapirau *from the Heaven of the Moon, that ſhe might repair the loſs of drowned mankind, and that then the goddeſs having ſet her feet on a Land, from which the waters were withdrawn, called* Calemphuy, (which was the ſame Iſland, whereof I have ſpoken heretofore, in the ſtreight of *Nanquin*, whereof *Antonio de Faria*
went

went on land) she was changed all into gold, and in that manner standing upright with her face looking up unto Heaven, she sweat out at her armpits a great number of children, namely males out of the right, and females out of the left, having no other place about her body whence she might bring them forth, as other women of the world have, who have sinned, and that for a chastisement of their sin, God by the order of nature hath subjected them to a misery full of corruption and filthiness, for to shew how odious unto him the sin was that had been committed against him. The goddess Amida having thus brought forth these creatures, which they affirm were thirty three thousand, three hundred, thirty and three, two parts of them females, and the other males, for so say they the world was to be repaired, she remained so feeble and faint with this delivery, having no body to assist her at her need, that she fell down dead in the place, for which cause the Moon at that time in memory of this death of hers, whereat she was infinitely grieved, put her self into mourning, which mourning they affirm to be those black spots we ordinarily behold in her face, occasioned indeed by the shadow of the earth, and that when there shall be so many years ran out, as the goddess Amida brought forth children, which were, as I have delivered, thirty three thousand, three hundred, thirty and three, then the Moon will put off her mourning, and afterwards be as clear as the day. With these and such like fopperies did the *Chineses* so turmoil us, as we could not chuse but grieve to consider how much those people, which otherwise are quick of apprehension, and of good understanding, are abused in matter of Religion with such evident and manifest untruths. After we were come out of this great place, where we saw all these things, we went unto another Temple of religious Votaries, very sumptuous and rich, where they told us the Mother of the then reigning King, named *Nhay Camisama*, did abide, but thereunto we were not permitted to enter, because we were strangers; From this place through a street, arched all along, we arrived at a Key, called *Hichario Topileu*, where lay a great number of vessels, full of pilgrims from divers Kingdoms, which came incessantly on pilgrimage to this Temple, for to gain, as they believe, plenary indulgences, which the King of *China*, and the *Chaems* of the Government, do grant unto them, besides many priviledges and franchises throughout the whole Country, where victuals are given them abundantly, and for nothing. I will not speak of many other Temples, or *Pagodes*, which we saw in this City whilest we were at liberty, for I should never have done to make report of them all, howbeit I may not omit some other particulars, that I hold very fit to be related before I break off this discourse; whereof the first were certain houses, in several parts of this City, called *Laginampurs*, that is to say, *The School of the poor*, wherein fatherless and motherless children, that are found in the streets, are taught to write and read, as also some trade, whereby they may get their living, and of these houses, or schools, there are about some five hundred in this City; Now if it happen that any of them through some defect of nature cannot learn a trade, then have they recourse to some means for to make them get their living according to each ones incommodity; As for example, if they be blind they make them labour in turning of handmils; if they be lame of their feet, they cause them to make laces, riband, and such like manufactures; if they be lame of their hands, then they make them earn their living by carrying of burdens; but if they be lame both of feet and hands, so that nature hath wholly deprived them of means to get their living, then they shut them up in great Convents, where there are a number of persons that pray for the dead, amongst whom they place them, and so they have their share of half the offerings that are made there, the Priests having the other half; if they be dumb, then they are shut up in a great house, where they are maintained with the amerciaments that the common sort of women, as oyster-wives, and such like, are condemned in for their scolding and fighting one with another; As for old queans, that are past the trade, and such of the younger sort as by the lewd exercise thereof are become diseased with the pox, or other filthy sickness, they are put into other houses, where they are very well looked unto, and furnished abundantly with all things necessary, at the charge of the other women that are of the same trade, who thereunto pay a certain sum monthly, and that not unwillingly, because they know that they shall come to be so provided for themselves by others, and for the collecting of this mony there are Commissioners expresly deputed in several parts of the City. There are also other houses, much like unto Monasteries, where a great many of young maids, that are Orphans, are bred up, and these houses are maintained at the charge of such women as are convicted of adultery; for say they it is most just, that if there be one which hath lost her self by her dishonesty, there should be another, that should be maintained by her vertue. Other places there are also, where decayed old people are kept at the charge of Lawyers, that plead unjust causes, where the parties have no right; and of Judges, that for favoring one more then another, and corrupted with bribes, do not execute justice as they ought to do; whereby one may see with how much order and policy these people govern all things.

§.2　　In the prosecution of my discourse it will not be amiss here to deliver the marvellous order and policy, which the Kings of *China* observe in furnishing their States abundantly with provisions and victuals, for the relief of the poor people, which may very well serve for an example of charity, and good government, to Christian Kingdoms and Commonwealths. Their Chronicles report, that a certain King, great Grandfather to him that then raigned in *China*, named *Chausi-Zarao Panagor*, very much beloved of his people for his good disposition and vertues, having lost his sight by an accident of sickness, resolved to do some pious work, that might be acceptable to God, to which effect he assembled his Estates, where he ordained, that for the relief of the poor there should be Granaries established in all the Towns of his Kingdom for wheat and rice, that in the time of dearth (which many times happened) the people might have wherewithall to nourish themselves that year, and to that purpose he gave the tenth part of the Duties of his Kingdom by a Grant under his hand, which when he came to signe accordingly with a golden stamp, that he ordinarily used because he was blind, it pleased God to restore him perfectly to his sight again, which he enjoyed still as long as he lived; By this example, if it were true, it seemed that our Lord Jesus Christ would demonstrate, how acceptable the charity that good men exercise towards the poor is to him, even though they be *Gentiles*, and without the knowledge of the true Religion; Ever since there have been always a great many of Granaries in this Monarchy, and that to the number of an hundred and fourteen thousand. As for the order which the Magistrates observe in furnishing them continually with corn, is such as followeth; A little before reaping time all the old corn is distributed forth to the inhabitants, as it were by way of love, and that for the term of two months, after this time is expired, they unto whom the old corn was lent, return in as much new, and withall six in the hundred over and above for waste, to the end that this store may never fail: But when it falls out to be a dear year, in that case the corn is distributed to the people without taking any gain or interest for it, and that which is given to the poorer sort, who are not able to repay what hath been lent to them, is made good out of the Rents, which the Countries pay to the King, as an alms bestowed on them by his special grace. Touching the Kings Revenues, which are paid in silver *Picos*, they are divided into three parts, whereof the first is for the maintenance of the King, and his State, the second for the defence of the Provinces, as also for the provisions of Magazines, and Armies, and the third to be laid up and reserved in a Treasury, that is in this City of *Pequin*, which the King himself may not touch, unless it be upon occasion for defence of the Kingdom, and to oppose the *Tartars, Cauchins*, and other Neighbouring Princes, who many times make grievous war upon him. This Treasure is by them called *Chidampur*, that is to say, *The Wall of the Kingdom*, for they say, that by means of this treasure, being well imployed and carefully managed, the King needs lay no impositions upon the people, so that they shall not be any ways vexed and oppressed, as it happens in other Kingdoms for want of this providence. Now by this that I have related one may see, how in all the great Monarchy the Government is so excellent, the Laws so exactly observed, and every one so ready and careful to put the Princes Ordinances in execution, that Father *Navier*, having well noted it, was wont to say, that if ever God would grant him the grace to return into *Portugal*, he would become a Suter to the King for to peruse over the rules and ordinances of those people, and the manner how they govern both in time of war and peace; adding withall that he did not think the *Romans* ever ruled so wisely in all the time of their greatest prosperity, and that in matter of policy the *Chineses* surpassed all other Nations of whom the Ancients have written.

CHAP. XXXVII.

The great number of Officers, and other people, which are in the King of China's Pallace; With our going to Quincay to accomplish the time of our Exile; and what befell us there.

Out of the fear I am in lest coming to relate in particular all those things which we saw within the large inclosure of this City of *Pequin*, they that shall chance to read them may call

them

them in question, and not to give occasion also unto detractors, who judging of things according to the little world they have seen, may hold those truths for fables, which mine own eyes have beheld, I will forbear the delivery of many matters, that possibly might bring much contentment to more worthy spirits, who not judging of the riches and prosperity of other Countres by the poverty and misery of their own, would be well pleased with the relation thereof. Howbeit on the other side I have no great cause to blame those, who shall not give credit to that which I say, or make any doubt of it, because I must acknowledge, that many times when I call to mind the things that mine eyes have seen, I remain confounded therewith, whither it be the Grandeurs of this City of *Pequin*, or the magnificence wherewith this *Gentile* King is served, or the pomp of the *Chaems*, and *Anchacys* of the Government, or the dread and awe wherein all men are of these Ministers, or the sumptuousness of their Temples and *Pagodes*, together with all the rest that may be there, for within the only inclosure of the Kings Pallace there are above a thousand Eunuchs, three thousand women, and 12 thousand men of his Guard, unto whom the King gives great entertainment and pentions : also twelve *Tutons*, dignities that are Soveraign above all others, whom, as I have already declared, the vulgar call, *The beams of the Sun* ; Under these twelve *Tutons*, there are forty *Chaems*, or Vice-roys, besides many other inferiour dignities, as Judges, Majors, Governours, Treasurers, Admirals, and Generals, which they term, *Anchacys, Aytaos, Ponchacy, Lauteas,* and *Chumbims*, whereof there are above five hundred always residing at the Court, each of them having at the least two hundred men in his train, which for the most part to strike the greater terror are of divers Nations, namely, *Megores, Persians, Curazens, Moems, Calaminhams, Tartars, Canchins,* and some *Braamas* of *Chaleu,* and *Tangun* ; for in regard of valour, they make no account of the Natives, who are of a weak and effeminate complection, though otherwise I must confess they are exceeding able and ingenious in whatsoever concerneth Mechanick Trades Tillage, and Husbandry ; they have withall a great vivacity of spirit, and are exceeding proper and apt for the inventing of very subtle & industrious things. The women are fair and chaste, and more inclined to labour then the men, The Country is fertile in victual, and so rich & abounding in all kind of good things, as I cannot sufficiently express it, & such is their blindness as they attribute all those blessings to the only merit of their King, and not to the Divine Providence, and to the goodness of that Soveraign Lord, who hath created all things. From this blindness and incredulity of these people are these great abuses, and confused superstitions derived, which are ordinary amongst them, and wherein they observe a world of diabolical ceremonies ; For they are so brutish and wicked as to sacrifice humane blood, offering it up with divers sorts of perfumes, and sweet savors ; Moreover they present their Priests with many gifts, upon assurance from these profane wretches, of great blessings in this life, and infinite riches and treasure in the other ; To which effects the same Priests grant them I know not what Certificates, as it were Bills of Exchange, which the common people call *Couchinnoces,* that after their death they may serve above in Heaven to procure for them a recompence of an hundred for one ; wherein these miserable creatures are so blinded, that they save the very meat & drink from their own mouths to furnish those accursed priests of Satan with all things necessary, believing that these goodly bills they have from them, will assuredly return them that benefit. There are also Priests of another Sect, called *Naustolins,* who contrary to those others preach, and affirm with great oaths, that reasonable creatures live and die like beasts, & therfore that they are to make merry & spend their goods jovially whiles life shall last, there being no other after this, as all but fools & ignorants are to believe. There is another Sect, named *Trimechau,* who are of opinion that so long time as a man shall live in this world, so long shall he remain under ground, until at length by the prayers of their priests his soul shall reassume the body of a child of seven days old, wherein he shall live again till he shall grow so strong, as to re-enter into the old body, which he hed left in the grave, and so be transported into the Heaven of the Moon, where they say he shal live many years, & in the end be converted into a star, which shall remain fixed above in the Firmament for ever. Another Sect there is called *Gyson,* who believe that only the beasts in regard of their sufferings, and the labour which they endure in this life, shall possess Heaven after their death, & not man, that leadeth his life according to the lusts of the flesh, robbing, killing, and committing a world of other offences, by reason whereof, say they, it is not possible for him to be saved, unless at the hour of death he leave all his estate to the *Pagodes,* and to the Priests, that they may pray for him ; whereby one may see that all the intentions of their diabolical Sects is not founded but upon a very tyranny, and upon the interests of the *Bonzes,* who are they that preach this pernicious doctrine

to

to the people, and perfwaded them with many fables to believe it; In the mean time thefe things feem fo true to thefe wretches that hear them, as they very willingly give them all their goods, imagining that thereby only they can be faved, and freed from thofe punifhments and fears, wherewithall they threaten them if they do otherwife. I have fpoken here of no more then thefe three Sects, omitting the reft of the two and thirty, which are followed in this great Empire of *China*, as well becaufe I fhould never have done (as I have faid heretofore) if I would relate them all at large, as for that by thefe it may be known what the others are, which are nothing better, but in a manner even the very fame ; wherefore leaving the remedy of fuch evils, and great blindnefs to the mercy and providence of God, unto whom only it appertains ; I will pafs on to the declarations of the miferies we indured during our exille in the Town of *Quancy*, until fuch time as we were made flaves by the *Tartars*, which happened in the year, 1544.

§. 2.   We had been now two months and an half in this City of *Pequin*, when as on *Saturday*, the thirteenth of *July*, 1554. we were carried away to the Town of *Quanfy*, there to ferve all the time that we were condemned unto : Now as foon as we arrived there, the *Chaem* caufed us to be brought before him, and after he had asked us fome queftions, he appointed us to be of the number of fourfcore Halberdiers, which the King affigned him for his Guard ; This we took as a fpecial favour from God, both in regard this imployment was not very painful, as alfo becaufe the entertainment was good, and the pay of it better, being affured befides that at the time we fhould recover our liberty. Thus lived we almoft a month very peaceably, and well contented for that we met with a better fortune then we expected, when as the divel, feeing how well all we nine agreed together (for all that we had was in common amongft us, and whatfoever mifery any one had we fhared it with him like true brothers,) he fo wrought that two of our company fell into a quarrel, which proved very prejudicial to us all ; This divifion fprung from a certain vanity too familiar with the *Portugal* Nation, whereof I can render no other reafon, but that they are naturally fenfible of any thing that touches upon honour : Now fee what the difference was, two of us nine falling by chance in conteft about the extraction of the *Madureyras* and the *Fonfecas*, for to know which of thefe two houfes was in moft efteem at the King of *Portugals* Court, the matter went fo far, that from one word to another they came at length to terms of oyfter-wives, faying one to the other, Who are you ? and again, who are you ? fo that thereupon they fuffered themfelves to be fo tranfported with choller, that one of them gave the other a great box on the ear, who inftantly returned him a blow with his fword, which cut away almoft half his cheek, this fame feeling himfelf hurt caught up an halbert, and therewith ran the other through the arm ; this difafter begot fuch part-taking amongft us, as of nine that we were feven of us found our felves grievoufly wounded ; In the mean time the *Chaem* came running in perfon to this tumult with all the *Anchacys* of Juftice, who laying hold of us gave us prefently thirty lafhes a piece, which drew more blood from us then our hurts ; This done, they fhut us up in a dungeon under ground, where they kept us fix and forty days with heavy iron collers about our necks, manacles on our hands, and irons on our legs, fo that we fuffered exceedingly in this deplorable eftate. This while our bufinefs was brought before the Kings Atturny, who having feen our accufations, and that one of the articles made faith, that there were fixteen witneffes againft us, he ftuck not to fay, *That we were people without the fear or knowledge of God, who did not confefs him otherwife with our mouths, then as any wild beaft might do if he could fpeak ; that thefe things prefuppofed it was to be believed, that we were men of blood, of a Language, of a Law, of a Nation, of a Country, and of a Kingdom, the inhabitants whereof wounded and killed one another moft cruelly, without any reafon or caufe, and therefore no other judgment could be made of us, but that we were the fervants of the moft gluttenous Serpent of the profound pit of fmoak, as appeared by our worke, fince they were no better then fuch as that accurfed Serpent had accuftomed to do, fo that according to the Law of the third Book of the will of the Son of the Sun,* called Mileterau, *we were to be condemned to a banifhment from all commerce of people, as a venemous and contagious plague ; fo that we deferved to be confined to the Mountains of* Chabaguay, Sumbor, *or* Lamau, *whither fuch as we were ufe to be exiled, to the end they might in that place hear the wild beafts howl in the night, which were of as vile a breed and nature as we.* From this prifon we were one morning led to a place, called by them *Pitau Calidan*, where the *Anchacy* fat in judgment with a majeftical and dreadful greatnefs ; He was accompanied by divers *Chumbims*, *Uppes*, *Lanteas*, and *Cypatons*, befides a number of other perfons;

                                                                                                          there

there each of us had thirty lashes a piece more given us, and then by publique sentence we were removed to another prison, where we were in better case yet then in that out of which we came, howbeit for all that we did not a little detest amongst our selves both the *Fonsecas*, and the *Madureyras*, but much more the divel, that wrought us this mischief. In this prison we continued almost two months, during which time our stripes were throughly healed, howbeit we were exceedingly afflicted with hunger, and thirst. At length it pleased God that the *Chaem* took compassion of us; for on a certain day, wherein they use to do works of charity for the dead, coming to review our sentence he ordained, *That in regard we were strangers, and of a Country so far distant from theirs, as no man had any knowledge of us, nor that there was any book or writing which made mention of our name, and that none understood our language; as also that we were accustomed, and even hardned to misery and poverty, which many times puts the best and most peaceable persons into disorder, and therefore might well trouble such, as made no profession of patience in their adversities, whence it followed, that our discord proceeded rather from the effects of our misery, then from any inclination unto mutiny and tumult; wherewith the Kings Atturny charged us; and furthermore representing unto himself what great need there was of men for the ordinary service of the State, and of the Officers of Justice; for which provision necessarily was to be made,* he thought fit, that the punishment for the crimes we had committed, should in the way of an alms bestowed in the Kings name be moderated, and reduced to the whipping which we had twice already had, upon condition nevertheless that we should be detained there as slaves for ever, unless it should please the Tuton otherwise to ordain of us. This sentence was pronounced against us, and though we shed a many of tears to see our selves reduced unto this miserable condition, wherein we were, yet this seemed not so bad unto us as the former. After the publication of this Decree we were presently drawn out of prison, and tied three and three together, then led to certain iron Forges, where we past six whole months in strange labours, and great necessities, being in a manner quite naked, without any bed to lie on, and almost famished. At last after the enduring of so many evils, we fell sick of a Lethargy, which was the cause, in regard it was a contagious disease, that they turned us out of doors for to go and seek our living, until we became well again. Being thus set at liberty we continued four months sick, and begging the alms of good people from door to door, which was given us but sparingly, by reason of the great dearth that then reigned over all the Country, so as we were constrained to agree better together, and to promise one another by a solemn oath, that we took, to live lovingly for the future, as good Christians should do, and that every month one should be chosen from amongst us to be as it were a kind of Chief, whom, by the oath we had taken, all the rest of us were to obey, as their Superior, so that none of us was to dispose of himself, nor do any thing, without his command, or appointment; and those rules were put into writing by us, that they might be the better observed; As indeed God gave us the grace to live ever afterward in good peace and concord, though it were in great pain, and extream necessity of all things.

We had continued a good while living in peace and tranquility, according to our fore-mentioned agreement, when as he, whose lot it was to be our Chief that month, named *Christovano Boralho*, considering how necessary it was to seek out some relief for our miseries by all the ways that possibly we could, appointed us to serve weekly two and two together, some in begging up and down the Town, some in getting water and dressing our meat, and others in fetching wood from the Forrest, both for our own use, & to sell. Now one day my self & one *Gaspar de Meyrelez* being enjoyned to go to the Forrest, we rose betimes in the morning, & went forth to perform our charge; And because this *Gaspar de Meyrelez* was a pretty Musician, playing well on a Cittern, whereunto he accorded his voice, which was not bad, being parts that are very agreeable to those people, in regard they imploy the most part of their times in the delights of the flesh, they took great pleasure in hearing of him, so as for that purpose they invited him very often to their sports, from whence he never returned without some reward, wherewith we were not a little assisted: As he and I then were going to the wood, and before we were out of the Town, we met by fortune in one of the streets with a great many of people, who full of jollity were carrying a dead corps to the grave with divers banners, and other funeral pomp, in the midst whereof was a Consort of musick and voices; Now he, that had the chief ordering of the Funeral, knowing *Gaspar de Meyrelez*, made him stay, and putting a Cittern into his hands, he said unto him, *Oblige me, I pray thee, by singing as loud as thou canst, so as thou mayst be heard by this dead man whom we are carrying to burial, for I swear unto thee, that he went away very sad for that he was separated from his wife and children, whom he*

§.3

dearly

dearly loved all his life time. Gaſpar de Meyrelez would fain have excuſed himſelf, alledging many reaſons thereupon to that end, but ſo far was the Governour of the *Funeral* from accepting them, that contrarily he anſwered him very angerly. *Truly, if thou wilt not deign to benefit this defunct with the gift, that God hath given thee, of ſinging, and playing on this inſtrument, I will no longer ſay, that thou art an holy man, as we all believed hitherto, but that the excellency of that voice which thou haſt comes from the inhabitants of the houſe of ſmoak, whoſe nature it was at firſt to ſing very harmoniouſly, though now they weep and wail in the profound lake of the night, like hunger-ſtarved dogs, that gnaſhing their teeth, and foaming with rage againſt men diſcharge the froth of their malice by the offences, which they commit againſt him, that lives in the higheſt of the Heavens.* After this ten or eleven of them were ſo earneſt with Gaſpar de Meyrelez, as they made him play almoſt by force, and led him to the place, where the deceaſed was to be burnt, according to the cuſtom of thoſe *Gentiles.* In the mean time ſeeing my ſelf left alone without my comrade I went along to the Forreſt for to get ſome wood according to my Commiſſion, and about evening returning back with my load on my back I met with an old man in a black damask Gown furred clean through with white Lamb, who being all alone, as ſoon as he eſpied me, he turned a little out of the way, but perceiving me to paſs on without regarding him, he cried ſo loud to me, that I might hear him, which I no ſooner did, but caſting my eye that way, I obſerved that he beckened to me with his hand, as if he called me, whereupon imagining there was ſomething more then ordinary, herein I ſaid unto him in the *Chineſe* Langnage, *Potauquinay*, which is, Doeſt thou call me ? whereunto returning no anſwer, he gave me to underſtand by ſignes that in effect he called me ; conjecturing then that there might be ſome thieves thereabouts, which would bereave me of my load of wood, I threw it on the ground to be the better able to defend my ſelf, and with my ſtaff in my hand, I went fair and ſoftly after him, who ſeeing me follow him began to double his pace athwart a little path, which confirmed me in the belief I had before that he was ſome thief, ſo that turning back to the place where I left my load, I got it up again on my back as ſpeedily as I could, with a purpoſe to get into the great high way, that led unto the City ; But the man gueſſing at my intention, began to cry out louder to me then before, which making me turn my look towards him, I preſently perceived him on his knees, and ſhewing me afar off a ſilver croſs about a ſpan long, or thereabout, lifting up withall both his hands unto Heaven ; whereat being much amazed, I could not imagine what this man ſhould be, in the mean time he with a very pitiful geſture ceaſed not to make ſignes unto me to come to him ; whereupon ſomewhat recollecting my ſelf, I reſolved to go and ſee who he was, and what he would have, to which end with my ſtaff in my hand I walked towards him, where he ſtayed for me ; when as then I came near him, having always thought him before to be a *Chineſe*, I wondred to ſee him caſt himſelf at my feet, and with tears and ſighs to ſay thus unto me, *Bleſſed and prayſed be the ſweet Name of our Lord Jeſus Chriſt, after ſo long an exile hath ſhewed me ſo much grace, as to let me ſee a Chriſtian man, that profeſſeth the Law of my God fixed on the Croſs.* I muſt confeſs that when I heard ſo extraordinary a matter, and ſo far beyond my expectation, I was therewith ſo ſurpriſed, that ſcarcely knowing what I ſaid, *I conjure thee,* anſwered I unto him, *in the Name of our Lord Jeſus to tell me who thou art ?* At theſe words this unknown man redoubling his tears, *Dear Brother,* replyed he, *I am a poor Chriſtian, by Nation a Portugal, and named* Vaſco Calvo, *brother to* Diego Calvo, *who was ſomtime Captain of* Don Nuna Manoel *his ſhip, and made a Slave here in this Country about ſeven and twenty years ſince, together with one* Tome Perez, *who* Loppo Soarez *ſent as Ambaſſador into this Kingdom of* China, *and that ſince died miſerably by the occaſion of a Portugal Captain.* Whereupon coming throughly to my ſelf again, I lifted him up from the ground where he lay weeping like a child ; and ſhedding no fewer tears then he, I intreated him that we might ſit down together, which he would hardly grant, ſo deſirous he was to have me go preſently with him to his houſe, but ſitting down by me he began to diſcourſe the whole ſucceſs of his travels, and all that had befallen him ſince his departure from *Portugal,* till that very time, as alſo the death of the Ambaſſador *Tome Perez,* and of all the reſt, whom Fernand Perez d' Amdrada had left at *Canton* to go to the King of *China,* which he recounted in another manner then our Hiſtorians have delivered it. After we had ſpent the remainder of the day in entertaining one another with our paſſed adventures, we went to the City, where having ſhewed me his houſe, he deſired me that I would inſtantly go and fetch the reſt of my fellows, which accordingly I did, and found them all together in the poor lodging where we lay, and

having

having declared unto them what had befallen me, they were much abashed at it, as indeed they had cause, considering the stratagems of the accident, so they went presently along with me to *Vasco Calvo's* house, who waiting for us, gave us such hearty welcome, as we could not chuse but weep for joy; Then he carried us into a Chamber where was his wife, with two little boys, and two girls of his; she entertained us very kindly, and with as much demonstration of love, as if she had been the mother or daughter to either of us; After this we sat down at the table, which he had caused to be covered, and made a very good meal of many several dishes provided for us: Supper done, his wife arose very courteously from the table, and taking a key which hung at her girdle, she opened the door of an Oratory, where there was an altar, with a silver cross, as also two candlesticks, and a lamp of the same, and then she and her four children falling down on their knees, with their hands lift up to Heaven, began to pronounce these words very distinctly in the *Portugal* tongue: *O thou true God, We wretched sinners do confess before thy Cross, like good Christians, as we are, the most sacred Trinity, Father, Son, and Holy Ghost, three Persons, and one God; and also We promise to live and dye in thy most Holy Catholique Faith, like good and true Christians, confessing and believing so much of thy holy truth, as is held and believed by thy Church; In like manner We offer up unto thee our souls, which thou hast redeemed with thy most precious bloud, for to be Wholly imployed in thy service all the time of our lives, and then to be yielded unto thee at the hour of our death, as to our Lord and God, unto Whom We acknowledge they appertain both by Creation and Redemption.* After this Confession *they said the Lords Prayer, and the Creed,* which they pronounced very distinctly, whereat we could not chuse but shed a world of tears to see these innocents, born in a Country, so far remote from ours, and where there was no knowledge of the true God, thus to confess his Law in such religious terms. This being done, we returned because it was three of the clock in the morning to our lodging, exceedingly astonished at that we had seen, as at a thing which we had great reason to admire.

C H A P. XXXVIII.

A Tartar Commander enters With his Army into the Town of Quincay, *and that which followed thereupon; With the* Nauticors *besieging the Castle of* Nixiamcoo, *and the taking of it by the means of some of us* Portugals.

§. I.

WE had been now eight months and an half in this captivity, wherein we endured much misery, and many incommodities, for that we had nothing to live upon but what we got by begging up and down the Town, when as one *Wednesday*, the third of *July*, in the year 1544. a little after midnight there was such a hurly burly amongst the people, that to hear the noise and cries which was made in every part, one would have thought the earth would have come over and over, which caused us to go in haste to *Vasco Calvo* his house, of whom we demanded the occasion of so great a tumult, whereunto with tears in his eyes he answered us, that certain news were come how the King of *Tartary* was fallen upon the City of *Pequin* with so great an Army, as the like had never been seen since *Adams* time; In this army, according to report, were seven and twenty Kings, under whom marched eighteen hundred thousand men, whereof six hundred thousand were horse, which were come by land from the Cities of *Luançama*, *Famstir*, and *Mecuy*, with fourscore thousand *Rhinocerots*, that draw the waggons, wherein was all the Bigage of the Army; as for the other twelve hundred thousand, which were foot, it was said that they arrived by Sea in seventeen thousand vessels, down through the river of *Batampina*; By reason whereof the King of *China* finding himself too weak for the resisting of such great forces, had with a few retired himself to the City of *Nanquin*. And that also it was reported for a certain, that a *Nauticor*, one of the chiefest *Tartar* Commanders, was come to the Forrest of *Malincataran*, not above a league and an half from *Quinçay*, with an Army of threescore and two thousand Horse, wherewith he marched against the Town, that in all likelihood he would be there within two hours at the furthest. These news so troubled us, that we did nothing but look one upon another, without being able to speak a word to any purpose, howbeit desiring to save our selves, we prayed *Vasco Calvo* to shew us what means he thought we might use to effect it, who sad and full of grief thus answered us; O that we were in our Country between *Laura* and *Carncha*, where I have often been, and should be there now in safety, but since it cannot be so, all that we can do for

the

the prefent, is to recommend our felves to God, and to pray unto him to afsift us; for I affure you that an hour ago I would have given a thoufand *Taeis* in filver to any one, that could have got me from hence, and faved me with my wife and children, but there was no poffibility for it, becaufe the gates were then all fhut up, and the walls round about invironed with armed men, which the *Chaem* hath placed there to withftand the enemy. So my fellows and I, that were nine in number, paft the reft of the night there in much affliction and unquietnefs, without any means of counfelling one another, or refolving on what we were to do, continually weeping for the extream fear we were in of what fhould become of us. The next morning a little before Sun-rifing the enemy appeared in a moft dreadful manner, they were divided into feven very great Battalions, having their Enfignes quartered with green and white, which are the colours of the King of *Tartaria*; marching in this order to the found of their Trumpets, they arrived at a *Pagode*, called *Petilau Nameioo*, a place of good receit, in regard of the many lodgings it had, which was not much diftant from the walls. In their Vantguard they had a number of Light-horfe, who ran confufedly up and down with their Lances in their Refts. Being in this fort come to the *Pagode*, they ftayed there about half an hour, and then marching on till they were within an harquebufe fhot of the walls, they fuddenly ran to them with fuch hideous cries, as one would have thought that Heaven and Earth would have come together, and rearing up above two thoufand Ladders, which for that purpofe they had brought along with them, they affaulted the Town on every fide with a moft invincible courage. Now though the befieged at the beginning made fome refiftance, yet was it not able to hinder the enemy from effecting his defigne, for by the means of certain iron rams broking up the four principal gates, they rendred themfelves Mafters of the Town after they had flain the *Chaem*, together with a great number of *Mandarins*, and Gentlemen, that were run thither to keep them from entring; Thus did thefe *Barbarians* poffefs themfelves of this miferable Town, whereof they put all the inhabitants they could meet withall to the fword, without fparing any; and it was faid that the number of the flain amounted to threefcore thoufand perfons, amongft whom were many women and maids of very great beauty, which appertained to the chiefeft Lords of the place. After the bloody Maffacre of fo much people, and that the Town was fired, the principal houfes overthrown, and the moft fumptuous Temples laid level with the ground, nothing remaining on foot during the diforder, the *Tartars* continued there feven days, at the end whereof they returned towards *Pequin*, where their King was, and from whence he had fent them to this execution, carrying with them a world of gold and filver only, having burnt all the Merchandife they found there, as well becaufe they knew not how to tranfport it away, as for that the *Chinefes* fhould not make any benefit of it. Two days after their departure they arrived at a Caftle, named *Nixianicoo*, where the *Nauticor* of *Luançama*, their General, pitched his Camp, and intrenched himfelf on all fides with an intention to take it by affault the next day to be revenged on the *Chinefes* there, for that upon his paffing by them towards *Quinçay*, they had cut off an hundred of his men by an Ambufcado.

§.2   After the Army was encamped, and intrenched, and that the General had placed fure Guards and Sentinels in all places, he retired to his Tent, whither he fent for the feventy Captains that commanded his Army, unto whom upon their arrival he difcovered his refolution, which being well approved of they fell into deliberation in what manner the Caftle fhould be affaulted the day following, which concluded on, the next morning as foon as it was light the fouldiers began to march towards the Caftle, divided into fourteen Bataillions; being come within a flight fhoot of it with the found of trumpets, and moft hideous cries, they reared up their Ladders againft the walls, and couragioufly mounted up; but in the heat of this affault, where every one fhewed his valour, the one in bravely attempting, and the other in well defending, the *Tartar* in lefs then two hours loft above three thoufand of his men, which made him found a retreat in great diforder, and he paft the reft of that day in burying the dead, and curing of the wounded, whereof, there being a great number, the moft part died not long after, for that the arrows wherewith they were hurt had been fmeared by the *Chinefes* with fo ftrange and deadly poifon, as there was no remedy to be found for it. In the mean time the *Tartar* Commanders feeing the ill fuccefs of this affault, and fearing the King would be offended at fo great a lofs for fo fmall an occafion, perfwaded the General to call another Councel, wherein it might be confidered, whether it would be moft expedient for the Kings honour to perfift in the Siege of that place, or to give it over, whereupon this affair coming accordingly into deliberation it was a long time debated with fuch diverfity of opinions, as they were not able to

con-

conclude upon any thing, so that it was thought fit, in regard it was then late to put off the Assembly till the next day; This resolution taken, every man retired to his quarter. Now we being led away amidst a great many of other slaves, with whom we had escaped out of the fire of the Town, it fell out, whether for our good, or for our greater misfortune, we could not then tell, that we were under the Guard, as prisoners of war, of one of that Assembly, a rich and honourable man, who returning to his tent with three other persons, of like quality to himself, whom he had invited to Supper, it chanced after they were risen from table that one of them espied us, where we stood chained in a corner of the tent, and perceiving us to weep was so moved, that he demanded of us what people we were? what the name of our Country was? and how we came to be slaves to the *Chineses*? whereunto we gave such an answer, as the *Tartar* ingaging himself further in this discourse, enquired of us whether our King was inclined to the wars, and whether we did use to fight in our Country? to whom one of our companions, named *Jorge Mendez*, replyed that we did, and that we had been trained up from our infancy in a military course of life; which so pleased the *Tartar*, that calling his two friends unto him, Come hither, said he, and have the patience to hear what these prisoners can say; for believe me they seem to be men of understanding; whereupon the other two came near, and hearing us relate some part of our misfortunes, it begat a desire in them to ask us other questions, wherein having satisfied them the best that we could, one of them that seemed more curious then the rest, addressing himself to *Jorge Mendez*, spake thus; *Since you have seen so much of the world, as you say, if there were ere a one amongst you that could find out any device, or stratagem of war, whereby the* Mitaquer *(for so was the* Nauticor *called) might take this Castle, I vow to you that he would become your prisoner, whereas you are his.* Then *Jorge Mendez*, never considering with what imprudence he spake, nor understanding what he said, nor into what danger he was putting himself, boldly answered him; *If my Lord* Mitaquer *will in the name of the King give it us under his hand, that we shall have a safe conduct to convey us by Sea to the Isle of* Ainan, *from whence we may freely return into our Country, possibly I may be the man that will shew him how he shall take the Castle with little ado.* This Speech being heard, and maturely considered by one of the three, a man in years, and of great authority, as having the honour to be much esteemed and beloved of the *Mitaquer*, *Think well of what thou sayest*, replyed he to Jorge Mendez, *for I assure thee if thou doest it, that whatsoever thou demandest shall be granted thee, I, and more too.* Hereupon the rest of us seeing what *Jorge Mendez* was going to undertake, as also how far he ingaged himself in his promise, and that the *Tartars* began already to ground some hope thereupon, we thought fit to reprehend him for it, and to tell him, that he was not to hazard himself so at random by promising a thing that might bring us into the danger of our lives. *I fear nothing less*, said he unto us, *for as for my life, in the estate where now I am, I make so little account of it, that if any of these* Barbarians *would play for it at* Primero, *I would with three of the worst cards in the pack venture it upon the first encounter, for I am confident that all the benefit they can expect from us will never oblige them to grant us either life or liberty, so that for my particular I had as lief die to day as to morrow, judg you only by that which you saw them do at* Quincay, *whether you are likely to be better dealt withall now.* The *Tartars* were much abashed to see us thus in contestation one with another, and to hear us talk so loud, which is not usual amongst them, wherefore they reprehended us very seriously, saying, *That it was for women to speak aloud, who could not put a bridle to their tongue, nor a key to their mouths, and not for men, that carry a sword, and are made for the wars:* Howbeit if it were so that Jorge Mendez *could execute what he had propounded, the* Mitaquer *could not refuse him any thing he could demand.* This said, the *Tartars* retired every one to his lodging, for that it was eleven of the clock at night, the first watch being newly past, and the Captains of the Guard beginning then to walk the round about the camp at the sound of divers instruments, as is the custom in semblable occasions.

The fame of the three *Tartar* Commanders, which I said before was so esteemed of by the *Mitaquer*, had no sooner learnt of *Jorge Mendez*, that he could tell how to take the Castle of *Nixiamcoo*, but that he went presently to acquaint the General with it, and making the matter greater then it was, he told him, that he could do no less then send for him to hear his reasons, which peradventure would perswade him to give credit unto him, and in case it proved not so, yet was there nothing lost thereby. The *Mitaquer* being well pleased with this advice, sent incontinently a Command to *Tileymay*, which was the Captain under whose

§.1.

Guard

Guard we were, for to bring us unto him, as presently he did. Being then arrived, chained as we were, at the *Mitaquers* Tent, we found him set in Council with the seventy Commanders of the Army about two hours after midnight ; At our coming he received us with an affable countenance, yet grave and severe, and causing us to approach nearer unto him, he commanded part of our chains to be undone, then asked us if we would eat, whereunto we answered most willingly, for that in three days together we had not so much as tasted a bit of any thing, whereat the *Mitaquer* was very much offended, and sharply reproving the *Tileymay* for it, willed two great platters of sodden rice, and Ducks cut in small pieces to be set before us, whereto we fell with such an appetite, like men that were almost famished, as those of the company, who took great pleasure to see us feed so, said to the *Mitaquer*, *When as you had nothing else, my Lord, but cause these to come before you for to slack their hunger, verily you had done very much for them, by saving them from a languishing death, which otherwise they could not have avoided, and so you might have lost these slaves, of whom the service or sale might have been some way profitable unto you, for if you will not make use of them at* Lancama, *you may sell them for a thousand* Taeis *at least.* Hereat some began to laugh, but the *Mitaquer* commanded more rice to be given us, together with some apples, and other things, conjuring us again to eat, as a thing which he took pleasure to see us do. wherein we most willingly gave him satisfaction. After we had fed well, he began to talk with *Jorge Mendez* about that which had been told him of him, and of the means that were to be used for taking the Castle, making him many great promises of honours, pentions, favour with the King, and liberty for all the rest of his fellows, with other such offers, as passed all measure : For he swore unto him that if by his means God should give him the victory, whereby he sought nothing but to be revenged on his enemies for the blood which they had shed of his men, he should every way be like unto himself, or at least to any of his children whichsoever : Herewith *Jorge Mendez* found himself somewhat perplexed, because he held it almost impossible for him to bring it to effect, howsoever he told him, that not to hold him longer in hand, he did not think but if he might view the Castle with his own eys, he might then peradventure let him know how it might be taken, wherefore if his Lordship pleased, he would the next morning consider it all about, and thereupon render him an account what course was to be taken therein. The *Mitaquer*, & all the rest, allowed very well of his answer, and greatly commending him for it sent us to be lodged in a Tent not far from his, where we spent the rest of the night under a sure Guard ; you may judg now in what fear we were, knowing that if the business did not succeed according to the desire of these *Barbarians*, they would cut us all in pieces, for that they were a people which for never so small a matter would not stick to kill twenty or thirty men, without any regard either of God, or any thing else. The next morning about eight of the clock, *Jorge Mendez*, and two of us, that were appointed to accompany him, went to survey the place with thirty horse for our safe-Guard ; when as *Jorge Mendez* had well observed the scituation thereof, as also that part whereby it might most commodiously be assaulted, he returned to the *Mitaquer*, that expected him with impatience, to whom he gave an acount of what he had seen, and facilitated the taking of the Castle with little hazard, whereat the *Mitaquer* was so overjoyed, that he presently caused the rest of our irons, and the chains, wherewith we were fastened by the neck and feet to be taken off, swearing to us by the rice he did eat, that as soon as he came to *Pequin*, he would present us to the King, and infallibly accomplish all that he had promised us, for the more assurance whereof he confirmed it by a Deed under his hand, that was written in letters of gold, to make it more authentical. That done, he sent for us to dinner, and would needs have us to sit with him at table, doing us many other honours according to their manner, which greatly contented us, but on the other side we were in no little fear, least this affair should not for our sins have a success answerable to that hope the *Mitaquer* had already conceived of it. The rest of this day the Commanders spent in resolving upon the order that was to be observed for assaulting the Castle, wherein *Jorge Mendez* was the sole Director : First of all then an infinite company of Bavins & Fagots was gotten together for to fill up the ditches; there were also three hundred Ladders made, very strong, and so large, that three men might easily mount up on them afront without incombring one another ; likewise there was a world of Paniers Dossers, and Baskets provided, together with a great multitude of Mattocks, and Spades, that were found in the Villages and Burroughs thereabout, which the inhabitants had deserted upon the bruit of this war, and all the souldiers of the Army made preparation of such things as they should need the next day when the assault was to be given :

In

In the mean time *Jorge Mendez* rode always by the *Mitaquers* side, who shewed him many great favours, which we perceived had begotten in him a stately carriage, far different from that he was wont to have, whereat we wondring, some of us (who envious of anothers good fortune, and out of an ill nature) could not chuse but murmur, saying one to another, as it were in disdain, and in a kind of jeering, *What think you of this dog? verily he will be the cause that either to morrow morning we shall be all cut in pieces, or if the business he hath undertaken succeed as we desire, it is probable that he will be in such credit with these Barbari-ans, that we shall account it for a happiness to be his servants*; and this was the talk which we had amongst us. The next day all the Army was put into order, and divided into twelve Battalli-ons, whereof they made twelve Files, and one Counterfile in the Vantguard, that incompas-sed the whole Camp in manner of an half moon: upon the wings were the foremost with all that Mass of Bavins, Ladders, Baskets, Mattocks, Spades, and other materials to fill up the ditch, and make it equal with the rest of the ground. Marching in this manner they arrived at the Ca-stle, which they found strongly mann'd, and with a number of Flags and Streamers waving upon the Battlements. The first Salutation between the besiegers and the besieged was with arrows, darts, stones, and pots of wild-fire, which continued about half an hour, then the *Tartars* presently filled the ditch with bavins and earth, and so reared up their ladders against the wall, that now by reason of the filling up of the ditch was not very high; The first that mounted up was *Jorge Mendez*, accompanied with two of ours, who as men resolved had set up their rest, either to die there, or to render their valour remarkable by some memorable act, as in effect it pleased our Lord that their resolution had a good success, for they not only entred first, but also planted the first colours upon the wall, whereat the *Mitaquer*, and all that were with him, were so amazed, as they said one to another, Doubtless if these people did besiege *Pequin*, as we do, the *Chineses*, which defend that City, would sooner lose their honour, then we shall make them to do it with all the forces we have; in the mean time all the *Tartars*, that were at the foot of the ladders, followed the three *Portugals*, and carried themselves so valiantly, what with the example of a Captain that had shewed them the way, as out of their own natural disposition, almost as resolute as those of *Japan*, that in a very short space above 5000 of them were got upon the walls from whence with great violence they made the *Chineses* to retire, whereupon so furious and bloody a fight ensued between either party, that in less then half an hour the business was fully decided, and the Castle taken, with the death of two thousand *Chineses* and *Mogores* that were in it, there being not above sixscore of the *Tartars* slain. That done the gates being opened, the *Mitaquer* with great acclamations of joy entred, and causing the *Chineses* colours to be taken down, and his own to be advanced in their pla-ces, he with a new ceremony of rejoycing at the sound of many instruments of war after the the manner of the *Tartars* gave rewards to the wounded, and made divers of the most vali-ant of his followers Knights, by putting bracelets of gold about their right arms; and then about noon he with the chief Commanders of his Army, for the greater triumph dined in the Castle, where he also bestowed bracelets of gold upon *Jorge Mendez*, and the other *Portu-gals*, whom he made to sit down at table with him; After the cloth was taken away, he went out of the Castle with all his company, and then causing all the walls of it to be dismantelled, he razed the place quite to the ground, setting on fire all that remained with a number of cere-monies, which was performed with great cries and acclamations to the sound of divers instru-ments of war; Moreover he commanded the ruines of this Castle to be sprinkled with the blood of his enemies, and the heads of all of them that lay dead there to be cut off; as for his own souldiers that were slain, he caused them to be triumphantly buried, and such as were hurt to be carefully looked unto; this done, he retired with a huge train, and in great pomp to his tent, having *Jorge Mendez* close by him on horsback; As for the other eight of us, together with many brave Noblemen and Captains, we followed him on foot. Being arrived at his tent, which was richly hung, he sent *Jorge Mendez* a thousand *Taeis* for a reward, and to us but an hundred a piece, whereat some of us, that thought themselves to be better qualified, were very much discontented, for that he was more respected then they, by whose means, as well as his, the enterprise had been so happily atchieved, though by the good success thereof we had all obtained honour and liberty.

A a

CHAP. XXXIX.

The Mitaquer *departs from the Castle of* Nixiamcoo, *and goes to the King of*
Tartary *his Camp before* Pequin; *with that which we saw till*
we arrived there; and the Mitaquers *pre-*
senting us unto the King.

§. 1 THe next day the *Mitaquer* having nothing more to do where he was, resolved to take
his way towards the City of *Pequin*, before which the King lay, as I have delivered before; To this effect having put his Army into battel aray, he departed from thence at eight of
the clock in the morning, and marching leasurely to the sound of his warlike instruments, he
made his first station about noon upon the bank of a river, whose scituation was very pleasant,
being all about invironed with a world of fruit trees, and a many goodly houses, but wholly
deserted, and bereaved of all things which the *Barbarians* might any way have made booty of.
Having past the greatest heat of the day there, he arose and marched on until about an hour in
the night that he took up his lodging at a pretty good Town, called *Lantimay*, which likewise
we found deserted, for all this whole Country was quite dispeopled for fear of the *Barbarians*,
who spared no kind of person, but wheresoever they came put all to fire and sword, as the
next day they did by this place, and many other along this river, which they burnt down to
the ground; and that which yet was more lamentable, they set on fire, and clean consumed to
ashes a great large plain, being above six leagues about, and full of corn ready to be reaped. This
cruelty executed, the Army began again to move, composed as it was of some threescore and
five thousand horse, (for as touching the rest they were all slain, as well at the taking of *Quin-*
çay, as in that of the Castle of *Nixiamcoo*,) and went on to a mountain, named *Pommitay*,
where they remained that night; The next morning dislodging from thence, they marched on
somewhat faster then before, that they might arrive by day at the City of *Pequin*, which was
distant about seven leagues from that mountain: At three of the clock in the afternoon we
came to the river of *Palamxitan*, where a *Tartar* Captain, accompanied with an hundred
horse, came to receive us, having waited there two days for that purpose; The first thing that
he did, was the delivering of a letter from the King to our General, who received it with a
great deal of ceremony; From this river to the Kings quarter, which might be some two leagues,
the Army marched without order, as being unable to do otherwise, partly as well in regard of
the great concourse of people, wherewith the ways were full in coming to see the Generals arrival, as for the great train which the Lords brought along with them, that over-spread all the
fields; In this order, or rather disorder, we arrived at the Castle of *Lautir*, which was the
first Fort of mine that the Camp had for the retreat of the Spies, there we found a young Prince,
whom the *Tartar* had sent thither to accompany the General, who alighting from his horse,
took his Scymitar from his side, and on his knees offered it unto him, after he had kissed the
ground five times, being the ceremony or compliment ordinarily used amongst them; The
Prince was exceedingly pleased with this honour done unto him, which with a smiling countenance, and much acknowledgment of words he testified unto him; This past, the Prince with
a new ceremony stept two or three paces back, and lifting up his voice with more gravity then before, as he that represented the Person of the King, in whose name he came, said unto him, *He, the border of whose rich vesture my mouth kisseth, and that out of an incredi-*
ble greatness mastereth the Scepters of the earth, and of the Isles of the Sea, sends thee word
by me, who am his slave, that thy honourable arrival is no less agreeable unto him, then the
Summers sweet morning is to the ground, when as the dew doth comfort and refresh our bodies,
and therefore would have thee without further delay to come and hear his voice mounted on
his horse, whose trappings are garnished with jewels taken out of his Treasury, to the end,
that riding by my side, thou mayest be made equal in honour to the greatest of his Court, and
that they which behold thee marching in this sort, may acknowledge that the right hand of him
is mighty and valiant unto whom the labours of war giveth this recompence. Hereupon the
Mitaquer prostrating himself on the earth, with his hands lifted up, answered him thus, *Let*
my head be an hundred times trampled on by the sole of his feet, that all those of my race may
be sensible of so great a favour, and that my eldest Son may ever carry it for a mark of ho-
nour. Then mounting on the horse, which the Prince had given him, trapped with gold and
precious stones, being one of those that the King used to ride on himself, they marched on with
a great

a great deal of State and Majesty. In this pomp were many spare horses led richly harnessed; there were also a number of Ushers, carrying silver Maces on their shoulders, and six hundred Halberdiers on horsback, together with fifteen Chariots, full of silver Cymbals, and many other ill tuned barbarous instruments, that made so great a din, as it was not possible to hear one another. Moreover in all this distance of way, which was a league and an half, there were so many men on horsback, as one could hardly pass through the croud in any part thereof. The *Mitaquer* being thus in triumph arrived at the first trenches of the Camp, he sent us by one of his Servants to his quarter, where we were very well received, and abundantly furnished with all things necessary for us.

Fourteen days after we arrived at this Camp, the *Mitaquer,* our General, sent for us to his §. 2 Tent, where in the presence of some of his Gentlemen, he said unto us; *To morrow morning about this time be you ready, that I may make good my word unto you, which is to let you see the face of him, whom we hold for our Soveraign Lord, a grace that is done you out of a particular respect to me; And this his Majesty doth not only grant unto you, but your liberty also, which I have obtained of him for you, and which in truth I am no less glad of, then of the taking of* Mixiancoo, *the particulars whereof you may relate unto him, if you come to be so happy as to be questioned by him about it. Withall I assure you that I shall take it for a great satisfaction, if when you shall return into your Country, you will remember that I have kept my word with you, and that therein I have shewed my self so punctual, as it may be I would not for that consideration demand of the King some other thing more profitable for me, that you may know this was that which I only desired: Also the King hath done me the honour to grant it me presently, and that with such exceeding demonstration of favour, as I must confess I am thereby more obliged unto you, then you are to me.* Having spoken thus unto us we prostrated our selves upon the ground, and in this sort answered him. *My Lord, the good which you have pleased to do us is so great, that to go about to thank you with words (as the world useth to do) in the state we now are in, would rather be an ingratitude, then a true and due acknowledgment; so that we think it better to pass it by in silence within the secret of that soul which God hath put into us; And therefore since our tongues are of no use to us herein, and that they cannot frame words, capable to satisfie so great an obligation, as this is, wherein all of us stand for ever so infinitely ingaged unto you, we must with continual tears and sighs beg of the Lord which made Heaven and earth, that he will reward you for it; for it is he that out of his infinite mercy and goodness, hath taken upon him to pay that for the poor, which they of themselves are not able to discharge; It is he then, that will throughly recompence you and your children for this good office you have done us, and whereby you merit to have a share in his promises, and to live long and happily in this world.* Amongst those which accompanied the *Mitaquer* at that time, there was one named *Bonquinuda,* a man in years, and of the principalest Lords of the Kingdom, who in this Army commanded over the strangers and *Rhinocerots,* that served for the Guard of the Camp; This same, unto whom more respect was born then to all the rest that were present, had no sooner heard our answer, but lifting up his eyes to Heaven he said, *O! who could be so happy, as to be able to ask of God the explication of so high a secret, whereunto the weakness of our poor understanding cannot arrive; for I would fain know from whence it comes, that he permits people so for esloigned from the knowledge of our truth, to answer on the suddain in terms so agreeable to our ears, that I dare well say, nay, I will venture my head on it, that concerning things of God, and Heaven, they know more sleeping, then we do broad awake, whence it may be inferred that there are Priests amongst them that understand the course of the Stars, and the motions of the Heavens, far better then our Bonzes of the house of* Lechuna. Whereupon all that were about him answered, *Your Greatness hath so much reason for it, that we were obliged to behold it as an Article of our faith, wherefore we think it were fit, that these strangers should not be suffered to go out of our Country, where, as our Masters and Doctors, they might teach us such things they know of the world.* That which you advise, replyed the *Mitaquer,* is not much amiss, and yet the King would never permit it for all the treasures of China, because if he should, he would then violate the truth of his word, and so lose all the reputation of his greatness, wherefore you must excuse me if I do not propound things unto him that cannot be; whereupon turning himself towards us, Go, get you gone, said he unto us, and to morrow morning fail not to be ready for to come again when I shall send for you. These words exceedingly contented us, as there was great cause they should; and accordingly the next day he sent us nine horses very well furnished, upon which we mounted, and so went to his Tent; He

in

in the mean time had put himself into a *Piambre* (that is somewhat like to a Litter) drawn with two horses richly harnessed; round about him for his Guard marched threescore Halberdiers, six pages apparelled in his Livery mounted on white Curtals, and we nine on horsback a little more behind. In this manner he went on towards the place where the King was, whom he found lodged in the great and sumptuous Edifice of the Goddess *Nacapirau*, by the *Chineses* called the Queen of Heaven, whereof I have spoken at large in the thirty fourth *Chapter*. Being arrived at the first trenches of the Kings Tent, he alighted out of his Litter, and all the rest likewise off from their horses, for to speak to the *Nautaran*, of whom with a kind of ceremony, after the fashion of the *Gentiles*, he craved leave to enter, which was presently granted him. Thereupon the *Mitaquer* being returned into his Litter, passed through the gates in the same manner as before, only we and the rest of his followers waited upon him on foot. When he came to a low and very long Gallery, where there was a great number of Gentlemen, he alighted again out of his Litter, and told us that we were to attend him there, for that he would go and know whether it were a fit time to speak with the King, or no. We stayed there then about an hour, during the which some of the Gentlemen that were in the Gallery observing us to be strangers, and such kind of people as they had never seen the like, they called us, and very courteously bid us to sit down by them, where having spent some time in beholding certain tumblers shewing feats of activity, we perceived the *Mitaquer* coming forth with four very beautiful boys, attired in long coats after the *Turkish* fashion, garded all over with green and white, and wearing about the small of their legs little hoops of gold in the form of irons and shackles. The Gentlemen that were present, as soon as they saw them rose up on their feet, and drawing out their Courtelasses, which they wore by their sides, they laid them on the ground with a new kind of ceremony, saying three times, *Let the Lord of our heads live an hundred thousand years.* In the mean while as we lay with our heads bending to the ground, one of those boys said aloud unto us; *You men of the other end of the world, rejoyce now, for that the hour is come, wherein your desire is to be accomplished, and that you are to have the liberty, which the* Mitaquer *promised you at the Castle of* Nixiamcoo, *wherefore arise from off the earth, and lift up your hands to Heaven, rendring thanks unto the Lord, who during the night of our peaceable rest, enammels the Firmament with Stars, seeing that of himself alone, without the merit of any flesh, he hath made you to encounter in your exile with a man that delivers your persons.* To this Speech, prostrated as we were on the ground, we returned him this answer by our truch-man, *May Heavens grant us so much happiness, as that his foot may trample on our heads*; whereunto he replied, *Your Wish is not small, and may it please God to accord you this gift of riches.*

§.3.   These four boys, and the *Mitaquer*, whom we followed, past through a Gallery, erected upon five and twenty pillars of brass, and entred into a great room, where there were a number of Gentlemen, and amongst them many strangers, *Mogores, Persians, Bordies, Calaminhams,* and *Bramaas*. After we were out of this room, we came unto another, where there were many armed men, ranged into five Files all along the room, with Courtelasses on their shoulders, that were garnished with gold. These stayed the *Mitaquer* a little, and with great complements asked him some questions, and took his oath upon the Maces the boys carried, which he performed on his knees, kissing the ground three several times, whereupon he was admitted to pass on into a great place, like a quadrangle; there we saw four ranks of Statues of brass, in the form of wild men, with clubs and crowns of the same mettal guilt: These Idols or Gyants, were each of them six and twenty spans high, and six broad, as well on the brest, as on the shoulders; their countenances were hideous and deformed, and their hair curled like to *Negroes*. The desire we had to know what these figures signified, made us to demand it of the *Tartars*, who answered us, that they were the three hundred and threescore gods, which framed the days of the year, being placed there expresly, to the end that in their effigies they might be continually adored, for having created the fruits which the earth produceth; and withall that the King of *Tartary* had caused them to be transported thither from a great Temple, called *Angicamoy*, which he had taken in the City of *Xipaton*, out of the Chappel of the Tombs of the Kings of *China*, for to triumph over them, when as he should happily return into his Country, that the whole world might know how in despight of the King of *China* he had captivated his gods. Within this place, whereof I speak, and amidst a plantation of Orange-trees, that was invironed within a fence of Ivy, Roses, Rosemary, and many other sort of flowers, which we have not in *Europe*, was a Tent pitched upon twelve Ballisters of the wood of Champhire, each

of

of them wreathed about with silver in the fashion of knotted card-work, bigger then ones arm. In this Tent was a low Throne in the form of an Altar, garnished with branched work of fine gold, and over it was a cloth of State, set thick with silver Stars ; where also the Sun and Moon were to be seen, as also certain clouds, some of them white, and others of the colour of which appear in the time of rain, all enammelled so to the life, and with such art, that they beguiled all those that beheld them, for they seamed to rain indeed, so as it was impossible to see a thing more compleat, either for the proportions or colours. In the midst of this Throne upon a bed lay a great Statue of silver called *Abicau Nilancor*, which signifies, *the God of the health of Kings*, that had been also taken in the Temple of *Angicamoy*. Now round about the same Statue were four and thirty Idols of the height of a child of five or six years old, ranged in two Files, and set on their knees, with their hands lifted up towards this Idol, as if they would adore him. At the entry into this Tent there were four young Gentlemen richly clad, who with each of them a Censer in his hand, went two and two about, then at the sound of a bell prostrated themselves on the ground, and censed one another, saying with a loud voice, *Let our cry come unto thee as a sweet perfume, to the end thou mayest bear us.* For the Guard of of this Tent, there were threescore Halberdiers, who at a little distance invironed it all about. They were clothed with guilt leather, and had Murrians on their heads curiously engraven ; all which were very agreeable and majestical objects. Out of this place we entred into another division, where there were four Chambers very rich and well furnished, in the which were many Gentlemen, as well strangers as *Tartars*. From thence passing on whith r the *Mitaquer*, and the young boys conducted us, we arrived at the door of a great low room, in form like to a Church, where stood six Ushers with their Maces, who with a new complement to the *Mitaquer* caused us to enter, but kept out all others. In this room was the King of *Tartaria*, accompanied with many Princes, Lords, and Captains, amongst whom were the Kings of *Pafua, Mecuy, Capinper, Raina Benan, Anchesacotay*, and others to the number of fourteen, who in rich attire were all seated some three or four paces from the foot of the Tribunal. A little more on the one side were two and thirty very fair women, who playing upon divers instruments of musick, made a wonderful sweet Consort. The King was set on his Throne under a rich Cloth of State, and had about him twelve young boys kneeling on their knees, with little Maces of gold like Scepters, which they carried on their shoulders ; close behind him was a young Lady extreamly beautiful, and wonderfully richly attired, with a Ventiloe in her hand, wherewith she ever and anon fanned him. This same was the sister of the *Mitaquer* our General, and infinitely beloved of the King, for whose sake therefore it was that he was in such credit and reputation throughout the whole Army : The King was much about forty years of age, full stature, somewhat lean and of a good aspect ; His beard was very short, his Mustaches after the *Turkish* manner, his eyes like to the *Chineses*, and his countenance severe and majestical ; As for his vesture, it was violet colour, in fashion like to a *Turkish* Robe imbroydered with pearl, upon his feet he had green Sandals wrought all over with gold purl, and great pearls among it, and on his head a sattin cap of the colour of his habit, with a rich band of diamends and rubies intermingled together : Before we past any farther, after we had gone ten or eleven steps in the room, we made our complement by kissing of the ground three several times, and performing other ceremonies, which the Truch-men taught us : In the mean time the King commanded the musick to cease, and addressing himself to the *Mitaquer* ; Ask these men of the other end of the world said he unto him, whether they have a King, what is the name of their Country, and how far distant it is from this Kingdom of *China* where now I am ? Thereupon one of ours speaking for all the rest, answered ; That our Country was called *Portugal*, that the King thereof was exceeding rich and mighty, and that from thence to the City of *Pequin* was at the least three years voyage. This answer much amazed the King, because he did not think the world had been so large, so that striking his thigh with a wand that he had in his hand, and lifting up his eyes to Heaven, as though he would render thanks unto God ; he said aloud, so as every one might hear him : *O Creator of all things ; are we able to comprehend the marvels of thy greatness, we that at the best are but poor worms of the earth?* Fuxiquidane, fuxiquidane, *let them approach, let them approach.* Thereupon beckening to us with his hand, he caused us to come even to the first degree of the Throne, where the fourteen Kings sat, and demanded of him again, as a man astonished, *Pucau, pucau*, that is to say, *how far, how far ?* whereunto he answered as before, that we should be at least three years in returning to our Country. Then he asked why we came not rather by Land, then by Sea, where so

many

many labours and dangers were to be undergon? Thereunto he replyed, that there was too great an extent of land, through which we were not affured to pafs, for that it was commanded by Kings of feveral nations. *What come you to feek for then,* added the King, *and wherefore do you expofe your felves to fuch dangers?* Then having rendred him a reafon to this laft demand with all the fubmiffion that might be, he ftayed a prety while without fpeaking, and then fhaking his head three or four times, he addreffed himfelfe to an old man that was not far from him, and faid, *Certainly we muft needs conclude, that there is either much ambition, or little juftice in the Country of thefe people, feeing they came fo far to conquer other Lands.* To this Speech the old man, named *Raia Benan,* made no other anfwer but that it muft needs be fo, for men, faid he, who have recourfe unto their induftry and invention to run over the Sea for to get that which God hath not given them, are neceffarily carried thereunto, either by extream poverty, or by an excefs of blindnefs and vanity, derived from much covetoufnefs, which is the caufe why they renounce God, and thofe that brought them into the world. This reply of the old man was feconded with many jeering words by the other Courtiers, who made great fport upon this occafion, that very much pleafed the King, in the mean time the women fell to their mufick again, and fo continued, till the King withdrew into another Chamber in the company of thefe fair Muficians, and that young Lady which fanned him, not fo much as one of thofe great Perfonages, daring to enter befides: Not long after one of thofe twelve boys, that carried the Scepters before mentioned, came to the *Mitaquer,* and told him from his fifter, that the King commanded him not to depart away, which he held for a fingular favour, by reafon this meffage was delivered to him in the prefence of thofe Kings and Lords that were in the room, fo that he ftirred not, but fent us word, that we fhould go unto our tent with this affurance, that he would take care the Son of the Sun fhould be mindful of us.

CHAP. XL.

The King of Tattaria's *raifing of his Siege from before* Pequin, *for to return into his Country, and that which paffed until his Arrival there.*

§.1. WE had been now full three and forty dayes in this Camp, during which time there paft many fights and skirmifhes between the befiegers and the befieged, as alfo two affaults in the open day which were refifted by them within with an invincible courage like refolute men as they were; In the mean time the King of *Tartaria,* feeing how contrary to his hope fo great an enterprife had been, wherein he had confumed fo much treafure, caufed his Councel of War to be affembled, in the which were prefent the feven and twenty Kings that accompanied him, and likewife many Princes, and Lords, and the moft part of the chief Commanders of the Army: In this Councel it was refolved, that in regard Winter was at hand, and that the rivers had already overflowed their banks with fuch force and violence, as they had ravaged and carried away moft of the Trenches and Pallifadoes of the Camp, and that moreover great numbers of the fouldiers died daily of ficknefs, and for want of victuals, that therefore the King could not do better then to raife his Siege, and be gone before Winter came, for fear left ftaying longer, he fhould run the hazard of lofing himfelf, and his Army: All thefe reafons feemed fo good to the King, that without further delay he refolved to follow this counfel, and to obey the prefent neceffity, though it were to his great grief. fo that incontinently he caufed all his Infantry and Ammunition to be imbarqued, then having commanded his Camp to be fet on fire, he himfelf went away by Land with three hundred thoufand Horfe, and twenty thoufand Rhinocerots: Now after they had taken an account of all the dead, they appeared to be four hundred and fifty thoufand, the moft of whom died of ficknefs, as alfo an hundred thoufand Horfes, and threefcore thoufand Rhinocerots, which were eaten in the fpace of two months and an half, wherein they wanted victual, fo that of eighteen hundred thoufand men wherewith the King of *Tartaria* came out of his Country to befiege the City of *Pequin,* before the which he lay fix months and an half, he carried home fome feven hundred and fifty thoufand lefs then he brought forth, whereof four and fifty thoufand died of ficknefs, famine, and war, and three hundred thoufand went and rendred themfelves unto the *Chinefes,* drawn thereunto by the great pay which they gave them, and other advantages of honour and prefents which they continually beftowed on them; whereat we are not to marvel, feeing experience doth fhew, how that alone is of far more power to oblige men, then all other things in the world.

world. After the King of *Tartaria* was gone from this City of *Pequin*, upon a *Munday*, the seventeenth of *October*, with three hundred thousand horse, as I have related before, the same day about evening he went and lodged near to a river, called *Quaytragun*, and the next morning an hour before day the Army began to march at the sound of the Drums, Fifes, and other instruments of war, according to the order prescribed them: In this manner he arrived a little before night at a Town, named *Guiiampea*, which he found altogether depopulated: After his Army had reposed thereabout an hour and an half, he set forth again, and marching somewhat fast he came to lodg at the foot of a great mountain, called *Liampeu*, from whence he departed towards morning. Thus marched he eight leagues a day for fourteen days together, at the end whereof he arrived at a good Town, named *Guauxitim*, which might contain about eleven or twelve thousand fires; There he was counselled to furnish himself with victuals, whereof he had great need, for which purpose therefore he begirt it round, and skaling it in the open day, he quickly made himself Master of it, and put it to the sack with so cruel a Massacre of the inhabitants, as my fellows and I were ready to swoond for very astonishment: Now after that the wood and fire had consumed all things, and that the Army was abundantly provided of ammunition and victual, he departed at the break of day; and though he past the next morning in the view of *Caixiloo*, yet would not he attaque it, for that it was a great and strong Town, and by scituation impregnable, having heard besides that there were fifty thousand men within it, whereof ten thousand were *Mogors*, *Cauchins*, and *Champaas*, resolute souldiers, and much more warlike then the *Chineses*. From thence passing on he arrived at the walls of *Singrachirau*, which are the very same, that, as I have said heretofore, do divide those two Empires of *China* and *Tartaria*; There meeting with no resistance he went and lodged on the further side of it at *Panquinor*, which was the first of his own Towns, and seated some three leagues from the said wall, and the next day he marched to *Psipator*, where he dismissed the most part of his people. In this place he stayed not above seven days, which he spent in providing pay for his souldiers, and in the execution of certain prisoners he had taken in that war, and brought along with him: These things thus expedited, he, as a man not very well pleased, imbarqued himself for *Lançame*, in sixscore *Lanlees*, with no more then ten or eleven thousand men: So in six dayes after his imbarquing, he arrived at *Lançame*, where not permitting any reception to be made him he landed about two hours within night.

The King abode in this City of *Lançame* until such time as all his forces, as well horse as foot, **S. 2** were arrived there, which was within six and twenty days, then having all his Army together, he went on to another City far greater and fairer, called *Tuymicoa*, where he was visited by some Princes his Neighbours, and by the Ambassadors of many other Kings and Soveraigns of more remoter Countrys, of which the chiefest were six great and mighty Monarchs, namely *Xataanai* the *Sophy* of *Persia*; *Siamon* Emperour of the *Gueos*, whose Country borders on that of *Bramaa*, and *Tangun*; the *Calaminham*, Lord of the indomptable force of the Elephant of the Earth, as I shall deliver hereafter, when I come to treat of him and his State; the *Sournau* of *Odiaa*, that names himself the King of *Siam*, whose dominion runs seven hundred leagues along the coast with that of *Tanauserin*, and on *Champaa* side with the *Malayos*, *Berdios*, and *Patanes*, and through the heart of the Country with *Passiloqua*, *Capioper*, and *Chiammay*, as also with the *Lauhos*, and *Gueos*, so that this Prince alone hath seventeen Kingdoms within his State, by reason whereof, for to make himself the more redoubted amongst the *Gentiles*, he causeth himself to be stiled, *The Lord of the white Elephant*; the fifth was the great *Mogor*, whose State is within the heart of the Country, near to the *Corazones*, a Province bordering upon *Persiu*, and the Kingdom of *Dely*, and *Chitor*; and the last an Emperour of a Country, named *Caran*, as we were informed there, the bounds of whose Soveraignty are at the Mountains of *Goncalidau*, sixty degrees further on, where a certain people live, whom they of the Country call *Moscovites*, whereof we have some in this City, which were fair of complection, well shapen, and apparelled with Breeches, Cassocks, and Hats, like to the *Flemings* which we see in *Europe*, the chiefest of them wearing Gowns lined with Sables, and the rest with ordinary furs. The Ambassador of this Emperor of *Caran*, was more remarkable in his entry, then all the rest: He had for his Guard about sixscore men, armed with arrows, and Partisans damasked with gold and silver, and all attired alike in violet and green; After them marched on horsback twelve Ushers, carrying silver Maces, before whom twelve horses were led, that had carnation clothes on them, bordered about with gold and silver; They

were

were followed by twelve huge tall men, that seemed to be Giants, clothed with Tygers skins as wild men are used to be painted of them holding in his hand a great Greyhound by a silver chain; Then appeared twelve little Pages, mounted on white Hackneys, having green velvet Saddles, trimmed with silver lace and frenge, they were all apparelled alike in crimson sattin Cassocks, lined with marterns, breeches, and hats of the same, and great chains of gold scarf-wise about them ; These twelve boys were all of one equal stature, so fair of face, so well favoured, and of so sweet a proportion of body, as I believe there have never been any seen more accomplished : For himself, he was seated in a Chariot with three wheels on each side, garnished all over with silver ; Round about this *Pirange*, (for so was this Chariot called) there were forty foot-men in jerkins, and breeches of green and red cloth, laced all over with carnation silk lace, having swords by their side above three fingers broad, with the hilts, handles, and chaps of silver, and hunting horns hanging in silver chains, bandrick-wise about them, and on their heads they wore caps, with feathers in them full of silver spangles : Thus was the equipage of this Ambassador so sumptuous and stately, that one might very well conclude he belonged to some very rich and mighty Prince. Now going one day as attendants on the *Mitaquer*, who went to visit him from the King, amongst other things that we saw in his lodging, we observed there for one of the greatest rarities in that Country, five Chambers hung all with very rich Arras, such as we have in Christendom ; and no question brought from thence : In each of these Chambers was a Cloth of State of gold or silver tinsel, and under it a Table with a Bason and Ewer of silver of a very costly fashion ; also a Chair of State of rich violet stuff trimmed with gold frenge, and at the foot of it a Cushion of the same, all upon an exceeding large foot-pace of tapestry ; There was also a chafingdish of silver, with a perfuming pot of the same, out of the which proceeded a most delicate odour ; At the door of each of those five Chambers stood two Halberdiers, who permitted persons of quality to enter that came thither to see them ; In another very great room in form like to a Gallery, there was upon a very high and large foot-pace a little table placed, covered with a damask table-cloth, edged about with gold-frenge, and upon a silver plate a napkin with a fork and a spoon of gold, as also two little salt-sellers of the same mettal : Now about ten or eleven paces on the one side from this table were two cupbards of plate of all kind of fashions, and other vessels of great value; Moreover at the four corners of this table were four cisterns about the bigness of a bushel, with their kettels fastened to them with chains all of silver, as also two very great candlesticks of the same with white wax candles in them but not lighted ; There were also at the door of the room twelve handsome Halberdiers, clothed in mantles like to *Irish* rug, with Scymitars by their sides, all covered over with plates of silver, which Guard (as ordinarily it is with them) were very haughty and rude in their answers to all that speak to them. Although this Ambassadour was come thither in the way of visit as the rest, yet the principal subject of his Ambassy was to treat of a marriage between the Emperour of *Caran*, and a sister of the *Tartar*, named *Meica vidau*, that is to say, a rich Saphir, a Lady about some thirty years of age, but very handsom, and exceeding charitable to the poor, whom we saw divers times in this City at the chiefest Feasts, which these people use to solemnize at certain times of the year, after the manner of the *Gentiles*. Howbeit setting aside all this, whereof I had not spoken but that it seemed more remarkable unto me then all the rest, I will return to my former discourse, as well concerning our liberty, as the voyage that we made even to the Islands of the Sea of *China*, whether the Emperour of *Tartaria* caused us to be conveighed, to the end that such as shall come after us may attain to the knowledge of a part of those things, whereof it may be they have never heard spoken until this present.

CHAP. XLI.

In what manner We were brought again before the King of Tartaria ; *with our departure from that Kingdom ; and all that we saw, and befell us in our voyage, till our arrival at the Court of the King of* Cauchinchina.

§. I.　AFter some time had been spent in the Celebrations of certain remarkable Feasts, that were made for joy of the conclusion of a marriage betwixt the Princess *Meica vidau*, the Kings sister, and the Emperour of *Caran*, the *Tartar* by the advice of his Captains resolved to return anew to the Siege of *Pequin*, which he had formerly quitted, taking the ill success cefs that he had there as a great affront to his perfon ; To this effect then he caufed all the Eftates of his Kingdom to be affembled, and alfo made a league with all the Kings and Princes bordering in his Dominions : whereupon confidering with our felves how prejudicial this might prove to the promife had been made us for the fetting of us at liberty, we repaired to the *Mitaquer*, and reprefented unto him many things that made for our purpofe, and obliged him to keep his word with us ; To the which he returned us this anfwer : Certainly you have a great deal of reafon for that you fay, and I have yet more not to refufe you that which you demand of me with fo much juftice; wherefore I refolve to put the King in mind of you, that you may enjoy your liberty, and the fooner you fhall be gone from hence, the fooner you fhall be freed from the labours which the time begins to prepare for us in the enterprife that his Majefty hath newly undertaken by the counfel of fome particulars, who for that they know not how to govern themfelves have more need to be counfelled, then the earth hath need of water to produce the fruits that are fowed in her ; but to morrow morning I fhall put the King in mind of you, and your poverty, and withall I fhall prefent unto him how you have poor fatherlefs children, as you have heretofore told me, to the end he may be thereby incted to caft his eyes upon you, as he is accuftomed to do in like cafes, which is none of the leaft marks of his greatnefs. Hereupon he difmiffed us for that day, and the next morning he went to *Pontiveu*, which is a place where the King ufeth to give audience to all fuch as have any fuit to him ; There befeeching his Majefty to think of us, he anfwered him, that as foon as he difpatched away an Ambaffador to the King of *Cauchenchina*, he would fend us along with him, for fo he had refolved to do : With this anfwer the *Mitaquer* returned to his houfe, where we were ready attending his coming, and told us what the King had promifed him, wherewithal not a little contented we went back to our lodging ; There in the expectation of the good fuccefs of this promife we continued ten days with fome impatience, at the end whereof the *Mitaquer* by the Kings exprefs command carried us with him to the Court, where caufing us to approach near to his Majefty, with thofe ceremonies of greatnefs which are obferved in coming before him, being the fame we ufed at *Pequin*, after he had beheld us with a gentle eye, he bid the *Mitaquer* ask of us whether we would ferve him, and in cafe we would, he fhould not only be very well pleafed with it, but he would alfo give us better entertainment, and more advantagious conditions then all the ftrangers that fhould follow him in this war. To this demand the *Mitaquer* anfwered very favourably for us, how he had often heard us fay, that we were married in our Country, and had a great charge of children, who had no other means to maintain them, but what we got with our labour, which was poorly enough God knows : The King heard this fpeech with fome demonftration of pity, fo that looking on the *Mitaquer* ; *I am glad*, faid he, *to know that they have fuch good caufe to return home as they fpeak of, that I may with the more contentmant acquit me of that which thou haft promifed them in my name.* At thefe words the *Mitaquer*, and all we that were with him, lifting up our hands, as to a teftimony of our thankfulnefs unto him, we kiffed the ground three times, and faid, *May thy feet reft themfelves upon a thoufand generations, to the end that thou mayft be Lord of the inhabitants of the earth.* Hereat the King began to fmile, and faid to a Prince that was near him, *Thefe men fpeak as if they had been bred amongft us* ; Then cafting his eyes on *Jorge Mendez*, who ftood before all us next to the *Mitaquer*, *And thou*, faid he unto him, *in what condition art thou, wilt thou go, or ftay ?* whereupon *Mendez*, who had long before premeditated his anfwer, *Sir*, replyed he, *for me, that have neither wife, nor children to bewail my abfence, the thing I moft defire in the world is to ferve your Majefty, fince you are pleafed therewith, whereunto I have more affection then to be Chaem of* Pequim *one thoufand years together.* At this the King fmiled again, and then difmiffed us, fo that we returned very well fatisfied to our lodging, where we continued three days in a readinefs to depart, at the end of which by the mediation of the *Mitaquer*, and means of his fifter, who, as I have faid before, was wonderfully beloved of the King, his Majefty fent us for the eight that we were two thoufand *Taeis*, and gave us in charge to his Ambaffadour, whom he fent to the City of *Uzamguee* in *Cauchenchina*, in the company of the fame King of *Cauchenchina's* Ambaffador : With him we departed from thence five days after, being imbarqued in the veffel wherein he went himfelf : But before our departure *Jorge Mendez* gave us a thoufand Duckets, which was eafie for him to do, for that he had already fix thoufand of yearly rent, withal he kept us company all that day, and at length took his leave of us, not without fhedding many a tear for grief that he had fo expofed himfelf to a voluntary exile.

Bb

Being

§.2   Being departed from this City of *Tuymican* on the ninth day of *May*, in the year one thousand, five hundred, forty and four, we came to lodg that night at a University in a *Pagode* called *Guatipanior*, where the two Ambassadors were very well entertained by the *Tnyxivau* of the house, which is as the Rector thereof, and the next morning when it was broad day, both of them continued their course down the river, each one in his own ship; besides other two wherein their stuff was; About two hours in the night we arrived at a little Town, named *Puxanguim*, well fortified with Towers and bulwarks after our manner, as also with very broad ditches, and strong bridges of hewed stone; there was likewise great store of Artillery, or Cannons of wood, made like unto the pumps of ships, behind the which they put boxes of iron, that held their charge, and were fastened unto them with iron bands; as for the bullets which they shot, they were like unto those of Falconets, and half black: Being much amazed to see this, we demanded of the Ambassador who it was that had invented those kind of guns? whereunto they answered, that it was certain men, called *Almains*, and of a Country named *Muscovy*, who by a very great lake of salt-water, came down to this Town in nine vessels rowed with oars, in the company of a widdow woman, Lady of a place, called *Gaytor*, who they said was chased out of her Country by a King of *Denmark*, so that flying for refuge with three sons of her, the great Grand-father of this King of *Tartaria* made them all great Lords, and gave them certain kinswoman of his in marriage, from whom are extracted the chiefest families of this Empire. The next morning we parted from this Town, and that night lay at another more nobler, named *Euxcau*: Five days after we continued our voyage down this river, and then we arrived at a great Temple, called *Singuafatur*, where we saw an inclosure of above a league in circuit, in which were builded an hundred, threescore, and four houses, very long and broad, after the fashion of Arcenals, all full up to the very tyles of dead mens heads, whereof there was so great a number, that I am afraid to speak it, for that it will hardly be credited. Without each of these houses were also great piles of the bones of these heads, which were three fathom higher then the ridges of them, so that the house seemed to be buried, no other part of them appearing but the frontispiece where the gate stood; not far from thence upon a little hill on the South-side of them was a kind of a platform, whereunto one went up by certain winding-stairs of iron, and through four several doors; Upon this platform was the tallest, the most deformed, and dreadful Monster that possibly can be imagined, standing upon his feet, and leaning against a mighty tower of hewed stone; he was made of cast iron, and of so great and prodigious a stature, that by guess he seemed to be above thirty fathom high, and more then six broad, notwithstanding the which deformity he was exceedingly well proportioned in all his limbs, only his head was somewhat too little for so great a body. This monster held in both his hands a bowl of the same iron, being six and thirty spans about. Beholding so strange and monstrous a thing, we demanded of the *Tartar* Ambassadour the explication thereof, who willing to satisfie our curiosity, *If you knew*, answered he, *what the power of this God is, and how needful it is for you to have him to friend, certainly you would think it well imployed if you presented him with all your means, how great soever they might be, and give them to him rather then to your own children; for you must know that this great Saint, which you see there, is the Treasurer of the bones of all those that are born into the world, to the end that at the last day, when men come to be born again he may give to every one the same bones which he had upon earth, for he knows them all, and can tell in particular to what body each of those bones belong: whereupon you are further to understand, that he, who in this life shall be so unadvised as not to honour him, nor present him with something, will be but in an ill case in the other world, for this Saint will then give him some of the rottenest bones he can meet withal, and one or two less then he should have, by means whereof he will become deformed, lame, or crooked, and therefore if you will follow my counsel, you shall make your selves of his fraternity, by offering something unto him, and you will find by experience the good that will redound to you thereof hereafter.* We desired also to know of him what the bowle which this Monster held in his hand, signified, whereunto he answered us, *That he held it to fling it at the head of the gluttonous Serpent, that lived in the profound Obism of the house of smoak, when he should come thither to steal away any of those bones.* After this we enquired of him how this Monster was called, and he told us that his name was, *Pachinavau du beculem Prinaufaque*, and that it was threescore and fourteen thousand years since he was begotten on a Tortois, called *Migama*, by a Sea-horse, that was an hundred and thirty fathom long, named *Tybrem vncam*, who had been King of the Giants of *Fanius*; he
told

told us likewise,many other brutish fooleries and absurdities, which those of that Country believe as their Creed, and wherewith the Divel precipitates them all into hell ; Moreover this Ambassadour assured us, that the gifts which were presented to this Idol, amounted to above two hundred thousand *Taeis* of yearly rent, without comprising therein what came from Chappels, and other foundations of obits from the principal Lords of the Country, the Revenue whereof was far greater then that of the gifts ; For a conclusion he told us, that this same Idol had ordinarily twelve thousand priests attending on his service, who were maintained with meat, drink, and clothing, only to pray for the dead, that is to say, for those unto whom these bones appertained; we were also assured,that these priests never went out of this inclosure without the permission of their Superiours, but that there was still without six hundred servants, who took care for the providing of all things necessary for them ; And further that it was not lawful for these priests, save once a year, to break within this inclosure the vow which they had made of chastity, but without the same they might whore their pleasure with whomsoever they would, without committing any sin ; There was also a *Serraglio* there, wherein many women, appointed for that purpose were shut up, whom their Governesses permitted to have to do with the priests of this beastly and diabolical Sect.

Continuing our voyage from this *Pagode*, or Monastery of *Gentiles*, whereof we have spoken,the next day we arrived at a very fair Town,called *Quanginau*, which stands on the bank of the river ; In this place the Ambassadours stayed three whole dayes for to furnish themselves with certain things they wanted, as also for to see the feastings and joy that was made at that time upon the entry of the *Talapicor* of *Echuna*, which is their Pope, who was going then unto the King for to comfort him about the ill success he had in *China*. Amongst other graces, which this *Talapicor* bestowed on the inhabitants of this Town, in recompence of the charge they had been at for his reception, he granted unto them, that they might be all Priests, and administer their sacrifices in what places soever they were, and likewise that they might therefore receive the same entertainment and gifts,that were accustomed to be given unto our Priests, without any difference between them and those that upon examination had been promoted to that dignity;Moreover he gave them power to grant Bills of Exchange for Heaven unto all such as should do them good here below. To the Ambassador of *Cauchinchina* he granted as a most singular favor,that he might legitimate any that would pay him for it,& also confer on the Lords of the Court titles, and marks of honour, as far forth as if he had been King, whereof the foolish Ambassador was so proud, as setting aside covetousnesse, though it were a vice he was naturally inclined unto, he imployed all that ever he had there in gifts upon those Priests, and besides not contented therewith, he for that end borrowed of us the two thousand *Taeis* the King had given us, which afterwards he paid us again with interest after fifteen in the hundred. After these matters the two Ambassadors resolved to continue their voyage, but before their departure they went to visit the *Talapicor* in a *Pagode* where he was lodged, for in regard of his greatness, and that he was held for a Saint, he might not abide with any man, but with the King only. Now as soon as he understood of the Ambassadors coming to him he sent them word not to go away that day, because he was to preach at the Church of certain religious women of the Invocation of *Pontimaqueu*; this they took for a great honour, and incontinently went to the *Pagode*, where the Sermon was to be: At their arrival they found such a concourse of people, that they were constrained to remove the Pulpit to another very great place, which in less then an hour was invironed with Scaffolds, hung about with silk stuff, whereon the one side were the Ladies, richly apparelled, and on the other the Princess, called *Vangœnarau*, with all the *Menigregues*, or religious women of the *Pagode*, being in number above three hundred. After the *Talapicor* was gone up into the Pulpit, and that he had made an exterior shew of much holiness, ever and anon lifting up his hands and eyes to Heaven, he began his Sermon in this manner, *Like as it is the property of water to clense all things, and of the Sun to warm all creatures, so it is the property of God through a cœlestial and divine nature to do good unto all ; wherefore we are all bound, as well in general and particular, to imitate this our Lord, who hath created, and doth nourish us, by doing that unto those, who stand in need of the good of this world, as we would that they should do unto us, for that by this work we are more pleasing unto him, then by any other whatsoever. For as the good Father of a Family rejoyceth to see his children made much of, and presents given to them, so our Heavenly Lord, who is the true Father of us all, rejoyceth at such time as with a zeal of charity we communicate one with another ; whereby it is evident, that the covetous man,*

who

who shuts his hand, when the poor ask something of him which they want, constrained thereunto by necessity, and that turns him another way without assisting them, shall be treated in the same manner by a just judgment of God, and driven down into the bottom of the sink of the night, where like a frog he shal croke without ceasing, being tormented by the hunger of his covetousness: This being so, I do advise and enjoyn you all, since you have ears to hear me, that you do that which the Law of the Lord obligeth you to do, which is, that you give of that whereof you have too much, to the poor, who have not wherewith to feed themselves, to the end God may not be wanting to you when you shall be at the last gasp of your life: Go to then, let this charity be so remarkable and universal in you, that the very fowls of the air may taste of your liberality; And this you ought to do to keep the poor, having need of what you possess in excess, from being forced by their necessity to rob other men of their goods, whereof you would be no less blameable, then if you killed an infant in the cradle; I commend also unto your remembrance that which is written in the Book of our truth, touching the good you are bound to do unto the Priests, that pray for you, to the end they may not perish for want of the good you ought to do unto them, which would be as great a sin before God, as if you should cut the throat of a little white heifer when she is sucking of her Dam, by the death of whom a thousand souls would die, which are buried in her as in a golden Tomb, in expectation of the day, which is to accomplish the promise, that was made unto them, wherein they shall be transformed into white pearls for to dance in Heaven, like unto the moats which are in the beams of the Sun. Having uttered these things, he added many others thereunto, and delivering a world of extravagancies and fooleries, he bestirred himself in such manner, as was a wonder to behold, so that we eight *Portugals* were exceedingly amazed at the extream devotion of these people, and how that in lifting up their hands to Hands to Heaven, they ever and anon repeated this word *Taiximida*, that is to say, *So we believe*; In the mean time one of our fellows, named *Vincent Morosa*, hearing the auditors so often use that word *Taiximida*, said in imitation of them, *Such may thy life be*; and that with such a grace, and so setled a countenance, not seeming any way to jeer him, that not one in the Assembly could forbear laughing: He in the mean while continued still firm, and more and more confirmed, seeming even to weep out of an excess of devotion; Now his eyes being always fixed on the *Talapicor*, he whensoever he chanced to look on him could not chuse but do as the rest did, so that upon the conclusion of his Sermon all that heard him fell to laughing out-right: The Prioress her self, and all the *Menigregues* of her Monastery could not contain themselves in their serious humour, imagining that the faces which the *Portugal* made, and his actions, were so many effects of his devotion, and good meaning; For if one had thought it to be otherwise, and that he had not done it out of derision, no question but he had been so chastised, as he should never have been able to mock again. When the Sermon was ended, the *Talapicor* returned to the *Pagod* where he lodged, being accompanied with the most honourable of all the Assembly, together with the Ambassadours, unto whom all the way as he went he ceased not to commend the devotion of the *Portugal*, *Look*, said he, *there is not so much as these people, who live like beasts, and without the knowledge of our truth, but see well enough that there is nothing but what is godly in that I have preached*; whereunto all answered that it was as he said.

§.4   The day after we parted from the Town of *Quanginau*, and continued our voyage down the river for the space of fourteen dayes, during the which we saw a number of Towns, and great Boroughs on either side of us, at the end whereof we arrived at a City, called *Lechuna*, the chiefest of the Religion of these *Gentiles*, and such it may be, as *Rome* is amongst us. In this City was a very sumptuous Temple, where there were many remarkable edifices, in the which seven and twenty Kings or Emperours of this Monarchy of *Tartaria* have been buried. Their Tombs are in Chappels, wonderful rich, as well for the excellency of their workmanship, which is of an infinite cost, as for that they are within covered all over with plates of silver, wherein there are divers Idols of different forms made also of silver. On the North side a little part from the Temple was an inclosure worthy the observation, both for its extent, and the fortification thereof; within it were two hundred and fourscore Monasteries, as well of men, as of women, dedicated to certain Idols, and for the service of all these *Pagodes*, or Temples there are ordinarily, as we were assured, two and forty thousand Priests and *Menigrepes*, not comprising therein those which were lodged without the inclosure for the service of these false priests. We observed that in these two hundred and fourscore houses there was an infinite company of pillars of brass, and upon the top of each pillar are idols of the same mettal

mettal guilt, befides thofe which likewife were there all of filver : Thefe Idols are the Statues of them, who in their falfe Sect they hold for Saints, and of whom they recount fuch fopperies, as would make a man wonder to hear them ; For they give unto each of them a Statua, more or lefs rich, and guilded, according to the degrees of vertue which they have exercifed in this life : And this they do exprefly, that the living may be incited to imitate them, to the end there may be as much done unto them when they are dead. In one of thefe Monafteries of the Invocation of *Quiay Frigau*, that is to fay, *The God of the moats of the Sun*, was a fifter of the Kings, the widdow of *Raia Benan*, Prince of *Pafua*, whom the death of her husband had made refolve to fhut her felf up in this Monaftery, with fix thoufand women that had followed her thither, and fhe had taken upon her, as the moft honourable Title fhe could think on, the name of, *the broom of the Houfe of God.* The Ambaffadors went to fee this Lady, and kiffed her feet as a Saint ; fhe received them very courteoufly, and demanded many things of them with great difcretion, whereunto they rendred fuch anfwers as became them ; but coming to caft her eye upon us, who ftood fomewhat far off, and underftanding that never any of our Nation was feen in thofe parts before, fhe enquired of the Ambaffadors of what Country we were ? They anfwered, that we were come from a place at the other end of the world, whereof no man there knew the name. At thofe words fhe ftood much amazed, and caufing us to come nearer, fhe queftioned us about many things, whereof we gave her fuch an account as greatly contented her, and all that were prefent ; In the mean time the Princefs wondring at the anfwers, which one of ours made her, *They fpeak*, faid fhe, *like men that have been brought up amongft people, who have feen more of the world then we have.* So after fhe had heard us talk a while of fome matters, that fhe had propounded unto us, fhe difmiffed us with very good words, and caufed an hundred *Taeis* to be given us in way of an alms. The Ambaffadors having taken their leave of her, continued their voyage down along the river, fo that at the end of five days we arrived at a great Town, called *Rendacalem*, fcituated on the uttermoft Confines of the Kingdom of *Tartaria* : Out of this place we entred upon the State of the *Xinaleygrau*, and therein we proceeded on four days together, until fuch time as we came to a Town, named *Voulem*, where the Ambaffadors were very well entertained by the Lord of the Country, and abundantly furnifhed with all things neceffary for their voyage, as alfo with Pilots to guide them in thofe rivers. From thence we purfued our courfe for feven days together, during the which we faw not any thing worthy of note, and at length came to a ftraight, called *Catencur*, whereinto the Pilots entred, as well to abridge their voyage, as to avoid the encounter of a famous Pirot, who had robbed thofe parts of moft of their wealth. Through this ftraight running Eaft, as alfo Eaft, North-eaft ; and fomtimes Eaft, and by Eaft, according to the windings of the water we arrived at the Lake of *Singapamor*, called by them of the Country *Cunebetea*, which was, as our Pilots affirmed, fix and thirty leagues in extent, where we faw fo many feveral forts of birds, that I am not able to recount them. Out of this Lake of *Singapamor* (which as an admirable Mafter-piece nature hath opened in the heart of this Country) do four very large and deep rivers proceed, whereof the firft is named *Ventrau*, that runneth Eaftward through all the Kingdoms of *Sornau* and *Siam*, entring into the Sea by the Bar of *Chiamtabuu*, in fix and twenty degrees ; The fecond, *Jangumaa*, that going South, and South-eaft, traverfeth alfo the greateft part of this Country, as likewife the Kingdom of *Chiammay*, the *Laos*, *Gueos*, and another part of *Danbambur*, difimboking into the Sea by the Bar of *Martabano*, in the Kingdom of *Pegu*, and there is in diftance from the one to the other by the degrees of this Climate, above feven hundred leagues ; The third, called *Pamphileu*, paffeth in the fame manner through all the Countries of *Capimper* and *Sacotay*, and turning above that fecond river runs quite through the Empire of *Monginoco*, and a part of *Meleytay*, and *Sovady*, rendring it felf into the Sea by the Bar of *Cofmim*, near to *Arracan* ; The fourth, which in all likelihood is as great as the reft, is not known by any name, neither could the Ambaffadors give us any reafon for it : but it is probable, according to the opinion of divers, that it is *Ganges* in the Kingdom of *Bengala*, fo that by all the difcoveries which have been made in thefe Oriental Countries it is conceived, that there is not a greater river then it : Having croffed this Lake we continued our courfe for the fpace of feven dayes, till we came to a place named *Caleyputa*, the inhabitants whereof would by no means permit us to land, for the Ambaffadors endeavouring to do fo, they entertained us with fuch ftore of darts and ftones from the fhore, as we thought us not a little happy in that we could fave our felves from the danger of it. After we had gotten out of this place, much vexed with the bad entreaty

we

we had received there, that which most afflicted us was to see our selves unprovided of things we were greatly in need of, but by the counsel of our Pilots we sailed by another river far larger then the straight which we had left, and that by the space of nine dayes, at the end whereof we arrived at a very good Town, called *Tarem*, the Lord of which was subject to the *Cauckin*, who received the Ambassadors with great Demonstrations of love, and furnished them abundantly with all that they wanted. The next day we departed from thence about Sun-set, and continuing our voyage down the river about seven days after we came to an Anchor in the Port of *Xolor*, which is a very fair Town, where all the enammelled purcelain, which is carried to *China*, is made. There the Ambassadors stayed five days, during which time they caused their ships, that were very heavy, to be haled ashore by the force of boats: That done, and provision made of all things necessary, they went to see certain Mines, which the King of *Cauchin* hath in that place, from whence great store of silver is drawn, and the Ambassadors being desirous to know how much silver those Mines yielded every year, they were answered, that the whole amounted to some six thousand *Picos*, which make eight thousand Quintals of our weight.

§.5.   After our departure from the Town of *Xolor* we still continued our course for five days together down that great river, and saw all along that while a many of great Boroughs, and goodly Towns; for in that Climate the Land is better then other where, very well peopled, and full of riches; withall the rivers are frequented with a world of vessels, and the fields very well tilled, and replenished with abundance of wheat, rice, all kind of pulse, and exceeding great Sugar-canes, whereof there is marvellous store in all that Country. The Gentlemen there are ordinarily clothed in silk, and mounted on horses handsomly furnished; as for the women, they are exceeding white and fair. Now it was not without much labour, pain, and danger, that we passed those two Channels. as also the river of *Ventinau*, by reason of the Pyrats that usually are encountred there, nevertheless we at the length arrived at the Town of *Manaquileu*, which is scituated at the foot of the Mountains of *Chomay*, upon the Frontiers of the two Kingdoms of *China*, and *Cauchenchina*, where the Ambassadors were both well received by the Governour thereof. The next morning departing from that place, they went and lay in a Town, named *Quinancaxi*, which appertained to an Aunt of the Kings, whom they went to visite; she gave them a very kind reception, and withall told them for news, that the King her Nephew, was newly returned from the War of the *Tinocouhos*, and wonderfully well pleased with his good success therein; whereunto she added many particularities, which they were glad to hear, especially when she assured them, that the King, after he had dismissed the forces that he had carried out with him, was gone with a small Train to the City of *Fanaugrem*, where he intended to spend some time in hunting & fishing, & then to go & winter at *Usamguee*, the capital City of this Empire of *Cauchim*. When as they had consulted a while upon these news, they resolved to send their four vessels away to *Usamguee*, and themselves to travel by land to *Fanaugrem*, where they understood the King was. This deliberation taken they put incontinently into execution, & that by the advice of this Princess, who for that purpose caused them to be furnished with horses for themselves, & their people, as also with eight Rhinocerots for the transportation of their baggage. They began their journy then about three days after, and having travelled fourscore & six leagues, in the space of thirteen days, and that with much toil & labour, by reason of certain mountains which they were to pass, that were of a long extent, and very rough and stony, in the end they arrived at a great lodging, called *Tarandachit*, seated upon the bank of a river; There they passed the night, and the next morning they parted thence for to go to a Town, named *Lindau Panoo*, where they were very well received by the Captain thereof, a kin man of the Ambassadors of *Cauchenchina*; who was come not about six days before from *Fanaugrem*, where the King remained still, being not more then fifteen leagues from that place. After that this Captain hath told this Ambassador his kinsman some other news of the Court, and of the success of the war, he further advertised him that a Son in law of his was dead, for the love of whom his daughter the wife of the deceased, had cast her self into a pile of flaming fire, where with her husbands body she was consumed to ashes, at which all her kinred exceedingly rejoyced, for that by so generous an end she had given proof of what she had ever been. The Ambassador himself, her father, testified also no little content for the same, saying; *Now it is, O my daughter, that I know assuredly thou art a Saint, and that thou servest thy husband in Heaven, wherefore I promise and swear to thee, that for so memorable an end, wherein thou hast given an infallible proof of the Royal blood whereof thou art descended, I will in memory of thy goodness build thee such a magnificent and honourable house, as shall*

make

make thee defire to come from were thou art, for to recreate thy felf in it, in imitation of thofe bleffed fouls, which we hold have heretofore done the like. This faid, he fel flat down with his face on the ground, and in that pofture continued till the day following, when as he was vifited by all the religious men of the place, who comforted him with full affurance that his daughter was a Saint, fo that all of them granted him permiffion to erect a Statue of filver unto her. Thefe fpeeches of the Priefts greatly pleafed the Ambaffador, who very much acknowledged the fame unto them, giving mony both to them, and to all the poor that were thereabout ; At this place we fpent nine days in celebrating the Funerals of the Defunct, and then departing we went the next day to a certain Monaftery, called *Latiparau,* that is to fay, *The remedy of the poor,* where the two Ambaffadors remained three days in expectation of news from the King, whom they had already advertifed of their arrival ; Now his anfwer to them was, that they fhould go to a Town, named *Agimpur,* three leagues from the place where they were, and but one from *Fanaugrem,* whither he would fend for them when time ferved.

CHAP. XLII.

The reception of the Tartarian *Ambaffador by the King of* Cauchenchina, *with the faid Kings going from thence to the City of* Uzam-guee, *and his triumphal Entry thereinto.*

THe King being advertifed by his Ambaffadour, that he brought another along with him §.1 from the King of *Tartaria,* fent for him not long after from *Agimpur* by the Brother of the Queen his wife, a very valiant and rich Prince : He was mounted on a Chariot with three wheels on a fide, adorned all within with plates of filver, and drawn by four white Horfes, whofe furniture was all imbroidered with gold; This Chariot, which they of the Country call *Piamber,* was waited on by threefcore footmen, half on the one fide, and half on the other, clothed in green leather, with Scymiters by their fides, whofe Scabberds were garnifhed with gold, and before them went twelve Ufhers bearing their Maces on their fhoulders ; After the footmen followed certain others carrying Halberts trimmed with filver, in gowns and breeches of green and white filk, and with Scymiters by their fides ; Thefe fellows feemed very haughty and proud, fo that by their outward behaviours, which in all their actions appeared to be like unto their furly difpofitions, they rendred themfelves fomewhat terrible to others ; Thirty pa-ces after this Guard marched fourfcore Elephants exceeding well furnifhed, with chairs and caftles adorned with filver which they carried on their backs, and on their teeth their Panores, or warlick Defences, together with many little bells of the fame mettal hanging about their necks ; Before thefe Elephants, which were faid to be the Kings Guard, rode a number of men at Arms in very good Equipage, and in the Vantgard of all this train went twelve Chari-ots with Cymbals of filver, and covered with filk. When this Prince was come in this ftately manner to the Ambaffador of *Tartaria,* who attended him, and that they had performed all fuch compliments one to another, as are ufual amongft them, the Prince gave the Ambaffador the Chariot wherein he came thither, and mounting on a gallant Courfer, he placed himfelf on the right hand of him, and the Kings Ambaffadour on the left : In this pomp, and with the fame order as before, as alfo with the found of divers inftruments of mufick, they arrived at the firft Court of the Kings houfe, where the *Broquem,* Captain of the Guard of the Pallace attended them, being accompanied with many Noble-men, befides a number on horsback, which ftood ranked in two files all along the Court. After they had with a new ceremony been com-plemented withall, they went on foot to the Pallace-gate, where they encountred with an old man, above fourfcore years of age, who was faid to be the Kings Uncle ; This fame, being waited upon by divers great Lords, was no fooner perceived by the Ambaffadors, but with a new kind of complement they kift the Scymiter that hung by his fide, whereupon he returned them the like, together with an honour, which is of no little eftimation amongft them, that was to hold his hand upon their heads, fo long as they were proftrated on the ground before him. Then having caufed the *Tartar* to rife, and to march even cheek by jole with him, he led him through a very long Hall to a door which was at the end thereof, where after he had knock-ed three times, one demanded of him, who he was, and what he would have? whereunto an-fwering very foberly, *Here is come,* faid he, *out of an ancient cuftom of true amity, an Am-baffador from the great* Xinarau *of* Tartaria, *to demand audience of* Prechau Guimian, *whom we all hold for the Lord of our heads.* This anfwer being returned, the door was opened, into
which

which they presently entred; the Prince marched fore-most with the Ambassador of *Tartaria*, whom he held by the hand, and a little behind them went the other belonging to the King, with the Captain of the Guard, then followed all the company by three and three. Having gone through that room, where there was none but certain of the Guard on their knees with Halberds in their hands, we went into another room far more spacious and fair then the former, in the which we saw threescore and four Statues of brass, and nineteen of silver, all tied by the neck with iron chains; At so extraordinary a thing as this being much abashed, we demanded of one of their *Grepes*, or priests, the reason of it, who answered us, That the Statues which we beheld there were the fourscore and three gods of the *Tinoconbos*, whom the King in the late war had taken from them out of a Temple, where they were placed; for, added he, there is nothing in the world held in more esteem, or for a greater honour by the King, then to triumph over the gods of his enemies, which he hath led away captive in despight of them: whereupon enquiring further of him, why they were set there, he replyed, that it was to have them in a readiness against the time that the King should make his entry into *Uzamguee*, whither he purposed shortly to go, for to make a shew of them so chained in his triumph as a special mark of the victory he had gained. After we were at the end of this room, where the Idols were, we entred into another very great one, where we saw a number of very fair women, who were set all along, some imployed in curious needle-works, and others singing and playing upon certain instruments of musick, very pleasing to hear. Passing on we arrived at the door of the Kings Chamber, where we found six women, which were as it were porters there, and carried silver Maces; In this room was the King, in the company of a few ancient men, and a great number of young women, to the tune of whose musick certain little girls sung very harmoniously: The King was set on a Throne of eight steps high in the manner of an Altar, over the which was a cloth of State supported by pillars, all covered over with gold engraven; near to him were six little children upon their knees with Scepters in their hands, and a little further off stood a woman reasonably well in years, which fanned him ever and anon, and had a great Garland about her neck. This Prince was about some five and thirty years of age, and of a goodly presence: He had full eyes, auborn hair and beard, a grave look, and in all points the countenance of a generous King. As soon as the Ambassadors came into the room they prostrated themselves three times on the ground, and at the third time the Kings lay still flat all along, whilest the *Tartar* passed on; who being come near to the first step of the Throne where the King sate, he said unto him with so loud a voice as all there present might hear him, *O thou the Prop of all the Forces of the Earth, and the breath of the High God which hath created all things, may the Majestical Being of thy greatness prosper for ever and ever, so that thy Sandals may serve for hairs to the heads of Kings, making thee like to the bones and flesh of the great Prince of the silver mountains, by whose commandment I come to visit thee, as thou mayst perceive by this his Letter sealed with his Royal arms.* When he had made an end of speaking thus, the *Cauchin* beholding him with a smiling countenance, *May the Sun*, answered he, *put a conformity between the desires of the King thy Master, and mine, and that by the sweet heat of his amorous rayes, to the end that the great amity, which is betwixt us, may endure and continue firm till the last noise the Sea shall make, that so the Lord may be eternally praised in his peace.* At these words all the Lords that were in the room answered with one voice, *So grant it may be O Lord Almighty, that givest a being to the night and the day.* Then the same women, which played before, beginning their musick again, the King used no further speech, but only in kindly entertaining the Ambassador, *I will*, said he, *read my brother* Xinarau's *Letter, and return an answer thereunto according to thy desire, to the end thou mayst go from me contented.* The Ambassador made him no reply, but prostrated himself again at the foot of the Royal Throne, laying his head three times on the uppermost step where the Kings feet stood. That done the Captain of the Guard took him by the hand, and led him to his house, where he lodged during the three days that he abode there, at the end whereof the King departed thence for to go to *Uzamguee*.

§.2. In regard of the Kings journy to *Uzamguee*, the *Tartar* Ambassador had audience but once by the way, in the which he moved him about our particular, according to the express commandment he had received from his Master for that purpose, and it was said that the King heard him very willingly, answering, that he would do what he desired, and therefore willed him to put him in mind of it, when the time should serve, to the end we might not lose the opportunity of the season for our voyage. With this good news the Ambassador acquainted us at his return, and demanded of us for this good office he had done us, that we would write him out some of those prayers which we made to our God, whose flave, he faid, he infinitely defired to be, in regard of the great excellencies which he had heard us deliver of him; This we not only granted him very readily, but alfo gave him infinite thanks befides for this his great favour fhewed unto us, which we made more account of then all the benefits that had been propounded unto us by the King of *Tartaria*, if we would have continued in his fervice. After the King was departed from the City of *Fanaugrem*, he proceeded on in his journy travelling but only fix leagues a day, by reafon of the great number of perfons that he carried along with him; The firft day he dined at a little Town, called *Benau*, where he ftayed until the evening, and then went to lodge at a Monaftery, named *Pamgatur*; The next morning he departed from thence, and fo with not above three thoufand horfe in his Train, he profecuted his journy for nine dayes together, paffing by many goodly Towns, at leaft they feemed to be fo, without permitting any reception to be made him by any of them; In this manner he arrived at the City of *Lingator*, feated on a river of frefh water, which for the bredth and deepnefs of it is frequented with much fhipping; There he abode five days, for that he found himfelf fomewhat indifpofed with the tedioufnefs of the journy: From this place he departed before day, taking no greater company with him then thirty horfe, and fo withdrawing himfelf from the communication of fo much people, as continually importuned him, he fpent moft part of the time as he went by the way in hawking and hunting; thofe of the Countryes by which he paft providing game always ready for him. In this fort going on he flept moft commonly amidft very thick woods in Tents pitched for him to that purpofe. Being arrived at the river of *Baguetor*, he paffed down the fame in certain veffels, called *Laulees* and *Jangoas*, which were there ready for him, till he came to a Town, named *Natibafoy*, where about evening he landed without any kind of pomp; The reft of his journy he made by land, fo that at the end of thirteen dayes he arrived at *Uzamguee*, where he had a moft magnificent reception. At his entry thereinto there marched before him, as it were in triumph, all the fpoyls which he had taken in the wars, whereof the principal, and thofe which he made moft reckoning of, were twelve Chariots laden with the Idols, of whom I have fpoken heretofore, and whereof the forms were different, as they ufe to have them in their *Pagods*. Of thefe Idols there were threefcore and four of brafs, which feemed to be Gyants, and nineteen of filver of the fame Stature, for, as I have delivered before, thefe people glory in nothing fo much, as to triumph over thofe idols, that fo they may fay, *That in defpight of their enemies he had made their gods his flaves*; Round about thefe twelve Chariots went divers Priefts by three and three weeping, and bound with iron chains; After them followed forty other Chariots, each of them being drawn by two Rhinocerots, and full from the bottom to the top of an infinite company of Arms, and trayled Colours; In the tayl of them there were twenty more, carrying each of them a very great Cheft, barr'd with iron, and wherein, as we were told, was the treafure of the *Tinooouhos*; In the fame order marched all other things, which are ufed to be moft efteemed of in fuch triumphant entries, as two hundred Elephants armed with Caftles, and warlike *Panoures*, which are certain fwords that are faftened to their teeth when they fight, and a great number of horfes laden with facks full of dead mens heads and bones; fo that in this entry this King of *Cauchin* prefented to the view of his people all that he had gained from his enemies in the battail he had given them. After we had been a full month in this City, during which time we had feen a world of ftately fhews, fports, and feveral forts of rejoycings, accompanied with moft coftly feafts and banquets, fet forth and made not onely by the greater perfons, but by the common people alfo, the *Tartar* Ambaffadour, that had brought us thither, moved the King again about our voyage, whereunto he gave us fo gracious an ear, that he prefently commanded we fhould be furnifhed with a Veffel for to carry us to the Coaft of *China*, where we hoped to meet with fome *Portugal* fhip, that might tranfport us to *Malaca*, and from thence to the *Indiaes*, which accordingly was done, whereupon without further delay we prepared all things neceffary for our departure.

CHAP.

CHAP. XLIII.

Our Departure from the City of Uzamguee, *and our adventures till our arri-*
vall at the Iſle of Tanixumaa, *which is the firſt Land of Jap-*
pon; with our going aſhore there.

§. 1 UPon the twelfth of *January* we departed from the City of *Uzamguee*, exceedingly rejoycing at our eſcape from ſo many labours and croſſes, which we before had ſuſtained,
and imbarqued our ſelves upon a river, that was above a league broad, down the which we
went ſeven dayes together, beholding in the mean time on either ſide thereof many fair Towns,
and goodly Boroughs, which by the outward appearance we believed were inhabited by very
rich people, in regard of the ſumptuouſneſs of the buildings, not only of particular houſes,
but much more of the Temples, whoſe ſteeples were all covered over with gold, as likewiſe
in regard of the great number of Barques and Veſſels, that were on this river, abundantly
fraught with all ſorts of proviſions and merchandiſe. Now when we were come to a very fair
Town, called *Quangeparuu*, containing ſome eighteen or twenty thouſand fires, the *Naude-*
lum, who was he that conducted us by the expreſs commandment from the King, ſtayed there
twelve dayes to trade in exchange of ſilver and pearl; whereby he confeſſed to us that he had
gained fourteen for one, and that if he had been ſo adviſed as to have brought ſalt thither, he
had doubled his mony above thirty times: we were aſſured that in this Town the King had
yearly out of the ſilver Mines above fifteen hundred *Picos*, which are forty thouſand Quintals
of our weight, beſides the huge revenue, that he drew out of many other different things:
This Town hath no other fortification then a weak brick wall, eight foot high, and a ſhallow
ditch ſome thirty foot broad; The inhabitants are weak and unarmed, having neither Artillery, nor any thing for their defence, ſo that five hundred reſolute ſouldiers might eaſily take it.
We parted from this place on *Tueſday* morning, and continued our courſe thirteen dayes, at
the end whereof we got to the Port of *Sanchan*, in the Kingdom of *China*. Now becauſe
there was no ſhipping of *Malaca* there, for they were gone from thence nine dayes before,
we went ſeven leagues further to another Port, named *Lampacau*, where we found two
Juncks of *Malaya*, one of *Patana*, and another of *Lugor*; And whereas it is the quality of
us *Portugals* to abound in our own ſence, and to be obſtinate in our opinions, there aroſe
amongſt us eight ſo great a contrariety of judgment about a thing, wherein nothing was ſo
neceſſary for us, as to maintain our ſelves in peace and unity, that we were even upon the point
of killing one another; But becauſe the matter would be too ſhamefull to recount in the manner as it paſt, I will ſay no more but that the *Necoda* of the *Lorche*, which had brought us
thither from *Uzamguee*, amazed at this ſo great barbarouſneſs of ours, ſeperated himſelf from
us in ſuch diſpleaſure, that he would not charge himſelf either with our meſſages or letters,
ſaying, that he had rather the King ſhould command his head to be cut off, then to offend God
in carrying with him any thing whatſoever that belonged to us. Thus different as we were
in opinions, and in very bad terms amongſt our ſelves, we lingered above nine dayes in this
little Iſland, during which time the three Juncks departed without vouchſafing to take us in,
ſo that we were conſtrained to remain in theſe ſolitudes, expoſed to many great dangers, out
of which I did not think that ever we could have eſcaped, if God had not been extraordinarily
merciful unto us; for having been there ſeventeen dayes in great miſery and want; it hapened
that a Pyrat, named *Samipocheca*, arrived in this place, who having been defeated, went flying from the Fleet of *Aytao* of *Chincheo*, that of eight and twenty Sayl, which this Pyrat
had, had taken ſix and twenty of them from him, ſo that he had with much ado eſcaped with
thoſe only two remaining, wherein the moſt part of his men were hurt, for which cauſe he
was conſtrained to ſtay there ſeven dayes to have them cured: Now the preſent neceſſity in-
forcing us to take ſome courſe whatſoever it were, we were glad to agree for to ſerve under
him until ſuch time as we might meet with ſome good opportunity to get unto *Malaca*. Thoſe
twenty dayes ended, wherein yet there was no manner of reconciliation between us, but ſtill
continuing in diſcord we imbarqued our ſelves with this Pyrat, namely three in the Junk
where he himſelf was, and five in the other, whereof he had made a Nephew of his Captain.
Having left this Iſland with an intent to ſail unto a Port, called *Lailoo*, ſome ſeven leagues from
Chincheo, we continued our voyage with a good wind all along the Coaſt of *Lamau* for the
ſpace of nine dayes, until that one morning when we were near to the river of ſalt, which is
about

about five leagues from *Chabaquea*, it was our ill fortune to be assailed by a Pirate, who with seven great Juncks fell to fighting with us from six in the morning till ten of the clock before noon, in which conflict we were so entertained with shot, and pots full of artificial fire, that at last th re were three Sail burnt, to wit, two of the Pirats, and one of ours, which was the Junck wherein the five *Portugals* were, whom we could by no means succour, for that then most of our men were hurt; But at length towards night being well refreshed by the afternoons gale, it pleased our Lord that we escaped out of this Pirats hands. In this ill equipage wherein we were we continued our course for three dayes together, at the end whereof we were invironed by so great and impetuous a Tempest, that the same night in which it seized us we lost the Coast, and because the violence of the Storm would never suffer us after to recover it again, we were forced to make with full Sail towards the Islands of the *Lequios*, where the Pirate, with whom we went, was well known, both to the King, and those of the Country; with this resolution we set our selves to sail through the Archipelage of these Islands, where notwithstanding we could not make land, as well for that we wanted a Pilot to steer the vessel, ours being slain in the last fight, as also because the wind and tide was against us; Amidst so many crosses we beat up and down with labour enough from one rhomb to another for three and twenty dayes together, at the end whereof it pleased God that we discovered land, whereunto approaching to see if we could descry any appearance of a Port, or good anchorage, we perceived on the South-coast near to the Horizon of the Sea a great fire, which perswaded us that there we might peradventure find some Borough, where we might furn sh our selves with fresh water, whereof we had very great need. So we went and rode just before the Island in seventy fathom, and presently we beheld two *Almedias* come towards us from the Land with six men in them, who being come close to the side of our Junck, and having complemented with us according to their manner, demanded of us from whence we came? whereunto having answered, that we came from *China* with merchandise intending to trade in this place if we might be suffered, one of the six replyed; That the *Nautaquim*, Lord of that Island, called *Tanixumaa*, would very willingly permit it upon payment of such customs as are usual in *Japan*, which is, continued he, this great Country that you see here before you: At these news, and many other things, which they told us, we were exceeding glad, so that after they had shewed us the Port, we weighed anchor, and went and put our selves under the lee-shoar of a creek, which was on the South-side, and where stood a great Town, named *Miay-gimaa*, from whence there came instantly abord of us divers *Paraoos* with refreshments, which we bought.

We had not been two hours in this Creek of *Miaygimaa*, when as the *Nautaquim*, Prince of this Island of *Tanixumaa* came directly to our Junck, attended by divers Gentlemen and Merchants, who had brought with them many Chests full of silver Ingots, therewith to barter for our commodities; so after ordinary complements past on either side, and that we had given our word for his easiest coming aboard of us; he no sooner perceived us three *Portugals*, but he demanded what people we were, saying, that by our beards and faces we could not be *Chineses*: Hereunto the Pirate answered, That we were of a Country called *Malaca*, whither many years before we were come from another Lend, named *Portugal*, which was at the further end of the world; At these words the *Nautaquim* remained much amazed, and turning himself to his followers; *Let me not live*, said he unto them, *if these men here be not the Chenchicogis, of whom it is written in our books, that flying on the top of the waters they shall from thence subdue the inhabitants of the earth, where God hath created the riches of the world, wherefore it will be a good fortune for us if they come into our Country as good friends.* Thereupon having called a woman of *Lequia*, whom he had brought to serve as an interpreter between him and the *Chinese*, Captain of the Junck; *Ask the Necoda*, said he unto her, *where he met with these men, and upon what occasion he hath brought them hither with him into our Country of* Jappon? The Captain thereunto replied, That we were honest men and Merchants, and that having found us at *Lampacau*, where we had been cast away, he had out of charity taken us in, as he used to do unto all such as he met withall in the like case, to the end that God might out of his gracious goodness be thereby moved to deliver him from the danger of such violent Tempests, as commonly they that sail on the Sea are subject to perish in. This saying of the Pirate seemed so reasonable to the *Nautaquim*, that he presently came abord of us, and because those of his Train were very many, he commanded that none but such as he named should enter in. After he had seen all the commodities in the Junck, he sate

§.2.

him

him down in a Chair upon the Deck, and began to queſtion us about certain things which he deſired to know, to the which we anſwered him in ſuch ſort, as we thought would be moſt agreeable to his humour, ſo that he ſeemed to be exceedingly ſatisfied therewith : In this manner he entertained us a good while together, making it apparent by his demands that he was a man very curious, and much inclined to hear of novelties, and rare things. That done he took his leave of us, and the *Necoda*, little regarding the reſt, ſaying, *Come and ſee me at my houſe to morrow, and for a preſent bring me an ample relation of the ſtrange things of that great World through which you have travelled, as alſo of the Countries that you have ſeen, and withall remember to tell me how they are called, for I ſwear unto you that I would far more willingly buy this commodity then any that you can ſell me.* This ſaid, he returned to Land, and the next morning as ſoon as it was day he ſent us to our Junck a great *Parao*, full of divers ſorts of refreſhments, as Reaſons, Pears, Melons, and other kinds of fruits of that Country ; In exchange of this preſent the *Necoda* returned him by the ſame meſſenger divers rich pieces of ſtuff, together with certain knacks and rarities of *China*, and withall ſent him word, that as ſoon as his Junck ſhould be at anchor, and out of danger of the weather, he would come and wait on him aſhore, and bring him ſome patterns of the commodities which we had to ſell ; as indeed the next morning he went on land, and carried us three along with him, as alſo ſome ten or eleven of the chiefeſt of the *Chineſes* of his Company, to the end that at this firſt ſight he might ſettle a good opinion of himſelf in this people for the better ſatisfaction of that vanity whereunto they are naturally inclined ; we went then to the *Nautaquims* houſe, where we were very well entertained, and the *Necoda* having given him a rich picture, ſhewed him the patterns of all the commodities he had, wherewith he reſted ſo contented, that he ſent preſently for the principal Merchants of the place, with whom the *Necoda* having agreed upon a price for his commodities, it was reſolved that the next day they ſhould be tranſported from the Junck unto a certain houſe, which was appointed for the *Necoda* and his people to remain in till ſuch time as he ſhould ſet ſail for *China* : After all this was concluded, the *Nautaquim* fell again to queſtioning of us about many ſeveral matters, whereunto we rendred him ſuch anſwers as might rather fit his humour, then agree with the truth indeed, which yet we did not obſerve but in ſome certain demands that he made us, where we thought it neceſſary to make uſe of certain particulars altogether fained by us, that ſo we might not derogate from the great opinion he had conceived of our Country. The firſt thing he propounded was, how he had learned from the *Chineſes* and *Lequios*, that *Portugal* was far richer, and of a larger extent, then the whole Empire of *China*, which we confirmed unto him. The ſecond, how he had likewiſe been aſſured, that our King had upon the Sea conquered the greateſt part of the world, which alſo we averred to be ſo ; The third, that our King was ſo rich in gold and ſilver, as it was held for moſt certain, that he had above two thouſand houſes full of it even to the very tops ; but thereunto we anſwered, that we could not truly ſay the number of the houſes, becauſe the Kingdom of *Portugal* was ſo ſpacious, ſo abounding with treaſure, and ſo populous, as it was impoſſible to ſpecifie the ſame. So after the *Nautaquim* had entertained us above two hours with ſuch and the like diſcourſe, he turned him to thoſe of his Train, and ſaid, *Aſſuredly not one of thoſe Kings, which at this preſent we know to be on the earth, is to be eſteemed happy, if he be not the vaſſal of ſo great a Monarch as the Emperour of this people here.* Whereupon having diſmiſſed the *Necoda* and his Company, he intreated us to paſſe that night on ſhore with him, for to ſatisfie the extream deſire that he had to be informed from us of many things of the world, whereunto he was exceedingly carried by his own inclination ; withall he told us, that the next day he would aſſigne us a lodging next to his own Pallace, which was in the moſt commodious place of the Town, and for that inſtant he ſent us to lie at a very rich Merchants houſe, who entertained us very bountifully that night.

CHAP. XLIV.

The great honour which the Nautaquim, *Lord of the Iſle, did to one of us for having ſeen him ſhoot with an Harquebuſe ; and his ſending me to the King of* Bungo ; *and that which paſſed till my arrival at his Court.*

§.1 THe next day the *Chineſe Necoda* diſimbarqued all his commodities, as the *Nautaquim* had enjoyned him, and put them into ſure rooms, which were given him for that purpoſe,
and

and in three dayes he fold them all, as well for that he had not many, as becaufe his good fortune was fuch that the Country was at that time utterly unfurnifhed thereof, by which means this Pirate profited fo much, that by this Sale he wholly recovered himfelf of the loffe of the fix & twenty Saile which the *Chinefe* Pirate had taken from him ; for they gave him any price he demanded, fo that he confeffed unto us, that of the value of fome five and twenty hundred *Taeis* which he might have in goods, he made above thirty thoufand. Now as for us three *Portugals*, having nothing to fell, we imployed our time either in fifhing, hunting, or feeing the Temples of thefe *Gentiles*, which were very fumptuous and rich, whereinto the *Bonzes*, who are their priefts, received us very courteoufly, for indeed it is the cuftome of thofe of *Jappon* to be exceeding kind and courteous. Thus we having little to do, one of us, called *Diego Zeimoto*, went many times a fhooting for his pleafure in an *Harquebufe* that he had, wherein he was very expert, fo that going one day by chance to a certain Marfh, where there was great ftore of fowl, he killed at that time about fix and twenty wild Ducks ; In the mean time thefe people beholding this manner of fhooting, which they had never feen before, were much amazed at it, infomuch that it came to the notice of the *Nautaquim*, who was at that inftant riding of horfes, and not knowing what to think of this novelty fent prefently for *Zeimoto*, juft as he was fhooting in the Marfh, but when he faw him come with his *Harquebufe* on his fhoulder and two *Chinefes* with him carrying the fowl, he was fo mightily taken with the matter, as he could not fufficiently admire it: for whereas they had never feen any Gun before in that Country, they could not comprehend what it might be, fo that for want of underftanding the fecret of the powder, they all concluded that of neceffity it muft be fome Sorcery ; Thereupon *Zeimoto* feeing them fo aftonifhed, and the *Nautaquim* fo contented, made three fhoots before them, whereof the effect was fuch, that he killed one Kite, and two Turtle Doves ; In a word then, and not to lofe time, by endeering the matter with much Speech, I will fay no more, but that the *Nautaquim* caufed *Zeimoto* to get up on the horfes croupper behind him, and fo accompanied with a great croud of people, and four Hufhers, who with Battoons headed with iron went before him, crying a along the ftreets, *Know all men, that the* Nautaquim, *Prince of this Ifland of* Tanixumaa, *and Lord of our heads, enjoyns and exprefly commands, That all perfons whatfoever, which inhabit the Land that lies between the two Seas, do honour this* Chenchicogim, *of the further end of the world, for even at this prefent and for hereafter he makes him his kinfman, in fuch manner as the* Jacharons *are, who fit next his Perfon ; and whofoever fhall not do fo willingly, he fhall be fure to lofe his head.* Whereunto all the people anfwered with a great noife ; *We will do fo for ever.* In this pomp *Zeimoto* being come to the Pallace gate, the *Nautaquim* alighted from his horfe, and taking him by the hand, whileft we two followed on foot a pretty way after, he led him into his Court, where he made him fit with him at his own table, and to honour him the more, he would needs have him lodg there that night, fhewing many other favours to him afterwards, and to us alfo for his fake. Now *Zeimoto* conceiving, that he could not better acknowledge the honour which the *Nautaquim* did him, then by giving him his *Harquebufe*, which he thought would be a moft acceptable prefent unto him; on a day when he came home from fhooting, he tendred it unto him with a number of Pigeons and Turtle-doves, which he received very kindly, as a thing of great value, affuring him that he efteemed of it more, then of all the treafures of *China*, and giving him withall in recompence thereof a thoufand *Taeis* in filver, he defired him to teach him how to make the powder, faying, that without that the *Harquebufe* would be of no ufe to him, as being but a piece of unprofitable iron, which *Zeimoto* promifed him to do, and accordingly performed the fame. Now the *Nautaquim* taking pleafure in nothing fo much as fhooting in this *Harquebufe*, and his Subjects perceiving that they could not content him better in any thing, then in this, wherewith he was fo much delighted, they took a pattern of the faid *Harquebufe* to make others by it, & the effect thereof was fuch, that before our departure (which was five months & an half after) there was fix hundred of them made in the Country ; nay I will fay more, that afterwards, namely, the laft time that the Vice-roy *Don Alphonfo de Noronha* fent me thither with a prefent to the King of *Bungo*, which happened in the year 1556. thofe of *Jappon* affirmed, that in the City of *Fucheo*, being the chief of that Kingdom, there were above thirty thoufand ; whereat finding my felf to be much amazed, for that it feemed impoffible unto me, that this invention fhould multiply in fuch fort, certain Merchants of good credit affured me that in the whole Ifland of *Jappon* there were above three hundred thoufand *Harquebufes*, and that they alone had tranfported of them in the way of trade to the Country of

the

the *Lequios*, at fix feveral times, to the number of five and twenty hundred; fo that by the means of that one, which *Zeimoto* prefented to the *Nautaquim* in acknowledgment of the honour and good offices that he had done him, as I have declared before, the Country was filled with fuch abundance of them, as at this day there is not fo fmall an hamlet but hath an hundred at the leaft; for as for Cities and great Towns they have them by thoufands; whereby one may perceive what the inclination of this people is, and how much they are naturally addicted to the wars, wherein they take more delight, then any other Nation that we know.

§.2. We had been now three and twenty dayes in the Ifland of *Tanixumaa*, where very contentedly we paft away the time, either in fishing, fowling, or hunting, whereunto thefe people of *Jappon* are much addicted, when as a veffel belonging to the King of *Bungo* arriving in that Port, in the which were divers men of quality, and certain Merchants, who as foon as they were landed went to wait upon the *Nautaquim* with their prefents, according to the ufual cuftom of the Country: Amongft them there was an ancient man, very well attended, and unto whom the reft carried much refpect, that falling on his knees before the *Nautaquim* prefented him with a letter, and a rich Courtelafs garnifhed with gold, together with a box full of ventiloes, which the *Nautaquim* received with a great deal of ceremony: Then having fpent fome time with him in asking of certain queftions, he read the letter to himfelf, and thereupon having remained a prety while as it were in fufpence, and difmiffed the bearer thereof from his prefence, with an exprefs charge unto thofe about him to fee him honourably entertained, he called us unto him, and commanded the Truchman that was there by, to ufe thefe words unto us, *My good Friends, I intreat you that you will hear this letter read, which is fent me from my Lord and Uncle, and then I will let you know what I defire of you*; So giving it to a Treafurer of his, he commanded him to read it, which inftantly he did, and thefe were the contents of it, *Thou right eye of my face, Hyafcarangoxo, Nautaquim of Tanixuma, I Orgemdoo, who am your Father in the true love of my bowels, as he from whom you have taken the name and being of your Perfon, King of Bungo and* Facataa, *Lord of the great Houfe of* Fiancima, Tofa, *and* Bandou, *Chief Soveraign of the petty Kings of the Ifands of* Goto, *and* Xamanaxequa, *I give you to underftand, my Son, by the words of my mouth, which are fpoken of your perfon, that fome dayes fince certain men, coming from your Country, have affured me, that you have in your Town three* Chenchicogims *of the other end of the world, men that accommodate themfelves very well with thofe of* Japan, *are clothed in filk, and ufually wear fwords by their fides, not like Merchants that ufe traffique, but in the quality of perfons that make profeffion of honour, and which by that only mean pretend to render their names immortal; Moreover I have heard for a truth, that thefe fame men have entertained you at large with all matters of the whole Univerfe, and have affirmed unto you on their faith that there is another World greater then ours, inhabited with black and tawny people, of whom they have told you things moft incredible to our judgment, for which caufe I infinitely defire you, as if you were my Son, that by* Fiangeandono, *whom I have difpatched from hence to vifit my daughter, you will fend me one of thofe three ftrangers, which I am told you have in your houfe; the rather for that you know my long indifpofition, accompanied with fo much pain and grief, hath great need of fome diverfion: Now if it fhould happen that they would not be willing thereunto, you may then affure them, as well on your own faith, as on mine, that I will not fail to return them back in all fafety; whereupon, like a good Son that defires to pleafe his Father, fo order the matter that I may rejoyce my felf in the fight of them, and fo have my defire accomplifhed. What I have further to fay unto you, my Ambaffadour* Fingeandono *fhall acquaint you with, by whom I pray you liberally import to me the good news of your perfon, and that of my daughter, feeing fhe is as you know the apple of my right eye, whereof the fight is all the joy of my face. From the houfe of* Fucheo *the feventh Mamoque of the Moon.* After that the *Nautaquim* had heard this letter read; The King of *Bungo,* faid he unto us, is my Lord, and my *Uncle,* the brother of my mother, and above all he is my good Father, for I call him by that name, becaufe he is fo to my wife, which is the reafon that he loves me no lefs then his own children, wherefore I count my felf exceedingly bound unto him, and do fo much defire to pleafe him, that I could now find in my heart to give the beft part of my Eftate for to be transformed into one of you, as well for to go unto him, as to give him the content of feeing you, which out of the knowledge I have of his difpofition, I am affured he will value more then all the treafures of *China*; Now having thus acquainted

acquainted you with his defire, I earneftly intreat you to render your felves conformable there-unto, and that one of you two will take the pains to go to *Bungo*, there to fee that King whom I hold for my Father, and my Lord, for as for this other to whom I have given the name and being of a kinfman, I am not willing to part with him till he hath taught me to fhoot as well as himfelf. Hereupon *Chriftovano Borralho*, and I, greatly fatisfied with the *Nautaquim's* courtefie, anfwered him, that we kiffed his Highnefs hands for the exceeding honour he did us in vouchfafing to make ufe of us, and feeing it was his pleafure fo to do, that he fhould for that effect make choice of which of us two he thought beft, and he fhould not faile to be fuddainly ready for the voyage. At thefe words ftanding a while in mufing to himfelf, he look-ed on me, and faid, I am refolved to fend him there, becaufe he feems not fo folemn, but is of a more lively humour, wherewith thofe of *Japon* are infinitely delighted, and may thereby cheer up the fick man, whereas the too ferious gravity of this other, faid he, turning him to *Borralho*, though very commendable for more important matters, would ferve but to enter-tain his melancholy in ftead of diverting it. Thereupon falling into merry difcourfe and jeft-ing with thofe about him, whereunto the people of *Japon* are much inclined, the *Fingeandono* arrived, unto whom he prefented me, with a fpecial and particular recommendation touching the affurance of my perfon, wherewith I was not only well fatisfied, but had my mind alfo cleared from certain doubts, which out of the little knowledge I had of thefe peoples humours, had formerly troubled me. This done, the *Nautaquim* commanded two hundred *Taeis* to be given me for the expence of my voyage, whereupon the *Fingeandono* and I imbarqued our felves in a veffel with Oars, called a Funce, and in one night having traverfed all this Ifland of *Tanixumaa*, the next morning we caft anchor in an Haven, named *Hiamangoo*, from whence we went to a good Town, called *Quanquixumaa*, and fo continuing our courfe afore the wind, with a very fair gale, we arrived the day enfuing at a very fweet place, named *Tanora*, whence the morrow after we went to *Minato*, and fo forward to a Fortrefs of the King of *Bungoes*, called *Ofquy*, where the *Fingeandono* ftayed fome time, by reafon that the Captain of the place (who was his Brother in law) found himfelf much indifpofed in his health. There we left the veffel in which we came, and fo went by land directly to the City, where being arrived about noon, the *Fingeandono*, becaufe it was not a time fit to wait upon the King, went to his own houfe. After dinner having refted a little, and fhifted himfelf into a better habit, he mounted on horfback, and with certain of his friends rode to the Court, carrying me along with him, where the King was no fooner advertifed of his coming, but he fent a Son of his a-bout nine or ten years of age to receive him, who accompanied with a number of Noble-men, richly apparelled, and his Ufhers with their Maces going before him, took the *Fingeandono* by the hand, and beholding him with a fmiling countenance ; *May thy entrance*, faid he unto him, *into this houfe of the King my Lord, bring thee as much content and honour as thy chil-dren deferve, and are worthy, being thine, to fit at table with me in the folemn Feafts.* At thefe words the *Fingeandono* proftrating himfelf on the ground; *My Lord*, anfwered he, *I moft humbly befeech them that are in Heaven above, which have taught thee to be fo cour-teous and fo good, either to anfwer for me, or to give me a tongue fo voluble, as may exprefs my thankfulnefs in terms agreeable to thy ears for the great honour thou art pleafed to do me at this prefent, for in doing otherwife I fhould offend no lefs, then thofe ingratefull wretches, which inhabit the loweft pit of the profound and obfcure houfe of fmoak:* This faid, he offered to kifs the Cuttelats which the young Prince wore by his fide, which he would by no means permit, but taking him by the hand, he led him to the King his Father, unto whom, lying fick in his bed, he delivered a letter from the *Nautaquim*, which after he had read, he commanded him to call me in from the next room where I ftaid attending, which inftantly he did, and pre-fented me to the King, who entertaining me very gracioufly. *Thy arrival*, faid he unto me, *in this my Country is no lefs pleafing to me, then the rain which falls from Heaven is profita-ble to our fields that are fowed with Rice.* Finding my felf fomewhat perplexed with the no-velty of thefe terms, and this manner of falutation, I made him no anfwer for the inftant, which made the King fay to the Lords that were about him, I imagine that this ftranger is daunted with feeing fo much company here, for that peradventure he hath not been accuftomed unto it, wherefore I hold it fit to remit him unto fome other time, when as he may be better acquaint-ed, and not be fo abafhed at the fight of people. Upon this Speech of the Kings I anfwered by my Truchman, that whereas his Highnefs had faid that I was daunted, I confeffed that it was true, not in regard of fo many folks as were about me, becaufe I had feen far many more,

but

but that my amazement proceeded from the consideration that I was now before the feet of so great a King, which was sufficient to make me mute an hundred thousand years, if I could live so long; I added further, that those which were present there seemed to me but men, as I my self was, but as for his Highness, that God had given him such great advantages above all, as it was his pleasure that he should be Lord, and that others should be meer servants, yea, and that I my self was but a silly Ant, in comparison of his greatness, so that his Majesty could not see me in regard of my smalness, nor I in respect thereof be able to answer unto his demands. All the Assistants made such account of this mad answer of mine, as clapping their hands by way of astonishment, they said unto the King, Mark I beseech your Highness how he speaks to purpose; verily it seems that this man is not a Merchant, which meddles with base things as buying and selling, but rather a *Bonzo*, that offers sacrifices for the people, or if not so, surely he is some great Captain that hath a long time scoured the Seas. Truly, said the King, I am of the same opinion, now that I see him so resolute; but let every man be silent, because I purpose that none shall speak to him but my self alone, for I assure you that I take so much delight in hearing him talk, that at this instant I feel no pain. At those words the Queen and her daughters, which were set by him, were not a little glad, and falling on their knees, with their hands lifted up to Heaven, they thanked God for this his great goodness unto him.

CHAP. XLV.

The great mishap that befel the King of Bungo's *Son, with the ex-*
tream danger that I was in for the same; and
what followed thereupon.

S.1 A Little after the King caused me to approach unto his bed, where he lay sick of the Gout, when I was near him, *I pree thee*, said he unto me, *be not unwilling to stay here by me, for it does me much good to look on thee, and talk with thee; thou shalt also oblige me to let me know whether in thy Country, which is at the further end of the world, thou hast not learn'd any remedy for this disease wherewith I am tormented, or for the lack of appetite, which hath continued with me now almost these two months without eating any thing to speak of.* Hereunto I answered, that I made no profession of physick, for that I had never learnt that art, but that in the Junck, wherein I came from *China*, there was a certain wood, which infused in water healed far greater sicknesses then that whereof he complained, and that if he took of it, it would assuredly help him; To hear of this he was very glad, insomuch that transported with an extream desire to be healed, he sent away for it in all haste to *Tanixumaa*, where the Junck lay, and having used of it thirty dayes together, he perfectly recovered of this disease, which had held him so for two years together, as he was not able to stir from one place to another. Now during the time that I remained with much content in this City of *Fuchea*, being some twenty dayes, I wanted not occasions to entertain my self withall; for sometimes I was imployed in answering the questions, which the King, Queen, Princes, and Lords asked of me, wherein I easily satisfied them, for that the matters they demanded of me, were of very little consequence. Other-whiles I bestowed my selfe in beholding their Solemnities, the Temples, where they offered up their prayers, their warlike Exercises, their naval Fleets, as also their fishing and hunting, wherein they greatly delight, especially in the high flying of Falcons, and Vultures. Oftentimes I past away the time with my *Harquebuse* in killing of Turtles, and Quailes, whereof there is great abundance in the Country. In the mean season this new manner of shooting seemed no less marvellous and strange to the inhabitants of this Land, then to them of *Tanixumaa*, so that beholding a thing which they had never seen before, they made more reckoning of it then I am able to express, which was the cause that the Kings second Son, named *Arichandono*, of the age of sixteen or seventeen years, and whom the King wonderfully loved, intreated me one day to teach him to shoot, but I put him off, by saying that there needed a far longer time for it then he imagined, wherewith not well pleased, he complained to his Father of me, who to content the Prince desired me to give him a couple of charges for the satisfying of his mind; whereunto I answered, that I would give him as many as his Highness would be pleased to command me. Now because he was that day to dine with his Father, the matter was referred to the afternoon, howbeit then too there was nothing done, for that he waited on his Mother to a Village adjoyning, whither they came from all parts on pilgrimage by reason of a certain feast, which was celebrated there for the health of

the

the King: The next day this young Prince came with only two young Gentlemen waiting on him to my lodging, where finding me asleep on a Mat, and my *Harquebuse* hanging on a hook by, he would not wake me till he had shot off a couple of charges, intending, as he told me afterwards himself, that these two shoots should not be comprised in them I had promised him: Having then commanded one of the young Gentlemen, that attended him, to go softly and kindle the Match, he took down the *Harquebuse* from the place where it hung, and going to charge it, as he had seen me do, not knowing how much powder he should put in, he charged the Piece almost two spans deep, then putting in the bullet, he set himself with it to shoot at an Orange tree that was not far off, but fire being given, it was his ill hap that the *Harquebuse* brake into three pieces, and gave him two hurts, by one of the which his right hand thumb was in a manner lost, instantly whereupon the Prince fell down as one dead, which the two Gentlemen perceiving, they ran away towards the Court, crying along in the streets that the strangers *Harquebuse* had killed the Prince; At these sad news the people flocked in all haste with weapons and great cries to the house where I was; Now God knows whether I was not a little amazed when coming to awake I saw this tumult, as also the young Prince lying along upon the floor by me weltring in his own blood without stirring either hand or foot; All that I could do then was to imbrace him in my arms, so besides my self, as I knew not where I was. In the mean time, behold the King comes in a Chair carried upon four mens shoulders, and so sad and pale, as he seemed more dead then alive; after him followed the Queen on foot leaning upon two Ladies, with her two daughters, and a many of women all weeping. As soon as they were entred into the Chamber, and beheld the young Prince extended on the ground, as if he had been dead, imbraced in my arms, and both of us wallowing in blood, they all concluded that I had killed him, so that two of the Company drawing out their Scymitars, would have slain me; which the King perceiving, *Stay, stay,* cried he, *let us know first how the matter goes, for I fear it comes further off, and that this fellow here hath been corrupted by some of those Traitors kinred, whom I caused to be last executed.* Thereupon commanding the two young Gentlemen to be called which had accompanied the Prince, his Son, thither, he questioned them very exactly; Their answer was, that my *Harquebuse* with the inchantments in it had killed him: This deposition served but to incense the Assistants the more, who in a rage addressing themselves to the King; What need, Sir, have you to hear more, cried they? here is but too much, let him be put to a cruel death: Therewith they sent in all haft for the *Jarabuca*, who was my Interpreter, to them; now for that upon the arrival of this disaster he was out of extream fear fled away, they brought him straightly bound to the King, but before they fell to examining of him, they mightily threatned him, in case he did not confess the truth; whereunto he answered trembling, and with tears in his eyes, that he would reveal all that he knew. In the mean time being on my knees, with my hands bound, a *Bonzo,* that was President of their Justice, having his arms bared up to his shoulders, and a Poynard in his hand dipped in the blood of the young Prince, said thus unto me, *I conjure thee, thou Son of some Divel, and culpable of the same crime, for which they are damned that inhabit in the house of smoak, where they lye buried in the obscure and deep pit of the Center of the earth, that thou confess unto me with a voice so loud, that every one may hear thee, for what cause thou haft with these sorceries and inchantments killed this young innocent, whom we hold for the hairs, and principal ornament of our heads.* To this demand I knew not what to answer upon the suddain, for that I was so far besides my self, as if one had taken away my life, I believe I should not have felt it; which the President perceiving, and beholding me with a terrible countenance, *Seeft thou not,* continued he, *that if thou doeft not answer to the questions I ask thee, that thou mayft hold thy self for condemned to a death of blood, of fire, of water, and of the blasts of the wind; for thou shalt be dismembred into the air, like the feathers of dead fowl, which the wind carries from one place to another, separated from the body with which they were joyned whilest they lived.* This said, he gave me a great kick with his foot for to rowse up my spirits, and cried out again, *Speak, confess who they are that have corrupted thee? what sum of mony have they given thee? how are they called? and where are they at this present?* At these words being somewhat come again to my self, I answered him, that God knew my innocence, and that I took him for witness thereof: But he not contented with what he had done began to menace me more then before, and set before my eyes an infinite of torments and terrible things; wherein a long time being spent, it pleased God at length that the young Prince came to himself, who no sooner saw the King his Father, as also his Mo-

ther

ther and Sifters diffolved into tears, but that he defired them not to weep, and that if he chanced to die, they would attribute his death to none but himfelf, who was the only caufe thereof, conjuring them moreover by the blood, wherein they beheld him weltring, to caufe me to be unbound without all delay, if they defired not to make him die anew : The King much amazed with this language, commanded the Manacles to be taken off which they had put upon me; whereupon came in four *Bonzoes* to apply remedies unto him, but when they faw in what manner he was wounded, & that his thumb hung in a fort but by the skin, they were fo troubled at it, as they knew not what to do ; which the poor Prince obferving, Away, away, faid he, fend hence thefe divels, and let others come that have more heart to judg of my hurt, fince it hath pleafed God to fend it me ; Therewith the four *Bonzoes* were fent away, and other four came in their ftead, who likewife wanted the courage to drefs him, which the King perceiving was fo much troubled as he knew not what to do, howbeit he refolved at length to be advifed therein by them that were about him, who counfelled him to fend for a *Bonzo*, called *Teixeandono*, a man of great reputation amongft them, and that l ved then at the City of *Facataa*, fome feventy leagues from that place ; but the wounded Prince not able to brook thefe delayes ; *I know not*, anfwered he, *what you mean by this counfel which you give my Father, feeing me in the deplorable eftate wherein I am, for whereas I ought to have been dreft already, you would have me ftay for an old rotten man, who cannot be here until one hath made a journy of an hundred and forty leagues, both in going and coming, fo that it muft be a month at leaft before he can arrive, wherefore fpeak no more of it, but if you defire to do me a pleafure, free this Stranger a little from the fear you have put him in, and clear the room of all this throng, he that you believe hath hurt me will help me as he may, for I had rather die under the hands of this poor Wretch, that hath wept fo much for me, then be touched by the Bonzo of Facataa, who at the age he is of, of ninety and two years, can fee no further then his nofe.*

CHAP. XLVI.

My curing the young Prince of Bungo ; *with my return to* Tanixumaa, *and imbarquing there for* Liampoo ; *and alfo that which hapened to us on land, after the fhipwrack we fuffered by the way.*

§. I.   THe King of *Bungo* being extreamly grieved to fee the difafter of his Son, turned himfelf to me, and beholding me with a very gentle countenance ; *Stranger*, faid he unto me, *try I pray thee if thou canft affift my Son in this peril of his life, for I fware unto thee if thou canft do it, I will make no lefs afteem of thee, then of him himfelf, and will give thee whatfoever thou wilt demand of me* : Hereunto I anfwered the King, that I defired his Majefty to command all thofe people away, becaufe the coyle that they kept confounded me, and that then I would fee whether his hurts were dangerous, for if I found that I was able to cure them, I would do it moft willingly : Prefently the King willed every one to be gone, whereupon approaching unto the Prince, I perceived that he had but two hurts ; one on the top of his forehead, which was no great matter, and the other on his right hand thumb, that was almoft cut eff : So that our Lord infpiring me, as it were, with new courage, I befought the King not to be grieved, for I hoped in lefs then a month to render him his Son perfectly recovered. Having comforted him in this manner, I began to prepare my felf for the drefsing of the Prince, but in the mean time the King was very much reprehended by the *Bonzoes*, who told him, that his Son would affuredly die that night, and therefore it was better for him to put me to death prefently, then to fuffer me to kill the Prince out-right, adding further, that if it fhould happen to prove fo, as it was very likely, it would not only be a great fcandal unto him, but alfo much alienate his peoples affections from him. To thefe fpeeches of the *Bonzoes* the King replyed, that he thought they had reafon for that they faid, and therefore he defired them to let him know how he fhould govern himfelf in this extremity ; You muft, faid they, ftay the coming of the *Bonzo Teixeandono*, and never think of any other courfe, for we affure you in regard he is the holieft man living he will no fooner lay his hand on him but he will heal him ftraight, as he hath healed many others in our fight : As the King was even refolved to follow the curfed counfel of thefe fervants of the Divel, the Prince complained that his wounds pained him in fuch fort as he was not able to indure it, and therefore prayed that any handfome remedy

medy might be inftantly applied to them, whereupon the King, much diftracted between the opinion of the *Bonzoes*, and the danger that his Son was in of his life, together with the extream pain that he fuffered, defired thofe about him to advice him what he fhould refolve on, in that exigent ; not one of them but was of the mind, that it was far more expedient to have the Prince dreft out of hand, then to ftay the time which the *Bonzoes* fpake of. This counfel being approved of the King, he came again to me, and making very much of me, he promifed me mighty matters if I could recover his Son ; I anfwered him with tears in my eyes, that by the help of God I would do it, and that he himfelf fhould be witnefs of my care therein : So recommending my felf to God, and taking a good heart unto me, for I faw there was no other way to fave my life, but that, I prepared all things neceffary to perform the cure. Now becaufe the hurt of the right hand thumb was moft dangerous, I begun with that, and gave it feven ftitches, whereas peradventure if a Chirurgion had dreft him, he would have giv n it fewer ; as for that of the forehead, I gave it but four, in regard it was much flighter then the other ; that done, I applied to them tow wet in the whites of eggs, and fo bound them up very clofe, as I had feen others done in the *Indiaes* : Five days after I cut the ftitches, and continued dreffing him as before, until that at the end of twenty days it plea ed God he was throughly cured, without any other inconvenience remaining to him, then a little weaknefs in his thumb ; For this caufe after that time the King and all his Lords did me much honour ; the Queen alfo, and the Princeffes her daughters prefented me with a great many Sutes of filks, and the chiefeft of the Court with Cymitars, and other things, b fides all which the King gave me fix hundred *Taeis*, fo that after this fort I received in recompence of this my cure above fifteen hundred Duckets, that I carried with me from this place. After things were paft in this manner, being advertifed by letters from my two Companions at *Tanixumaa*, that the *Chinefe* Pirate, with whom we came thither, was preparing for his return to *China*, I befought the King of *Bungo* to give me leave to go back, which he readily granted me, and with much acknowledgement of the curing of his Son he willed a Funce to be made ready for me, furnifhed with all things neceffary, wherein commanded a man of quality, that was attended by twenty of the Kings fervants, with whom I departed one *Saturday* morning from the City of *Fucheo*, and the *Friday* following about Sun-fet I arrived at *Tanixumaa*, where I found my two Comrades, who received me with much joy. Here we continued fifteen days longer, till fuch time as the Junck was quite ready, and then we fet Sail for *Liampoo*, which is a Sea-port of the Kingdom of *China*, whereof I have fpoken at large heretofore, and where at that time the *Portugals* traded. Having continued our voyage with a profperous wind, it pleafed God that we arrived fafe at our defired Port, where it is not to be believed how much we were welcome by the Inhabitants of the place. Now becaufe it feemed ftrange unto them, that we had voluntarily fubmitted our felves in that fort to the bad faith of the *Chinefes*, they asked of us from what Country we came, and where it was that we imbarqued our felves with them ? whereupon we freely declared unto them the truth of all, and gave them an account of our Voyage, as alfo of the new Land of *Japon* that we had difcovered, the great abundance of filver that was there, and the exceeding profit that might be made by carrying the commodi ies of *China* thither ; wherewith they were wonderfully contented, and inftantly ordained a general Proceffion to be made by way of thankfgiving unto God for fo great a bleffing : But withall covetoufnefs began in fuch fort to feize upon the hearts of moft of the Inhabitants, every one ftriving to be the foremoft in this voyage, as they came to divide themfelves into troops, and to make feveral parties, fo that even with weapons in their hands they went thronging to buy up the commodities of that Country, which made the *Chinefe* Merchants, upon the fight of our unruly avarice, fet fo high a price upon their wares, that whereas a *Pico* of filk was at firft not worth forty *Taeis*, it rofe before the end of eight dayes to an hundred and threefcore, at which rate too the Merchants feemed to part with it very willingly. Thus by the means of this unreafonable defire of gain nine Juncks, which were then in the Port, were in fifteen days ready to fet Sail, though to fay the truth they were all in fuch diforder, and fo unprovided, that fome amongft them had no other Pilots then the Mafters themfelves, who had but little underftanding in Navigation. In this bad order they departed all in company together one *Sunday* morning, notwithftanding that they had the wind, the feafon, the fea, and all things elfe contrary, not fuffering themfelves to be guided by reafon, or the confideration of the dangers which they are fubject unto that commit themfelves to this Element ; For they were fo obftinate and fo blinded as they would not reprefent any inconvenience to themfelves, and I my felf was fo infortunate,

that

that I went along with them in one of their Vessels. In this manner they sailed all that same day as it were groping between the Islands and the firm Land, but about midnight there arose in the dark so mighty a Storm, accompanied with such horrible rain, that suffering themselves to be carried at the mercy of the wind, they ran upon the Sands of *Gotem*, whereof the nine Juncks two only, as it were by miracle, were saved, so that the other seven were left, out of which not so much as one man escaped. This loss was thought to amount unto above three hundred thousand Crowns in commodities, besides the greater, which was of six hundred persons that left their lives there, whereof there were an hundred and forty *Portugals*, all rich men, and of quality. As for the other two Juncks in one of the which by good hap I was, joyning in consort together, they followed the course they had begun, until such time as they arrived at the Island of the *Lequios*; There we were beaten with so furious a North-east wind, which increased by the conjunction of the new Moon, that our vessels were seperated in such sort as we could never see one another again: After dinner the wind turned to West North-west, whereby the Sea was so moved, and the waves rose with such fury, as it was a most dreadful thing to behold; whereupon our Captain, named *Gaspar Melo*, a very couragious Gentleman, seeing the greatest part of the prow of the Junck to be half open, and that there was nine spans water in the bottom of her, he resolved by the advice of all the Officers to cut down the two Masts, whose weight was the cause of the opening of the Junck, howbeit this could not be done with such care, but that the main Mast in its fall overwhelmed fourteen persons, whereof five were *Portugals*, which were all crushed in pieces, a spectacle so lamentable to behold that it exceedingly grieved every mans heart. Now forasmuch as the Storm increased more and more, we were constrained to let our selves be carried at the mercy of the Sea even until Sun-set, at which time the Junck made an end of splitting quite asunder, whereupon our Captain and every one of us, seeing the deplorable estate whereunto our sins had reduced us, fell to preparing our selves for our last end. Having in this sort past away half of the night, about the first quarter of the watch we struck upon a Shelf, where at the first blow the Junck broke all to pieces, the event whereof was so lamentable that threescore and two men left their lives there, some of which were drowned, and the rest squeezed to death under the Keel of the Vessel.

§.2.   There were but four and twenty of us, besides some women, that escaped from this miserable Shipwrack; Now as soon as it was day we perceived by the sight of the Island of fire, and of the Mountain of *Taydacano*, that the Land where we were was the great *Lequio*, whereupon with tears in our eyes recommending our selves to God, and marching up to the brest in water, we swam over certain deeper places, and so went five dayes together in great pain, not finding in all that time any thing to eat but the slime which the Sea cast up on the mud; Howbeit at length by the mercy of God we got to land, where going into the woods we sustained our selves with a certain herb like unto Sorrel, whereof there was great plenty along these Coasts, which was all the nourishment that we had for three days space that we were there, until at last we were espyed by a boy that was keeping of cattel, who as soon as he had discovered us, ran to the next Village, which was some quarter of a league off, for to give notice of it to the inhabitants there; who presently thereupon with the sound of Drums and Cornets assembled all their Neighbours round about them, so that within three or four hours they were a Company of about two hundred men, whereof there were fourteen on horsback. As soon as they descried us a far off, they made directly towards us, whereupon our Captain, seeing the wretched estate whereunto we were reduced, fell down upon his knees, and began to encourage us with many good words, desiring us to remember, *That nothing in the world could fall out without the Providence of God, and therefore like good Christians we should assure our selves it was his pleasure, that this should be the last hour of our lives, so that we could not do better then to conform our selves to his holy will, and with patience imbrace this pitiful end, which came from his Almighty hand, craving pardon from the bottom of our hearts for all our sins past; and that for himself he had such confidence in his mercy, that we duly repenting us according as we were obliged by his holy Commandments, he would not forget us in this our extremity.* Having made us this Exhortation, and lifted up his hands to Heaven, he cried out three times together with abundance of tears, *Lord have mercy upon us,* which words were reiterated by all the rest, but with such sighs and groans of true Christians, and so full of devotion and zeal, that I may truly say, the thing which then we feared least was that which naturally is most abhorr'd. As we were in this grievous agony six horsmen came unto

us,

us, and beholding us in a manner naked, without arms, on the ground upon our knees, and two women lying as it were dead before us, they were so moved with compassion, that four of them turning back to the footmen, which were coming on, made them all to stay, not suffering them to approach us; Howbeit a little after they came to us again, bringing with them six footmen, which seemed to be some of the Officers of Justice, who by the commandment of the horsmen tied us, three and three together, and with some shew of pity bid us, *That we should not be afraid, for that the King of the Lequios was a man greatly fearing God, and very well inclined to the poor, upon whom he continually bestowed much alms:* Moreover they swore unto us by their Law, that we should receive no hurt, yet could we not by any means be perswaded thereunto, for at that time we had so little hope of life, that if persons worthy of credit had assured us of it we should hardly have believed them, much less those cruel and detestable *Gentiles*, who neither had Religion, nor any knowledg of God: When they had tied us together, the footmen placed us in the midst of them, whilest those on horsback coursed up and down on every side, as though they had gone the round; now we no sooner began to march, but that the three women, which were with us more dead then alive, fell down on the place in a swoon, partly through their natural weakness, and partly through the fear they were in, so that the footmen were forced to take them up in their arms, and each one to carry them in his turn, howbeit for all that before we could arrive at the place whither they were leading us, two of the three died, and were left in the Wood for a prey to the Wolves, Foxes, and other Wild-beasts, whereof we saw great plenty thereabout. At length after we had marched a good while we arrived about Sun-set at a great Borough where we were presently put into a *Pagode* or Temple of theirs, which was invironed with very high walls, and yet for the more security they placed an hundred men about it to guard us all that night, who with their cries and beating of their Drums, kept us waking till the next morning, for the noise thereof, and the consideration of our present misery, would not suffer us to take any rest.

Chap. XLVII.

The carrying of us to the Town of Pungor, *and presenting us to the* Broquen, *Governour of the Kingdom; With that which ensued upon it.*

AS soon as it was morning the next day the chiefest women of the Town came to visit us, and in way of charity brought us a quantity of Rice, boyled fish, and certain fruits of the Country for us to eat, shewing themselves to be much moved with our misery, as well by their words, as by their tears; and seeing the extream need we stood in of clothes, for that we had little, or scarce any upon our bodies, six amongst them, which for that purpose were chosen by the rest, went a begging for us through all the streets of the Town, saying; *O good folks, good folks, which make profession of the Law of the Lord, whose property it is, if one may say so, to shew himself prodigal towards us by communicating his benefits unto us, come forth of your houses to behold the flesh of our flesh, which the wrath of the hand of the Lord Almighty hath touched, and succour them with your alms, to the end the mercy of his greatness may not abandon you, as it hath done them.* These words were of such force to stir up their charity, as within less then an hour we were abundantly furnished with all things necessary for us: But about three of the clock in the afternoon came a Post to this Borough with letters to the *Xivalon* of the place, that is the Captain thereof, who had no sooner read them, but he caused two Drums to beat an Alarum, at the sound whereof all the people assembled together in a great *Pagode* or Temple, where out of a window he spake unto them, and gave them to understand that the *Broquen*, the Governour of the Kingdom, had commanded us to be brought to the Town of *Pungor*, which was some seven leagues from thence. The most part of them at first refused to obey this command, so that there was great contention about it, in such sort that nothing could be agreed upon all that day, by means whereof the Post was returned to the *Broquen* with a relation of that which had past, and so we were left there till eight of the clock the next morning, at which time two *Peretandaos*, who are as it were Judges, came accompanied with divers Burgesses, and some twenty horsmen unto us, and after many writings drawn up by certain publique Registers concerning us, they sent us away the same day to a Town, called *Gondexilau*, where we were put into a dungeon, made in the fashion of a Cistern,

remaining

remaining there till the next day up to the middle in filthy standing water, that was full of horsleeches, which made us all gore blood : As soon as it was morning they carried us towards *Pungor*, where we arrived about four of the clock in the afternoon, now because it was late the *Broquen* would not see us till the day following, and then bound together as we were, he caused us to be led through four of the principal streets of the City, where the people thronging from all parts to behold us, seemed much to pity our misery, chiefly the women ; In this manner we were brought to a Court of Justice, where there was a great many of Officers, amongst whom we continued a long time waiting for the coming of the Judge, at length upon the thrice striking of a clock, a door that stood just against the place where we attended, was presently opened, by which we entred into a very spacious Hall, where the Governour sat upon a Throne all adorned with rich tapestry, and under a Cloth of State of silver tinsel ; round about him were six Ushers upon their knees, carrying Maces on their shoulders, and all along the room stood a Guard with Halberds in their hands, damasked with gold and silver ; All the rest of the Hall was full of people of divers Nations, the like whereof we had not seen in those Countries. After silence was imposed on all that were present, we prostrated our selves before the Throne of the *Broquen*, and weeping said unto him, *Sir, we beseech thee by that God which hath made Heaven and Earth, and on whose power we all of us depend, to take pity of our miserable fortune, for since the waves of the Sea hath brought us to the lamentable estate, and wretched condition wherein thou seest us, we most humbly desire thee that thy goodness will be pleased to put us into a better before the King, to the end he may be incited to have compassion on us poor strangers, that are destitute of all succour and favour of the world, for so it hath pleased God to have it in regard of our sins.* At these words the *Broquen* looking on them that were about him, and shaking his head, *What think you of these people,* said he unto them, *verily here is one of them that speaks of God as a man which hath the knowledge of his truth, so that we may conclude without all doubt, that there is another great world whereof we have no notice, wherefore since these men know the Source of all good, it is reasonable that we should proceed with them according to the request they have made unto us with so many tears.* Whereupon turning him towards us, who all this while lay prostrated on the ground, with our hands lifted up, as if we were worshipping God ; *I must confess,* said he unto us, *that I have so great compassion of your misery, and am so grieved to see you so poor as you are, as I assure you in all verity, that I had rather, if it were the good pleasure of the King, be like unto one of you, as wretched as you are, then to see my self in this office, which questionless was conferred on me for my sins: wherefore I would be loth to offend you, but the duty of my place obliging me thereunto, I must desire you as friends not to be troubled, if I ask you some questions, which are necessary for the good of Justice ; and as touching your deliverance, if God affords me life, be assured you shall have it, for I am most confident that the King my Masters inclination to the poor is truly Royal.* These promises exceedingly contented us, and to thank him for them we had recourse to our tears, which we shed in abundance, for our hearts were so full, as we could not possibly bring forth a word to answer him.

§.2.   The *Broquen* caused four Registers, the two *Peretandaos* of the Court aforesaid, and some eleven or twelve other Officers of Justice, to come immediately before him ; Then rising on his feet, he began with a severe countenance, and a naked Scymitar in his hand, to examine us, speaking so loud as every one might hear him ; *I Pinaquila,* said he, *Broquen of this City of Pungor by the good pleasure of him whom we all hold for the hairs of our heads, King of the Nation of the Lequios, and of all this Country of the two Seas, where the fresh and salt waters divide the Mynes of his treasures, do advise and command you by the rigour and force of my words, to tell me clearly, and with a clean heart, what people, and of what Nation you are, as also where your Country is, and how it is called?* To this demand we answered according to the truth, that we were *Portugals*, Natives of *Malaca. It is well,* added he, *but what adventure brought you into this Country, and whither did you intend to go when as you suffered shipwrack?* We replied thereunto, That being Merchants, who make no other profession then of traffique, we had imbarqued our selves in the Kingdom of *China*, for to go from the Port of *Liampoo* to *Tanixumaa*, where we had formerly been, but that arriving near to the Island of Fire we were surprized by a mighty tempest, so that not able to oppose the violence of the Sea, we were constrained to lie at the mercy of the winds for the space of three dayes and three nights together ; and that at the end thereof our Junck ran her self upon the Sands of *Taydican*, where, of ninety and two persons

that

that we were, threescore and eight were drowned, no more escaping of that great number but these four and twenty of us which stood before him all covered over with wounds, that were saved as it were by miracle through the special grace of God. At these words standing a little in suspence, *By what tytle,* replied he, *did you possess so much riches, and so many pieces of silk which were in your Junck, and that were worth above an hundred* Taeis, *as I am informed? Truly, it is not credible that you could get so much wealth any other way then by theeving, which being a great offence against God, is a thing proper to the servants of the Serpent of the house of smoak, and not to those of the house of the Sun, where they that are just, and of a pure heart, do bathe themselves amidst perfumes in the great Pool of the most Almighty:* We answered hereunto, that assuredly we were Merchants, and not thieves, as he was pleased to charge us, because the God in whom we believed forbad us by his holy Law, either to kill or to rob. Hereupon the *Broquen* beholding them which were about him; *Doubtless,* continued he, *if that which these men affirm be true, we may well say that they are like unto us, and that their God is much better then all others, as me thinks may be inferred from the truth of their words.* Then turning himself towards us, he examined us as before with a stern countenance, and the behaviour of a Judg that exerciseth his charge with integrity: In this examination he bestowed almost an hour, and in the last place said unto us; *I would fain know why those of your Country, when as heretofore they took* Malaca, *carried thereunto by extream avarice, did kill our men with so little pity? which is still made good by divers wiadows who in these Countries have survived their husbands.* To this we made answer, how that hapned rather by the chance of war, then out of any desire of robbing, which we had never used to do in any place wheresoever we came; *What is this you say,* replied he, *can you maintain that he that conquers, doth not rob? that he which useth force, doth not kill? that he which shews himself covetous, is not a thief? that which he oppresseth, performs not the action of a Tyrant? and lo, all these are the goodly qualities which are given to you, and whereof you are said to be culpable, and that by the affirmation of verity it self: Whence it is manifest, that Gods abandoning of you, and permitting the waves of the Sea to swallow you up, is rather a pure effect of his justice, then any injury that is done to you.* This said he arose out of the Chair where he was set, and commanded the Officers to return us back to prison, promising to give us audience according to the grace which it should please the King to shew us, and the compassion that he would have of us; wherewith we were very much afflicted, and in great dispair of our lives. The next day the King was advertised, as well of our imprisonment, as of the answers we had made, by the *Broquens* letters, wherein he had intermingled something in favour of us, by means whereof he did not cause us to be executed, as it was said he had resolved to have done upon certain false reports which the *Chineses* had made to him of us. In this prison we continued very near two months with much pain, never hearing in all that time so much as any word spoken of that first proceeding against us. Now forasmuch as the King desired to be more amply informed concerning us by other more particular inquiries then the letters of the *Broquen,* he sent a certain man unto us, named *Randinaa,* for to come secretly to the prison where we were, to the end that under the pretext of being a Merchant-stranger, he might exactly learn the cause of our arrival in that place, and that upon the report he should make thereof to the King, he might proceed to do that which should seem just unto him. Howbeit though this was closely carried, yet was it our good fortune to be advertised of it the day before his coming to us, so that we had time enough to arm our selves outwardly with all the apparances of misery and affliction we could possibly devise, and counterfeit; which expedient next to Gods assistance stood us in more stead then any other we could have thought upon. This man then came one morning well accompanied to the prison, and after he had viewed us all one after another, he called to him the *Jurabaca,* who served to interpret for him; *Ask these men,* said he, *what is the cause that the mighty hand of God hath so abandoned them, as to permit their lives through an effect of his Divine Justice to be subjected to the judgement of men, without having so much remorse of conscience, as to set before their eyes the terrour of that dreadful vision, which doth use to fright the soul at the last gasp of a mans life, for it is to be believed that they, who have done that which I observe in them, have heaped sin upon sin.* We answered him thereunto, that he had a great deal of reason for what he spake, in regard it was very probable that the sins of men were the principal cause of their sufferings, howbeit that God, as the Soveraign Lord of all, did nevertheless in that case accustome to take pity of them, with sobs and tears continually called upon him, and that it was also

his

his bounty wherein all our hope was placed, to the end he would be pleased to inspire the Kings heart with a will to do us justice according to our works, for that we were poor strangers destitute of all favour, a thing whereof men make most account in this world. *That which you say*, replyed he, *is very well, provided that your hearts be conformable to your words, and then you are not to be found fault with, for it is most certain, that he, which enammels all that our eyes do behold for the beautifying of the night, and that hath likewise made whatsoever the day doth shew us for the sustenance of man, who are but worms of the earth, will not refuse you your deliverance, seeing you beg of him with so many sighs and tears; Wherefore I intreat you not to dissemble with me, but truly to confess what I desire to understand from you at this present; namely, what people you are? of what Nation? in what part of the World you live in, and how the Kingdom of your King is named? whereunto you shall adde the cause that hath brought you hither, and to what place you were going with so much riches, which the Sea hath cast up on the shoars of* Taydican, *whereat all the Inhabitants have so wondred, as they were perswaded that you were Masters of all the Trade of* China. To these, and other like questions, which this Spie asked of us, we returned him such answers, as was most behoofull for us to give him, wherewith he was so contented, that making us many offers, he promised to move the King for our deliverance. In the mean time he spake not a word to us of the occasion for which he was sent, but still fained himself to be a stranger, and a Merchant like one of us. Howbeit when he went away, he carefully recommended us to the Jaylour, and willed him not to let us want any thing, promising to satisfie him for it to his content; In acknowledgment whereof we gave him many humble thanks with tears in our eyes, whereby he was greatly moved to compassion, so that he gave us a Bracelet of gold, that weighed thirty Duckats, and also six sacks of Rice, and withall desired us to excuse him for the smalness of the present he had given us. After this he returned back to the King, unto whom he rendred an account of all that had past with us, assuring him that we were not such as the *Chineses* had made him to believe, and offered for proof thereof to pawn his life an hundred times, if need were, which was the cause that the King abated much of the suspicion wherewithall they had inveighed him about our manner of lying. But as he was resolving to give order for our enlargement, as well upon the report of this man, as in regard of the letter which the *Broquen* had written him, there arrived at the Port a *Chinese* Pyrat with four Juncks, unto whom the King gave his Country for a place of Retreat, upon condition that he should share with him the moity of the booty which he should take, by means whereof he was in great favour with the King, and all them of the Country. Now forasmuch as our sins would have it, that this Pyrate was one of the greatest enemies the *Portugals* had at that time, by reason of a fight that we had had with him a little before in the Port of *Lamau*, where *Lancerote Pareyra*, born at *Lyma*, commanded in chief, and in which he had two Juncks burnt, and three hundred of his men slain; this dog was no sooner advertised of our imprisonment, and how the King was resolved to free us, but that he imbroyled the business in a strange manner, and told him so many lies of us, that he lacked but little of perswading him, that ere long we would be the cause of the loss of his Kingdom: For he assured him that it was our custom to play the Spies in a Country under pretence of trading, and then to make our selves Masters of it like robbers as we were, putting all to the sword that we met withall in it; which wrought so powerfully with the King, that he revoked all that he had resolved to have done, and changing his mind he ordained that in regard of what had been told him, we should each of us be dismembred into four quarters, and the same set up in the publique streets, that all the world might know we had deserved to be used so.

CHAP. XLVIII.

The King of the Lequios *sending a cruel Sentence against us to the* Broquen *of the Town, where we were prisoners, to the end he should put it in execution; and that which hapened unto us, till our arrival at* Liampoo.

§. I.   AFter that this cruel Sentence of death had been pronounced against us, the King sent a *Peretanda* to the *Broquen* of the City, where we were prisoners, to the end that within four dayes it should be executed upon our persons. This *Peretanda* departed presently away, and upon his arrival at the City, he went and lodged himself at a certain widows house,

that

that was his fifter, a very honourable woman, and from whom we had received much alms; This
fame man having fecretly imparted unto her the caufe of his coming, & how he was not to return
but with a good Certificate unto the King of the performance of this execution, fhe went ftrait-
way, and acquainted a Niece of hers with it, who was daughter to the *Broquen* of the City, in
whofe houfe lay a *Portugal* woman, the wife of a Pilot who was a prifoner with us, and two
children of hers, defiring then to comfort her, fhe difcovered unto her all that fhe had learnt,
which fhe had no fooner underftood, but that extreamly afflicted at fo fad a news, fhe fell inftantly to the ground in a fwoon, wherein fhe continued a long time fpeechlefs; At length
being come to her felf again, fhe fell to tearing of her cheeks fo cruelly with her nails, that all
her face was nothing but gore bloud, which, for that it was a new and extraordinary thing in
that Country, was incontinently fpread abroad throughout all the City, infomuch that all the
women being frighted with it, the moft part of them went forth with their children in their
hands to the *Broquens* daughters houfe, where the *Portugal* woman was, more ready to die, then
to anfwer to the queftions one or another of them asked her, & being exceedingly moved with pity
to behold her, fo lamentably taking on, drowned all in tears and blood, which paffion & grief had
drawn from her, they all refolved to write a letter in favour of us to the old Queen, the Kings
Mother, as accordingly they did, and the contents of it were thefe; *Sacred pearl, congealed in
the greateft fhell of the profoundeft depth of the waters; thou Star, enammelled with rayes
of fire; thou trefs of golden hair, intermixed with a Garland of rofes, whofe feet are fo replenifhed with greatnefs that they reft upon the top of our heads, like to rubies enchaced in
gold, whereof the price is ineftimable: We that are no other then the leaft and pooreft of
thy creatures, the daughters and kinfwomen of the* Broquens *wife, together with the reft of
thy captives that have fet their hands to thefe prefents, do make our moan unto thee concerning a thing which we have feen with our eyes, that is a poor woman, a ftranger, who feems
to have neither flefh nor face, drowned as fhe is in a pool of blood, beating her breft with fuch
cruelty, as would ftir up even wild beafts in the Forreft to compaffion, and ftrike fear into e-
very one; Moreover we have heard her cry fo loud, as we affure thee by the Law of all verity, that if God fhould lend an ear unto her, as we believe he will, becaufe he doth ufually
affift the poor, that are defpifed of the world, it is to be feared that fome great chaftifement of
famine and fire will fall upon us; Wherefore the extream apprehenfion, which we have of
thefe things, caufeth us to joyn all our voyces together, like little children hungry after their
mothers, and humbly befeech thee, that cafting thine eyes upon the foul of the deceafed King,
thy Hufband, for whofe fake we beg this of thee, thou wilt vouchfafe to make thy felfe like
the Saints, fetting afide all refpect of the flefh; For the more thou fhalt do for God, the greater thou fhalt be in his houfe, where we verily believe thou fhalt find the King thy Hufband,
finging to the found of the harp of thofe children, that have never finned, the fong of this charitable alms, which for Gods fake, and his, we pray thee to obtaine of the King, thy Son:
And this we hope fhall be a means to move him, both for the love of God, and of thy felf, as
alfo by the force of our tears and cries, to take pity on thefe ftrangers, and freely pardon them
all the faults, wherewith they are unjuftly charged, fince, as thou knoweft, they are not the
Saints of Heaven that ufe to accufe us, but men, that are infamous, and of an evil life, to
whom we are forbidden to lend an ear.* Conchenilau, the fair Gentlewoman, and well born,
but above all more honourable then all thofe of this City, for having been bred up in thy fervice by her Aunt, fhall reprefent unto thee on the behalf of God, and the King thy Hufband,
for the love of whom we prefer this requeft unto thee, all the other particularities of this affair, as alfo the grievous tears and groans of thefe poor folks, and the extream fadnefs and
fear of all the inhabitants of this place, who moft earneftly befeech thee to prefent their humble Suit to the King, thy Son, cherifhed above all others, on whom may it pleafe the Lord of
all good to beftow fo much thereof, as with that, which only fhall be refting to him, all thefe
people, that inhabit the Land, and Iflands of the Sea, may be replenifhed.* This letter, figned by above an hundred of the chiefeft women of the City, was fent by a Gentlewoman, the
daughter of the *Mandarin Comanilau,* Governour of the Ifland of *Bancaa,* which is on the
the South-fide of that of the *Lequios,* and good luck would have it that this young Da-
mofel came thither, but three dayes before the Sentence of death was to be put into
execution upon us, in the company of two of her brothers, and ten or eleven Gentlemen,
her kinfmen.

  This Gentlewoman being arrived at the City of *Bintor,* where the King and the Queen his S. 2.
                    E e   Mother

Mother were, she went to the house of an Aunt of hers, the chief Lady of honour to the Queen, and that infinitely loved her, to whom she rendred an account of the occasion of her coming, and withall represented unto her how much it imported both her honour and credit, seeing all the rest had made choice of her for this affair, that her Highness should grant her the grace which all of them together made such suit unto her for: The Lady having given her Neece the best welcome that possibly she could by all demonstrations of her affection, she said unto her, that since she perceived this business so much concerned her honour, she would labour by all the means she could that she should not return discontented, and frustrated of the hope of her request, the rather for that the thing was just in it self, and so earnestly sought for by so many great Ladies; whereupon the Gentlewoman, having given her very humble thanks, besought her to dispatch the business with as much speed as might be, in regard we had but two dayes more to live, according to the tenour of our Sentence, after which time all help would be in vain. *Since it is so,* answered her Aunt, *and that for want of requisite diligence the poor wretches are like to suffer the punishment, whereunto the King hath destined them upon the* Chineses *report, I will go and lay my self at the Queens feet, as soon as she awakes, which will be within an hour at the furthest, to the end that this novelty, not having done so these six years by reason of my indisposition, may draw her to demand of me the cause of it.* Having said this, she left her Neece behind her, and went and opened a Gallery door, whereof she alone had the key, and so entred into the Chamber where the Queen lay; A while after the Queen awaking, found her lying at her feet, whereupon she said unto her; *How now* Nhay Meicamur, *(for so was this Lady called) what is it hath brought you hither at this time? certainly it is some extraordinary matter.* Madam, answered she, *that which your Majesty sayes, is very true, and I assure my self that it will seem no less strange in your ears, then it was to me to see my Neece arrive here lately with so much sorrow and grief, that I am not able to express it in words.* The Queen having then commanded her to call her in, she presently fetched her; The first thing that this young Gentlewoman did, was to prostrate her self before the Queen, who was in her bed, and so told her weeping the occasion that brought her thither, and therewithall presented her with the letter, which the Queen commanded her to read, as accordingly she did; and it is said the Queen was so moved with compassion at it, that not induring to have her make an end of reading it, she said many times unto her with tears in her eyes; *Enough, enough, I will hear no more of it at this time, and since the business stands in the terms you speak of, God, and the Soul of the King my Husband, for whose sake all these Ladies beg this boon of me, forbid, that these poor wretches should lose their lives so unjustly: The false reports which the* Chineses *have made of them, together with the miseries they have indured at Sea, may serve them instead of great punishments; wherefore rely upon me for your request, and in the mean space withdraw your selves til to morrow morning betimes, when we will go all three to the King my Son before it be day, and then you shall read this letter to him, as you have read it to me, that being incited to pity he may make no difficulty to grant us that which we demand of him with so much reason.* This resolution taken, the Queen was no sooner up the next day, but carrying along with her only her chief Lady, and the Gentlewoman her Neece, she past through a Gallery to the Chamber of the King her son, whom she found still in bed, and having rendred him an account of occasion of her coming, she commanded the Gentlewoman to read the letter, as also to tell by word of mouth all that had happened in that affair, which the Gentlewoman performed very exactly, but not without mingling her tears with those of her Aunts, as we knew afterwards: In the mean time the King looking on his Mother, Madam, answered he unto her, *I must needs confess, that I dream'd this night how I saw my self before a very angry Judge, who carying his hand three times to his face, as if he had threatned me, I promise thee, said he unto me, that if the blood of these strangers doth cry unto me for vengeance, thou and thine shall satisfie my justice, which makes me believe, that assuredly this vision comes from God, for whose sake I will do this alms to his praise, giving them both life and liberty, that so they may go where they will, and moreover I will cause a vessel to be provided for them, furnished with all things they shall need, all at mine own charge.* The Queen gave the King her Son thanks for this his great grace unto them, and withall commanded her Lady and the Gentlewoman to kiss his feet, as instantly they did, and so the Queen retired to her own lodging. Hereupon the King sent for the *Chumbim* to command him that the Sentence against us might be revoked, telling him all that had past, as well concerning his dream, as the request the Queen his Mother had made unto him, which he had granted her. Then the Officers of Justice commending

ing

ing the King much for this action, revoking the former, drew up another Sentence in favour of us, which contained words to this effect, *Broquen of my City of Pungor, I, the Lord of seven Generations, and of the hairs of thy head, do send thee the smiles of my mouth, that thy reputation may be thereby augmented. Considering the information which the Chineses had given me of the pernicious manner of living of these strangers, assuring me by a solemn oath, and upon the faith they owe unto their Gods, that infallibly they were Pyrats and robbers, who used no other trade then to steal away other mens goods, and bathe their hands in the blood of those that would defend their own according to reason, as they said was manifest to all the world, which they have run over, not leaving any Island, Port of the Sea, River, nor Land, that they have not invaded with fire and sword, committing such enormous and horrible crimes, as for fear of offending God, I may not mention. All which things have at first sight seemed unto me most worthy to be punished in justice according to the Laws of my Kingdom; wherefore I sent their Proces to the principal officers of my Crown, who all with one common consent swore unto me that these strangers deserved not only one, but many deaths, if it were possible, so that relying upon their advice, I wrote unto* Nhay Peretanda, *that he should enjoyn thee from me not to fail within four dayes to put that Sentence of mine in execution. Now forasmuch as the chiefest Dames of your City, whom I hold for my kinswomen, have been Suiters unto me since, that I would be pleased to bestow their lives upon them by way of an alms, alledging many reasons in their letters to that purpose, whereby I might be induced not to deny, but rather to accord them that grace; the fear which I have least their cries should in case of refusal arrive at the highest of the Heavens, where that Lord liveth raigning, whose property it is to have pity on the tears, which are truly shed by those that have a right zeal to his holy Law, hath wrought so with me, that freeing my self from that blind passion, whereunto the flesh rendred me inclined, I would not let my choller prevail over the blood of those wretches. For which reasons I command thee, that as soon as this fair Gentlewoman, who is of noble extraction, and my kinswoman, shall present thee these letters, signed with my hand, wherewith I confess, I am well contented, in regard of the persons that have made this Suite unto me, thou go unto the prison, whither thou hast committed these strangers, and that without all delay thou set them at liberty, as also that thou furnish them with a vessel at my charge, giving them moreover such alms as the Law of the Lord commandeth thee to bestow on them, and that too with a liberal hand; whereupon thou shalt tell them, that they may go away without seeing my Person, for which I will dispense with them, as well because that labour would be to no purpose, as for that, performing as I do the Office of a King, it is not fit for me to behold men, who have a great knowledge of God, and yet seem to make little account of his Law, in that they accustom themselves to rob others of their goods. Given at* Bintor *in the third* Chavequa *of the first* Mamoquo *of the Moon, in the presence of the Queen my Mother, the Source of my right eye, and Lady of all my Kingdom.* And signed a little below, *Hira Pitau, Xinancor, Ambulec, the firm prop of all Justice.* As soon as the Gentlewoman had this Letter of the Kings in her hands, she was never at quiet, till she had left her Aunt, and put her self upon her journey, which she continued with such diligence, that in a short space she arrived at the City, and delivered the Letter to the *Broquen*, who presently upon the reading of it caused all the *Peretandas, Chumbims*, and other Officers of Justice to assemble together, and then went with them directly to the Prison, where we were at that instant under a sure guard; we no sooner saw them enter, but all of us cried out three or four times together, *Lord have mercy upon us*, wherewith the *Broquen*, and all that accompanied him, whereof the prison was full, were so moved, as some of them could not forbear weeping, out of the compassion they had of us: In the mean time the *Broquen* fell to comforting us in such kind and loving terms, as well expressed the greatness of his charity: Withall he commanded the irons to be taken off from our hands and feet, and drawing us into an outward Court, he recounted unto us all that had past in our business, whereof we had not any knowledge at all, in regard of the strict watch that was set upon us all the while; Then having caused the Kings Letters to be published: *My friends*, said he unto us, *now that God hath shewed you so much grace, to deliver you as you see, I have one request to make unto you, which is, that for my sake, you will thank him from the bottom of your heart, and praise him for it; for if you make this acknowledgement unto him, he will communicate to you from above, whence all good doth proceed, an agreeable repose, which is a thing far more convenient for us then to live three or four days in the miseries of this world, where there is nothing but labour, grief,*

great

great affliction, and above all poverty, which is the accomplishment of all evils, and whereby ordinarily our souls are wholly consumed in the deep abyss of the house of smoak.

§.3.   The *Broquen* moreover caused two Paniers full of clothes to be brought to that place, and distributed to them amongst us according to each ones need ; That done he carried us home to his house, where all the Ladies of the Town came to see us, testifying by their countenances that they greatly rejoyced at the good success of our deliverance : They comforted us also with great demonstration of pity, which is an effect of the good nature of the women of this Country, that is common to them all ; and not contented therewith they entertained us in their houses, one after another during all the time we were there until our departure, for we continued in this City afterwards the space of forty six dayes, in which time we were furnished with all things necessary for us, and that in such abundance, as there was not one of us but carried above an hundred Duckets away with him. As for the *Portugal* woman, of whom I spake before, she had above a thousand, as well in mony, as in other gifts which were given her, by which means her husband in less then an year recovered himself of all the losses he had sustained. After we had with a great deal of contentment past those forty six dayes there, the season proper for our voyage being come, the *Broquen* procured us passage in the Junck of a *Chinese*, which was bound for the Port of *Liampoo* in the Kingdom of *China*, according to the commandment that he had received of the King for that purpose, but first he caused the Captain of the Junck to put in good security for the safety of our persons during all the time of the voyage. In this manner we departed from *Pangor* the capital City of the island of *Lequios*, of which I will here make a brief relation, to the end that if it shall one day please God to inspire the *Portugal* Nation, principally for the exaltation and increase of the Catholick faith, and next for the great benefit that may redound thereof, to undertake the Conquest of this Island, they may know where first to begin, as also the commodities of it, and the easiness of this Conquest. We must understand then that this island of *Lequios*, scituated in nine and twenty degrees, is two hundred leagues in circuit, threescore in length, and thirty in bredth. The Country is almost like that of *Japon*, saving that it is a little more mountainous in certain parts, but in the middle it is plainer and more fertile. It is rendred very agreeable by many large Plains, that are watred with divers rivers of fresh water, and from whence are gathered great provisions especially of Rice and Wheat. It hath Mountains out of which is drawn such quantity of copper, as in regard of the abundance thereof it is so common among those people, that whole Ships are laden with it from thence in way of traffique to all the Ports of *China, Laman, Sumbor, Chabaquea, Tosa, Miacoo,* and *Japon,* as likewise to all the other Islands on the South-side thereof, as those of *Sesirau, Goto, Fucanxi,* and *Pollem :* Moreover in all this Country of the *Lequios,* there is also great store of iron, steel, lead, tin, allum, salt-peeter, brimstone, hony, wax, sugar, and ginger, far better then that which comes from the *Indiaes.* It hath withall a world of Angelin-wood, Chestnuts, Trees, Oak, and Cedar, wherewith thousands of Ships may be made. On the East-side it hath five very great Islands, where many Mynes of Silver are found, as also Pearls, Amber, Frankincense, Silk, Ebony, Brasil, and a great abundance of a certain wood fit for Carpentry, called *Poytan ;* It is true that there is not such store of Silk there, as in *China.* The Inhabitants of all this Country do as the *Chineses* cloth themselves, with Linnen, Cotten, Silk, and a kind of Damask-stuff, which comes to them from *Nanquin ;* They are great eaters, very much addicted to the delights of the flesh, little inclined to arms, and altogether unfurnished of them ; which induceth me to believe that they might be easily conquered, and the rather for that in the year, a thousand, five hundred, fifty and six, a *Portugal* arrived at *Malaca,* named *Pero Gomez a' Almeyda,* servant to the Grand Master of *Santiago,* with a rich Present, and Letters from the *Nautaquim,* Prince of the Island of *Tanixumaa,* directed to King *John* the third ; the Substance and Contents of his request was, to have five hundred *Portugals* granted to him, to the end that with them, and his own Forces, he might conquer the Island of *Lequio,* for which he would remain tributary to him at fivethousand Kintals of Copper, and athousand of Lattin yearly; which Ambassy came to no effect, because the Messenger was lost in the Gallion, where *Manael de Souza de Sepulveda,* also perished. A little further to the Northward of this Island of *Lequio,* there is a great Archipelago of small Islands, from whence is drawn a great quantity of silver, which in my opinion, & by what I gathered out of a petition which *Ruy Lopez de Vilhalobos* General of the *Castillians* presented to *Jorge de Castro,* at that time Captain of *Ternate,* should be those whereof the Inhabitants
had

had some knowledge, and which they called the Islands of Silver; and yet I cannot see with what reason that may be, because both by what I have observed, and read, as well in the writings of *Ptolomie*, as other Geographers, not any one of them hath pierced into the Kingdom of *Siam*, and the Island of *Sumatra*, only our Cosmographers, since the time of *Alphonso d' Albuquerque* have passed a little further, and treated of the *Selebres*, *Pasuaas*, *Mindanaus*, *Champas*, as also of *China*, and *Japon*, but not of the *Lequios*, or other *Archipelagoes*, which are to be discovered within the vast extent of that Sea. From this brief relation which I have made of the Island of *Lequios*, may be inferred, both out of what I have heard and seen, that with two thousand men only this Island might be taken, together with all the rest of these *Archipelagoes*, whence more profit might be drawn then from the *Indiaes*, and they might be conserved with less charge, as well in regard of men, as otherwise; for we spake there with Merchants, who assured us, that the sole Revenue of three Custom-houses, and of the Island of *Lequios*, amounted unto one million and an half of gold, not comprising therein either the Mass of the whole Kingdom, or the Mynes of Silver, Copper, Iron, Steel, Lead, and Tin, which are of a far greater revenue, then the Customs. I will not speak further of other particularities of this Island, which I might here insert, for that I hold this sufficient to awaken the courages of the *Portugals*, and incite them to an Enterprise, of so much service for our King, and profit for themselves.

CHAP. XLIX.

My sayling from Liampoo *to* Malaca, *from whence the Captain of the Fortress, sent me to the* Chaubainhaa *at* Martabano; *and all that befel us in our voyage thither.*

BEing arrived at *Liampoo*, we were very well received by the *Portugals*, that lived there, §.1 From whence within a while after I imbarqued my self in the Ship of a *Portugal*, named *Tristano de Gaa*, for to return unto *Malaca*, with an intention once more to try my fortune, which had so often been contrary to me, as may appear by that which I have delivered before. This Ship being safely arrived at *Malaca*, I went presently unto *Pedro de Faria*, Governour of the Fortress, who desiring to benefit me somewhat before the time of his Government was expired, he caused me to undertake the voyage of *Martaban*, which was usually very profitable, and that in the Junck of a *Mahumetan*, named *Necoda Mamude*, who had wife and children at *Malaca*. Now the principal designe of this voyage was, to conclude a peace with the *Chaubainhaa*, King of *Martabano*, as also to continue the commerce of those of that Country with us, because their Juncks did greatly serve for the provisions of our Fortress, which at that time was unfurnished thereof by reason of the success of the Wars of *Jaoa*. Besides I had a designe in this my voyage of no less consequence, then the rest, which was to get one, called *Lancarote Guerreyro*, to come thither, who was then on the Coast of *Tanaucarim* with an hundred men in four Foists, under the name of a Rebel or Mutiner; I was to require him to come to the succour of the Fortress, in regard it was held for certain, that the King of *Achem* was suddainly to fall upon it; so that *Pedro de Faria*, seeing himselfe destitute of all that was necessary for him to sustain a Siege, and of men likewise; found it fit to make use of these hundred men, the rather for that they were nearest, and so might be the sooner with him. In the third place he sent me upon another important occasion, namely to give advice to the Ships of *Bengala*, that they should come all carefully in consort together, lest their negligence in their Navigation should be the cause of some distaster. This voyage then I undertook very unwillingly, and parted from *Malaca* upon a *Wednesday*, the ninth day of *January*, in the year, one thousand, five hundred, forty and five; being under Sail I continued my course with a good wind to *Pullo Pracelar*, where the Pilot was a little retarded by means of the Shelves, which cross all that Channel of the firm Land, even unto the Island of *Sumetra*; When we were got forth with much labour we passed on to the Islands of *Pullo Sambillam*, where I put my self into a *Manchua*, which I had very well equipped, and sayling in it the space of twelve days, I observed, according to the order *Pedro de Faria* had given me for it, all the Coast of that Country of *Malaya*, which unto *Juncalan* contains an hundred and thirty leagues, entring by all the Rivers of *Bartnhaas*, *Salangor*, *Panaagim*, *Quedam*, *Parles*, *Pendan*, and *Sambilan*, *Siam*, without so much as hearing any news at all of his enemies in any of them: So continuing the same course nine days more, being the three and

twen-

twentieth of our voyage, we went and cast anchor at a little Island, called *Pisandurea*, where the *Necoda*, the *Mahometan* Captain of the Junck, was of necessity to make a cable, and furnish himself with wood and water ; With this resolution going on shore every man applyed himself to the labour he was appointed unto, and therein spent most part of the day ; Now whilest they were thus at work the Son of this *Mahometan* Captain came and asked me whither I would go with him, and see if we could kill a Stag, whereof there was great plenty in that Island ; I answered him that I would accompany him with all my heart, so that having taken my *Harquebuse*, I went along with him athwart the wood, where we had not walked above an hundred spaces, but that we espied a many of wild boars, that were rooting in the earth near to a pond ; Having discovered this game, we got as near to them as we could, and discharging amongst them, we carried two of them to the ground : Being very glad of this good success we presently gave a great shout, and ran straight to the place we had seen them rooting. But so dreadful to behold, in this place we found above a dozen bodies of men digged out of the earth, and some nine or ten others half eaten. Being much amazed at this object, we withdrew a little aside by reason of the great stanch, which proceeded from these dead bodies. Hereupon the *Sarrazin* told me, that he thought we should do well to advertise his father of this, to the end we might instantly surround this Island all about for to see whether we could discover any vessels with Pirats ; for, said he, there may be some lye hidden behind yonder poynt, whereby we may very well run the hazard of our lives, as it hath often befallen other ships, where many men have been lost by the carelesness of their Captains. This advice of the *Sarrazin* seemed so good unto me, that we presently returned back unto the Rode, where he gave an account to his father of that we had seen. Now for that the *Necoda* was a very prudent man, and scalded (as one may say) with the like inconveniences, he straightway gave order to have the Island surrounded, then causing the women, children, and linnen, although it were but half washed, to be imbarqued, he himself being followed by forty men, armed with Harquebuses and Lances, went directly to the place where we had discovered those bodies, and viewing them one after another, with stopping our noses by reason of the stench, which was insupportable, he was so moved to compassion, that he commanded the Marriners to dig a great pit for to bury them in ; But as they were about to render them this last duty, and looking over them again, there was found upon some of them little daggers garnished with gold, and on others bracelets : Whereupon the *Necoda*, understanding well this mystery, wished me with all speed to dispatch away the roving vessel that I had to the Captain of *Malaca*, for that, as he assured me, those dead men, which they saw there, were *Achems*, who had been defeated near to *Tanauçarim*, whither their Armies ordinarily retired because of the war which they had with the King of *Siam*. The reason he alledged to us for this was, that those which we saw there lying dead, having golden bracelets about them, were Captains of *Achem*, who had caused themselves to be buried without permitting them to be taken away, and that he would lose his head if it were not so. For a greater proof whereof, he further added, that he would make some more of them to be dis-enterred, as incontinently he did, and having digged some seven and thirty of them out of the earth, there was found about them sixteen bracelets of gold, twelve very rich daggers, and many jewels, so that thinking of no other but hunting, we got a booty worth above a thousand Duckats, which the *Necoda* had, besides what was concealed ; but the truth is, this was not altogether to our advantage, for the most part of our men became sick with the extream stench of those bodies. At the very instant I dispatched away the rowing vessel that we had to *Malaca*, and advertised *Pedro de Faria* of the whole success of our voyage ; Withall I certified him what course we had held, as also into what Ports, and into what Rivers we had entred, without hearing any other news of his enemies, then that it was suspected they had been at *Tanauçarim*, where by the appearances of those dead bodies, it was to be believed that they had been defeated, whereunto I added for a conclusion, that if I could light on any more assured news concerning them, I would presently acquaint him with it, in what part soever I were.

§.2.   After I had dispatched away the rowing Vessel to *Malaca*, with the Letters which I had directed to *Pedro de Faria*, and that our Junck was furnished with all things necessary for her, we sayled towards the Coast of *Tanauçarim*, where, as I said before, I had order to land for to treat with *Lancerote Guerreyro*, that he, and the rest of the *Portugals* of his Company might come to the succour of *Malaca*, which the *Achems* intended to besiege, according to the report that went of it. Being under Sail then we arrived at a little Island, a league in circuit,

circuit, called *Pulho Hinhor*, where a *Parao* came unto us, in the which were six tawny Moors, poorly clad, with red Bonets on their heads; their Boat being come close to our Junck, which was then under Sayl, they saluted us in a way of peace, whereunto we answered in the like manner; That done they demanded of us if there were any *Portugals* amongst us? we told them that there were, but mistrusting it, they desired to see one or two of them upon the hatches, because, added they, it imports much that it should be so. Whereupon the *Necoda* prayed me to come up, which incontinently I did, though at that time I was shut up in my Cabbin below somewhat indisposed in my health; when I was on the deck I called to them that were in the *Parao*, who had no sooner seen me, and known me to be a *Portugal*, but they gave a great shout, and clapping their hands for joy they came abord our Junck. Then one of them, who by his countenance seemed to have more Authority then the rest, began to say unto me; *Signior, Before I crave leave of thee to speak, I desire thee to read this Letter, to the end it may induce thee the more readily to believe that which I am to say unto thee.* Thereupon out of an old filthy clout he took a Letter, wherein after I had opened it, I found this written: *Signiors Portugals, which are true Christians, this honourable man, that shall shew you this Letter, is King of this Island, newly converted to the Faith, and called* Dom Lancerote; *He hath rendred many good Offices, not only to them, who have subscribed this writing, but to us also that have navigated on these Coasts: For he hath given us very important advertisements of the treasons, which the* Achems *and* Turks *have plotted against us, so that by the means of this honest man we have discovered all their designes: Withall God hath made use of him for to give us not long since a great victory against them, wherein we have taken from them one Gally, four Galliots, and five Foists, with the death of above a thousand Sarrazins. Wherefore we intreat you, by the wounds of our Lord Jesus Christ, and by the merits of his holy passion, not only to keep him from all wrong, but to assist him with all your power, as the manner is of all good* Portugals, *that it may serve for an example to those which shall know this, to do the like in imitation of you; And so we kiss your hands this thirteenth day of* November, 1544. This Letter was signed by more then fifty *Portugals*, amongst whom were the four Captains that I sought for, namely, *Lançerote Guerreyra, Antonio Gomez, Pedro Ferreyra,* and *Cosmo Bernaldes.* When I had read this Letter, I made a tender of my person to this petty King, for otherwayes my power was so small, as it could not reach further then to the giving him a bad dinner, and a red Bonnet I had on, which all worn as it was, was yet better then his own. Now after this poor King had made some Declaration to me of himself, and of his miseries, lifting up his hands to Heaven, and shedding abundance of tears; *Our Lord Jesus Christ,* said he unto me, *whose slave I am, doth know what great need I have now of the favour and succour of some Christians, for because I am a Christian, as they are, a* Mahometan *slave of mine about four months ago, reduced me to that extremity, wherein I behold my self at this instant, being not able in the state I am in to do any other then cast up mine eyes to Heaven, and lament my misfortune, with much sorrow, and little remedy. And I assure thee by the verity of that holy and new Law, whereof I now make profession, that only for being a Christian, and a friend to the* Portugals, *I am persecuted in this sort. Now for that being alone, as thou art, it is not possible for thee to assist me; I beseech thee, Signior, to take me along with thee, to the end that this Soul which God hath put into me may not perish, and in recompence thereof I promise to serve thee as a slave all the dayes of my life.* Lo this is that which this poor King said with so many tears, as it was great pity to behold it, in the mean time the *Necoda*, who was of a good disposition, and charitably inclined, was very much moved with the disaster of this unfortunate King, so that he gave him a little Rice, and some linnen to cover himself withall, for he was so ragged, that one might see his naked skin every where about him. After he had informed himself from him of certain particulars, the knowledge whereof concerned him, he demanded him where his enemy was, and what forces he had? Whereunto he answered, That he was a quarter of a league from thence, in a Cabbin covered with straw, having not above thirty fisher-men with him, who were most of them without Arms. Hereupon the *Necoda* cast his eye upon me, and seeing me sad, for that I was not able of my self to succour this poor Christian, thinking withall that he should much oblige me thereby, *Signior*, said he unto me, *if thou wert now Captain of this Junck, as I am, what remedy wouldst thou give to the tears of this poor man, wherewith also thy eyes do participate?* I knew not what reply to make him, for that I was greatly moved to behold my Neighbour, a Christian like my self, to suffer in that manner, which the

14

Nece-

Necoda's son perceiving, who was, as I have said, a young man of a good spirit, and brought up amongst the *Portugals*, and guessing at the shame and sorrow I was in, he desired his father to lend him twenty Mariners of his Junck, that by their means he might re-establish this poor King, and chase the Thief out of the Island; To this the *Necoda* answered, That if I would demand so much of him, he would do it very willingly; whereupon casting my self at his feet and embracing him, which is the humblest complement used amongst them, I told him with tears in my eyes, that if he would do me this favour I would be his slave whilest I lived, and that both he and his children should find how ready I would be always to acknowledg the same; He presently granted my request, so that causing the Junck to approach near the shoar, he prepared himself in three Boats with one Faulcon, three Bases, and threescore Men, *Jaos* and *Lesons*, all well armed, for thirty of them carried Harquebuses, the rest Lances, and Bows and Arrows, besides Grenadoes, and other such like Fireworks, as we thought were convenient for our design.

§.3.   It was about two of the clock in the afternoon when we landed, and so we went directly to the Trench where the Enemies were. The *Necoda's* son led the Vauntgard, consisting of forty men, whereof twenty were armed with Harquebuses, and the rest with Bows and Arrows; The *Necoda* himself brought on the Rere, wherein were thirty Soldiers, carrying a Banner, which *Pedro de Faria* had given him at his parting from *Malaca*, with a cross painted in it, to the end he might be known for a Vassal to our King, in case he should encounter any of our Ships. Marching in this order by the guiding of this petty King, we arrived where the Rebel was with his men set in order, who by their shouting and cries seemed in shew not to make any reckoning of us. They were in number about fifty, but weak, unarmed, and utterly destitute of all things necessary for their defence, having for all their Arms but Staves, ten or eleven Lances, and one Harquebuse. As soon as we had discovered them we gave fire to the Faulcon and Bases, discharging withall twenty Harquebuses, whereupon the Theeves betook themselves presently to flight, being in great disorder, and most of them hurt; We pursued them then so close, that we overtook them on the top of a little hill, where they were defeated in the space of two *credoes*, not one of them escaping with life save only three, whom we spared for that they said they were Christians. That done, we went to a Village, where there were not above twenty poor low Cabbins, covered with straw; in it we found some threescore and four women, with a many of little children, who no sooner perceived us, but all of them with tears fell a cryed out, *Christian, Christian, Jesus, Jesus.* At these words being fully perswaded that they were Christians, I desired the *Necoda* that he would cause his son to retire, and not suffer any of them to be killed because they were not Gentiles, which he presently yielded unto, and yet for all that he could not keep the Cabbins from sacking, though in them all there was not found the value of five Duckets. For the people of this Island are so poor, that scarce one of them is worth a groat; they feed on nothing but a little fish, which they take with angling, and eat it broiled on the coals without salt, yet are they so vain and presumptuous, that not one almost amongst them but terms himself a King of some vile piece of ground, whereon there is little more then one poor Cabbin; besides, neither the men nor the women have wherewithall to cover their nakedness. After the slaughter of the rebellious *Sarrazin* and his followers, and the re-establishment of the poor Christian King, putting him in possession of his wife and children, whom his Enemy had made slaves, together with above threescore and three Christian Souls, we ordeined a kind of Church amongst them, for the instruction of those that were newly converted; And then returning to our Junck, we presently set sail, and continued our course towards *Tanauçarim*, where I was perswaded I should find *Lancerote Guerreyra*, and his companions, for to treat with them about the business, whereof I have formerly spoken: But for as much as in the Letter, which the petty King shewed me, the *Portugals* made mention of a Victory which God had given them against the *Turks* and *Achems* of this Coast, I hold it not amiss to relate here show that hapned, as well for the content the Reader may take therein, as to shew that there is no enterprize which valiant Soldiers at a need may not bring to pass, in regard whereof it imports much to cherish, and make esteem of them. For eight months and more our hundred *Portugals* had scoured up and down this Coast in four well rig'd Foists, wherewith they had taken three and twenty rich Ships, and many other lesser Vessels, so that they which used to sail in those parts were so terrified with the sole name of the *Portugals*, as they quitted their

Commerce

Commerce without making any further use of their shipping : By this surcease of Trade the Custom-houses of the Ports of *Tanauçarim*, *Junçalan*, *Merguim*, *Vagaruu*, and *Tavay*, fell much in their Revenue, in so much that those people were constrained to give notice of it to the Emperor of *Sornau*, King of *Siam*, and soveraign Lord of all that Country, beseeching him to give a remedy to this mischief, whereof every one complained. Instantly whereupon, being then at the City of *Odiaa*, he sent with all speed to the Frontire of *Lauhos* for a Turkish Captain of his, named *Heredrin Mahomet*, the same who in the year one thousand five hundred thirty and eight came from *Suez* to the Army of *Soliman* the *Bashaw*, Vice-roy of *Cairo*, when as the great *Turk* sent him to invade the *Indiaes* ; but it fell out that this man slipping from the body of the Army arrived in a Gally on the Coast of *Tanauçarim*, where he was entertained by the *Sornau* King of *Siam*, and for a Pention of twelve thousand Duckets by the year served him as a General of that Frontire. Now for that the King held this *Turk* for invincible, and made more account of him then of all others, he commanded him from the place where he was, with three hundred *Janizaries* that he had with him, and giving him a great sum of mony he made him General of all the Coast of this Sea, to the end he might free those people from our incursions, withall he promised to make him Duke of *Banchaa*, which is an estate of great extent, if he could bring him the heads of four *Portugal* Captains. This proud *Turk*, becomming more insolent by the reward and promises which the King made him posted presently away to *Tanauçarim*, where being arrived he rigged forth a Fleet of ten Sails for to fight with us, being so confident of vanquishing us, as in answer of certain Letters, which the *Sornau* had written unto him from *Odiaa*, these words was found in one of them. *From the time that my head was esloigned from the feet of your Highness for to execute this small enterprize, wherein it seems you are pleased I should serve you, I continued my Voyage till at the end of nine days I arrived at* Tanaucarim, *where I presently provided my self of such Vessels as were necessary for me, and indeed would have had but only two, for I hold it most infallible that those would suffice to chase away these petty Thieves ; howbeit not to disobey the Commission, which* Combracalon *the Governor of the Empire hath given me under your great Seal, I have made ready the great Gally, as also the four little ones, and the five Foists, with which I purpose to set forth with all speed ; For I fear lest these Dogs should have news of my coming, and that for my sins God should be so much their friend, as to give them leasure to fly, which would be so great a grief unto me, that the very imagination thereof might be my death, or through an excess of despair render me like unto them ; but I hope that the Prophet* Mahomet, *of whose Law I have made profession from mine infancy, will not permit that it should so happen for my sins.* This *Heredrin Mahomet* being arrived at *Tanauçarim*, as I have delivered before, presently made ready his Fleet, which was composed of five Foists, four Galliots, and one Gally Royal : Within these Vessels he imbarqued eight hundred *Mahometans*, men of combat (besides the Mariners,) amongst the which were three hundred *Janizaries*, as for the rest they were *Turks*, *Greeks*, *Malabares*, *Achems*, and *Mogores*, all choyce men, and so disciplined, that their Captain held the Victory already for most assured ; Assisted with these Forces he parted from the Port of *Tanauçarim* for to go in the quest of our men, who at that time were in this Island of *Pulbo Hinhor*, whereof the foresaid Christian was King. Now during those levies of men of War, this petty King going to the Town for to sell some dryed fish there, as soon as he perceived what was intended against us, he left all his Commodities behind him, and in all haste returned to this Island of his ; where finding our men in great security, as little dreaming of that which was in hand against us, he related it all unto them, whereat they remained so much amazed, as the importance of the matter did require ; In so much that the same night and the next day having well caulked their Vessels which they had drawn ashore, they lanched them into the Sea, after they had imbarqued their provisions, their water, their artillery, and ammunition. So falling to their oars, with a purpose (as I have heard them say since) to get to *Bengala*, or to *Racan*, for that they durst not withstand so great an Army ; but as they were unresolved thereupon, and divided in opinion, behold they saw all the ten Sails appearing together, and behind them five great Ships of *Guzarates*, whose Masters had given *Heredrin Mahomet* thirty thousand Duckets for to secure them against our *Portugals*. The sight of these fifteen Sails put our men into a very great confusion, and because they were not able at that time to make to Sea for that the wind was contrary, they put themselves into a Creek, which was on the South-side of the Island, and invironned

ronned

ronned by a Dowh, or Hill, where they resolved to attend what God would send them: In the mean time the five *Guzarat* Ships shewed themselves with full sails at Sea, and the ten Sails with oars went directly to the Island, where they arrived about Sun-set. Presently thereupon the *Turkish* Captain sent out Spies to the Ports, where he was advertised that they had been, and entered by little and little into the mouth of the Haven, that so he might render himself more assured of the prize which he pretended to make, with hope that as soon as it was day he should take them all, and so bound hand and foot present them to the *Sornau* of *Siam*, who in recompence thereof had promised him the State of *Banchaa*, as I have said before. The *Manchua*, which had been at the Port to spy them out, returned to the Fleet about two hours within night, and told *Heredin* for news, that they were fled and gone, wherewith it is said this Barbarian was so afflicted, that teering his hair, *I always feared,* said he weeping, *my sins would be the cause that in the execution of this enterprize God would shew himself more a Christian, then a Sarazin, and that Mahomet would be like to these Dogs, of whom I go in quest.* This said, he fell down all along in the place, and so continued a good while without speaking a word. Nevertheless being come again to himself he gave order, like a good Captain, to all that was necessary. First of all then he sent the four Galliots in quest of them to an Island, called *Taubasoy*, distant from that of *Pulho Hinhor* about seven leagues, for he was perswaded that our men were retired thither, because this was a better Harbor then that of the Island from whence they were gone. As for the five Foists he divided them into three, whereof he sent two to another Island, named *Sambilan*, and other two to those which were nearest to the firm Land, for that all these places were very proper to shelter one in; As for the fifth Foist, in regard she was fleeter then the rest, he sent her along with the four Galliots, that she might before it was day bring him news of that which should happen, with promise of great reward for the same; but during these things our men, who had always a watchful eye, seeing the *Turk* had rid himself of his greatest Forces, and that there was no more remaining with him but the Gally wherein he was, they resolved to fight with him, and so sallying out of the Creek, where they had shrouded themselves, they rowed directly to her. Now in regard it was past midnight, and that the Enemies had but weak Sentinels, for that they thought themselves most secure, and never dreamt of any body lying in wait to attaque them there, our four Foists had the opportunity to board her all together, and threescore of their lustiest men leaping suddenly into her, in less then a quarter of an hour, and before the Enemies knew where they were for to make use of their Arms, they killed above fourscore *Turks*, as for the rest they cast themselves all into the Sea, not one man remaining alive: The dog *Heredin Mahomet* was slain amongst the rest, and in this great action God was so gracious to our men, and gave them this Victory at so cheap a rate, that they had but one young man killed, and nine *Portugals* hurt. They assured me since, that in this Gally in so short a time, what by water, and the sword, above three hundred *Mahometans* lost their lives, whereof the most part were Janizaries of the Gold Chain, which among the *Turks* is a mark of honor. Our *Portugals* having past the rest of the night with much contentment, and always keeping good watch, it pleased God that the next morning the two Foists arrived from the Island whither they had been sent, who altogether ignorant of that which had past, came carelesly doubling the point of the Haven, where the Gally lay, so that the four Foists made themselves Masters of them in a little space, and with the loss of but a few men. After so good a success they fell diligently to work in fortifying the Gally and the two Foists, which they had taken, and then flanked the South-side of the Island with five great Pieces of Ordnance to defend the entry into the Haven. Now about evening the other two Foists arrived, making to Land with the same indiscretion as the others, and although they had much ado to reach them, yet were they constrained at length to render themselves, with the loss only of two *Portugals*. Hereupon our men resolved to attend the four Galliots that remained, and which had been sent to the next Island, but the next day so great a wind arose from the North, that two of them were cast away upon the Coast, not one that was in them escaping. As for the other two about evening they discovered them very much in disorder, destitute of oars, and separated above three leagues the one from the other; But at last about Sun-set one of them came to the Port, and ran the same fortune as the former, without saving any one of the *Sarazins* lives. The next morning an hour before day, the wind being very calm, our men discovered the other Galliot, which for want of oars was not able to recover the Port, in

regard

regard whereof our men refolved to go and fetch her in, as accordingly they did, and coming fomewhat near her with two Cannon fhot, they killed the moft part of them that were in her, and fo bording her took her very eafily ; Now becaufe all her men were either flain, or hurt, they drew her to land by force of other Boats ; fo that of the ten Sail of this Fleet, our men had the Gally, two Galliots, and four Foyfts ; as for the other two Galliots, they were caft away on the Ifle of *Taubafoy*, as I have delivered before, and touching the fift Foyft, no news could be heard of her, which made it credible that fhe alfo fuffered fhipwrack, or that the wind had caft her upon fome of the other Iflands. This glorious victory, which it pleafed God to give us, was obtained in the month of *September*, one thoufand, five hundred, forty and four, on *Michaelmas* Eve, which rendred the name of the *Portugals* fo famous through all thofe Coafts, that for three years after there was nothing elfe fpoken of, fo that the *Chaubainhaa*, King of *Martabano* hearing of it, fent prefently to feek them out, and promifed them great advantages if they would fuccour him againft the King of *Bramaa*, who at that time was making preparation in his City of *Pegu*, for to go and befiege *Martabano*, with an Army of feven hundred thoufand men.

CHAP. L.

The Continuance of our voyage to the Bar of Martabano ; *and certain memorable particularities hapening there.*

BEing departed, as I faid, from the Ifland of *Pulho Hinbor*, we continued our courfe towards the Port of *Tarnaffery* for the affair, of which I have fpoken, but upon the approach S. I. of the night, the Pilot defiring to avoid certain fands that were to the Prow-ward of him, put forth to Sea, with an intention as foon as it was day to return towards land with the Wefterly wind, which at that inftant blew from the *Indiaes* by reafon of the Seafon. We had now held this courfe five dayes, running with much labour by many different roombs, when as it pleafed God that we accidentally difcovered a little veffel, and for as much as we thought it to be a Fifher-boat, we made to it, for to be informed from them in her whereabouts we were, and how many leagues it was from thence to *Tarnaffery*, but having paffed clofe by her, and haled her without receiving any anfwer, we fent off a Shallop well furnifhed with men for to compel her to come abord us : Our Boat then going directly to the veffel, we entred her, but were much amazed to find in her only five *Portugals*, two dead, and three alive, with a Coffer, and a fack full of *Tangues*, and *Larius*, which is the mony of that Country, and a fardle, wherein there were Bafins and Ewers of filver, and two other very great Bafins. Having laid up all this fafely, I caufed the *Portugals* to be brought into our Junck, where looking very carefully unto them, yet could I not in two dayes get one word from them ; But at length by the means of yolks of egs, and good broaths, which I made them take, they came again to themfelves, fo that in fix or feven dayes they were able to render me a reafon of their accident. One of thofe *Portugals* was called *Chriftovano Doria*, who was fince fent into this Country for a Captain to faint *Tomé* ; the other *Luys Tabo da*, and the third *Simano de Brito*, all men of credit, and rich Merchants. Thefe fame recounted unto us, that coming from the *Indiaes* in a veffel belonging to *Jorge Manhoz*, that was married at *Goa*, with a purpofe to go to the Port of *Charingan*, in the Kingdom of *Bengala*, they were caft away in the fands of *Rucano* for want of taking heed, fo that of fourfcore perfons, that they were in the veffel, onely feventeen being faved, they had continued their courfe all along by the Coaft for five dayes together, intending if poffibly they could to recover the river of *Cofmira* in the Kingdom of *Pegu*, there to fhip themfelves for the *Indiaes* in fome veffel or other that they fhould meet with in the Port ; but whileft they were in this refolution, they were fo driven by a moft impetuous Wefterly wind, that in one day and a night they loft the fight of Land, finding themfelves in the main Sea without Oars, without Sayls, and all knowledge of the wind, they continued in that State fixteen dayes together, at the end whereof their water coming to fail, all died but thofe three he faw before him. Upon the finifhing of this relation we proceeded on in our courfe, and within four days after we met with five *Portugal* veffels, which were fayling from *Bengala* to *Malaca*. Having fhewed them *Pedro de Faria's* Order, I defired them to keep in confort together for fear of the *Achems* Army, that ranged all over the Coaft, left through their imprudence they fhould fall into any mifchief, and thereof I demanded a Certificate from them, which they willingly

granted,

granted, as also furnished me very plentifully with all things necessary. Having made this dispatch we continued our course, and nine days after we arrived at the Bar of *Martabano*, on a *Friday*, the seven and twentieth of *March*, one thousand, five hundred, forty and five, having past by *Tarnassery*, *Tovay*, *Merguin*, *Juncay*, *Pullo*, *Camuda*, and *Vagaruu*, without hearing any tidings of those hundred *Portugals*, in search of whom I went, because that before that they had taken pay in the service of the *Chaubainhaa*, King of *Martabano*, who, according to report, had sent for them to assist him against the King of *Bramaa*, that held him besieged with an Army of seven hundred thousand men, as I have declared before; howbeit they were not at this time in his Service, as we shall see presently.

§.2.   It was almost two hours within night, when we arrived at the mouth of the River, where we cast anchor with a resolution to go up the next day to the City; Having continued some time very quiet, we ever and anon heard many Cannon shot, whereat we were so troubled, as we knew not what to resolve on; As soon as the Sun rose, the *Nicoda* assembled his men to Councel, for in Semblable occasions he always used so to do, and told them, that as sure as they were all to have a share in the peril, so it was fit that every one should give his advice about it; Then he made them a Speech, wherein he represented unto them that which they had heard that night, and how in regard thereof he feared to go unto the City. Their opinions upon it were very different, howbeit at length they concluded, that their eyes were to be witnesses of that whereof they stood in such doubt: To this end we set Sail, having both wind and tyde, and doubled a point, called *Mounay*, from whence we discovered the City, invironed with a world of men, and upon the River almost as many vessels, and although we suspected what this might be, because we had heard something of it, yet left we not off from sayling to the Port, where we arrrived with a great deal of care, and having discharged our Ordnance according to the usual manner in signe of peace, we perceived a vessel very well furnished, came directly to us from the shore, wherein there was six *Portugals*, at which we exceedingly rejoyced; These presently came abord our Junck, where they were very well entertained, & having declared unto us what we were to do for the safety of our persons, they councelled us not to budge from thence for any thing in the world, as we had told them our resolutiono was to have fled that night to *Bengala*, because if we had followed that designe, we had assuredly been lost, and taken by the Fleet which the King of *Brama* had in that place, consisting of seventeen hundred Sayls, wherein were comprised an hundred Gallies very well furnished with strangers. They added withall, that they were of opinion I should go ashore with them to *Joan Cayeyro*, who was Captain of the *Portugals*, for to give him an account of the cause that brought me thither, the rather for that he was a man of a sweet disposition, and a great friend of *Pedro de Faria*'s, to whom they had often heard him give much commendation, as well for his noble extraction, as for the goodly qualities that were in him; besides they told me that I should find *Lançarote Gueyreyro*, and the rest of the Captains with him, unto whom my aforesaid Letters were directed, and that I should do nothing therein prejudicial to the Service of God, and the King. This counsel seeming good unto me, I went presently to land with the *Portugals* to wait on *Joano Cayeyro*, to whom I was exceeding welcome, as likewise to all the rest that were in his quarters, to the number of seven hundred *Portugals*, all rich men, and of good esteem. Then I shewed *Joano Cayeyro* my Letters, and the Order that *Pedro de Faria* had given me; Moreover I treated with him about the affair that led me thither: whereupon I observed that he was very instant with the Captains, to whom I was addrest, who answered him that they were ready to serve the King in all occasions that should be presented, howbeit since the Letter of *Pedro de Faria*, Governour of *Malaca*, was grounded on the fear that he was in of the Army of the *Achems*, composed of an hundred and thirty Sayl, whereof *Bijaya Sora* King of *Pedir*, was General, and it having fallen out, that his Admiral had been defeated at *Tarnasery* by those of the Country, with the loss of seventy *Lanchares*, and six thousand men, it was not needful they should stir for that occasion; for according to what they had seen with their own eyes, the Forces of that enemy were so mightily weakned, as they did not think he could in ten years space recover again the loss he had sustained. To this they added many other reasons, which made them all to agree, that it was not necessary they should go to *Malaca*. After these things I desired *Joano Cayeyro* to make me a Declaration of all that had past in this business, that it might serve me as it were for a Certificate at my return to our Fortress, determining as soon as I had it to get me from this place, for that I had nothing more to do there. With this resolution I stayed there with *Joano Cayeyro*, in

continual

continual expectation to be gone when the Season should serve for the Junck to depart, and remained with him at this Siege the space of six and forty days, which was the chief time of the King of *Bramaa* his abode there, of whom I will say something here in a few words, because I conceive the curious would be well content to know what success the *Chaubainhaa*, King of *Martabano*, had in this war. This Siege had lasted now six months and thirteen dayes, in which space the City had been assaulted five times in plain-day, but the besieged defended themselves always very valiantly, and like men of great courage: Howbeit in regard they were insensibly consumed with length of time, and the success of war, and that no succour came to them from any part, their enemies were without comparison far more in number then they, in such sort as the *Chaubainhaa* found himself so destitute of men, as it was thought he had not above five thousand souldiers left in the City, the hundred and thirty thousand which were said to be there at the beginning of the Siege, being consumed by Famine, or the Sword, by reason whereof the Councel assembling for to deliberate what was to be done thereupon, it was resolved that the King should sound his enemy by his Interest, which he presently put in execution: For that effect he sent to tell him, that if he would raise the Siege he would give him thirty thousand Bisses of silver, which is in value a million of gold, and would become his Tributary at threescore thousand Duckets by the year. The answer made by the King of *Bramaa* hereunto was, that he could accept of no conditions from him, if he did not first yield himself to his mercy. The second time he propounded unto him, that if he would suffer him to depart away with two ships, in one of the which should be his Treasure, and in the other his Wife and Children, that then he would deliver him the City, and all that was in it. But the King of *Bramaa* would hearken no more to that then the former. The third Proposition which he made him was this, That he should retire with his Army to *Tagalaa*, some six leagues off, that so he might have liberty to go away freely with all his, and thereupon he would deliver him the City, and the Kingdom, together with all the Treasure belonging to the King his Predecessour, or that in lieu thereof he would give him three millions of gold: But he also refused this last offer, insomuch that the *Chaubainhaa* utterly dispairing of ever making his peace with so cruel an enemy, began to meditate with himself what means he might use to save himself from him; Having long thought upon it he found no better an expedient then therein to serve himself of the succour of the *Portugals*, for he was perswaded that by their means he might escape the present danger. He sent them secretly to tell *Joano Cayero*, that if he would imbarque himself in the night in his four ships, and take him in, with his wife, and children, and so save them, he would give him half his treasure. In this affair he very closely imployed a certain *Portugal*, named *Paulo de Seixas*, born in the Town of *Obidos*, who at that time was with him in the City; This same having disguised himself in a *Pegu* habit, that he might not be known, stole one night to *Cayeroy's* Tent, and delivered him a Letter from the *Chaubainhaa*, wherein this was contained: *Valiant and faithful Commander of the* Portugals, *through the Grace of the great King of the other end of the world, the strong and mighty Lion, dreadfully roaring, with a Crown of Majesty in the House of the Sun, I the unhappy* Chaubainhaa, *heretofore a Prince, but now no longer so, finding my self besieged in this wretched and infortunate City, do give thee to understand by the words pronounced out of my mouth, with an assurance no less faithful then true, that I now render my self the Vassel of the great King of* Portugal, *Soveraign Lord of me, and my children, with an acknowledgement of homage, and such tribute as he at his pleasure shall impose on me: Wherefore I require thee on his behalf, that as soon as* Paulo Seixas *shall present this my Letter unto thee, thou come speedily with thy Ships to the Bulwark of the* Chappel-key, *where thou shalt find me ready attending thee, and then without taking further counsel, I will deliver my self up to thy mercy, with all the treasures that I have in gold, and precious stones, whereof I will most willingly give the one half to the King of* Portugal, *upon condition that he shall permit me with the remainder to leavy in his Kingdom, or in the Fortresses which he hath in the* Indies, *two thousand* Portugals, *to whom I will give extraordinary great pay that by their means I may be re-established in this State, which now I am constrained to abandon; since my ill fortune will have it so. As for that which concerns thee, and thy men, I do promise them by the faith of my verity, that in case they do help to save me, I will divide my treasure so liberally among them, that all of them shall be very well satisfied and contented; And for that time, will not suffer me to enlarge any further;* Paulo de Seixas, *by whom I send this unto thee, shall assure thee both of that which he hath seen, and of the rest*

which

which I have communicated unto him. Joano Cayeyro had no sooner received this Letter, but he presently caused the chief of his followers secretly to assemble together in Councel. Having shewed them the Letter, he represented unto them how important and profitable it would be for the service of God and the King to accept of the offer, which the Chaubain-haa had made them ; Whereupon causing an Oath to be given to Paulo de Seixas, he willed him freely to declare all his knowledg of the matter, and whether it were true that the Chaubainhaa his Treasure was so great, as it was reported to be. Thereunto he answered by the Oath that he had taken, That he knew not certainly how great his Treasure was, but that he was well assured how he had often seen with his own eyes, an house in form of a Church, and of a reasonable bigness, all full up to the very tyles of bars and wedges of Gold, which might very well lade two great Ships : He further said, That he had moreover seen six and twenty Chests bound about with strong cords, wherein according to the Chaubain-haa his own report was the Treasure of the deceased Bresaguean King of Pegu, which said Treasure containing an hundred and thirty thousand Bisses, and every Bis in value five hundred Duckets, made up all together the sum of threescore Millions of Gold : He said also, That he knew not certainly the number of the wedges of Gold which he had seen in the Temple of the God of Thunder, but he was most assured notwithstanding that they would fully lade four good Vessels : And for a conclusion he told them, That the same Chaubain-haa had shewed him the golden Image of Quiay Frigau, which was taken at Degum, all full of such rich and resplendent stones, as it was thought the like again were not in the whole world ; So that this Declaration which this man made upon Oath astonished them so that heard it, as they could not possibly beleeve it to be true. Howbeit after they had sent him out of the Tent, they entered into consultation about this affair, wherein nothing was resolved, of which I verily beleeve our sins were the cause, for there were in this Assembly as many different opinions, as Babel had diversities of Languages, which proceeded especi-ally from the envy of six or seven men there present, who would needs perswade the rest, that if this affair should happen to have such success, as was hoped for, Ioano Cayeyro (unto whom they all bore no good will) would go then into Portugal with so much honor and reputation, as it would be a small matter for the King to make him an Earl, or a Marquis, or at least recompence him with the Government of the Indiaes ; so that after these Mini-sters of the Devil had alledged many reasons wherefore it might not be done, which I think was but the mask of their weakness and ill nature, though it may be they did it out of the fear they were in of losing both their goods and lives if this matter should come to be dis-covered to the King of Bramaa; howsoever they would not agree to accept of this offer, but contrariwise they threatened Juano Cayeyro, that if he desisted not from his purpose, which was to comply with the Chaubainhaa, they would disclose it to the Bramaa, so that Cayeyro was constrained to abandon this business, lest if he should persist therein the Portugals them-selves would discover him, as they threatened to do, without either fear of God, or regard of men.

§.3. Joana Cayeyro, seeing he could not possibly bring his desire to pass, wrote a Letter to the Caubainhaa, wherein he used many weak excuses for not performing that which he de-manded of him, and giving it to Paulo de Seixas, he speedily dispatched him away with it, so that departing about three hours after midnight he arrived safe at the City, where he found the Caubainhaa attending him in the same place which he had named in his Letter, unto whom he delivered the Answer he had brought ; After he had read it, and thereby found that he could not be succored by our men, as he always thought he should, it is said that he remained so confounded, that for very grief and sorrow he sunk down to the ground like a dead man, and continuing a pretty while in that manner, at length he came again to himself, and then beating his brest, and bewailing his miserable fortune, *Ah Portugals,* said he with tears in his eyes, *how ill do you acknowledg that which I have done for you, ima-gining that thereby I should make acquisition of your friendship, as of a treasure, to the end that like faithful men you would be assisting to me in so great a necessity as this is which now I am in, whereby I desired no other thing then to save my childrens lives, inrich your King, and state you in the number of my chiefest friends ? And would it had pleased him, who raigns in the beauty of these stars, that you had merited before him the doing me this good office, which only for my sins you have refused me, for in so doing you had by my means augmented his Law, and I been saved in the promises of his truth.* Thereupon sending away Paulo de Seixas, with a
young

young Wench, by whom he had had two sons, he gave him a pair of Bracelets, and said unto him, *I desire thee not to think of this little which now I give thee, but of the great love I have always born thee; above all, forget not to tell the Portugals, with how much cause and grief I complain of their extream ingratitude, whereof I will render them culpaple before God at the last and dreadful day of Judgment.* The night following *Paul de Seixas* came back to the *Portugals,* with two children, and a very fair young Damosal their Mother, with whom he married afterwards at *Coromandel,* and shewed to *Simon de Binto,* and *Pedro de Bruges,* Lapidares, the Bracelets which the *Chaubainhaa* had given him, who buying them of him payd six and thirty thousand Duckets for them, and had afterwards fourscore thousand for them of *Trimira Raia* Governor of *Narsingua.* Five days after *Paulo de Seixas* coming to the Camp, where he recounted all that I have related before, the *Chaubainhaa,* seeing himself destitute of all humane remedy, advised with his Councel what course he should take in so many misfortunes, that dayly in the neck of one another fell upon him, and it was resolved by them to put to the sword all things living that were not able to fight, and with the blood of them to make a Sacrifice to *Quiay Nivandel,* God of Battels, then to cast all the treasure into the Sea, that their Enemies might make no benefit of it, afterward to set the whole City on fire, and lastly that all those which were able to bear arms should make themselves *Amoucos,* that is to say, men resolved either to dye, or vanquish, in fighting with the *Bramaas.* The *Chaubainhaa* very much approved this counsel, and concluding of it accordingly they fell presently to the demolishing of houses, and were preparing all other things for the effecting of their design, when as one of the three principal Commanders of the City, apprehending that which was to follow the next day, fled the night ensuing to the Enemies Camp, and there rendered himself with four thousand men under his leading to the *Bramaa;* Hereupon the courages of all the rest were so abated by such a strange infidelity and flight, that not one of them cared afterwards either to keep watch, maintain the breaches, or do any other service whatsoever, but contrarily all that remained stuck not to say publiquely, that if the *Chaubainhaa* would not suddenly resolve to yield himself to the *Bramaa,* they would open the gates and let him in, for that it would be better for them to dye so, then to languish and consume away like rotten beasts as they did; The *Chaubainhaa* seeing them stifly bent thereunto for to appease them answered, that he would perform their desire, howbeit withall he caused a review to be made of those that would fight, but he found them to be not above two thousand in all, and they too so destitute of courage, as they could hardly have resisted feeble women: Beholding himself then reduced to the last cast, he communicated his mind to the Queen only, as having no other at that time by whom he may be advised, or that indeed could advise him; The only expedient then that he could rest on, was to render himself into the hands of his Enemy, and to stand to his mercy, or his rigor. Wherefore the next day about six of the clock in the morning he caused a white flag to be hung out over the wall in sign of peace, whereunto they of the Camp answered with another like banner; Hereupon the *Xenimbrum,* who was as it were Marshal of the Camp, sent an horseman to the bulwark, where the flag stood, unto whom it was delivered from the top of the wall, That the *Chaubainhaa* desired to send a Letter to the King, so as he might have a safe-conduct for it, which being signified to the *Xenimbrum,* he instantly dispatched away two of good quality in the Army with a safe-conduct, and so these two *Bramaas* remaining for hostages in the City, the *Chaubainhaa* sent the King a Letter by one of his Priests, that was fourscore years of age, and reputed for a Saint amongst them. The contents of this Letter were these: *The love of children hath so much power in this house of our weakness, that amongst us, who are fathers, there is not so much as one that for their sakes would not be well contented to descend a thousand times into the deep pit of the house of the Serpent, much more would expose his life for them, and put himself into the hands of one that useth so much clemency towards them that shall do so: For which reason I resolved this night with my wife and children, contrary to the opinions that would disswade me from this good, which I hold the greatest of all others, to render my self unto your Highness, that you may do with me as you think fit, and as shall be most agreeable to your good pleasure. As for the fault, wherewith I may be charged, and which I submit at your feet, I humbly beseech you not to regard it, that so the merit of the mercy, which you shall shew me, may be the greater before God and men. May your Highness therefore be pleased to send some presently for to take possession of my person, of my wife, of my children, of the City, of the Treasure, and of all the Kingdom; all which I do*

even

even now yield up unto you, *as to my Soveraign Lord, and lawful King. All the request that I have to make unto you thereupon with my knees on the ground, is, that we may all of us with your permission finish our days in a Cloister, where I have already vowed continually to bewail and repent my fault past ; For as touching the honors and estates of the world, wherewith your Highness might inrich me, as Lord of the most part of the Earth, and of the Isles of the Sea, they are things which I utterly renounce for evermore. In a word, I do solemnly swear unto you before the greatest of all the Gods, who with the gentle touch of his Almighty hand makes the Clouds of Heaven to move, never to leave that Religion which by your pleasure I shall be commanded to profess, where being freed from the vain hopes of the world, my repentance may be the more pleasing to him that pardoneth all things. This holy* Grepo, *Dean of the golden House of Saint* Quiay, *who for his goodness and austerity of life hath all power over me, will make a more ample relation unto you of what I have omitted, and can more particularly tell you that which concerns the offer I make you of rendring my self, that so relying on the reality of his Speech, the unquietness wherewith my soul is incessantly troubled may be appeased.* The King of *Bramaa* having read this Letter instantly returned another in answer thereunto full of promises and oaths to this effect, *That he would forget all that was past, and that for the future he would provide him an estate of so great a Revenue, as should very well content him :* Which he but badly accomplished, as I shall declare hereafter. These news was published throughout all the Camp with a great deal of joy, and the next morning all the Equipage and Train that the King had in his quarter was set forth to view : First of all there were to be seen fourscore and six Field-Tents, wonderful rich, each of them being invironed with thirty Elephants, ranked in two Files, as if they had been ready to fight, with Castles on their backs full of Banners, and their *Panores* fastened to their Trunks, the whole number of them amounted unto two thousand, five hundred, and fourscore : Not far from them were twelve thousand and five hundred *Bramaas,* all mounted on horses, very richly accoustred ; with the order, which they kept, they inclosed all the Kings quarter in four Files, and were all armed in Corslets, or Coats of Mayl, with Lances, Cymitars, and guilded Bucklers. After these Horse followed four Files of Foot, all *Bramaas,* being in number above twenty thousand. For all the other Souldiers of the Camp there were so many as they could not be counted, and they marched all in order after their Captains. In this publique Muster were to be seen a world of Banners, & rich colours, & such a number of Instruments of war sounded, that the noise thereof, together with that which the Souldiers made, was most dreadful, and so great as it was not possible to hear one another. Now for that the King of *Bramaa* would this day make shew of his greatness in the reddition of the *Chaubainhaa,* he gave express Command, that all the Captains which were strangers, with their men, should put on their best clothes, and Arms, and so ranged in two Files, they should make as it were a kind of street, through which the *Chaubainhaa* might pass ; this accordingly was put in execution ; and this street took beginning from the City gate, and reached as far as to the Kings Tent, being in length about three quarters of a League, or better : In this street there were six and thirty thousand strangers of two and forty different Nations, namely *Portugals, Grecians, Venetians, Turks, Janizaries, Jews, Armenians, Tartars, Mogores, Abyssins, Raizbutos, Nobins, Coracones, Persians, Tuparaas, Gizares, Tanacos, Malabares, Jaos, Achems, Moens, Siams, Luffons* of the Island *Borneo, Chacomas, Arracons, Predins, Papuaas, Selebres, Mindancas, Pegus, Bramaas,* and many others whose names I know not. All these Nations were ranked according to the *Xemimbrums* order, whereby the *Portugals* were placed in the Vantgard, which was next to the gate of the City where the *Chabainhaa* was to come ; After them followed the *Armenians,* then the *Janizaries* and *Turks,* and so the rest.

CHAP. LI.

In what manner the Chaubainhaa *rendred himself to the King of* Bramaa, *and the cruel proceeding against the Queen of* Martabano, *and the Ladies, her Attendants.*

ABout one of the clock in the afternoon a Cannon was shot off, which was the Signal for § 1 the instant opening of the gates of the City, whereupon first of all issued out the Souldiers, whom the King had sent thither for the guard of it, being four thousand *Siams* and *Bramaas*, all Harquebusiers, Halberdiers, and Pikemen, with above three hundred armed Elephants; all which were commanded by a *Bramaa*, Uncle to the King, named *Monpocasser*, *Bainha* of the City of *Melietay*; Ten or eleven paces after this Guard of Elephants marched divers Princes, and great Lords, whom the King had sent to receive the *Chaubainhaa*, all mounted on Elephants, richly harnessed, with Chairs upon their backs, plated over with gold, and Collars of precious stones about their necks; Then followed at some eight or nine paces distance the *Rolim* of *Monnay*, Soveraign *Talapoy* of all the Priests of the Kingdom, and held in the reputation of a Saint, who went alone with the *Chaubainhaa*, as a Mediatour between the King and him; immediately after them came in a close Chair, carried upon mens shoulders, *Nhay Canatoo*, the daughter of the King of *Pegu*, from whom this *Bramaa* had taken his Kingdom, and wife to the *Chaubainhaa*, having with her four small children, namely, two boyes, and two girls, whereof the eldest was not seven years old; round about her and them went some thirty or forty young women of noble extraction, and wonderful fair, with cast down looks, and tears in their eyes, leaning upon other women: After them marched in order certain *Talagrepos*, which are amongst them as the *Capuchins* with us, who bare-foot and bare-headed went along praying, holding beads in their hands, and ever and anon comforting those Ladies the best they could, and casting water in their faces for to bring them to themselves again, when as they fainted, which they did very often; A spectacle so lamentable, as it was not possible to behold it without shedding of tears: This desolate Company was attended by another Guard of Foot, and five hundred *Bramaas* on Horse-back. The *Chaubainhaa* was mounted on a little Elephant, in signe of poverty and contempt of the world, conformable to the Religion which he intended to enter into, being simply apparelled in a long Cassock of black velvet, as a mark of his mourning, having his beard, head, and eyebrows shaven, with an old cord about his neck, so to render himself to the King; In this Equipage he appeared so sad and afflicted, that one could not forbear weeping to behold him; As for his age, he was about some threescore and two yeers old, tall of Stature, with a grave and severe look, and the countenance of a generous Prince. As soon as he was arrived at a place, which was near to the gate of the City, where a great throng of women, children, and old men waited for him, when they saw him in so deplorable an estate, they all made seven times one after another so loud and dreadful a cry, as if Heaven and earth would have come together. Now these lamentations and complaints were presently seconded with such terrible blows, that they gave themselves without pity on their faces with stones, as they were most of them all of a gore blood; In the mean time things so horrible to behold, and mournful to hear, so much afflicted all the Assistants, that the very *Bramaas* of the Guard, though men of war, and consequently but little inclined to compassion, being also enemies to the *Chaubainhaa*, could not forbear weeping. It was likewise in this place, where *Nhay Canatoo*, and all the other Ladies that attended on her, fainted twice, by reason whereof they were fain to let the *Chaubainhaa* alight from his Elephant for to go and comfort her; whereupon seeing her lying upon the ground in a swoon with her four children in her arms, he kneeled down on both his knees, and looking up to Heaven with his eyes full of tears. *O mighty Power of God,* cryed he, *who is able to comprehend the righteous judgements of thy divine Justice, in that thou, having no regard to the innocency of these little creatures, givest way to thy wrath, which passeth far beyond the reach of our weak capacities! but remember; O Lord, who thou art, and not what I am:* This said, he fell with his face on the ground, near to the Queen his wife, which caused all the Assembly, who were without number, to make another such loud and horrible cry, as my words are not able to express it; The *Chaubainhaa* then took water in his mouth, and spurted it on his wife, by which means he brought her to her self again, and so taking her up in his arms, he fell a comforting her with speeches so full of zeal and devotion, as any one that heard him would have taken him rather for a Christian, then a

G g

Gen-

Gentile. After he had employed about half an hours time therein, and that they had remounted him on his Elephant, they proceeded on their way in the same order as they held before, and as soon as the *Chaubainhaa* was out of the City gate, and came to the streets which was formed of the several Companies of the strangers, ranked in two Files, he by chance cast his eye on that side, where the seven hundred *Portugals* were, all of them in their best clothes, with their buffe-coats, great feathers in their Caps, and their Harquebuses on their shoulders, as also *Joano Cayeyro* in the middest of them, in a Carnation Satin Suit, and a guilt Parisan in his hand, wherewith he made room; the afflicted Prince no sooner knew him, but he presently fell down on the Elephant, and there standing still without passing on, he said with tears in his eyes, to those that were about him; *My brethren, and good friends, I protest unto you, that it is a less grief unto me to make this sacrifice of my self, which the divine Justice of God permits me to make him this day, then to look upon men so wicked and ingrateful as these same here are; either kill me then, or send these away, for otherwise I will not stir a foot further.* Having said so he turned away his face three times that he might not behold us, thereby shewing the great spleen that he bore us; and indeed all things well considered there was a great deal of reason that he should carry himself in that sort towards us in regard of that which I have related before: In the mean time the Captain of the Guard seeing the stay which the *Chaubainhaa* had made, and understanding the cause why he would not go on, though he could not imagine wherefore he complained so of the *Portugals*, yet he hastily turned his Elephant towards *Cayeyro*, and giving him a scurvy look: *Get you gone,* said he, *and that instantly, for such wicked men as you are do not deserve to stand on any ground that bears fruit, and I pray God to pardon him which hath put it in the Kings head that you can be any ways profitable unto him; It were fitter for you therefore to shave away your beards that you may not deceive the World as you do, and we will have women in your places that shall serve us for our money.* Whereupon the *Bramaas* of the Guard, being incensed against us, drove us away from thence with a great deal of shame and contumely. And truly, not to lye, never was I so sensible of any thing as this in respect of the honour of my Country-men. After this, the *Chaubainhaa* went on till he came to the Tent of the King, who attended him with a Royal Pomp: for he was accompanied with a great number of Lords, amongst the which there were fifteen *Bainhaas,* who are as Dukes with us, and of six or seven others, that were of greater dignity then they: As soon as the *Chaubainhaa* came near him, he threw himself at his feet, and so prostrated on the ground he lay there a good while, as it were in a swoon, without speaking a word, but the *Rolim* of *Mounay,* that was close by him, supplyed that defect, and like a religious man, as he was, spake for him to the King, saying; *Sir, Here is a Spectacle able to move thy heart to pity, though the crime be such as it is; Remember then that the thing most pleasing to God in this World, and whereunto the effects of his mercy is soonest communicated, is such an action, and voluntary submission, as this is, Which here thou beholdest: It is for thee now to imitate his clemency, and so to do thou art most humbly intreated by the hearts of all them that are mollified by so great a misfortune as this is; Now if thou grantest them this their request, Which with so much instance they beg of thee, be assured that God will take it in good part, and that at the hour of thy death he will stretch forth his mighty hand over thee, to the end thou mayst be exempted from all manner of faults.* Hereunto he added many other speeches, whereby he perswaded the King to pardon him; at least-wise he promised so to do, wherewith the *Rolim,* and all the Lords there present, shewed themselves very well contented, and commended him exceedingly for it, imagining that the effect should be answerable to that which he had ingaged himself for before all. Now because it began to be night, he commanded the most of them that were about him to retire, as for the *Chaubainhaa,* he committed him into the hands of a *Bramaa* Commander, named *Xemin Commidau,* and the Queen his wife, with his children, and the other Ladies were put into the custody of *Xemin Ansedaa,* as well because he had his wife there, as for that he was an honourable old man, in whom the King of *Bramaa* much confided.

§.2.   The fear which the King of *Bramaa* was in lest the men of war should enter into the City of *Martabano,* and should pillage it now that it was night before he had done all that, which I am hereafter to relate, was the cause that he sent to all the gates of the City, being four and twenty, *Bramaa* Captains for to guard them, with express Commandment, that upon pain of death no man should be suffered to enter in at any of them, before he had taken order for the performance of the promise, which he had made to the strangers to give them the

spoyl

spoil of it; howbeit he took not that care, and used such diligence for the consideration he spake of, but onely that he might preserve the *Chaubainhaas* treasure, to which effect he spent two whole days in conveighing it away, it being so great that a thousand men were for that space altogether imployed therein; At the end of these two days the King went very early in the morning to an hill, called *Beidao*, distant from his quarters some two or three flight shoot, and then caused the Captains that were at the Guard of the gates to leave them, and retire away; whereupon the miserable City of *Martabono* was delivered to the mercy of the Souldiers, who at the shooting off of a Cannon, which was the signal thereof, entred presently into it pell-mell, and so thronging together, that at the entring into the gates, it is said above three hundred were stifled, for as there was there an infinite company of men of War of different Nations, the most of them without King, without Law, and without the fear and knowledge of God, they went all to the Spoile with closed eyes, and therein shewed themselves so cruel minded, that the thing they made least reckoning of was to kill an hundred men for a crown; And truly the disorder was such in the City, as the King himself was fain to go thither six or seven times in Person for to appease it. The Sack of this City endured three days and an half, with so much avarice and cruelty of these barbarous enemies, as it was wholly pillaged, without any thing left that might give an eye-cause to covet it. That done, the King with a new ceremony of Proclamations caused the *Chaubainhaas* Pallaces, together with thirty or forty very fair rich Houses of his principal Lords, and all the *Pagods* and Temples of the City to be demolished, so that according to the opinion of many, it was thought that the loss of those magnificent Edifices amounted to above ten millions of gold: wherewith not yet contented he commanded all the buildings of the City that were still a foot, to be set on fire, which by the violence of the wind kindled in such manner, as in that onely night there remained nothing unburnt, yea the very Walls, Towers, and Bulwarks were consumed even to the foundations. The number of them that were killed in this Sack was threescore thousand persons, nor was that of the prisoners much less. There were an hundred and forty thousand houses, and seventeen hundred Temples burnt, wherein also were consumed threescore thousand Statues, or Idols of divers mettals, during this Siege they of the City had eaten three thousand Elephants. There was found in this City six thousand pieces of Artillery, what of brass and iron, an hundred thousand Quintals of Pepper, and as much of Sanders, Benjamin, Lacre, Lignum Aloes, Camphire, Silk, and many other kinds of rich Merchandise, but above all an infinite number of commodities, which were come thither from the *Indiaes* in above an hundred vessels of *Cambaya*, *Achem*, *Melinda*, *Ceilam*, and of all the Streight of *Mecqua*, of the *Lequios*, and of *China*. As for the gold, silver, precious stones, and jewels, that were found there, one knows not truly what they were, for those things are ordinarily concealed; wherefore it shall suffice me to say, that so much as the King of *Bramaa* had for certain of the *Chaubainhaas* Treasure, amounted to an hundred Millions of gold, whereof, as I have said before, our King lost the Moitie, as well for our sins, as through the malice and envy of wicked dispositions. The next day after the City was pillaged, demolished, and burnt, there was seen in the morning upon the hill where the King was, one and twenty pair of Gallows, twenty of the which were of an equal height, and the other a little lower erected on pillars of stone, and guarded by an hundred *Bramaa* Horsmen; There were also round about the place very large Trenches, where a great many Banners spotted with drops of bloods were planted. As this Novelty promised somewhat which no man had heard of before, six of us *Portugals* ran thither to learn what the matter might be, and as we were going along we heard a great noise made by the men of War from the Camp, whereupon we saw come out of the Kings Quarter a number of Horsmen, who with Lances in their hands prepared a great Street, and cried out aloud; *Let no man upon pain of death appear in Armes, nor utter that with his mouth which he thinks in his heart.* A pretty way off from these Horse was the *Xemimbrum*, with an hundred armed Elephants, and a good many Foot; after them went fifteen hundred *Bramaas* on Horsback, cast into four Orders of Files, each of them six in a rank, whereof the *Talanagybras*, Viceroy of *Tangu*, was Commander: Then marched the *Chauseroo Siammon* with three thousand *Siammes*, armed with Harquebuses and Lances, all in one Battalion: In the midst of these was an hundred and twenty women tyed and bound four and four together, and accompanied with *Talagrepos*, men of great Austerity, and are such as the *Capachins* amongst us, who laboured all they might to comfort them in this last act of life;

Behind them were twelve Ushers with Maces, that went before *Nhay Canatoo*, Daughter to the King of *Pegu*, from whom this *Bramaa* Tyrant had usurped his Kingdom, and wife to the *Chaubainhaa*, with four children of hers, which were carried by so many Horsmen: all these sufferers were the wives or daughters of the principal Commanders that the *Chaubainhaa* had with him in the City, upon whom in the way of a strange revenge this *Bramaa* Tyrant desired to wreak his spight, and the hatred that he had alwayes born unto women. The most of these poor wretches were between seventeen and five and twenty years of age, all of them very white and fair, with bright auborn hair, but so weak in body, that oftentimes they fell down in a swoon, out of which certain women upon whom they leaned, endeavoured still to bring them again, presenting them Comfits, and other such things fit for that purpose, but they would take none of them, for that they were, as I have said, so feeble and benummed, as they could scarce hear what the *Talegrepos* spake unto them, only they now and then lifted up their hands to Heaven. After this Princess marched threescore *Grepos*, in two Files, praying with their looks fixed on the ground, and their eyes watered with tears, saying ever and anon in a doleful tone; *Thou which holdest thy Being of none but thy self, so justifie our works, that they may be agreeable to thy Justice.* Whereunto others answered weeping; *Grant, Lord, that it may be so, that through our fault we lose not the rich gifts of thy promises.* After these *Grepos* followed a procession of three or four hundred little children, quite naked from the Girdle-sted downwards, having in their hands great white wax lights, and cords about their necks; These, like the others, with a sad and lamentable voice, which moved every one to compassion, uttered these words: *We most humbly beseech thee, O Lord, to give ear unto our cries and groans, and shew mercy to these thy Captives, that with a full rejoycing they may have a part of the graces and benefits of thy rich treasures;* and much more they said to that purpose in favour of these poor sufferers: Behind this Procession was another Guard of Footmen, all *Bramaas*, and armed with Lances, Arrows, and some Harquebuses. As for the Rear-ward, it consisted of an hundred Elephants, like to them that marched first of all, so that the number of the men of War that assisted at this Execution, as well for the Guard, as for the Pomp thereof, was ten thousand Foot, and two thousand Horse, besides the two hundred Elephants, and a world of other people, both Strangers and Natives, that came thither to behold the end of so mournful and lamentable and action.

CHAP.

CHAP. LII.

In what sort the sentence of Death was executed on the person of the Chaubainhaa, *King of* Martaban, Nhay Canatoo *his wife, and an hundred and forty Women ; with that which the King of* Bramaa *did after his return to* Pegu.

THese poor sufferers having been led in the order before mentioned clean through the S.r. Camp, they came at last to the place of Execution, where the six Ushers with a loud voyce made this Proclamation: *Let all manner of people see and observe the bloody justice, which is here to be done by the living God, Lord of all truth, and our King the Soveraign of our Heads, who of his absolute power doth command that these hundred and forty Women be put to death, and thrown into the ayr, for that by their counsel and incitement their Fathers and Husbands stood out against us in this City, and at times killed twelve thousand Bramaas of the Kingdom of* Tangu. Then at the ringing of a Bell all the Officers and Ministers of Justice pel-mell together with the guards, made such a cry, as was most dreadful to hear; whereupon the cruel Hangmen being ready to put the sentence of Death in execution, those poor wretches embraced one another, and shedding abundance of tears they addressed themselves to *Nhay Canatoo,* who lay at that time almost dead in the lap of an old Lady, and with their last complements one of them spake for all the rest unto her in this manner ; *Excellent Lady, that art as a crown of Roses upon our Heads, now that we thy humble servants are entering into those mournful Mansions where Death doth reside, comfort us we beseech thee with thy dear sight, that so we may with less grief quit these bodies full of anguish for to present our selves before that Almighty just Judg, of whom we will for ever implore his justice for a perpetual vengeance of the wrong that is done us.* Then *Nhay Canatoo* beholding them with a countenance more dead then alive, answered them with a feeble voyce, that could scarce be heard, *Go not away so soon, my Sisters, but help me to sustain these little children.* That said, she leaned down again on the bosom of that Lady, without speaking a word more, whereupon the Ministers of the Arm of Vengeance, so they term the Hangmen, layd hold on those poor women, and hanged them up all by the feet, with their heads downwards, upon twenty Gibbets, namely seven on each one : now so painful a death as this was, made them give strange and fearful groanes and sobs, until at length the blood stifled them all in less then an hour. In the mean time *Nhay Canatoo* was conducted by the four women, upon whom she leaned, directly to the Gallows whereon she and her four children were to be hanged, and there the *Rolim* of *Mounay,* who was held amongst them for a holy man, used some speeches unto her for to encourage her the better to suffer death, whereupon she desired them to give her a little water, which being brought unto her, she filled he mouth with it, and so sputted it upon her four children, whom she held in her arms ; then having kissed them many times, she said unto them weeping, *O my Children, my Children, whom I have conceived anew within the interior of my Soul, how happy would I think my self if I might redeem your lives with the loss of mine own a thousand times over if it were possible ! for in regard of the fear and anguish wherein I see you at this present, and wherein every one sees me also, I should receive Death with as good an heart from the hand of this cruel Enemy, as I willingly desire to see my self in the presence of the Soveraign Lord of all things, within the repose of his celestial Habitation.* Then turning her to the Hangman, who was going to bind her two little boys, *Good Friend,* said she, *be not I pray thee so voyd of pity, as to make me see my children dye, for in so doing thou wouldst commit a great sin : wherefore put me first to death, and refuse me not this boon which I crave of thee for Gods sake.* After she had thus spoken she took her children again in her arms, and kissing them over and over in giving them her last farewell, she yielded up the ghost in the Ladies lap upon whom she leaned, not so much as once stirring ever after, which the Hangman perceiving, ran presently unto her and hanged her as he had done the rest, together with her four little children, two of each side of her, and she in the middle. At this cruel and pitiful spectacle there arose from amongst all this people so great and hideous a cry, that the Earth seemed to tremble under the feet of them that stood upon it, and withall there followed such a Mutiny throughout the whole Camp, as the King was constrained to

fortifie

fortifie himfelf in his quarter with fix thoufand *Bramaa* Horfe, and thirty thoufand Foot, and yet for all that he thought not himfelf fecure enough from it, had not the night come, which onely was able to calm the furious motions of thefe men of war; For of feven hundred thoufand which were in the Camp, fix hundred thoufand were by Nation *Pegu's*, whofe King was the Father of this Queen, that was thus put to death; but this Tyrant of *Bramaa* had fo difarmed and fubjected them, as they durft not fo much as quich upon any occafion. Behold in what an infamous manner *Nhay Canatoo* finifhed her days, a Princefs every way accomplifhed, wife to the *Chaubainhaa* King of *Martabano*, and the daughter of the King of *Pegu*, Emperor of nine Kingdoms, whofe yearly Revenue amounted unto three millions of Gold. As for the infortunate King her Husband, he was the fame night caft into the River with a great ftone tyed about his neck, together with fifty or threefcore of his chiefeft Lords, who were either the Fathers, Husbands or Brothers of thofe hundred and forty Ladies, that were moft unjuftly put to fuch an ignominious death, amongft the which there were three, whom this King of *Bramaa* had demanded in marriage at fuch time as he was but a fimple Earl, but not one of their Fathers would condefcend unto it, whereby one may fee how great the revolutions of time and fortune are.

§.2.   After the Tyrant of *Bramaa* had caufed this rigorous Juftice to be done, he ftayed there nine whole days, during the which many of the Inhabitants of the City were alfo execued; At laft he departed for to go to *Pegu*, leaving behind him *Bainhaa Chaque*, Lord Steward of his Houfe, to take order for all things that might conduce to the pacifying of that Kingdom, and to provide for the repairing of what the fire had confumed, to which purpofe he placed a good Garifon there, and carryed with him the reft of his Army; *Joano Cayeyro* followed him alfo with feven hundred *Portugals*, not above three or four remaining behind in the ruines of *Martabano*, and thofe too not very confiderable, except it were one, named *Gonçalo Falcan*, a Gentleman well born, and whom thefe *Gentiles* commonly called *Crifna Pacan*, that is to fay, *Flower of Flowers*, a very honorable Title amongft them, which the King of *Bramaa* had given him in recompence of his fervices: Now for as much as at my departure from *Malaca*, *Pedro de Faria* had given me a Letter directed unto him, whereby he defired him to affift me with his favor, in cafe I had need of it in the affair for which he fent me thither, as well for the fervice of the King, as for his own particular; as foon as I arrived at *Martabano*, where I found him refident, I delivered him this Letter, and withall gave him an account of the occafion that brought me thither, which was to confirm the ancient league of Peace that the *Chaubainhaa* had made by his Embaffadors with them of *Malaca*, at fuch time as *Pedro de Faria* was firft Governor of it, and whereof he could not chufe but have fome knowledg; adding moreover, how to that effect I had brought the *Chaubainhaa* Letters full of great proteftations of amity, and a Prefent of certain very rich Pieces of *China*, Hereupon this *Gonçalo Falcan* imagining that by means hereof he might infinuate himfelf much more into the good grace of the King of *Bramaa*, to whofe fide he turned at the fiege of *Martabano*, quitting that of the *Chaubainhaa*, whom formerly he ferved, he went three days after the Kings departure to his faid Governor, and told him that I was come thither, as Embaffador from the Captain of *Malaca* to treat with the *Chaubainhaa*, unto whom the Captain fent an offer of great Forces againft the King of *Bramaa*, in fo much that they of the Country were upon the point of fortifying themfelves in *Martabano*, and chafing away the *Bramaas* out of the Kingdom; whereunto he added fo many other fuch like matters, that the Governor fent prefently to apprehend me, and after he had put me into fafe cuftody, he went directly to the Junck, in which I came from *Malaca*, and feized upon all the goods that were in her, which were worth above an hundred thoufand duckets, committing the *Necoda*, Captain and Mafter of the Junck, to prifon, as alfo all the reft that were in her, to the number of an hundred threefcore and four perfons, wherein comprized forty rich Merchants, *Malayes*, *Menancabo's*, *Mahumetans*, and *Gentiles*, Natives of *Malaca*. All thefe were incontinently condemned to a confifcation of their goods, and to remain the Kings prifoners, as well as I, for being complices in the Treafon, which the Captain of *Malaca* had plotted in fecret with the *Chaubainhaa* againft the King of *Bramaa*. Having thus caufed them to be put into a deep Dungeon, he made them to be fo cruelly fcourged, that within a month after their imprifonment, of an hundred fixty four of them, which they were, there dyed nineteen, either of a Lethargy, or of hunger, or thirft. As for the reft, they were put into a
miferable

miserable Shallop without Sails or Oars, wherein they were exposed down the River: Being delivered in this sort to the mercy of Fortune, they were cast by the wind into a defart Island, called *Pulho Canuida*, seated twenty leagues within the Sea of this Bar, where they furnished themselves with some Sea-fish, and such fruits as they found in the woods, and in this necessity making a kind of sail of the clothes they had, and with two Oars, which it may be they met withall there, or made themselves, they took their course all along by the Coast of *Junçalan*, and from thence to another place, wherein they employed the space of two months, arriving at length at the River of *Parles* in the Kingdom of *Queda*, where they all dyed of certain Impostumes, which rose in their throats like unto Carbuncles, two onely excepted, who came to *Malaca*, and recounted to *Pedro de Faria* the whole success of this sad Voyage, and how that I was condemned to dye, as indeed I expected every hour to be led to execution, when as it pleased God to deliver me miraculously; for as soon as the *Necoda* and the Merchants were banished in the manner that I have declared, I was committed to another prison farther off, where I remained six and thirty days laden with chains and irons in a most cruel and insupportable manner; During all that time the Traytor *Gonçalo* exhibited against me dayly new and false allegations, wherein he charged me with a world of things, which I never so much as thought of, and that to no other intent but to procure my death, that so he might rob me, as he had done all the rest that were in the Junck: To which end, having questioned me three several times in Judgment, I never answered any thing to his Interrogatories that was to purpose, whereat he and other of my Enemies were much enraged, saying, that I did it out of pride, and in contempt of Justice, so that for a punishment thereof they caused me to be openly whipped, and a great deal of lacre, which is like unto hard wax, to be dropped scalding hot upon me, whereof the pain was such, as it had almost killed me, and indeed all that were by, held me for a dead man. Now because for the most part I knew not what I spake, but talked like a desperate man, I happened three or four times to say, that for to rob me of my goods I had all these false accusations put upon me, but that Captain *Joano Cayeyro*, who was at *Pegu*, would ere it were long acquaint the King with this cruel usage of me, which was the cause of saving my life; for even as this wicked Governor was going to have the sentence executed, which was given against me, some of his friends counselled him to forbear, saying, that if he put me to death, no doubt but that all the *Portugals*, which were at *Pegu*, would complain of him to the King, and tell him, that for to rob me of an hundred thousand duckets, which I had there in Commodities, appertaining to the Captain of *Malaca*, he had most unjustly taken away my life: And that this being so, the King would demand an account of him of all those Commodities, or of the Mony for them, and that if he rendered him even all that he had taken from me, yet would not that content him, imagining still there was somewhat more, whereby he would so put himself out of the good grace of the King, as he would never recover it again, which would be the cause of the utter overthrown both of himself and his children, besides the dishonor that would redound to him over and above. This dog the Governor *Bainhaa Chaque*, fearing left that should come to pass which they had said, desisted from his former obstinacy, and correcting the sentence he had given, he ordained, That I should not dye, but that my goods should be confiscated, and my self arrested for the Kings prisoner; As indeed so soon as I was healed of the hurts, which the burning of the lacre, and the stripes of the whips had made upon me, I was conducted in chains to *Pegu*, and there as a prisoner was put into the hands of a *Bramaa*, Treasurer to the King, named *Diosoray*, who had also in his custody eight other *Portugals*, whose sins had procured them the same misfortune, which mine had caused unto me; for it was now full six months since these poor wretches had been in his power, being taken in the ship of *Don Anrique Deça* of *Cananor*, which by a tempest was cast on that Coast. Now seeing that hitherto I have discoursed of the success of my Voyage to *Martabano*, and of the benefit that redounded to me by my going thither for the service of the King, which was no other then the loss of my goods, and the imprisonment of my person; before I engage my self further in these relations, I am resolved to intreat of the divers Fortunes, which I ran in that Kingdom for the space of two years and an half that I travelled therein, being the time of my Captivity, as also of the several Countries through which I was carryed by my crosses and mishaps, as holding it altogether necessary for the declaration of that which I am going on withall. I say then, that after

15

this

this King of *Bramaa* was departed from the City of *Martabano*, as I have related before, he journeyed so long that at length he came to *Pegu*, where, before he dismissed his Commanders, he caused a Muster to be made of his Army, and found that of seven hundred thousand men, which he had carryed along with him to the besieging of the *Chaubainhaa*, there was fourscore and six thousand of them wanting: And for as much as he had about that time some inckling how the King of *Avaa*, confederated with the *Savadis* and *Chaleus*, would give entry unto the *Sianmon* (whose Country borders on the West and Northwest side on the *Calaminhan*, Emperor of the indomptable Forces of the Elephants of the Earth, as I will shew hereafter when I speak of him) to the end he might win from this *Bramaa* the chiefest strengths of his Kingdom, he like a good Captain as he was, and very cunning in matter of War, before he passed on further, caused men to be levyed, with whom, as also with all other necessary things he furnished those principal Fortresses from whence his greatest fear proceeded. Then having resolved to go and besiege the City of *Prom*, he retained the Army, which he had already a foot, and made new and great preparations throughout the Kingdom, using such diligence therein, as in six months time he had got together the number of nine hundred thousand men, whom he imbarqued in twelve thousand rowing Vessels, whereof two thousand were *Seroos*, *Laulers*, *Caturos*, and *Foists*. Now all this great Fleet set forth from *Pegu* the ninth day of *March*, 1545. and going up the River of *Ansedaa*, it went to *Danapluu*, where it was furnished with all such provisions as was necessary. From this place following on their way through a great River of fresh water, called *Picau Malacou*, which was above a league broad, at length upon the thirteenth of *April* they came within view of *Prom*. There, by some whom they took that night, they learned, that the King was dead, and how he had left for his successor to the Kingdom a son of his of thirteen years of age, whom the King his Father before he dyed had marryed to his wives sister, the Aunt of the said young Prince, and Daughter to the King of *Avaa*. This young King was no sooner advertised of the King of *Bramaa* his coming to besiege him in his City of *Prom*, but he sent presently away to the King his Father-in-law for succor, which he instantly granted, and to that end speedily raised an Army of 30000 *Mons*, *Tarees*, and *Chalems*, choyce men and trained up in the Wars, of whom he made a son of his, and brother to the Queen, General. In the mean time the *Bramaa*, having intelligence thereof, used all possible diligence for to besiege the City before so great a succor might arrive. To which purpose, having landed his Army in a plain, called *Meigavotau*, some two leagues below the City, he continued there five days in making ready such preparations as were needful; Having given order for all things, he caused his Army to march one morning before day directly to the City, with the sound of Drums, Fifes, and other such instruments of War; where being arrived about noon without any opposition, he began presently to settle his Camp, so that before it was night, the whole City was environed with Trenches, and very great Ditches, as also with six rows of Cannons, and other Pieces of Ordnance.

CHAP. LIII.

That which passed between the Queen of Prom, *and the King of* Bramaa, *together with the first Assault that was given to the City and the Success thereof.*

THe King of *Bramaa* had been now five days before the City of *Prom*, when as the S.1 Queen that governed the State in the place of her Husband, seeing her self thus besieged, sent to visit this her enemy with a rich jewel of precious stones, which was presented unto him by a *Talagrepo*, or religious man, of above an hundred years old, who was held amongst them for a Saint, together with a Letter, wherein this was written; *Great and mighty Lord, more favoured in the House of fortune then all the Kings of the earth, the force of an extream power, an increasing of the Salt-seas, whereinto all lesser rivers do render themselvos a Shield full of very fair devices, Processor of the greatest States, upon the Throne whereof thy feet do repose with a marvellous Majesty: I* Nhay Nivolau, *a poor woman, Governess, and Tutress of my Son, an Orphan, do prostrate my self before thee with tears in mine eyes, and with the respect which ought to be rendred unto thee; I beseech thee not to draw thy Sword against my weakness, for thou knowest that I am but a silly woman, which can but only cry unto God for the wrong that is done me, whose property also it is to succour with mercy, and to chastice with justice the States of the World be they never so great, trampling them under his feet with so redoubted a power, that the very Inhabitants of the profound house of smoak do fear and tremble before this Almighty Lord: I pray and conjure thee not to take from me that which is mine, seeing it is so small a thing, as thou shalt not be the greater for it when thou hast it, nor yet the less if thou hast it not; whereas contrarily, if thou, my Lord, wilt shew thy self pitiful to me, that act of clemency will bring thee such reputation, as the very Infants themselves will cease from sucking the white breasts of their Mothers for to praise thee with the pure lips of their innocency, and likewise all they of my Country, and Strangers will ever remember such thy charity towards me, and I my self will cause it to be graven on the Tombs of the dead, that both they and the living may give thee thanks for a thing, which I do beg of thee with so much instance from the bottom of my heart. This holy man,* Avenlachim, *from whom thou shalt receive this Letter, written with mine own hand, hath Power and Authority to treat with thee in the Name of my Fatherless Son, concerning all that shall be judged reasonable touching the tribute and homage which thou shalt think fit to have rendred unto thee, upon condition that thou wilt be pleased to let us enjoy our houses, so that under a true assurance thereof we may bring up our children, and gather the fruit of our labours for the nourishment of the poor Inhabitants of this paltry Town, who will all serve thee, and I to with a most humble respect in all things, wherein thou shalt think good to imploy us at thy pleasure.*

The *Bramaa* received this Letter and Ambassage with a great deal of authority, and entertained the Religious man, that delivered it into him, with much honour, as well in reguard of his age, as for that he was held as a Saint amongst them; withall he granted him certain things which were at first demanded, as a Cessation of Arms till such time as Articles should be agreed on, as also a permission for the Besieged to converse with the Besiegers, and other such things of little consequence; In the mean time judging with himself that all those offers, which this poor Queen made him, and the humble submissions of her Letter proceeded from weakness and fear, he would never answer the Ambassadour clearly, or to purpose: Contrarily he caused all the places there abouts that were weak and unarmed, to be secretly ransaked, and the poor Inhabitants thereof to be unmercifully butchered by their barbarous enemies, whose cruelty was so great, that in five dayes, according to report, they killed fourteen thousand persons, the most part whereof, were women, children, and old men, that were not able to bear Arms. Hereupon the *Rolim*, who brought this Letter, relying no longer on the false promises of this Tyrant, and discontented with the little respect he used towards him, demanded leave of him to return to the City, which the *Bramaa* gave him, together with this answer; That if the Queen would deliver up her self, her Treasure, her Kingdom, and her Vassals to him, he would recompence her another way for the loss of her State: but withall that she was to return him a peremptory answer to this proposition of his the very same day, which was all the time I could give her, that so he might upon the knowledge of her resolution determine upon what he had to do. The *Rolim* went herewith back to the City, where he gave the Queen an account of all things, saying, That this Tyrant was a man without faith, and replete with damnable intentions, for proof whereof he represented unto her the Siege of *Martabano*, the usage of the *Chaubainhaa* after he rendred himself unto him upon his word, and how he had put him, his wife, his children, and the chiefest Nobility of his Kingdom to a most shamefull death. These things considered it was instantly concluded, as well by the Queen, as by all those of her Councel, that she should defend the City, till such time as succour came from her Father, which would be within fifteen days at the furthest: This resolution taken, she being of a great courage without further delay took order for all things, that were thought necessary for the defence of the City, animating to that end her people with great prudence, and a man-like Spirit, though she was but a woman; Moreover, as she liberally imparted to them of her Treasure, so she promised every one throughly to acknowledg their services with all manner of recompences and honours, whereby they were mightily encouraged to fight: In the mean space the King of *Bramaa*, seeing that the *Rolim* returned him no answer within the time prefixt, began the next day to fortifie all the Quarters of his Camp with double rows of Cannon, for to batter the City on every side; and for assaulting of the walls he caused a great number of Ladders to be made, publishing withall throughout his whole Army, that all Souldiers upon pain of death should be ready within three days to go to the Assault; The time then being come, which was the third of *May*, 1545. About an hour before day the King went out of his Quarter, where he was at anchor upon the river with two thousand vessels of choice men, and giving the Signal to the Commanders which were on Land, to prepare themselves, they altogether in one Body assailed the walls, with so great a cry, as if Heaven and earth would have come together, so that both sides falling to encounter pell-mell with one another, there was such a conflict betwixt them, as within a little while the air was seen all on fire, and the earth all bloody, whereunto being added the clashing of weapons, and noise of guns, it was a spectacle so dreadful, that we few *Portugals*, who beheld these things, remained astonished, and almost besides our selves: This fight indured full five hours, at the end whereof the Tyrant of *Bramaa* seeing those within defend themselves so valiantly, and the most part of his Forces to grow faint, he went to land with ten or eleven thousand of his best men, and with all diligence re-inforcing the Companies, that were fighting, the Bickering renewing in such sort, as one would have said it did but then begin, so great was the fury of it. The second trial continued till night, yet would not the King desist from the fight, what counsel soever was given him to retire, but contrarily he swore not to give over the Enterprise begun, and that he would lie that night within the inclosure of the City walls, or cut off the heads of all those Commanders that were not wounded at their coming off; In the mean time this obstinacy was very pejudicial to him, for continuing the Assault till the Moon was gone down, which was two hours past midnight, he was then forced to sound a Retreat, after he had lost in this Assault, as was the next day found upon a Muster, fourscore thousand of his men, besides those which were hurt, which were thirty thousand at the least, whereof many died for want of dressing, whence issued such a plague in the Camp, as well through the corruption of the air, as the water of the river, that was all tainted with blood and dead bodies, that thereby about fourscore thousand more perished, amongst whom were five hundred *Portugals*, having no other buriall then the bellies of Vultures, Crows, and such like birds of prey, which devoured them all along the Coast where they lay.

§.2.   The King of *Bramaa*, having considered that this first Assault having cost him so dear, would no more hazard his men in that manner, but he caused a great Terrace to be made with Bavins, and above ten thousand Date-trees, which he commanded to be cut down, and on that he raised up a platform so high, as it over-topped the walls of the City two fathom, and more, where he placed fourscore pieces of Ordnance, and with them continually battering the City for the space of nine dayes together, it was for the most part demolished with the death of fourteen thousand persons, which quite abated the poor Queens courage, especially when she came to understand that she had but six thousand fighting men left, all the rest, which consisted of women, chidren, & old men, being unfit & unable to bear Arms. The miserable besieged, seeing themselves reduced to such extreamity, assembled together in Councel, and there by the advice of the chiefest of them, it was concluded, That all in general should anoint themselves with the Oile of the Lamps of the Chappel of *Quiay Nivandel*, God of Battail of the field *Vitau*, and so

cffering

offering themselves up in sacrifice to him, set upon the platform, with a determination either to dye, or to vanquish, in vowing themselves all for the defence of their young King, to whom they had so lately done homage, and sworn to be true and faithful Subjects. This resolution taken, which the Queen and all her Nobility approved of for the best and most assured, in a time wherein all things were wanting to them for the longer defending themselves, they promised to accomplish it in the manner aforesaid by a solemn Oath, which they all took ; Now there being no further question but to see how they should carry themselves in this affair, they first of all made an Uncle of the Queens the Captains of this resolute Band, who assembling these six thousand together, the same night, about the first quarter of the watch, made a sally out of the two gates that were nearest to the Terrace and platform, and so taking courage from their despair, and resolution to dye, they fought so valiantly, that in less then half an hour the whole Camp was put in disorder, the Terrace gained, the fourscore pieces of Cannon taken, the King himself hurt, the Pallisado burnt, the Trenches broken, and the *Xenimbram*, General of the Army, slain, with above fifteen thousand men more, amongst the which were five hundred *Turks* ; there were moreover forty Elephants taken, besides those that were killed, and eight hundred *Bramaas* made prisoners, so that these six thousand resolute men did that, which an hundred thousand, though valiant enough, could hardly have effected. After this they retreated an hour before day, and upon a review they found, that of six thousand which they were, there was but seven hundred slain. This bad success so grieved and incensed the King of *Bramaa*, as attributing the cause thereof to the negligence of some of his Captains in the ill guarding of the Terrace, that the day following he caused two thousand *Pegu*'s to be beheaded, which had stood sentinel that night. This adventure rendred things quiet for the space of twelve days, during which the besieged stirred not ; in the mean time one of the four principal Captain of the City, named *Xemim Meleytay*, fearing that which all others in general misdoubted, namely, that they could not escape from falling into the hands of so cruel an Enemy, treated secretly with the Tyrant, and upon condition that he would continue him in his charge, not meddle with any of the houses of his friends, and make him *Xemin* of *Ansedaa* in the Kingdom of *Pegu*, with all the Revenue which the *Bainhaa* of *Malacou* had there, being thirty thousand Duckats a year, he would deliver him up the City by giving him entrance into it through the gate which he commanded : The King of *Bramaa* accepted hereof, and for a gage of performance on his part, he sent him a rich Ring from off his finger. This Treason so concluded, was effected on the three and twentieth of *August*, in the year 1545. wherein this Tyrant of *Bramaa* carryed himself with all the barbarousness and cruelty that he used to practise in the like cases. And for as much as I conceive that I should never have done, if I should recount here at large how this affair past, I will say no more, but that the gate was opened, the City delivered up, the Inhabitants all cut in pieces, without so much as sparing one ; the King and Queen made prisoners, their Treasurers taken, the Buildings and Temples demolished, and many other inhumanities exercised with such outragiousness, the belief whereof is beyond the imagination and thought of man, and truly I never represent unto my self in what manner it was done, as having seen it with mine own eyes, but that I remain as it were astonished and besides my self at it. For as this Tyrant was touched to the quick with the affront he had lately received, so he executed all the cruelties he could imagine against those miserable Inhabitants, for to be revenged of the ill success he had had in the siege, which could not proceed from any other but a base mind and vile extraction, for it ordinarily falls out, that barbarousness finds place in such kind of people, rather then in generous and valiant hearts ; Whereunto may be added, that he was a man without faith, and of an effeminate disposition, though he was nevertheless an Enemy to women, albeit there were in that Kingdom, and in all the others whereof he was Lord, those that were very white and fair. After the bloody ruine of that wretched City, the Tyrant entred into it in great pomp, and and as it were in triumph, through a breach that was made of purpose in the wall, and by his express commandment. When he was arrived at the young Kings pallace, he caused himself to be crowned King of *Prom*, and during the Ceremony of this Coronation, he made that poor Prince, whom he had deprived of his Kingdom, to continue kneeling before him, with his hands held up, as if he adored some God, and ever and anon they constrained him to stoup down and kiss the Tyrants feet, who in the mean time made shew as if he were not pleased therewith. This done, he went into a Balcone, which looked on a great Market place, whither he commanded all the dead children, that lay up and down the streets, to be brought, and then causing them to be hacked very small, he gave them, mingled with Bran, Rice, and Herbs, to his Elephants to eat. Afterward, with a strange kind of ceremony, at the sound of Trumpets, Drums, and other such like Instruments, there was above an hundred Horses led in, loaden with the quarters of men and women, which also he commanded to be cut small, and then cast into a great fire, kindled expresly for it. These things so done, the Queen was brought before him, that was wife to the poor little King, who, as I said before, was but thirteen years of age, and she thirty and six, a woman very white, and well-favored, Aunt to her own Husband, Sister to his Mother, and Daughter to the King of *Avaa*, which is the Country from whence the Rubies, Saphirs, and Emeralds do come to *Pegu*; and it was the same Lady, whom this *Bramaa* had sent to demand in marriage of her Father, as it was then spoken, but that he refused him, saying to his Embassador for an answer, That the thoughts of his Daughter soared a pitch higher then to be the wife of the *Xemim* of *Tanguu*, which was the family whence this Tyrant was issued: But now that she was fallen into his hands as his slave, whether he used her so, either out of a revenge of that affront, or out of scorn and contempt, so it was that he made her to be publiquely stript stark naked, and to be torn and mangled with whipping, and then in that manner to be led up and down all the City, where amidst the cries and hooting of the people, he exposed her to other cruel torments, wherewith she was tortured till she gave up the ghost; When she was dead, he made her to be bound to the little King her Husband, who was yet living, and having commanded a great stone to be tyed about their necks, they were cast into the River, which was a kind of cruelty very dreadful to all that beheld it. To these barbarous parts he added many others so inhumane, as it is not likely that any other but he could imagine the like; And for a conclusion of his cruelties, the next day he caused all the Gentlemen that were taken alive, being some three hundred, to be impaled, and so spitted like rosted Pigs, to be also thrown into the River, whereby may be seen how great and unheard of the injustice of this Tyrant was, which he exercised on these miserable wretches.

CHAP. LIV.

The King of Bramaa *his besieging of the Fortress of* Meleytay, *with his going from thence to* Avaa; *and that which passed there.*

§. I. FOurteen days were past since the doing of these things, during the which the Tyrant employed himself in fortifying the City with a great deal of diligence and care, when as his spies, whom he had sent out, brought him word, that from the City of *Avaa* a Fleet of four hundred rowing Vessels was come down the River of *Queitor*, wherein there were thirty thousand *Siamon* Soldiers, besides the Mariners, of which the King of *Avaas* son, and brother to the poor Queen, was General; for this Prince having received advertisement of the taking of the City of *Prom*, and of the death of his sister and brother-in-law, went and lodged in the Fortress of *Meleytay*, which was some twelve leagues up the River from *Prom*. This news much troubled the Tyrant, howbeit he resolved to go himself in person against his Enemies before that other succors came to joyn with them, as indeed the report went, that fourscore thousand, all *Mons* by Nation, and led by the King of *Avaa*, were on their way thither: With this resolution the Tyrant of *Bramaa* set forth towards *Meleytay* with an Army of three hundred thousand men, namely two hundred thousand by Land alongst the Rivers side, whereof the *Chaumigrem* his Foster-brother was Commander in chief, and the other hundred thousand under his own conduct, being all choyce men, and imbarqued in two thousand *Seroos*; Being come within sight of *Meleytay*, the *Avaas* desiring to shew that the resolution wherewith they were come thither, was of far more power with them, then any fear they could have, and that also their Enemies might not receive any benefit by their Fleet which lay on the River, and do them an affront besides by taking of it, they set all their Vessels on fire, and burnt them every one; Then, without any dread of that which the flesh doth naturally most fear, they got all into

the

the field, and ranged themselves into four Battalions, in three of which, whereof each one made ten thousand men, were the thirty thousand *Mons* ; and in the the other, that were somewhat bigger, were all the Mariners of the four hundred Vessels they had burnt : These same they placed in the Vaunt-guard, with an intention that they should weary the Enemies, with whom they made a cruel fight, which lasted about half an hour, wherein all these Mariners were cut in pieces ; presently after them the thirty thousand *Mons*, close compacted together in three Battalions, presented themselves, and with wonderful violence set upon their Enemies, between whom and them followed so extraordinary and cruel a battel, as not longer to insist upon it, nor to recount in particular how things past, which also I cannot well do, it shall suffice me to say, that of the thirty thousand *Mons*, eight hundred only escaped out of it, who being routed, made their retreat into the Fortress of *Meleytay* ; but that which was most memorable herein was that of the King of *Bramaas* two hundred thousand men, an hundred and fifteen thousand lay dead in field, and all the rest for the most part were wounded. In the mean time the Tyrant, which came along on the River in the two thousand *Seroos*, arrived at the place of Battel, where beholding the strange massacre which the *Mons* had made of his people, he became so enraged at it, that dis-imbarquing his Forces, he instantly layd siege unto the Fortress, with a purpose, as he said, to take all those eight hundred that were in it alive. This siege continued seven whole days together, during the which those without gave five assaults to it, and the besieged defended themselves always very valiantly, howbeit seeing that the last hour of their life was come, and that they could no longer hold that place for their King, as they had hoped they might, by reason of the fresh Forces which the King of *Bramaa* had landed, like couragious men as they were they resolved to dye in the field, as their companions had done, and valiantly revenge their deaths with that of their Enemies, whereunto they were the more willingly carryed, because they perceived well that if they continued still in the place, they should never make use of their valor, as they desired to do, for that the Tyrants Ordnance would by little and little consume them : This resolution taken, they under the favor of a very dark and rainy night sallyed forth, and first of all fell upon the two first Courts of guard that were on the Lands side, cutting all in pieces that they met withall ; Then following their design they passed on like desperate men, and whether they did it, either to shew that they regarded not death which threatened them, or for the desire they had to gain honor, so it was that they behaved themselves so couragiously, and pressed the Tyrant so neer, as they forced him to leap into the River, and swim for his life, in so much that all the Camp was in disorder, and broken through in I know not how many places, with the death of above twelve thousand men, amongst whom were fifteen hundred *Bramaas*, two thousand strangers of divers Nations, and all the rest *Pegu*. This fight last not above half an hour, in which time the eight hundred *Mons* were all slain, there being not so much as one of them that would yield upon any composition whatsoever: Hereupon the Tyrant of *Bramaa* seeing the fight ended, and all things quiet, went and reassembled his Forces together, and so entered into the Fortress of *Meleytay*, where he presently commanded the *Xemims* head to be cut off, saying, that he was the sole cause of that disaster, and that he who had been a Traytor to his King, could not be faithful unto him : behold the recompence which this Tyrant made him for delivering up the City of *Prom* unto him, howsoever it justly belonged unto him for a punishment of his perfidiousness, that carryed him to betray his King and his own Country into the power of his Enemies : After this they fell to dressing of the hurt men, which were in very great number.

We past all this night with much apprehension, always keeping good watch, and the §. 2. next morning as soon as it was day, the first thing that we did was to rid away the dead bodies, which were in so great number all over the Camp, that the ground was quite covered with them ; After this we took a view of those that were killed, as well on the one, as the other party, and we found that on the *Bramaas* side there were an hundred and fourscore thousand, and on the Prince of *Avaas* forty and two thousand, wherein were comprized the thirty thousand *Mons*. That done, after the Tyrant had fortified the City of *Prom*, as also the Fort of *Meleytay*, and made two other Forts upon the bank of the River, in such places as he judged to be most important for the safety of that Kingdom, he went up the River of *Queitor* in a thousand rowing *Seroos*, wherein were imbarqued

seventy

seventy thousand men. In this Voyage his intention was to go in his own person, for to observe the Kingdom of *Avaa*, and to see the City himself, the better to consider the strength of it, and thereby judg what Forces he should bring for to take it ; So he proceeded still on for the space of eight and twenty days, and during that time passed by many goodly places, which within the Kingdom of *Chaleu* and *Jacuçalaon* were upon the bank of the River : At length he arrived at the City of *Avaa* the thirteenth of *October* the same year, a thousand five hundred forty and five ; Being come to the Port, he remained there thirteen days, and that while burned between two and three thousand Vessels that he found there ; Moreover he set fire on many Villages thereabout, which cost him not so little but that he lost in all these degasts eight thousand of his men, amongst the which were threescore and two *Portugals*. Now whereas this City was very strong, as well in regard of the scituation of it, as of the Fortifications which were newly made there, it had besides within it twenty thousand *Mons*, who it was said were come thither some five days before from the Mountains of *Pondalou*, where the King of *Avaa*, by the permission of the *Siamon*, Emperor of that Monarchy, was levying above fourscore thousand men for to go and regain the City of *Prom* : for as soon as that King had received certain news of the death of his daughter and son-in-law, perceiving that he was not strong enough of himself to revenge the wrongs this Tyrant had done him, or to secure himself from those which he feared to receive of him in time to come, namely the depriving him of his Kingdom, as he was threatened, he went in person with his wife and children and cast himself at the *Siamons* feet, and acquainting him with the great affronts he had received, and what his desire was, he made himself his Tributary at threescore thousand *Bisses* by the year, which amount to an hundred thousand Duckets of our mony, and a *gueta* of Rubies, being a measure like to our pynt, therewith to make a jewel for his wife, of which Tribute it was said, that he advanced the payment for ten years beforehand, besides many other precious stones, and very rich Plate, which he presented him with, estimated in all at two millions, in recompence whereof the *Siamon* obliged himself to take him into his protection, yea and to march into the field for him as often as need should require, and to re-establish him within a year in the Kingdom of *Prom*, so as for that effect he granted him those thirty thousand men of succor, which the *Bramaa* defeated at *Meleytay*, as also the twenty thousand that were then in the City, and the fourscore thousand which were to come to him, over whom the said King of *Avaa* was to be the General. The Tyrant having intelligence thereof, and apprehending that this, above all other things he could fear, might be the cause of his ruine, he gave present order for the fortifying of *Prom* with much more care and diligence then formerly : howbeit before his departure from this River where he lay at anchor, being about some league from the City of *Avaa*, he sent his Treasurer, named *Dioçory* (with whom we eight *Portugals*, as I have related before, remained prisoners) Embassador to the *Calaminhan*, a Prince of mighty power, who is seated in the midst of this region in a great and spacious extent of Country, and of whom I shall say something when I come to speak of him. The subject of this Embassage was to make him his Brother in Arms by a League and Contract of new amity, offering for that effect to give him a certain quantity of Gold and precious stones, as also to render unto him certain Frontier Lands of his Kingdom, upon condition that the Spring following he should keep the *Siamon* in war for to divert him from succoring the King of *Avaa*, and thereby give him means the more easily to take his City from him, without fear of that assistance which that King hoped should serve for an obstacle to his design. This Embassador departed then after he had imbarqued himself in a *Laulea*, that was attended on by twelve *Seroos*, wherein there were three hundred men of service, and his guard, besides the Watermen and Mariners, whose number was little less. The Presents which he carryed to the *Calaminhan* were very great, and consisted in divers rich pieces, as well of Gold as of precious stones, but above all in the Harness of an Elephant, which according to reports was worth above six hundred thousand Duckets, and it was thought that all the Presents put together amounted to a Million of Gold. At his departure, amongst other favors, which the King his Master conferred on him, this same was not the least for us, that he gave us eight unto him for to be his perpetual slaves ; Having clothed us then very well, and furnished us abundantly with all things necessary, he seemed to be exceedingly contented with having us along with him in this Voyage, and ever after he made more account of us, then of all the rest that followed him.

CHAP.

CHAP. LV.

Our going with the King of Bramaa's *Ambassadour to the* Calaminham, *with the Course which we held until we arrived at the Temple or* Pagod *of* Timagoogoo, *and a Description thereof.*

IT seems fit unto me, and conformable to that which I am relating, to leave for a while this §. 1. Tyrant of *Bramaa*, to whom I will return again when time shall serve, for to intreat here of the way we held for to go into *Timplan*, the capital City of the Empire of the *Calaminham*, which signifies, *Lord of the world*, for in their language *Cala* is Lord, and *Minhan* the world; This Prince also entitles himself, *The absolute Lord of the indomptable force of the Elephants of the Earth*; And indeed I do not think that in all the world there is a greater Lord then he, as I shall declare hereafter. This Ambassadour then departing from *Avaa* in the month of *October*, a thousand, five hundred, forty and five, took his course up the river of *Queitor*, steering West, South-East, and in many places Eastward by reason of the winding of the water, and so in this diversity of rhombes we continued our voyage seven days together, at the end whereof we arrived at a Channel, called *Guampanoo*; through which the *Rhobamo*, who was our Pilot, took his course, that he might decline the *Siamons* Country, being so commanded to do by the express Order of the King: A while after we came to a great Town, named *Gataldy*, where the Ambassadour stayed three days to make provision of certain things necessary for his voyage. Having left this place we went on still, rowing up through his Channel eleven dayes longer, during which time we met not with any place that was remarkable, only we saw some small villages, the houses whereof were covered with thatch, and peopled with very poor folks, and yet for all that the fields are full of Cattel, which seemed to have no Master, for we killed twenty and thirty of them in a day in the sight of those of the Country, no man so much as finding fault with it, but contrarily they brought them in courtesie to us, as if they were glad to see us kill them in that sort. At our going out of this Channel of *Guampanoo* we entred into a very great river, called *Angegumaa*, that was above three Leagues broad, and in some places six and twenty fathom deep, with such impetuous currents, as they drove us often-times from our course; This river we coasted above seven dayes together, and at length arrived at a pretty little walled Town, named *Gumbim*, in the Kingdom of *Jangromaa*, invironed on the Lands side for five or six leagues space with Forrests of *Benjamin*, as also with Plains of Lacre, wherewith they ordinarily traded to *Martabano*, and do also lade there many vessels with those commodities for to transport them into divers Countries of the *Indiaes*, as to the Streight of *Mecqua*, to *Alcoçer*, and *Judaa*. There is also in this Town great store of Musk, far better then that of *China*, which from thence is carried to *Martabano* and *Pegu*, where those of our Nation buy of it therewith to traffique at *Narsingua*, *Orixaa*, and *Masulepatan*. The women of this Country are all very white and well-favoured; They apparel themselves with Stuffs made of Silk and Cotten-wool, wear links of gold and silver about their legs, and rich Carcanets about their necks; The ground there is of it self exceeding fertile in Wheat, Rice, Millets, Sugar, Wax, and Cattel: This Town with ten leagues of circuit about it, yields every year to the King of *Jangomaa* threescore Altars of gold, which are seven hundred thousand Duckets of our mony. From thence we coasted the river Southward, for the space of above seven dayes, and arrived at a great Town, named *Catammas*, which in our language signifies, *the golden Crevice*, being the Patrimony of *Raudiavaa Tinhau*, the *Calaminhams* second Son. The *Naugator* of this Town gave good entertainment to the Ambassadour, and sent him many sorts of refreshments for his followers; withall he gave him to understand that the *Calaminham* was at the City of *Timplan*. We departed from this place on a *Sunday* morning, and the day after about evening we came to a Fortress, called *Campalagor*, built in the midst of the river in the form of an Island upon a rock, and invironed with good free-stone, having three Bulwarks, and two Towers seven stories high, wherein, they told the Ambassador, was one of the four and twenty Treasures, which the *Calaminham* had in this Kingdom, the most part whereof consisted in Lingots of silver, of the weight of six thousand *Candins*, which are four and twenty thousand Quintals, and it was said, that all this silver was buried in wells under ground. After this we still continued our course for the space of thirteen days, during the which we saw on both sides of the river

many

many very goodly places, whereof the moſt were fair Towns, and the reſt ſtately high Trees, delicate Gardens, and great Plains full of Corn, as alſo much Cattel, red Deer, Shamoiſes, and Rhinocerots, under the keeping of certain men on horsback who looked to them whileſt they fed. On the river there were a great number of veſſels, where in much abundance was all things to be ſold which the earth produceth, wherewith it hath pleaſed God to enrich theſe Countries more then any other in the world. Now foraſmuch as the Ambaſſadour fell ſick here of an Impoſtume in his ſtomack, he was councelled to proceed no further till he was healed, ſo that he reſolved to go with ſome of his Train for to be cured to a famous Hoſpital, ſome twelve Leagues from thence, in a *Pagode*, named *Tinagoogoo*, which ſignifies *the God of thouſand Gods*, and ſo departing at the ſame inſtant he arrived there on *Saturday* about night.

§.2.   The Ambaſſadour being ſet on ſhore was the next day led to an Hoſpital, called *Chipano-can*, whither the greateſt Lords uſed to repair when they were ſick, and where there were two and forty ſeveral Lodgings very neat and convenient, in one of the which he was placed by the expreſs command of the *Puitaleu*, who was as it were Governour of the Hoſpital: There care was taken that he wanted for nothing, but was furniſhed in abundance with all that was neceſſary for him: I will omit the odours, the neatneſs, the care of attendance, the veſ-ſels, the robes, the exquiſite meats, the delicacies, and all the delights that may be imagined, which were to be had there with as much perfection and curioſity, as more cannot be deſired. Thither likewiſe came twice a day to him exceeding fair women, who ſung to the Tune of Inſtruments of Muſick, and at certain hours repreſented Playes, or Comedies before him, that were very pleaſant, and finely ſet forth. Now that I may not trouble my ſelf in recount-ing here at length the infinite number of things, which I could ſpeak of concerning this Sub-ject, I will paſs over many of them in ſilence, whereof, other perſons that could better ex-preſs them then my ſelf, would peradventure make great eſteem. After we had been eight and twenty days there, by which time the Ambaſſador was perfectly cured, we departed from thence for to go to a Town, named *Meidur*, twelve leagues further up the river of *Angeguma*; But that I may not be blamed for failing in the promiſe which I made heretofore of ſpeaking of this *Pagods* of *Tinagoogoo*, I will here leave the Ambaſſadour to his Voyage, and return me to the *Pagode*, that of ſo many things which we ſaw there I may deliver ſome one, for to ſhew how little we Chriſtians do to ſave our ſouls, in compariſon of that much theſe wret-ches do to loſe theirs. During the eight and twenty dayes which the Ambaſſadour imployed in recovering his health, we nine *Portugals* that waited on him not knowing what to do, or how to beſtow our time in the mean while, no more then the reſt, we paſt it away in di-vers things, according to each ones fancy and delight, for to that purpoſe we wanted no com-modities. Thus ſome applied themſelves to the hunting of Stags and Wild-boars, whereof there is great ſtore in that Country; Some to the purſuing of Tygers, Rhinocerots, Ounces, Zeores, Lions, Buffles, Wild-bulls, and of many other ſuch kind of beaſts which we have not heard ſpoken of in our *Europe*; ſome to ſhooting at Wild-ducks, Geeſe, and ſuch like Water-fowl; ſome to hawking with Vultures and Faulcons; and ſome to fiſhing for Trowts, Mackarels, Chevins, Mullets, Soles, and many other ſorts of fiſh, where-of there is great abundance in all the rivers of this Empire. In this manner we be-ſtowed our time, now in one thing, and then in another, but that which we gave our ſelves moſt unto was to hear, and ſee, as alſo to enquire after the Laws of the Coun-try, the *Pagodes*, and Sacrifices which we beheld there with much terrour and aſtoniſh-ment: Howbeit I purpoſe not to make any relation here more then of a few of them, which I conceive may ſuffice to draw out the conſequences of thoſe that I ſhall not diſ-courſe of. I ſay then that one of thoſe ſacrifices was made on the day of the new Moon of *December*, namely on the ninth of that Month, which is a time wherein theſe blinded peo-ple are accuſtomed to celebrate a Feaſt, called by thoſe of the Country *Maſſunterivoo*; by thoſe of *Jappon*, *Ferioo*; by the *Chineſes Maneioo*; by the *Lequios Champas*, and *Cauchins*, *Ampatilor*; by the *Siamens*, *Bramaas*, *Paſuas*, and *Sacotays*, *Sanſaporau*; ſo that though all theſe names through the diverſity of thoſe languages are different, yet do they in our tongue ſignifie all one thing, that is, *The memorial of all the dead*. This was then the Feaſt which we ſaw celebrated here with ſo much diverſity of things that we never dreamt of, as I know not where to begin; for ſuch a multitude of people of all the Nations of theſe Countries came flocking to this place, as is not to be expreſſed, howbeit

beit the chiefeft caufe of their repair thither in fuch numbers, is a Fair, which is kept all the time of the Feaft, being fifteen dayes, namely from the new to the full Moon. In this Fair are all things to be fold, which Nature hath created on the earth, or in the Sea, and that in fo high a degree of abundance, as there is not any one kind of thing, whereof there are not whole Streets of Houfes, Cabbins, or Tents, fo long that one can hardly fee from one end to the other. All thefe ftreets are replenifhed with very rich Merchants, befides an infinite company of other people, who are lodged all along the River, which is above two Leagues broad, and planted about with feveral forts of Trees, as Walnuts, Chefnuts, Cocos, and Dates, whereof every one takes what he pleafeth, becaufe it doth all belong to the *Pagode*. The Temple of this Idol is a very fumptuous Edifice, fcituated in the midft of a Plain upon a little round hill, more then half a league in circuit: It is built all flope fifteen fathom high, and from thence upward it hath a wall of free-ftone of fome three fathom, with its Bulwarks, and Towers, after the fafhion of ours. Within the inclofure of this wall there is a platform made level with Battlements, a ftones caft in bredth, which together with the wall extends round about the hill, fo that at firft fight one would take it for a Gallery. There are likewife all along an hundred and threefcore Hofpitals, in each whereof are above an hundred houfes, which are low, but very neat and convenient, where the Pilgrimes, *Fucateus*, and *Daroezes* are entertained, which come thither in troops, like the Gipfies in our *Europe*, with their Captains, each company of them having two or three thoufand perfons, fome more, fome lefs, according as the Kingdoms from whence they refort are nearer or further off; now it is known of what Country they are by the devices which they carry in their Banners. From the top to the bottom it is all invironed with Cyprefs-trees, and Cedars, where many fountains of moft excellent water do continually flow forth, and on the higheft part of this hill, almoft a quarter of a league in circuit, there are four Convents, and in them very fumptuous and rich Temples, namely two of men, and as many of women, in each of which, as we were affured, were very near five hundred perfons. In the midft of thefe four Monafteries there is a Garden, compaffed about with three inclofures of Ballifters of Lattin, having very fair Arches, of curious Mafons-work, and Steeples guilt all over, with a number of little filver bels in them, which ting continually with the moving of the air. This Chappel of the Idol *Tinagoogoo* is of a round form, all overlaid on the in-fide with plates of filver wrought in flowers, and garnifhed with a great many Branches for lights of the fame mettal. This Monfter, of whom we could not judge, whether he were gold, wood, or copper guilt, ftood upright on his feet, with his hands lifted up to Heaven, and a rich Crown on his head; round about him were many other little Idols on their knees, and beholding him as it were amazed: Below were two men made of brafs, in the fafhion of Gyants, feven and thirty fpans high, and very ugly and deformed, whom they held for the Gods of the twelve months of the year. Without this place alfo there were an hundred and forty Gyants, who ranked in two Files inclofed it round about, and were made of caft iron, holding Halberds in their hands, as if they had been the Guard of it; fo that all the Marvels of this Edifice put together made it appear fo ftately, that looking upon it one could not fufficiently efteem the riches and fumptuoufnefs thereof. But fetting afide for this prefent the relation I could make of the buildings of this *Pagode*, becaufe that which I have faid of it may, me thinks, fuffice for the underftanding of the reft, I will intreat here of the Sacrifices which we faw to be made there on a feftival day, called by them, *Xipatilan*, fignifiing, *The refrefhing of good people.*

CHAP. LVI.

The great and sumptuous Procession made in this Pagode, together with their Sacrifices; and other particularities.

§.1. WHilest this Feast of these *Gentiles*, as also the Fair, which was kept all the time thereof, endured for the space of fifteen days, with an infinite concourse of Merchants and Pilgrims, that came flocking thither from all parts, as I have declared before, there were many Sacrifices made there with different ceremonies, not a day passing without some new thing or other. For amongst many of great charge, and very worthy of observation, one of the chiefest was a *Jubile* after their manner, which was published the fifth day of the Moon, together with a Procession, that was above three leagues in length, as we could guess; It was the common opinion of all, that in this Procession there were forty thousand Priests of the four and twenty Sects, which are in this Empire, most of them were of different dignities, and called *Grepos, Talagrepos, Roolims, Neepois, Bicos, Sacareus*, and *Chanfarauhos*; Now by the ornaments they wear, as also by the devices and ensigns which they carry in their hands, they may be distinguished, and so every of them is respected according to his dignity; Howbeit these went not on foot as the other ordinary Priests, for that they were as this day forbidden upon pain of great sin to tread upon the ground, so that they caused themselves to be born in *Pallaquins*, or Arm-chairs, upon the shoulders of other Priests their inferiors, apparelled in green Sattin, with their Stoles of Carnation Damask. In the midst of the ranks of this Procession were all the inventions of their Sacrifices to be seen, as also the rich Custodes of their Idols, for the which each of them had a particular Devotion; They that carryed them were clothed in yellow, having each of them a big wax candle in his hand, and between every fifteen of those Custodes went a triumphant Charet, all which Charets put together were in number an hundred twenty and six: All these Charets were four, and some five stories high, with as many wheels on either side; In each of them there were at the least two hundred persons, what with the Priests and the Guards, and on the top of all an Idol of Silver, with a Miter of Gold on its head, and all of them had rich chains of Pearl and precious stones about their necks; round about every Charet went little Boys, carrying Silver Maces on their shoulders, and behind them were a many of Caskets full of exquisite perfumes, as also divers persons with Censors in their hands, who ever and anon censed the Idol to the tune of certain Instruments of Musick, saying three times with a lamentable voyce, *Lord, asswage the pains of the dead, to the end they may praise thee peaceably*; whereunto all the people answered with a strange noise, *Such may thy pleasure be, and so may it come to pass every day wherein thou shewest us the Sun.* Each of these Charets was drawn by above three thousand persons, who for that purpose made use of very long coards, covered with silk, and thereby gained to themselves plenary remission of their sins, without restitution to be made of any thing at all: Now that many might participate of this absolution by drawing the coard, they set their hands to it one after and close to another, continuing doing so to the very end, in such sort that the whole coard was covered with hands, and nothing else to be seen; but that they also which were without might gain this indulgence, they helped those that had their hands on the coard by putting theirs about their shoulders, then they that were behind them did the like, and so consequently all the rest: In this manner throughout the whole length of the coard there were six or seven Ranks or Files, and in each of them above five hundred persons. This Procession was environed with a great number of Horsemen, that carryed staves with pikes at both ends, who riding all about, went crying to the people, which were infinite in number, that they should make way, and not interrupt the Priests in their prayers: Many times also they struck those so rudely whom they first met withall, as they beat down three or four together, or hurt them grievously, no man daring to find fault with, or so much as speak a word against it. In this order this mervelous Procession passed through above an hundred streets, which to that end were all adorned with boughs of Palms and Myrtle, amongst the which were many Standarts and Banners of Silk planted; There were also many Tables set up in divers places, where all that desired it for Gods sake were admitted to eat of free-cost, yea and in other parts they had clothes

and

and mony given them ; There likewise Enemies reconciled themselves one to another, and the rich men forgave them their debts which were not able to pay. In a word, so many good works were done there, more proper for Cristians, then for Gentiles, as I must needs conclude, that if they had been done with Faith and Baptism for the love of our Lord Jesus Christ, and without any mixture of the things of this world, assuredly they would have been acceptable to him. But alas ! the best was wanting to them, and that both for theirs and our sins. Whilest this Procession, together with the Charets wherein the Idols were, passed along in this manner, and that with a dreadful noise of Drums, and other such instruments, behold where out of certain wooden Sheds made expresly for that purpose, six, seven, eight, or ten men, all besmeared with odors, and wrapped up in silk, wearing Gold Bracelets about their wrists, start forth all at once, and room being instantly made them by the people, after they had saluted the Idol which was on the top of the Charet, they went and layd themselves down athwart on the ground, so that the wheels coming to go over them crush'd them all to pieces, which the assistants beholding, cryed out aloud together, *My Soul be with thine :* Presently whereupon nine or ten of the Priests descending from the Charet took up these blessed, or rather accursed, creatures, that sacrificed themselves in this sort, and putting the head, bowels, and all the other members so crushed in pieces into great bowls made for that purpose, they shewed them to the people from the highest part of the Charet where the Idol stood, saying with a pitiful voyce, *Miserable sinners, fall ye to praying, that God may make you worthy to be a Saint, as this here is, who hath now offered himself up as a sweet smelling Sacrifice.* Whereunto all the people prostrated on the ground answered with a fearful noise, *We hope that the God of a thousand Gods will permit to be so.* In this manner many other of these wretches sacrificed themselves, to the number, as we were told by certain Merchants worthy of credit, of six hundred and more. After these followed other Martyrs of the Devil, whom they called *Xixaporaus,* which sacrificed themselves before the said Charets, by most mercilesly slashing themselves with sharp Rasors, that to behold them how they did it, one could not think but that they were altogether insensible ; for they cut off great gobbets of their flesh, and holding them on high at the end of Arrows, as if they would shoot them up to Heaven, they said, *That they made a Present thereof to God for the Souls of their Fathers, of their Wives, of their Children, or of such a one, for whose sake they did this wicked work.* Now wheresoever this gobbet of flesh chanced to fall, there ran so much people to catch it up, as oftentimes many were stifled in the press, for they held it as a very great relique. In this sort these miserable wretches stood upon their feet, all bathed in their own blood, without Noses, without Ears, and without any resemblance at all of man, until at length they fell down stark dead on the Earth, then came the *Grepos* in all haste down from the top of the Charet, and cutting off their heads, shewed them to all the people, who kneeling on the ground, and lifting up their hands to Heaven cryed out with a loud voyce, *Let us, O Lord, live to that time, wherein for thy service we may do as this same here hath done.* There were others also whom the Devil drew thither after another manner ; These same craving an Alms, said, *Give me an Alms for Gods sake, or if thou dost it not, I will kill my self.* So that if they were not presently contented, they would instantly cut their own throats with Rasors which they held in their hands, or stab themselves in to the belly, and so drop down stark dead ; whereupon the *Grepos* ran suddenly to them, and having cut off their heads, shewed them, as before, to the people, who reverenced them prostrated on the ground. We likewise saw some, named *Nucaramons,* men of a very ill look, clothed with Tygers skins, and carrying in their hands certain pots of Copper full of excrements, and filthy corrupted urine, the stench whereof was so horrible and insupportable, as it was not possible for any nostril to endure it ; These craving an Alms of the people, said ; *Give me an Alms, and that instantly, otherwise I will eat this ordure which the Devil eats, and bespatter thee with it, that so thou mayst be accursed as he is.* They no sooner uttered these words, but that all ran hastily to give them an Alms, for if they stay'd never so little, they straightway set the pot to their mouths, and taking a great sup of that stinking stuff, they therewith all to bedashed such as they pleased ; in the mean time all others that beheld them so drest, holding them accursed, fell upon them, and entreated them in such a strange fashion, as the poor wretches knew not which way to turn themselves ; for there was not a man of the company that drove them not away with blows, and that railed not at them, saying ; *That they were accursed for having been the cause that*

this

this holy man had eaten of that beastly filth which the Devil feeds upon, and therefore was become stinking before God, so that he could neither go into Paradise, nor live amongst men. Behold how strange the blindness of this people is, who otherwise have judgment and wit enough. I will pass by much other beastliness committed by them, which is so far esloigned from all reason, as they serve for a great motive unto us, to render thanks without ceasing unto God for the infinite mercy and goodness that he shews us, in giving us the light of true Faith for the saving of our Souls.

§.2.   Of the fifteen days that this Feast was to last, nine being past, all the people, which were there assembled, feigning that the gluttonous Serpent of the House of Smoke (who is their *Lucifer,* as I have said elsewhere) was come for to steal away the ashes of them that were dead in these several Sacrifices, and so to keep their Souls from going into Heaven, there arose among them so great and dreadful a noise, as words are not able to express it ; for to the confused voyces that were heard from every part, there was adjoyned such a ringing of Bells and Basins, beating of Drums, and winding of Horns, as it was not possible to hear one another, and all this was done to fright away the Devil. Now this noise endured from one of the clock in the afternoon till the next morning, and it is not to be believed what a world of lights and Torches were spent that night, besides the infinite number of fires that were kindled every where ; the reason hereof was, as they said, *For that* Tinagoogoo, *the God of thousand Gods, was gone in quest of the gluttonous Serpent, for to kill him with a Sword which had been given him from Heaven.* After the night had been past thus amidst this infernal noise and tumult, as soon as it was day the whole Hill, whereon the Temple was built, appeared full of white Banners, which the people beholding, they fell straight to giving thanks unto God, and to that end they prostrated themselves on the ground with great demonstrations of joy, and then began to send presents one to another for the good news they received from the Priests by the shew of those white Banners, an assured sign that the gluttonous Serpent was killed. So all the people, transported with incredible gladness, fell to going up the hill, whereon the Temple stood, by four and twenty several accesses that there were unto it, for to give thanks unto the Idol, and chaunt his praises for the victory he had the night past obtained over the gluttonous Serpent, and cutting off his head : This throng of people continued three days, and three nights, so that during that time it was not possible to break through the press on the way, but with much pain. Now we *Portugals* having little to do, resolved to go thither also for to see those abuses, wherefore we went to ask leave of the Embassador, but he denyed us for the present, willing us to stay till the next day, and that then we should wait on him thither, for in his last sickness he had vowed to visit it ; hereat we were very glad, because we thought that by this means we should the more easily see all that we desired : The morrow after, which was the third day of this Assembly, the greatest croud being over, we went along with him to the Temple of *Tinagoogoo,* and at length arrived, though with much ado, at the Hill whereon it was built. There we saw six very fair long streets, all full of Scales hanging on great Rods of Brass ; In these Scales a number of people weighed themselves, as well for the accomplishment of the vows they had made in their adversities and sickness, as for the remission of all the sins they had committed till that present, and the weight which each of them layd in the other Scale was answerable to the quality of the fault they had done : So they that found themselves culpable of gluttony, and had not all that year used any abstinence, weighed themselves with Hony, Sugar, Eggs, and Butter, which were things not displeasing to the Priests, from whom they were to receive absolution ; They that were addicted to sensuality weighed themselves with Cotton wool, Feathers, Cloth, Apparel, Wine, and sweet Odors, because, say they, those things incite a man to that sin : They that were uncharitable to the poor weighed themselves with Coyn of Copper, Tin, and Silver, or with pieces of Gold ; The slothful with Wood, Rice, Coals, Pork, and Fruit ; and the envious, because they reap no benefit by their maligning the prosperity of others, expiated their sin by confessing it publiquely, and suffering a dozen boxes on the ear to be given them in the memory and praise of the twelve Moons of the year : As for the sin of pride, it was satisfied with dryed fish, Brooms, and Cow-dung, as being the basest of things ; And touching them that had spoken ill of their Neighbors, without asking them forgiveness, they put for that a Cow into the Scale, or else an Hog, a Sheep, or a Stag : so that infinite was the number of those which weighed themselves in the Scales that were in those six

streets,

ſtreets, from whom the Prieſts received ſo much Alms, as there were great piles of all ſorts of things made up all along. Now for the poor that had nothing to give for the remiſſion of their ſins, they offered their own hair, which was preſently cut off by above an hundred Prieſts, who for that effect ſat in order one by another on low ſtools, with Sizzars in their hands; There alſo we ſaw great heaps of that hair, whereof other *Grepos*, which were a thouſand at leaſt, and ranked alſo in order, made Wreathes, Treſſes, Rings, and Bracelets, which one or another bought for to carry home to their houſes, even as our Pilgrims uſe to do, that come from *Santiago de Compoſtella*, or other ſuch places. Our Embaſſador, being amazed at the ſight of theſe things, enquired further of the Prieſts concerning them, who beſides other particulars told him, that all thoſe alms, and other offerings which were given there during the fifteen days of this Aſſembly, amounted to a great Revenue, and that even of the hair of the poor alone there was raiſed every year above an hundred thouſand *pardanis* of Gold, which are fourſcore and ten thouſand Duckets of our Mony, whereby one may judg what a world of wealth was made of all the reſt. After that the Embaſſador had ſtay'd ſometime in the ſtreets of the Scales, he paſſed on through all the other quarters, where were Comedies, dancing, wraſtling, and excellent conſorts of all kinds of muſick, till at length we arrived at *Tinagoogoo*, but with much labor and pain, becauſe the throng was ſo great, as one could hardly break through it. This Temple had but one Iſle, that was very long and ſpacious, and full of great wax lights, each of them having ten or eleven wieks in it, ſet up all about in Silver Candleſticks; there was alſo great ſtore of perfumes of Aloes and Benjamin : As for the Image of *Tinagoogoo*, it was placed in the midſt of the Temple upon a ſtately Tribunal in the form of an Altar, environed with a number of Silver Candleſticks, and a many of Children attired in purple, which did nothing but cenſe it at the ſound of Inſtruments of muſick, whereon the Prieſts played reaſonable well : Before this Idol danced, to the tune of the ſaid Inſtrument, certain Ladies, which were wonderful fair, and richly clad, to whom the people preſented their alms and offerings, which the Prieſts received for them, and then layd them before the Tribunal of the Idol with a great deal of ceremony and complement, ever and anon proſtrating themſelves on the ground. The Statue of this Monſter was ſeven and twenty ſpans high, having the face of a Gyant, the hair of a Negro, wide diſtorted noſtrils, mighty great lips, and a very ſowre and ill-favored countenance ; He had in his hand an Hatchet in the form of a Coopers Addis, but with a far longer handle : With this Addis, as the Prieſts made the people believe, *this Monſter the night before killed the gluttonous Serpent of the Houſe of Smoke, for that he would have ſtoln away the aſhes of thoſe that ſacrificed themſelves.* There alſo we ſaw the Serpent amidſt the place before the Tribunal in the form of an Adder, more horrible to behold then the wit of man can imagine, and done ſo to the life, as all that looked on it trembled for fear ; It was layd all along, with the head cut off, being eight fathom long, and the neck of it as thick as a Buſhel, ſo lively repreſented, that though we knew it to be an artificial thing, yet could we not chuſe but be afraid of it. In the mean time all the aſſiſtants ran thronging about it, ſome pricking it with the points of their Halberds, and ſome with their Daggers, every one with railing ſpeeches curſing, and calling it, *Proud, preſumptuous, accurſed, infernal Mannor, Pool of Damnation, envious of Gods goodneſs, hunger-ſtarved Dragon, in the midſt of the night,* and many other names, which they delivered in ſuch extraordinary terms, and ſo fitted to the effects of this *Serpent*, as we could not but admire them. That done, they put into Baſins which ſtood at the foot of the Idols Tribunal a world of alms, of Gold, Silver, Jewels, pieces of Silk, fine Callicoes, Mony, and hundred other things in very great abundance. After we had ſeen all theſe things, we continued following the Embaſſador, who went to ſee the Grots of the Hermits or Penitents, which were at the utmoſt end of the Wood, all cut out of the hard Rock, and in ſuch order, as one would have thought that Nature, rather then the hand of man, had labored in it. There were an hundred forty and two of them, in ſome of the which remained divers men, whom they held for Saints, and that did very great and auſtere pennance ; They in the firſt Grots wore long Robes like the *Bonzes* of *Japan*, and followed the Law of an Idol, that had ſometimes been a man, called *Situmpor michay*, who during his life enjoyned thoſe of his Sect to lead their lives in great auſterity, aſſuring them that the only and true way to gain Heaven, was to ſubdue the fleſh, and that the more they labored to afflict themſelves, the more liberally God would grant them all they could demand of him. They which accompanyed

companyed us thither, told us, that they seldom eat any thing but herbs boyled, a few Beans of Aricot roſted, and wilde fruit, which were provided for them by other Prieſts, who as the Purveyors of a Cloiſter took care to furniſh theſe Penitents with ſuch things as were conſortmable to the Law whereof they made profeſſion. After theſe we ſaw in a Grot others of a Sect of one of their Saints, or rather of a Devil, named *Angemacur*, theſe lived in deep holes, made in the midſt of the Rock, according to the Rule of their wretched order, eating nothing but Flies, Ants, Scorpions, and Spiders, with the juyce of a certain Herb growing in abundance thereabout, much like to ſorrel; Theſe ſpent their time in meditating day and night, with their eyes lifted up to Heaven, and their hands cloſed one within another, for a teſtimony that they deſired nothing of this world, and in that manner dyed like beaſts, but they are accounted greater Saints then all the reſt, and as ſuch, after they are dead, they burn them in fires, whereinto they caſt great quantities of moſt precious perfumes; the Funeral pomp being celebrated with great ſtate, and very rich offerings, they have ſumptuous Temples erected unto them, thereby to draw the living to do as they had done, for to obtain this vain glory, which is all the recompence that the world gives them for their exceſſive pennance. We likewiſe ſaw others of a Sect altogether diabolical, invented by a certain *Gileu Mitray*; Theſe have ſundry orders of pennance, and are not much different in their Opinions from the *Abiſſins* of *Ethiopia*; Now that their abſtinence may be the more agreeable to their Idol, ſome of them eat nothing but filthy thick ſpitings and ſnot, with Graſhoppers and Hens dung; others clots of blood drawn from other men, with bitter fruits and herbs brought to them from the wood, by reaſon whereof they live but a ſhort time, and have ſo bad a look and colour, as they fright thoſe that behold them. I will paſs by them of the Sect of *Godomem*, who ſpend their whole life in crying day and night on thoſe mountains, *Godomem*, *Godomem*, and deſiſt not from it until they fall down ſtark dead to the ground for want of breath: Neither will I ſpeak of them, which they call *Taxilacons*, who dye more brutiſhly then the reſt, for they ſhut themſelves up in certain Grots made of purpoſe for it, that are very little and cloſe, ſtopped on all ſides, and then burning green thiſtles and thorns in them, they choke themſelves with the ſmoke thereof; Whereby one may ſee how by ſuch rude and different ways of living theſe miſerable creatures render themſelves the Devils Martyrs, who in reward thereof gives them everlaſting Hell-fire; and verily it is a pitiful thing to behold the great pains which theſe wretches take to loſe themſelves, and the little that we do to be ſaved.

CHAP.

CHAP. LVII.

What we saw in the continuing of our voyage, until we arrived at the City of Timplan.

AFter we had seen all these things with wonder enough, we departed from this *Pagod* of §.1.
Tinagoogoo, and continued on our way for thirteen days together, at the end whereof
we arrived at two great Towns, scituated on the Bank of the river, just opposite the one a-
gainst the other, about the distance of a stones cast, one of the which was called *Manavedia*,
and the other *Singilapau*; In the midst of this same river, which was there somewhat nar-
row, there was an Island by nature formed round, and in it a rock six and thirty fathom high,
and a Cross-bow shoot broad; upon this rock was a Fort built, with nine Bulwarks and five
Towers; without the rampire of the wall it was invironed with two rows of great iron gates,
and from the Bulwarks to the other side of the river ran a huge Chain of iron, to keep vessels
from passing along, so that nothing could possibly enter there: At one of these two Towns,
which was called *Singilapau*, the Ambassadour landed, where he was exceedingly well entertained by the *Xemimbrum*, or Governour of it, who likewise furnished all his Train with
great store of refreshments. The next morning we left this place, accompanied with twenty
Laulès, wherein there were a thousand men and better, and about evening we arrived at the
Custom-houses of the Kingdom, which are two strong places, and from the one to the other
run five mighty great chains of Latten all atwart the whole bredth of the river, so that nothing can pass in and out without leave; Hither came a man in a swift *Seroo* to the Ambassadour, and told him that he was to go ashore at *Campalagro*, which was one of the two
Castles on the South-side, for to shew the Letter which this King had sent by him to the *Calaminham*, to see if it were written in the form that was required in speaking to him, as was
usually observed. The Ambassadour presently obeyed, and being come to land he was led into
a great Hall, where were three men set at a table, with a great many Gentlemen, who gave
him good entertainment, and demanded of him the occasion of his coming thither, as they
that knew nothing of it; Whereunto the Ambassadour answered; *That he came thither
from the King of* Bramaa, *Lord of* Tanguu, *and that he had a message to deliver unto the
holy* Calaminham *concerning matters greatly importing his Estate.* Then having made further
answer to other questions, which were put to him in a way of ceremony by the three principal
persons that were at the Table, he shewed them the letter, wherein they corrected some words,
which were not of the style wherewith they were accustomed to speak to the *Calaminham*;
together with this letter the Ambassadour shewed them the present which he had brought
for him, whereat they very much wondred, especially when they saw the Chair for an Elephant of gold and precious stones, which in the judgments of divers Lapidaries was worth
above six hundred thousand Duckets, besides the other rich pieces that he carried him also, as
I have before related. After we had our dispatch from this first Custom-house, we went to
the other, where we found more venerable men then the former, who with another new Ceremony looked likewise on the Letter, and the present, and put to all the several parcels of it
strings of wreathed carnation silk, with three Seals in Lacre, which was as the conclusion of the receiving of the Ambassy by the *Calaminham*. The same day there came
a man from the next Town of *Queitor*, sent by the Governour of the Kingdom to visit the
Ambassadour with a present of refreshments of flesh, fruit, and other such things after their
manner. During nine dayes that the Ambassadour stayed in this place he was abundantly furnished with all things necessary, both for his own Person, and his Train, and withall was entertained with sundry sports of hunting and fishing, as also with Feasts, accompaied with musick and Comedies represented by very beautiful women, and richly attired: In the mean time
we *Portugals* went with the permission of the Ambassadour to see certain things, which they
of the Country had much commended unto us, namely very antique buildings, rich and sumptuous Temples, very fair Gardens, Houses and Castles, that were all along the side of this river, made after a strange fashion, well fortified, and of great charge, amongst the which there
was an Hospital for to lodge pilgrims in, called *Manicafaran*, signifying in our tongue, *The
Prison of the Gods*, which was above a League in bredth; Here we saw twelve streets, all
vaulted over, and in every one of them two hundred and forty houses, namely, sixscore on

each

each side, which made in all two thousand, eight hundred, and fourscore, all full of pilgrims, who the whole year throughout came thither in pilgrimage from divers Countries; for, as they told, this pilgrimage ought to be of far greater merit then all others, because that these Idols imprisoned by strangers have need of company. All these pilgrims, which, as they of the Country say, are all the year long without discontinuing above six thousand, have meat given them the whole time of their abode there, at the charge, and out of the revenue of the house: They are served by four thousand Priests of *Manicafaran*, who with many others reside within the same inclosure in sixscore religious houses, where there are also as many women that serve in the like manner. The Temple of this Hospital was very great, with three Isles after the fashion of ours, in the midst whereof was a remarkable Chappel built round, and invironed with three very big Ballisters of Latten; within it there were fourscore Idols of men and women, besides many other little gods, that lay prostrated on the ground, for the fourscore great Idols only stood upright, and were all tied together with chains of iron; As for the little ones, they were, as I said, laid along on the pavement, as the children of these greater, and tied six to six by the middle with other slighter chains: Moreover without the Ballisters in two Files there stood two hundred, forty and four Giants of brass, six and twenty spans high, with their Halberds and Clubs upon their shoulders, as if they had been set there for the Guard of the captive Gods. There was over-head upon iron rods, that traversed the Isles of the Temple, great store of Lamps hanging, having seven or eight Matches apiece in them, in the fashion of Candlesticks, like to them of the *Indiaes*, all varnished without, as also the walls were, and every thing else that welsaw there, in token of mourning, by reason of the captivity of these Gods. Being amazed as well at that which I have recounted, as at many other things which I pass over in silence, and not able to comprehend what they meant by the imprisonment of these gods, we demanded the signification of it of the Priests, whereunto one amongst them, that seemed of more authority then the rest, made us this answer; *Since I see that being Strangers, you desire to learn of me that which I know very well, and which you have never heard spoken, nor read of in your Books, I will declare the matter unto you as it past, according as it is truly delivered by our Histories. Know then, that it now seven thousand, three hundred, and twenty Moons, which make six hundred and ten years after the supputation of other Nations, since the time that an holy Calaminham, named* Xixivarem Melentay, *commanding over the Monarchy of the six and twenty Kingdoms of this Crown, waged wars with the* Siamon, *Emperour of the Mountains of the Earth, insomuch that there assembled what on the one part and the other threescore and two Kings, who putting themselves into the Field, fought so cruel and bloody a battail, as it endured from an hour before day till night, and there was slain on both sides sixteen Laquesaas of men, each of which makes an hundred thousand; At length the victory remaining to our* Calaminham, *without any more resting alive of his Forces then two hundred and thirty thousand, he ruined in four months space all the enemies Countries, with such a destruction of people, as if credit may be given to our Histories, or to what any other besides have assured, there died fifty Laquesaas of persons. This battail was fought in the first of the said seven thousand, three hundred, and twenty Moons, in the renowned Field* Vitau, *where* Quiay Nivandel *appeared to the* Calaminham, *sitting in a Chair of Wood, who acquired unto himself in this place a greater and more famous Title of honour, then all the other Gods of the* Mons *and* Siammes, *in regard whereof so often as they that inhabit the earth desire to make oath of things which pass the belief of men, they use for the more authorizing thereof to swear by the holy* Quiay Nivandel *God of Battails of the field* Vitau. *Now in a great City named* Sarocatam, *where five hundred thousand persons were slain, all these Gods, which here you see before you, were made prisoners in despight of the Kings that believed in them, and the Priests that served them with perfumes in their sacrifices. Thus by reason of so glorious a victory all those people became subject to us, and tributaries to the Crown of the* Calaminham, *who at this day holds the Scepter of this Monarchy, whereunto he was not raised but with much labour, and the shedding of a world of blood, during the threescore and four rebellions made by the said people since that time until this present; who not able to endure the captivity of their gods, for that, to say the truth, it is a mighty affront unto them, they do still in memory of so unhappy a success continue making great demonstrations of sorrow for it, renewing every year the vow they have made not to celebrate any Feast, nor to rejoyce in any kind of sort whatsoever, until they have provided for the deliverance of these*
                                                                                        prisoners:

prisoners; which also is the cause that no Lamps are seen in their Temples, and that they are resolved to light up none during the captivity of their Idols. Some of us seeming to doubt the verity hereof, because it seemed strange unto them, the *Grepo* swore that it was most true, and that also there had been killed at sundry times about the deliverance of these Gods, whom there we saw captive, above three millions of men, besides those that fell in precedent Battails; whereby one may clearly see in what a strange manner the Devil keeps these poor blinded wretches subjected unto him, and with how much abuse and extravagancy he precipitates them into hell. When we had well observed all the singularities of this Temple, we went to see another, called *Urpanesendoo,* to speak of which I desire to be excused, that I may not be forced to treat of infamous and abominable matters, wherefore omitting the great abundance of riches, and other things which we saw there; it shall suffice me to say, that this Temple is served by none but women, who are all of them the daughters of Princes, and of the principal Lords of the Kingdom, which dedicates them from their infancy to offer up their honour in sacrifice there; Now this filthy and sensual sacrifice is performed with so great charge, that many of them bestow above ten thousand Duckets in it, besides the offerings which are made to this Idol *Urpanesendoo,* to whom they sacrifice their honour. This Idol is in a Chappel that is round, and guilt all over; it is made of silver, and set upon a Tribunal in form of an Altar, invironed over-head with a great number of Candlesticks, which are all of silver likewise, every light in them having six wieks: Round about this Tribunal are many other Idols guilded over, of very comely and well-favoured women, who with their knees on the ground, and hands lifted up, adore this Idol; These same, as the Priests told us, are the holy souls of certain young Ladies, which finished their dayes there to the great honour of their parents, who made more esteem of that then of all the King could give them. They assured us that the Revenue belonging to the Idol, was three hundred thousand Duckets by the year, besides the offerings and rich ornaments of their abominable sacrifices, which was yet worth more. In this Diabolical Temple were shut up within many religious houses that we saw above five thousand women, being all of them old, and for the most part exceeding rich, so that coming to dy, they make a donation of all their wealth to the *Pagode,* wherefore it is no marvel, if it have the revenue I spoke of. From this place we went to see the companies of the strangers, which came thither in pilgrimage in the manner that I have declared. These Companies were forty and six in number, every one of an hundred, two hundred, three hundred, four hundred, or five hundred persons; nay, some of them were more, and were all lodged along by the river, as if it had been a Camp. Amidst these troops of strangers we met by chance with a *Portugal* woman, whereat we wondred more then at all we had seen before, so that desiring to know of her the reason of so strange an accident, she told us with tears, who she was, what occasion had brought her thither, and how she was at that instant the wife of one of those Pilgrims, to whom she had been married three or four and twenty years; whereunto she further added, that not daring to go and live amongst Christians because of her sin, she continued still in her wickedness, but that she hoped God would at length be pleased to bring her into some Country, where before she ended her dayes, she might repent her of her life past, and that although we found her in the company of people devoted to the service of the Devil, yet she left not for all that to be still a true Christian: we remained much amazed at so strange a relation, and not a little sorrowful also to see and understand to what a point of misfortune this poor woman was reduced, so that we told her our opinion, and what we thought was fit for her to do, whereupon she concluded to go along with us to *Timplam,* and so to *Pegu,* and from thence to set sail for *Coromandel,* there to finish her days in the Island of *St Thomé.* Having vowed unto us to do thus we quitted her, not doubting that she would lose so good an opportunity to retire her self out of the errors wherein she was, and to restore her self to an estate wherein she might be saved, since it had pleased God to permit her to meet with us in a Country so far distant from that which she could hope for: Howbeit she performed nothing, for we could never see nor hear of her afterwards, which made us to believe, that either some thing was befallen her that kept her from coming to us, or that through the obstinacy of her sins, she deserved not to make her profit of the grace which our Lord had offered to her out of his infinite goodness and mercy.

CHAP. LVIII.

The Magnificent Reception of the King of Bramaa *his Ambassadour, at the City of* Timplam; *and that which passed betwixt the* Calaminham, *and him.*

§.1. NIne dayes after the King of *Bramaa* his Ambassadour had reposed himself there by way of ceremony, according to the fashion of the Coutry, for the more honour of his Ambassage, one of the Governours of the City, called *Quampanogrem*, came to fetch him, accompanied with fourscore *Seroos* and *Laulees*, very well eqipped, and full of lusty able men: Throughout this Fleet they played on so many barbarous and ill accorded instruments, as Bels, Cymbals, Drums, and Sea-cornets, that the din thereof coming to joyn with the noise, which the Rowers made, terrified all those that heard it; and indeed one would have thought it at first to be some inchantment, or to say better, a musick of hell, if there be any there. Amidst this stir we drew near to the City, where we arrived about noon; Being come to the first Key, that was named *Campalarraia*, we saw a great many men, both Horse and Foot, all richly accoutred, as also a number of fighting Elephants, very well harnessed, having their chairs and fore-head pieces garnished with silver, and their warlike *Panores* fastened to their teeth, which rendred them very terrible. The Ambassadour was no sooner come on shore, but the *Campanogrem* took him by the hand, and falling on his knees, presented him to another great man that attended for him at the Key in great pomp; This same was called *Patedacan*, one of the chiefest of the Kingdom, as we were told; After he had with a new complement of courtesie received the Ambassadour, he offered him an Elephant furnished with a Chair and harness of gold, but whatsoever the *Mandarin* could do to make the Ambassadour accept of it, he could by no means draw him thereunto, whereupon he caused another almost as well furnished to be brought, and gave it to him. As for us nine *Portugals*, and fifty or threescore *Bramaas* they provided Horses, on which we mounted: In this manner we departed from that place, having his Chariots before us full of men, that amidst the acclamations of the people played upon divers kinds of instruments; namely on silver Cymbals, Bells, and Drums; Thus we were conducted through many long Streets, whereof nine were invironed with Ballisters of Lattin, and at the entrance into them, there were Arches very richly wrought, as also many Chapters of pillars guilt, and great Bells, which like unto clocks struck the hours, nay the quarters of the hour of the day, whereby the people were ordinarily directed. After that with much ado, by reason of the great press of people that was in the streets, we were come to the outward Court of the *Calaminham's* Pallace, which was as long, or little less, as a Faulcons shot, and broad proportionable thereunto, we saw in it above six thousand Horses, all trapped with silver and silk, and those that were mounted on them were armed with Cosslets of Lattin and Copper, head-pieces of silver, carrying Ensigns in their hands of divers Colours, and Targets at their Saddle-bows. The Commander of these Troops was the *Quietor* of Justice, who is as the Super-intendent over all the other Civil and Criminal Ministers, which is a Jurisdiction seperate by it self, from whence there is no appeal. The Ambassadour being come near unto him, who was also advanced to receive him, and the two Governours, they all prostrated themselves on the ground three times, which is amongst them a new kind of Compliment, whereupon the *Quietor* spake not a word to the Ambassadour, but onely laid his hand on his head, and then gave him a rich Scymitar that he wore by his side, which the Ambassadour accepted of very thankfully, and kissed it thrice; That done the *Quietor* set the Ambassadour on his right hand, and leaving the two *Mandarins* a little behind, they past along through two ranks of Elephants, which made a kind of Street of the length of the outward Court, they being fifteen hundred in number, all furnished with Castles, and rich Chairs of divers inventions, as also with a great many of silk Banners, and gorgeous Coverings; round about were a great Company of Halberdiers, and many other shews of Greatness and Majesty, which made us believe that this Prince was one of the mightiest of the Country. When we were come to a great Gate, that stood between two high Towers, two hundred men which guarded it no sooner saw the *Quietor*, but they all fell down on their knees. Through this Gate, we entred into another very long outward Court, where the Kings second Guard was, composed of a thousand men,

who

who were all in guilt Arms, their Swords by their fides, and on their heads Helmets wrought with gold and filver, wherein ftuck gallant plums of feveral colours. After we had paft through the middle of all this Guard we arrived at a great Hall, where there was a *Mandarim*, Uncle to the King, called the *Monvagarus*, a man of above feventy years of age, accompanied with a great number of Nobity, as alfo with many Captains and Officers of the Kingdom; About him were twelve little boyes richly clad, with great Chains of gold three or four times double about their necks, and each of them a filver Mace upon his fhoulder: As foon as the Ambaffadour was come near him, he touched him on the head with a *Ventiloe* that he held in his hand, and beholding him, *May thy entrance*, faid he, *into this Palace of the Lord of the World, be as agreeable to his eyes, as the rain is to our fields of Rice, for fo fhall he grant thee all that thy King demands of him.* From thence we went up an high pair of ftairs, and entred into a very long room, wherein there were many great Lords, who feeing the *Monvagaruu* ftood up on their feet, as acknowledging him for their Superiour; Out of this room we entred into another, where there were four Altars, very well accommodated with Idols of filver; upon one of thefe Altars we faw the Statue of a woman as big as a Giant, being eighteen fpans high, and with her arms all abroad looking up to Heaven: This Idol was of filver, and her hair of gold, which was very long, and fpread over her fhoulders; There alfo we faw a great Throne, incompaffed round about with thirty Giants of brafs, who had guilded Clubs upon their fhoulders, and faces as deformed as thofe they paint for the Divel. From this room we paft into a manner of a Gallery, adorned from the top to the bottom with a number of little Tables of Ebony, inlayed with Ivory, and full of mens heads, under every one of the which the name of him to whom it belonged was written in letters of gold; At the end of this Gallery there were a dozen of iron Rods guilt, whereon hung a great many filver Candlefticks of great value, and a number of perfuming Pans, from whence breathed forth a moft excellent odour of Amber, and Calambuco, or Lignum Aloes, but fuch as we have none in *Chriftendom*. There on an Altar invironed all about with three rows of Balliſters of filver, we faw thirteen Kings viffages of the fame mettal, with golden Mitars upon their heads, and under each of them a dead mans head, and below many Candl fticks of filver, with great white wax lights in them, which were ftuffed ever and anon by little boys, who accorded their voyces to thofe of the *Grepos* that fung in form of a Letany, anfwering one another. The *Grepos* told us that thofe thirteen dead mens heads which were under the viffages were the skulls of thirteen *Calaminhams*, which in times paft gained this Empire from certain ftrangers, called *Roparons*, who by Arms had ufurped the fame upon them of the Country; As for the other dead mens heads which we faw there, they were the skuls of fuch Commanders, as by their Heroick deeds had honourably ended their dayes in helping to recover this Empire, in regard whereof it was moft reafonable, that though death had deprived them of the recompence which they had merited by their action, yet their memory fhould not be abolifhed out of the world. When we were gone out of this Gallery, we proceeded on upon a great Bridg, that was in the form of a Street, rayled on either fide with Balliſters of Lattin, and beautified with a many of Arches curioufly wrought, upon which were Scutchions of Arms, charged with feveral devices in gold, and the Crefts over them were filver Globes, five fpans in circumferences, all very ftately and majeftical to behold. At the end of this bridge was another building, the doors whereof we found fhut, whereupon we knocked four times, they within not deigning to anfwer us, which is a ceremony obferved by them in fuch occafions; At the length after we had rung a bell four times more as it were in hafte, out comes a woman of about fifty years of age, accompanied with fix little girls, richly attired, and Scymitars upon their fhoulders garnifhed with flowers wrought in gold: This ancient woman having demanded of the *Monvagaruu* why he had rung the bell, and what he would have, he anfwered her with a great deal of refpect, *That he had there an Ambaffadour from the King of* Bramaa, *the Lord of* Tanguu, *who was come thither to treat at the feet of the* Calaminham *about certain maſters much importing his fervice.* By reafon of the great authority which this woman was in fhe feemed little to regard this anfwer, whereat we wondred much, becaufe he that fpake to her was one of the chiefeft Lords of the Kingdom, and Uncle to the *Calaminham*, as it was faid; Neverthelefs one of the fix girls that accompanied her, fpake thus in her behalf to the *Monvagaruu, My Lord, may it pleafe your Greatnefs to have a little patience till we may know whether the time be fit for the kiffing of the foot of the Throne of this Lord of the World, and advertifing him of the coming of this ftranger, and fo according to the*

grace

grace which our Lord will shew him therein, his heart may rejoyce, and we with him. That said, the door was shut again for the space of three or four Credoes, and then the six Girls came and opened it, but the ancient woman that at first came along with them, we saw no more, howbeit in stead of her there came a Boy of about nine years of age, richly apparelled, and having on his head an *hurfangua* of Gold, which is a kind of Myter, but that it is somewhat more closed all about, and without any overture, he had also a Mace of Gold, much like a Scepter, which he carryed upon his shoulder : this same, without making much reckoning of the *Monvagaruu*, or of any of the other Lords there present, took the Embassador by the hand, and said unto him, *The news of thy arrival is come unto the feet of* Binaigaa *the Calaminhan, and Scepter of the Kings that govern the Earth, and is so agreeable to his ears, that with a smiling look he now sends for thee to give thee audience concerning that which is desired of him by thy King, whom he newly receives into the number of his brethren, with a love of the son of his entrals, that so he may remain powerful and victorious over his Enemies :* Thereupon he caused him, together with the Kings Uncle, and the other Governors that accompanyed him, to come in, l aving all the rest without ; the Embassador then seeing none of his Train follow him, looked three or four times back, seeming by his countenance to be somewhat discontented, which the *Monvagaruu* perceiving, spake to the *Queitor*, who was a little behind, that he should cause the strangers to be let in, and none else ; the doors being then opened again, we *Portugals* began to go in with the *Bramaas*, but such a number of others came thrusting in amongst us, as the Gentlemen Ushers, who were above twenty, had much ado to keep the doors, striking many with Battouns which they had in their hands, and of those some that were persons of quality, and yet could they not therewith, neither with their cries, nor menaces, stop them all from entering : Thus being come in, we past along through the midst of a great garden, made with such art, and where appeared so many goodly things, so divers, and so pleasing to the eye, as words are not able to express them : For there were there many Alleys environed with Ballisters of Silver, and many Arbors of extraordinary scent, which we were told had so much sympathy with the Moons of the year, that in all seasons whatsoever they bare flowers and fruits ; withall there was such abundance and variety of Roses and other flowers, as almost passeth belief. In the midst of this Garden we saw a great many young women, very fair, and well clad, whereof some past away their time in dancing, and others in playing on sundry sorts of Instruments much after our manner, which they performed with so much harmony, as we were not a little delighted therewith : some also bestowed themselves in making of curious Needle-works and Gold-strings, some in other things, whilest their companions gathered fruit to eat ; and all this was done so quietly, and with such order and good behavior, as made us admire it. At our going out of this Garden, where the *Monvagaruu* would needs have the Embassador to stay awhile, that he might there observe something worthy to entertain his King with at his return to *Pegu*, we went into a very great Antichamber, where many Commanders and Lords were sitting, as also some great Princes, who received the Embassador with new ceremonies, and complements, and yet not one of them stirred from his place ; Through this Antichamber we came to a door, where there were six Gentlemen Ushers with Silver Maces, by which we entered into another room very richly furnished : in this was the *Calaminhan* seated on a most majestical Throne, encompassed with three rows of Ballisters of Silver ; At the foot of the degrees of his Throne sat twelve women that were exceeding beautiful, and most richly apparelled, playing on divers sorts of Instruments, whereunto they accorded their voyces ; On the top of the Throne, and not far from his person, were twelve young Damsels about nine or ten years old, all of them on their knees round about him, and carrying Maces of Gold in the fashion of Scepters ; amongst them there was also another that stood on her feet, and fanned him. Below, all along the whole length of the room, were a great many of old men, wearing Myters of Gold on their heads, and long Robes of Sattin and Damask, curiously embroidered, every one having Silver Maces on their shoulders, and ranked in order on either side against the walls : Over all the rest of the room were sitting, upon rich *Persian* Carpets, about two hundred young Ladies, as we could guess, that were wonderful fair, and exceeding well favored. Thus did this room, both for the marvelous structure of it, and for the excellent order that was observed therein, represent so great and extraordinary a Majesty, as we heard the Embassador say afterwards

talk-

talking of it, that if God would grant him the grace to return to *Pegu*, he would never speak of it to the King, as well for fear of grieving him, as of being taken for a man that reports things which seem altogether incredible.

As soon as the Embassador was entred into the room where the *Calaminhan* was, accompanyed with the four Princes that conducted him, he prostrated himself five times on the ground, with ut so much as daring to behold the *Calaminhan*, in sign of the great respect he carryed towards him, which the *Monvagaruu* perceiving, willed him to advance forward, so that being arrived neer to the first degree of his Throne, with his face still bending downward, he said to the *Calaminhan*, with so loud a voyce as every one might hear him; *The Clouds of the Ayr, which recreate the fruits whereof we eat, have published over the whole Monarchy of the World the great Majesty of thy Power, which hath caused my King, desiring to be honored with thy amity, as with a rich pearl, to send me for that purpose, and to tell thee from him, that thou shalt much oblige him, if thou pleasest to accept of him for thy true Brother, with the honorable obedience which he will always render to thee, as to him that is the elder, as thou art: And for that end it is, that he sends thee this Letter, which is the jewel of all his treasure that he prizes most, and wherein his eyes take more pleasure, for the honor and contentment they receive by it, then in being Lord of the Kings of* Avaa, *and of all the precious stone of the mountain of* Falent, *of* Jatir, *and* Pontau. Hereunto the *Calaminhan* made him this answer following, and that with a grave and severe countenance; *For my part I accept of this new amity, thereby to give full satisfaction to thy King, as to a son newly born of my intrals.* Then began the women to play on Instruments of Musick, and six of them danced with little children for the space of three or four credoes; After that, other six little girls danced with six of the oldest men that were in the room, which seemed to us a very pretty fantasticalness. This dance ended, there was a very fine Comedy represented by twelve Ladies, exceeding beautiful, and gorgeously attired, wherein appeared on the Stage a great Sea-monster, holding in his mouth the daughter of a King, whom the fish swallowed up before them all, which the twelve Ladies seeing, went in all haste weeping to an Hermitage, that was at the foot of a Mountain, from whence they returned with an Hermit, who made earnest supplications to *Quiay Patureu*, God of the Sea, that he would bring this Monster to the shore, so as they might come to bury the Damsel according to her quality; The Hermit was answered by *Quiay Patureu*, That the twelve Ladies should change their lamentations and complaints into so many consorts of musick, that were agreeable to his ears, and he would then command the Sea to cast the fish upon the strand to be done withall as they thought good; whereupon comes on the Stage six little Boys with wings and crowns of Gold upon their heads, in the same manner as we use to paint Angels, and naked all over, who falling on their knees before the Ladies, presented them with three Harps and three Viols, saying, that *Quiay Patureu* sent them these Instruments from the Heaven of the Moon, therewith to cast the Monster of the Sea into a sleep, that so they might have their desire on him, whereupon the twelve Ladies took them out of the hands of the little Boys, and began to play upon them, tuning them unto their voyces with so lamentable and sad a tone, and such abundance of tears, that it drew some from the eyes of divers Lords that were in the room; Having continued their musick about half a quarter of an hour, they saw the Monster coming out of the Sea, and by little and little as it were astonished, making to the shore where these fair Musicians were; all which was performed so properly, and to the life, that the Assistants could hardly imagine it to be a Fable, and a matter devised for pleasure, but a very truth, besides the Scean was set forth with a world of state and riches. Then one of the twelve Ladies drawing out a Poignard, all set with precious stones, which she wore by her side, ripped up the fish, and out of the belly of it drew the Infanta alive, which presently went and danced to the tune of their Instruments, and so went and kissed the *Calaminhans* hand, who received her very graciously, and made her sit down by him; It was said, that this young Lady was his Niepce, the Daughter of a Brother of his; as for the other twelve, they were all the Daughters of Princes, and of the greatest Lords of the Country, whose Fathers and Brothers were there present. There were also three or four Comedies more like this, acted by other young Ladies of great quality, and set forth with so much pomp and magnificence, as more could not be desired. About evening the *Calaminhan* retired into another room, accompanyed with women onely, for all the rest they went along with the *Monvagaruu*, who

took

took the Embassador by the hand, and led him back to the outermost room of all, where with many complements after their manner, he took his leave of him, and so committed him to the Queitor, who straightway carryed him to his House, where he lodged all the while that he was there, being two and thirty days, during which time he was feasted by the principal Lords of the Court in a splendid and sumptuous manner, and continually entertained with several sports of fishing, hunting, hawking, and other such like recreations ; As for us *Portugals*, we took a singular content in observing, over all the City and about it, the excellent structure of very sumptuous and magnificent edifices, of stately Pagodes or Temples, and of houses adorned with goodly workmanship, and of inestimable value. Now amongst all these Buildings there was not in the whole City a more majestical one then that which was dedicated to *Quiay Pimpocau*, who is *The God of the Sick*: In it serve continually a number of Priests, apparelled in grey Gowns, who being of greater knowledg then all the rest of the four and twenty sects of this Empire, do distinguish themselves from the others by certain yellow strings, which serve them for girdles ; they are also by the vulgar people in a soveraign degree of honor called ordinarily, *Perfect men*. The Embassador himself went five times to their Temple, as well to see very marvelous things, as to hear the doctrine of those that preached there, of which, and of all that concerns the extravagancies of their Religion, he brought a great volume to the King of *Bramaa*, which was so pleasing to him, as he afterward commanded the said Doctrine to be preached in all the Temples of that Kingdom, which is to this day exactly observed in all his states. Of this Book I brought a Translation into the Kingdom of *Portugal*, which a *Florentine* borrowed of me, and when I asked him for it again, he told me that it was lost, but I found afterward that he had carryed it to *Florence*, and presented it to the Duke of *Tuscany*, who commanded it to be printed under this Title, *The new Belief of the Pagans of the other end of the World*. Upon a day as the Embassador was talking in this Pagode with one of the *Grepos*, who professed much kindness unto him, for indeed they are all of a good nature, easie of access, and communicating themselves to strangers freely enough, he demanded of him, how long it was since the Creation of the World, or whether those things had a beginning which God doth shew so clearly to our eyes, such as the Night, the Day, the Sun, the Moon, the Stars, and other Creatures that have neither Father nor Mother, and of whom no reason can be rendered in Nature how they began : The *Grepo* relying more on his own knowledg, then on the others that were about him made this answer to his Question ; *Nature*, said he, *had no other Creation but that which proceeded from the Will of the Creator, Who in a certain time, determined in his divine Counsel, manifested it to the Inhabitants of Heaven, created before by his soveraign power, and according to that which is written thereof, it was fourscore and two thousand Moons, since the Earth was discovered from under the Waters, When as God created therein a very fair Garden, where he placed the first man, Whom he named Adaa, together with his wife Bazagon, them he expresly commanded, for to reduce them under the yoke of obedience, that they should not touch a certain fruit of a tree, called Hisfloran, for that he reserved the same for himself ; and in case they came to eat thereof, they should for a chastisement of their fault prove the rigor of his Justice, whereof they and their descendants should feel the dire effects : This being known to the great Lupantoo, Who is the gluttonous Serpent of the profound House of Smoke, and perceiving how by this commandment, God Would for mans obedience on Earth give him Heaven for a reward, he Went to Adaas Wife and bid her eat of that fruit, and that she should also make her Husband eat thereof, for he assured her that in so doing they should both of them be more excellent in knowledg then all other creatures, and free from that heavy nature whereof he had composed them, so that in a moment their bodies should mount to Heaven. Then Bazagon, hearing What Lupantoo had said unto her, Was so taken With a desire of enjoying that excellent prerogative of knowledg which he promised her, as to attain thereunto she eat of the fruit, and made her Husband likewise to eat of it, Whence it insued, that they were both of them by that unhappy morsel subjected to the pains of death, of sorrow, and of poverty. For God seeing the disobedience of these two first creatures, made them feel the rigor of his Justice, by chasing them out of the Garden Where he had placed them, and confirming the punishments upon them wherewith he had threatened them before ; Wherefore Adaa, fearing lest the divine Justice should proceed further against him, gave himself up for a long time to continual tears ; Whereupon God sent him Word, that if he continued in his repentance he would forgive him,*

his

his sin. Whilest the *Grepo* was speaking thus, the Embassador wondering at his discourse, which was a great novelty to him, *Certainly,* said he unto him, *I am well assured that the King my Master hath never heard the like of this from the Priests of our Temples; for they in recompence of our works propound no other thing unto us but the possession of riches in this life; for, as they say, there is no guerdon after death, and that we must finish our lives as all the beasts of the field do, except the Cows, which for a remaind of the milk they have given us, are converted into other Sea-cows, of the apples of whose esasure pearls ingendred:* At these words the *Grepo,* puffed up with vanity for that which he had said to the Embassador, *Think not,* answered he unto him, *that there is any one in all this Country can let thee understand so much as I have done, unless it be one Grepo, who is as learned as my self:* With this fume of presumption he chanced to cast his eye on us *Portugals,* that were behind the Embassador, and as the Minister of the Devil, believing that we esteemed him as much as he did himself, *Verily,* said he unto us, *I should be glad, that you, who as strangers have no knowledg of this truth, would come more often to hear me, for to understand how God hath created all these things, and how much we are bound to him for the benefit of this Creation:* Then one of our company, named *Gaspar de Meyrelez,* shewing himself therein more curious then the rest, after he had thanked the *Grepo* in the name of us all, he prayed him to give him leave to ask him something which he desired to know of him; Whereunto the *Grepo* made answer, that he was very well contented; *For,* added he, *it is as well the property of a wise and curious man to enquire for to learn, as of an ignorant to hear, and not be able to answer:* whereupon *Gaspar de Meyrelez* demanded of him, whether God, after he had created all these things whereof he spake, had not done some heroical works upon Earth, either by his Justice, or by his Mercy. To this the *Grepo* replyed, that he had, *it being evident, that as long as man lived in this flesh, he could not chuse but commit sins which would render him punishable, nor God be without a great desire to pardon him;* and he added further, *That the sins of men coming to be multiplyed on Earth, God had overwhelmed the whole World, by commanding the Clouds of Heaven to rain upon it, and to drown all living things, except one just man with his Family, which God put into a great House of wood, from whom issued afterwards all the Inhabitants of the Earth.* The *Portugal* again enquired, whether God after this chastisement had not sent some other. *God did not,* answered he, *send any, which taken in general, was like unto that; but it is true, that in particular he chastiseth Kingdoms and People with Wars, and other scourges which he sendeth them, as we see that he punisheth men with infinite afflictions, labors, diseases, and above all with extream poverty, which is the last and extreamest of all evils.* The *Portugal* continuing in his demands, desired him to tell him, whether he had any hope that God would one day be appeased, so as men might have entrance into Heaven; Whereunto the *Grepo* replyed, *That he knew nothing thereof, but that it was an evident thing, and to be believed as an Article of Faith, that even as God was an infinite good, so he would have regard to the good which men did upon Earth for his sake.* Hereupon he demanded of him, whether he had not heard it said, or found written, That after all those things, whereof he spake, a man was come into the World, who dying on the Cross, had satisfied God for all men; or whether there was not among them some knowledg thereof: Whereunto the *Grepo* answered, *None can make satisfaction to God but God himself, although there be in the world holy and vertuous men, which satisfie for themselves, and for some of their friends, such as are the Gods of our Temples, as the* Grepos *do assure us; But to say, that one alone hath satisfied for all, is a thing which we have never heard of till now, besides, on Earth, which is so base of it self, a Ruby of so high a price cannot be ingendred:* It is true nevertheless, that in times past so much was certified to the Inhabitants of this Country by a man, named John, who came into this City, and was held for an holy man, having been the Disciple of another, called Tomé Modeliar, the Servant of God, whom those of the Country put to death, because he went publiquely preaching, That God was made man, and that he had suffered death for mankind; which at first wrought such a Division amongst the people of this Nation, as many believed it for a very truth, and others opposed it, and formed a contrary party against it, incited thereunto by the Grepoes of the Law of Quiay Figrau, God of the Atomes of the Sun; so that they reproved all that this stranger said, by reason whereof He was banished from this City to the Kingdom of Bramaa, and from thence for the

same

same cause to the Town of Digan, *where he was put to death for preaching publiquely, as I said before, That God became man, and was crucified for men.* Upon these speeches *Gaspar de Meyrelez* and we, said, that this man had preached nothing in this Country which was not most true; wherewith the *Grepo* was so taken, that he fell down on his knees before all that were present, and lifting up his hands and eyes to Heaven, he said with tears in his eyes, *Lord, of whose beauty and goodness the Heavens and the Stars do give testimony, I with all my heart do beseech thee to permit, that in our times the hour may come, wherein the People of the other end of the World may give thee thanks for so great a Grace.* After that these matters were past in this manner, and many others besides, which well deserved to be related, if my gross wit were able to describe them, the Embassador took his leave of the *Grepo* with many complements and words of courtesie, whereof they are nothing sparing, as being much accustomed to practise them one with another.

CHAP.

CHAP. XLIX.

An ample relation of this Empire of the Calaminham, *and of the Kingdomes of* Pegu, *and* Bramaa, *with the continuance of our voyage, and what we saw among the same.*

A Moneth after our arrivall at this City of *Timphan*, where the Court then was, the Ambassador demanded an answer to his Ambassie, and it was immediately granted him by the *Calaminham*, with whom he spake himself, and being graciously entertained by him, he referred him for his dispatch to the *Monuagaruu*, that was, as I have heretofore delivered, the chief man in governing the Kingdome, who gave him an answer on the behalf of the *Calaminham*, as also a present in exchange of that which the King of *Bramaa* had sent him, withall he wrote him a Letter, that contained these words, *Thou arm of a clear Ruby, which God hath newly enchaced into my body, and whose flesh is fitly fastned to me, as that of my brother, by that new league and amity now accorded unto thee, by me* Prechau Guimiam, *Lord of the seven and twenty Crownes of the Montaignes of the earth, inherited by a lawfull succession from him, who these two and twenty moneths hath not set his feet upon my head; for so long it is since he left me, never to see me again, by reason of the sanctification which his soul doth now enjoy in feeling the sweet heat of the beams of the Sun. I have seen thy Letter, dated the fifth chaveca of the eighth moon of the year, whereunto I have given the true credit of a brother, and as such a one I accept of the party thou dost present me with, obliging my self to render thee the two passages of Savady free, that so thou mayest without fear of the Siamon be King of Avaa, as thou desirest me by thy Letter: And as for the other conditions, whereof thy Ambassador hath made some mention unto me, I will make answer thereunto by one of mine own, whom I will send unto thee from hence e're it be long, to the end thou mayest have a good successe in the pleasure thou seemest to take in making war upon thine enemies.* The Ambassador having received this Letter, departed from the Court the third day of *November*, in the year one thousand five hundred forty and six, accompanied with certain Lords, who by the expresse commandement of the *Calaminham* went along with him to *Bidor*, where they took their leave of him, after they had made him a great feast, & presented him with divers gifts. But before I intreat of the way which we held from this place till we came to *Pegu*, where the King of *Bramaa* was, I think it convenient and necessary to make a relation here of certain things which we saw in this country, wherein I will acquit my self as succinctly as I can, as I have done in all other matters whereof I have spoken heretofore; for if I would discourse in particular of all that I have seen, and of that which hath past as well in this Empire, as in other Kingdomes, where I have been during my painfull voyages, I had then need to make another volume far bigger then this same, and be indued with a wit much above that I have: howbeit that I may not wholly conceal things so remarkable, I am contented to say so much thereof as my grosse stile will permit me to deliver. The Kingdome of *Pegu* hath in circuit an hundred and forty leagues, is scituate on the South side in sixteen degrees, and in the heart of the Country towards the rhomb of the East it hath an hundred forty leagues, being invironed all above with an high ground, named *Pangavirau*, where the Nation of the *Bramaas* doth inhabit, whose country is fourscore leagues broad, and two hundred long. This Monarchy was in times past one sole Kingdome, which now it is not, but is divided into thirteen estates of Soveraignes, who made themselves masters of it by poysoning their King in a banquet which they made him in the City of *Chaleu*, as their histories relate: of these thirteen estates, there are eleven that are commanded by other Nations, who by a tract of another great country are joyned to all the bounds of the *Bramaas*, where two great Emperors abide, of which the one is called the *Siamon*, and the other the *Calaminham*, who is the same I purpose only to treat of. According to report, the Empire of the Prince is above three hundred leagues bredth, and as much in length, and it is said that antiently it contained seven and twenty Kingdomes, the inhabitants whereof spake all one language: within this Empire we saw many goodly Cities, exceedingly well peopled, and abounding with all provisions necessary for mans life, as flesh, fresh water, fish, corn, pulse, rice, pastures, vines, and fruits; the chief of all these Cities is *Tymphan*, where this Emperor, the *Calaminham*, with his Court commonly resides: it is seated along by a great river, named *Pituy*, and invironed all about with two broad walls of earth, made up with strong stone

on

on either side, having very broad ditches, and at each gate a Castle with high Towers; certain Merchants affirmed unto us, that this City had within it some four hundred thousand fires, and albeit the houses are for the most part not above two stories high, yet in recompense thereof they are built very stately, and with great charge, especially those of the Nobility, and of the Merchants, not speaking of the great Lords, which are separated by great inclosures, where are spacious outward Courts, and at the entring into them arches after the manner of *China*, as also gardens, and walks planted with trees, and great ponds, all very handsomely accommodated to the pleasures and delights of this life, whereunto these people are very much inclined: We were also certified, that both within the inclosure of the City, and a league about it, there were six and twenty hundred *Pagodes*, some of which, wherein we had been, were very sumptuous and rich, indeed for the rest the most of them were but petty houses in the fashion of Hermitages: These people follow four and twenty Sects, all different one from another, amongst the which there is so great a confusion of errors, and diabolicall precepts, principally in that which concerns their bloudy Sacrifices, as I abhor to speak of them; but the Idol which is most in vogue amongst them, and most frequented, is that whereof I have already made mention, called *Quiay Frigau*, that is to say, *The God of the Moats of the Sun*, for it is in this false God that the *Calaminham* believes, and does adore him, and so do all the chiefest Lords of the Kingdome, wherefore the *Grepos*, *Menigrepos*, and *Talagrepos* of this false god are honored far more then all others, and held in the retation of holy personages; their superiours, who by an eminent title are called *Cabizondos*, never know women, as they say, but to content their bruitish and sensuall appetites they want not diabolicall inventions, which are more worthy of tears then recital: during the ordinary Fairs of this City, called by them *Chandubas*, we saw all things there that nature hath created, as iron, steel, lead, tin, copper, lattin, saltpeter, brimstone, oyl, vermillion, honey, wax, sugar, lacre, benjamin, divers sorts of stuffes and garments of silk, pepper, ginger, cinamon, linnen cloth, cotton wool, alum, borax, cornalines, christall, camphire, musk, yvory, cassia, rhubarbe, turbith, scamony, azure, woad, incense, cochenill, saffron, myrrhe, rich porcelain, gold, silver, rubies, diamonds, emerauds, saphirs, and generally all other kind of things that can be named, and that in so great abundance, as it is not possible for me to speak that which I have seen, and be believed; women there are ordinarily very white and fair, but that which most commends them is, that they are of a good nature, chast, charitable, and much inclined to compassion: The Priests of all these four and twenty Sects, whereof there are a very great number in this Empire, are cloathed in yellow, like the *Roolims* of *Pegu*, they have no money either of gold or silver, but all their commerce is made with the weight of *eates*, *caeis*, *maazes*, and *conderins*. The Court of the *Calaminham* is very rich, the Nobility exceeding gallant, and the revenue of the Lords and Princes very great, the King is feared and respected in a marvellous manner; he hath in his Court many Commanders that are strangers, unto whom he giveth great pensions to serve him for the safety of his person, our Ambassador was assured, that in the City of *Timphan*, where most commonly the Court is, there are above threescore thousand horse, and ten thousand Elephants: the gentlemen of the country live very handsomely, and are served in vessels of silver, and sometimes of gold, but as for the common people they use porcelain & lattin; in summer they are apparelled in sattin, damask, and wrought taffeties, which come from *Persia*, & in winter in gowns furred with marterns; there is no going to Law amongst them, nor does any man enter into bond there, but if there be any difference among the common people, certain Magistrates, like to our Aldermen of Wards, do decide it, and if contention happens to arise between persons of an higher quality, then they submit to the judgment of certain religious men, who are expresly deputed for that purpose, and from them matters passe on in manner of appeal to the Queitor of Justice, which is as the superintendent thereof, from whose sentence there is no appeal, how great and important soever the businesse be: The Monarchy of these seven and twenty Kingdomes hath seven hundred Provinces, that is six and twenty in every Kingdome; and in the capitall town of each of those Provinces doth a Governor preside, all of them being of like and equall power. Now on every new Moon, each Captain is bound to muster the souldiers that are under his charge, which ordinarily are two thousand foot, five hun

dred

dred horse, and fourscore fighting Elephants, one of the which is called by the name of the capitall town of the same Province, so that if one should make a just computation of all those men of war that are in those seven hundred companies of those Provinces, they would appear to be seventeen hundred and fifty thousand, whereof there are three hundred and fifty thousand horse, and five and fifty thousand Elephants; for in regard of the great number that there are of those beasts in that country; this Emperor stiles himself in his titles, Lord of the indomptable force of Elephants. The revenue which the Monarch draws from his Royall Prerogatives, by them called, *the price of the Scepter*, as also from his Mines, amounts to twenty millions of gold, without comprising therein the presents which are given him by the Princes, Lords and Captains, and a great quantity of money that is distributed amongst the men of war, according to every ones merit, which are not of that accompt. In all this country, pearl, amber, and salt are very much esteemed of, because they are things that come from the Sea; which is far distant from the City of *Timplan*, but of all other commodities they have infinite store: The Country of it self is very healthy, the ayr very good, and likewise the waters. When they sneeze they use to say, *the God of truth is three and one*, whereby one may judge that these people have had some knowledge of the Christian Religion.

Being departed from the town of *Bidor*, we held on our course down the great river of *Pituy*, and the same day at night we went and lodged at a certain *Abby* of the land of *Quiay Jarem*, the God of married folks; this Abby is seated on the bank of the river in a plain, where are a great many of trees planted, and very rich buildings, here the Ambassador was well entertained by the *Cabizondo* and the *Talagrepos*; then continuing our voyage seven dayes longer, we arrived at a town named *Pavel*, where we staid three dayes to furnish our vessells with some provisions which we needed; in this place the Ambassador bought divers knacks of *China*, and other commodities that were sold there at a very cheap rate, as musk, fine porcelains, wrought silks, Ermins, and many other sorts of furs, which are much used in that country, because it is extreme cold there; these wares were brought thither by great troops of Elephants and Rhinocero's from a certain far distant Province, as the Merchants told us, called *Frioucaranian*, beyond the which, they said, was a kind of people called *Calogens* and *Funcaos*, tawny men, and great Archers, having their feet like unto Oxen, but hands like unto other men, save that they are exceeding hairy, they are naturally inclined to cruelty, and have below at the end of the backbone a lump of flesh as big as ones two fists; their dwelling is in mountains that are very high and rough on some parts, where there are mighty deep pits or caves, from whence are heard in winter nights most dreadfull cries, and dolefull lamentations: We were told likewise, that not far from these people there were others, called *Calonhos*, *Timpates*, and *Bugems*, and a good way beyond them some, named *Oquens* and *Magores*, who feed on wild beasts which they catch in hunting, and eat raw, as also on all kind of contagious creatures, as lizards, serpents, and adders; they hunt those wild beasts mounted on certain animalls, as big as horses, which have three horns in the midst of their foreheads, with thick short legs, and on the middle of their backs a row of prickles, wherewith they prick when they are angry, and all the rest of the body is like a great lizard; besides they have on their necks, instead of hair, other prickles far longer and bigger then those on their backs, and on the joynts of their shoulders short wings like to the fins of fishes, wherewith they fly, as it were, leaping the length of five or six and twenty paces at a jump: These creatures are called *Banazes*, upon which these savage ride into the country of their enemies, with whom they hold continuall war, and whereof some pay them tribute in salt, which is the thing they make most account of, in regard of the need they have of it, for that they are very far distant from the Sea: We spake also with other men called *Bumioens*, who live on high mountains, where there are Mines of Alum and Lacre, and great store of wood; of this Nation, we saw a troop conducting of above two thousand oxen, on whom they had put pack-saddles, and so made them to carry their Merchandise; these men were very tall, and had eys and beards like the *Chineses*: We saw others likewise, that had reasonable long beards, their faces full of freckles, and their ears and nostrills pierced, and in the holes thereof small threds of gold made into clasps, these were called *Ginaphogaas*, and the Province whereof they were Natives *Surobosay*, which within the mountains of the

Lauhos are bounded with the lake of *Chiammay*, and are cloathed with hairy skins, going bare-foot and bare-headed, certain Merchants told us that these had great riches, and that all their traffique was in silver, whereof they had great store. We spake also with another sort of men, called *Tuparoens*, who are tawny, great eaters, and much addicted to the pleasures of the flesh; these gave us better entertainment then all the rest, and oftentimes feasted us. Now because in a certain banquet, where we nine *Portugals* were with the Ambassador; one of us, named *Francisco Temuda*, challenged them to drink, they taking it for a great affront, caused the feast to continue the longer for the recovery of their honor, but the *Portugal* set on them so lustily, twenty that they were, as he laid them all along drunk on the ground, himself remaining still sober; when they were out of their drink, the *Sapiton*, that was their Captain, and in whose house the feast had been made, called his company together, which were above three hundred, and whether the *Portugal* would or no made him to mount upon an *Elephant*, and so lead him through all the town, accompanied with a great multitude of people that followed him at the sound of trumpets, drums, and other such instruments; the Captain himself, as also the Ambassador, and the rest of us, together with all the *Bramaas*, marching on foot after him, with boughs in our hands, and two men before him on horseback, that rode crying, *O all ye people, praise with gladness the beams which proceed from the midst of the Sun, who is the God that makes our rice to grow, for that you have lived to see a man so holy, that knowing how to drink better then all the men of the world, hath laid on the ground twenty of the principall drinkers of our troop, to the end his renown may be daily more and more augmented.* Whereunto all the crowd of people that accompanied him, answered with such cries and acclamations, as the very noyse thereof frighted all that heard it. In this equipage they lead the *Portugal* to the Ambassadors house, where they set him down with a great deal of respect and many complements, then on their knees they rendred him to the Ambassador, desiring him to have a care of him as of an holy man, or the son of some great King, for, said they, it cannot be otherwise, seeing God hath bestowed so great a gift on him, as to know how to drink so well. Whereupon having made a gathering for him, they got together above two hundred lingots of silver, which they gave him, and untill the time that we departed he was continually visited by the inhabitants, whereof many presented him with rich pieces of silk, and other gifts, as if they had made an offering to some Saint upon a solemn day of his invocation. After these we saw other men that were very white, named *Pavilens*, great archers, and good horsemen, apparrelled in cassocks of silk like those of *Japon*, and that carried their meat to their mouths with little sticks, after the manner of the *Chineses*; these same told us that their Coyntry was called *Binagorem*, and that it was distant from thence about two hundred leagues up the river, their merchandize was store of gold in powder, like to that of *Menancabo*, of the Island of *Sumatra*, as also lacre, aloes, musk, tin, copper, silk, and wax, which they exchanged for pepper, ginger, salt, wine, and rice: the wives of these men which we saw there are very white, of better conversation then all the rest of those countryes, well natured, and exceeding charitable, demanding of them what was their Law, and what was the divinity that they adored they answered us, *That their Gods were the Sun, the heaven, and the stars, for that from them they received by an holy communication all the good that they enjoyed upon earth; and furthermore, that the soul of man was but a breath which ended in the death of the body, and that afterwards tumbling up and down in the ayr she mingled her self with the clouds, untill such time as coming to be dissolved into water, she died again upon the earth, as the body had done before.* I omit an infinite many of such extravagances which were told us, and that gave us good cause to wonder at the blindness and confusion of these wretches, and doth also oblige us to render thanks continually unto God for delivering us from these errors, and this false belief. Now from the diversity of these unknown Nations, which we saw in these parts, it is easie to infer, that in this Monarchy of the world there are many countries yet undivided, and unknown to us.

CHAP.

CHAP. LX.
Our arrivall at Pegu, *with the death of the* Roolim *of* Mounay.

COntinuing our course from this town of *Pavel*, we came the next day to a village, §. 1. called *Luncor*, invironed about the space of three leagues, with a great number of trees of *Benjamin*, which from this place is transported into the Kingdoms of *Pegu*, and *Siam*. From thence we sailed for nine daies together down that great river, all alongst the which we saw many goodly towns, and then we arrived at another river, called *Ventrau*, thorough the which we continued our voyage to *Penauchin*, the first Borough of the Kingdome of *Jangumaa*, where the Ambassador registred his vessells, and all that were within them, because such was the custom of the country. Being departed from thence, we went and lay that night at the *Randitens*, which are two strong places belonging to the Prince of *Poncanor*. Five days after we came to a great town, called *Magdaleu*, which is the country from whence lacre is brought to *Martabano*; the Prince thereof, during the time that we stayed there, shewed the Ambassador a generall muster of all the men of war that he had levied against the King of the *Laubos*, with whom he was at difference, because he had repudiated a daughter of his, which he had married three years before, intending to espouse a gentlewoman by whom he had had a son that he had legitimated, and made choice of for heir of his Kingdom, thereby frustrating his Nephew (by his daughter) of his right. Passing on then thorough the streight of *Madur*, wherein we sailed five days, we arrived at a village called *Mouchell*, the first place of the Kingdome of *Pegu*; there one *Chalagonim*, a famous Pyrat, that went up and down robbing in this place with thirty *Ceroos*, well equipped, and full of warlike men, assailed us one night, and fighting with us till it was almost day, he handled us in such sort, as it was the great grace of God that we escaped out of his hands, neverthelesse it was not without the loss of five of the twelve vessells that we had, together with an hundred and fourscore of our men, whereof two were *Portugals*: The Ambassador himself had a cut on one of his arms, and two wounds besides with arrow shot, which had almost cost him his life; all of us likewise were cruelly hurt, and the Present which the *Calaminham* sent to the King of *Bramaa*, being worth above an hundred thousand duckats, was taken by the Pyrat, together with a great deal of rich merchandize that was in the five vessells, whereof he had made himself master. In this sad equipage we arrived three days after at the City of *Martabano*, from whence the Ambassador wrote the King a letter, wherein he rendred him an accompt of all that had happened to him in his voyage, as also in his disaster. Whereupon the King sent presently away a Fleet of sixscore *Ceroos*, with a number of choice men, amongst which were an hundred *Portugals* in quest of this Pyrat. This Fleet having by good fortune discovered him, found that he had put on shore his thirty *Ceroos*, wherewith he had assailed us, and was with all his forces retired into a fortress, which was full of divers prizes that he had taken in severall parts thereabout; our men immediately attacqued the place, and carried it easily at the very first assault, only with the loss of some few *Bramaas* and one *Portugal*, howbeit many were hurt with arrows, but they recovered in a short time without the maiming of any one. As soon as the fortress was gained, all that were found within it were put to the sword, not sparing the life of any, but that of the Pyrat, and sixscore others of his company which were led alive to the King of *Bramaa*, who caused them to be cast to his Elephants, that instantly dismembred them. In the mean time the taking of this fortress was so advantagious to the *Portugals* that were sent thither, as they returned from thence all very rich; and it was thought that five or six of them got each of them the value of five and twenty, or thirty thousand duckats apiece, and that he which had least, had the worth of two or three thousand for his share: After that the Ambassador was cured at *Martabano* of the hurts which he had received in the fight, he went directly to the City of *Pegu*, where, as I have declared, the King of *Bramaas* Court was at that time, who being advertised of his arrivall, and of the letter which he brought him from the *Calaminham*, whereby he accepted of his amity, and allied himself with him, he sent the *Chaumigrem*, his foster-brother, and brother-in-law, to receive him; to which end he set forth, accompanied with all the Grandees of the Kingdom, and four battalions of strangers, amongst the which were a thousand *Portugals* commanded

manded by *Antonio Ferreira*, born in *Braguenca*, a man of great understanding, and to whom this King gave twelve thousand duckats a year penfion, befides the Prefents which he beftowed on him in particular, that came to little lefs. Hereupon the King of *Bramaa* feeing that by this new league God had contented his defire, he refolved to fhew himfelf thankfull for fo great a favour, wherefore he caufed great feafts to be made amongft thefe people, and a number of Sacrifices to be offered in their Temples, where there was no fpare of perfumes, and wherein it was thought there were killed above a thoufand, ftags, cows, and hogs, which were beftowed for an alms among the poor, befides many other works of charity, as the cloathing of five thoufand poor folks, and imploying great fums of money in the releafing of a thoufand prifoners which were detained for debt. After that thefe feafts had continued feven whole days together, with a moft ardent zeal, and at the incredible charge of the King, Lords, and people, news came to the City of the death of the *Aixquendoo, Roolim* of *Mounay*, who was as it were their Soveraign Bifhop, which caufed all rejoycings to ceafe in an inftant, and every one to fall into mourning, with great expreffions of forrow: The King himfelf retired, the fairs were given over, the windows, doors, and fhops were fhut up, fo that no living thing was feen to ftir in the City, withall their Temples and Pagods were full of penitents of all forts, who with inceffant fhedding of tears, exercifed fuch an exceffe of repentance, as fome of them died therewith. In the mean time the King departed away the fame night for to go to *Mounay*, which was fome twenty leagues from thence, for that he was neceffarily to be affiftant at this funerall pomp, according to the antient cuftom of the Kings of *Pegu*; he arrived there the next day fomewhat late, and then gave order for all that was neceffary for his funerals, fo that the next day every thing being in a readinefs, the body of the deceafed was about evening brought from the place where he died, and laid on a Scaffold that was erected in the midft of a great place, hung all about with white velvet, and covered over head with three cloths of Eftate of gold and filver tinfell; in the middle of it was a Throne of twelve fteps afcent unto it, and an hearfe almoft like unto ours, fet forth with divers rich works of gold and pretious ftones; round about hung a number of filver candlefticks, and perfuming pots, wherein great quantities of fweet odours were burnt, by reafon of the corruption of the body, which already began to have an ill favour. In this manner they kept it all that night, during the which was no little ado, and fuch a tumult of cries and lamentations made by the people, as words are not able to exprefs; for the only number of the *Bicos, Grepos, Menigrepos, Talagrepos, Guimons*, and *Roolims*, who are the chiefeft of their Priefts, amounted to above thirty thoufand, that were affembled together there, befides a world of others which came thither every hour. When divers inventions of forrow, that were well accommodated to the fubject of this mourning, had been fhown, there came fome two hours after midnight out of a Temple, called *Quiay Figrau*, god of the Motes of the Sun, a proceffion, wherein were feen five hundred little boys ftark naked, and bound about the neck and the middle with cords, and chains of iron; upon their heads they carried bundles of wood, and in their hands knives, finging in two Quires with a tone, fo lamentable and fad, as few that heard them could hardly forbear crying: In the mean time one amongft them went, faying in this manner, *Thou that art going to enjoy the contentments of heaven, leave us not prifoners in this exile*; whereunto another Quire anfwered, *To the end we may rejoyce with thee in the bleffings of the Lord*: then continuing their fong in manner of a Letany, they faid many other things with the fame tone. After that, when they were all fallen on their knees before the Scaffold where the body lay, a *Grepo* above an hundred years old, proftrated on the ground with his hands lifted up on high, made a fpeech to him in the name of thefe little boys whereunto another *Grepo*, who was neer the hearfe, as if he had fpoken in the perfon of the deceafed, came to anfwer thus, *Since it hath pleafed God by his holy will to form me of earth, it hath pleafed him alfo to refolve me into earth, I recommend unto you, my children, the fear of that hour, wherein the hand of the Lord fhall put us into the balance of his juftice*; whereupon all the reft with a great cry replied in this fort, *May it pleafe the moft Almighty high Lord that raigns in the Sun, to have no regard to our works, that fo we may be delivered from the pains of death*: Thefe little boys being retired, there came others about the age of ten or eleven years, apparrelled in white Sattin robes, with chains

of

of gold on their feet, and about their necks many rich jewels and pearls: After they had with much ceremony done a great deal of reverence to the dead body, they went and florished naked scymitars which they had in their hands all about the hearse, as if they would chace away the divell, saying aloud, *Get thee gone, accursed as thou art, into the bottom of the house of smoke, where dying with a perpetuall pain, without making an end of dying, thou shalt pay, without making an end also of paying the rigorous justice of the Lord above.* This said, they withdrew, as if they would shew that by this action they had left the body of the deceased exempt from the power of the divell, which besieged it before; In the place of these same came in six and twenty of their principall *Talagrepos*, being fourscore years old and upwards, apparrelled in robes of violet coloured damask, and carrying silver censors in their hands, before whom for the greater gracing of them marched twelve gentlemen Ushers with Maces of the same metall; as soon as these Priests had censed the hearse four severall times with many ceremonies, they all prostrated themselves with their faces on the ground, and then one of them began to say, as if he had spoken to the dead man, *If the clouds of heaven were able to tell our grief unto the beasts of the field, they would forsake their pasture for to help us to wail thy death, and the great extremity whereunto we are reduced; or els they would beseech thee Lord, to imbarque us with thee into this deadly house, where thou seest not us, because we are not worthy of so great a favour, but that all this people may be comforted in thee before the tomb shall hide thy body from us, shew us, Lord, by figures of earth, the peaceable joy, and sweet contentment of thy repose, that we may be all awaked out of the heavy sleep, wherein the obscurities of the flesh doth wrap us, and that we miserable wretches may be incited to imitate thee, and follow thy steps, for to behold thee in the joyfull house of the Sun at the last gasp of our lives.* To these words, the people having made a very dreadfull cry, answered incontinently, *The Lord grant us this grace.* Then the twelve gentlemen Ushers that carried the Maces, going on afore to make way thorough the press, though with much ado, because the people would not withdraw, there came forth of an house on the right side of the Scaffold four and twenty little boys richly apparrelled, with chains of gold and pretious stones about their necks, who playing after their manner on divers instruments of musick, and falling down on their knees in two ranks before the hearse, they continued playing on their instruments, to the tune whereof there were only two of them that sung, whereunto five others answered from time to time in such a dolefull manner, as made all the assistants shed abundance of tears, yea some of them were so sensible of it, as they could not forbear plucking of their hair, and knocking their heads against the steps of the Throne where the hearse stood. During this and many other ceremonies there performed, six young gentlemen *Grepos* sacrificed themselves, by drinking out of a golden cup a certain yellow liquor, so venemous, that before they had made an end of their draught, they fell down stark dead on the ground; this action of theirs brought these Martyrs of the divell into the number of their Saints, so as they were envied by every one for it, and presently their bodies were carried with a solemn procession to be burnt in a great fire, that was made of Sanders, Aloes, and Benjamin, where they were quickly reduced unto ashes. The next morning the Scaffold was disgarnished of all the richest pieces about it, and the hearse, but the cloths of estate, the hangings and banners, as also many other moveables of great worth were not stirred, and so with divers ceremonies, fearfull cries and lamentations, and a strange noyse of severall sorts of instruments, they set fire on the Scaffold, and all that was upon it, anoynting it often with odoriferous liquors, and confections of great price. Thus was the body consumed to ashes in a very short time, but whilst it was burning, the King and all the Grandees of his Court which were then present, cast in by way of alms many pieces of gold, pretious stones, jewels, and chains of pearl of exceeding great value, all which so ill imployed were instantly consumed by the fire, together with the body and bones of that wretched dead man, so as we were certainly informed afterward, that this funerall pomp cost above an hundred thousand duckets, besides the garments which the King and the Grandees of the country gave to thirty thousand Priests that were assisting at it, wherein was imployed an incredible quantity of stuffes of severall sorts, witnesse the *Portugals*, who mightily profited by so lucky an occasion, because they sold at what price they would such as they brought from *Bengala*, for which they were paid in lingots of gold and silver.

CHAP.

CHAP. LXI.

The election of the new Roolim *of* Mounay *, the grand* Talagrepo *of these Gentiles of the Kingdome of* Pegu.

§. 1.

THe next day between seven and eight in the morning, which was the time when the ashes of the deceased began to be cold, the King and all the great Lords of the Court came unto the place where the body had been burnt, marching all in order after the manner of a stately procession, and assisted by all the *Grepos*, amongst whom there were an hundred and thirty with silver censors, and fourteen with miters of gold on their heads; they were apparrelled in long robes of yellow sattin, as for all the rest, to the number of ten thousand, they were cloathed with taffeta of the same colour, and with a kind of surpliss of fine linnen, which was not done without a very great charge, by reason of the number of them. Being arrived at the place where the *Roolim* had been burnt, after some ceremonies performed, as is usuall with them, according to the time and sence that every one had of it, a *Talagrepo* of the *Bramaa* Nation, and Uncle to the King, as Brother to his Father, whom the people held for the ablest of them all, having been chosen to preach that day, went up into the Pulpit for that effect: The beginning of his Sermon was an Elegy touching the defunct, whose life he commended with many speeches that made for his purpose, wherein he grew so earnest and hot, as turning himself to the King with tears in his eys, and lifting up his voice somewhat louder, to the end he might hear him the better, he said unto him, *If the Kings in these times wherein we live do consider how little a time they have to live, and with what rigour of justice they shall be chastised by the Almighty hand of the most high God for the crimes of their tyrannicall lives, possibly it would be better for them to feed in the open fields like bruit beasts, then to be so absolute in their will, and to use it with so little reason, even as to be cruel to the good, and slack in punishing the wicked, whom by their soveraign power they have put into greatnesse and authority; and truly they are much to be lamented, whose good fortune hath raised them up to an estate so dangerous, as is that of Kings at this day, by reason of the insolence and liberty wherein they continually live, without so much as the least apprehension of any fear or shame. But you must know, O ye blinded of the world, that God hath made you Kings to use clemency towards men, to give them audience, to content, to chastise them, but not to kill them tyrannically: Nevertheless, O ye bad Kings, in the condition whereunto you are raised, you oppose your selves to the nature which God hath indued you with, and take upon you many other different forms, in apparrelling your selves every hour with some such livery as seems best unto you, to the end you may be to the one very bloud-suckers, that incessantly suck from them their goods and their lives, never leaving them so long as they have one drop of bloud in their veins; and to others you are dreadfull roaring Lions, who to give a mask and a colour to your ambition and avarice, cause supreme Laws of death to be published for the least faults, and all for to confiscate other mens goods, which is the main end of your pretensions. Contrarily if there be any that you love, and unto whom you, or the world, or I know not what, have given the name of* Grandees, *you are so negligent in chastising their proud humors, and so prodigall in inriching them with the spoils and undoing of the poor, whom you have left naked, and even flayed to the very quick, as you cannot doubt but that they will one day accuse you before God for all these things, when you will have no excuse to make, so that there will be nothing left you but a dreadfull confusion to trouble you, and to put you into an horrible disorder.* To these he added so many other remonstrances in favour of the poor subjects, cried out so mainly, and shed so many tears in their behalf, as the King remained almost besides himself, and was touched so neerly therewith, that he instantly called *Brazagaran*, the Governor of *Pegu*, unto him, and commanded him without all delay to dismisse all the Deputies of the Provinces of the Kingdome, whom he had caused to be assembled in the Town of *Cosmin*, for to demand of them a great sum of money, that he might set upon the Kingdom of *Savady*, on which he had newly resolved to make war. Withall he sware publikely on the ashes of the defunct, that during his raign he would never charge his subjects with imposts, nor would make them to serve by force, as he had formerly done; yea, and that for the future he would have a most speciall care to hear the poor, and to do them justice against the misdemeanours of the great ones, conformable to the merit of every one, together with many other things very

just

just and good, which might well serve for a lesson to us that are Christians. This Sermon being finished, the ashes of the defunct, which had been gathered up, was distributed as a relique into fourteen golden basons, whereof the King himself took up one on his head, and the *Grepos* of chiefest quality carried the rest; so the Procession going from thence in the same order as it came thither, those ashes were conveyed into a very rich Temple, which might be some slight shot from that place, and named *Quiay Docco*, that is, *the god of the afflicted of the earth*, there they were put into a shallow grave, without other pomp or vanity, for so had *Aixequendoo*, the late *Roolim*, commanded. This grave then was invironed about with three iron grates, and with two of silver, and one of latten, and upon three iron rods that crossed the whole bredth of the chappell, hung seventy and two lamps of silver, namely four and twenty on each of them, all of great value, and fastened together with great silver chains. Furthermore, there were placed about the steps, whereby one descended into the grave, thirty and six little perfuming pots, with Benjamin, Aloes, and other confections, wherein was great store of Ambergreece, all which was not finished till it was almost night, by reason of the many ceremonies used in this funerall; all that day long they freed an infinite number of birds which had been brought thither in above an hundred cages, these Gentiles being of the opinion that they were so many souls of deceased persons, which before times had passed out of this life, and that were deposited as it were in the bodies of those birds, till the day of their deliverance should come, at which time they were in all liberty to accompany the soul of the defunct: The like they did with a great many of little fishes which had been transported thither also in certain vessells full of water, so that to set them at liberty, they cast them into the river with another new ceremony, to the end they might serve the soul of him whose ashes were then buried: There was also brought thither all kind of venison and foul, which was distributed as an alms to all the poore that were present there, whereof the number was almost infinite. These ceremonies, and other such like which were performed in this action being finished, the King in regard it was neer night retired into his quarter, where he had caused tents to be pitched for to lodge in, and that in sign of mourning, the like did all the great ones, so that all the Assembly by little and little withdrew. The next morning as soon as it was day, the King made it to be proclaimed, that all persons of what condition soever they were, should upon pain of death dislodge speedily out of the Island, and that they which were Priests should return to the attendance of their cures, with this penalty, in case of contravention to be degraded from their dignity. Whereupon all the Priests went presently out of the Island, ninety of them excepted, who were deputed for the election of him that was to succeed in the place of the defunct. These same then assembled in the house of *Gangiparo* to acquit themselves of their charge, and for that in the two first daies, which was the term limited to make this election, it could not succeed by reason of the diversity of opinions, and great contrariety that was found amongst them, which were to give their votes; the King thought fit, that out of those deputed ninety, there should nine be chosen, who alone should make the election. This resolution being taken, these nine continued five daies, and as many nights together in continuall prayer; in the mean time a world of offerings were made, and alms given; a great number of poor people were also cloathed, and tables prepared, where all men that would might eat of free cost, and all this was accompanied with processions in every quarter. At last these nine being agreed in conformity of votes, elected for *Roolim* one *Manicha Monchan*, who at that time was a *Capizondo*, or Prelate in the town of *Digum* of a *Pagode*, called *Quiay Figrau*, that is to say, *god of the atomes of the Sun*, of whom I have oftentimes spoken; he was a man of about threescore and eight years of age, accounted amongst them for an holy personage, very knowing in the customes and lawes of those Sects of the Gentiles, and above all exceeding charitable to the poor: With this election the King and all the great ones of the Court remained very well satisfied: The King then speedily dispatched away the *Chaumigrem* his foster-brother, to whom he gave thereupon the title of *Contalanhaa*, which signifies, the Kings brother, to the end he might be the more honorably qualified with an hundred *Lauleas*, wherein was the Flower of all the *Bramaa* Nobility, together with the nine Electors, for to go and fetch him which had been newly chosen to the dignity of *Roolim*: And having brought

Bbb

him

him nine dayes after with a great deal of respect and honor to a place called *Tagalaa*, some five leagues from the Isle of *Mounay*, the King met him with all the great men of the Court, besides a world of other people, and above two thousand vessells with oars. When he was come in this equipage where the new *Roolim* was, he prostrated himself before him, and kissing the ground three times, *O thou holy pearl*, said he unto him, *which art in the midst of the Sun, breath forth upon me by an agreeable inspiration of the Lord of uncreated power, that I may not dread upon earth the insupportable yoke of mine enemies*: At these words the new *Roolim* putting forth his hand to raise him from the ground, spake thus unto him, *Labour my Son that thy works may be pleasing to God, and I will pray for thee without ceasing*. Hereupon the King rising up, the *Roolim* made him sit down by him, and stroked him three times with his hand on the head, which the King took for the greatest honor he could do him; then having said something unto him which we could not hear, for that we were a little too farr off, he blowed three times on the Kings head, whilest he was on his knees again before him, and all the people laid flat on the earth. This done, he parted from that place amidst the applauses that were given him from all parts, and the sound of bells and instruments of musick, and imbarqued himself in the Kings *Laulea*, where he was seated in a rich chair of gold, set with precious stones, and the King at his feet, which was also taken for a great honor done him by the *Roolim*; round about, and a little distant from him were twelve little boys attired in yellow sattin, with scarfes of silver Tinsell, golden Maces, and Scepters in their hands: All along the sides of the vessell, instead of Mariners, stood the Lords of the Kingdom with guilt oars by them; and as well in the Poop as the Prow were two Quires of young striplings, apparrelled in carnation sattin, and having divers sorts of instruments in their hands, to the tune whereof they sung the praises of God. Some of our company observed, that one of their songs said thus; *Children of a pure heart, praise this admirable and divine Lord, for as for me being a sinner I am not worthy to do it; and if that too be not permitted unto you, let your eys weep before his feet, that so you may render your selves agreeable unto him*. In the same manner they sung many other songs to the tune of their instruments, and with so much ardor and zeal, as if they had been Christians; it would have been able to have stirred up the devotion of them that heard them. After that the *Roolim* was in this sumptuous sort arrived at the City of *Martabano*, he did not go to Land, as it had been resolved, because it was night, for it was not lawfull for him at any hand to touch the ground with his feet, in regard of the great dignity of his person, but stayed till the next morning, at which time the King disimbarqued him first of all upon his own shoulders, and so too did the Princes and great Lords of the Kingdom carry him alternatively to the Pagode of *Quiay Ponnedea*, as being the greatest and most sumptuous of the whole City, in the midst whereof was a Theater richly set forth of yellow sattin, which is the livery of that soveraign dignity. There, out of a new ceremony, being laid all along upon a little bed of gold, he made as though he were dead, and then at the sound of a bell which gave three toles, the *Bonzes* prostrated themselves all with their faces on the ground for the space of half an hour, during which time, all the assistants for a sign of sadnesse held their hands before their eys, in saying aloud, *Lord recall this thy servant to a new life, to the end we may have one to pray for us*. Instantly thereupon they took him from thence, and put him into a Tomb adorned with the same livery, then chanting out certain, I know not what, very sorrowfull words with tears in their eys, they left him, after they had surrounded the Temple thrice, in a grave made expresly for that purpose, covered over with a cloth of black velvet, and invironed about with dead mens heads. This done, they said certain prayers after their manner, weeping, which very much moved the King; and then all the throng of people that made a strange noyse, being commanded to silence, they gave three toles with a great bell, for a sign to all the rest of the bells in the City to answer them, as they did with so horrible and dreadfull a din, that the earth even trembled therewith: After the ceasing of this noyse, two *Talagrepos*, men of great reputation amongst them, and very well versed in their Laws, went up into two Pulpits, prepared expresly for them, and that were hung with rich Turky Carpets, where they entertained their Auditors with the subject of this ceremony, and gave them the explication of every thing, making an ample relation unto them of the life and death of the deceased *Roolim*,

and

and of the election of this same; together with the excellent qualities with which he was indued for to be raised to so high a charge whereunto he was called by a particular grace of God; to this they added many other things wherewith the people were exceedingly satisfied and contented; then the same bell having tolled three times more, the two Priests descended from their Pulpits, which together with all their furniture were presently burned with another new kind of ceremony, whereof I will forbear here making a relation, because it seems unnecessary to me to lose time in these superfluities, having said but too much already thereof. After all things were peaceable and quiet, and that for the space of five or six Credoes nothing had been spoken, there appeared coming from the next Temple, which was about a flight shot off, a very rich and sumptuous Procession of little children, attired all in white taffeta, for a mark of their innocency and purenesse; they had about their necks a number of jewells, chains of gold upon their legs in form of bracelets, white wax lights in their hands, and upon their heads bonnets imbroydered with silk and gold, and set with Pearls, Rubies, and Saphirs; in the middle of this Procession was a rich Canopy of cloth of gold, which twelve of those little children carried, invironed round about with perfuming pans and censors of silver, from whence breathed forth excellent odors most pleasing to the sent. These little children played on divers instruments of musick, and went on singing praises to God, and praying him to resuscitate this defunct to a new life. When they were arrived at the place where the *Roolim* lay, they drew to the shrine, and taking away the cloth wherewith it was covered, there came out of it a little child, which could not be above three or four years old, and although he was naked, yet was not his nakednesse seen, because he was all covered over with gold and pretious stones, and appeared in the same fashion as we are accustomed to paint Angells; he had also golden wings, and a very rich Crown upon his head: Whenas he was come from out the shrine, the Assistants being prostrated on the ground, fell to saying aloud with a voice that made those to tremble which heard them, *Thou Angel of God, sent from heaven for our salvation, pray for us when thou returnest thither again.* The King went instantly to this child, and having taken him in his arms with a great deal of respect, and a strange ceremony, as if he would shew that he was not worthy to touch him, in regard he was an Angell sent from heaven, he set him on the brink of the grave, where after the child had taken away the cloth of black Velvet that covered him, whilest all were on their knees, with their hands and eys lift up to heaven, he said aloud, as if he had spoken to him, *Thou which hast been conceived in sin, amidst the misery and filthinesse of the flesh, God commands thee by me, who am the least of his servants, that thou do resuscitate to a new life which may be agreeable unto him, alwayes dreading the chastisement of his mighty hand, to the end that at the last gasp of thy life thou mayest not stumble like the children of the world; and that from this place where thou art extended stark dead, thou do rise up presently, because it hath been so decreed by the greatest of the greatest in the Temple of the earth, and come after me, and come after me, and come after me.* The King thereupon took this child again in his arms, and then the *Roolim* rising up in the grave where he was, as it were amazed with this vision, fell on his knees before the child whom the King held, and said, *I accept of this new grace from the hand of the Lord, conformably to that which thou hast told me from him, obliging my self to be even till death an example of humility, and the least of all his, to the end the toads of the earth may not lose themselves in the abundance of the world.* This said, the child rid himself again out of the Kings arms, and going directly to the grave, he lent the *Roolim* his hand to help him out of it. Now he was scarce come forth, whenas they gave five toles with a Bell, which was a sign for all the people to prostrate themselves on the ground the second time, saying, *Blessed be thou, O Lord, for so great a grace;* whereupon all the bells in the City began to ring, and all the Ordnance that were on the land to shoot of, as also those of above two thousand vessells that rode at Anchor in the Port, from whence proceeded so strange a noyse, as was most insupportable to the ears of them that heard it.

CHAP.

CHAP. LXII.

In what manner the Roolim was conducted to the Isle of Mounay, and put into possession of his dignity.

THe new *Roolim* was conducted from that place in a chair of gold exceeding rich, and set with Pretious Stones, which the principall Lords of the Kingdome carried upon their shoulders; the King in the mean time marched on foot before him, bearing a rich Scymitar upright in his hand. In this equipage he accompanied him to his Palace, which was gorgeously furnished, and where he was lodged three dayes, during which time the preparations necessary for his entry was made in the Isle of *Mounay*. Now whilest he abode in the City of *Martabano* there were many sorts of inventions of great charge made by the Princes, Lords, and Inhabitants; In two of those feasts the King himself was present in person, with a most sumptuous entertainment, which I shall not describe, because to say the truth I do not know how it did passe. The day being arrived, wherein the new *Roolim*, who is (as I have already declared) their Soveraign High Priest, was to make his entry into the Isle of *Mounay*, the whole Fleet of *Seroos*, *Jangoas*, *Lauleas*, and such other vessells of divers sorts which were upon the river, to the number of two thousand and better, were ranked in two files, some a league and half in length, being the space between the City & the Island; so that of all those vessels joyned together was formed a street, the fairest that possibly could be seen, for every vessell was covered with boughs full of several dainty fruits, together with all kind of flowers, Tangets, Standards, and banners of silk, each one striving in emulation of another to gain their pretended Jubilee, and a plenary indulgence and absolution of all the robberies they had formerly committed, without being subject to the restitution of any thing whatsoever. This they did also to be absolved from an infinite of other abuses of their abhominable lives, which I passe by in silence, as a matter unfit for devout ears, but conformable to their diabolicall Sects, and the damnable intentions of those which have instituted them, for their whole manner of living is nothing but dissolution and excesse in the lasciviousnesse of the flesh, as in like manner are all other infidells, and arch-heretiques. In the *Roolims* company there were not above thirty *Lauleas*, who were replenished with a great number of the Nobility; as for him he was in a rich *Seroo*, seated in a Throne of silver, under a cloth of State of cloth of gold, and the King at his feet, as not being worthy to sit in a more eminent place; round about him were thirty children on their knees attired in Crimson Sattin, with silver Maces on their shoulders, and twelve standing on their feet cloathed with white Damask, having censors in their hands, from whence breathed forth most delicate perfumes. In the rest of the shipping followed two hundred of the most honorable *Talagrepos*, such as Archbishops and other Prelates may be amongst us, in the number of whom were also six or seven young Princes, all the Sons of Kings, comprehended. Now because these Vessells were so full of people as one could not row, they had fifteen *Lauleas*, or little *Skiffes*, wherein the Supreme religious men of those nine Sects did row, to bring them the sooner to land. In this equipage, and in this order the new *Roolim* parted from the City of *Martabano* two hours before day, and continued his course amidst these Vessells, which made, as I have delivered, a kind of street, and forasmuch as it was not yet day, there were a great number of Lanterns of different fashions placed amongst the boughs. As soon as he began to set forth, a Canon was shot off three times, at which sign there was such a noyse of Bells, and great Ordnance, as also of divers sorts of very strange Instruments intermingled with the cries and acclamations of the people, as one would have thought that heaven and earth would have come together. When he was arrived at the *Kay*, where he was to land, he was received with a solemn Procession by certain religious men that live in solitary places, and are called *Menigrepos*, which are like to the *Capucins* in *France*, whom these Gentiles infinitely respect, by reason of their manner of living, for according to the rule which they observe, they use more abstinence by far then all the rest; These same, being some six or seven thousand in number, were all bare foot, and cloathed with black Mat, to shew their contempt of the world: upon their heads they wore the sculls and bones of dead men, and great cords about their necks, having all their faces dawbed over with dirt, and a writing hanging upon them which contained

these

these words, *Mire, mire, do not cast thine eye on thy basenesse, but on the recompenses which God hath promised to those that vilifie themselves to serve him.* When as they were very neer to the *Roolim,* who received them very affably, they prostrated themselves with their faces down to the ground, and after they had continued so some time, the chiefest amongst them looking on the *Roolim, May it please him,* said he, *from whose hand thou hast newly received so great a blessing, as to be the Head of all on the earth, to render thee so good and so holy a man, that all thy works may be as pleasing unto him, as the innocency of children which hold their peace when their mother gives them the dug.* Whereunto all the rest answered with a great noyse of confused voices, *Permit O Lord Almighty that it may be so.* Passing on then, accompanied with this Procession, which the King for the greater honor governed himself, together with some of the principall personages, whom he called unto him for that purpose, he went directly to the place where the dead *Roolim* lay buried, and being arrived at his Tomb, he fell down flat with his face upon it, then having shed a great many tears, he said with a sad and dolefull voice, as if he had spoken to the deceased, *May it please him, who raigns in the beauty of the Stars, to make me deserve the honor to be thy Slave, to the end, that in the house of the Sun, where now thou recreatest thy self, I may serve as a broom to thy feet, for so shall I be made a Diamond of so high a price, as the world, and all the riches thereof together, shall not be able to equall the value of it:* whereunto the *Grepos* answered, *God grant it.* Thereupon taking a pair of Beads which had belonged to the deceased, and that was upon the Tomb, he put it about his neck as a relique of great worth, giving as an Almes, six Lamps of silver, two Censors, and six or seven pieces of violet coloured Damask. This done, he retired unto his Palace, accompanied still with the King, the Princes, and great Lords of the Kingdome, as also with the Priests that were there assistant, from whom he presently rid himself, and then from out of the window he threw down upon the Assembly handfulls of Rice, as amongst the Papists they use to cast Holy Water, which all the people received upon their knees, with their hands lifted up. This Ceremony ended, which lasted very neer three hours, they gave three toles with a Bell, upon which Signal the *Roolim* retired for altogether, and so did the Vessells, and they that came in them, wherein all that day was wholly bestowed. About evening the King took his leave of the *Roolim,* and returned to the City, making directly the next morning towards *Pegu,* which was some eighteen leagues from thence, where he arrived the day following two hours within night, without making any entry or shew, to testifie the extreme griefe he was in for the death of the late *Roolim,* whom it was said, he greatly affected.

CHAP. LXIII.

That which the King of Bramaa *did after his arrivall at the City of* Pegu, *together with his besieging of* Savady.

TWo and twenty daies after the King of *Bramaa* arrived at the City of *Pegu,* he perceived by the Letter which his Ambassador brought him from the *Calaminham,* that he had concluded the League with him against the *Siamon,* yet in regard the season was not fit for him, either to commence that war, or to assail the Kingdome of *Avaa,* as he desired, he resolved to send his Foster-brother, unto whom, as I have already declared, he had given the title of lawfull Brother, to the siege of *Savady,* which was some hundred and thirty Leagues from thence to the North-East. Having assembled an Army then of an hundred and fifty thousand men, amongst whom were thirty thousand strangers of divers Nations, and five thousand fighting Elephants, besides three thousand others that carried the baggage, and the victualls, the *Chaumigrem* departed from *Pegu* with a Fleet of thirteen hundred rowing Vessells, the fifteenth of the moneth of *March.* Fourteen daies after he arrived in the sight of *Savady,* and having cast Anchor neer to a great Plain, called *Gumpalaor,* he remained there six daies in attending the five thousand Elephants which were to come to him by land, who were no sooner arrived, but he began to besiege the Town, so that having begirt it round, he assaulted it three times in the open day, and retreated still with very great losse, as well in regard of the notable resistance which they within made against him, as of the extreme trouble his

people

people were at in planting their ladders againſt the walls, by reaſon of their bad ſcitu-ation, which was all of Slate; whereupon conſulting with his Commanders about what he ſhould do, they were all of opinion to have it battered with the Canon on the weakeſt ſide, untili that by the overthrow of ſome part of the wall, a breach might be made, whereby they might enter with more eaſe and leſſe danger. This reſolution was as ſoon executed as taken, ſo that the Ingineers fell to making of two manner of bull-works on the outſide upon a great Platform, compoſed of great beams and bavins, which in five daies they raiſed up to ſuch an height, as it ſurpaſſed the wall two fathom at the leaſt. This done, they planted on each bulwark twenty great pieces of Ordnance, wherewith they began to batter the Town ſo violently, that in a little time they beat down a pane of the wall; and beſides thoſe pieces of battery, there were above three hundred Falcons that ſhot inceſſantly, with an intention only to kill thoſe that were in the ſtreets, as indeed they made a great havock, which was the cauſe that ſeeing them-ſelves ſo ill-intreated, and their people ſlain in that manner, they reſolved, like valiant men as they were, to ſell their lives as dearly as they could, ſo that one morning having ſallied forth by the ſame breach of the wall which the Canon had made, they gave ſo valiantly upon thoſe of the Camp, that in leſſe then an hour they almoſt routed the *Bramaas* whole Army. Now becauſe it began to be day, the *Savadis* thought it fit to re-enter into the Town, leaving eight thouſand of their enemies dead on the place. After this they repaired the breach in a very little time by the means of a rampire of earth, which they made up with bavins and other materialls, that was ſtrong enough to reſiſt the Canon. Hereupon the *Chaumigrem* ſeeing the bad ſucceſſe he had had, re-ſolved to make war, both upon the places neer about, as alſo upon the frontiers that were furtheſt off from the Town, for which purpoſe he ſent *Dioſaaay*, high Treaſurer of the Kingdome, whoſe Slaves we *Portugals* were, Colonel of five thouſand men to ſpoil a certain Borough, called *Valeutay*, which furniſhed the beſieged Town with pro-viſions; but this voyage was ſo infortunate unto him, that before his arrivall at the de-ſigned place, his forces were by two thouſand *Savadis*, whom he incountred by the way, all cut in pieces in leſſe then half an hour, not one eſcaping with life that fell into the enemies hands. Neverthelesſe it pleaſed our Lord that amidſt this defeat we ſaved our ſelves by the favour of the night, and without knowing whither we went, we took the way of a very craggy mountain, where we marched in exceeding great pain three daies and an half, at the end whereof we entred into certain Mooriſh Plains, where we could meet with no path or way, nor having other company then Tygers, Serpents, and other ſavage beaſts, which put us into a mighty fear. But as our God, whom inceſſantly we invoked with tears in our eys is the true guide of travellers, he out of his infinite mercy permitted, that at length we perceived one evening a certain fire towards the Eaſt, ſo that continuing our courſe towards that place where we ſaw this light, we found our ſelves the next morning neer to a great Lake, where there were ſome Cottages, which in all likelyhood were inhabited by very poor people; howbeit not daring to diſcover our ſelves as yet, we hid us all that day in certain hanging pre-cipices that were very boggy, and full of Horſleeches, which made us all gore blood. As ſoon as it was night we fell to marching again untill the next morning, whenas we arrived neer to a great river, all alongſt the which we continued going for five daies to-gether. At laſt with much pain we got to another Lake, that was far greater then the former, upon the bank whereof was a little Temple in the form of an Hermitage, and there we found an old Hermite, who gave us the beſt entertainment that poſſibly he could: This old man permitted us to repoſe our ſelves two daies with him, during which time we demanded many things of him that made for our purpoſe; whereunto he alwaies anſwered according to the truth, and told us, that we were ſtill within the Territories of the King of *Savady*, that this Lake was called *Oregnauter*, that is to ſay, *the opening of the night*, and the Hermitage, *the God of ſuccour*. Whereupon being deſi-rous to know of him the ſignification of this abuſe, he laid his hand on an horſe of braſſe, that ſtood for the Idoll upon the Altar, and ſaid that he often read in a book, which intreated of the foundation of the Kingdome, that ſome two hundred, thirty, and ſeven years before; this Lake being a great Town, called *Ocumhalen*, a King that was named *Avaa* had taken it in war, that in acknowledgement of this victory, his

Prieſts

Priefts, by whom he was wholly governed, counselled him to facrifice unto *Quiay Guator*, the God of war, all the young male children which had been made captives; and in cafe he did not fo, they would when they became men regain the Kingdome from him. The King apprehending the event of this threatning, caufed all thefe children, being fourfcore and five thoufand in number, to be brought all into one place, and fo upon a day that was kept very folemn amongft them, he made them to be put moft inhumanely to the edge of the fword, with an intent to have them burned the next morning in Sacrifice; but the night following there came a great earthquake, and fuch lightning and fire fell from heaven upon the Town, as within leffe then half an hour it was quite demolifhed, and all that was in it reduced to nothing, fo that by this juft judgement of God, the King, together with all his were ftrucken dead, not fo much as one efcaping, and befides them thirty thoufand Priefts in like manner, who ever fince during all the New Moons are heard to cry and roar fo dreadfully, that all the inhabitants thereabouts were ready to go befides themfelves with fear, by reafon whereof the Country was utterly depopulated, no other habitation remaining therein, fave only fourfcore and five Hermitages, which were erected in memory of the fourfcore and five thoufand children, whom the King had caufed to be butchered through the evill counfell of his Priefts.

CHAP. LXIIII.

A continuation of the fucceffe which we had in this voyage, with my departure from Goa to Zunda, and what paffed during my abode there.

WE paft two daies in this Hermitage, where, as I declared before, we were very well entertained by the Hermite; the third day after betimes in the morning we S. 1. took our leave of him, and departed from thence not a little afflicted with that which we had heard, and fo all the fame day and the night following we continued on our way along by the river; the next morning we arrived at a place where were a great many of fugar canes, of which we took fome, for that we had nothing els to nourifh us withall. In this manner we marched ftill along by this river, which we kept for a guide of our voyage, becaufe we judged that how long foever it were, yet would it at laft ingulfe it felf in the Sea, where we hoped that our Lord would raife us up fome remedy for our miferies. The day enfuing we arrived at a village called *Pommiferay*, where we hid our felves in a very thick wood from being defcried by paffengers, and two hours within night we continued our defign in following the current of this river, being refolved to take our death in good part, if it fhould pleafe God to fend it us, for to put an end to fo many fufferings as we had undergone day and night; and without lying, the apprehenfion and vifions of this laft end troubled us more then death it felf, wherewith we imagined our felves to be already enfnared. At the end of feventeen daies, that this painfull and fad voyage had lafted, God fhewed us fo much grace, that during the obfcurity of a very rainy night, we difcovered a certain light little more then a Faulcon fhot before us, the fear we were in at the firft that we were neer fome Town, made us to ftand ftill for a good fpace, without knowing what to refolve upon, untill we obferved that this light feemed to move, whereby we conjectured that it was fome Veffell which went from one port to another; as indeed half an hour after we perceived one, wherein there were nine perfons, who approaching to the bank of the river, neer to the place where we were, landed all in a Creek that was there in the form of an Haven, and prefently making a fire, they began to prepare their fupper, which was no fooner ready, but they fell to eating with great demonftrations of mirth, wherein they beftowed a pretty good time. At length when they were well replenifhed with meat and drink, it happened that all nine of them, amongft whom there were three women, fell faft afleep; whereupon feeing that we could not find a more favourable occafion to make our benefit of this adventure, we went all eight of us very foftly into the barque, that ftuck half in the Ouze, and was tyed faft to a great ftake, which pufhing forth with our fhoulders we fet aflote, and then imbarquing our felves in it with all fpeed, we began to row down the river with as little noyfe as poffibly we could make. Now in regard the current of the water and the wind were both very favourable

unto

unto us, we found our selves the next morning above ten leagues from the place vvhence vve parted, namely neer to a *Pagode*, called *Quiay Hinarel*, that is to say, *the God of Rice*, vvhere vve met but only vvith one man and seven and thirty vvomen, the most of them old, and Religionaries of this Temple, vvho received us vvith a great deal of charity, although in my opinion they did it rather out of fear of us, then any vvill that they had to do us good. Having questioned them about many things vvhich served for our purpose, they could give us no pertinent ansvver thereunto, alledging still, that they vvere but poor vvomen, vvho upon a solemn vovv had renounced all things in the vvorld, and confined themselves into this inclosure, vvhere they bestovved all their time in continuall prayer to *Quiay Ponuedea*, vvhich moves the clouds of heaven, that he vvould be pleased to give them rain, vvhereby their grounds might be made fruitfull to produce them abandance of Rice. In this place vve spent all the day in caulking our barque, and furnishing our selves at these religious vvomens cost, vvith Rice, Sugar, French Beans, Onyons, and some smoak-dried flesh, vvherevvith they vvere sufficiently provided. Being parted from hence about an hour vvithin night, vve continued our course vvith our Oars and Sails for seven vvhole days together, vvithout so much as once daring to touch the Land, so much vvere vve in fear of some disaster that might easily arrive to us from those places vvhich vve savv all alongst the river: But as it is impossible to avoid that here belovv vvhich is determined there above, just at the instant, as vve vvere continuing on our course, all confused as vve vvere, and in a perpetuall alarm, by reason of the danger that vvas alvvays present before our eys, as vvell for that vvhich vve savv, as for that vve vvere in doubt of, our ill hap vvould have it, that an hour before day, as vve past thorough the mouth of a Channell, three *Paraos* of Pyrats assaulted us vvith such violence, and vvith so many different sorts of Darts, vvhich they showred upon us, that within less then two *Credoes*, they had killed three of our companions; as for us five that remained, vve cast our selves into the Sea all bloudy as we vvere vvith the vvounds vvhich vve had received, vvhereof tvvo others died a little after: When as vve vvere got ashore vve hid our selves in the vvoods, vvhere vve past all that day in lamenting our present mishap after so many fortunes as vve had run thorough before time. Thus vvounded as vve vvere, parting from thence in more hope of death then life, vve proceeded on our vvay by Land, vvith so much pain and irresolution concerning vvhat vve vvere to do, as vve fell many times a vveeping, vvithout being able to comfort one another, in regard of the small likelyhood there vvas of saving our lives by any humane means. As vve vvere reduced to this deplorable estate, vvith tvvo of our companions ready to die, it pleased our Lord (vvhose succour doth ordinarily supply our defects) that in a place vvhere vve found our selves upon the bank of the vvater, there chanced to pass by a Vessell, vvherein there vvas a Christian vvoman, named *Violenta*, vvho vvas married to a *Pagan*, to vvhom this Vessell appertained, vvhich he had laden vvith Cotton Wooll to sell off at *Cosmin*; this vvoman no sooner perceived us, but moved vvith pity at the sight of us, *Iesus*, cried she, *these are Christians which I behold*! that said, she caused the Vessell vvherein she vvas to come to the shore, and leaping on Land, together vvith her husband, they fell both of them to imbracing us vvith tears in their eys, and then made us to be imbarqued vvith them; presently whereupon this vertuous Dame took a care to have our vvounds drest, and provided us of cloaths the best that she could, rendring us many other good offices of a true and charitable Christian: Then setting aside all fear, vve parted from this place vvith all speed, & five days after thorough Gods grace vve arrived safely at the Tovvn of *Cosmin*, vvhich is a part of the Sea in the Kingdome of *Pegu*, vvhere in the house of this good Christian vvoman vve vvere as vvel looked unto, that in a short time vve found our selves thoroughly cured of all our hurts. Now vvhereas there is never any vvant in the grace vvhich God doth to his creatures, it pleased him that at that very time vve met in this Port vvith a ship, vvhereof *Luis de Montorrayo* vvas Master, vvho vvas upon the point of setting sail for *Bengala*, so that after we had taken our leave of our Hostess, to whom we rendred many thanks for all the benefits vvhich we had received of her, we imbarqued our selves vvith the said *Luis de Montarroyo*, who likewise intreated us exceeding well, and furnished us abundantly with all that was necessary for us. At our arrivall at the Port of *Chatigan* in the Kingdome of *Bengala*, where there was at that time many

Portugals,

Portugals, I instantly imbarqued my self in the foist of a certain Merchant, called *Fernando Caldeyra*, who was bound for *Goa*, where it pleased God I arrived in good health. There I found *Pedro de Faria*, who had been Captain of *Malaca*, and by whom I had been sent as Ambassador to the *Chaumbanhaa* of *Martabano*, as I have declared heretofore. To him I rendred an exact accompt of all that had past, for which he shewed himself very sorrowfull, and accommodated me with divers things, whereunto his conscience and generosity obliged him, in regard of the goods which I had lost for his occasion. A little after, that I might not lose the oportunity of the season, I imbarqued my self with an intention to go to the Southward, and once more to try my fortune in the Kingdomes of *China* and *Japan*, to see if in those countries where I had so many times lost my coat, I could not find a better then that I had on.

Being imbarqued at *Goa* in a Junck that belonged to *Pedro de Faria*, which was bound §. 2. in way of trade for *Zunda*, I arrived at *Malaca* the same day that *Ruy vas Pereyra*, termed *Marramaque* died, who was then Captain of the fortresse there. Being departed from that place to go to *Zunda*, at the end of seventeen dayes I arrived at *Banta*, where the *Portugals* are accustomed to traffique. And because there was at that time great scarcity of pepper over all the country, and that we came thither of purpose for it, we were constrained to passe the winter there, with a resolution to go for *China* the year following. We had been almost two moneths in this Port, where we exercised our commerce very peaceably, whenas from the King of *Demaa*, Emperor of all the Islands of *Jaoa*, *Angenia*, *Bala*, *Madura*, and of the rest of the Islands of that *Archipelago*, there landed in this country a widdow woman, named *Nbay Pombaya*, about the age of threescore years, who came as Ambassador to *Tagaril*, King of *Zunda*, that was also his Vassall as well as all the rest of that Monarchy, for to tell him that he was within the term of six weeks to be in person at the town of *Japara*, where he was then making preparation to invade the Kingdome of *Passaruan*. When this woman arrived in this Port, the King went in person to the Vessell where she was, from whence he carried her to his Palace with great pomp, and put her into the company of his wife for her better entertainment, whilest he himself retired to another lodging farther off to do her the more honor. Now that one may know the reason wherefore this ambassage was executed rather by a woman then a man, you must note, that it hath alwayes been the custome of the Kings of this Kingdome to treat of the most important matters of their State by the mediation of women, especially when it concernes peace, which they observe not only in particular messages that are sent by the Lords to their Vassalls, such as this was, but also in matter of publique and generall affairs, which is performed by ambassage from one King to another, and all the reason they give for it, is; *That God hath given more gentlenesse and inclination to courtesie, yea and more authority to women then to men, who are severe, as they say, and by consequent lesse agreeable to those unto whom they are sent*. Now it is their opinion, that every one of those women which the Kings are accustomed to send about affaires of importance, ought to have certain qualities for well executing of an ambassage, and worthily discharging the Commission which is granted to them: for first of all, they say, *That she must not be a Maid, for fear she chance to lose her honor in going out of her house, because that even as with her beauty she contents every one, so by the same reason she may be a motive of discord and unquietnesse in matters where unity is required, rather then an accesse to concord, and the peace which is pretended unto. To this they adde, that she must be married, or at leastwise a widdow after a lawfull marriage; that if she have had children, she must have a Certificate how she hath given them all suck with her own breasts, alledging thereupon, that she who hath borne children, and doth not nourish them if she can, is rather a carnall, voluptuous, corrupted, and dishonest woman, then a true mother*. And this custome is observed so exactly over all this country, principally amongst persons of quality, that if a mother hath a child which she cannot give suck unto for some valuable consideration, she must make an attestation thereof, as of a thing very serious, and much importing her honor. That if being young too she happens to lose her husband, and becomes a widdow, she must for the better testifying of her verrue enter into Religion, to the end she may thereby shew, that she did not formerly marry for the pleasure which she expected from her marriage, but to have children, according to the pure and honest intention, wherewith

Ccc

God

God joyned together the first married couple in the terrestiall Paradise. Furthermore, that there might be nothing to be found fault with in the purity of their marriage, and that it might be altogether conformable to the Law of God, they say, that after a woman is with-child, she ought no longer to have the company of her husband, because the same could not then be but dishonest and sensuall. To these conditions they add many others which I will passe over in silence, for that I think it unreasonable to use prolixity in matters that I hold worthy of excuse, if I do not relate them at length. In the mean time after that *Nhay Pombaya* had delivered her Embassage to the King of *Zunda*, as I have declared before, and treated with him about the occasion which brought her thither, she presently departed from this Towne of *Banta*; whereupon the King having speedily prepared all things in readinesse, he set sail with a Fleet of thirty *Calaluzes*, and ten *Juripangoes*, well furnished with ammunition and victuall, in which forty vessells there were seven thousand fighting men, besides the Mariners and Rowers. Amongst this number were forty *Portugalls*, of six and forty that we were in all, in regard whereof they did us many particular favours in the businesse of our Merchandize, and publikely confessed, that they were much obliged to us for following them as we did, so that we should have had little reason to have excused our selves from accompanying them in this war.

CHAP. XLIV.

The expedition of the Pangueyran, *Emperor of* Jaoa, *and King of* Demaa, *against the King of* Passeruan, *and all that which passed in this war.*

§. I. THe King of *Zunda* being departed from the Port of *Banta* the fifth day of *January*, in the year one thousand five hundred forty and six, arrived on the nineteenth of the same at the Town of *Japara*, where the King of *Demaa*, Emperor of this Island of *Jaoa*, was then making his preparatives, having an army on foot of eight hundred thousand men. This Prince being advertised of the King of *Zundaes* coming, who was his brother-in-law and vassall, he sent the King of *Panaruca*, Admirall of the Fleet, to receive him, who brought along with him an hundred and threescore *Calaluzes*, and ninety *Lanchares*, full of *Luffons* from the Isle of *Borneo*: With all this company he arrived where the King of *Zunda* was, who entertained him very courteously, and with a great deal of honor. Fourteen daies after our coming to this Town of *Japara*, the King of *Demaa* went and imbarqued himself for the Kingdome of *Passaruan* in a Fleet of two thousand and seven hundred sails, amongst the which were a thousand high-built Juncks, and all the rest were Vessells with oars. The eleventh of *February* he arrived at the river of *Hicandurea*, which is at the entrance of the bar; and because the King of *Panaruca*, Admirall of the Fleet, perceived that the great Vessells could not passe unto the Port, which was two leagues off, by reason of certaine shelves of sand that were in divers parts of the river, he caused all those that were in them to be disimbarqued, and the other Vessells with oars to go and anchor in the road before the Town, with an intention to burn the Ships that were in the Port, which indeed was accordingly executed. In this Army was the Emperor *Pangueyran* in person, accompanied with all the grandees of the Kingdome; the King of *Zunda*, his brother-in-law who was Generall of the Army, went by land with a great part of the forces, and being all arrived at the place where they meant to pitch their Camp, they took care in the first place for the fortifying thereof, and for placing the Canon in the most commodious places to batter the Town, in which labour they bestowed the most part of the day. As for the night ensuing it was spent in rejoycings, and keeping good watch untill such time as it was day, whenas each Captain applied himself to that whereunto his duty obliged him, all in generall imploying themselves according to the ingineers directions, so that by the second day the whole Town was invironed with high *Pallisadoes*, and their Platformes fortified with great beames, whereupon they planted divers great pieces of Ordnance, amongst the which were Eagles and Lions of metall, that the *Achems* and *Turks* had cast by the invention of a certain *Renegado*, born in the Kingdome of *Algarues*, appertaining to the Crown of *Portugal*, and by reason this wicked wretch had changed his belief, he called himself *Coia Geinal*, for as for the name which he had before
before

fore when he was a Christian, I am contented to passe it over in silence for the honor of his Family, being indeed of no mean extraction. In the mean time the besieged having taken notice how ill-advised they had been in suffering the enemies to labour two whole daies together peaceably in fortifying of their Camp, without any impeachment of theirs; and taking the same for a great affront, they desired their King to permit them to fal upon them the night following, alledging how it was probable that men wearied with labour could not make any great use of their arms, nor be able to resist this first impetuosity. The King, who at that time commanded the Kingdom of *Passaruan*, was young, & indued with many excellent qualities which made him to be exceedingly beloved of all his subjects, for as it was reported of him, he was very liberal, no manner of Tyrant, exceedingly affable to the common people, a friend to the poor, and so charitable towards Widows, that if they acquainted him with their necessities, he relieved them instantly, and did them more good then they asked of him. Besides these perfections that were so recommendable, he possessed some others so conformable to mens desires, as there was not any one that would not have exposed his life a thousand times for his service if need had been. Furthermore he had none but choice men with him, even the flower of all his Kingdome, besides many strangers, upon whom he conferred much wealth, honor, and many graces, which he accompanied with good words, that being indeed the means whereby the minds both of great and small are so strongly gained, that they make them Lions of sheep, whereas carrying ones self other wayes, of generous Lions, they are made fearfull hares. This King then examining the request which his people made unto him, and referring himself to the advice of the antientest and most prudent Councellors of his State which were with him, there was a great contention about the successe that the affairs might have, but in the end, by the counsell of all in generall, it was concluded, *That in case Fortune should be altogether adverse unto them in this sally which they meant to make against their enemies, yet would it be a much lesse evill, and lesse considerable affront, then to see the King so besieged by vile people, who against all reason would reduce them by force to quit their beliefe, wherein they had been bred by their Fathers, to imbrace another new one by the suscitation of the* Farazes, *who place their salvation in washing their parts behind, in not eating of swines flesh, and marrying of seven wives, whereby the best advised may easily judge, that God was so much their enemy, as he would not assist them in any thing, seeing that with so great offence they would under pretext of Religion, and with reasons so full of contradiction, compell their King to become a* Mahometan, *and render himself tributary to them.* To these reasons they added many others, which the King, and they that were with him found to be so good, as they all with one common consent agreed thereunto, which is en evident mark, that it is a thing no lesse naturall for a good Subject to expose his life for his King, then for a vertuous wife to conserve her chastity for the husband which God hath given her: This being so, said they, a matter of so great importance was no longer to be deferred, but we all in generall, and each one in particular, are by this sally to make demonstration of the extreme affection which we bear to our good King, who we are assured will never be unmindfull of them that shall fight best for his defence, which is all the inheritance we desire to leave to our children. Whereupon it was resolved that the night following they should make a sally upon their enemies.

Whereas the joy, which this designed sally brought to all the inhabitants of the Town was generall, they never stayed till they were called, but two hours after midnight, and before the time which the King had appointed, they assembled all in a great place, which was not far from the Royall Palace, and where they of the country had accustomed to keep their Fairs, and to solemnize their most remarkable feasts on those principall dayes which were destined to the invocation of their *Pagodes*. The King in the mean time, wonderfully content to see such heat of courage in them, of seventy thousand inhabitants which were in the Town, drew out twelve thousand only for this enterprise, and divided them into four companies, each of them containing three thousand, whereof an Unkle of the Kings was Generall, a man whom experience had rendred very knowing in such undertakings, and that marched in the head of the first company. Of the second was Captain another of the principall *Mandarins*; Of the third a stranger, a *Champaa* by Nation, and born in the Island of *Barneo*; and of the fourth one called *Panbaealnio*; all of them good Commanders, very valiant, and exceeding expert in matters of war. When they were all ready, the King made them a Speech, whereby he succinctly represented unto them the confidence which he had in them touching this enterprise. After which, the better to incourage them, and assure them of his love, he took a cup of gold and drunk to them all, causing the chiefest of them to pledge him, and craving pardon of the rest, for that the time would not permit them to do the like. This gracious carriage of his so incouraged the souldiers, that without further delay the most part of them went and annoynted themselves with *Minhamundi*, which is a certain confection of an odoriferous oyle, wherewith these people are accustomed to frote themselves with, when they have taken a full resolution to die, and these same are ordinarily called *Amacos*. The hour being come wherein this sally was to be made, four of twelve gates that were in the Town were opened, thorough each of the which sallied forth one of the four Captaines with his company, having first sent out for Spies into the Camp six *Orobalons*, of the most valiant that were about the King, whom he had honored with new titles, and with such speciall favours, as use to give courage to them that want it, and to increase it in them that are indued with some resolution. The four Captains marched a little after the six Spies, and went and joyned all together in a certain place, where they were to fight with the enemies: whereupon falling into the midst of them with a marvellous impetuosity, they fought so valiantly, that in lesse then an houres time, which the fight indured, the twelve thousand *Passaruans* left above thirty thousand enemies upon the place, besides those that were wounded, which were in a far greater number, and whereof many died afterwards. Furthermore they took prisoner three Kings, and eight *Pates*, which are as the Dukes amongst us, the King of *Zunda* too, with whom we forty *Portugalls* were, could not so save himselfe, but that he was hurt with a Lance in three places, a number being killed in defending him. Thus was the Camp put in so great disorder, as it was almost destroyed, the *Pangueyran* himself being wounded with a dart, and constrained to leap into the water, where little lacked but that he had been drowned. Whereby one may see what the force of a number of resolute and fearlesse men is against such as are surprised when least they think of it; for before that the enemies could know what they did, or the Commanders could put their souldiers into order, they were twice routed. The next morning, as soon as the day gave them leave to know the truth of the businesse, the *Passeruans* retired into the Towne, where they found that they had not lost above nine hundred of their men, nor more then two or three thousand hurt.

S. 3.   It is scarcely to be believed how much the King of *Demaa* was grieved with the disaster of the former day, as wel for the affront which he received from those within by the losse of his people, as for the bad successe of the beginning of this siege, whereof he seemed in some sort to impute the fault unto our King of *Zunda*, saying that this fortune had happened by the bad directions he had given to the Centinells. Now after he had commanded that the wounded should be drest, and the dead buried, he called to Councell all the Kings, Princes, and Captains of the forces that he had, both by Land and Water, unto whom he said, *That he had made a solemn vow, and oath upon the Mozapho of Mahomet, which is their Alcoran, or the book of their Law, never to raise the siege from before this Town, untill he had utterly destroyed it, or lost his own State therein.* Whereunto he added, *That he protested he would put to death whomsoever should oppose this resolution of his, what reason soever he could alledge thereupon*; which begot so great a terror in the minds of all that heard him, as there was not one that durst contradict his will, but contrarily they infinitely approved and commended it. He used then all kind of diligence for the new fortifying of the Camp with good ditches, strong Pallisadoes, & divers Bulworks made of stone and timber, garnished on the inside with their Platformes, where he caused a great many of Canons to be planted, so that by this meanes the Camp was stronger then the Towne it selfe, in regard whereof the besieged did often times jeere the Centinells without, telling them, *That it must needs be concluded they were notorious cowards, since instead of besieging their enemies like valiant men, they besieged themselves like feeble women, wherefore they bid them returne home to their houses, where it was fitter for them to fall to spinning, then to make war.* These were the jeers which they ordinarily

put

put upon the befiegers, who vvere greatly offended vvith them. This Tovvne had been almoſt three moneths befieged, and yet had the enemies advanced but little, for during all that time, vvherein there had been five batteries, and three aſſaults given to it, with above a thouſand ladders planted againſt the vvalls, the befieged defended themſelves ſtill like valiant and couragious men, fortifying themſelves vvith counter-mires which they oppoſed to the breaches, vvhich they made vvith pieces of timber taken from the houſes; ſo that all the power of the *Pangueyran,* which(as I have declared) was about eight hundred thouſand men, whereof the number was much diminiſhed, was not able to give him entrance into it. Hereupon the principall Ingineer of the Camp, who was a Renegado of *Maillorque,* ſeeing that this affair had not a ſucceſſe anſwerable to what he had promiſed the King, he reſolved to take another far different courſe. To that ef-fect, with a great amaſſe of earth and bavins he framed a kind of a Platform, which he fortified with ſix rows of beames, and wrought ſo, that in nine dayes he raiſed it a fa-thom higher then the wall; that done, he planted forty great pieces of Canon upon it, together with a number of Baſes and Faulconets, wherewith he fell to battering the Town in ſuch ſort, as the befieged were therewith mightily damnified, ſo that the King perceiving that this invention of the enemy was the only thing in the world that could moſt incommodate him in the Towne, he reſolved by the meanes of ten thouſand Vo-lunteers, who had offered themſelves unto him for that purpoſe, and to whom for a mark of honor he gave the title of *Tygers of the world,* to attacque this Fort, and they that were upon it; this matter was no ſooner reſolved upon, but was preſently put in execution, and for the better incouragement of them, the King himſelfe would be their Captaine, albeit this whole enterpriſe was governed by the four *Panarieons,* which had formerly commanded in the firſt ſally. Having put themſelves into the field then with the riſing of the Sun, they fought ſo valiantly without any fear at all of the dreadfull Ordnance; which were planted on the Platform, as in leſſe then two *Credoes* they got to the top of it, and there ſetting on the enemies, who were thirty thouſand in num-ber, they defeated them all in a very ſhort time. The *Pangueyran* of *Pate* ſeeing his forces thus routed, ran thither in perſon with twenty thouſand choice ſouldiers, intend-ing to beat the *Paſſeruans* from the place which they had gained, but they defended it ſo couragiouſly, as is not poſſible to expreſſe it in words. This bloudy battell having in-dured till evening, the *Paſſeruan,* who had loſt the moſt part of his men, made his re-treat into the Towne by the gate that was next to the Platforme, whereunto having firſt ſet fire in ſix or ſeven places, it took hold of ſome barrells of powder, whereof there was great ſtore there, which inflamed it ſo terribly in ſeverall parts, as it was not poſſible to approach unto it by the ſpace of a flight ſhoot; this accident was very favour-able to the befieged, becauſe the enemies were thereby kept from joyning together, and ſo the Towne was for this time preſerved from the great danger wherewithall it was threatned; howbeit the *Paſſeruans* ſcap't not ſo ſcot-free, but that of the ten thouſand Volunteers imployed in this ſervice, ſix thouſand remained dead on the top of the Plat-forme. True it is, that in the *Pangueyran* part there vvas above forty thouſand killed, amongſt the vvhhich vvere three thouſand ſtrangers of divers Nations, the moſt part *A-chems, Turks,* and *Malabares,* as alſo twelve *Pates,* or Dukes, five Kings, with many o-ther Commanders, and men of quality.

All this night was ſpent on both ſides in lamentations and complaints, as alſo in dreſſing the vvounded, and caſting the dead into the river. The next morning as ſoone as it was day the *Pangueyran* of *Pata* ſeeing the bad ſucceſſe which his enterpriſe had had untill that preſent, could not for all that be dravvn to deſiſt from it, ſo that he cauſed all his ſouldiers to prepare themſelves for a nevv aſſaulting of the Tovvne, being perſvvaded that the befieged had no great force left to defend them vvithall, conſidering their vvalls vvere overthrovvn in many places their ammunition ſpent, the moſt part of their people ſlaine, and their King dangerouſly hurt, at leaſtvviſe it vvas ſo reported. Novv the better to be aſſured thereof, he cauſed ſome of his forces to be laid in ambuſh in certain avenues, by vvhich he had been advertiſed, that divers of the frontizing inhabitants vvould paſſe, to bring unto the Tovvne Eggs, Pullaine, and o-ther ſuch like things neceſſary for the recovery of ſick perſons. Novv they, vvhom he had ſent for that purpoſe, arrived at the Camp a little before day, and brought nine

§. 4.

priſoners

prisoners with them, amongst the which there was one *Portugal*. After then that they had racked and tortured the other eight, & were come to do as much to the *Portugal*, who was the last, he imagined that it may be they would shew him some favour if he declared unto them what he was, so that upon the first torment he cried out, *That he was a Portugal*, he not knowing hitherto any thing of us, nor we of him: Our King of *Zunda* no sooner heard this Declaration of his, but he commanded him to be taken from the rack, and instantly sent for us to know whether that which this wretch delivered was true; whereupon six of us that were the least hurt went unto him, and at the first sight we judged him by his countenance to be a *Portugal*, so that prostrating our selves before the King, we besought him to give us this man, representing unto him, that in regard he was of our Nation we were bound to make this suit for him, which he very willingly granted us, and so we in way of thankfullnesse kissed his feet. After we had received him, we carried him to the place where our companions lay wounded, and then we would needs understand of him whether he were a *Portugal* indeed, because he looked so strangely as we could not well know him, no not by his speech; but after he was a little come to himselfe, and that he had shed a many of teares, *My Masters*, said he unto us, *I assure you that I am a Christian, and a Portugal, both by father and mother, although as you see I do not weare the habit of one; my country is Penamocor, and my name* Nuno Rodriguez Taborda; *I went out of Portugal in the year one thousand five hundred and thirteen, after I had inrolled my self in the Marshalls Army, and in the Ship called the S. Joano, whereof* Ruy Diaz Pereyra *was Captaine. Now because in those first beginnings I shewed my self in all occasions a worthy man,* Alphonso d'Albuquerque *made me Captain of the four brigandines which he had in the Indiaes at that time; afterwards I was present with him at the taking of Goa and Malaca; withall I laboured in the foundations of Ormuz and Calecut, never failing in any of the services performed in those times by that famous Commander, to whom so many different Nations do at this day give the title of Great. I continued the same proof of my courage during the Governments of Lopo, Suarez, of Diego, Lopez de Siqueyra, and of other Governors of the Indiaes, even unto Don Anriaque de Menesez, who succeeded to that charge by the death of the Vice-Roy Vasco de Gama; who at the entrance into his Government made Francisco de Sa Generall of a Fleet of twelve Vessells, wherein were three hundred men which he was to make use of for the building of a Fort at Zunda, in regard of the feare they were then in of the Spaniards, who at that time went to the Moluccaes by the new way which Magellan had discovered unto them; in this Fleet I was made Captain of a Brigandine, called the S. Jorge, where I commanded over six and twenty very couragious and valiant men. We departed then from the bar of Bintan, whenas Pedro de Mascarenhas destroyed it; but when we arrived at the Isle of Lingua, we were beaten with so furious a tempest, that unable to resist it, we were forced to make towards Jaoa, where of seven rowing Vessells that we were, six were lost, and my sins would have it that mine was one of that number; besides for my greater infortune, the tempest cast my Brigandine upon the coast of this Country, where I have now remained these three and twenty years, not one of all that were in the Vessell escaping, save three of my companions, who are every one dead but my self, and would to God it had pleased him to shew me the grace that I had been so too, that so I might not have offended him as I have done since, for seeing my self continually pressed by these Gentiles to follow their pernicious errors, I withstood them a long time, but whereas the flesh is fraile, being very poor, far from my country, and without hope of liberty, my sins made me at their intreaties to yeeld to that which they desired of me with so much importunity; by reason whereof this Kings Father did me many great favours; and being sent for yesterday from a place where I was to look unto two of the chiefest Gentlemen of this country, it pleased God that I fell into the hands of these dogs, to the end I should no longer be one, for which the Lord be blessed for evermore.* This mans discourse exceedingly astonished us, and as much as the novelty of so strange an accident required, so that having comforted him as well as we could in such termes as we thought were necessary for the time wherein we were, we asked him whether he would go with us to *Zunda*, and from thence to *Malaca*, where God might shew him the grace to die in his service like a good Christian. Whereunto having made answer, that he desired nothing more, and that he had never had other design, we gave him another habit, because he was cloathed like a Pagan, and kept him alwayes with us as long as the siege lasted.

The

CHAP. XLV.

The death of the King of Demaa by a very ftrange accident, and that which arrived thereupon.

TO come again now to our hiſtory, you are to underſtand, that the *Pangueyran of* §. 1. *Pata*, King of *Demaa*, being certified by ſome of the enemies, whom his men had taken priſoners, of the piteous eſtate whereunto the beſieged were reduced, the moſt part of them dead, their ammunition failing, and their King dangerouſly hurt; all theſe things together carried him more ardently then ever to the aſſault, which he had purpoſed with himſelf to give to the beſieged Town. He reſolved then to ſcale it in plain day, and to aſſault it with more violence then before, ſo that inſtantly great preparations were made over all the Camp, where divers Serjeants at Armes, on horſeback, and carrying Maces on their ſhoulders, went proclaiming aloud, after the men of war had been made to aſſemble together with the ſound of trumpets, *The* Pangueyran of Pata *by the power of him who hath created all things, Lord of the Lands which inviron the Seas, being willing to diſcover unto all in generall the ſecret of his ſoul, doth let you know, that nine daies hence he will have you be in a readineſs, to the end that with the courages of Tygers, and re-doubled forces, you aſſiſt him in the aſſault which he intends to give unto the Town, for a re-compence whereof he liberally promiſeth to do great favours, as well in money, as in honorable and remarkable titles, thoſe to the five ſouldiers, which firſt of all ſhall plant colours on the enemies walls, or that ſhall perform actions which ſhall be agreeable to him. Whereas contra-rily, they which do not carry themſelves valiantly in this enterpriſe, conformably to his plea-ſure, ſhall be executed by the way of juſtice, without any regard had to their condition.* This Ordinance of the Kings, full of menaces, being publiſhed over every part of the Camp, put them into ſuch an alarm, as the Commanders began incontinently to make them-ſelves ready, and to provide all things neceſſary for this aſſault, without ſcarce taking a-ny reſt either day or night, making withall ſo great a noyſe, by intermingling their hues and cries with the ſounds of drums, and other inſtruments of war, as it could not be heard without much terror. In the mean time, whereas of the nine daies, deſtined for the purpoſe aforeſaid, ſeven were already paſt, ſo as there reſted no more but two, at the end whereof an aſſault was to be given to the Towne, one morning as the *Pan-gueyran* ſate in Councell, to reſolve of the affairs of this ſiege with the principall Lords of his Army, as alſo of the means, of the time, and places, whereby they were to aſ-ſault the Town, and of other neceſſary things, it was ſaid, that from the diverſity of o-pinions, which the one and the other had, there aroſe ſo great a contention amongſt them, as the King was conſtrained to take every ones advice in writing. During this time, whereas he had alwayes neer about him a young Page, who carried *Bethel*, an herb whoſe leaves are like unto Plantain, which theſe Pagans are accuſtomed to chaw, becauſe it makes them have a ſweet breath, and alſo purges the humours of the ſtomack; he aſk-ed this Page then for ſome of it, who at firſt ſeemed not to hear him, being much about twelve or thirteen years old, for I hold it fit to make mention of his age, in regard of that I am to ſay of him hereafter. Now to return to the *Pangueyran*, as he vvas conti-nuing his diſcourſe vvith his Councell of War; thorough much ſpeaking, and ſomevvhat in choler, his mouth became dry, ſo that he aſked the Page again for ſome *Bethel*, which he ordinarily carried in a little box of gold, but he heard him no more this ſe-cond time, then he had done the firſt; inſomuch as the King having aſked him for ſome the third time, one of the Lords that vvas neere to the Page pulled him by the ſleeve, and bid him *give the King ſome Bethel*, vvhich immediately he did, and falling on his knees he preſented him vvith the box vvhich he had in his hands; the King then took tvvo or three leaves of it, as he uſed to do, and vvithout being othervviſe angry, giving him a light touch vvith his hand on the head, *art thou deaf,* ſaid he unto him, *that thou couldſt not hear me?* and thereupon re-entred into diſcourſe vvith them of his Coun-cell. Novv becauſe theſe *Jaoas* are the moſt punctillious and perfidious Nation of the vvorld, and that vvithall they of this country hold it for the greateſt affront that can be done them, vvhen one gives them a touch on the head, this young Page imagining that the King had touched him ſo out of a mark of ſo great a contempt, as he ſhould thereby be made infamous for ever, though indeed none of the company took notice of

18

it,

it, he went aside weeping and sobbing by himself, and in the end resolved to revenge the injury which the King had done him, so that drawing out a little knife which he wore at his girdle, he stabbed the King with it into the midst of the left pap, and so because the blow was mortall, the King fell instantly down on the ground, not able to say any more then these two or three words; *I am dead*: wherewithall those of the Counsell were so frighted, as it is not possible to expresse it.   After that this emotion was a little calmed, they fell first unto looking to the King, to see if some remedy might not be applied to his wound; but because he was hurt just in the heart there was no hope of recovery, so that he died within a very short time after: Presently they seized on the Page, whom they put to torture, by reason of some suspition which they had upon this accident, but he never confessed any thing, and said nought els, save, *That he had done it of his own free will, and to be revenged of the blow which the King had given him on his head by way of contempt, as if he had struck some dog that was barking up and down the streets in the night, without considering that he was the son of the* Pate Pondan, *Lord of* Surebayaa.   The Page then was impaled alive, with a good big stake, which was thrust in at his Fundament, and came out at the nape of his neck. As much was done to his Father, to three of his brothers, and to threescore and twelve of his kinsmen, so that his whole Race was exterminated, upon which so cruell and rigorous an execution, many great troubles ensued afterwards in all the country of *Iaoa*, and in all the Islands of *Bale, Tymor,* and *Madura,* which are very great, and whereof the Governors are Soveraigns by their Lawes, and from all antiquity.   After the end of this execution, question was made what should be done with the Kings body, whereupon there were many different opinions amongst them, for some said, that to bury him in that place was as much as to leave him in the power of the *Paffernans;* and others, that if he were transported to *Demaa,* where his Tomb was, it was not possible but that it would be corrupted before it arrived there; whereunto was added, that if they interred him so putrified and corrupted, his soul could not be received into *Paradiso,* according to the Law of the country, which is that of *Mahomet,* wherein he died. After many contestations thereupon, in the end they followed the counsell which one of our *Portugals* gave them, that was so profitable to him afterwards, as it was worth him above ten thousand duckats, wherewith the Lords rewarded him as it were in vye of one another for a recompence of the good service which he did then to the deceased. This counsell was, that they should put the body into a Coffin full of Lime and Camphire, and so bury it in a Junck also full of earth; so that albeit the thing was not so marvellous of it self, yet left it not to be very profitable to the *Portugals,* because they all found it very good, and well invented, as indeed the successe of it was such, as by means thereof the Kings body was carried to *Demaa,* without any kind of corruption or ill favour.

§. 2.   As soon as the Kings body was put into the *Junck* appointed for it, the King of *Zunda,* Generall of the Army, caused the great Ordinance and the ammunition to be imbarqued, and with the least noyse that might be, committed to safe custody the most precious things the King had, together with all the treasures of the Tents. But whatsoever care and silence was used therein, the enemy could not be kept from having some inkling of it, and from understanding how things went in the Camp, so that instantly the King marched out of the Town in person, with only three thousand souldiers of the past confederacy, who by a solemn vow caused themselves to be annoynted with the oyle which they call *Minhamundi,* as men resolved, and that had vowed themselves to death. Thus fully determined as they were, they went and fell upon the enemies, whom finding busie in truffing up their baggage, they intreated so ill, as in lesse then half an hours space, for no longer lasted the heat of the fight, they cut twelve thousand of them in pieces. Withall they took two Kings, and five *Pates,* or *Dukes* prisoners, together with above three hundred *Turks, Abyssines,* and *Achems,* yea and their *Caeifmoubana,* the Soveraign dignity amongst the *Mahometans,* by whose counsell the *Pangueyran* was come thither. There were also four hundred ships burnt, wherein were the hurt men, so that by this means all the Camp was neer lost. After this the King retreated into the Town with his men, whereof he lost but four hundred: In the mean time the King of *Zunda* having caused the remainder of the Army to be re-imbarqued with all speed the same day, being the nineth of *March,* they set saile directly

directly for the City of *Demaa*, bringing along with them the body of the *Pangueyran*, vvhich upon the arrivall thereof vvas received by the people vvith great cries, and strange demonstrations of a universall mourning. The day after a revievv vvas taken of all the men of vvar, for to knovv hovv many vvere dead, and there vvas found missing an hundred and thirty thousand; vvhereas the *Passeruans*, according to report, had lost but five and tvventy thousand; but be it as it vvill, and let fortune make the best market that she can of these things, yet they never arrive, but the field is died vvith the bloud of the vanquishers, and by a stronger reason vvith that of the vanquished, to vvhom these events do alvvayes cost far dearer, then to the others. The same day there vvas question of creating a nevv *Pangueyran*, vvho, as I have said heretofore, is Emperor over all the *Pates* and Kings of that great Archipelago, vvhich the *Chineses*, *Tartar*, *Japon*, and *Lequio*, Historians are vvont to call *Raterra Vendau*, that is to say, *the eye-lid of the world*, as one may see in the Card, if the elevation of the heights prove true. Novv because that after the death of the *Pangueyran*, there vvas not a lavvfull successor to be found that might inherit this Crovvn, it vvas resolved that one should be made by election; for vvhich effect by the common consent of all, eight men vvere chosen, as heads of all the people, to create a *Pangueyran*. These same assembled then together in a house, and after order had been taken for the pacifying of all things in the City, they continued seven vvhole daies together vvithout being able to come to any agreement about this election; for vvhereas there vvere eight pretendents of the principall Lords of the Kingdome, there vvere found amongst these Electors many different opinions, vvhich proceeded from this, that the most part, or all of them, vvere meetly allied to these eight, or to their kinsmen, so that each one laboured to make him *Pangueyran*, vvhich vvas most to his mind. Whereupon the inhabitants of the City, and the souldiers of the Army, making use of this delay to their advantage, as men vvho imagined that this affair vvould never be terminated, and that there vvould be no chastisement for them, they began shamelessly to break out into all kind of actions full of insolency and malice. And forasmuch as there vvas a great number of Merchants Ships in the Port, they got aboard them, and fell pell-mell to rifling both of strangers, and those of the country, vvith so much licentiousnesse, as it vvas said, that in four daies they took an hundred Juncks, vvherein they killed above six thousand men; vvhereof notice being given to the King of *Panaruca*, Prince of *Balambuam*, and Admirall of the Sea of this Empire, he ran thither with all speed, and of the number of those which were convicted of manifest robbery, he caused fourscore to be hanged all along the shore, to the terror of those that should behold them. After this action, *Quiay Ansedeaa*, *Pate* or Duke of *Cherbom*, who was Governor of the Towne, and greatly in authority, taking this which the King of *Panaruca* had done for a manifest contempt, because he had, said he, little respected his charge of Governor, was so mightily offended at it, as having instantly got together about six or seven thousand men, he went and fell upon this Kings Palace, with an intent to seize upon his person; but the *Panaruca* resisted him with his followers, and as it was said, he endeavoured with many complements to justifie himself to him all that ever he could; whereunto *Quiay Ansedeaa* was so far from having any regard, as contrarily entring by force into his house he slew thirty or forty of his men; in the mean time so many people ran to this mutiny as it was a dreadfull thing to behold. For whereas these two heads were great Lords, one Admirall of the Fleet, the other Governor of the Town, and both of them allied to the principall families of the Country, the devill sowed so great a division amongst them, as if night had not separated the fight, it is credible that not one of them had escaped; neverthelesse the difference went yet much farther, and ended not so; for the men of war, who were at that time above six hundred thousand in number, coming to consider the great affront which *Quiay Ansedeaa*, Governor of the Town, had done to their Admirall, they to be revenged thereof went all ashore the same night, the *Panaruca* not being of power enough to keep them from it, notwithstanding he laboured all that he could to do it. Thus all of them animated and transported with wrath, and a desire of revenge, went and set upon *Quiay Ansedeaa* house, where they slew him, and ten thousand men; wherewith not contented, they assaulted the Town in ten or eleven places, and fell to killing and plundering all that ever they met with, so that they carried themfelves therein with fo much violence, as in three daies alone, which was as long as the fiege of this Town lafted, nothing remained that was not an infupportable object to the fight. There was withall fo great a confufion of howling, weeping, and heavy lamentation, as all that heard it could think no other but that the earth was going to turn topfie turvy. In a word, and not to lofe time in aggravating this with fuperfluous fpeeches, the Town was all on fire, which burnt to the very foundations, fo that according to report there were above an hundred thoufand houfes confumed, above three hundred thoufand perfons cut in pieces, and almoft as many made prifoners, which were led away flaves, and fold in divers countries. Befides, there was an infinite of riches ftollen, whereof the value, as it was faid, only in filver and gold, amounted even to forty millions, and all put together, to an hundred millions of gold. As for the number of prifoners, and of fuch as were flain, it was neer five hundred thoufand perfons; and all thefe things arrived by the evill counfell of a young King, bred up amongft young people like himfelf, who did every thing at his own pleafure, without any body contradicting him.

CHAP. LXVI.

That which befell us, untill our departure towards the Port of Zunda, *from whence we fet fail for* China, *and what afterwards happened unto us.*

§.1. THree daies after fo cruell and horrible a mutiny, whenas all things were peaceable, the principall Heads of this commotion fearing as foon as a *Pangueyran* fhould be elected, that they fhould be punifhed according to the enormity of their crime, they all of them fet fail without longer attending the danger which threatned them. They departed away then in the fame Veffels wherein they came, the King of *Panaruca*, their Admirall, being not poffibly able to ftay them, but contrarily was twice in jeopardy of lofing himfelfe in endeavouring to do it with thofe few men that were of his party. Thus in the fpace of two daies only, the two thoufand failes which were in the Port went away, leaving the Town ftill burning, which was the caufe that thofe few Lords, which remained, being joyned together, refolved to paffe unto the Towne of *Iapara*, fome five leagues from thence towards the Coaft of the Mediterranean Sea. This refolution being taken, they put it prefently in execution, to the end that with the more tranquillity (for the popular commotion was not yet well appeafed) they might make election of the *Pangueyran*, which properly fignifies *Emperor*; As indeed they created one, called *Pate Sudayo*, Prince of *Surubayaa*, who had been none of thofe eight Pretendents of whom we have fpoken; but this election they made, becaufe it feemed to them neceffary for their common good, and the quiet of the Country: All the inhabitants too were exceedingly fatisfied with it, and they immediately fent the *Panaruca* for him to a place fome dozen leagues from thence, called *Pifammenes*, where he at that time lived. Nine dayes after he was fent for, he failed not to come, accompanied with above two hundred thoufand men, imbarqued in fifteen hundred *Calaluzes* and *Juripangos*. He was received by all the people with great demonftrations of joy, and a little after he was crowned with the accuftomed ceremonies, as *Pangueyran* of all the countries of *Jaoa*, *Bala*, aud *Madura*, which is a Monarchy that is very populous, and exceeding rich and mighty. That done, he returned to the Towne of *Demaa*, with an intent to have it rebuilt anew, and to reftore it to its former eftate. At his arrivall in that place, the firft thing he did was to give order for the punifhing of thofe which were found attainted and convicted of the facking of the Town, who proved not to be above five thoufand, though the number of them was far greater, for all the reft were fled away, fome here, fome there. Thefe wretches fuffered onely two kinds of death, fome were impaled alive, and the reft were burned in the very fame fhips wherein they were apprehended; and of four daies, wherein this juftice was executed, there paft not one without the putting to death of a great number, which fo mightily terrified us *Portugals* that were there prefent, as feeing the commotion very great ftill over the whole country, and no likelyhood that things would of a long time be peaceable, we humbly defired the King of *Zunda* to give us leave to go to our fhip which lay in the Port of *Banta*, in regard the feafon for the voyage to *China* was already come. This

King having easily granted our request, with an exemption of the customes of our Merchandise, presented every one of us besides with an hundred duckats, and to each of the heirs of fourteen of ours, which were slain in the war, he gave three hundred, which we accepted of as a very honorable reward, and worthy of a most liberall, and good natured Prince. Thus went we presently away very well satisfied of him to the Port of *Banta*, and there we remained twelve whole daies together, during the which vve made an end of preparing our selves for our voyage. After this, vve set saile for *China* in the company of other four ships, vvho vvere bound for the same place, and vve took along vvith us the same *Joano Rodriguez*, vvhom vve incountred at *Passervan*, as I have before declared, that had made himself a Brachman of Pagode, called *Quiay Nacorel*, and as for him he had named himself *Gauxitan Facalem*, vvhich is as much to say as, *the Councell of the Saint*. The same *Joano Rodriguez* no sooner arrived at *China*, but he imbarqued himselfe for *Malaca*, vvhere (through the grace of God) he vvas reconciled anevv to the Catholike faith, and after he had continued a year there, he died vvith great demonstrations of a good and true Christian, vvhereby it seems vve may believe that our Lord received him to mercy, since after so many years profession of an infidell, he reserved him to come and die in his service, for vvhich be he praised for evermore. Our five ships then, vvith vvhich vve parted from *Zunda*, being arrived at *Chincheo*, vvhere the *Portugals* at that time traded, vve abode three moneths and an half there vvith travell and danger enough of our persons; for vve vvere in a country, vvhere nothing but revolts and mutinies vvere spoken of. Withall, there vvere great armies afoot all alongst the Coast, by reason of many robberies vvhich the Pyrats of *Japon* had committed thereabout, so that in this disorder there vvas no meanes to exercise any commerce, for the Merchants durst not leave their houses to go to Sea. By reason of all this vve vvere constrained to passe unto the Port of *Chabaqua*, vvhere vve found at anchor sixscore *Juncks*, vvho having set upon us, took three of our five Vessells, vvherein four hundred Christians vvere killed, of which fourscore and two vvere *Portugals*. As for the other tvvo Vessells, in one of the vvhich I vvas, they escaped as it vvere by miracle. But because vve could not make to Land, by reason of the Easterly vvinds vvhich vvere contrary to us all that same moneth, vve vvere constrained (though to our great grief) to regain the Coast of *Java*. At length after vve had continued our course by the space of tvvo and tvventy daies vvith a great deal of travell and danger, vve discovered an Island called *Pullo Condor*, distant eight degrees, and one third of heighth from the bar of the Kingdome of *Camboya*. Whereupon as we were even ready to reach it, so furious a storm came from the South Coast, as we were all in jeopardy to be cast away. Neverthelesse driving along we got to the Isle of *Lingua*, where a tempest surprised us at *West* and *South-West*, with so impetuous a wind, as strugling against the billow, it kept us from making use of our sails: so that being in fear of rocks and shelves of sand, which were on the Prow side, we steered the other way, untill that after some time the Forekeel of our Poup opened within nine hand-bredths of the water, which was the cause, seeing our selves so neer unto death, that we were inforced to cut down our two masts, and to cast all our Merchandises into the Sea, whereby our Ship was somwhat eased. This done, vvhereas vve had left our ship the rest of the day, and a good part of the night to the mercy of the Sea, it pleased our Lord out of an effect of his divine justice, that without knowing how, or without seeing any thing, our ship ran her self against a rock, with the death of seventy and tvvo persons. This miserable successe so deprived us of all our understanding and forces, that not so much as one of us ever thought of any way saving himself, as the *Chineses*, whom we had for Mariners in our Junck had done, for they had so bestirred themselves all the night long, that before it was day they had made a raft of such planks and beams as came to their hands, tying them together in such sort with the cordage of their sails, that forty persons might abide upon it with ease. Now whereas we were all in an imminent danger, and in a time wherein (as they say) the father does nothing for the son, nor the son for the father, no man took care but for himselfe alone, whereof we had a fair example in our *Chinese*-Mariners, whom we accounted but as our slaves; for *Martin Estevez*, the Captain and Master of the Junck, having intreated his own servants, vvho vvere upon the raft, to receive him amongst them, they ansvvered him, that they could not do it at any hand, vvhich

Ddd2

coming

coming to the ears of one of ours called *Ruy de Moura*, whereas he could not indure that these perfidious villains should use us with so much discourtesie and ingratitude, he got him up on his feet from a place where he lay hurt, and made unto us a short speech, whereby he represented unto us, *That we were to remember how odious a thing cowardice was*; and withall, *how absolutely it imported us to seize upon this raft for the saving of our lives.* To these words he added many other such like, which so incouraged us, that with one accord, and with one and the same resolution, whereunto the present necessity obliged us, being but eight and twenty *Portugals*, we set upon the forty *Chineses* which were upon the raft. We opposed our swords then to their iron hatchets, and fought so lustily with them, as we killed them all in the space of two or three *Credoes*. It is true indeed, that of us eight and twenty *Portugals*, sixteen were slain, and twelve escaped, but so wounded, that four of them died the next day. This was an accident, whereof no doubt the like hath seldome been heard of, or seen, whereby one may clearly perceive how great the misery of humane life is, for it was not twelve hours before, when as we all imbraced each other in the ship, and behaved our selves like right brethren, intending to die for one another, and so soon after our sins carried us to such great extremity, as hardly sustaining our selves upon four scurvy planks, tied together with two ropes, we killed one another with as much barbarisme, as if we had been mortall enemies, or something worse. It is true, that the excuse which may be alledged thereupon is, that necessity, which hath no law, compelled us thereunto.

§. 2.   Whenas we were were Masters of this raft, which had cost us and the *Chineses* so much bloud, we set upon it eight and thirty persons of us that we were, of which there were twelve *Portugals*, some of their children, our servants, and the remainder of those that were hurt, whereof the most part died afterwards. Now forasmuch as we were so great a number upon a very little raft, where we floated at the mercy of the waves of the Sea, the water came up to our middles, and in this fashion we escaped from that dangerous and infortunate rock, one Saturday, being Christmas day, one thousand five hundred forty and seven, with one only piece of an old counter-point, which served us for a sail, having neither needle nor compasse to guide us: True it is, that we supplied this defect with the great hope which we had in our Lord, whom we invoked incessantly with groans and sighs, that were accompanied with abundance of tears. In this pitifull equipage we navigated four whole dayes without eating any thing, so that upon the fitth day necessity constrained us to feed on a *Caphar* which died amongst us, with whose body we sustained our selves five dayes longer, which made up the nineth of our voyage, so that during other four, wherein we continued in this case, we had nothing els to eat but the foam and slime of the Sea; for we resolved to die with hunger rather then feed on any of those four *Portugals* which lay dead by us. After we had wandred thus at the mercy of the Sea, it pleased our Lord out of his infinite goodness to let us discover land on the twelfth day, which was so agreeable a sight to us, as the joy of it proved mortall to some of ours, for of fifteen of us that were still alive, four died suddainly, whereof three were *Portugals*; so that of eight and thirty persons which had been imbarqued on the raft, there was but eleven that escaped, namely seven *Portugals*, and four of our boyes. In the end having got to land, we found our selves in a shallow rode, fashioned much like to an Haven, where we began to render infinite thanks to God for having thus delivered us from the perills of the Sea, promising our selves also, that through his infinite mercy he would draw us out of those of the land. Having then made provision of certain shell-fish, as oysters, and sea-crabs to nourish our selves withall, because we had observed how all this country was very desert, and full of Elephants and Tygers, we got up into certain trees, to the end we might avoid the fury of these beasts, and some others which we saw there; then when as we thought that we might proceed on our way with less danger, we gathered us together, & went on thorough a wood, where to secure our lives, we had recourse to loud cries, and hollowings. In the mean time, as it is the property of the divine mercy never to forsake the poore sufferers that are upon the earth, it permitted us to see coming along in a channell of fresh water, that ran ingulphing it selfe into the Sea, a little barque, laden with timber and other wood, wherein were nine *Negroes*, *Jaoas*, and *Papuas*. As soon as these men saw us, imagining that we were some devills, as they confessed to us afterwards, they leapt

into

into the vvater, and quite left the Veſſell, not ſo much as one of them abiding in her But vvhen they perceived vvhat vve vvere, they abandoned the fear they vvere in before, and coming unto us they queſtioned us about many particulars, vvhereunto vve anſvvered according to the truth, and vvithall, deſired them for Gods ſake to lead us vvhitherſoever they vvould, and there to ſell us as ſlaves to ſome that would carry us to *Malaca*; adding that we were Merchants, and that in acknowledgement of ſo good an office, they ſhould get a great deal of money for us, or as much in commodities as they would require. Now whereas theſe *Jaoas* are naturally inclined to avarice, when they heard us talk of their intereſt, they began to be more tractable, and gave us better words, with hope of doing that which we deſired of them, but theſe courteſies laſted no longer but till ſuch time as they could get again into their barque, which they had quitted; for as ſoon as they ſaw themſelves aboard her, they put off from the land, and making as though they would part without taking us in, they told us, that to be aſſured of what we had ſaid to them they would have us before they proceeded any further, to yeeld up our armes to them, whereas otherwiſe they would never take us in, no not though they ſaw us eaten up with Lions. Seeing our ſelves thus conſtrained by neceſſity, and by a certain diſpair of finding any other remedy to our preſent extremity, we were inforced to do all that theſe men required of us; ſo that having brought their barque a little neerer, they bid us ſwim to them, becauſe they had never a boat to fetch us from the ſhore, which we preſently reſolved to do. Whereupon two boys and one *Portugal*, leapt into the Sea to take hold of a rope, which they had thrown out to us from of the poup of the barque; but before they could reach it, they were devoured by three great Lizards, nothing of the bodies of all theſe three appearing to us, but only the bloud, wherewith the Sea was all died. Whileſt this paſſed ſo, we the other eight that remained on the ſhore were ſo ſeized with fear and terror, as we were not our ſelves a long time after, wherewith thoſe dogs which were in the barque were not awhit moved; but contrarily clapping their hands together in ſign of joy, they ſaid in a way of jeering, *O how happy are theſe three, for that they have ended their daies without pain!* Then whenas they ſaw that we were half ſunk up into the Ouze, without ſo much ſtrength as to get our ſelves out of it, five of them leaped aſhore, and tying us by the middle, drew us into their barque, with a thouſand injuries and affronts. After this ſetting ſail they carried us to a village called *Cherbom*, which was ſome dozen leagues from thence, where they ſold all eight of us, namely ſix *Portugals*, one *Chineſe* boy, and a *Caphar*, for the ſum of thirteen *Pardains*, which are in value three hundred realls of our money. He that bought us was a Pagan Merchant of the Iſle of *Zelebres*, in whoſe power we continued five or ſix and twenty daies, and without lying, we had no lack with him, either of cloaths or meat. The ſame Merchant ſold us afterwards for twelve Piſtolls to the King of *Calapa*, who uſed ſo great a magnificence towards us, as he ſent us freely to the Port of *Zunda*, where there were three *Portugal* Veſſells, whereof *Jeronimo Gomez Surmento* was Generall, who gave us a very good reception; and furniſhed us abundantly with all that was neceſſary for us, untill ſuch time as he put to Sea from the Port, to ſail to *China*.

CHAP. XLVII.

My paſſing from Zunda *to* Siam, *where in the company of the* Portugals *I went to the War of* Chiammay; *and that which the King of* Siam *did, untill he returned into his Kingdome, where his Queen poyſoned him.*

AFter we had been very neer a moneth in this Port of *Zunda*, where a good number of *Portugals* were aſſembled together, ſo ſoon as the ſeaſon to go to *China* was come, the three Veſſells ſet ſail for *Chincheo*, no more *Portugals* remaining aſhore, but only two, who went to *Siam* in a Junck of *Patana* with their Merchandiſe. I bethought me then to lay hold on this occaſion, and put my ſelf into their company, becauſe they offered to bear my charges in this voyage, yea and to lend me ſome money for to try fortune once more, and ſee whether by the force of importuning her, ſhe would not uſe me better then formerly ſhe had done. Being departed then from this place, in ſix and twenty daies we arrived at the City of *Odiaa*, the Capitall of this Empire of *Sarnau*, which they of this country do ordinarily call *Siam*, where we were wonderfully

S. 1.

fully well received and intreated by the *Portugals*, which we found there. Now having been a moneth and better in this City, attending the season for the voyage to *China*, that so I might passe to *Japon* in the company of six or seven *Portugals*, who had imbarqued themselves for that purpose, I made account to imploy in commodities some hundred duckats, which those two, with whom I came from *Zunda*, had lent me. In the mean time very certain news came to the King of *Siam*, who was at that time with all his Court at the said City of *Odiaa*, that the King of *Chiammay*, allied with the *Timocouhos, Laaos*, and *Gueos*, people which on the North-East hold the most part of that country above *Capimper* and *Passiloeo*, and are all Soveraignes, exceeding rich and mighty in Estates, had laid siege to the Town of *Quitiruan*, with the death of above thirty thousand men, and of *Oyaa Capimper*, Governor and Lievtenant Generall of all that Frontire. The King remained so much appalled with this news, that without further temporising, he passed over the very same day to the other side of the river, and never standing to lodge in houses, he went and incamped under Tents in the open field, thereby to draw others to do the like in imitation of him: Withall he caused Proclamation to be made over all the City, *That all such as were neither old nor lame, and so could not be dispensed with for going to this war, should be ready to march within twelve daies at the uttermost, upon pain of being burned alive, with perpetuall infamy for themselves, and their descendants, and confiscation of their Estates to the Crown*: To the which he added many other such great and dreadfull penalties, as the only recitall of them struck terror, not into them of the country, but into the very strangers, whom the King would not exempt from this war, of what Nation soever they were; for if they would not serve, they were very expresly enjoyned to depart out of his Kingdome within three daies. In the mean time so rigorous an Edict terrified every one in such sort, as they knew not what counsell to take, or what resolution to follow. As for us *Portugals*, in regard that more respect had alwayes been carried in that country to them, then to all other Nations, this King sent to desire them that they would accompany him in this voyage, wherein they should do him a pleasure, because he would trust them onely with the guard of his person, as judging them more proper for it then any other that he could make choice of; and to oblige them the more thereunto, the message was accompanied with many fair promises, and very great hopes of pensions, graces, benefits, favours, and honors, but above all, with a permission which should be granted them to build Churches in his Kingdome, which so obliged us, that of an hundred and thirty *Portugals* which we were, there were sixscore of us that agreed together to go to this war. The twelve daies limited being past, the King put himself into the field with an Army of four hundred thousand men, whereof seventy thousand were strangers of divers Nations: They imbarqued all in three hundred *Seroos, Laulias*, and *Iangas*, so that on the nineth day of this voyage the King arrived at a Frontire Town, named *Suropisem*, some twelve or thirteen leagues from *Quitiruan*, which the enemies had besieged. There he abode above seven daies to attend four thousand Elephants which came to him by Land. During that time, he was certified that the Town was greatly prest, both on the rivers side, which the enemies had seized upon with two thousand Vessels, as also towards the Land, where there were so many men, as the number of them was not truly known, but as it was judged by conjecture, they might be some three hundred thousand, whereof forty thousand were horse, but no Elephants at all. This news made the King hasten the more, so that instantly he made a review of his forces, and found that he had five hundred thousand men, for since his coming forth many had joyned with him by the way, as also four thousand Elephants, and two hundred carts with field pieces. With this Army he parted from *Suropisem*, and drew towards *Quitiruan*, marching not above four or five leagues a day. At the end of the the third, then he arrived at a valley called *Siputay*, a league and an half from the place where the enemies lay. Then all these men of War, with the Elephants, being set in battell array by the three Masters of the Camp, whereof two were *Turks* by Nation, and the third a *Portugal*, named *Domingos de Seixas*, they proceeded on in their way towards *Quitiruan*, where they arrived before the Sun appeared. Now whereas the enemies were already prepared, in regard they had been advertised by their Spies of the King of *Siams* forces, and of the design which he had, they attended him resolutely in the plain field, relying much on their

forty

forty thousand horse. As soon as they discovered him, they presently advanced, and with their vant-guard, which were the said forty thousand horse, they so charged the King of *Siams* rearward, composed of threescore thousand foot, as they defeated them in lesse then a quarter of an hour, with the losse of three Princes that were slaine upon the place. The King of *Siam* seeing his men thus routed, resolved not to follow the order which he had formerly appointed, but to fall on with the whole body of his Army, and the four thousand Elephants joyned together. With these forces he gave upon the battalion of the enemies with so much impetuosity, as at this first shock they were wholly discomfited, from whence ensued the death of an infinite company of men; for whereas their principall strength consisted in their horse, as soone as the Elephants, sustained by the harquebuses, and the field pieces, fell upon them, they were defeated in lesse then an half hour, so that after the routing of these same, all the rest began instantly to retreat. In the meane time the King of *Siam*, following the honor of the victory, pursued them to the rivers side, which the enemies perceiving, they formed a new Squadron of all those that remained of them, wherein there were above an hundred thousand men, as well sound as hurt, and so past all the same day there, joyned together in one entire body of an Army, the King not daring to fight with them, by reason he saw them fortified with two thousand ships, wherein there were great numbers of men. Neverthelesse as soon as it was dark night the enemies began to march away with all speed all along by the river, wherewith the King was nothing displeased, because the most part of his souldiers being hurt, they were necessarily to be drest, as indeed that was presently executed, and the most part of the day and the night following imployed therein.

After the King of *Siam* had obtained so happy a victory, the first thing that he did §. 2. was to provide with all diligence for the fortifications of the town, and whatsoever els he thought to be necessary for the security thereof. After that he commanded a generall muster to be made of all his men of war, that he might know how many he had lost in this battell; whereupon he found that some fifty thousand were wanting, all men of little reckoning, whom the rigor of the Kings Edict had compelled to serve in this war, ill provided, and without defensive arms: As for the enemies, it was known the next day that an hundred and thirty thousand of them had been slain. As soon as the hurt men were recovered, the King having put into the principall places of this frontier such guards as seemed requisite to him, was counselled by his Lords to make war upon the Kingdom of *Guibem*, which was not above fifteen leagues from thence on the North side, to be revenged on the Queen of *Guibem*, for having given free passage thorough her dominions to those of *Chiammay*, in regard whereof he attributed to her the losse of *Oyaa Capimaer*, and the thirty thousand men that had been killed with him. The King approving of this advice, parted from this town with an army of foure hundred thousand men, and went and fell upon one of this Queens towns, called *Fumbacor*, which was easily taken, and all the inhabitants put to the sword, not one excepted. This done, he continued his voyage till he came to *Guitor*, the capitall town of the Kingdom of *Guibem*, where the Queen then was, who being a widdow governed the State under the title of Regent, during the minority of her son, that was about the age of nine years: At his arrivall he laid siege to the Town, and forasmuch as the Queen found not her self strong enough to resist the King of *Siams* power, she fell to accord with him to pay him an annuall tribute of five thousand *Turmes* of silver, which are threescore thousand Duckats of our money, whereof she paid him five years advance in hand. Besides that, the young Prince her son did him homage as his vassall, and the King led him away with him to *Siam*. Hereupon he raised his siege from before the Town, and passed on towards the North-East to the Town of *Taysiran*, where he had news that the King of *Chiammay* was fallen off from the league aforesaid. In the mean time, whereas he had been six daies march in the enemies territories, he sacked as many places as he met withall, not permitting the life of any male whatsoever to be saved. So proceeding onward, he arrived at the Lake of *Singipamor*, which ordinarily is called *Chiammay*, where he stayed six and twenty daies, during the which he took twelve goodly places, invironed with ditches and bullworks after our fashion, all of brick and mortar, without any stone or lime in them, because in the country it is not the custome to build so;

but they had no other Artillery then some Faulconets, and certain muskets of brasse. Now forasmuch as winter began to approach, and that it was very rainy weather, the King too feeling himself not very well, he retired back again to the Town of *Quitiruan*, where he tarried three and twenty daies and better, in which space he made an end of fortifying it with walls, and many broad and deep ditches, so that having put this Town into an estate of being able to defend it self against any attempt, he imbarqued his Army in the three thousand vessells which brought him thither, and so returned towards *Siam*. Nine daies after he arrived at *Odiaa*, the chiefe City of his whole Kingdome, where for the most part he kept his Court. At his arrivall the inhabitants gave him a stately reception, wherein they bestowed a world of money upon divers inventions, which were made against his entry. Now whereas during the six moneths of the Kings absence, the Queen his wife had committed adultery with a Purveyor of her house, named *Uquumcheniraa*, and that at the Kings return she found her selfe gone four moneths with-child by him, the fear she was in lest it should be discovered, made her, for the saving of her self from the danger that threatned her, resolve to poyson the King her husband, as indeed without further delaying her pernitious intention, she gave him in a messe of milk, which wrought that effect, as he died of it within five daies after; during which time he took order by his Testament for the most important affairs of his Kingdome, and discharged himself of the obligation wherein he stood ingaged to the strangers which had served him in this war of *Chiammay*. In this Testament, whenas he came to make mention of us *Portugals*, he would needs have this clause added thereunto, *It is my intent that the sixscore* Portuga's, *which have alwayes so faithfully watched upon the guard of my person, shall receive for a recompence of their good services, half a years tribute which the* Queen *of* Guibem *gives me; and that in my custome houses, their Merchandise shall pay no custome for the space of three years:* Moreover my *intent is, that their Priests may throughout all the Townes of my* Kingdome *publish the* Law *whereof they make profession, namely of a* God made man for the salvation of mankind, *as they have many times assured me.* To these things he added many others such like, which well deserve to be reported here, though I passe them under silence, because I hope to make a more ample mention of them hereafter. Furthermore, he desired all the Grandees of his Court which were present with him, that they would give him the consolation before he died, to make his eldest Son be declared King, which was incontinently executed. For which effect, after that all the *Oyaas, Conchalis,* and *Monteos,* which are Soveraign dignities over all the rest of the Kingdome, had taken the oath of Allegeance to this young Prince, they shewed him out at a window to all the people, who were in a great place below, and they set upon his head a rich Crovva of gold in the form of a Miter, and put a svvord into his right hand, and a pair of balances into his left, a custome vvhich they alvvays observe in such a like ceremony. Then *Oya Passilico*, who was the highest in dignity in the Kingdome, falling on his knees before this new King, said unto him with tears in his eyes, and so loud that every one might hear him, *Blessed child, that in so tender an age doest hold from the good influence of thy Star the happinesse to be chosen by heaven there above for Governour of this Empire of* Sornau; *see how God puts it into thy hand by me who am thy vassall, to the end thou mayest take thy first oath, whereby thou doest protest to hold it with obedience from his divine will, as also to observe justice equally to all the people, without having any regard to persons, whether it be in chastising or recompencing the great or small, the mighty or the humble, that so in time to come thou mayest not be reproached for not having accomplished that which thou hast sworn in this solemn action. For if it shall happen, that humane considerations shall make thee swarve from that which for thy justification thou art obliged to do before so just a Lord, thou shalt be greatly punished for it in the profound pit of the house of smoke, the burning lake of insupportable stench, where the wicked and damned howl continually with a sadnesse of obscure night in their entrails. And to the end thou mayest oblige thy selfe to the charge which thou takest upon thee,* say now Xamxaimpom, *which is as much as to say amongst us,* Amen. The *Passilico* having finished his speech, the young Prince said weeping *Xamxaimpom,* which so mightily moved all the Assembly of the people, as there was nothing heard for a good while together, but sighing and wailing. At length, after that this noyse was appeased, the *Passilico* proceeding on with his discourse in looking on the young King; *This Sword,*

said

said he unto him, *which thou holdest naked in thy hand, is given thee as a Scepter of Sove-*
raign power upon earth for the subduing of the rebellious, which is also to say that thou art
truly obliged to be the support of the feeble and poor, to the end that they which grow lofty
with their power, may not overthrow them with the puffe of their pride, which the Lord doth
as much abhor, as he doth the mouth of him that blasphemeth against a little infant which
hath never sinned: And that thou mayest in all things satisfie the fair enamelling of
the stars of heaven, which is the perfect, just, and good God, whose power is admirable over all
things of the world, say once again Xamxaimpom; whereunto the Prince answered twice
weeping, *Maximau, Maximau,* that is to say, *I promise so to do.* After this, the *Passilico*
having instructed him in divers other such like things, the young Prince answered seven
times *Xamxaimpom,* and so the ceremony of his Coronation was finished; onely there
came first a *Talagrepo,* of a soveraign dignity above all the other Priests, named *Quiay*
Ponuedea, who it was said was above an hundred years old: This same prostrating himself at the feet of the Prince, gave him an oath upon a golden bason full of rice, and
that done, they put him into it, after they had created him thus anew, for time would
not permit them to hold him there longer, in regard the King his Father was at the
point of death, besides there was so universall a mourning amongst the people, that
in every place there was nothing heard but lamentations and wailing.

CHAP. XLVIII.

The lamentable death of the King of Siam, *with certain illustrious and memorable*
things done by him during his life, and many other accidents that ar-
rived in this Kingdome.

WHenas the day and the night following had been spent in the manner that I S. 1.
have related, the next morning about eight of the clock the infortunate King
yeelded up the Ghost in the presence of the most part of the Lords of his Kingdome,
for the which all the people made so great demonstrations of mourning; as every
where there was nothing but wailing and weeping. Now forasmuch as this Prince had
lived in the reputation of being charitable to the poor, liberall in his benefits and recompences, pitifull and gentle toward every one, and above all incorrupt in doing of
justice, and chastising the wicked; his subjects spake so amply thereof in their lamentations, as if all that they said of it was true, we are to believe, that there was never a better King then he, either amongst these Pagans, or in all the countries of the world.
Howbeit, whereas I cannot assure, that those things which they affirmed in their complaints were true, because I did not see them, I will only insist upon those which past
concerning him, in the time whilest I was trading in this Kingdome, whereof I will report three or four amongst many others, which I have seen him do, from the year 1540.
untill 1545. The first was, that in the year 1540. *Pedro de Faria,* being Governour of
Malaca, King *Joano* the *John,* the third of glorious memory wrote him a letter, whereby
above all things he recommended unto him his using allpossible means for the redeeming
of a certain *Domingos de Seixas,* who for the space of three and twenty years had been a
slave in the Kingdome of *Siam,* adding that the doing thereof would be very important for Gods service and his, in regard he was informed, that from him, rather then
from any other he might be certified of the great things which were recounted to him
of this Kingdome; and in case he could redeem this Christian, that he should send him
incontinently to *Don Garcia,* the Vice-Roy of the *Indiaes,* to whom he had also written, that he should imbarque him in the ship which was to part that year for to returne
into *Portugal. Pedro de Faria* had no sooner received this letter, but seeing with how
much care the King his Master recommended this affair unto him, he sent us his Ambassador to *Siam* one *Francisco de Crasto,* a noble and very rich man, to the end he should
treat about the ransome of this *Domingos de Seixas,* and other sixteen *Portugals,* which
were also slaves there as well as he. According to this Commission *Francisco de Castro*
came to the City of *Odiaa,* whilest I was there, where he delivered his letter to the
King of *Siam,* who gave him a very good reception, and after he had read it, and questioned him concerning many new and curious things, he answered him presently,
which was a thing he did not usually do to any Ambassador, his answer contained this
much, *As for* Domingos de Seixas, *whom the Captain of* Malaca *sends to me for; adverti-*

sing

sing me that I shall do the King of Portugal *a great pleasure in releasing him*, *I do most willingly grant to do it, as also to deliver all the rest that are with him.* Whereupon *Francisco de Crasto*, having had this dispatch from the King, gave him most humble thanks for it, and prostrated himself three severall times before him, with his head bowed down to the ground, as the custome was to do unto this King, in regard he was more absolute then others. Whenas then the season permitted *Francisco de Castro* to return to *Malaca*, the King sent to fetch *Domingos de Seixas* from the Town of *Goutaleu*, where he was at that time Generall of the Frontire, having under his charge thirty thousand foot, five thousand horse, and eighteen thousand duckats pension by the year: With him also he caused to be brought the other sixteen *Portugals*, and consigned them all into the hands of *Francisco de Castro*, who gave him thanks again for the grace which he did him. A little after, whenas *Domingos de Seixas* and his companions went to take their leave of this King, he caused a thousand turmes of silver to be given to them, which are in value twelve thousand duckats of our money, and desired them to pardon him for giving them so little. Another time, which was in the year a thousand five hundred forty and five, *Simano de Melo*, being Captain of the same fortresse of *Malaca*, one *Luys de Montarroyo* coming from *China* to go to *Patana*, it happened that the ship wherein he was, being beaten with a furious tempest, was cast away in the Port of *Charir*, some five leagues from *Lugor*, where all his good were seized upon by the *Xabandar* of the country, after that the Sea had cast him ashore, and withall, he himself was made a prisoner, together with all the rest which were saved, to the number of four and twenty *Portugal*, and fifty boys, which made in all seventy and four persons; the goods too that were saved out of this Shipwrack, amounted at least to fifteen thousand duckats. Now the reason which the *Xabandar* alledged for this same was, that by the antient custom of the Kingdome all these goods belonged unto him, whereof *Luis de Montarrayo* having advertised certain *Portugals* which were at that instant in the City, they concluded amongst themselves to make an *Odiaa*, or present of some rich pieces, to the value of a thousand duckats, and therewith to go unto the King, upon the day which was named *of the white Elephant*, that was ten daies after, and on the which, in regard it was a very solemn feast, this Prince was accustomed to do many graces to such as were suitors to him for them. So on the solemnity of this day, which they call *Onidaypileu*, that is to say, *the rejoycing of goodmen*, all the *Portugals*, who were threescore and odd, placed themselves in a certain passage of one of the three principall streets, thorough which the King was to passe with a great deal of pomp and Majesty, and whenas they saw the King come by, they prostrated themselves all upon the ground, as the inhabitants of *Siam* use to do, and one of them, being deputed thereunto, recounted unto the King the whole businesse of *Luis de Montarrayo* and his companions, just as it had past, beseeching him he would do them so much grace, as to command the releasement of those poor prisoners, without speaking of the goods which the *Xabandar* had seized upon, because it seemed not reasonable unto them. But the King, who presently understood their demand, was so moved with the tears which he saw some of them shed, as he caused the white Elephant whereon he was mounted to stay, then casting his eye on the *Portugals*, and the Present that some of them held out in their hands, which he knew they intended to offer unto him; *My friends*, said he unto him, *I take that for received which you would present me with, and do thank you for it; for in so solemn a day as this is I do not use to take any thing of any body, but to give, and oblige every one with benefits; wherefore I desire you for the love of your God, whose servant I am, and ever will be, to bestow this Present upon such of your company as are in most need of it; for you shall do far better in gaining thereby the recompence of this Almes, which you shall give for his sake then you could get by all that which I should confer on you in acknowledgement of this Present, it being most certain that before him I am but a poor worm of the earth. As for the prisoners which you demand of me, it is my pleasure to bestow them as an Almes upon you, that so in all liberty they may return unto Malaca; and further, I command that all the goods which they say have been taken from them, be restored to them again; for things which are done for Gods sake, ought to be accomplished with much more liberality then the need of the poor requires, especially when they crave it with tears in their eys.* Hereupon the *Portugals* prostrated themselves all before him, and the next day the King by his Letters Patents ordained,

That

That within the term of ten daies the prisoners should be brought to the City, together with all that which had been taken from them; which incontinently was executed very exactly, for there were restored unto them all the goods which had been saved out of the ship, amounting, as I have already said, to fifteen thousand duckats, which the King freely gave them. Two or three moneths after, in the same year one thousand five hundred forty and five, it greatly importing this King of *Siam* to go in person and repulse the King of *Tuparahos*, who on *Passilicans* side had invaded his country, and sacked some of the weakest places, with an intent to besiege the fortresse of *Xinau* and *Lauter*, whereon depended the whole safety of this state, he resolved to go against him in person. Wherefore he sent certain Colonells over all the Kingdome to levy men, with an expresse Commission to return within twenty daies with their men of war to the City of *Odiaa*, for it was his intention to set forth from thence about that time. Withall he enjoyned his Commanders upon pain of a rigorous chastisement not to dispense with a man that could fight, from this war, except it were such as were any way impotent, and above threescore years of age, whereupon each of these Colonells was assigned the Province wherein he should make his levies: It happened then that one *Quiay Raudinaa*, a man of quality, and one that the King made oftentimes use of, had for his lot the frontier of *Blanchaa*, where the most part of the inhabitants being very rich, as well in money, as other wayes, gave themselves to the delights of the flesh, and spent the most part of their time in feasts, in sports, and other such like pleasures of this life, so that when they saw that *Quiay Raudinaa* would compell them to go to this war, as he was enjoyned to do, they took it for too heavy a yoke, and too insupportable a burthen, and that did not well agree with the manner of life which they were wont to lead, and therefore the richest of the country assembled together, and resolved to get a dispensation from this voyage by the means of a great sum of money which they made up amongst themselves, and carried to the Colonel. Now whereas there is no place where money is not powerfull enough to overthrow all things, and from which a man can hardly defend himself, the Colonel *Raudinaa* suffered himself to be overcome with such a masse of coyn as these men presented him with, and consented that they should not budge from their homes. In this sort he was constrained to take up in their steads most of the poor impotent and old men of the country, without any regard had to the Kings expresse Injunction to the contrary. Being arrived with this goodly company of souldiers at the City of *Odiaa*, he was commanded to make a shew of them before the King, as all the Colonels did of theirs; as soon as this Prince cast his eye from a window where he was, upon men so wretched, old, and poorly clad, he caused one file of them to come before him; then having asked of them how old they were, and why they presented themselves before him in so bad an equipage; one amongst them speaking for the rest, recounted unto him the whole businesse as it had past, which put the King into such choler, that having presently commanded *Quiay Raudinaa* to be brought before him, and reviled him publikely for his villany and basenesse, he caused him to be bound hand and foot, and having given order for the melting of five *Turmes* of silver, he made it to be powred into his mouth in his presence, whereof he died instantly. Whereupon beholding him lie dead before him; *If it be so*, said he unto him, *that there needed but five Turmes of silver to kill thee, how could'st thou imagine that the threescore thousand duckats which thou tookest of the cowards of Banchaa for to dispense with them from the war, should not be capable of sending thee into the other world? God forgive thee thy avarice, and me the little punishment I have inflicted on thee for the same.* After this, he sent presently to search his house, where the five thousand *Turmes* he had taken were found, which were immediately brought to the King, who caused this money to be distributed in his presence to those old and impotent poor wretches which *Raudinaa* had brought thither, being in number above three thousand; that done he sent them home to their houses, willing them to pray unto God for him. As for those effeminate men, who to be exempted from going to the war had given the five thousand *Turmes* to the Colonell, he commanded them to be attired like women, and so banished them into an Island called *Pulho Caton*; wherewith yet not contented, he confiscated all their estates, which he ordered should be bestowed on such as behaved themselves best in the war. And not long after, observing that one of the hundred and threescore *Portugals*,

which

which went along with him in this expedition, hung back in a certain attempt, which the reſt of his fellows went upon, where they carried themſelves ſo valiantly, and with ſuch courage, as they regained the principall Fort which the enemy had taken in the Town of *Lautor*, he commanded him to return to *Siam*, ſeeing he was not like his other companions, and that as long as he continued there, he ſhould neither offer to go out of the houſe where he was, nor take upon him the name of a *Portugal*, on paine of having his beard ſhaven off, and uſed like thoſe of *Banchaa*, ſince he was as cowardly as they; whereas contrarily to all the reſt of the *Portugals* he ſent treble pay, and exempted them from all duties that were to be paid for their Merchandize, as alſo gave them power to build Churches in any part of his Kingdome for the adoring of the name of the God of the *Portugals*. By theſe and many other examples which I could produce here, it is manifeſt how great and commendable the inclinations of this Prince were, who notwithſtanding that he was a Gentile, was of a wonderfull good nature, and exceedingly addicted to vertuous actions.

§. 2.   It is not to be believed with what infinite ſorrow, both all the great Lords, and generally all the ſubjects of this Kingdome bewailed the death of their good King; but at length an Aſſembly was made of all the Prieſts of this City, who as it was ſaid, were twenty thouſand in number, by whoſe direction the principall perſons of the Kingdom concluded upon the funerall pomp, and ceremonies which were to be uſed thereabout, according to the cuſtome of the conntry: whereupon a mighty great pile was forthwith erected, made of Sandal, Aloes, Calembaa, and Benjamin, on the which the body of the deceaſed King being laid, fire was put to it, with a ſtrange ceremony: during all the time that the body was a burning, the people did nothing but wail and lament beyond all expreſſion, but in the end, it being conſumed to aſhes, they put them into a ſilver ſhrine, which they imbarqued in a *Laulea* very richly equipped, that was accompanied with forty *Seroos* full of *Talagrepos*, which are the higheſt dignity of their Gentile Prieſts, and a great number of other Veſſels, wherein there was a world of people; after them followed an hundred ſmall barques laden with divers figures of Idolls, under the formes of Adders, Lizards, Tygers, Lions, Toads, Serpents, Bats, Geeſe, Bucks, Dogs, Elephants, Cats, Vultures, Kites, Crows, and other ſuch like creatures, whoſe figures were ſo well repreſented to the life, as they ſeemed to be living. In another very great ſhip was the King of all theſe Idolls, which they called, *The gluttonous Serpent of the profound pit of the houſe of ſmoke*. This Idoll had the figure of a monſtrous Adder, was as big about as an hogſhead, and vvrithed into nine circles, ſo that whenas it was extended, it was above an hundred ſpans long, it had the neck ſtanding upright, and out of the eyes, throat, and breaſt iſſued flames of artificiall fire, which rendred this monſter ſo dreadfull and furious, as all that beheld it trembled for fear. Now upon a Theater three fathom high, and richly guilt, was a very beautiful little boy, about four or five years old, covered all over with pearls, and chains, and bracelets of precious ſtones, having wings, and a buſh of hair of fine gold, much after the manner as we uſe to paint Angells. This child held a rich Curtelas in his hand, by which invention theſe Pagans would give to underſtand, *That it was an Angell of heaven ſent from God to impriſon all thoſe many devills, to the end they ſhould not ſteal away the Kings ſoul, before it ſhould arrive at the place of reſt, which was prepared for it there above in glory, for a recompence of the good works which he had done below in the world*. In this order all theſe Veſſells got to land at a Pagode, called *Quiay Poutor*, where after that the ſilver ſhrine, in which the Kings aſhes were, was placed, and the little boy taken from thence, fire was put to all that infinite number of Idolls, juſt in the manner as they ſtood in the Barques; and this was accompanied with ſo horrible a din of cries, great Ordnance, Harquebuzes, Drums, Bells, Cornets, and other different kinds of noyſe, as it was impoſſible to hear it without trembling. This ceremony laſted not above an hour, for whereas all theſe figures were made of combuſtible ſtuffe, and the Veſſells filled with pitch and rozen, ſo dreadfull a flame enſued preſently thereupon, as one might well have ſaid that it was a very pourtraiture of hell; ſo that in an inſtant the Veſſells, and all that vvere in them vvere ſeen to be reduced to nothing. Whenas this, and many other very lively inventions, which had coſt a great deal of money, vvere finiſhed, all the inhabitants, vvhich vvere come thronging thither, and vvhereof the number ſeemed to be infinite, retired back to their houſes,

where

where they remained with their doors and windows shut, not one appearing in the streets for the space of ten daies, during which time all places were unfrequented, and none were seen stirring but some poor people, who in the night went up and down begging with strange lamentations. At the end of the ten daies wherein they had shut themselves up so, they opened their doors and windows, and their *Pagodes*, or Temples, were adorned with many Ensigns of rejoycing, together with a world of hangings, standards, and banners of silk. Hereupon there went through all the streets certain men on horseback, apparelled in white Damask, who at the sound of very harmonious instruments, cried aloud with tears in their eys, *Ye sad inhabitants of this Kingdome of* Siam, *hearken, hearken to that which is made known to you from God, and with humble and pure hearts praise ye all his holy name, for the effects of his divine justice are great; withall laying aside your mourning, come forth of your abodes wherein you are shut up, and sing the praises of the goodnesse of your God, since he hath been pleased to give you a new King, who fears him, and is a friend of the poor.* This Proclamation being made, all the Assistants, with their faces prostrated on the ground, and their hands lifted up, as people that rendred thanks to God, answered aloud weeping; *We make the Angells of heaven our Attorneys, to the end they may continually praise the Lord for us.* After this, all the inhabitants of the City coming out of their houses, and thinking of nothing but dancing and rejoycing, went to the Temple of *Quiay Fanarel,* that is to say, *the God of the joyfull,* where they offered sweet perfumes, and the poorest sort, fruits, pullen, and rice, for the entertainment of the Priests. The same day the nevv King shewed himself over all the City with a great deal of pomp and Majesty, in regard whereof the people made great demonstrations of joy and gladnesse. And forasmuch as the King was but nine years old, it was ordained by the four and twenty *Bracalons* of the Government, that the Queen his mother should be the Protector or Regent of him, and that she should beare rule over all the Officers of the Crown. Things past thus for the space of four moneths and an half, during the which there was no manner of disorder, but all was peaceable in the Kingdome; howbeit at the end of that time, the Queen coming to be delivered of a Son which she had had by her Purveyor, being displeased with the bad report that went of her, she resolved with her self to satisfie her desire, which was to marry with the Father of this new Son, for that she was desperately in love with him: And further, she wickedly enterprised to make away the new King, her lawfull child, to the end that by this means the Crown might passe to the bastard by right of inheritance. Now to execute this horrible design of hers, she made shew that the excesse of her affection to the young King her Son, kept her always in fear, lest some attempt should be made upon his life; so that one day having caused all the Councell of the State to be assembled, she represented unto them, that having but this only pearl enchaced in her heart, she desired to keep it from being plucked from thence by some disaster; for which effect she thought it requisite, as well to secure her from her apprehensions, as to prevent the great mischiefs which carelessenesse is wont to bring in such like cases, that there should be a guard set about the Palace, and the person of the King. This affair was immediately debated in the Councell, and accorded to the Queen, in regard the matter seemed good of it self. The Queen seeing then that her design had succeeded so well, took instantly for the guard of the Palace, and the person of her Son, such as she judged were proper for the executing of her damnable enterprise, and in whom she most confided. She ordained a guard then of two thousand foot, and five hundred horse, besides the ordinary guard of her house, which were six hundred *Caubins* and *Lequios,* and thereof she made Captain one called *Tileubacus,* the cozen of the same Purveyor, by whom she had had a child, to the end that by this mans favour she might dispose of things as she pleased, and the more easily bring to passe her pernicious design. Whereupon relying on the great forces which she had already on her party, she began to revenge her self upon some of the great ones of the Kingdome, because she knew they despised her, and held her not in that esteem she desired, The two first whom she caused to be laid hands on were two Deputies of the Government, making use of this pretext, that they held secret intelligence with the King of *Chiamway,* and were to give him an entry into the Kingdome thorough their lands, so that under colour of justice she caused them to be both executed, and confiscated their estates, whereof she gave the one to her Favorite, and
the

the other to a brother-in-law of his, who (it was said) had been a Smith : But in regard this execution had been done precipitously, and without any proof, the greatest part of the Lords of the Kingdom murmured against the Queen for it, representing unto her the merit of them whom she had put to death, the services they had rendred to the Crown, the qualitie of the persons, and the nobility and antiquity of their extractions, as being of the blond royall, and lineally descended from the Kings of *Siam*, howbeit she made no reckoning thereof, but contrarily a little after making show as if she had not been well, she in a full Councill renounced her regency, and conferred it on *Uquumcheniraa*, her Favorite, to the end that by this means bearing rule over all others, he might dispose of the affairs of the kingdom at his pleasure, and give the most important charges thereof to such as would be of his party, which he thought to be the most assured way for him to usurp this Crown, and make himself absolute Lord of the Empire of *Sornau*, whereof the revenue was twelve millions of gold, besides other comings in, which amounted to as much more. With all these inventions this Queen used so great diligence for the contenting of the desire which she had to raise her Favorite to the Royalty, to marry her self to him, and to make the illegitimate son, which she had had by him, successor of the Crown, as within the space of eight moneths, fortune favouring her designes, and hoping more fully to execute her wicked plot, shee caused most of the great men of the kingdom to be put to death, and confiscated all their lands, goods and treasures, which she distributed amongst such of her creatures as she daily drew to her party. Now forasmuch as the young King her son served for the principall obstacle to her intentions, this young Prince could not escape her abominable fury, for she her self poysoned him even as she had poysoned the King his father. That done, she married with *Uquumcheniraa*, who had been one of the Purveyors of her house, and caused him to be crowned King in the city of *Odiaa*, the eleventh of November in the yeare one thousand five hundred forty five. But whereas Heaven never leaves wicked actions unpunished, the year after, one thousand five hundred forty and six, and on the fifteenth day of January, they were both of them slain by *Oyaa Passilico*, and the King of *Cambaya*, at a certain banquet which these Princes made in a Temple, that was called *Quiay Figrau*, that is to say, *the god of the atoms of the Sun*, whose solemnity was that day celebrated: So that, as well by the death of these two persons, as of all the rest of their party, whom these Princes also killed with them, all things became very peaceable, without any further prejudice to the people of the kingdom ; onely it is true, that it was despoyled of the most part of the Nobility, which formerly it had, by the wicked inventions, and pernicious practices, whereof I have spoken before.

CHAP. LXIX.

The King of Bramaa's *enterprize upon the Kingdom of* Siam ; *and that which past untill his arrivall at the city of* Odiaa, *with his besieging of it, and all that ensued thereupon.*

§. 1.   THe Empire of *Siam* remaining without a lawfull successor, those two great Lords of the Kingdom, namely, *Oyaa Passilico*, and the King of *Cambaia*, together with four or five more of the trustiest that were left, and which had been confederate with them, thought fit to chuse for King, a certain religious man, named *Pretием*, in regard he was the naturall brother of the deceased Prince, husband to that wicked Queen of whom I have spoken ; whereupon this religious man, who was *Talagrepo* of a *Pagode*, called *Quiay Mitrau*, from whence he had not budg'd for the space of thirty years, was the day after drawn forth of it by *Oyaa Passilico*, who brought him on the seventeenth day of January into the city of *Odiaa*, where on the nineteenth he was crowned King with a new kind of ceremony, and a world of magnificence, which (to avoid prolixity) I will not make mention of here, having formerly treated of such like things. Withall passing by all that further arrived in this Kingdom of *Siam*, I will content my self with reporting such things as I imagine will be most agreeable to the curious. It happened then that the King of *Bramaa*, who at that time reigned tyrannically in *Pegu*, being advertised of the deplorable estate whereinto the Empire of *Sornau* was reduced, and of the death of the greatest Lords of the Country, as also that the new King of this Monarchy was a religious man, who had no knowledge either of arms or war, and withall of a cowardly difpofition, a tyrant, and ill beloved of his fubjects, he fell to confult there-upon with his Lords in the town of *Anaplen*, where at that time he kept his Court. Defiring their advice then upon fo important an enterprize, they all of them told him, that by no means he fhould defift from it, in regard this Kingdome was one of the beft of the world, as well in riches, as in abundance of all things; thereunto they added, that the feafon which was then fo favourable for him, promifed it to him at fo good a rate, as it was likely it would not coft him above the revenue of one only year, what expence foever he fhould make of his treafure; befides, if he chanced to get it, he fhould remain Monarch of all the Emperors of the world, and therewithall he fhould be honored with the fovcraign title of *Lord of the white Elephant*, by which means the feventeene Kings of *Capimper*, who made profeffion of his Law, muft of neceffity render him obedience. They told him moreover, that having made fo great a conqueft, he might, thorough the fame territories, and with the fuccour of the Princes his Allies, paffe into *China*, where was that great City of *Pequin*, the incomparable pearl of all the world, and againft which the great *Cham* of *Tartaria*, the *Siamon*, and the *Calaminham*, had brought fuch prodigious Armies into the field. The King of *Bramaa*, having heard all thefe reafons, and many others which his great Lords alledged unto him, wherein his intereft was efpecially concerned, which alwayes works powerfully on every man, was perfwaded by them, and refolved to undertake this enterprife. For this effect he went directly to *Martabano*, where in leffe then two moneths and an half, he raifed an Army of eight hundred thoufand men, wherein there were an hundred thoufand ftrangers. and amongft them a thoufand *Portugals*, which were commanded by *Diego Suarez d' Albergaria*, called *Galego* by way of nick-name. This *Diego Suarez* departed out of the Kingdome of *Portugal* in the year one thoufand five hundred thirty and eight, and went into the *Indies* with the Fleet of the Vice-Roy, *Don Garcia de Noronha*, in a Junck, whereof *Joano de Sepulveda* of the town of *Enora* was Captain; but in the time of which I fpeak, namely in the yeare one thoufand five hundred forty and eight, he had of this King of *Bramaa* two hundred thoufand duckats a yeare, with the title of his brother, and Governor of the Kingdome of *Pegu*. The King departed then from the Town of *Martabano* the Sunday after Eafter, being the feventh of *April* 1548. His Army, as I have already faid, was eight hundred thoufand men, whereof only forty thoufand were horfe, and all the reft foot, threefcore thoufand of them being Harquebuziers; there were moreover five thoufand warlike Elephants; with whom they fight in thofe countries, and alfo a world of baggage, together with a thoufand pieces of Canon, which were drawn by a thoufand couple of Buffles and Rhinocerots; withall, there was a like number of yoke of oxen for the carriage of the victualls. Having taken the field then with thefe forces, he caufed his Army to march ftill on, untill at length he entred into the Territories of the King of *Siam*, where after five days he came to a fortreffe called *Tapuran*, containing fome two thoufand fires, commanded by a certain *Mogor*, a valiant man, and well verft in matters of war. The King of *Bramaa* having invefted it, gave three affaults to it in the open day, and laboured to fcale it with a world of ladders which he had caufed to be brought thither for that purpofe; but not being able to carry it, in regard of the great refiftance of them within, he retreated for that time. But having by the counfell of *Diego Suarez*, who was Generall of the Camp, and by whom he was wholly governed, caufed forty great pieces of Ordnance, whereof the moft of them fhot bullets of iron, to be planted againft it, he fell to battering it with fo much fury, as having made a breach in the wall twelve fathom wide, he affaulted it with ten thoufand ftrangers, *Turks*, *Abyffins*, *Moors*, *Malavares*, *Achems*, *Jaaos*, and *Malayos*; whereupon enfued fo terrible a conflict between the one and the other, that in leffe then half an hour, the befieged, which were fix thoufand *Siamites*, were all cut in pieces, for not fo much as one of them would render himfelf. As for the King of *Bramaa*, he loft above three thoufand of his men, whereat he was inraged, as to be revenged for this loffe he caufed all the women to be put to the fword, which no doubt was a ftrange kind of cruelty: After this execution, he drevv directly tovvards the Tovvn of *Sacotay*, vvhich vvas nine leagues beyond, defiring to make himfelf mafter of that, as vvell as of the other. He arrived in the fight of this Tovvn one Saturday about Sun-fet, and incamped all along the river of *Lebrau*, vvhich is one of the three that iffue

19   OUT

out of the Lake of *Chiammay*, vvhereof I have formerly made mention, vvith a defign to march thorough it directly to *Odiaa*, the Capitall City of the Empire of *Sornau*; for he had already been advertifed that the King vvas there in perfon, and that he vvas making preparation to fight vvith him in the field; he no fooner received this advice, but his Lords counfelled him to make no tarrying in any place, as vvell that he might not lofe time, as that he might keep himfelf from infenfibly confuming his forces, in lying before places vvhich he pretended to take, that vvere fo vvell fortified, as they vvould coft him dear if he amufed himfelf about them, fo that at his arrivall at *Odiaa* he vvould find the moft part of his men vvanting, and his victualls quite fpent. The King having approved of this advice, caufed his Army to march avvay the next day thorough vvoods that vvere cut dovvn by threefcore thoufand Pioners, vvhom he had fent before to plane the paffages and vvays; vvhich vvith much ado they performed. When he vvas come to a place, called *Tilau*, vvhich is befides *Juncalan*, on the South-Eaft Coaft, neere to the Kingdome of *Quedea*, an hundred and forty leagues from *Malaca*, he took guides that were very well acquainted with the way, by whofe means in nine daies journey he arrived in the fight of *Odiaa*, where he pitched his Camp, which he invironed with trenches and ftrong Pallifadoes.

§. 2.   During the firft five daies that the King of *Bramaa* had been before the City of *Odiaa*, he had beftowed labour and pains enough, as well in making of trenches and Pallifadoes, as in providing all things neceffary for this fiege, in all which time the befieged never offered to ftir, whereof *Diego Suarez*, the Marfhall of the Camp being aware, as alfo of the little reckoning which the *Siamites* made of fo great a power as was there affembled, and not knowing whereunto he fhould attribute the caufe of it, he refolved to execute the defign for which he came, to which effect, of the moft part of the men which he had under his command, he made two feparated Squadrons, in each of which there were fix battalions of fix thoufand a piece. After this manner he marched in battell array, at the found of many inftruments, towards the two points which the City made on the South-fide, becaufe the entrance there feemed more facile to him then any other where. So upon the nineteenth day of *June*, in the year one thoufand five hundred forty and eight, an hour before day, all thefe men of war, having fet up above a thoufand ladders againft the walls, endeavoured to mount up on them; but the befieged oppofed them fo valiantly, that in leffe then half an hour there remained dead on the place above ten thoufand on either part. In the mean time the King, who incouraged his fouldiers, feeing the ill fucceffe of this fight, commanded thefe to retreat, and then made the wall to be affaulted afrefh, making ufe for that effect of five thoufand Elephants of war which he had brought thither, and divided into twenty troops, of two hundred and fifty apiece, upon whom there were twenty thoufand *Moens* and *Chalens*, choice men, and that had double pay. The wall then was affaulted by thefe forces with fo terrible an impetuofity, as I want words to expreffe it. For whereas all the Elephants carried wooden Caftles on their backs, from whence they fhot with muskets, braffe culverins, and a great number of harquzes a crock, each of them ten or twelve fpans long, thefe guns made fuch an havock of the befieged, that in leffe then a quarter of an hour the moft of them were beaten down; the Elephants withall fetting their trunks to the target fences, which ferved as battlements, and wherewith they within defended themfelves, tore them down in fuch fort, as not one of them remained entire, fo that by this means the wall was abandoned of all defence, no man daring to fhew himfelf above. In this fort was the entry into the City very eafie to the Affailants, who being invited by fo good fucceffe to make their profit of fo favourable an occafion, fet up their ladders again which they had quitted, and mounting up by them to the top of the wall, with a world of cries and acclamations, they planted thereon in fign of victory a number of Banners and Enfigns. Now becaufe the *Turks* defired to have therein a better fhare then the reft, they befought the King to do them fo much favour as to give them the vantguard, which the King eafily granted them, and that by the counfell of *Diego Suarez*, who defired nothing more then to fee their number leffened, always gave them the moft dangerous imployments. They in the mean time extraordinarily contented, and proud to fee themfelves preferred before fo many other Nations as were in the Camp, refolved to come off with honor from this fervice which they had undertaken. For which purpofe

pofe having formed a Squadron of twelve hundred men, wherein fome *Abyffins* and *Janizaries* were comprifed, they mounted with great cries by thofe ladders up to the top of the wall, which as I have declared, was at that time in the power of the King of *Bramaaes* people. Thefe *Turks* then, whither more rafh, or more infortunate then the reft, fliding down by a pane of the wall, defcended thorough a bullwork into a place which was below, with an intent to open a gate, and give an entrance unto the King, to the end they might rightly boaft, that they all alone had delivered to him the Capitall City of the Kingdome of *Siam*, and fo might gain the recompence vvhich they might well expect for fo brave an action; for the King had before promifed to give unto whomfoever fhould deliver up the City unto him, a thoufand biffes of gold, which in value are five hundred thoufand duckats of our money. Thefe *Turks* being gotten down, as I have faid, laboured to break open a gate with two rammes which they had brought with them for that purpofe; but as they were occupied about it, upon a confidence that they alone fhould gain the thoufand biffes of gold, which the King had promifed to whomfoever fhould open him the gates, they faw themfelves fuddainly charged by three thoufand *Jaos*, all refolute fouldiers, who fell upon them with fuch fury, as little more then a quarter of an hour, there was not fo much as one *Turk* left alive in the place, wherewith not contented, they mounted up immediately to the top of the wall with a wonderfull courage, and fo flefht as they were, and covered over with the bloud of the *Turks*, whom they had newly cut in pieces, they fet upon the *Bramaaes* men which they found there, and fought with them fo valiantly, that they durft not make head againft them, fo that moft of them were there flain, and the reft tumbled down over the vvall. The King of *Bramaa* redoubling his conrage more then before, would not for all that give over this affault, but contrarily refolved to undertake it anew, fo as imagining that thofe Elephants alone would be able to give him an entry into the City, he caufed them once again to approach unto the wall. At the noyfe hereof, *Oyaa Paffilico*, Captain Generall of the City, ran in all haft to this part of the wall, accompanied with fifteen thoufand men, whereof the moft part were *Luzons*, *Borneos*, and *Champaaes*, with fome *Menancabos* among, and caufed the gate to be prefently opened, thorough which the *Bramaa* pretended to enter, and then fent him word, that whereas he was given to underftand how his Highneffe had promifed to give a thoufand biffes of gold to whomfoever fhould open him the gates, that fo he might thereby enter into the City, he had now performed it, fo that he might enter if he would, provided that like a great King as he was, he would make good his word, and fend him the thoufand biffes of gold which he ftayed there to receive. The King of *Bramaa* having received this jeer, would not vouchfafe to return an anfwer, thereby to fhew his contempt of *Oyaa Paffilico*; but inftantly he commanded the City to be affaulted, which was prefently executed with a great deal of fury; for the fight became fo terrible, as it was a dreadfull thing to behold, the rather for that the violence of it lafted above three whole hours, during the which time the gate vvas tvvice forced open, and twice the Affailants got an entrance into the City, which the King of *Siam* no fooner perceived, and that all vvas in danger to be loft, but he ran fpeedily to oppofe them vvith his follovvers, vvhich vvere about thirty thoufand in number, and the beft fouldiers that were in all the City; whereupon the conflict grew much better then before, and continued half an hour and better, during the which I do not know what paft, nor can fay any other thing, fave that we favv ftreams of bloud running every vvhere, and the ayr all of a light fire; there vvas alfo on either part fuch a tumult and noyfe, as one would have faid the earth had been tottering; for it was a moft dreadfull thing to hear the difcord and jarring of thofe barbarous inftruments, as bells, drums, and trumpets, intermingled with the noyfe of the great Ordnance and fmaller fhot, and the dreadfull yelling of fix thoufand Elephants, whence enfued fo great a terror, that it took from them that heard it both courage and fenfe; withall, that place at the City gate, whereof the *Bramaa* had been Mafter, was all covered over with bodies drowned in bloud, a fpectacle fo horrible, that the very fight of it put us almoft befides our felves. *Diego Suarez* then, feeing their forces quite repulfed out of the City, the moft part of the Elephants hurt, and the reft fo feared with the noyfe of the great Ordnance, as it was impoffible to make them return

un-

unto the vvall; as also that the best men of those that had fought at the gate were slain, and that the Sun was almost down, came to the King, and counselled him to sound a retreat, whereunto the King yeelded, though much against his will, because he observed, that both he and the most part of the *Portugals* were wounded, but it was with a purpose to returne to the same enterprise againe the next morning.

§. 2.   The King being retired to his quarter, found himself wounded with the shot of an arrow which he received in that daies conflict, and which he felt not untill then, by reason of the heat of the fight. This accident hindered the executing of the resolution he had taken to give another assault to the City the next day; for he was constrained to keep his bed twelve daies together, but at seventeen days end, when he was fully cured of his hurt, he undertook again the prosecution of his design, and to effect that which he had so resolved upon, namely, not to raise his siege from before the City untill he had made himself Master of it, though it cost him both his life and his whole State. He gave then a second assault unto the City, which proved like unto the former, for he lost a vvorld of men in it, so that he was forced to retreat; but his wilfullnesse was such, as nothing daunted with the great slaughter of his men, he gave five assaults more to it in the open day, wherein he made use of many warlike stratagems, which a *Greek* Ingineer daily invented for him; but whatsoever he could do, he was always fain to retire with losse, whereat he was greatly troubled. In the mean time, whereas the siege of this City had already indured four moneths and an half, he commanded a generall muster of his souldiers to be made, and he found that an hundred and forty thousand of them were wanting. Whereupon seeing to what estate he was reduced, for the putting of an end to the businesse, he resolved to assault the City again with another nevv invention, and this assault was the eighth he had already given to it, during the siege, which he enterprised by the Councell of war, and that under the favour of the night; for they alledged unto him, that darknesse would make the assault lesse dangerous, and the scaling of the walls more facile. This resolution taken, he instantly commanded all preparations necessary for this design to be made, so that in seventeen days they built up six and twenty Castles of strong pieces of timber, whereof each one was set upon six and twenty wheels of iron, which facilitated the motion of so great a frame. Every Castle was fifty foot broad, threescore and five long, and five and twenty high, and all of them were reinforced with double beams, covered over with sheets of lead: Moreover each of them was full of wood, and had fastned to them before great iron chains, and that were very long in regard of the fire. Things thus prepared, one Friday about midnight, being very dark and rainy, the King of *Bramaa* caused three times one after another all the great Ordnance of the Camp to be discharged, which, as I remember, I have already said, consisted of an hundred and threescore great pieces, vvhereof the most part shot iron bullets, besides a many of Falconets, bases, and muskets, to the number of fifteen hundred, so that from all these guns shot off together three times one after another, proceeded so horrible and dreadfull a noyse, as I cannot think that any vvhere but in hell the like could be; for on whatsoever the imagination can be fixt, it cannot meet with any thing that may be rightly compared thereunto. At this time, it vvas not only the great pieces of Ordnance, whereof I have spoken before, and the small ones too, which were shot off, but the like was done by all the guns which were both within the City, and without in the Camp, of what bignesse soever they vvere, being at least an hundred thousand in all, for whereas there were, as I have already said, threescore thousand Harquebuziers in the King of *Bramaaes* Army, there vvere thirty thousand also in the City, besides seven or eight thousand Falconets and Bases; so that to hear all these shot off continually for the space of three hours together, and intermingled with thunder, lightning, and the tempest of the night, was, to say the truth, a thing which was never seen, read of, or imagined, and such indeed as put every one almost besides himself; for some fell flat on the ground, some crept behind walls, and others got into walls. During the greatest violence of this horrible and furious tempest, they set fire on the six and twenty Castles which they had before brought close to the walls, so that by the force of the wind, which vvas at that time very great, and

by

by the means of barrels of pitch that had been put into them, they fel a flaming in such a strange manner, as there was anew to be seen so dreadfull a picture of hell(for it is the only name that can be given it, because there is nothing upon earth that may rightly be resembled unto it) that if even those which were without trembled at it, I leave you to think vvith hovv much more reason vvere they to fear it vvhom necessity constrained to abide the violence of it. Hereupon began a most bloudy conflict on either part, they without falling to scale the walls, and the besieged, who took no less care for all things then they, valiantly to defend themselves, so that no advantage was to be found on either side, but rather both of them were in a condition to be utterly destroyed; for whereas the one and other reinforced themselves continually with fresh supplies, and that the King of *Bramaaes* obstinacy vvas such, as he went himself in person amongst his souldiers, incouraging them with his speeches, and the great promises that he made them, the fight proceeded so far, and increased so mightily, as being unable to deliver the least part of that which passed therein, I leave it to the understanding of every one to imagine what it might be. Four hours after midnight, the six and tvventy Castles being quite burned to the ground, with so terrible a blaze, as no man durst come within a stones cast of it, the King of *Bramaa* caused a retreat to be sounded, at the request of the Captains of the strangers, for there vvere so many hurt men amongst them, as all the day, and most part of the night following was imployed in dressing of them.

CHAP. LXX.

The King of Bramaaes *raising his siege from before the City of* Odiaa; *with a description of the Kingdome of* Siam; *and the fertility thereof.*

THe King of *Bramaa*, seeing that neither the great Ordnance vvherevvith he had **S. 1.** battered the City, nor the assaults vvhich he had given unto it, nor his inventions of Castles, accompanied vvith so many artifices of fire, whereon he had so much relied, had served him to any purpose for the execution of that which he had so mightily desired, and being resolved not to desist from the enterprise vvhich he had begun, he ca'led a Councell of War, vvherein all the Princes, Dukes, Lords, and Commanders that vvere in the Army were present. Having then propounded his desire and intention unto them, he required them to give him their advice thereupon; immediately the affair being put into deliberation, and thoroughly debated on either part, they concluded in the end, that the King vvas by no means to raise this siege, in regard this enterprise was the most glorious, and most profitable of all that ever might be offered unto him; they represented moreover unto him the vvorld of treasure that he had imployed therein, and that if he continued battering the City without desisting from his assaults, at length the enemies would be spent, because it vvas apparent (as they vvere informed) that they vvere no longer able to vvithstand the least attempt that should be made against them. The King being exceedingly contented, for that their opinions proved to be conformable to his desire, testified the great satisfaction that he received thereby, so that he gave them many recompences in money, and vovved to them, that if they could take the City, he vvould confer upon them the greatest commands of the Kingdome, vvith very honorable titles and revenues. This resolution being taken, there was no further question but of considering in vvhat manner the businesse should be carried; whereupon by the counsell of *Diego Suarez*, and of the Ingineer, it was concluded, that vvith bavins and green turfe a kind of Platform should be erected higher then the vvalls, and that thereon should be mounted good store of great Ordnance, wherewith the principall fortifications of the City should be battered, since that in them alone consisted all the enemies defence. Order then vvas presently given for all that vvas judged necessary thereunto, and the threescore thousand Pioners vvhich vvere in the Camp vvere imployed about it, vvho in tvvelve days brought the Fort or Platform into the estate vvhich the King desired. There vvere already planted on it then forty pieces of Canon for the battering of the City the day ensuing, vvhenas a Post arrived vvith Letters to the King, vvhereby he vvas advertised, *That the* Zemindoo *being risen up in the King-*

dome

dome of Pegu, *had cut fifteen thousand Bramaaes there in pieces, and had withall seized on the principall places of the country.* At these news the King was so troubled, that without further delay he raised the siege, and imbarqued himself on a river, called *Pacarau*, where he stayed but that night, and the day following, which he imployed in retiring his great Ordnance and ammunition. Then having set fire on all the Pallisadoes, and lodgings of the Camp, he parted away one Tuesday, the fifteenth day of *October*, in the year a thousand five hundred forty and eight, for to go to the Town of *Martabano*. Having used all possible speed in his voyage, at seventeen days end he came thither, and there was amply informed by the *Chalagonim*, his Captain of all the *Zemindoos* proceedings, in making himself King, and seizing on his treasure; by killing fifteen thousand *Bramaaes*, and that in divers places he had lodged five hundred thousand men, with an intention to stop his passage into the Kingdome. This news very much perplexed the King of *Bramaa*, so that he fell to thinking with himself what course he should take for the remedying of so great a mischief as he was threatned with: In the end he resolved to tarry a while at *Martabano*, to attend some of his forces that were still behind, and then to go and fight a battell with his enemy; but it was his ill luck, that in the space of fourteen days only which he abode there, of four hundred thousand men which he had, fifty thousand quitted him: For whereas they were all *Pegues*, and consequently desirous to shake off the *Bramaaes* yoke, they thought it best to side with the new King the *Zemindoo*, who was a *Pegu* as well as they; and they were the rather induced thereunto, by understanding, that this Prince was of an eminent condition, liberall, and so affable to every one, that he thereby won most men to be of his party. In the mean time the King of *Bramaa*, fearing lest the defection of his souldiers should daily more and more increase, was advised by his Councell to stay no longer there, in regard the longer he should tarry, the more his forces would diminish, for that a great part of his Army was *Pegues*, which were not likely to be very faithfull unto him. This counsell was approved of by the King, who presently marched away towards *Pegu*, neer unto which he was no sooner arrived, but he was certified that the *Zemindoo*, being advertised of his coming, was attending ready to receive him. So these two Kings being in the view of one another, incamped in a great Plaine, some two leagues from the City of *Pegu*, the *Zemindoo* with six hundred thousand men, and the *Bramaa* with three hundred and fifty thousand. The next day these two Armies being put into battell array, came to joyn together one Friday the sixteenth of *November*, the same year, a thousand five hundred forty and eight. It was about six of the clock in the morning when first they began their incounter, which was performed with so much violence, as a generall defeat ensued thereupon, yet fought they with an invincible courage on either part; but the *Zemindoo* had the worse, for in lesse then three hours his whole Army was routed, with the slaughter of three hundred thousand of his men, so that in this extremity he was forced to save himself only with six horse in a fortress, called *Batteler*, where he stayed but one hour, during the which, he furnished himself with a little Vessell, wherein he fled the night ensuing up the river to *Cedaa*. Let us leave him now flying, untill we shall come to him again whenas time shall serve, and return to the King of *Bramaa*, who exceedingly contented with the victory which he had gotten, marched the next morning against the City of *Pegu*; where as soon as he arrived, the inhabitants rendred themselves unto him, on condition to have their lives and goods saved. Whereupon he took order for the dressing of them that were hurt; as for those that he lost in this battell, they were found to be threescore thousand in number, amongst the which were two hundred and fourscore *Portugals*, all the rest of them being grievously wounded.

§. 2.   Having already intreated of the successe which the King of *Bramaas* voyage had in the kingdom of *Siam*, and of the rebellion of the Kingdom of *Pegu*, me thinks it will not be amisse for me to speak here succinctly of the scituation, extent, abundance, riches, and fertility which I saw in this kingdom of *Siam*, and in this Empire of *Sornau*, to shew that the conquest thereof would have been far more utile unto us, then all the estates which now we have in the *India's*, and that we might obtain it with a great deal lesse charge.

charge. This kingdom, as may be seen in the Map, is seven hundred leagues in length, and a hundred and threescore in bredth; the most part of it consists in great plaines, where are a world of corn grounds, and rivers of fresh water, by reason whereof the Country is exceeding fertile, and abundantly stored with cattell and victualls. In the most eminent parts of it are thick Forests of *Angelin* wood, whereof thousands of ships might be made; there are also many mines of Silver, Iron, Steel, Lead, Tin, Saltpetre, and Brimstone; likewise great abundance of Silk, Aloes, Benjamin, Lacre, Indico, Cotton wooll, Rubies, Saphires, Ivory and gold: There is moreover in the woods marvailous store of Brasill and Ebony, wherewith an hundred Juncks are every year laden, to be transported to *China, Hainan,* the *Lequios, Camboya* and *Camphaa*; besides Wax, Honey, and Sugar, which divers places there do yeeld very plentifully. The Kings yearly revenue is ordinarily twelve millions of gold, over and above the presents which the great Lords make him, that comes to a great matter. In the jurisdiction of his territories there are six and twenty hundred populations, which they call *Prodon*, as cities and towns amongst us, besides villages and small hamlets, whereof I have no reckoning. The most part of those populations have no other fortifications or walls, then palisadoes of wood, so that it would be easie for any that should attaque them to make themselves masters thereof; the rather for that the inhabitants of those places are naturally effeminate, and destitute of arms offensive and defensive. This coast of this kingdom joyns upon the two North and South Seas; on that of the *Indiaes* by *Juncalo* and *Tanaucarim*, and on that of *China* by *Monpolocata, Cuy, Lugor, Chintabu,* and *Berdio*. The capitall City of all this Empire is *Odiaa*, whereof I have spoken heretofore; it is fortified with walls of brick and mortar, and contains, according to some, foure hundred thousand fires, whereof an hundred thousand are strangers of divers countries of the world: for whereas the country is very rich of it self, and of great traffick, there passes not a yeare whereunto from the Provinces and Islands of *Iaoa, Bale, Madoura, Angenio, Birneo,* and *Solor*, there sailes at the least a thousand Iuncks, besides other smaller vessells, wherewith all the rivers and all the harbors are full. The King naturally is no way given to tyranny. The customs of all the Kingdome are charitably destinated for the maintenance of certain *Pagodes*, where the duties that are paid are very easie; for whereas the religious men are forbidden to trade with money, they take no more of Merchants then what they will give them out of almes. There are in this Country twelve Sects of Gentiles, as in the Kingdome of *Pegu*; and the King for a sovcraigne title causeth himself to be called *Prechau Salou* which in our tongue signifies, *A holy member of God*. He shewes not himself to the people save only twice in the year, but then with so much riches and majesty, as he hath power and greatnesse, and yet for all this that I say, he lets not to acknowledge himself the vassall and tributarie to the King of *China*, to the end that by means thereof his subjects Iuncks may be admitted into the port of *Combay*, where ordinarily they exercise their commerce. There is also in this Kingdome a great quantity of Pepper, Ginger, Cinamon, Camphire, Allume, Cassia, Tamarinds and Cardamon; so as one may truly affirm that, which I have often heard say in those parts, namely, that this Kingdom is one of the best countries in the world, and easier to be subdued then any other Province, how little soever. I could here report likewise many more particularities of things which I have seen only in the city of *Odiaa*, but I am not minded to make mention of them, that I may not beget in them that shall read this the same grief which I have for the losse which we made of it through our sins, and the gain we might make in conquering this Kingdom.

CHAP. LXXI.

A continuation of that which happened in the Kingdome of Pegu, *as well during the life, as after the death of the King of* Bramaa.

§.I.　TO return now unto the history which heretofore I have left, you must know, that after the King of *Bramaa* had obtained that memorable victory neer to *Pegu*, as I have declared heretofore, by means whereof he remained peaceable possessor of the whole Kingdom, the first thing he imployed himself in was to punish the offendors, which had formerly rebelled; for which effect he cut off the heads of a great many of the Nobility, and Commanders, all whose estates were confiscated to the Crown, which (according to report) amounted unto ten millions of gold, besides plate and jewells, whereby that common Proverb, which was common in the mouths of all, was verified, namely, *That one mans effence cost many men very deare.* Whilest the King continued more and more in his cruelties, and injustice, which he executed against divers persons during the space of two moneths and a half, certain newes came to him, that the city of *Martabano* was revolted, with the death of two thousand *Bramaas*, and that the *Chalogomin*, Governour of the same city, had declared himself for the *Xemindoo*. But that the cause of this revolt may be the better understood by such as are curious, I will (before I proceed any further) succinctly relate, how this *Xemindoo* had been of a religious order in *Pegu*, a man of noble extraction, and (as some affirmed) neer of kin to the precedent King, whom this *Bramaa* had put to death twelve years before, as I have already declared. This *Xemindoo* had formerly to name *Xoripam Xay*, a man of about forty five years of age, of a great understanding, and held by every one for a Saint: he was withall very wel verst in the Laws of their Sects & false Religion, and had many excellent parts, which rendered him so agreeable unto all that heard him preach, as he was no sooner in the Pulpit, but all the assistants prostrated themselves on the ground, saying at every word that he uttered, *Assuredly God speaks in thee.* This *Xemindoo*, seeing himself then in such great credit with the people, spurred on by the generosity of his nature, and the occasion which was then so favourable unto him, resolved to try his fortune, and see to what degree it might arrive. To this end, at such time as the King of *Bramaa* was fallen upon the kingdom of *Siam*, and had laid siege to the city of *Odiaa*, the *Xemindoo* preaching in the temple of *Conquiay* at *Pegu*, which is as it were the Cathedrall of all the rest, where there was a very great assembly of people, he discoursed at large of the losse of this Kingdom, of the death of their lawfull King, as also of the great extortions, cruell punishments, and many other mischiefs which the *Bramaas* had done to their Nation; with so many insolencies, and with so many offences against God, as even the very houses which had been founded by the charity of good people, to serve for Temples wherein the Divine Word might be preached, were all desolated and demolished; or if any were found still standing, they were made use of, either for stables, lay-stalls, or other such places accustomed to lay filth or dung in. These, and many other such like things, which the *Xemindoo* delivered, accompanied with many sighs and tears, made so great an impression in the minds of the people, as from thenceforward they acknowledged him for their lawfull King, and swore allegeance unto him; so that instead of calling him, as they did before, *Xoripam Xay*, they named him *Xemindoo*, as a soveraigne title which they gave him above all others. Seeing himself raised then to the dignity of King, the first thing during the heat and fury of this people, was to go to the King of *Bramaas* palace, where having found five thousand *Bramaas*, he cut them all in pieces, not sparing the life of one of them; the like did he afterwards to all the rest of them that were abiding in the most important places of the State, and withall he seized on the Kings treasure, which was not small. In this manner he slew all the *Bramaas* that were in the Kingdom, which were fifteen thousand, besides the women of that Nation of what age soever, and seized on the places where they resided, which were instantly demolished; so that in the space of three and twenty dayes onely he became absolute possessor of the Kingdom, and prepared a great Army to fight with the King of *Bramaa*, if he should chance to return upon the bruit of this rebellion, as indeed he

fought

fought with him to his great damage, being defeated by him, as I have heretofore declared. And thus having methinks said enough for the intelligence of that which I
am to recount, I will come again to my first discourse. This King of *Bramaa* being
advertised of the revolt of the Town of *Martabano*, and of the death of those two
thousand *Bramaaes*, gave order immediately to all the Lords of the Kingdome for
their repair unto him with as many men as they could levy, and that within the term
of fifteen daies at the furthest, in regard the present necessity would not indure a
longer delay. This done, he parted the day following with a small train from the
City of *Pegu*, to give example to others to do the like, and went and lodged at a
Town called *Mouchan*, with an intention to tarry there those fifteen days he had limited the Lords to come unto him. Now whenas six or seven of them were already
past, he was advertised that *Xemin de Satan*, Governor of a Town so named, had
secretly sent a great sum of gold to the *Zemindoo*, and had withall done him homage
for the same Town where he commanded. This news somewhat troubled the King
of *Bramaa*, who devising with himself of the means which he might use to meet
with the mischief that threatned him, he sent for *Xemin de Satan*, who was then in
the said Town of his Government, with a purpose to cut off his head; but he, betaking himself to his bed, and making shew of being sick, answered, that he would
wait upon the King as soon as he was able to rise. Now in regard he found himself
to be guilty, and misdoubting the cause wherefore he was sent for, he communicated this affair to a dozen of his kinsmen that were there present with him, who all
of them concluded together, how since there was no better way to save himself then
in killing the King, that without further delay it was to be put in execution, so that
all of them offering secretly to assist him in this enterprise, they speedily assembled
all their Confidents, without declaring unto them at first the occasion wherefore
they did it; and withall, drawing others unto them with many fair promises, they
made up of all being joyned together a company of six hundred men. Whereupon
being informed that the King was lodged in a certain *Pagode*, they fell upon it with
great violence, and fortune was so favourable unto them that finding him almost a-
lone in his chamber, they slew him without incurring any danger. That done, they
retired into an outward Court, where the Kings Guard having had some notice of
this treason, set upon them, and the conflict was so hot between them, that in half an
hours space, or thereabout, eight hundred men lay dead in the place, whereof the
most part were *Bramaaes*. After this *Xemin de Satan* making away with four hundred of his followers, went to a place of a large extent, called *Poutel*, whither all
those of the country round about resorted unto him, who being advertised of the
death of the King of *Bramaa*, whom they mortally hated, made up a body of five
thousand men, and went to seek out the three thousand *Bramaaes* which the King
had brought thither with him: And forasmuch as these same were dispersed in severall places, they were all of them easily slain, not scarce so much as one escaping.
With them also were killed fourscore of three hundred *Portugals* that *Diego Suarez* had with him, who, together with all the rest which remained with their lives
saved, rendred themselves upon composition, and were received to mercy, upon condition that for the future they should faithfully serve *Xemin de Satan*, as their proper
King, which they easily promised to do. Nine days after this mutiny, the Rebell seeing himself favoured by fortune, and such a multitude of people at his devotion,
which were come to him out of this Province, to the number of thirty thousand
men, caused himself to be declared King of *Pegu*, promising great recompences to
such as should follow and accompany him, untill he had wholly gained the Kingdome, and driven the *Bramaaes* out of the country. With this design he retired
to a fortresse called *Tagalaa*, and resolved to fortifie himself there out of the feare
he was in of the forces which were to come to the succour of the deceased King,
thinking to find him alive, having been advertised that many were already set forth
from the City of *Pegu* for that purpose. Now of those *Bramaaes* which *Xemin de
Satan* had slain, one by chance escaped, and cast himself all wounded as he was into
the river, and swimming over, never left travelling all that night, and the day following

lovving, for fear of the *Pegues*, untill he arrived at a place, called *Contafarem*, where he incountred with the *Chaumigrem*, the deceafed Kings Fofter-brother, vvho vvas incamped there vvith an army of an hundred and fourfcore thoufand men, vvhereof there vvere but only thirty thoufand *Bramaaes*, all the reft *Pegues*; finding him then upon the point of parting from thence, in regard of the heat that vvould be vvith-in tvvo hours after, he acquainted him vvith the death of the King, and all that had paft befides. Now though this news greatly troubled the *Chaumigrem*, yet he diffem-bled it for the prefent with fo much courage and prudence, as not one of his follow-ers perceived any alteration in him: But contrarily, putting on a rich habit of Car-nation Sattin, imbroidered with gold, and a chain of precious ftones about his neck, he caufed all the Lords and Commanders of his Army to affemble before him, and then fpeaking to them with the femblance of a joyfull man, *Gentlemen*, faid he, *this fellow which you faw come to me but now in fuch haft, hath brought me this Letter, which I have here in my hand, from the King, my Lord and yours; and although by the contents thereof he feemeth to blame us for our careleffeneff in lingering thus, yet I hope e're long to render him fuch an accompt of it, as his Highneffe fhall give us all thanks for the fervice we have done him. By this letter too he certifies me, that he hath very certaine intelligence, how the* Zemindoo *hath raifed an army, with an intent to fall upon the Towns of* Cofmin *and* Dalaa, *and to gain all along the rivers of* Digon *and* Meidoo, *the whole Province of* Danapluu *even to* Anfedaa; *wherefore he hath exprefly enjoyned me, that as foon as poffibly I may, I put into thofe places (as the moft important) fuch forces as fhall be able to refift the enemy; and that I take heed nothing be loft through my negligence, becaufe in that cafe he will admit of no excufe. This being fo, it feems to me very impor-tant and neceffary for his fervice, that you my Lord* Xemimbrum *go inftantly without all delay, and put your felf with your forces into the Town of* Dalaa; *and your brother-in-law* Bainhaa Quem *into that of* Digon, *with his fifteen thoufand men; as for Colonel* Gi-pray *and* Monpocaffer, *they fhall go with their thirty thoufand fouldiers into* Anfedaa, *and* Danapluu, *and* Ciguamcan, *with twenty thoufand men fhall march along to* Xaraa, *and fo to* Malacou; *moreover* Quiay Brazagaran, *with his brethren and kinfmen, fhall go for Generall of the Frontier, with an Army of fifty thoufand men, to the end that affifted with thofe forces, he may in perfon give order wherefoever need fhall be. Behold, what the King hath written to me, whereof I pray you let us make an agreement, and all fign it to-gether, for it is no reafon that my head fhould anfwer for your want of care, and impru-dence.* His Commanders prefently obeyed him, and without longer tarrying there, each of them went ftraight to the place, whither his Commiffion directed him. The *Chaumigrem*, by means of this fo cunning and well diffembled a fleight, rid himfelf in leffe then three hours of all the hundred and fifty thoufand *Pegues*, who he knew, if once they came to hear of the Kings death, would fall upon the thirty thoufand *Bramaaes* that he had there with him, and not leave one of them alive. This done, as foon as it was night, turning back to the City, which was not above a league from thence, he feized with all fpeed on the deceafed Kings Treafure, which amounted, according to report, unto above thirty millions of gold, befides jewells that were not to be eftimated; and withall, he faved all the *Bramaaes* wives and children, and took as many arms and as much ammunition as he could carry away. After this, he fet fire on all that was in the Magazines, caufed all the leffer Ordnance to be rived a-funder, and the greater, which he could not ufe fo, to be cloyed. Furthermore, he made feven thoufand Elephants that were in the country to be killed, referving only two thoufand for the carriage of his treafure, ammunition, and baggage. As for all the reft, it was confumed with fire, fo that neither in the Palace, where were cham-bers all feeked with gold, nor in the Magazines and Arfenalls, nor on the river, where were two thoufand rowing Veffells, remained ought that was not reduced to afhes. After this execution, he departed in all haft, an hour before day, and drew di-rectly towards *Tangau*, which was his own country, from whence he came fome fourteen years before to the conqueft of the Kingdome of *Pegu*, which in the heart of the country was diftant from thence about an hundred and threefcore leagues. Now whereas fear commonly adds wings to the feet, it made him march with fuch

fpeed,

speed, as he and his arrived in fifteen days at the place whither they were a going. In the mean time, whereas the *Chaumigrem* had cunningly sent away the hundred and fifty thousand *Pegues*, as I have declared already, it happened that two days after they understood how the King of *Bramaa* was dead : Now in regard they were mortall enemies of that Nation, sixscore thousand of them in one great body turned back in hast for to go in quest of the thirty thousand *Bramaaes*, but when they arrived at the City, they found that they were gone from thence three days before; this making them to follow in pursuit of them with all the speed that possibly they could, they came to a place, called *Guinacoutel*, some forty leagues from the City whence they came; there they were informed, that it was five days since they passed by, so that dispairing of being able to execute the design which they had of cutting them in pieces, they returned back to the place from whence they were parted, where they consulted amongst themselves about that which they were to do and resolved in the end, since they had no lawfull King, and that the Land was quite freed of the *Bramaaes*, to go to *Xemin de Satan*, as incontinently they did, who received them, not only with a great deal of joy and good entertainment, but promised them mighty matters, and much honor, by raising them to the principall commands of the Kingdome, as soon as time should serve, and that he was more peaceably setled. Thereupon he went directly to the City of *Pegu*, where he was received with the magnificence of a King, and for such crowned in the Temple of *Comquiay*, which is the chief of all the rest.

CHAP. LXXII.

That which arrived in the time of Xenim de Satan, *and an abominable case that befell to* Diego Suarez ; *together with the* Xemindoos *expedition against* Xenim de Satan ; *and that which insued thereupon.*

THree moneths and nine dayes had this Tyrant *Xenim de Satan* already peaceably possessed the city and kingdome of *Pegu*, whenas without fearing any thing, or being contradicted by none, he fell to distributing the treasure and revenues of the Crown to whomsoever he pleased, whereupon great scandalls insued, which were the cause of divers quarrells and divisions amongst many of the Lords, who for this cause, and the injustice which this tyrant did them, retyred into severall foraigne Countries and Kingdoms. Some also went and sided with the *Xemindoo*, who began at that time to be in reputation again: For after he had fled from the battell onely with six horse, as I have declared heretofore, he got into the Kingdom of *Ansedaa*, where as well by the efficacy of his Sermons, as by the authority of his person, he won so many to his devotion, as assisted by the favour and forces of those Lords as adhered to him, he made up an army of threescore thousand men, with which he marched to *Meidoo*, where he was very well received by those of the Country. Now setting aside what he did in those parts, during the space of foure moneths, that he abode there, I will in the mean time passe to a strange accident which in a few dayes fell out in this city, that one may know what end the good fortune of the great *Diego Suarez* had, who had been Governour of this Kingdom of *Pegu*; and the recompence which the world is accustomed to make at last unto all such as serve and trust in it, under the semblance of a good countenance which she shews them at first. The matter past in this sort ; There was in this city of *Pegu* a Merchant, called *Manbagoaa*, a rich man, and that of good reputation in the country : This same resolved to marry a daughter of his to a young man, the son of a worshipfull and very rich Merchant also, named *Manicaniandarim*, about that time that *Diego Suarez* was in the greatest height of his fortune, and termed the Kings brother, and in dignity above all the Princes and Lords of the Kingdom. So the fathers of these young couple being agreed on this marriage, and of the dowry that was to be given, which by report was three hundred thousand duckats; when as the day was come wherein the nuptialls were celebrated with a great deal of state and magnificence, and honoured with the presence of most of the gentlemen of chiefest quality in the city, it happened

Ggg   that

that *Diego Suarez*, being come a little before Sun-set from the royall palace, with a great train both of horse and foot, as his manner was to be alwayes well accompanied, passed by *Mambogoaas* door, where hearing the musick and rejoycing that was in the house, asked what the matter was, whereunto answer being made him, that *Mambogoaa* had married his daughter, and that the wedding was kept there, he presently caused the Elephant on which he was mounted to stay, and sent one to tell the father of the bride, that he congratulated with him for this marriage, and wished a long and happy life to the new married couple; to these words he added many others by way of complement, yea and made him many offers if he would make use of him; wherewith the old father of the bride finding himself so exceedingly honored, as not knowing how to acknowledge it, in regard the person who did him so much honor, was no lesse then the King himself in greatnesse and dignity, the desire which he had to satisfie this obligation in part, if he could not wholly do it, made him go and take his daughter by the hand, accompanied with many Ladies of quality, and so leading her to the street door, where *Diego Suarez* was, he prostrated himself on the ground with a great deal of respect, and with many complements after his manner, thanked him for the favour and honor that he had done him. Thereupon the new married bride, having taken from off her finger a rich ring, presented it on her knees by her fathers expresse commandement, to *Diego Suarez*; but he that naturally was sensuall and lascivious, instead of using civility, whereunto the Laws of generosity and friendship obliged him, having taken the ring which the maid presented unto him, he reached out his hand, and plucked her to him by force, saying, *God forbid that so fair a maid as you should fall into any other hands but mine*; whereupon the poor old man seeing *Diego Suarez* hale his daughter so rudely, lifting up both his hands to heaven, with his knees on the ground, and tears in his eys, *My Lord*, said he unto him, *I humbly beseech thee for the love and respect of the great God, whom thou adorest, and which was conceived without any spot of sin in the Virgins womb, as I confesse and believe, according to that which I have heard thereof, that thou wilt not forcibly take away my daughter; for if thou doest so, I shall assuredly die with griefe and displeasure at it; but if thou desire of me that I should give thee her dowry, together with all that is in my house, and that I deliver up my self unto thee for thy slave, I will instantly do it, provided thou wilt permit that her husband may possesse her, for I have no other good in the world but she, nor will I have any other as long as I live.* Whereupon offering to lay hold on his daughter, *Diego Suarez* making no answer to him, turned himself about to the Captain of his guard, who was a Turk by Nation, and said unto him, *kill this dog.* The Turk presently drew out his Scymitar to kill the poor old man, but he suddainly fled away, leaving his daughter with her hair all about her ears in *Diego Suarez* his hands. In the mean time the Bridegroom came running to this tumult, with his cheeks all bedeawed with tears, but he was scarcely arrived there, whenas these Barbarians slew him, and his Father too, with six or seven other of his kinsmen. Whilest this past so, the women made such fearfull cries in the house, as terrified all those that heard them, so that even the earth and the ayr seemed to tremble at it, or to say better, they demanded vengeance of God for the little respect which was had to his divine justice, and for so great a violence as this was; and truly if I do not more amply report the particularities of so black and so abhominable an action, I desire to be excused, in regard I passe them by for the honor of the *Portugal* Nation. Wherefore it shall suffice me to say, that this poor Maid seeing her self upon the point to be forced, strangled her self with a string that she wore about her middle for a girdle, which she chose rather to do, then suffer this sensuall and bruitish man to carry her away with him by force; but he was therewith so displeased, as he was heard to say, that he repented him more for that he had not enjoyed her, then for using her in that sort as he did. Now from the day of this abhorred act, till four years after, the good old man, the Father of the Bride, was never seen to go out of his house; but at length to give a greater demonstration of his sorrow, and to shew his extreme resentment of the matter, he covered himself with an old tattered mat, and in that sad equipage went up and downe, begging an alms of his very slaves,

never

never eating any thing, but lying all along naked, and his face fixed on the ground. Thus continued he in so sad a manner of life, untill in the end he saw that the season invited him to have recourse unto justice, which he demanded in this sort; perceiving that in the Kingdome there was another King, other Governors, and other Jurisdiction, alterations which time ordinarily produceth in every country, and in all kind of affairs, he went out of his house in the wretched fashion he had so long used, having a big cord about his neck, and a white beard, reaching almost down to his girdle, and got him into the midst of a great place, where stood a Temple called *Quiay Fantaren*, that is to say, *the God of the afflicted*; there he took the idoll from off the Altar, and holding it in his armes, he returned out of the Temple, to the said great place, where having cried out aloud three times to draw the people together, as accordingly they came flocking in unto him, he said with teares in his eys; *O ye people, ye people! who with a cleane and peaceable heart make profession of the truth of this God of the afflicted, which you see here in my armes, come forth like lightning in a dark and rainy night, and joyn with me in crying so loud, that our cryes may pierce the heavens, to the end the pitifull ear of the Lord may be drawn to hear our heavy lamentations, and by them he may know the reason we have to demand justice against this accursed stranger, as the most wicked man that ever was born into the world; for this abhominable wretch hath not been contented with spoiling us of our goods, but hath also dishonored our families; wherefore whosoever shall not with me accompany the God which I hold in my hands, and water with my tears, in detesting so horrible a crime, let the gluttonous Serpent of the profound pit of smoke abridge his dayes miserably, and tear his body in pieces at midnight.* This old mans words so mightily terrified the Assistants, and made so deep an impression in their minds, that in a short time fifty thousand persons assembled in that place, with so much fury and desire of revenge, as was wonderfull to behold. Thus the number of the people still more and more increasing, they ran thronging strait to the Kings Palace, with so horrible a noyse, as struck terror into all that heard them. In this disorder, being arrived at the outward Court of the Palace, they cried out six or seven times with a dreadfull tone; *O King come out of the place wherein thou art shut up, to hearken to the voice of thy God who demands justice of thee by the mouth of thy poor people.* At these cries the King put forth his head out of the window, and affrighted with so strange an accident, would needs know of them what they would have? whereunto they all answered unanimously with such loud cries, as seemed to pierce the heavens, *Justice, justice against a wicked infidell, who to spoil us of our goods hath killed our fathers, our children, our brothers, and our kinsmen.* The King having thereupon inquired of them who it was, *it is*, answered they, *an accursed thief, participating with the works of the Serpent, who in the fields of delight abused the first man that God created.* Is it possible, said he unto them, *that there should be any such thing as you tell me?* whereunto they all replied, *This same is the most accursed man that ever was born on the earth, and is so out of his wicked nature and inclination, wherefore we all of us beseech thee in the name of this God of the afflicted, that his veins may be as much emptied of his bloud, as hell is filled with his wicked works.* At these words the King turning towards them that were about him, *What do you think hereof*, said he unto them? *What am I to do? and how am I to carry my self in so strange and extraordinary a matter?* To which they all answered, *My Lord, if thou wilt not hearken to that which this God of the afflicted comes to demand of thee, it is to be feared that he will take care no longer to aid thee, and will refuse to support thee in thy dignity.* Then the King turning himself again to the multitude that were below in the Court, *bad them go to the place where the great Market was kept, and he would give order that the man whom they required should be delivered unto them to be disposed of at their pleasure.* Whereupon having sent for the *Chirca of justice*, who is as the Soveraign Superintendent thereof above all others, he commanded him to go and apprehend *Diego Suarez*, and deliver him bound hand and foot to the people, that they might do justice upon him, for he feared if he did otherwise, that God would execute it upon him.

The

§. 2.

The *Chirca* of Juſtice vvent immediately to *Diego Suarez* his houſe, and told him that the King had ſent for him ; he in the mean time was ſo troubled to ſee the *Chirca* come for him, that he remained a pretty while not able to anſwer him , as a man that was always beſides himſelf, and had loſt his underſtanding ; but at length being ſomewhat come to himſelf again; *He earneſtly deſired him to diſpenſe with him at this time for going with him, in regard of a great pain that he had in his head, and that in acknowledgement of ſo good an office, he would give him forty biſſes of gold.* Whereunto the *Chirca* replied, *The offer which thou makeſt me is too little for me to take upon me that great pain which thou ſyeſt thou haſt in thy head, wherefore thou muſt go along with me , either by fair means or by force, ſince thou obligeſt me to tell thee the truth.* *Diego Suarez* then, ſeeing that there was no means to excuſe him, would have taken along with him ſix or ſeven of his ſervants, and the *Chirca* not permitting it; *I muſt,* ſaid he unto him, *fulfill the Kings command, which is, that thou ſhalt come alone, and not with ſix or ſeven men, for the time is now paſt wherein thou wert wont to go ſo well accompanied, as I have oftentimes ſeen thee do ; all thy ſupport is gone by the death of the Tyrant of* Bramaa, *who was the quill wherewith thou blowedſt up thy ſelf to an unſupportable pride, as is apparent by the wicked actions which thou haſt committed, which at this preſent accuſe thee before the juſtice of God.* This ſaid, he took him by the hand , and led him along with him, invironed with a guard of three hundred men, whereat we remained very much diſmayed. Thus marching from one ſtreet to another, he arrived in the end at the *Bazor,* which was a publike place where all kind of wares was ſold; but as he was going thither, he met by chance with *Balthazar Suarez* his ſon , who came from a Merchants houſe, whither his Father had ſent him that morning to receive ſome money that was owing to him. The Son, ſeeing his Father in this plight, alighted preſently from his horſe, and caſting himſelf at his feet; *What means this, my Lord,* ſaid he unto him with tears in his eys, *and whence comes it that you are led along in this ſort?* *Ask it of my ſins,* anſwered Diego Suarez, *and they will tell thee, for I proteſt unto thee my Son, that in the caſe I am in, all things ſeem dreams unto me.* Thereupon imbracing one another, and mingling their tears together, they continued ſo, untill ſuch time as the *Chirca* commanded *Balthazar Suarez* to get him gone, which he would not do, being loth to part from his father, but the Miniſters of juſtice haled him away by force, and puſhed him ſo rudely, as he fell and broke his head, yea and withall they gave him many blows beſides , whereat his Father fell into a ſwoun. Being come again to himſelf, he craved a little water, which he had no ſooner taken, but lifting up his hands to heaven, he ſaid with tears in his eys, *Si iniquitates obſervaberis Domine, Domine quis ſuſtinebit?* *But, O Lord,* added he , *out of the great confidence I have in the infinite price of thy precious bloud, which thou haſt ſhed for me upon the croſſe, I may ſay with more aſſurance , Miſericordias Domini in æternum cantabo.* Thus altogether deſolated as he was in this laſt affliction, when he was come in ſight of the place, whither the King had commanded him to be conducted, it is ſaid, that perceiving ſo many people, he remained ſo exceedingly diſmayed, that turning himſelf to a *Portugal,* who was permitted to accompany him , *Jeſus,* ſaid he unto him, *have all theſe accuſed me to the King?* whereunto the *Chirca* made him this anſwer, *It is no longer time for thee to think of that, for thou haſt wit enough to know, that the people are of ſo unruly a humour, that they always follow evill whereunto they are naturally inclined.* It is not that, replied *Diego Suarez* with tears in his eys, *for I know that if there be any unrulineſſe in them, it proceeds from my ſins. Thou ſeeſt thereby,* ſaid the *Chirca, that this is the ordinary recompence which the world is accuſtomed to give to them, who during their life, have loſt the memory of the divine juſtice, as thou haſt done, and God give thee the grace that in this little time thou haſt to live, thou mayeſt repent thee of the faults thou committed, which poſſibly may avail thee more then all the gold that thou leaveſt behind thee, for an inheritance to him, who peradventure is the cauſe of thy death.* Here *Diego Suarez* falling down on his knees, and lifting up his eyes to heaven, *O Lord Jeſus Chriſt,* cried he, *my true Redeemer, I beſeech thee by the pains which thou*

haſt

haſt ſuffered upon the Croſſe, to permit that the accuſation of theſe hundred thouſand hunger-ſtarved dogs againſt me, may ſerve to ſatisſie the chaſtiſement of thy divine juſtice in my behalf, to the end that the ineſtimable price which thou haſt imployed for the ſalvation of my ſoule, without any merit of mine, may not be unproſitable unto me. This ſaid, he aſcended the ſtaires which led to the market place, and the *Portugal* that aſſiſted him, told mee, how at every ſtep he kiſſed the ground, and called upon the name of *JESVS*; at length when he was come to the top, the *Manbogoaa*, who held the Idoll in his armes, animating the people with great cries, ſaid unto them, *Whoſoever ſhall not for the honour of this God of the affliſted, whom I have here in my armes, ſtone this accurſed Serpent, let him for ever be miſerable, and let the braines of his children be conſumed in the midſt of the night, to the end that by the puniſhment of ſo great a ſinne, the righteous judgement of the Lord above may be juſtiſied in them.* He had no ſooner made an end of ſpeaking thus, but there fell ſo great a ſhowre of ſtones on *Diego Suarez*, as in leſſe then a quarter of an houre he was buried under them, and they that ſlung them at him, did it ſo indiſcreetly, as the moſt part of them hurt one another therewith. An houre after they drew forth the poore *Diego Suarez* from under the ſtones, and with another new tumult of cries and voices they tore him in pieces, with ſo much fury and hatred of the whole people in generall, as there was not he which did not believe that he did a charitable and holy work in giving a reward to the moſt mutinous amongſt thoſe, which dragged his members and entrailes up and downe the ſtreets. This execution done, the King willing to confiſcate his goods, ſent men to his houſe for that purpoſe, where the diſorder was ſo great, in regard of the extreme avarice which theſe hungry dogs had, they left not a tile unmoved; and becauſe they found not ſo much as they expected, they put all his ſlaves and ſervants to torture, with ſuch an exceſſe of cruelty, as eight and thirty of them remained dead in the place, amongſt which were ſeventeen *Portugals*, who bore the pain of a thing whereof they were not guilty. In all this ſpoile there were no more then ſix hundred biſſes of gold found, which are in value three hundred thouſand duckats, beſides ſome pieces of rich houſhold-ſtuffe, but no precious ſtones, nor jewells at all, which perſwaded men that *Diego Suarez* had buried all the reſt; howſoever it could never be found out, notwithſtanding all the ſearch that was made for it, and yet it was verified by the judgement of ſome who had ſeene him in his proſperity, that he had in meanes above three millions of gold, according to the ſupputation of the country. Behold what was the end of the great *Diego Suarez*, whom fortune had ſo favoured in this Kingdome of *Pegu*, as ſhe had raiſed him up to the degree of the Kings Brother, the higheſt and moſt abſolute title of all others, and given him withall two hundred thouſand duckats yearely rent, vvith the charge of Generall of eight hundred thouſand men, and Soveraigne over all the other Governours or Vice-Royes of fourteene Kingdomes, which the King of *Bramaa* had at that time in his poſſeſſion. But it is the ordinary courſe of the goods of this world, eſpecially of ſuch as are ill gotten, alwayes to ſerve for a way to diſgraces and misfortunes.

I

§. 3.   I return now to the *Xemindoo*, of whom I have not spoken a long time. Wheras that Tyrant and avaritious King *Xenim de Satan* gave daily new increases to the cruelties and tyrannies which he exercised against all sorts of persons, never ceasing killing and robbing indifferently those, who were thought to have money; nor sparing any thing on which he could lay his hands, his rapines proceeded so far, as it was that in the space of seven moneths only, wherin he was peaceable possessor of this Kingdom of *Pegu*, he put to death six thousand very rich Merchants, besides many ancient Lords of the Country, who by way of right of inheritance held their estates from the Crown. These extortions rendered him so odious, as the most part of those that were with him abandoned him to side with the *Xemindoo*, who had for him at that time the towns of *Digon*, *Meidoo*, *Dalaa*, and *Coulam*, even to the confines of *Xaraa*, from whence he parted in hast to go and besiege this Tyrant with an army of two hundred thousand men, & five thousand Elephants.   When he was arrived at the city of *Pegu*, where *Xemin de Satan* then kept his Court, he invested it round about with palisadoes and very strong trenches, yea and gave some assaults to it, but he could not enter it so easily as he believed, in regard of the great resistance he found from them within; wherefore judging it requisite for him to alter his mind, being prudent as he was, he came very subtilly to a truce of twenty dayes with the Tyrant upon certain conditions, whereof the principall was, that if within the terme of those twenty dayes he gave him a thousand bisses of gold, which are in value five hundred thousand Duckats, he would desist from the pretension and right which he had to this Kingdome; and all this he did (as I have already said) cunningly, hoping by this means to bring him to his bow with lesse perill.   So the time of the truce beginning to run on, all things remained peaceable on either side, and the besiegers fell to communicate with the besieged.   During this pacification every morning two houres before day, they of the *Xemindoos* Camp played after their manner upon divers sorts of instruments very melodiously, at the sound whereof all they of the city ran to the walls to see what the matter was. Whereupon those instruments ceasing to play, a Proclamation was made by a Priest, accounted by every man a holy personage, who said these words with a very sad voice, *O ye people, ye people! unto whom Nature hath given eares to hear, hearken to the voice of the holy Captain the* Xemindoo, *of whom God will make use for the restoring you to your liberty and former quiet; in order wherunto he admonisheth you from* Quiay Niuandel, *the god of battells of the field* Vitau, *that none of you be so hardy as to lift up your hand against him, nor against this holy assembly which he hath made, out of a holy Zeal towards these people of* Pegu, *as brother, that he is, to the least of all the poor: Otherwise whosoever shall come against the army of these servants of God, or shall have the will to do them any harm, let him be accursed for it, and as deformed and vile as the children of the night, who foaming with poyson make horrible cries, and be delivered into the burning jawes of the dragon of discord, whom the true Lord of all the Gods hath cursed for ever; whereas contrarily, to those, that shall be so happy as to obey this Proclamation, as his holy brethren and allies, shall be granted in this life a perpetuall peace, accompanied with a great deale of wealth and riches; and after their death their souls shall be no lesse pure and agreeable to God, then those of the Saints which goe dancing amidst the beams of the Sun in the celestiall repose of the Lord Almighty.*   This publication made, the musick began to play again with a

great

great noife as before, which made fuch an impreffion in the hearts of them that heard it, as in feven nights that it continned above threefcore thoufand perfons went and rendred themfelves to the *Xemindoo*; for moft of them which heard thofe words gave as mnch credit thereunto, as if an Angell from heaven had fpoken them. In the meane time the befieged Tyrant, feeing that thefe fecret Proclamations of the enemy were fo prejudiciall unto him, as they could not chufe but turn to his utter ruine, brake the truce at twelve dayes end, and deliberated with his Councell what he fhould do, who advifed him by no means to fuffer h mfelf to remaine any longer befieged, for feare left the inhabitants fhould mutinie, and fall from him to the enemy; and that the beft and fureft way was to fight with the *Xemindoo* in the open field, before he grew to any further ftrength. This refolution being approved of by *Zenim de Satan*, he prepared himfelf for the execution of it; to which effect he two dayes after before it was day fallied out at five gates of the city with fourfcore thoufand men, which then he had, and charged the enemies with ftrange fury. They then in the meane time, who alwayes ftood upon their guard, received them with a great deale of courage, whereupon infued fo cruell a conflict between them, that in leffe then halfe an houre, for fo long lafted the heat of the fight, there fell on both fides above forty thoufand men; but at the end of that time the new King *Zenim* was born from his Elephant by an harquebuze fhot, difcharged at him by a Portugall, named *Gonçalo Neto*, which caufed all the reft to render themfelves, and the city likewife, upon condition that the inhabitants fhould have their goods and lives faved. By this means the *Xemindoo* entred peaceably into it, and the very fame day, which was a Saturday the three and twentieth of February, a thoufand five hundred fifty and one, he caufed himfelf to be crowned King of *Pegu* in the greateft Temple of the city. As for *Gonçalo Neto*, he gave him in recompence for killing the Tyrant twenty Biffes of gold, which are ten thoufand Duckats; and to the other Portugalls, being eighty in number, he gave five thoufand Duckats, befides the honors and prſviledges which they had in the country; he alfo exempted them for three years from paying any cuftome for their merchandize, which was afterwards very exactly obferved.

CHAP.

CHAP. LXXIII.

That which the Xemindoo *did, after he was Crowned King of* Pegu, *with the* Chaumigrems ; *the King of* Bramaaes *Foster-Brothers coming against him, with a great Army ; and divers other memorable things.*

THe *Xemindoo* seeing himself Crowned King of *Pegu*, and peaceable Lord of all the kingdome ; began to have thoughts far different from those which *Xemin de Satan* had had, being raised to the same dignity of King ; for the first and principal thing wherein he imployed himself with all his endeavour, was to maintain his Kingdome in peace, and to cause Justice to flourish ; as indeed he established it with so much integritie, as no man how great so ever he was, durst wrong a lesser then himself : withall in that which concerned the government of the Kingdome, he proceeded with so much vertue and equity, as it filled the strangers that were there with admiration, so that one could not without marvel consider the peace the quiet, and union of the wills of the people ; during the happy and peaceable estate of this Kingdome, which continued the space of a year, and better ; at the end whereof the *Chaumigrem*, foster-brother to the same King of *Bramaa*, whom *Xemin de Satan* had slaine, as I have before declared, having received advertisement, that by reason of the rebellions and warres, which since his departure from thence had happened in the Kingdome of *Pegu* ; the principall men of the State there, had lost their lives ; and the *Xemindoo* who then raigned, was unprovided of all things necessary for his defence ; he resolved once again to adventure upon the same enterprise, which had formerly been undertaken by his late King. With this design, he entertained into his pay a mighty Army of strangers, unto whom he gave a Tincall of gold by the month, which is five dackets of our mony ; when as he had prepared all things in a readinesse, he departed from *Tanguu*, the place of his birth : On the ninth day of March, a thousand, five hundred, fifty and two, with an Army of three hundred thousand men, whereof only fifty thousand were *Bramaas*, and all the rest *Moas, Chalens, Calaminhams, Sauinis, Pamerus,* and *Auaas.* In the mean time the *Xemindoo*, the new King of *Pegu*, having certain intelligence of these great forces, which were coming to fall upon him, made preparation to go and meet them, with a design to give them battle ; for which effect, he assembled in the same City where he was ; a huge Army of nine hundred thousand men, which were all *Pegues* by nation, and consequently of a weake constitution, and lesse warlick then all the others, whereof I have spoken ; and on Tueseday the fourth of April, about noone, having received advice that the enemies Army was incamped all along the river of *Meleytay* some twelve leagues from thence, he used such expedition, as the same day, and the next night all his Souldiers were put into battle array, for whereas they had prepared every thing long before, and had also been trayned by their Capt. there needed no great ado to bring them into order. The day ensueing, all these men of warre begun about nine of the clock in the morning, to march at the sound of an infinite company of warlick instruments, and went and lodged that night some two leagues from thence neer to the river *Potarcu.* The next day, an hour before Sun-set the *Bramaa Chaumigrem* appeared with so great a body of men, as it took up the extent of a league and an half of ground ; his Army being composed of seaventy thousand horse, of two hundred and thirty thousand foot, and six thousand fighting elephants, besides as many more which carried the baggage and victuals ; and in regard it was almost night, he thought fit to lodge himself all along by the mountain, that he might be in the greater safety. Thus the night past with a good guard, and a strange noise that was made on either part. The day following, which was a Saturday, the seventh of Aprill in the year one thousand, five hundred, fifty and three, about five of the clock in the morning, these two Armies began to move, but with different intentions ; for the designe of the *Bramaa* was to passe the foard, and recover an advantageous peece of ground, which lay neer to another river ; and the *Xemindoo* had a desire to keep him from it, and to stop his passage ; upon this contention, some skirmishes ensued, which continued most part of the day, and wherein about five hundred men on the one side, and the other were slain,

how-

howbeit the advantage remained with the *Chaumigrem*, becauſe he gained the place whereunto he pretended, and paſſed all the night there in banquetting, and making great bonfires for this good ſucceſſe. The next day betimes in the morning the *Xemnidoo*, King of *Pegu*, preſented the battail to his enemyes, who did not refuſe it ; ſo that they incountred one another with all the fury that a cruel hatred is accuſtomed to kindle in ſuch like caſes ; the two vantgards then, vvho vvere the beſt Soldiers a-mongſt them, fell ſo luſtily unto it, that in leſſe then half an hour, all the Field was covered with dead bodies, and the *Pegues* began to lack courage. Wherupon the *Xemin-doo* ſeeing his men give ground, came to ſuccor them with a body of three thouſand elephants, wherewith he ſet upon the ſeventy thouſand horſe ſo couragiouſly, and to the purpoſe, as the *Bramaaes* loſt all that they had gained, ; which perceived by the *Chaumigrem*, who was better experienced in matters of Warre, knowing full well what he was to doe, to recover all again ; made ſhew of retyring, as if he had been vanquiſhed ; the *Xemindoo* thereupon, who underſtood not this ſtratagem, and that thought of nothing but the victory, purſued his enemie about a quarter of a league : but incontinently the *Bramaa* facing about with all his forces, fell upon his enemy with ſuch violence and horrible cryes, as not only men, but even the very earth, and all the other elements ſeemed to tremble at it. By this meanes the conflict renewed in ſuch ſort, as in a little time the ayre was ſeen all on fire, and the ground watered all over with bloud ; for the *Pegu* Lords and Commanders, beholding their King ſo farre ingaged in the battle, and likely to loſe the day, ran inſtantly to his ſuccor ; the like did the *Panonſaray*, the *Bramaaes* brother, on his ſide, with fourty thouſand men, and two thouſand elephants ; ſo that there enſued betwixt them, ſo bloudy and dreadfull a fight, as words are not able to expreſſe the truth of it ; wherefore I ſhall ſay no more, but that half an hour, or there about, before Sun-ſet, the Army of nine hundred thouſand *Pegues* was utterly diſcomfited ; and as it was ſaid, four hundred thouſand of them were left dead on the place, and all the reſt, or the moſt part of them, grievouſly wounded ; which the *Xemindoo* ſeeing, fled out of the field, and ſo eſcaped. Thus did the victory remain unto the *Chaumigrem*, who thereupon cauſed himſelf to be crowned King of *Pegu*, with the ſame royal Enſignes, magnificence, and triumph, as the other King of *Bramaa*, whom *Xemin de Satan* ſlew, had formerly been. And in regard it was already night, they beſtowed the time in no other thing, but in dreſſing the hurt men, and keeping good watch in the Camp.

The next day, as ſoon as it was light, all the victorious ſouldiers, as wel wound- *Sect.* 1. ed as unwounded, ran to the ſpoil of the dead bodies ; wherewith divers amongſt them were mightily enriched ; for they found there great ſtore of Gold and Jewels, by reaſon the cuſtome of thoſe Gentiles is, (as I think, I have heretofore delivered) to carry all their wealth about them to the War. The ſouldiers being well ſatisfied in this particular, the new King of this miſerable Kingdome parted forthwith from the place where he had gotten the Victory, and marched towards the Citie of *Pegu*, di-ſtant ſome three leagues from thence. Now foraſmuch as hee would not that day enter into it, for certain conſiderations which I will relate hereafter, hee ſet himſelf down in the view of it, about half a league off, in a Plain, called *Sunday Patir* : and after he had thus encamped his Army, hee gave order for the guard of the four and twenty gates thereof, by placing at each of them a *Bramaa* Commander with five thouſand Horſe. In this manner hee remained there five dayes, without being able to reſolve to enter into the Citie, out of the fear he was in, leſt the ſtrangers ſhould require of him the pillage of it, as indeed, he was obliged to grant it to them by the promiſe which he had made them for it at *Tanguu*. Now the cuſtom of men of War, who live but upon their pay, being to have regard to nothing but their intereſts, theſe ſix Nations ſeeing the King thus defer his entry into the Citie, which they could not brook, began to mutinie, and this by the inſtigation of a *Portugal*, named *Chriſto-nano Surnento*, a man of a turbulent ſpirit, but otherwiſe a good and valiant Com-mander ; and this mutinie proceeded ſo far, as the King of *Bramaa* for his own ſafety was conſtrained to retire into a *Pagode*, where he fortified himſelf with his *Bramaaes*, untill that the next morning about nine of the clock hee came to a truce with them, and cauſing them to aſſemble together, from the top of a wall he ſpake to them in this fort, *My worthy Friends, and valiant Commanders, I have caufed you to come to this holy refting place of the dead, to the end that with a folemn Oath I may difcover unto you my intentions ; whereof, with my knees on the ground, and my eyes lift up unto heaven, I take to witnefs* Quiay Nivandel, *the God of Battel of the field* Vitau, *befeeching him to be Judg of this between you and me, and to ftrike me dumb, if I do not tell you the truth. I very well remember the promife I made you at* Tanguu, *which was, to give you the pillage of this tumultuous Citie ; as well becaufe I believed your valor would be as it were the minifter of my revenge, as in fome fort to fatisfie your avarice, whereunto I know you are naturally very much inclined : Now having given you this promife for a gage of my faith, I acknowledg that I am altogether obliged not to break my word with you. But when on the other fide, I come to confider the great inconveniences which may accrue to me thereby, and the ftrict account which I fhall one day render for it before the equitable and rigorous juftice of the Lord above, I muft confeffe unto you, that I am very much affraid of charging my felf with fo heavie a burthen : wherefore Reafon advifes me to render my felf faulty towards men, rather then to fall into the difpleafure of God : Befides, it is not reafonable that the innocent fhould pay for the guilty, and of whom I am fufficiently fatisfied with the death which they have received in this laft battell by your hands. Behold, how I earneftly intreat you, as children that you are of my bowels, that having regard to my good intention, you will not kindle this fire wherein my foul will be burnt, fince you fee well enough how reafonable that is which I defire of you, and how unjuft it would be for you to refufe it me. Neverthelefle, to the end you may not remain altogether without recompenfe, I do here promife you to contribute thereunto all that fhall feem reafonable to you, and to fupply this default in part with my own goods, with my Perfon, with my Kingdom, and with my State.* Hereupon the Commanders of thofe fix Nations hearing the Kings juftification, and the promife which hee made them, yeelded to agree unto whatfoever he would do : howbeit, they prayed him above all things to have regard unto fouldiers pretenfions, who were not at any hand to be difcontented, but greatly to be made account of. Whereunto the King replyed, *That they had reafon, and that in all things he would endeavour to conform himfelf to whatfoever they fhould judg reafonable.* In the mean time, to avoid difputes which might enfue hereupon, it was concluded, that they fhould referr themfelves to Arbitrators : for which effect the Mutiners were to name three on their fide, and the King three others on his, which made fix in all, whereof three were to be Religious men, and the reft Strangers, that fo the judgment might be given with leffe fufpicion. This refolution being taken between them, they agreed together, that the three Religious men fhould be the *Menigrepos* of a *Pagode*, that was named *Quiay Hifaron*, that is to fay, the God of Povertie ; and that for the other three Strangers, the King and the Mutiners fhould caft lots, to fee who fhould chufe one or two of them on his fide. This Election being fallen to the King, he made a choice of two *Portugals*, of an hundred and forty that were then in the Citie ; whereof the one was *Gonçalo Pacheco*, the King our Mafters Factor for Lacre, a worthie man, and of a good confcience ; and the other a worfhipful Merchant, named *Nuno Fernandez Teixeyra*, whom the King held in good efteem, as having known him in the life time of the deceafed King. By the fame means the Commanders of the Mutiners elected another ftranger, whofe name I do not know. Things thus concluded, the Judges deftined for the refolution of this Affair, were fent for, becaufe the King was not willing to ftirre out of the place where he was, untill the matter was determined ; to the end he might difmiffe them all peaceably before he entred into the Citie, for fear left if they entered with him, they fhould not keep their word. For this purpofe then the King about midnight fent a *Bramaa* on horfeback to the *Portugals* quarter, who were in no leffe fear then the *Pegues* of being plundered and killed. After that the *Bramaa* vvas come into the Citie, and that hee had asked aloud (for fo they ufe to do vvhen they come from the King) vvhere the Captain of the *Portugals* vvas, he vvas prefently conducted to his Lodging, vvhere being arrived, *It is a thing* (faid he to the Captain) *as proper to the nature of that Lord above, who hath created the firmament and the whole heavens, to make good men for the converfion of the wicked, as it is ordinary with the pernicious Dragon to nourifh in his bofome fpirits of commotion and tumult, to*

bring

bring aisorder *unto the peace which conserves us in the holy Law of the Lord.* I mean *hereby* (continued he) *that amongst all those of your Nation there is one wicked man found, vomiting out of his infernall stomack flames of discord and sedition, by means wherof he hath caused the three strange Nations of the* Chalons, Meleytes *and* Savadis *to mutinie in the King my Masters Army, whereupon hath ensued so great a mischief, that besides almost the utter ruine of the Camp, three thousand Bramaaes have been slain, and the King himself hath been in such danger, as he was fain to retire into a Fort, where hee hath remained three dayes, and still is there, not daring to come out, because he cannot put any trust in those strangers. Howbeit, for a remedy of so great unquietnesse, it hath pleased God, who is the true Father of concord, to inspire the Kings heart with patience to endure this injurie, being prudent as he is, to the end hee may by that means pacifie the tumult and rebellion of these three turbulent Nations, who inhabit the most desert parts of the mountains of* Mons, *and are the most accursed of God amongst all people. Now, to make an entry into this peace and union, a Treaty hath been had between the King and the Commanders of the Mutiners, whereby it hath been concluded on either part with an Oath, That to exempt this Citie from the plundering which had been promised to the Souldiers, the King shall give them out of his own estate, as much as six men, deputed for that purpose, shall award; of which number there are already four, so that to make up the whole six, there wants none but thee, whom the King hath chosen for him; and another Portugal, whose name is written in this paper, whereby thou shalt be ascertained of that which I have said unto thee.* Thereupon he delivered a Letter unto him from the King of *Bramaa*; which *Gonçalo Pacheco* received upon his knees, and laid upon his head, with exterior complements so full of civilitie and courtesie, as the *Bramaa* remained very much contented and satisfied therewith, and said unto him, *Surely, the King my Master must needs have a great knowledg of thee, in that hee hath chosen thee for a Judg of his Honour and Estate.* Hereupon *Gonçalo Pacheco* read the Letter aloud before all the *Portugals,* who heard it standing, with their hats in their hands: The contents of it were to this effect, *Captain* Gonçalo Pacheco, *my dear Friend, and that appears before my eyes like a precious Pearl, as being no lesse vertuous in the tranquillitie of thy life, then the holyest Menigrepos which live in the Deserts; I, the ancient* Chaumigrem, *and new King of fourteen States, which God hath now put into my hands by the death of the holy King my Master, do send thee a smile of my mouth, to the end thou mayest be as agreeable to me, as those whom I cause to sit at my table in a day of joy and feasting: Know then, that I have thought good to take thee for a Judg of the Affair that is in question, and therefore have sent for thee, together with my good Friend,* Nuno Fernandez Teixeyra, *to come presently unto me, for to give an end to this businesse, which I wholly commit unto your trust. And for so much as concerns the security of your persons, in regard of the fear you may be in of the late Mutinie, I do engage my word, and swear to you by the faith which a King ought to have, whom God himself hath annointed, that I will take you, and all those of your Nation, with all others that beleeve in your God, into my protection.* After that this Letter was read, to the great astonishment of all us that heard it, we could beleeve no other, but that by Divine permission it came from Heaven for the assurance of our lives, whereof we stood in very great doubt until then. *Gonçalo Pacheco* and *Nuno Fernandez,* with ten other *Portugals* which were chosen for that purpose, instantly prepared a Present of divers rich Pieces to carry to the King, unto whom they went that very same night an hour before day, in the company of the *Bramaa* who brought the Letter, in regard the haste the King was in would brook no delay.

Gonçalo Pacheco, Nuno Fernandez, and the other *Portugals,* arrived at the camp an hour before Sun-rising, and the King sent to receive them one of the chiefest *Bramaa* Commanders that he had, and in whom he very much confided, who was accompanied with above an hundred horse, and six Serjeants at armes that carried maces. This same received the *Portugals,* and lead them to the King, who did much honour unto *Gonçalo Pacheco,* and *Nuno Fernandez*; and after he had talked with them of divers matters, he put them in mind of the importance of the businesse for which he had sent for them, and willed them by any means to leane rather to the Commanders then to him, assuring them that he should be very well contented there-

with,

with, and said many things to them to that purpose. Then he caused them to be conducted by the same *Bramaa* Lord to the Tent, where the other four Arbitrators were with the high Treasuror and two Registers ; when as they had commanded silence to all that were without, they fell to debating of the businesse for which they were assembled together ; whereupon there were many opinions, which took up the most part of the day, but at last all six came to conclude, That albeit on the one side the King, by the promise which he had made at *Tangu* to the forraigne Souldiers, for to give them the spoil or pillage of the places which he should take by force, was exceedingly obliged to the performance thereof, yet seeing that on the other side this promise was of great and notable prejudice to the innocent, because it could not be put in execution without greatly offending God ; these things considered, they ordained by their award ; *That the King, in regard of the promise which he had made them, should pay unto them a thousand bisses of gold out of his own treasure ; and that upon the Souldiers receiving thereof, they should passe over to the other side of the River, and retire directly into their countries ; but that they should first be also paid all that was due to them before this mutiny began, and that they should be furnished with victuals sufficient for twenty daies.* This award being published, was received with much content to either party ; So that the King commanded it to be instantly and punctually executed ; and for a greater testimony of his liberality, after he had paid them all this sum of mony, he bestowed upon the Commanders and Officers of each Company many bountifull rewards, wherewith they were all of them very well pleased, and satisfied. In this sort were these three mutinous nations discharged ; for the King would by no meanes trust, or make use of them any longer : Howbeit, he would not suffer these strangers to go all away together, but caused them to be divided into troups ; each of them consisting of a thousand men, to the end that by this means, they should give the lesse suspicion in their returne, and should be lesse able to plunder the open townes, by which they were to passe ; and thus the next day they departed. As for *Gonçalo Pacheco*, and *Nuno Fernandez Teixyra*, the King gave them ten bisses of gold, for being his Arbitrators in this affair, whereunto he added a passport written with his own hand, whereby the *Portugals* were permitted to retire freely into the *Indies*, without paying any custome or duty for their marchandize; whereof we made more account then of all the mony could have been given us, because that for three years before the precedent Kings had retayned us in this country, with exceeding much vexation and tyranny, whereby we were oftentimes in great danger of our lives, by reason of the successe of that which I have spoken heretofore. This done, there were Proclamations made by men on horseback, to give notice that the day following, the King would enter into the City in a peaceable manner, threatning all such as should do the contrary, with a cruell death. Accordingly, the next morning at nine of the clock the King parted from the *Pagode*, whither he had retired himself ; and about an hour after arrived at the City, whereinto entring by the chiefest gate, he was received by an assembly (in form of a *Procession*) of six thousand Priests of all the twelve Sects which are in this Kingdome ; by one of whom, called *Capizundo*, an oration was made unto him, whereof the preface was thus, *Blessed and praised be that Lord, who ought truly to be acknowledged of all men for such, in regard of the holy works which he hath made with his Divine hands, testified to us by the light of the day, the shining of the night, and all the other magnificenses of his mercy which he hath produced in us ; Praised be he, I say, for that by the effects of his infinite power, which are agreeable unto him, he hath been pleased to establish thee on the earth above all the Kings that govern it ; and seeing we hold thee for his favorite, we humbly beseech thee our Lord, that thou wilt never more remember the faults and offences which we have committed against thee, to the end that these thy afflicted people may be comforted with the promise thereof, which they hope thy Majesty will make them at this present.* This same request was likewise made unto him by the six thousand *Grepos,* all prostrated on the ground, and with their hands lifted up to heaven, who with a dreadful tumult of voices said unto him ; *Grant, our Lord and King, peace and pardon for that is past to all the people of this thy Kingdome of Pegu, to the end they may not be troubled with the feare of their offences, which they confesse publikely before thee.* The King answered them, that he

was

was contented fo to do, and fwore to them by the head of *Quiay Nivandel*, the God of Battel of the field *Vitau*, for the confirmation thereof. Upon this promife all the people proftrated themfelves with their faces on the ground, and faid unto him ; *God make thee to profper for infinite years in the victory over thy enemies, that thou mayeft trample their heads under thy feet.* Hereupon for a token of great gladneffe, they fel to playing on divers inftruments after their manner, though very barbaroufly, and untunably ; and the *Grepo Capizondo* fet on his head a rich Crown of gold and precious ftones of the fafhion of a Miter, wherewith the King made his entry into the City, with a great deal of ftate and tryumph, caufing to march before him all the fpoile of the elephants and chariots, as alfo the ftatue of the *Xemindoo*, whom he had vanquifhed, bound with a great yron chain, and forty Colours trayled on the ground ; As for him, he was feated on a very mighty elephant, harneffed with gold, and invironed with forty Serjeants at armes bearing Maces : there marched likewife all the great Lords and Commanders on foot with their Scymitars covered with plates of gold, which they carried on their fhouldiers, and three thoufand fighting elephants, with their Caftles of divers inventions, befides a world of other people, as well foot as horfe, which followed him without number.

CHAP. LXXIV.

The finding of the Xemindoo, *and bringing of him to the King ; with the manner of his execution and death ; and other particularities concerning the fame.*

AFter that the King of *Bramaa* had continued peaceably in this Citie of *Pegu* for the fpace of fix and twenty daies, the firft thing he did was to make himfelf Mafter of the principal places of this Kingdome, which not knowing the defeat of the *Xemindoo*, held ftill for him : To this purpofe, having given Commiffion to fome Commanders for it, hee wrote to the inhabitants of thofe places divers courteous Letters, wherein he called them his dear children, and gave them an abolition of all that was paft : He alfo promifed them by a folemn oath, to maintain them in peace for the time to come, and alwayes to minifter juftice to them, without any Impofts or other oppreffion ; but that hee would contrarily do them new favours, as to the very *Bramaas* which ferved him in the Warres. To thefe words hee added many others, very well accommodated to the time and his defire ; for the better crediting whereof, they that were already reduced under his obedience, wrote their Letters alfo unto them, wherein they made an ample relation of the Franchifes and Immunities which the King had granted to them. All this, accompanied with the fame which ran thereof in all parts, wrought fo great an effect, as all thofe places rendred unto him, and put themfelves under his obedience : fo that in imitation of them all the other Cities, Towns, States and Provinces that were in the Kingdom did the like. For my part, I hold, that this Kingdome whereof the King of *Bramaa* made at this time a new Conqueft, is the beft, the moft abundant, and richeft in Gold, in Silver, and precious Stones that may be found in any part of the world. Things being thus accomplifhed, to the great advantage of the *Bramaa*, he difpatches divers Horfemen with all fpeed into all parts, to go in queft of the *Xemindoo*, who (as I have already declared) had efcaped from the paft Battel, and was fo unhappy, that he was difcovered in a place named *Faulen*, a league from the Town of *Potem*, which feparates the Kingdom from *Aracam* : Prefently whereupon, he was lead with great joy by a man of bafe condition, to this King of *Bramaa*, who in recompence thereof, gave him thirty thoufand Duckats of yeerly rent. Being brought before him, bound as he was with an iron coller, and manacles, he faid unto him in way of derifion, *Thou art welcome (King of* Pegu) *and maift well kiffe the ground which thou feeft ; for I affure thee, I have fet my foot on it ; whereby thou mayeft perceive how much I am thy Friend, fince I do thee an honour which thou couldft never imagine.* To thefe words the *Xemindoo* made no anfwer ; fo that the King falling to jeer this miferable man anew, who lay before him with his face on the ground, faid unto him, *What means this ? Art thou amazed to fee me, or to fee thy felf in fo great honour ? Or what is the matter, that thou doft not anfwer to that which I demand of thee ?* After this affront, the *Xemindoo*, whether it were

that

that he was troubled with his misfortunes, or ashamed of his dishonour, answered him in this sort, *If the clouds of Heaven, the Sun, the Moon, and the other creatures, which cannot expresse in words that which God hath created for the service of man, and for the beautifying of the Firmament, which hides from us the rich treasures of his power, could naturally with the horrible voice of their dreadfull Thunder explain to them which now look upon me, the estate whereunto I see my self reduced before thee, and the extreme affliction which my soul doth suffer, they would answer for me, and declare the cause I have to be mute in the condition wherein my sins have set me : and whereas thou canst not be Judg of that which I say, being the party that accusest me, and the minister of the execution of thy designe, I hold my self for excused, if I do not make thee an answer, as I would do before that blessed Lord, who, how faulty soever I could be, would have pitie on me, moved with the least tear that I should shed.* This said, he fell down with his face on the ground, and twice together asked for a little water : Whereupon the King of *Bramaa,* the more to afflict him, commanded that the *Xemindoo* should receive this water from the hand of a Daughter of his, (held by him as a slave) whom he exceedingly loved, and had at that time of his defeat promised to the Prince of *Nautir,* Son to the King of *Avaa.* The Princesse no sooner saw her Father lying in that manner on the ground, but she cast her self at his feet, and straitly embracing him, after shee had kissed him thrice, she said to him with her eyes all bathed in tears, *O my Father, my Lord, and my King, I intreat you, for the extreme affection which I have alwayes born you, and for that also which you have at all times shewed to me, that you will be pleased to lead me with you, thus imbracing you as I do, to the end that in this sad passage you may have one to comfort you with a cup of water, now that for my sins the world refuses you that respect which is due unto you.* It is said, that the Father would fain have answered to these words, yet could not possibly do it, so much was he oppressed with grief and anguish of minde, to see this Daughter whom he so dearly loved, in such a taking; but fell as it were in a swoun, and so continued a good while; wherewith some Lords that were there present were so moved, as the tears came into their eyes; which observed by the King of *Bramaa,* and that they were *Pegues,* who had formerly been the *Xemindoo's* Subjects, fearing lest they should betray him in time to come, he caused their heads to be presently strucken off, saying with a disdainfull and fierce countenance, *Seeing you have so great pitie of the* Xemindoo *your King, get you before and prepare a lodging for him, and there he will pay you for this affection which you testifie to have for him.* After this, his wrath redoubled in such sort, as instantly he caused this very Daughter to be killed in her Fathers arms; which truly was more then a bruitish and savage cruelty, in seeking to hinder the affections which nature hath imprinted in us. Then no longer enduring the sight of the *Xemindoo,* he commanded him to be taken from thence, and to be carried to a close prison, where he passed all the night following under a sure guard.

The next morning, Proclamation was made over all the City, for the people to be present at the death of the unhappy *Xemindoo;* now, the chiefest reason why the *Bramaa* did this, was, that the inhabitants seeing him dead, might for ever lose all hope of having him for their King, as all generally desired; for whereas he was their Countryman, and the *Bramaa* a Stranger, they were in extreame fear, least the *Bramaa* should become in time like unto him whom *Xemin de Satan* slew, and that had been during his raign a mortall enemy to the *Pegues;* intreating them with such extraordinary cruelty, as their scarcely passed a day, wherein he did not execute hundreds of them; and all for matters of small importance, and which deserved no punishment, had they been proceeded against, by the waies of true Justice. About ten of the clock, the unfortunate *Xemindoo* was drawn out of the dungeon where he was, in the manner ensuing. Before him marched through the Streets, by which he was to passe, forty men on horseback with lances in their hands, to prepare and clear the waies; there were as many behind as before him, which carried naked swords, crying aloud to the people, whereof the number was infinite, to make roome : After them followed about fifteen hundred harquebusiers with their matches lighted; next to these last, which they of the country use to call, the *avant coureurs* of the Kings wrath, went an hundred and threescore elephants armed with their Castles, and covered with silk tapestry,

peſtry, marching by five and five in a rank ; after them rode in the ſame order by five in a rank, fifteen men on horſeback, which carried black enſignes all bloudy; crying aloud, as it were by way of Proclamation; *Let thoſe miſerable wretches, which are the ſlaves of hunger, and are continually perſecuted by the diſgrace of fortune, hearken to the cry of the arm of wrath, executed on them that have offended their King, to the end that the aſtoniſhment of the pain, which is ordained them for it, may be deeply imprinted in their memory.* Behind theſe ſame were other fifteen, clothed with a kind of bloudy garment, which rendred them dreadfull and of a bad aſpect ; who at the ſound of five Bells, which they rung in haſte, ſaid with ſo lamentable a voice, as they that heard them were moved to weep : *This rigorous Juſtice is done by the living God, the Lord of all truth, of whoſe holy body, the hairs of our heads are the feet ; It is he that will have the* Xemindoo *put to death, for uſurping the Eſtates of the great King of Bramaa, Lord of Tanguu.* Theſe Proclamations were anſwered by a troupe of people, which marched thronging before with ſuch loud cryes, as made one tremble to hear them, ſaying theſe words; *Let him die without having pity on him, that hath committed ſuch an of-fence* : Theſe were followed by a company of five hundred *Bramaa* horſe, and after them came another of foot, whereof ſome held naked ſwords and bucklers in their hands, and the reſt were armed with corſelets, and coats of maile ; In the midſt of theſe, came the poor patient, mounted on a lean ill-favored jade, and the hangman on the crupper behind him, holding him up under both the armes. This miſerable Prince was ſo poorly clad, that his naked skinne was every where ſeen; withall, in an exceeding deriſion of his perſon, they had ſet upon his head a Crowne of ſtraw, like unto an Urinall caſe ; which Crowne was garniſhed with muſcle-ſhells, faſtned toge-ther with blew thred ; and round about his yron coller were a number of onions tyed : Howbeit, though he was reduced to ſo deplorable an eſtate, and that his face was ſcarce like to that of a living man, yet left he not for all that, from having ſomething of I know not what in his eyes, which maniſeſted the condition of a King. There was beſides obſerved in him, a majeſticall ſweetneſſe, which drew tears from all that beheld him. About this guard which accompanied him, there was another of above a thouſand horſe men, intermingled with many armed elephants ; Paſſing thus tho-row the twelve principall ſtreets of the City, where there was a world of people he arrived at laſt at a certain ſtreet called *Cabam Bainhaa,* out of which he went but two and twenty days before, to go and fight with the *Bramaa,* in ſuch pomp and greatneſſe, as by the report of them that ſaw it, and of which number I was one, it was without doubt, one of the moſt marvellous ſights that ever hath been ſeen in the world; whereof notwithſtanding I will make no mention here, either in regard I cannot promiſe to recount rightly how all paſt, or for that I fear ſome will receive theſe truths for lies ; neverthelesſe mine eyes having been the witneſſes of theſe two ſucceſſes, if I do not ſpeak of the greatneſſe of the firſt, I will at leaſtwiſe declare the miſeries of the ſecond, to the end that by theſe two ſo different accidents, happening in ſo ſhort a time, one may learn what little aſſurance is to be put in the proſperities of the earth, and in all the goods which are given us by inconſtant and deceitful Fortune. Whenas the poor Pati-ent had paſt that ſtreet of *Cabam Bainhaa,* he arrived at a place where *Gonçalo Pacheco* our Captain was, with above an hundred Portugals in his Company ; amongſt the vvhich there was one of a very baſe birth, and of a minde yet more vile, vvho having been robbed of his goods ſome yeers before, as he ſaid, at ſuch time as the Patient raign-ed, and complained to him of thoſe who had done it, he vvould not vouchſafe to give him audience ; ſo that thinking to be revenged on him for it now, vvith extravagant and unſeemly ſpeech ; as ſoon as this poor Prince came where *Gonçalo Pacheco* was, with all the other Portugals, the witleſſe fellow ſaid aloud to him, that all might hear him. O Robber *Xemindoo, remember how when I complained to thee of thoſe that had robbed me of my goods, thou wouldſt not do me juſtice ; but I hope that now thou ſhalt ſa-tisfie what thy works deſerve : for I will at ſupper eat a piece of that fleſh of thine, where-unto I will invite two dogs that I have at home.* The ſad Patient having heard the vvords of this hair-brain'd fellow, lifted up his eyes to heaven, and after he had continued a while penſive, turning himſelf vvith a ſevere countenance towards him that uttered them, *Friend,* ſaid he unto him, *I pray thee, by the great goodneſs of that*

God

God in whom thou believest, to pardon me that for which thou accusest me, and to remember that it is not the part of a Christian, in this painful estate wherein I see my self at this present, to put me in mind of that which I have done heretofore; for besides that, thou canst not thereby recover the loss which thou sayest thou hast sustained, it will but serve to afflict and trouble me the more. Pacheco having heard what this fellow said, commanded him to hold his peace, which immediately he did; whereupon the Xemindoo with a grave countenance made shew that this action pleased him, so that seeming to be more quiet, it made him to acknowledge that with his mouth, which he could not otherwise requite, *I must confess,* said he unto him, *that I could wish, if God would permit it, I might have one hour longer of life to profess the excellency of the faith wherein you Portugals live; for, as I have heretofore heard it said, your God alone is true, and all other gods are lyers.* The Hangman had no sooner heard these words, but he gave him so great a buffet on the face, that his nose ran out with bloud, so that the poor Patient stooping with his hands downward, *Brother* (said he unto him) *suffer me to save this bloud, to the end thou maist not want some to fry my flesh withall.* So passing on in the same order as before, he finally arrived at the place where he was to be executed, with so little life as he scarcely thought of any thing: When he was amounted on a great Scaffold, which had been expresly erected for him, the Chirca of Justice fell to reading of his Sentence from an high Seate, where he was placed; the contents whereof were in few words these; *The living God of our heads, Lord of the Crown of the Kings of Avaa, commands, that the perfidious Xemindoo be executed as the Perturbator of the people of the earth, and the mortal enemy of the Bramaa Nation.* This said, he made a sign with his hand, and instantly the Hangman cut off his head at one blow, shewing it to all the people, which were there without number, and divided his body into eight quarters, setting his bovvels and other interior parts vvhich vvere put together, in a place by themselves; then covering all vvith a yellovv cloth, vvhich is a mark of mourning amongst them, they vvere left there till the going dovvn of the Sun, at vvhich time they vvere burnt in the manner ensuing.

Sect. 2.   The eight quarters of the Xemindooes body vvere exposed from mid-day till three of Clock in the afternoon to the view of all the people, whereof there was an infinite company there, for every one came thronging thither, as well to avoid the punishment wherewith they had been threatned, as to gain in so doing, the Plenary indulgence called by them *Axiperan,* which their Priests gave them of their sins, without restitution of any thing of all the Theeveries by them formerly committed. After then, that the tumult was appeased, and that certain men on horseback had imposed silence on the people by making certain publications, whereby the Transgressors therein were threatned with terrible punishments, a bell was heard to toll five several times; upon this signal twelve men clothed in black robes, spotted all over with bloud, having their faces covered, and bearing silver Maces on their shoulders, came out of a house of wood, made expresly for that purpose, and distant some five or six paces from the Scaffold; after them followed twelve Priests, which they call *Talagrepos,* being, as I have said, the most eminent Dignities amongst these Pagans, and held by them as Saints; then appeared the *Xemin Pocasser,* the King of *Bramaaes* Uncle, who seemed to be near an hundred years old, and was as the rest, all in mourning, and invironed with twelve little boyes richly apparelled, carrying on their shoulders Courtelasses curiously Damasked. After that the *Xemin* had with a great deal of Ceremonie prostrated himselfe three times on the ground, in way of extraordinary reverence; *O holy flesh* (said he) *which art more to be esteemed then all the Kingdomes of* Avaa, *thou orient Pearle of as many Carats as there be Atomes in the beams of the Sun, whom God hath placed in an height of Honour, with a Scepter of Soveraign power above that of Kings, I that am the least of thy meiny, and so unlike thee through my baseness, as I can scarcely see my self, so little I am, do most humbly beseech thee, O thou Lord of my head, by the fresh Meadow where thy soul doth now recreat thy self, to hear that with thy sorrowful ears which my mouth sayes to thee in publick, to the end thou maist remain satisfied for the offence which hath been done thee in this world.* Oretanan Chaumigrem, *thy brother,* Prince *of* Savady *and* Tanguu, *sends to intreat thee by me thy slave, that before he departs out of*

this

this life thou wilt pardon him that which is past if he have given thee any discontent, and withall that thou wilt take possession of all his Kingdomes, because he doth even now yeild them up unto thee, without reserving the least part thereof for himself; withall he protests unto thee by me thy vassal, that he makes this reconciliation with thee voluntarily, to the end that the complaints which thou maiest prefer against him there above in heaven, may not be heard of God: Moreover, for a punishment of the displeasure he hath done thee, he offers to be for thee during this pilgrimage of life, the Captain and Guardian of this thy Kingdome of Pegu, for which he does thee homage, with an oath to accomplish alwaies upon earth whatsoever thou shalt command him from heaven above; upon condition that thou wilt bestow the profit which shall arise thereof upon him as an almes for his entertainment; for he knowes very well, that otherwise he should not be permitted to possess the Kingdome, neither would the Menigrepos ever consent thereunto, nor at the hour of death give him absolution for so great a sinne. Upon these words, one of the Priests that was present, and that seemed to have more authoritie then all the rest, made him answer, as if the deceased himself had spoken; Since I see, O my Sonne, that thou doest now confesse thy past faults, and cravest pardon of me for them in this publick assembly, I do grant it thee with all my heart; and it pleases me to leave thee in this Kingdome for the pastor of this my flock, on condition that thou dost not violate the faith thou hast given me by this oath; which would be as great an offence, as if thou shouldst now come to lay hands on me without the permission of Heaven. All the people having heard these words, answered thereunto with joyfull voices; Perform so much, my Lord, my Lord. After this, the Priest being got into the pulpit, began to speak thus to the assistants; Present me with part of the teares of your eyes for the entertainment of my soul, because of the good newes I now bring you, which is, that by the wil of God this Country is setled on our King Chaumigrem, without being tyed to make any restitution thereof, for which you have all of you good cause to rejoyce, like good and faithfull servants as you are. He had scarcely made an end of speaking thus, when as all those of the assembly clapping their hands, gave great demonstrations of joy, and cryed out in a way of thanksgiving, Be thou praised, O Lord. All this ceremony ended, the Priests full of devotion and zeal immediately took all the parts of this poor King, dismembred in that sort, and with great veneration carried them to a place below, where a great fire was kindled of Sandal, Aloes, and Benjamin, which cost a great deal; then three of them taking up of the body of the deceased, with the bowels, and all the rest, threw it into it, and afterwads with a strange ceremony offered many sacrifices unto him, whereof the most part were of sheep. The body burned all that night untill the next morning, and the ashes thereof was put into a silver urne, wherein, with a very solemn assembly of above ten thousand Priests, it was carried to a Temple, called The God of thousand Gods, and there was buried in a rich tomb within a Chappel guilt all over. Behold what was the end of the great and mighty Xemindoo King of Pegu, unto whom his subjects bore so great respect and honour, during the time of his raign, which was so flourishing, that it seemed there was no other Monarch greater then he on the earth; but such is the course of all the world.

CHAP. LXXV.
My imbarking in the Kingdome of Pegu to go to Malaca, and from thence to Japan; and a strange accident which arrived there.

THe death of the good King of Siam, and the adulterie of the Queen his wife, whereof I have spoken at large heretofore, were the root and beginning of so many discords, and of so many crueil warres, which hapning in those two Kingdomes of Pegu and Siam, indured three years and an half, with so much expence of mony and bloud, as is horrible to think of. Now the end of all those warres was, that the Chaumigrem, King of Bramaa, remained absolute Lord of the Kingdome of Pegu: howbeit for the present I will speak no further of him, but will deliver that which arrived in other Countries, untill such time as the same Chaumigrem King of Bramaa returned upon the Kingdome of Siam, with so mighty an Army, as never any King whatsoever in the Indiaes brought a greater into the field, as consisting of seventeen hun-

dred thousand men, and of sixteen thousand elephants ; whereof nine thousand were
for the carriage of the Baggage, and seven thousand for fighting ; an enterprize that
was so dammageable for us, as I learned afterwards, that it cost us two hundred
and four score Portugals.   I come now again to my designe, from which I have wan-
dered a good while.   After that these commotions, whereof I have spoken heretofore, were all appeased, *Gonçalo Pacheco* departed from the City of *Pegu*, with all
us the rest of the Portugals which remained there, and whom the new King of *Bramaa* had delivered, as I have already declared, causing their merchandize to be restored unto them, and obliging them with many other courtesies, as well of Honour, as
of Liberty :   So we, an hundred and three score Portugals as we were, imbarqued
our selves in five vessels, which were at that time in the Port of *Cosmin*, one of the
principal Townes of that Kingdom ;   and there we divided our selves as pilgrims and
travellers to the Indiaes, for to go into divers Countries , according as each of us
thought to be most convenient for him.   As for me, I set sail for *Malaca*, with six and
twenty of my companions ;   where when we were arrived, I sojourned there one
month only, and then imbarqued my self again to go to *Japan* with one *Jorge Alvarez*, who in a Sip belonging to *Simono de Mello*, Captain of the Forttesse, went to
traffick.   Now having been already six and twenty dayes under sail, in continning our
course with a good winde, according to the season, wee came in sight of an Iland,
called *Tanixumaa*, some nine Leagues South towards the point of the Land of *Japan*;
so that turning our prow that vvay, vve vvent and rode the next day in the midst of
the haven of *Ganxiroo*: In this place the *Nantaquin*, who was Governour thereof,
had the curiositie to come unto us for to see a thing which he had never seen before ;
to which effect he got aboard of us, where amazed with the fashion and equipage of our
vessel, as being the first that ever arrived in that Country, he seemed to be infinitely
glad of our coming, yea, and was very earnest vvith us to have us trade in that place
with him :   but *Jorge Alvarez* and the Merchants excused themselves, saying, that
this port was not safe for their Ship, if any contrary winde should happen to arise.
The day following, being parted from this place, to go to the Kingdom of *Bungo*,
from whence vve vvere distant some hundred leagues to the Northward ;   in five
dayes after our departure it pleased God that we arrived in the port of the Town of
Fucheo, where we were vvell received, as vvell by the King as the people, vvho greatly favoured us in that vvhich concerned the duties of our Merchandize ;   and the King
had yet more obliged us, if in the little time that vve abode there he had not been
miserably slain by a Vassal of his named *Fucarandono*, a mighty Prince, Lord of many
Subjects, and exceeding rich ; a disaster, which hapned as followeth.   At the time
when we arrived there, there was in the King of *Bungo's* Court a young man, called
Axirandoo, Nephew to the King of *Arimaa*, vvho in regard of the ill intreaty vvhich
he had received from the King his Uncle,   had retired himself into this Court, and
continued there above a yeer, with an intent never to return into his Country again :
but his good fortune was such, as his Uncle coming to die, and having no other to
succeed him, he declared him for his Heir.   Whereupon the *Fucarandono*, of whom
I lately made mention, desiring to marry this Prince to a Daughter of his, intreated
the King to mediate this marriage for him, which he easily condescended unto.   For
vvhich effect the King one day invited the Prince to go a hunting with him into a
Wood, which was some two leagues off, and where there was great store of game, vvhich
he much delighted in.   When they were there in private together, he moved this
Marriage unto him, and certified how exceedingly it vvould content him that hee
vvould accept of it ; vvhich accordingly he did ; vvherewith the King seemed to be
extremely satisfied ; so that upon his return unto the Town, hee sent for the *Fucarandono*, and told him how he had prevailed for the Marriage of his Daughter vvith
the King of *Arimaa*, and therefore vvilled him to go and acknowledg unto him
vvith all thankfulnesse this grace and honour which he did him ; for he assured him
on the vvord of a King, that he himself had desired him for his Son-in-Law.   Hereupon the *Fucarandono* cast himself presently at the Kings feet, and in convenient terms
for so great an obligation, kissed them, with much sense of so extraordinary a favour
as he had shewed him.   That done, he went home to his Palace, where, with much
                                                                                        joy

joy and contentment, he gave an account of this Affair to his Wife, to his Sons, and his kinsmen, who shewing themselves exceedingly satisfied therewith, congratulated one another for it, as they commonly use to do in such honourable Matches as this. In the mean time, the Mother of the Bride, as she that had the best part in this Joy, went unto a chamber where her Daughter was sowing, with divers other young Maids that served her; and taking her by the hand, lead her into the room, where her Father, Brethren, and kinsmen were, who rejoyced with her for so happy a fortune, and honoured her with the Title of *Highnesse*, as being already *Queen* of the Kingdome of *Arimaa*; and so all that day was spent in Feasts, Banquets, visits of Ladies, and presenting her with many rich Gifts. But whereas the good or evill of such like Affairs consists more in that which followeth, then in the original thereof, upon the good and joyfull beginning of this Marriage, such great disasters ensued, as they almost equalled them of the Kingdom of *Siam*, whereof I have spoken heretofore: which I stick not to say, in regard I can affirm it with truth, as having seen these two Successes with mine own eyes, and been present at them wich danger enough of my person. All this day was spent in the visits of the principal persons of the Kingdom; But in this publick rejoycing there was none save the Bride alone that was discontented, in regard she was desperately in love with a young Gentleman, the son of one *Groge Arum*, who was as a Baron amongst us, but very much different in extraction and quality from the *Fucarandono*, the Father of the Bride: who, as soon as it was night, compelled by the violence of the love which she bore to him, sent him word by her whom she had alwayes secretly made use of in this Affair, that she would have him come and steal her away out of her Fathers house before some other mischief arrived. Whereupon the young man, who was no more free from this passion then shee, failed not to come to her to a place in which they used to meet together, where his Mistresse importuned him in such manner, as he was constrained to carry her away from her Fathers house, and put her into a Monastery of Religious women, whereof an Aunt of hers was as it were the Abbesse; in which she continued nine dayes concealed, without the knowledg or privity of any body. The next morning her Governesse went into her chamber where she had left her the night before; but not finding her there, she presently repaired to her Mothers chamber, imagining that she was gone thither to trick up her self extraordinarily, in regard of the time, or for some other such like occasion; and missing of her there too, she returned to her bed-chamber, where she found one of the windows that looked into a garden, open, together with a sheet fastned to one of the barrs, and one of her sandals lying below on the ground. Presently misdoubting the businesse, she went without farther delay to impart the sad news unto her Mother, who was still in her bed, out of which in all haste she arose, and diligently searching all the women chambers, where she conceived she might be, and not finding her, it was said, that she was so overcome with grief, as she fell down dead in the place. In the mean time, the *Fucarandono*, who as yet understood nothing of the matter, hearing the noise which the women made, ran in haste to know the cause thereof: Whereupon, being assured of the flight of his Daughter, he sent with all speed to acquaint his kinsmen therewith; who amazed with the novelty of so unfortunate and unexpected an accident, came instantly unto him: Having consulted then amongst themselves what they should do in this Affair, they resolved to proceed therein with all the rigour that possibly could be used; so that presently beginning with the women of the house, they cut off I know not how many of their heads, under pretext of being complices of this rape or flight. After this execution, being of different opinions touching the place where this maid might be, they were all of the minde not to proceed any further, untill they had first acquainted the King with the businesse; which instantly they did, and withall, very earnestly besought him to permit them to go and search the houses of some whom they named unto him, where they beleeved she was: Which the King refusing, as well to exempt the Masters of them from such an affront, as also to prevent the tumult which this disorder might cause; the *Fucarandono* offended for that the King did not grant him his request, returned with his kinsmen to his Palace, where he resolved with them to do therein all that in such a case he thought was for his honour, alledging that it was onely for men of little worth, and bafe mindes, to proceed by way of juftice in matters which might be carried by force.   This refolution taken, as it is the cuftome of thefe people of *Japan* to be more ambitious of honour then all the Nations of the world, he determined to bring his defigne to paffe at any price whatfoever, without regard to any thing that might arrive thereupon ; fo that giving intelligence thereof to all his friends and kinfmen that were in the Court, they came all to him that night, and approved of this his refolution, after he had declared it unto them ; infomuch that they went without further delay to the houfes of them where they were perfwaded this Maid lay hid : but they being already fortified and furnifhed with men, upon notice given them before-hand of their intent, fuch a great and terrible uproar enfued thereupon, as there were above twelve thoufand perfons killed that night.   To this diforder the King ran in perfon with his guard, to fee if he could pacifie it ; but the quarrell grew fo hot betwixt them, as it was impoffible to appeafe it : fo that after they had loft the refpect which they owed to the King, they turned all their fury againft him, and flew the moft part of them that were with him, fo that he was conftrained to retire unto his Palace, where he gathered unto him as many as poffibly he could upon a fudden ; but all that ferved him to little purpofe, for they purfued him thither, and killed him, together with very neer all them that he had drawn to his defence, amounting to the number of feven or eight thoufand men ; amongft the which were fix and twenty *Portugals* of forty that were with the King.   But thefe minifters of Satan, not contented with having committed fo horrible a Treafon, went directly to the Queens lodging, where having found her fick in her bed, they moft mercilefly butchered her with three of her Daughters, and all the women they could meet withall.   After this, with an inraged fury, they fet fire on the Town in fix or feven places, which kindling by the violence of the vvinde, that was very high at that time, it took hold of it in fuch fort, as in leffe then two hours it was almoft burnt down to the ground.   Whereupon, vve feven and twenty *Portugals* that remained, retired with much adoe to our Veffel, vvhere we faved our felves as it vvere by miracle, leaving our anchor in the fea, and fetting fail with all the fpeed we could.   The next morning the mutiners, who were about ten thoufand, having facked the Town, divided themfelves into two troops, and retired to a hill, called *Canaphamaa* ; there they fortified themfelves, with an intent to create a new Head that fhould govern them, becaufe the *Fucarandono* had been flain with the ftroak of a lance, which he had received in his throat, together with all the reft of his kinfmen, which had given a beginning to this Mutinie.

Æt.1. The fame day, after the end of this diforder, advertifement was given thereof to the Prince, the Kings Son, who was at that time in the fort of *Ofquy*, fome feven leagues from the town of *Fucheo*.   This young Prince, extremely afflicted with this newes, would prefently have gone to the town with fome of his favorites, which were all the company that he had then with him ; but the *Fingeindono* his governor, was utterly againft it, alledging many reafons to perfwade him not to budge from that place, until he had been more amply informed in what termes this affair ftood ; for it was very credible, that they who durft kill his father, would not ftick to difpatch him out of the way too, fince it lay in their power fo to doe, he not being in a condition to defend himfelf : Wherefore he advifed him to affemble all the forces he could, to the end he might by their means fubdue and chaftife his enemies.   The Prince approved of this counfell, and having taken order for that which he judged was moft neceffary according to the eftate wherein he was, he commanded fome that were about him, to go and wind the horn, a thing obferved in *Japan*, which caufed fuch a hurly burly over all the country, as words are not able to expreffe it.   Now the better to underftand this fame, you muft know, that by an ancient cuftome of this Kingdome of *Japan*, all the inhabitants, in whatfoever place they lived, from the leaft to the greateft, are bound to have in their houfes a horn of a great fea-winckles fhell, which they are forbidden at any time to winde upon pain of great punifhment, fave in one of thefe four cafes, namely, a tumult, a fire, a robberie, and a treafon ; fo that if one winds a horn, the caufe of it is prefently known ; becaufe if it be a tumult, one winds it once ; if a fire, twice ; if a robberie, thrice ; and if it be a treafon, four times ; infomuch,

that

that at the firſt winding of the horne, all others are bound upon pain of death to wind theirs, and in ſuch ſort as the firſt hath winded his, to the end that it may be diſtinctly known what it is, and that there may be no confuſion. Now, becauſe this ſignal of treaſon is not ſo ordinary as the others, which arrive very often ; when it happens to be given, all the people are ſo affrighted with it, as without further delay, they run thronging to the place where the horn was firſt winded ; ſo that by this means, the bruit paſſeth from one to another with ſuch ſpeed, as within leſſe then an hour, one is advertiſed thereof above twenty leagues about. But to return to that which I ſaid but now; as ſoon as the Prince had given order for that particular, he retired into a Monaſtery of Religious perſons, which ſtood in the midſt of a wood ; there he remained ſhut up three daies, during the which, he did nothing but bewail his Father, Mother, and Siſters ; and that with exceeding demonſtrations of ſorrow, teſtified by his ſighs, and tears. At the end of that time, in regard great numbers of his ſubjects were aſſembled unto him, he went out of that Monaſtery to provide for that which he judged neceſſary, as well for the ſafety of his kingdome, as for the chaſtiſement of the rebels; whoſe goods and eſtates were immediately confiſcated, their houſes demoliſhed, and ſuch terrible Proclamations publiſhed againſt them, as could not be heard without trembling. Seven daies after this deplorable event, the Prince was counſelled, in regard he had, as already I have ſaid, great numbers come unto him, to go and beſiege the ten thouſand Mutiners in the place of their retreat : Whereupon he parted from the fort of *Oſquy*, and marched directly to the town with his Army, which it was ſaid, conſiſted of very neer an hundred and thirty thouſand men, whereof ſeventeen thouſand were horſe, and the reſt foot, all luſty and well armed, and capable of executing any high enterpriſe. Being arrived at the town, he was wonderfully well received by the people, who teſtified a great deal of reſentment for the death of the late King his father : He would not go at firſt to the Roiall Palace, but went before he paſt any further to the *Pagode*, where his father was buried ; there he took care to make him a funerall Pomp, with a great deal of coſt and honor, according to the manner of the country, which laſted the two nights following. In concluſion, he was ſhewed the ſame robe all bloudy, that his father had on when he was killed ; upon which he took a ſolemn oath, never to pardon any of them that ſhould be found guilty, no not if they were *Bonzes*; and to burn all the Temples whereinto thoſe traitors had fled for ſanctuary. The fourth day after his entry into the town, he was proclaimed King, though but with little ceremony and magnificence, in regard of the general mourning. That done, accompanied as he was, with an hundred and threeſcore thouſand men, he marched directly to the place, whither the mutiners were retired : Now to the end he might the more eaſily take them, and keep them from flying away ; he beſieged them in the mountain where they were, and that for the ſpace of nine daies : But whereas they ſaw that they could hold out no longer for lack of victuals, and that they had no hope of ſuccor, they thought it was better for them to die like valiant men, then to let themſelves be beſieged like cowards ; with this reſolution, under the favor of a very dark and rainy night, they deſcended from the mountain by four ſeverall waies, and falling on the Kings Army, which was ready to receive them in battel array, as having been advertiſed of their deſign, there enſued ſo dreadfull and furious a fight betwixt them, as it laſted two hours within day, but at length the conflict ended with the death of ſeven and thirty thouſand men ; amongſt the which, the ten thouſand Mutiners were ſlain, not one of them deigning to ſave himſelf upon any termes whatſoever. In the mean time, the death of his men greatly afflicted the King, who after this puniſhment of the rebels, retyring to the town, the firſt thing he did was to provide for the curing of the hurt men, wherein he ſpent a good time, in regard they were very many, and whereof a great number died afterwards.

CHAP.

CHAP. LXXVI.

Our passing from the Town of Fucheo, *to the Port of* Hiamangoo; *and that which befell us there; together with my departure from* Malaca, *and arrival at* Goa.

After that this revolt had taken an end by the death of so many men on the one and the other side, we few *Portugals* that remained, as soon as time would permit us, got to the port of the town, where seeing the Country desolated, the merchants fled away, and the King resolved to leave the town, we lost all hope of selling our comodities, yea and of being safe in this harbour, which made us set sail, and go ninety leagues further to another Port, called *Hiamangoo*, which is in the bay of *Canguexumaa*; there vve sojourned tvvo months and an half, not able to sell any thing at all, because the country vvas so full of *Chinese* comodities, as they fell above half in half in the price: for there vvas not a Port or Read in all this Iland of *Japan*, vvhere there were not thirty or forty *Juncks* at anchor and in some places above an hundred; so that in the same very year, at least two thousand merchants ships came from *China* to *Japan*. Now most of this merchandise consisted in Silk, which was given at so cheap a rate, that the peece of Silk which at that time was worth an hundred Taies in *China*, was sold in *Japan* for eight and twenty, or thirty at the most, and that too with much adoe; besides, the prices of all other commodities were so low, as holding our selves utterly undone, we knew not what resolution or counsell to take. But whereas the Lord doth dispose of things according to his good pleasure, by waies which surpasse our understanding; he permitted, for reasons only known to himself, that on the new moon in December, being the fifth day of the month, there arose so furious a tempest of wind and rain, as all those vessels saving a few perished, in it : so that the losse caused by this storm, amounted unto a thousand, nine hundred, and seventy two *Juncks*; amongst the which, were six and twenty Portugals ships, wherein five hundred and two of our nation were drowned; besides, a thousand Christians of other Countries, and eight hundred thousand duckets worth of goods cast away. Of *Chinese* vessels, according to report, there were a thousand, nine hundred, thirty and six lost, together with above tvvo millions of gold, and an hundred and threescore thousand persons. Now from so miserable a ship-wrack, not above ten or eleven ships escaped, of which number, was that wherein I was imbarqued, and that almost by miracle; by reason whereof these same sold their commodities at what price they would. As for us, after we had uttered all ours, and prepared our selves for our departure, we put to sea on a twelfth day in the morning; and although we were well enough contented in regard of the profit we had made, yet were we not a little sad, to see things fall out so to the cost of so many lives and riches, both of those of our nation, and of strangers; But when we had weighed anchor, and hoisted our sailes for the prosecution of our course, the ties of our main sail brake; by which means, the sail yard falling down upon the 　　　　　　　　of the ship, brake all to peices; so that we were constrained by this accident, to recover the port again, and to send a shallop on shore to seek for a sail yard, and shipwrights to fit it for us. To this effect, we sent a present to the Captain of the place, that he might suddenly give us necessary succor, as accordingly he did; so that the very same day, the ship was put into her former estate, and better then before : Neverthelesse, as we were weighing anchor again, the cable of our anchor broke, and because we had but one more in the ship, we were forced to indeavor all that we might for the recovery thereof; by reason of the great need we stood in of it; now, to do this, we sent to land for such as could dive, who in consideration of ten duckets that we gave them, fell to diving into the sea, where they found our anchor in six and tvventy fathome depth, so that by the means 　　　　　　　　which we fastned unto it, vve hoysted it up, though vvith a great deal of labour, vvherein vve all of us bestovved our selves, and spent the most part of the night. As soon as it vvas day, vve set saile, and parting from this river of *Hiamangoo*, it pleased God, that in fourteen daies, vvith a good vvind, vve arrived at *Chincheo*, vvhich is one of the most renovvned and richest Ports of the Kingdome of *China*; there vve vvere advertised, that at the entrance of this river, there
lay

lay at that time a famous Pirate, called *Cheopocheca*, vvith a mighty fleet, vvhich put us into such a fear, that in all hast vve got avvay to *Lamau*, vvhere vve made some provision of victuals, vvhich lasted us untill our arrivall at *Malaca*.

Having stayed some time at *Malaca*, for the dispatch of certain affaires that I had there, I imbarqued my self for *Goa*, vvith an intent ot length, to return into *Portugal*, if I could meet vvith shipping ready to depart from thence at that time ; but some fevv daies after my arrivall there it happened, that a *Portugal* named *Antonio Ferreyra*, brought a present of very rich peeces to the Vice-Roy *Don Pedro Mascarenhas*, which the King of *Bungo* sent him from *Japan*, to getherwith a letter, whereof the contents were these, *Illustrious Lord, and of great majesty, Vice-Roy of the limits of the Indiaes, the dreadfull Lion in the flouds of the sea, by the force of thy ships and artillerie: I* Yacataaandono *King of* Bungo, Facataa, Omangucha, *and the Countries of the two seas, Lord of the petty Kings of the Ilands of* Tosa, Xemenarequa, *and* Miaygimaa, *do give thee to understand by this my letter, that Father* Francisco Xavier *having been not long since in this Country, preaching to them of* Omangucha *the new law of the Creator of all things, I secretly promised to him, that at his return into my Kingdome I would receive from his hand the name and water of holy Baptism, howsoever the noveltie of so unexpected a thing might put me into bad terms with my subjects, Whereupon, he also promised me on his side, that if God gave him life, he would come back again unto me as speedily as he could. And forasmuch as his return hath been longer then I looked for, I have sent thus expresly to know both of him, and of you, the cause of this retardment of his. Wherefore my Lord, I desire you, that he may hasten away to me with all the speed that the first season which shall be proper for navigation, will permit. For besides, that his arrivall in my Kingdome is greatly important for the service of God, it will be also very profitable to my self, for the contracting of a new leagne with the great King of* Portugal, *to the end that by this amitie, my country and his may hereafter be but one thing, and that his subjects may in all our ports and rivers be as free as they are in your* Cochim *where you are ; wherefore your Lordship shall exceedingly oblige me by sending one unto me, that may be witnesse of the desire I have to serve your King ; for I will do it as willingly, as the Sun is ready to hasten his course from the morning to the night. Moreover,* Antonio Ferreyra *will give thee the very same armes wherewith I vanquished the Kings of* Fiangaa *and* Xemenarequa, *and which I wore in the day of battel. I am ready in all things to obey my elder Brother, that invincible King of the other end of the world, Lord of the treasures of great* Portugal. The Vice-Roy having read this Letter, sent for one father *Belquior*, Rector of the Colledg of the Jesuits, and having imparted unto him the King of *Bungoes* desire, he told him, that in regard Father *Xavier* was dead, he could wish that he would in his stead undertake this voyage to *Japan*, which in all probalitie would very much redound to the service of God, and the propogation of the Christian faith. The Rector upon the hearing hereof, willingly imbraced the imployment, wherewith the Vice-Roy was exceedingly well pleased, and very much commended him for such his good and pious resolution. After this, the Vice-Roy consulting with some of his friends about the chusing of a man, that in qualitie of his Ambassador, might accompany the Father in this expedition ; I was nominated unto him, as the fittest he could fix upon, in regard of the knowledg I had, both of the Country and of the then King thereof : whereupon, I was immediatly also sent for, and the Vice-Roy acquainting me with the great desire he had, that I should take this negotiation upon me, which he said, did so much import the honor of God, and the King our Masters service ; he prest me so earnestly to it, that I knew not how to refuse him, although I must confesse, I was very unwilling thereunto : So that consenting to what I could not well avoide, he commanded that all things necessary for our voyage should with all convenient speed be prepared.

21

CHAP.

CHAP. LXXVII.

Father Belquior's *and my departure from the Indiaes to go to* Japan, *and that which befell us till our arrivall at the Island of* Champeiloo.

FOurteen dayes after, namely on the sixteenth of *April*, One thousand five hundred fifty and four, Father *Belquior* and I set sail for *Malaca* in a ship, wherein also was *Don Antonio de Noronha*, Son to *Don Garcia de Noronha*, who had been Vice-Roy of the Indiaes, that was going to take possession of the Government of the Fortresse there; from the which the Vice-Roy had sent order to displace *Don Alvaro de Tayda*, who was Captain of it, as well for that he would not obey his Commands, as for many other misdemeanors which he had committed, whereof I will not speak in particular here, because they are altogether from my purpose at this time. The fifth day of June following, we and the new Captain arrived at *Malaca*, where the Licentiat *Gasper Jorge* Superintendant Generall of the Indiaes, who was the man that prosecuted this businesse, caused the people of the Town to assemble together upon the tolling of a Bell; and having read unto them the Vice-Roys Letters Patents, whereby he displaced *Don Alvaro*, he examined him upon divers Interrogatories, whereof two Registers made a verbal procesf, which was signed both by them and the said Superintendent, and the new Captain. After all this, *Don Alvaro* was deposed from his Government, made a prisoner, and all his estate confiscated: the like was done to all his partakers who had favoured him in the imprisoning of *Gamboa*, Superintendent of the Treasure, and in disobeying the Vice-Roys Commissions, as also in many other disorders that had been committed thereupon: which was executed with so much rigour, as the most part fled to the *Mahometans*, whereby the Fortresse remained so bare of men, as it was in danger of being undone, had not the new Captain provided for it with a great deal of prudence, granting a general Abolition unto all, although they returned for all that but with an ill will. These revolutions, and this excesse of justice, which put all the Country into an uproar, were the cause that Father *Belquior* and I could not this year pass unto *Japan*, as we had resolved; so that we were constrained to winter at *Malaca* until *April* following, in the year One thousand five hundred fifty and five, which was ten months. During that time, the Auditor *Gaspar Jorge* continuing the rigorous executions which he exercised day by day, was a subject of great scandal to all the Country; wherewith not yet contented, and relying on the large Commission which the Vice-Roy had given him, he would needs intermeddle with the Captain *Don Antonio's* Jurisdiction; and indeed, he incroached so far on his Authority, as *Don Antonio* had no more but the name of it, and was no other then as a guard of the Fortress. Now though he was very sensible of this affront, yet he did dissemble and endure it with a great deal of patience: But these excessive rigours of this Auditor continuing for the space of four months; during the which there were many discontentments, whereof I will not treat here in particular, because the discourse of it would be infinite. One day *Don Antonio*, seeing the time proper for the execution of that which he had formerly resolved on, caused some, whom he had destined for it, to seise on him in the Fortress, and carry him to a private house; where (according to report) he was stript stark naked, and his hands and feet being bound with cords, he was grievously whipped: After which, having drop'd scalding oyl on his bare flesh, (which had almost killed him) and clapt irons on his legs, and manacles on his hands, they pluck'd off all the hair of his beard, leaving him not so much as one, and did many other such like things unto him, as it was publickly spoken: so that the poor Licentiat *Gaspar Jorge*, who termed himself Auditor Generall of the *Indiaes*, great Provisor of the deceased and Orphelins, and Superintendent of the Treasure of *Malaca*, and or the Countries of the South, for the King our Soveraign Lord, was thus handled by *Don Antonio*, if the report of it be true. Finally, when the season of Navigation was come, he was sent, so manacled as he was, to the *Indiaes*, with an infamous verball procesf; which the Parliament of *Goa* annulled afterwards: And *Don Antonio* had thereupon an expresse Commandment

from

from the Vice-Roy *Don Pedro de Mascarenhas*, who governed the State of the *Indiaes* at that time, to appear personally before him as a Prisoner, for to be confronted in judgment with *Gaspar Jorge*, and render an account of his proceeding against him; as indeed *Don Antonio* failed not in making his appearance at *Goa* accordingly : where being about to justifie himself for that which had past, he was ordered to answer within three dayes to an ignominious Libel, which *Gaspar Jorge* had exhibited a-gainst him : But forasmuch as *Don Antonio* was naturally an enemy of Justifica-tions by Answers and Replyes, whereby it was said, the Councellors of the Parlia-ment intended to surprize him, the report went (at least wise such was the say-ing of Detractors; for as for me, I neither saw nor am assured of it) that in stead of imploying the three dayes which had been given him, in making answer to this Libell, hee vvithin four and twenty hours having met accidentally vvith *Gaspar Jorge*, sent him to prosecute his Suit in the other World, laying him so sure on the ground, as he never rose again. Howbeit, there are those vvhich recount this Affair quite otherwise, and that say, how in a Feast, vvhereunto he was invited, hee vvas poysoned. By this death of his all this difference vvas decided, and this businesse vvholly ceased, so that *Don Antonio* vvas by Sentence absolutely clear-ed, and sent back to his Government : wherein he continued not above two months and a half, at the end vvhereof he died of a bloody Flux : and so vvere all the storms of envie and discord vvherewith the Fortresse of *Malaca* had been beaten, appeased.

When the season was come vvherein vve might continue our Voyage, on the first day of *April*, in the year One thousand five hundred fifty and five, wee par-ted from *Malaca*, after vvee had imbarqued our selves in a Carvel belonging to the King our Soveraign Lord, which *Don Antonio*, the Captain of the Fortresse gave us by the expresse command of the Vice-Roy. Three dayes after our putting to sea, we arrived at an Island called *Pulho Pisan*, at the entering into the Streight of *Sincaapura*, where the Pilot having never navigated that way before, ran us with full sails so dangerously on certain Rocks, as we thought our selves to be utterly lost, without all hope of recovery : In regard whereof, by the advice of all the rest, the Father and I were constrained to get into a Manchua, for to go and demand succour of one *Luis Dalmeida*, who two hours before had passed by us in a Vessell of his, and lay at anchor two leagues off us, by reason the winde was against him : So the Father and I made to him with peril enough. For whereas all that Country, which appertained to the King of *Jantana*, Grand-childe to him that had been King of *Malaca*, our mortall Enemy, were at that time in arms, his *Balons* and *Lanchares*, that were assembled in a Fleet of Warr, continually gave us chase, with an intention to take us; but by Gods providence we escaped them. At length, af-ter we had got to this ship, with no little fear and trouble, he that was Captain of her furnished us with a Boat and Mariners, and so we returned to our Carvel as speedily as we could, for to succour and draw her out of the danger wherein we had left her : But it pleased the Lord that we found her the day after deli-vered from it; though it is true, that she took in water abundantly in the prow's side ; but in the end we stanched it at *Patana*, where we arrived seven dayes af-ter. There I went ashore with two others, to see the King; unto whom I deliver-ed a Letter from the Captain of *Malaca* : and being received very graciously by him, he read it over, whereby he understood, that the cause of our coming thi-ther was to provide our selves of victuals, and some other things which we had not taken in at *Malaca* ; as also that we were resolved to proceed on in our course directly to *China*, and from thence to *Japan*, where Father *Belquior* and others with him were to preach the Christian Law to the Gentiles : vvhich the King of *Patana* having read, after he had mused a little, he turned to them that were a-bout him, and said smiling to them, *O how much better were it for these men, since they expose themselves to so many travels, to go to* China *and inrich themselves there, then to recount tales in strange Countreys ?* Whereupon, calling the *Xabandar* to him, *Be sure,* said he unto him, *that thou givest these men here all that they shall demand of thee, and that for the love of the Captain of* Malaca, *who hath greatly re-*

Kkk   *com-*

commended them unto mee: and above all remember, That it is not my custome to command a thing twice. When we had taken leave of the King, exceedingly contented with the good reception he had given us, we fell presently to buying of Victuals, and other such things as we stood in need of; So that in eight dayes we were abundantly furnished with whatsoever was necessary for us. Being departed from this Haven of *Patana*, we sailed two dayes together with a South-east winde along by the coast of *Lugor* and *Siam*, traversing the Barr of *Cuy*, to go to *Pulho Cambim*, and from thence to the Islands of *Canton*, with an intent there to attend the conjunction of the new Moon: But it was our ill fortune to be surprized by East and South-east winde, (which raign in that Coast the most part of the year) whereof the violence was so great, that we were in fear to be cast away: so that to decline the event thereof, we were forced to tack about again to the Coast of *Malaya*; and arriving at an Island, called *Pullo Timan*, we ran into great danger there, as well by reason of the tempest which we had upon the sea, as in regard of the great treason of the people of the Country. Now after five dayes that we had continued there, without having either fresh water or victuals, because for the easing of our Vessell we had cast out all into the Sea, it pleased God that wee encountred with three *Portugal* Ships which came from *Sunda*, by whose arrivall we were very much comforted in our travels: Whereupon Father *Belquior* and I began to treat with the Captains of those Vessels about that which they thought was requisite we should do; and all were of the opinion, that we should send back the Carvel wherein wee were, to *Malaca*; saying, that there was no likelihood wee should be able to make so long a Voyage in her as that of *Japan*. Having approved of this counsel, we presently imbarqued our selves in the Ship of one *Francisco Toscano*, a Worshipfull and rich man, who defrayed our charge during all our Voyage, yea, and most part of the time that vve were in *China*, not permitting any of our Company to spend a peny. From this Island *Pullo Timan* we put to sea on Friday the seventh of *June* in the same yeer One thousand five hundred fifty and five, and discovering the firm land of the Kingdome of *Champaa*, we sailed along the Coast with a North-West winde, and in twelve dayes we arrived at an Island called *Pullo Champeiloo*, in the Straght of *Cauchenchina*, where we took in fresh vvater at a River which descended from an high Mountain. There amongst the Rocks we perceived a very fair Cross graven on a great free Stone, and under it 1 5 1 8, with six letters abbreviated, which said, *Duart Coelho*: We observed also towards the River, and on the South-side, two flight shot off, threescore and two men hanged on trees alongst the Strand, besides others that lay on the ground half eaten; a thing which seemed to have been done not above six or seven dayes before. Upon another tree there hung a great Banner, wherein these vvords vvere seen in *Chinese* letters, *Let every Ship or Junck which shall arrive in this place, be sure to dislodg quickly from thence after shee hath furnished her self with fresh water, whether shee hath time, or hath it not; on pain of incurring the same justice as these wretches have done, whom the fury of the arm of the son of the Sun hath overwhelmed.* Wee were mightily surprised vvith so strange an accident, so that vvee could make no other judgment of it, but that some *Chinese* Army had arrived there, and meeting with those vvretches, had (as Pirats use to do) intreated them as vve saw, under the specious pretext of Justice.

CHAP. LXXVIII.
Our departure from the Iland of Champeiloo, *and our arrivall at that of* Lampacau; *With a relation of two great disasters which hapned in* China *unto two Portugal Colonies; and of a strange accident that befell in the Country.*

WHen we were parted from the Iland of *Champeiloo*, we got to the Ilands of *Canton*, so that on the fifth day of our voyage, it pleased God that we arrived at one of them, called *Lampacau*, where at that time the *Portugals* excercised their commerce with the *Chineses*, which continued untill the year One thousand five hundred

dred

dred, fifty and feven; when as the *Mandarins* of *Canton*, at the requeſt of the Merchants of the Country, gave us the port of *Macao*, where the trade now is; of which place (that was but a deſert Iland before) our country men made a very goodly plantation, wherein there were houſes worth three or four thouſand Duckats, together with a Cathedral Church: Moreover, this Colony hath its Governor, Auditor, and Officers of Juſtice; whereunto I ſhal add, that the inhabitants of this place are in as great ſafety there, as if they were in the quieteſt part of *Portugal*. But God grant of his infinite mercy, and goodneſſe, that this Colony may be of longer durance then that of *Liampoo*, which was another of the Portugals, and whereof I have ſpoken at large heretofore, being two hundred leagues from this ſame on the North Coaſt. But ill fortune would, that by the diſorder of one Portugal, it was demoliſhed in a very little time; in which diſaſter, I my ſelf was preſent, and can ſay, that the loſſe which was made there, as well of people, as of riches, was ineſtimable. For in this plantation, were three thouſand men, whereof twelve hundred were *Portugals*, and the reſt Chriſtians of divers nations. Yea, and I have heard many ſay, which ſpoke like knowing men thereof, that the Portugals traffick there, exceeded three millions of gold: Now, the moſt part of this traffick was in lingots of ſilver of *Japan*, which had been found out not above two months before, and was ſuch as a man doubled his mony three or four times by the commodities which he ſent thither. In this Colony, there was a Governor, who reſided in the Country; there were alſo an Auditor, Judges, Sheriffs, Aldermen, a Proviſor of the deceaſed and Orphelins, a town Clark, and all other Officers that are uſually in a Commonwealth; together with four publick Notaries, and ſix Regiſters, each of whoſe offices were ſold for three thouſand duckats; yea, and there were ſome farre dearer. There were alſo two Hoſpitals, wherein above thirty thouſand duckats was ſpent every year, and the Town houſe had in revenue ſix thouſand *per annum*; So that it was generally ſaid, that this Colony was the richeſt, and beſt peopled, of any that was in the Indiaes; beſides, for matter of extent, it had not its fellow in all *Aſia*. Furthermore, when the Regiſters or Secretaries paſſed any Grant, or when the publick Notaries made any writings, they ordinarily uſed theſe termes; *In this moſt noble and alwaies faithfull town of* Liampoo, *for the King our Soveraign Lord.* Now, having ſaid ſo much of it, I hold it not amiſſe to tell you, how and wherefore ſo noble and rich a Colony was deſtroyed, which arrived in this ſort. There was living there a man of a good extraction and rank, named *Lancerote Pereyra*, born at *Pont de Lima*, a town in *Portugal*; it is ſaid, that this ſame had lent ſome thouſand duckats to certain *Chineſes*, who were not men ſolvent, but became bankrupts, and never paid him any thing, nor could he hear any newes of them afterwards; which was the cauſe that deſiring to make good this loſſe, and to recover it of them which were not the occaſion of it, he aſſembled for that effect ſome eighteen or twenty *Portugals*, idle fellows, and of lewd diſpoſitions, with whom, under the favor of the night, he fell upon a village, ſome two leagues from thence, where he robbed eleven or twelve labouring men; and withall, ſeizing on their wives and children, killed about half a ſcore perſons, without any reaſon at all ſo to do. In the mean time, the Alarum being taken up by the whole country round about, by reaſon of this violence, the inhabitants went and complained to the *Chumbin* for Juſtice; and having made a verball proceſſe of the buſineſſe, they preſented it in the name of the people to the *Chaem* of the Government, which is as one of the Vice-Roys of the Kingdome; who immediately thereupon, diſpatched away an *Haitau*, who is as an Admirall amongſt us, with an Army of three hundred Juncks, and four ſcore Vançons with Oares; wherein there were threeſcore thouſand men, which being all made ready in ſeventeen daies, came and fell on this misfortunate Colony, and the matter paſſed in ſo ſtrange a manner for them, as I muſt confeſſe, I have not capacity enough to recount it ſufficiently, neither underſtanding enough to imagine it; only it ſhall ſuffice me to ſay, as one who ſaw it, that in leſſe then the ſpace of five hours, which this dreadfull chaſtiſement of the hand of God indured; theſe cruell enemies, left not any thing at all in *Liampoo* to which one could give a name, for they demoliſhed and burnt all that they could find; they put to death withall twelve hundred Chriſtians, amongſt the which, were eight hundred *Portugals*, who were all burned alive in five and twenty ſhips,

and

and two and forty Juncks.   It is said, that in this common ruine, there was lost to the value of two millions of Gold, as well in Lingots, Pepper, Sandal, Cloves, Mace, and Nutmeggs, as in other Commodities ; and all these desasters arrived by the ill conscience, and little judgment of an avaricious *Portugal*.   Now, from this misfortune, was another farre greater derived ; which was, that we lost our credit and reputation so mightily over all the Country, as the inhabitants would no longer endure the sight of us ; saying, that we were divels incarnate, ingendred by the malediction of the wrath of God, for the punishment of sinners.   This hapned in the year, one thousand, five hundred, forty and two, *Martim Alfonso de Sousa* being Governor of the *Indiaes*, and *Ruy Vaz Pereyra Marramaque* Captain of *Malaca*.   Two years after, the *Portugals* desiring to make another new Colony in a Port, called *Chincheo*, in the same Kingdome of China, five leagues lower then *Liampoo*, with an intention to settle their trade there , the Merchants of the Country coming to consider what great profit would redound to them thereby, intreated the *Mandarins* to make shew of permitting it, and obliged them thereunto with many great presents ; we had commerce then with those of the Country about two yeares and an half, untill such time as by the expresse command of *Simano de Mello*, Captain of the Fortresse, there was sent into this place another man of the same humor as *Lancerote Pereyra* was of, unto whom the said *Simano de Mello* gave a commission to be Governor of this Port of *Chincheo*, and Provisor of the Deceased : but the bruit went of him, that the extream covetuousnesse wherewith he was possest, made him lay hands on all things, without any the least respect to ought whatsoever.   It hapned then that in his time there arrived in the Port of *Chincheo* a stranger, by nation an *Armenian*, who was held by every one for a very good Christian :   This man, who had an estate of ten or twelve thousand duckets, and being a Christian, as I have said, and a stranger, as we were, passed out of a *Mahometans* Junck, wherein he was, into the ship of a *Portugal*, named *Luis de Montaroyo*.   Now having lived some six or seven months very peaceably amongst us, and much respected and favored of every one, he chanced to fall sick of a feaver, whereof he died ; but before he gave up the Ghost, he declared by his Testament, that he had a wife and children in a town of *Armenia*, called *Gaborem*, and that of his twelve thousand duckets estate he left two thousand to the Hospitall at *Malaca* ; and for the rest, he desired it might be kept in safe hands, untill there were an opportunity to have consigned it unto his children, as to his lawfull heirs ; and in case they were dead, he left it to the Hospitall.   Behold, what was the Testament of this faithfull Christian, who was no sooner buried, but *Ayrez Botelho de Sousa*, Provisor of the dead, seized on all his estate, without making any Inventorie, or other kind of accompt, saying, that before any farther proceeding therein, they were to send to make enquiry in *Armenia*, which was above two thosand leagues from thence, to see whether there were not some ingagements, or seizure of Justice upon it :   There arrived also at the same time, two *Chinese* Merchants, who had to the value of three thousand duckets in silk, peeces of damaske, musk, and porcelaines, appertaining to the deceased *Armenian* : the Provisor arrested them all, and not contented therewith, he would needs make the *Chineses* beleeve, that all the merchandise which they had, belonged also unto the *Armenian* ; so that under the pretext thereof, he took eight thousand duckets from them, and bid them go to *Goa* and there demand justice of the Provisor Generall, by reason he could do no otherwise then he did ; for that, he was obliged to deal in that sort by the duty of his Charge.   Now, not to stand upon the delivering of the reasons, which in vain were alledged by them against this injustice of his ; I will only say, that these two Merchants returning home without any of their merchandise, went with their Wives and Children, and casting themselves at the *Chaems* feet, represented unto him in a Petition the whole businesse, as it past : informing him, moreover, that we were men quite void of the fear of God. The *Chaem* willing to do justice then to these Merchants, and to many others which had formerly complained against us, caused it to be every where proclamed, that no man on pain of death should converse with us ; whereupon, the scarcity of victuals came to be so great amongst us, as that which was wont to be bought for six blanks, was then worth above a ducket; so that necessity constrained us to go unto certain hamlets;

where-

whereupon enfued fuch diforders, as all the Country rofe up againft us with fo much hatred and fury, that fixteen daies after we were fet upon by an Army of an hundred and twenty very great Juncks, which intreated us in that manner for our fins, as ofthirteen fhips which we had in the Port, there was not one that was not burnt; and of five hundred *Portugals* which were abiding in the Country, thirty only efcaped, who had not the worth of a penny left them. From thefe two fad hiftories, recounted by me, I inferre, that it feemes the Affairs which we have now in *China,* and the tranquillity and confidence wherewith we live there, (fuppofing that the treaties of peace which we have with them be firm and affured) wil laft but til our fins fhal ferve for motives to the inhabitants of the Country to mutine againft us, which God of his infinite mercy, permit not for the time to come. To return again now to my former difcourfe, you muft underftand, that after we were arrived at the Port of *Lampacau,* as I have declared before, we could not meet with any veffel that was bound for *Japan*; fo that we were conftrained to paffe another year too in this Port, with a defign in May following, which was ten months off, to continue our voyage as we had refolved.

Sect. 2

Father *Belquior* and I perceiving that there was no hope of going to *Japan* this yeare, as well for that the feafon was paft, as for other inconveniences that fell out, we were forced to ftay in this Iland till the time fhould ferve for us to make our voyage thither. Having continued there then til the feventeenth of Feb. following, certain news came to us from *Cantan,* that on the third day of the fame month the Province of *Sanfy* had been fwallowed up in the manner enfuing. The firft day of Frebruary, the earth fel a trembling from eleven til one of the clock at night, and the next day from midnight til two in the morning; as alfo the day following from one til three: During this trembling it was a dreadful thing to hear the terrible noife which the ftormes and thunder made: After all this fuch an horrible inundation of waters borke forth out of the center of the earth, as in an inftant, all the Country about, was fwallowed up threefcore leagues round, without the faving of any living creature from perifhing, but only of one child of feven years of age, and which was for a great wonder prefented to the King of *China.* In the mean time this news was no fooner come to the City of *Cantan,* but all the inhabitants thereof were terrifyed with it, yea and all ours were fo amazed at it, that holding it for an unpoffible thing, fourteen of our company would needs go thither to know the truth thereof; which they immediately put in execution, and at their return affirmed, that the matter was very certain, whereof an atteftation was made, figned by fourteen ocular witneffes, who had been upon the place; which atteftation was afterwads fent by *Francifco Tofcano* to the King of *Portugal, Don Joano* the third of glorious memory. This prodigious event fo affrighted the inhabitants of the City of *Cantan,* that all of them generally teftified a world of repentance; and although they were Gentiles, yet muft it be acknowledged that they confounded us Chriftians, who faw how far their devotion extended. For on the firft day when the newes thereof arrived there, Proclamations were made throughout all the Principall ftreets of the City by fix men on horfeback, who in long mourning robes, and with a fad and lamentable voice, rode crying out thefe words; *Miferable creatures as you are, that ceafe not from offending day by day, the Lord of all things: Heare, O heare, the moft lamentable and dreadfull adventure that ever was; For you are to know, that for our fins God hath drawn the fword of his Divine Juftice againft all the people of* Cuy *and* Sanfy, *overwhelming pell mell with water, fire, and tempefts from Heaven all that great Province of* China, *none being faved but one only Child which is carried to the Son of the Sun.* And thereupon, they rung a little bell thrice, which they had in their hands; Then all the people proftrating themfelves on the ground, faid with fearfull cryes, *God is Juft in all that he doth.* After this was paft, all the inhabitants retired into their houfes, which were fhut up for five daies together, fo that the City was fo defolate, as there was not a living creature feen ftirring in it. At the end of the five daies, the *Chaem* and the *Anchaffis* of the government, together with all the reft of the people (wherein the men only vvere comprehended, for as for the vvomen, they hold them incapable of being heard of God, by reafon of the difobedience of the firft finne committed by *Eve*) vvent as it vvere in proceffion

fion, thorow the principall Streets of the Citie, while their Priefts, vvhich vvere above five thoufand in number, cryed with a loud voyce that pierced the very skies, *O marvellous and'pitifull Lord, have no regard to our wickedneffe; for if thou takeft account of them, we fhall remain dumb before thee*. Whereunto all the people with an other fearfull cry, anfwered, *Lord, we confeffe our faults before thee*. And fo the Proceffion continuing, ftill going on, they at length arrived at a magnificent Temple, called *Nacapyrau*, whom they hold for the Queen of Heaven, as I have heretofore related. From thence they went the next day to another Temple, called *The God of Juftice*: and in this fort they continued fourteen dayes; during which, were great Alms generally beftowed, and many prifoners freed; alfo divers Sacrifices were made of the odoriferous perfumes of Aloes and Benjamin: There were many others too, wherein there was good ftore of blood fhed, and wherein many Kine, Stags and Swine vvere offered, vvhich were all diftributed in almes to the poor. In purfuance whereof, during the three months that we abode there, they continued in doing many other good works, which were performed vvith fo much charge and charity, as it is to be beleeved, that if the Faith of Jefus Chrift had been added thereunto, they would have been acceptable unto him. We heard afterwards, and this report was univerfall over all the Country, that during the three dayes of that Earth-quake at *Sanfy*, it had ftill rained blood in the City of *Pequin*, vvhere the King of *China*'s Court was at that time, vvhich made the moft part of the inhabitants to forfake it, and the King to fly to *Nanquin*, vvhere, it was faid, he gave great alms, and fet at liberty an infinite many of Slaves; amongft the which were five *Portugals*, vvho had been retained prifoners in the Town of *Pocaffer* above twenty yeers together. When thefe came to *Cantan*, they recounted unto us divers marvellous things; and amongft others, they told us, that the almes which the King had given upon this occafion, amounted to fix hundred thoufand Duckats, befides the magnificent Temples which he built to appeafe the vvrath of God; amongft the which hee made one in that very City, very fumptuous, and of great majefty, under the title of *The Love of God*.

CHAP. LXXIX.
Our arrival in the Kingdome of Bungo, and that which pafs'd there.

THe feafon being come vvherein vve might continue our Voyage, vve parted from this Ifland of *Lampacau* the feventh day of *May*, One thoufand five hundred fifty and fix, after vve had imbarqued our felves in a Ship, vvhereof *Don Francifco de Mafcarenhas*, furnamed *Pallia*, vvas Captain. So vve proceeded on in our courfe for fourteen dayes together; at the end whereof vve difcovered the fi ft Iflands, at the height of five and thirty degrees; and vvhich by gradat on regard the Weft, North-vveft of *Tanixumaa*: vvhereupon, the Pilot knowing that it vvas ill failing there, fteered to the South-vveft, to finde out the point of the Mountain of *Minatoo*: We coafted *Tanoraa* then, and ftill ran along this coaft to the Port of *Finugaa*. And forafmuch as in this Climate the windes are Northerly, and that the current of the vvater vvas contrary to them, the Pilot had a very bad opinion of his Navigation; fo that vvhen he came to know his fault, although out of an accuftomed obftinacy of Mariners, he vvould not confefs it, vve vvere already paft threefcore leagues beyond the Port vvhere vve meant to arrive; by reafon vvhereof, we vvere fain to tack about for the recovery of it fifteen dayes after, though with travell enough, for that the vvindes were croffe; and (without lying) our goods and lives were in no little jeopardy, by reafon all this Coaft was rifen up againft the King of *Bungo* our Friend, and the inhabitants, who vvere greatly inclined to the Law of the Lord, vvhich had formerly been preached unto them. At length, after that by the mercy of God vve had got to the Town of *Fucheo*, vvhereof I have oftentimes fpoken, which is the capitall of the Kingdom of *Bungo*, where the chiefeft Chriftians of all *Japan* do now flourifh; all they of the Ship thought it requifite that I fhould go to the Fortreffe of *Ofquy*, where we heard the King then was: Now though I feared to undertake this Journey, in regard the Country was all up, yet I
resolved

resolved for it, at the perswasion of them of the ship, who all in generall intreated me very earnestly unto it. Having prepared my self then, and received a Present worth five hundred Crowns, which *Don Francisco*, Captain of the Ship sent to the King, I took one of my companions with me, and so went away. After I was landed at the Town Key, the first thing I did was to go to the house of the Admirall of the Sea, who received me with great demonstrations of friendship, and confirmed me against the fear I was in; whereupon, having given him an account of the cause of my coming thither, I desired him to give me horses and men that might conduct me to the King; which most willingly he did, and more freely then I required. Being departed from this Town, the next morning about nine of the clock I arrived at a place called *Fingau*, which might be a quarter of a league from the Fortresse of *Osquy*; There I sent one of those of *Japan*, which I had with me, to let the Captain of the place understand that I was arrived, and that I had an Embassie to deliver to his Highnesse from the Vice-Roy of the *Indiaes*: In which regard, I intreated him *to appoint me such a time as he pleased, that I might speak with him.* Hereunto he returned me this answer by a Son of his, *That my Companions and I were very welcome, and that the King was in the Isle of* Xequa, *where he was entertaining himself in the catching of a great Fish, whereof the name was not known, and which was come thither from the bottom of the Sea, with a great number of many other little fishes: and that having cooped him up in a Channel there, it was likely that he would spend all the day in that sport, and not return till night: But that he would howsoever immediately advertise him of my arrivall.* Thereupon he sent me to repose my self in a better lodging which he gave me, where I was abundantly furnished with all that was necessary for mee; yea, and he told me by way of Complement, that all this Country was no lesse the King of *Portugals*, then *Malaca*, *Cochin* and *Goa*. Then one of his Followers, whom he had appointed to wait on us, gave us an extraordinary good reception in a *Pagode*, whereof the *Bonzes* made us a very sumptuous Feast. In the mean time, the King having notice of my arrivall, dispatched away from the Island where hee was catching that great Fish, three light Galleys, and in them his Chamberlain, a great Favourite of his, named *Oretandano*, who about evening came to me to the place where I was, and having told me that by word of mouth which the King had enjoyned him, he drew forth a Letter, and having kissed it with the Ceremonies and Complements used amongst them, he delivered it unto me, wherein I found this written, *Being at this present imployed in an exercise which is very pleasing unto me, I have been advertised of thy arrival in my Country, wherewith I am so contented, that I protest unto thee, I would have come away presently unto thee, had I not sworn that I would not part from hence, till I had killed a great Fish which I hold coop'd up here: Wherefore I intreat thee, as my good Friend, since by reason thereof I cannot go to thee, that thou wilt come thy self to me in this Vessel which I have sent for thee: for on thy coming, and on the death which I hope to give to this Fish, my perfect content depends.* Having read this Letter, I instantly imbarked my self in the Galley wherein *Oretandono* came for me, and my followers in the other two, with the Present they carried. And forasmuch as those Galleys were very swift, we arrived within lesse then an hour at the Island, which was some two leagues and an half off. Now we came thither at such time as the King, with above two hundred men in boats, with darts in their hands, was pursuing a prodigious Whale, which was altogether unknown and strange to them, as having never seen such a Fish before in all that Country. After they had killed and drawn it to land, the King was so pleased therewith, that to recompence all the fishermen that were imployed in the action, he exempted them from a certain Tribute which they had accustomed to pay before: as also conferred new Honours on some Gentlemen whom he loved, and that were there with him, and gave a thousand *Taeis* in silver to his Pages: withall, he received me with a smiling countenance, and questioned me very exactly about many particulars; whereunto I answered the best that I could, alwayes adding something of mine own thereunto, as judging it necessary for the increasing of the Portugals reputation, and of the great

esteem

esteem vvherein we vvere at that time in the Country; for all the inhabitants held it for moſt certain, that the King of *Portugal* was indeed the only Prince, which might terme himſelf the Monarch of the world, as well for the large extent of his territories, as for his power, and mighty treaſure; in regard whereof chiefly they of theſe Countryes made great account of our amitie. Theſe things done, the King vvent from this Iland towards *Oſquy*, and about an hour within night he arrived at his Caſtle, vvhere he was received with a great deal of rejoycing, and applaued by every one for ſo honourable an exploit, as that of killing the Whale, attributing to him alone, that which all the reſt had done; whereby one may ſee, that this pernicious vice of flattery raigns ſo abſolutely in the Courts of Princes, as it hath eſtabliſhed its ſelf a place even amongſt the very Gentiles and Infidels. The King having diſmiſſed all them that had accompanied him, vvent to Sup with his Wife and Daughters, and would not then be attended on by any body, becauſe the feaſt was made at his vvives charge. And whereas vve vvere then at a Treaſurers houſe of his, where vve vvere appointed to lodg, he ſent for us all five, and intreated us that vve ſhould eat in his preſence after the manner of our Country, adding, that the Queen did infinitely deſire it. Then having cauſed a table to be covered for us, and on it placed ſtore of excellent good meat and vvell dreſt, vvhich vvas ſerved up by very fair vvomen; vve feil to eating after our manner, of all that vvas ſet before us, vvhileſt the jeaſts vvhich the Ladies broke upon us, in ſeeing us feed ſo vvith our hands, gave more delight to the King and Queen, then all the Comedies that could have been repreſented before them: for thoſe people being accuſtomed to feed yvith tvvo little ſticks, as I have declared elſevvhere, they hold it for a great incivilitie, to touch the meat with ones hand, as we uſe to do. Hereupon the Kings Daughter, a marvellous fair Princeſſe, and not above fourteen or fifteen years of age, craved leave of the Queen her Mother, that ſhe and ſix or ſeven of her companions might preſent a certain Play before them concerning the ſubject in queſtion; which the Queen with the Kings conſent granted her. That done, they withdrew into another room, where they ſtayed a pretty while, during the which, they that remained in the place, drove away the time at our coſt, by jeering and gibing at us, who were much aſhamed, eſpecially my four companions, which were but novices in the Country, and underſtood not the language; for as for me, I had before ſeen ſuch a like Comedy acted at *Tainxuman* againſt the *Portugals*. As we were thus miniſtring matter for the Company to laugh at us, and ſetting the beſt face on it that poſſibly we could amidſt theſe affronts, in regard of the great pleaſure which we obſerved the King and Queen took therein, we ſaw the young Princeſſe come out of the other room diſguiſed like a Merchant, wearing a Sycmiter by her ſide, covered all over with plates of gold; and the reſt of her habit anſwerable to the perſon which ſhe repreſented. In this equipage falling down on her knees before the King her father, with the reſpect ſhe owed to him, *Moſt mighty Lord and King* (ſaid ſhe unto him) *albeit this my boldneſſe be worthy of great chaſtiſement, in regard of the inequalitie which it hath pleaſed God to put between your greatneſſe and my baſeneſſe; yet the neceſſity whereunto I find my ſelf reduced, makes me ſhut my eyes againſt all that may happen to me thereby; For being old as I am, and charged with many Children, which I have had by ſeverall Wives, with whom I have been married, my extream poverty, and the deſire I have not to leave them deſtitute of means, hath made me have recourſe to my friends for help, which they have granted me; So that having employed the mony which they have lent me, in a certain Commoditie, which I cannot ſell in all* Japan; *I have reſolved to barter it away for any other whatſoever it be: And having complained hereof to ſome freinds that I have at* Meacoo, *they have aſſured me that your Highneſſe may doe me ſome good. Wherefore, my Lord, I humbly beſeech you, that in conſideration of theſe white haires, and feeble age, as alſo for that I have many Children, and am poor, you will be pleaſed to aſſiſt me in my need, which will be an almes very well beſtowed, and moſt agreeable to the* Chenchicos, *which are lately arrived here in their Ship; for this commoditie of mine will accommodate them better then any other, in regard of the want they have continually thereof.* Whileſt this diſcourſe laſted, the

the King and Queen could not forbear laughing, to see that this old Merchant, who had so mony children, and so many incommodities, was the Princesse their Daughter, very young, and exceeding beautifull : But the King forbearing a little from laughing, answered her with a great deal of gravity, that shee should shew some samples of the Merchandize which she had, and if it were such as would accommodate us, he would desire us to buy it. At these words, the pretended Merchant having made a very low obeysance, retired into the other room again. In the mean time, we were so confounded with what we heard and saw, as we could not tell what to think, or what should be the event of it ; whilest the vvomen which were in the room, being about three score in number, (for there were no other men but we five there) fell to jogging one another, and laughing at us. Hereupon, the Merchant comes in again,, bringing with her six fair young maids, richly clad, and disguised also like Merchants, carrying samples of the Merchandize they had to sell : They had Scymiters and Daggers by their sides all guilt, with grave countenances and high looks, being all of them Daughters to the greatest Lords of the Kingdom, whom the Princesse had expresly chosen to act this Play with her. Each of these six Damsels bare on her shoulder a fardle of green Taffata, and all of them together, seeming to be Merchants sons, danced a Ball to the tune of two Harps and a Viol, and ever and anon sung in verse with a very sweet and melodious voyce, words of this substance, *High and mighty Lord, by the riches which thou possessest, we pray thee to think of our poverty ; we are miserable creatures in this strange Country, and consequently despised by the inhabitants thereof, which exposeth us to great affronts : wherefore we beseech thee by that which thou art, be mindfull of our poverty.* After that these young Merchants had finished their Dance and Song, they fell all on their knees before the King, and then the eldest of them having rendred him most humble thanks for the favour he did them, in helping them away with their Merchandize, they untied all their fardles, and let fall in the midst of the room a great number of woodden arms with hands, the said eldest of them saying with a very good grace, *Since that Nature for our sins hath subjected us to so villanous a misery, that our hands must of necessity smell always of flesh or fish, or of such other meat as wee eat with them, this Merchandize will greatly accommodate us, to the end that whilest we make use of one sort of hands, the other may be washed.* The King and Queen fell heartily a laughing at this Speech ; vvhereas in the mean time we five were so ashamed, as the King perceiving it, desired us to take it in good part, saying, That the Princesse his Daughter had done this to no other end, but for the better entertainment of us, vvhom she respected as her Brothers. Whereunto vve made answer, That *we hoped God our Master would reward his Highnesse for this honour and grace that he did us ; which we confess'd was very great, and for such wee would publish it over all the world as long as we lived :* Wherewith the King, Queen and Princesse shewed themselves very vvell satisfied, giving us thanks vvith many complements after their manner : yea, and the Princesse said to us moreover, *If your God would take me for his servant, I should endeavour the best I could to please him : but I hope he will not forget me.* At these vvords vve prostrated our selves on our knees before her, and kissing the hem of our garment, vve answered her, *That we hoped no lesse of her, and that in case shee became a Christian, we should see her Queen of Portugal :* Whereupon the Queen her Mother and she fell a laughing. Having taken leave then of the King, vve returned to our lodging, and the next morning as soon as it vvas day, he sent for us again, and questioned us very exactly about the coming of Father *Belquior*, the intention of the Vice-Roy, the Letter which I had brought from him ; our Ship, and the goods that were in her ; and many other things, wherein we spent four hours at the least ; after which he dismissed us, saying, that within six dayes he would be at the Town, and that there he would receive the Letter, see the Father, and make answer to all.

CHAP. LXXX.

My reception by the King of Bungo, *as Ambassador from the Vice-Roy of the* Indiaes.

AFter the six daies were past the King parted from *Osquy* to go to the town of *Fucheo*, accompanied with a great number of Nobilitie, and a guard of six hundred foot, and two hundred horse, which made a goodly shew. Being arrived there, he was received by the people with great demonstrations of joy, with Shewes, Interludes, and many other inventions after their manner, that were very costly; after which, he went to his Palace, an exceeding fair and magnificent structure, whither the next day he sent for me, and bid me bring him the Vice-Roys Letter, as being come for no other end but to receive it, and that after he had read it, he would speak with Father *Belquior* touching the matters that were most important. Whereupon I presently returned to my lodging, and having made ready all that was necessary for me, about two of the clock in the afternoon, the King sent the Captain of the town, and four other of the chiefest men of the Court for me; who conducted me to the Palace, accompanied with forty *Portugals*, which marched all on foot, because it is the custome of the Country so to do. All the streets thorow which we past, were very handsomly set forth, and there was such a world of people, as the officers had much adoe to make way for us. Three *Portugals* on horseback, carried each of them a peece of the present; and a little after them followed two curious Spanish Gennets, with rich Saddles and Trappings, and with such Armes as are used in Justs. Upon our arrival at the first court of the Palace, we found the King there on a scaffold, which had been erected expresly for him, accompanied with all the Lords of the Kingdome, amongst whom, were the Ambassadors of three strange Princes, namely the first of the King of the *Lequios*, the second of the King of *Chauchim*, and Isle of *Tosa*, and the third of the Emperor of the *Miacoo*; and round about as far as the court extended, there were above a thousand harquebuziers, and four hundred men mounted on good horses, besides a multitude of people without number. After that the forty *Portugals* and I were come to the Scaffold where the King was, we performed all the ceremonies and complements which are used to be done to him in such cases; and then approaching a little neerer to him, I delivered him the Letter from the vice-Roy, which he would not receive but standing. Then being set down again in his place, he gave it to one about him, that was as his Secretary who read it aloud that every one might hear. After it was read, the King questioned me before the three strange Ambassadors, and the great Lords with whom he was accompanied, about certain things which he was curious to know touching our *Europe*; whereof one was, how many men, armed *cap-a-pe*, and mounted on such horses as those were that I saw there, the King of *Portugal* could bring into the field? Whereupon fearing least I should blush if I came to tell a lie; I must confesse, that I was much troubled how to answer, which one of my companions who was neer me, perceiving, speaking for me, made answer; That he could bring an hundred or sixscore thousand; a matter whereat the King was much abashed, and I too: But the King taking pleasure as it seemed, in the marvellous answer, which this *Portugal* gave him, bestowved above an hours time in asking him questions. In the mean season, even the King himself, and all they that were present with him, being exceedingly amazed to hear such great and strange things delivered, he turned to them and said; *I sware truly unto you, that I should desire nothing so much in the world, as to see the Monarchy of this great Country, whereof I have heard such wonderfull things, as well concerning the immence treasures, and the infinite number of ships which he hath; for could I but once do this, I should live very well contented the rest of my daies.* Thereupon having sent me, and those that accompanied me, away, he said unto me, *When thou shalt think it a fit time, thou maiest bid the Father come unto me, for he shall find me ready here to receive him.*

After

After I was retired to my lodging, 1 gave Father *Belquior* an accompt of the Kings good reception of me, together with all that had past besides, and how desirous he was to see him; in regard whereof I held it fit, since all the *Portugals* were then together, and in their best clothes, that he should go to him out of hand, which he liked very well of. Having furnished himself then with certain things necessary for the better setting forth of his person, he and I went avvay, accompanied with forty *Portugals*, all very well apparrelled, and wearing chaines of gold Scarfe-wise; and four pretty boyes in cassocks, and hats of white taffata, and silken crosses on their brests, together with a converted *Japanois*, Christened *Joana Fernandez*, to serve for Interpreter. When wee were arrived at the first Court of the Kings Palace, we found some Lords attending us there, who with a great deal of courtesie and demonstrations of friendship brought the Father and me up to a chamber where the King stayed for him, who having taken him by the hand with a joyfull countenance, said unto him; *Beleeve me, Father, this day is the only one that I can call mine, in regard of the extreme pleasure I take to see thee before mine eyes, because, me thinks, I see Father* Xavier, *to whom I wished as well as to mine own person*: Then leading him into another inner chamber, that was richlyer furnished, he set him down by him, and made very much of the four little Boyes, for that it was a new thing to him, and never seen in that Country before. The Father rendred him thanks conformable to the great honor he did him, and after that manner which they are wont to use amongst themselves, and which *Joana Fernandez* had taught him. After this, he entertained him with the principall cause of his coming, which was, that the Vice-Roy had sent him expresly to serve him, and to shew him the assured way of salvation; which the King seemed to like of, by his action of bowing down of his head: The Father going on, made an holy speech somewhat like unto a Sermon unto him, agreeable to the businesse in hand; and which, he had directly studied for that purpose. Whereunto the King made this answer, *Good Father, I know not how to expresse the great content which I take in seeing thee in this house, and in learning all that which my ears have heard thee say; which I ao not answer for the present, in regard the affaires of my State are such, as thou maiest peradventure have heard: Wherefore, I earnestly intreat thee, since God hath brought thee hither, that thou wilt repose thee a while from the travel which thou hast endured for his service. And as for that which the Vice-Roy hath written to me, touching the businesse which I sent to him about by* Antonio Ferreyra, *I still avow it; but the Affaires of the present time, are reduced to that passe, as I am much afraid, if my subjects see any change in me, that they will approve of the Bonzoes counsel; Besides, I make no question but the Christians which are here, have told thee the great danger I run in this Country, by reason of the mutinies that have past here, during the which, I have been in as great jeopardy as any other; so that for the safety of my person, I have been inforced to execute in one morning thirteen of the Principallest Lords of my Kingdome, together with sixteen thousand persons of their faction and league, besides as many more which I have banished. Bat if it ever happens, that God shall grant me that which my soul desires of him, I shall hold it a small matter, to consent to what the Vice-Roy advises me by his Letter.* Hereunto, the Father replied, *That he was greatly satisfied with his holy resolution; but he was to remember, that his life was not in the hands of men, because they were mortall; and that if he should chance to die before he effected it, what would then become of his soul?* To which he answered smiling, *God knows.* The Father seeing that he could receive no other satisfaction from the King at that present but good words, without making any conclusion on a matter that was so important for him, dissembled with him, and changing discourse, talked to him of other things, wherein he knew he took more pleasure. So, having spent the most part of the night with the Father, in questioning him about divers novelties, whereunto he was much affected, he dismissed him in very plausible termes, with hope that he would become a Christian, but not so soon; a thing which was then well enough understood, and that sufficiently discovered his intention. The next day about two a clock in the afternone the Father went to see the

King

King again, and fetting afide his kind welcoming of him, this Prince never anfwe-ed him to purpofe; and within a while after returned to his Fortreffe of *Ofquy*, from whence he fent to defire him to continue abiding where he was, and to come fome times and fee him, for that he took extream pleafure in talking with him of the great things of God, and perfection of his Law. In the mean fpace, above two months and an half paft away, without giving in all that time any other fruit of himfelf, then certain kind of hopes, accompanied ever and anon with fome excu-fes, which did not much content the Father : fo that he thought it requifite for him to return to *Goa*, as well for the difcharging of the duty of his charge there, as for many other reafons that moved him thereunto. Being refolved then for our depar-ture, I went to the Fortreffe of *Ofquy* to the King, to demand an anfwer of the Letter I brought him from the Vice-Roy of the *Indiaes*, which he prefently gave me, having made it ready againft my coming; and in exchange of the Prefent he had received, he fent him very rich Armes, together with two Scymitars garnifhed with gold, an hundred Ventiloes of the Country of the *Lequios*. In the Letter which he himfelf had written, were thefe words contained : *Lord Vice-Roy of bo-norable Majeftie, that art feated in the Throne of thofe Which render Juftice by the power of the Scepter : I Yaretandono, King of Bungo, give thee to underftand, that Ferdinand Mendez Pinto is come to me, with a Letter from thy Royall Lordfhip, and a prefent of Armes, and other peeces very agreeable to my defire, and Which I ve-ry much efteem, for that they are of a Country in the other end of the world, which We call* Chenchicogim, *where through the power of great Armies, compofed of divers Nations, raignes the Crowned Lion of* Portugal, *Whofe fervant and fubject I do by thefe prefents declare my felf to be : Wherefore I pray thee, that as long as the Sun fhall not fwerve from the effect for which God hath created him, nor the waters of the fea ceafe from ri-fing and falling on the fhoares fide, thou wilt not forget this homage, Which hereby I make to your King, whom I acknowledg for my elder Brother; to the end, that there-by this my obedience may remain the more honorable, as I am confident it fhall alwaies be : And I defire thou wilt daign to accept of thefe Armes which I fend thee, as a gage and affurance of my faith. From this my Fortreffe of* Ofquy, *the ninth Mamocos of the third Moon, in the thirtie and feventh year of our age.* With this Letter, and his prefent I returned to our fhip, which rode at anchor fome two leagues off in the Port of *Zequa*, where I found Father *Belquior*, and all the reft of our company, already imbarqued, and from thence we fet fail the day after, being the fourteenth of November, One thoufand five hundred fifty and fix.

CHAP. LXXXI.

What paft after our departure from Zequa, *till my arrivall in the* Indiaes, *and from thence into the Kingdome of* Portugal.

FRom this Port of *Zequa* we continued our courfe with Northerly vvinds, which were favourable unto us in this feafon; and on the fourth of December vve ar-rived at the Port of *Lampacau*, vvhere we met with fix *Portugal* fhips, vvhereof was Generall a certain Merchant, called *Francifco Martinez*, the creature of *Francifco Barreto*, at that time Governour of the State of the Indiaes in the place of *Don Pedro Mafcarenhas*. And becaufe that then the feafon for Navigation into *India* was almoft paft, our Captain *Don Francifco Mafcarenhas* ftayed no longer there then was neceffary for providing of victuall. We departed then from this Port of *Lampacau* a little before *Chriftmaffe*, and arrived at *Goa* the feventeenth of February. The firft thing I did there was to go to *Francifco Barreto*, unto whom I gave an account of the Letter which I brought from the King of *Japan*: but he having referred it to the day following, I failed not to deliver it to him the next morning, together with the Arms, the Scymitars, and the other Prefents which
that

that Pagan King had sent. Whereupon, after he had seen all at leasure, addresfing himself unto me, *I assure you,* said he unto me, *that I prize these Arms which you have brought me, as much as the Government of India: for I hope that by the means of this Present, and this Letter from the King of* Japan, *I shall render my self agreeable to the King our Soveraign Lord, that I shall be delivered from the fortune of Lisbon, where almost all of us that govern this State, do go and land for our sins.* Then, in acknowledgment of this Voyage, and the great expence I had been at, he made me many large offers, which I would by no means accept of at that time : Neverthelesse I was well contented to justifie before him by attestations, and acts past expresly for it, how many times I had been made a slave for the service of the King our Master ; and how many times also I had been robbed of my Merchandize : for I imagined that this would suffice to keep me at my return into my Country, from being refused that, which I believed was due to me for my services ; as indeed, the Vice-Roy past me an Act of all these things, adding thereunto the Certificates which I presented unto him: withall, he gave me a Letter, addrest to the King, wherein he made so honourable a mention of me and my Services, that relying on these hopes, grounded as they were on such apparant reasons as I had on my side, I imbarqued my self for to return into the Kingdom of *Portugal* ; so contented with the Papers which I carried along with me, that I counted them the best part of my estate; at leastwise, I beleeved so, because I was perswaded that I should no sooner ask a recompence for so many services, but wont it be presently granted me. Upon this hope being put to sea, it pleased our Lord, that I arrived safely at the Citie of *Lisbon,* the two and twentieth day of September, in the Year One thousand five hundred fifty and eight, at such time as the Kingdome was governed by Madam *KATHERINA,* our Queen of happy memory. Having delivered her the Letter then from the Vice-Roy of the *Indiaes,* I told her by word of mouth all that I thought was important for the good of my businesse : whereupon she referred mee to the Minister of her State, who had the charge of dealing in her Affairs : At first he gave me very good words, but far better hopes, as indeed I held them for most assured, hearing what he said unto me : But in stead of letting me see the effect thereof, he kept me these miserable papers of mine four years and an half, at the end of which, all the fruit I reaped thereby was no other, then the labor and pains which to no purpose I had imployed in these vain sollicitations, and which had been more grievous unto me, then all the troubles I had suffered during my voyages : Wherefore seeing of what little profit all my past services were unto me, notwithstanding all the suit I could make ; I resolved to retire my self, and remain within the terms of my miserie, which I had brought along with me, and gotten by the means of many misfortunes, which was all that was resting to me of the time and wealth which I had bestowed in the service of this Kingdome, leaving the judgment of this processe to the divine Justice. I put this design of mine then in execution, not a little grieved that I had not done it sooner, because I might thereby peradventure have saved a good peece of mony. For a conclusion, behold what the services have been which I have done for the space of one and twenty years, during which time, I was thirteen times a slave, and sold sixteen times, by reason of the unlucky events of so long and painfull a voyage, whereof I have made mention amply enough in this Book. But although this be so, yet do I not leave to beleeve, that the cause why I remained without the recompence whereunto I pretented for so many services and travels, rather proceeded from the Divine providence, which permitted it to be so for my sins, then from the negligence and fault of him, whom the duty of his charge seemed to oblige to do me right. For it being true, that in all the Kings of this Kingdome who are the lively source from whence all recompence do flow, though many times they ranne thorow pipes more affectionate then reasonable, there is alwaies found an holy and acknowledging zeal, accompanied with a very ample and great desire, not only to recompence those which serve them, but also to confer great estates on them which render them no service at all ; whereby it is evident, that if I, and others, have not

been

been satisfied, the same happens by the only fault of the pipes, and not of the source; or rather it is a work of the Divine Justice, which cannot fail, and which disposeth of all things for the best, and as is most necessary for us, in regard whereof, I render infinite thanks to the King of Heaven, whose pleasure it hath been, that his divine will should be this way accomplished, and do not complain of the Kings of the earth, since my sins have made me unworthy of meriting more.

FINIS.

ERRATA.

PAg. 4.l.17. *read* first Vice-Roy. p.10.l.36. r. victual and ammunition. p.21.l.*ult.* r. of a Pagan. p.60. l.*ult.* r. shrewd. p 77.l.33. r. speech. p.80.l.30. r. lands aside. p.83.l.7. r. equalled. p.95.l.8. r. remorse of conscience. l 49. *for* deserved, r. demanded. p.100.l.28. r. poor folks. p.103.l.33. *for* Chaucer r. Chautir. p.104.l.48. *for* as, r. us. p.111.l.20. r. picos of silver. p.121.l.10. *for* levied, r. lived. p.123.l.8. r. render. p.124.l.44. r. many light. p.125.l.3. r. canals. l.12. r. praises. p.127.l.18. r. conservation. p.128. l.19. r. allegations. p.129.l.1. *for* constrained, r. painted. p.130 l.2. r. standish. l.17. *for* ye are, r. yea are. l.32. r. valuable. l.40 r. who being able. p.132.l.*ult.* r. Paquin. p.133.l.19. r. balisters. p.137. l.30. r. Ushers. l.44. *for* righly r. richly. p.136.l.12. r. remarkable. l.48. r. antiquitie. p.137.l.10. r. Piatzaes. l.46. r. so extravagant. p.138.l.5. r. Exiles: l.9. r abutting on. p.139.l.1. r. plenary. p.141.l.23. r. arches or vaults. p.142.l.15. *for* entertained, r. infolded. p.144.l.25. *for* love, r. lone. p.149.l.2. *for* stratagems r. strangenesse. p.150.l.21. r. breaking. p.155.l.16. r. Nixiancoo. p.155. r obliged to hold. p.163.l.13. r. at their pleasure. p.241.l.1. r. Timpian. l.46. r. this Prince. l.47. r. leagues in bredth. p.242.l. 21. r. reputation. p.244.l.*ult.* *for* undivided, r. undiscovered. p.248.l.14. r. Elogie. p.243. r. savages.